CRIMINAL JUSTICE IN AMERICA

CRIMINAL JUSTICE IN AMERICA
A Critical Understanding

EDITED BY
RICHARD QUINNEY

LITTLE, BROWN AND COMPANY   BOSTON

Library of Congress Catalog Card Number: 73–13297

Second Printing,

Published simultaneously in Canada
by Little, Brown & Company (Canada) Limited

Printed in the United States of America

PREFACE

Criminal law in the United States — according to conventional wisdom — is bound by the ideal of justice. In its formulation, enforcement, and administration, criminal law is based on such notions as impartiality and equality before the law. We are to assume that whenever legal order prevails, justice is being obtained. However, given this ideal, we know from experience that justice in practice is indeed problematic.

The concern in this book is with more than the possibilities of criminal justice, in the legal sense, in American society. Initially, we seek to understand the nature of American criminal justice. But going beyond this, our purpose is to critically examine the larger context within which criminal justice operates in the United States. Our objective is to provide the understanding necessary for the creation of an authentic human existence — an understanding that requires a much broader concept of criminal justice.

In my opinion, Karl Marx proposed the strongest alternative to the juridical concept of justice. Since the state and its legal order are an expression of the prevailing mode of production, and given that capitalist production is destructive of a human existence, the legal system supporting this kind of social and economic order is not capable of promoting justice. To accept the more traditional legal point of view is to adopt a mystified conception of reality. Thus, a critical understanding of social reality requires a frame of reference that goes beyond the notion of justice.

This book develops a Marxist understanding of crime and justice in America. At the beginning, after reviewing the various theoretical approaches to criminal law, I provide the outlines for a Marxist theory of criminal law. The framework is used in a critical examination of American criminal justice throughout the remainder of the book.

The book was started as a revision of my earlier *Crime and Justice in Society*. I soon realized, however, that more is required than further empirical studies of criminal justice following mainly positivist and liberal assumptions of method and reality. What we do need is a *critical* understanding of criminal justice and the social, economic, and political order on which it rests. The most appropriate intellectual tradition for this approach is Marxism.

Therefore, this book is totally different from the earlier one. The selections provide a critique of aspects of criminal justice in America, advancing our understanding more than ever possible by the accumulation of empirical studies based on what I believe are misconceptions of our reality. Whenever possible I have selected writings that are clearly Marxist. Because of the underdevelopment of Marxist theory and research in the United States, the writings are critical while also being supportive of Marxist assumptions. The result is an understanding that goes beyond our conventional wisdom and gets to the deeper meaning of criminal justice in America.

I want to note my indebtedness and appreciation to friends who in recent years have been working toward Marxist theory and practice. In a struggle that upsets the traditional sources of reward and security, we find support in each other. I hope this text will be a source of encouragement to those working for the advancement of Marxist criminology. As a socialist movement is built, our reach is to all who work together to create a new world.

CONTENTS

CRIMINAL JUSTICE IN AMERICA

Chapter One

A CRITICAL THEORY
OF CRIMINAL LAW

An understanding of crime is necessarily based on assumptions about the meaning
of human existence. Even our initial conception of crime depends on our views
regarding the nature of our being. For instance, a definition of crime focusing
on the acts of persons who transgress some code involves assumptions quite different
from those that underlie a definition focusing on the codes or laws themselves.
In either case, some idea about human life and the union of persons into community
is presupposed. An understanding of crime is not possible without these assumptions.

Moreover, explanations of crime are based on the larger consideration of human
essence — on the ideal of what may be achieved in our human existence. No
matter how much the explanations claim to be free of values, they contain some
notions about human possibilities. Indeed, it is the concept of justice that commonly
incorporates many of these ideals. Whether questions are raised about the treatment
of the offender, the administration of the law, the proper role of law, or the
necessity of law itself, ideas about justice are being entertained. Criminologists
and citizens alike are bound by some ideal of justice.

In addition to considerations of existence and essence, there is the position
that any explanation of crime takes in regard to the existing social order. Some
theories, given their particular notions about human existence and essence, support
established arrangements, whereas other theories are either amelioristic or seek
to transcend (in both thought and action) the existing order. No understanding
of crime can proceed without a recognition of the existing order and how it relates
to a higher ideal. In fact, the ultimate purpose of criminological theory is either
to support or to change in some way the existing order. All explanations of crime
are both moral and political. An understanding of crime that is not moral and
political is no understanding at all.

Finally, all theories of crime involve ways of structuring fact and truth; all theories have an epistemology governing procedure. The procedure may be as simple as a naive faith in discovering the real world; or it may be a more elaborate scheme containing explicit notions about the relation of thought to an objective world. The history of criminological theory can be traced according to such considerations.

In this introduction we will examine the various kinds of theories regarding crime and criminal law. My objective is to develop a critical understanding of crime — one that aims at the achievement of what is authentic to our being through a critique of our current existence. The recognition that our age is dominated by the capitalist social and economic order is the beginning of a critical analysis. To resolve the contradiction between our current existence and our ultimate essence should be the goal of all our endeavors. My contention is that a theory of crime and law — a critical theory — must serve the advancement of human possibilities. Past theories and current explanations can be evaluated according to this goal. Within this critical framework we can understand criminal justice in America.[1]

Classical and Positivistic Criminology

The two oldest traditions of thought in modern criminology are the classical and the positivistic. The "classical school," an extension of eighteenth-century rationalism, was formulated by such scholars as Cesare Beccaria, Jeremy Bentham, and Samuel Romilly. Their objective, in reaction to contemporary legal practices, was to reform criminal law so as to achieve criminal justice. The "positive school," beginning in the middle of the nineteenth century, was an attempt to apply the newly developing scientific methods to the study of crime. The founders of the school, particularly the Italian criminologists Cesare Lombroso, Enrico Ferri, and Raffaelle Garofalo, turned their attention to the offender (and away from the law) and sought to protect society from criminal violations. Whereas the classical school represented a new naturalistic approach to crime, in contrast to earlier supernaturalistic theories, the positive school carried the movement into the new realms of science. These two criminological traditions mark the beginnings of modern criminology.[2]

Classical and positivistic thought continued to differ sharply from each other in several important ways. To begin with, they differed fundamentally in their assumptions about human nature. The classical school was based on the doctrine of free will, the belief that individuals act rationally and are capable of choosing

---

[1]Portions of this chapter and the introductions are adapted from my book, *Critique of Legal Order: Crime Control in Capitalist Society* (Boston: Little, Brown and Company, 1974), with permission of the publisher.

[2]See C. Bernaldo de Quirós, *Modern Theories of Criminality*, trans. Alfonso de Salvio (Boston: Little, Brown and Company, 1911). For the larger social and economic context, see George Rusche and Otto Kirchheimer, *Punishment and Social Structure* (New York: Columbia University Press, 1939).

between right and wrong. More specifically, human beings were held to be utilitarian in acting to maximize pleasure and minimize pain. The positivists, on the other hand, assumed that human behavior is determined by causes beyond an individual's will.

These two opposing assumptions about human nature were associated with divergent criminal policies and practices. Following classical thought, criminal codes were revised according to rational schemes of relating the seriousness of the offense to the degree of punishment, the reasoning being that people would be deterred from conduct that resulted in pain greater than the pleasure of committing the act. Justice was in the certainty and equality of punishment — a definite penalty for each crime, with no judicial allowance for individual differences. In contrast, positivist thought led to programs based on the causes of an offender's behavior. Justice was individualized — for the protection of society.

> The Positive School rejected the doctrine of *nulla poena sine lege* — no punishment without a law. The Positive School emphasized individualized treatment and the protection of society against the criminal. The punishment must fit the criminal. A man was sentenced, not according to the seriousness of the offense, but according to the factor or factors which motivated him to commit a crime.[3]

The positive school not only shifted the criminologist's attention from the criminal law to the criminal but had important consequences for official policies of crime control as well. Positivists emphasized the protection of the state or society. Criminal laws, preferably indefinite laws to allow a maximum of discretion and individualized justice, would serve to protect society from the offender. Society would be maintained at the expense of human expression and liberation. The criminal would be reformed in a way that would prevent him from committing the offense again, while the existing social order remained unaltered.

Classical thought offered reforms in the criminal code that would support the interests of the rising bourgeoisie against those of the aristocracy. Positivist thought, however, served the interests of the existing social and economic order, as it continues to do today. It is not surprising, therefore, to learn that two of the leading positivists, Ferri and Garofalo, adapted themselves to Mussolini's Fascist regime. Their political alignment was not accidental or a matter of practical compromise but reflects the affinity between positivism and authoritarian rule. George B. Vold has written:

> The end of Ferri's career, assent to Fascism, highlights one of the implications of positivistic theory, namely, the ease with which it fits into totalitarian patterns of government. It is centered on the core idea of the superior knowledge and wisdom of the scientific expert, who, on the basis of his studies, decides what kind of human beings his fellow men are who commit crime, and who, on the basis of this knowledge and scientific insight, prescribes appropriate

---

[3]C. Ray Jeffery, "The Historical Development of Criminology," *Journal of Criminal Law, Criminology and Police Science*, 50 (June, 1959), p. 14.

treatment without consent from the person so diagnosed (i.e., the criminal). There is an obvious similarity in conception of the control of power in society between positivism and the political reality of centralized control of the life of the citizen by a government bureaucracy indifferent to democratic public opinion.[4]

Positivistic criminology is an ideology and a technology for the ruling class.

The classical school, although overshadowed for many years by positivism, has inspired criminologists at various times to return to criminal law for an understanding of crime. Moreover, the recent proposals by lawyers and criminologists for reform of criminal law embody some of the ideas and assumptions of the classical criminologists.[5] But it is positivism that has dominated criminology for over a century.

The positivist approach to crime was shared by the nineteenth-century criminologists in England and in parts of continental Europe, as well as by the criminologists in Italy. While the Italian positivists were applying scientific methods to the biological study of criminals, other criminologists were applying similar methods to sociological studies.[6] For example, Adolphe Quételet in Belgium studied the social nature of crime as reflected in crime statistics; H. M. Guerry analyzed the crime rates for various regions of France; and such English investigators as R. W. Rawson and Henry Mayhew studied crime statistics and observed criminal life. Similar studies were being conducted in the United States in the last part of the nineteenth century.

The deterministic concept of human existence and the search for scientific explanation have pervaded most twentieth-century American criminological studies. The major differences in the research have been in respect to whether causation is sought in the characteristics of the individual or in the society. Individualistic and multiple factor explanations have largely given way to sociological theories of criminal behavior. Nevertheless, positivistic assumptions have continued to dominate both theory and practice. From the early criminological research by sociologists at the University of Chicago to the later research and theoretical formulations embodied in the work of Edwin H. Sutherland, the approach to crime has been positivistic. Even when criminal law has been the focus of attention, rather than the criminal, the same assumptions have been followed.

What we clearly lack today in criminology is a critical approach to the study of crime. Such an approach is now emerging, however, and its emergence is the subject of this book. Only in the development of this approach, combined with political practice, can we free ourselves from the existing order. And in

---

[4]George B. Vold, *Theoretical Criminology* (New York: Oxford University Press, 1958), pp. 35–36.

[5]For example, see Norval Morris and Gordon Hawkins, *The Honest Politician's Guide to Crime Control* (Chicago: University of Chicago Press, 1970); and Herbert L. Packer, *The Limits of the Criminal Sanction* (Stanford: Stanford University Press, 1968).

[6]For a discussion of these and other developments in criminology, see Richard Quinney, *The Problem of Crime* (New York: Dodd, Mead, 1970), pp. 43–100.

so doing we can truly understand crime in American society and act in a way to create a truly democratic society.

Sociological Jurisprudence

The contemporary rapprochement of law and social science finds its origins not only in classical criminology but also in the development of a legal philosophy known as "sociological jurisprudence." Around the turn of this century several legal scholars began to consider the social nature of law. An Austrian, Eugen Ehrlich, in particular, distinguished between the "positive law" and the "living law."[7] According to Ehrlich, the positive law can only be effective when it corresponds to the living law, that is, when legal codes are based on underlying social norms. In other words, law is to be understood in relation to the social order.

Similar thoughts were developing in the United States after the turn of the century. The early American sociologists, for example, were incorporating law into their theoretical frameworks. E. A. Ross referred to law as "the most specialized and highly furnished engine of control employed by society."[8] Lester F. Ward, an advocate of government control and social planning, foresaw a day when legislation would undertake to solve "questions of social improvement, the amelioration of the condition of all the people, the removal of whatever privations may still remain, and the adoption of means to the positive increase of the social welfare, in short the organization of human happiness."[9] The possibility of social reform, through legal means available to the state, was also emphasized by Albion W. Small.[10]

The ideas of the early sociologists directly influenced the development of the school of legal philosophy that became a major force in American legal thought — sociological jurisprudence. Roscoe Pound, the principal figure in sociological jurisprudence, drew from the early sociologists in asserting that law should be studied as a social institution.[11] Pound saw law as a specialized form of social control which brings pressure to bear upon each man "in order to constrain him to do his part in upholding civilized society and to deter him from anti-social conduct, that is, conduct at variance with the postulates of social order."[12]

[7]Eugen Ehrlich, *The Fundamental Principles of the Sociology of the Law*, trans. W. Moll (Cambridge: Harvard University Press, 1936).

[8]E. A. Ross, *Social Control* (New York: Macmillan, 1922), p. 106. Originally published in 1901.

[9]Lester F. Ward, *Applied Sociology* (Boston: Ginn, 1906), p. 339.

[10]Albion W. Small, *General Sociology* (Chicago: University of Chicago Press, 1925).

[11]The relation between early American sociologists and the development of Pound's sociological jurisprudence is discussed in Gilbert Geis, "Sociology and Jurisprudence: Admixture of Lore and Law," *Kentucky Law Journal*, 52 (Winter, 1964), pp. 267–293. Also see Edwin M. Schur, *Law and Society* (New York: Random House, 1968), pp. 17–50.

[12]Roscoe Pound, *Social Control Through Law* (New Haven: Yale University Press, 1942), p. 18. Earlier statements by Pound are found in Roscoe Pound, *An Introduction to the Philosophy of Law* (New Haven: Yale University Press, 1922); Roscoe Pound, *Outline of Lectures on Jurisprudence* (Cambridge: Harvard University Press, 1928).

Pound argued that law is not merely a complex of rules and procedures; he called for the study of "law in action" as distinguished from the study of law in the books. For some purposes it may be useful to view law as autonomous within society, developing according to its own internal logic and proceeding along its own lines. But law also operates simultaneously as a reflection of society and as an influence in society. Thus, in a social sense, law is both social product and social force. In Pound's juristic approach, however, law as both a product and a force was viewed in a very special way reflecting the consciousness of the total society. This *consensus* model of law, as applied to criminal law, holds that: "The state of criminal law continues to be — as it should — a decisive reflection of the social consciousness of a society. What kind of conduct an organized community considers, at a given time, sufficiently condemnable to impose official sanctions, impairing the life, liberty, or property of the offender, is a barometer of the moral and social thinking of a community."[13]

Central to Pound's sociological jurisprudence was his theory of interests, according to which the law functions to accomplish socially worthwhile purposes. In this theory of interests, he looked upon law as reflecting the needs of the well-ordered society. In fact, the law was a form of "social engineering" in a civilized society:

> For the purpose of understanding the law of today I am content to think of law as a social institution to satisfy social wants — the claims and demands involved in the existence of civilized society — by giving effect to as much as we may with the least sacrifice, so far as such wants may be satisfied or such claims given effect by an ordering of human conduct through politically organized society. For present purposes I am content to see in legal history the record of a continually wider recognizing and satisfying of human wants or desires through social control; a more embracing and more effective securing of social interests; a continually more complete and effective elimination of waste and precluding of friction in human enjoyment of the goods of existence — in short, a continually more efficacious social engineering.[14]

The interests Pound had in mind were those which would maintain and, ultimately, improve the social order. His was a teleological as well as consensus theory of interests: There are interests which must be fulfilled for the good of the whole society; these interests are to be achieved through law. In Pound's theory, only the right law could emerge in a civilized society.

Sociological jurisprudence has generally utilized a *pluralistic* model with respect to law as a social force in society. Accordingly, law regulates social behavior and establishes social organization. Law orders human relations by restraining individual actions and by settling disputes in social relations. In recent juristic language, law functions "first, to establish the general framework, the rules of the game so to speak, within and by which individual and group life

---

[13]Wolfgang Friedmann, *Law in a Changing Society* (Harmondsworth, England: Penguin Books, 1964), p. 143.
[14]Pound, *An Introduction to the Philosophy of Law*, pp. 98–99.

shall be carried on, and secondly, to adjust the conflicting claims which different individuals and groups of individuals seek to satisfy in society."[15] For Pound, the law adjusts and reconciles conflicting interests: "Looked at functionally, the law is an attempt to satisfy, to reconcile, to harmonize, to adjust these overlapping and often conflicting claims and demands, either through securing them directly and immediately, or through securing certain individual interests, or through delimitations or compromises of individual interests, so as to give effect to the greatest total of interests or to the interests that weigh most in our civilization, with the least sacrifice of the scheme of interests as a whole."[16]

In Pound's theory of interests, therefore, it is assumed that the legal order is created in society to regulate and adjust conflicting desires and claims. Law provides the general framework within which individual and group life is carried on according to the postulates of social order. Moreover, as a legal historian has written, "The law defines the extent to which it will give effect to the interests which it recognizes, in the light of other interests and of the possibilities of effectively securing them through law; it also devises means for securing those that are recognized and prescribes the limits within which those means may be employed."[17] In the interest theory of sociological jurisprudence, the law is regarded as an instrument which controls interests according to the requirements of social order.

Pound's theory of interests included a threefold classification of interests: (1) individual interests, (2) public interests, and (3) social interests. "Individual interests are claims or demands or desires involved immediately in the individual life and asserted in the title of that life. Public interests are claims or demands or desires involved in life in a politically organized society and asserted in the title of that organization. They are commonly treated as the claims of a politically organized society thought of as a legal entity. Social interests are claims or demands or desires involved in social life in a civilized society and asserted in the title of that life. It is not uncommon to treat them as the claims of the whole social group as such."[18] Though Pound delineated three kinds of interests secured by the legal order, he warned that the types are overlapping and interdependent and that most claims, demands, or desires can be placed in all the categories, depending upon one's purpose. However, he argued that it is often expedient to put claims, demands, and desires in their most general form, that is, into the category of social interests.

Surveying the claims, demands, and desires found in legal proceedings and

---

[15]Carl A. Auerbach, "Law and Social Change in the United States," *U.C.L.A. Law Review*, 6 (July, 1959), pp. 516–532. Similarly, see Julius Stone, *The Province and Function of Law* (Cambridge: Harvard University Press, 1950), Part III; Julius Stone, *Social Dimensions of Law and Justice* (Stanford: Stanford University Press, 1966), chaps. 4–8.

[16]Roscoe Pound, "A Survey of Social Interests," *Harvard Law Review*, 57 (October, 1943), p. 39.

[17]George Lee Haskins, *Law and Authority in Early Massachusetts* (New York: Macmillan, 1960), p. 226.

[18]Pound, "A Survey of Social Interests," pp. 1–2.

in legislative proposals, Pound suggested that the most important social interest appears to be the interest in security against actions that threaten the social group. Other social interests consist of the interest in the security of social institutions, including domestic, religious, economic, and political institutions; the interest in morals; the interest in conservation of social resources; the interest in general progress, including the development of human powers and control over nature for the satisfaction of human wants; and the interest in individual life, especially the freedom of self-assertion. According to Pound, the nature of any legal system depends upon the way in which these interests are incorporated into law.

In spite of the impact of Pound's thought on legal philosophy, and although Pound's assumptions have been accepted by sociologists, there have been few attempts to revise Pound's theory of interests. A critical revision would have to move beyond the pluralist assumptions of Pound's theory. It would identify, following research on the power elite, a ruling class that imposes its interests on the society in spite of some diversity of interests among various groups.[19] In addition, law would have to be viewed as a consequence of interests rather than merely as an instrument that functions outside of interests to resolve conflicts between interests. Law is the tool of the ruling class. Criminal law, in particular, is a device made and used by the ruling class to preserve the existing order. In the United States, the state — and its legal system — exists to secure and perpetuate the capitalist interests of the ruling class. A critical theory of criminal law would develop these ideas.

Legalistic Criminology

Although naturalistic (nonlegal) definitions of crime have dominated American criminology, there has nevertheless been a steadily growing body of thought based on a legalistic concept of crime. The need for returning to a legal conception of crime was noted dramatically in the early 1930s with a report by Jerome Michael and Mortimer J. Adler on the state of knowledge in criminology.[20] Critical of the past research directed toward the etiology of criminal behavior, Michael and Adler suggested that it was the criminal law that defined the scope and boundaries of criminology. They wrote: "If crime is merely an instance of conduct which is proscribed by the criminal code it follows that the criminal law is the formal cause of crime. That does not mean that the law produces the behavior which it prohibits, although, as we shall see, the enforcement or administration of the criminal law may be one of the factors which influence human behavior, it means only that the criminal law gives behavior its quality of criminality."[21]

---

[19]The first steps toward a ruling class theory of crime were taken in a revision of Pound's theory of interests in my introduction ("Toward a Sociology of Criminal Law") to Richard Quinney (ed.), *Crime and Justice in Society* (Boston: Little, Brown and Company, 1969), pp. 26–30. A revision of this theory is presented in the present chapter in the form of a *critical theory of criminal law*.

[20]Jerome Michael and Mortimer J. Adler, *Crime, Law and Social Science* (New York: Harcourt, Brace, 1933).

[21]*Ibid.*, p. 5.

Michael and Adler forcefully observed that "the most precise and least ambiguous definition of crime is that which defines it as behavior which is prohibited by the criminal code" and, further, that "this is the only possible definition of crime."[22]

A strong adherent of a legal definition of crime was the legally trained sociologist Paul W. Tappan. Though he advocated explaining an offender's behavior, Tappan warned, "Our definitions of crime cannot be rooted in epithets, in minority value judgments or prejudice, or in loose abstractions."[23] Tappan recognized that a person is a criminal only because his behavior has been defined as criminal by the state. In answering his own question, "Who is the Criminal?" Tappan went so far as to propose that "only those are criminals who have been adjudicated as such by the courts."[24]

Several criminologists subsequently have called for a legalistic conception of crime. C. Ray Jeffery, after reviewing diverse definitions of crime, suggested that crime should be studied within the framework of the criminal law.[25] From the criminal law we would be able to ascertain under what conditions behavior becomes defined as criminal and how legal codes interact with other normative systems. Jeffery's concluding statement succinctly expressed his concern for a sociology of criminal law, following a legalistic concept of crime:

> The sociology of criminal law would provide us with a framework for the study of crime, and at the same time it would enable us to differentiate between the criminal and the non-criminal. The legal criterion is the only standard that differentiates the two groups. Further studies of the personality makeup of the offender, of the type engaged in for the past fifty years, are never going to furnish a differential. An explanation of criminal behavior is going to depend upon an explanation of behavior. Such an explanation necessarily involves many non-sociological factors. It is to be questioned at this time whether the sociologist would do better to be more concerned with group reactions to certain types of behavior. The study of social structure is sociological; the study of human motivation is only quasi-sociological. A study of social systems in relation to the topic "law and society" would eventually lead to a theory of crime.[26]

Vold illustrated how important criminal law is to the study of crime in observing that there exists a dual problem of explanation in criminology: "Crime always involves both human behavior (acts) and the judgment or definitions (laws, customs, mores) of fellow human beings as to whether specific behavior is appropriate and permissible, or is improper and forbidden. Crime and criminality lie in the area of behavior that is considered improper and forbidden. There is, there-

---

[22]*Ibid.*, p. 2.

[23]Paul W. Tappan, *Crime, Justice and Correction* (New York: McGraw-Hill, 1960), p. 10.

[24]Paul W. Tappan, "Who Is the Criminal?" *American Sociological Review*, 12 (February, 1947), p. 100.

[25]C. Ray Jeffery, "The Structure of American Criminological Thinking," *Journal of Criminal Law, Criminology and Police Science*, 46 (January–February, 1956), pp. 658–672.

[26]*Ibid.*, p. 672.

fore, always a dual problem of explanation — that of accounting for the behavior, *as behavior*, and equally important, accounting for *the definitions* by which specific behavior comes to be considered as crime or non-crime."[27]

In considering this dual problem further, Austin T. Turk observed that the problem that is distinctly criminological is the study of criminality.[28] He argued that the criminal law determines the criminal status of persons and behavior, and only an explanation of such criminality is an explanation of crime. Thus, because the legal definition of behavior determines what is regarded as criminal, it is necessary for the criminologist to study how criminal law is formulated and administered.[29]

The question today in the development of a critical theory of criminal law is whether or not the legalistic concept of crime limits the criminologist to the existing social and legal order. The argument has been advanced that a legalistic concept prevents the criminologist from examining — or even questioning — the established order.[30] There is, indeed, the danger that a sole reliance on the state's definition of crime can lead to the acceptance of the existing order. Criminologists have continually allied themselves closely with the state and the ruling class. As ancillary agents of power, criminologists provide the kinds of information that governing elites use to manipulate and control those who threaten the established system.[31]

Nevertheless, for some criminologists, a legalistic concept of crime has allowed us to critically examine the legal system. Rather than taking the law for granted, we have examined it according to the radical assumptions about human nature and society. The result is the emergence of a criminology that serves the needs of the people rather than the interests of the state and the ruling class. Such a criminology is on the side of liberation — opposing repression and oppression of all kinds, social and legal.

Sociology of Criminal Law

Meanwhile sociologists and other social scientists have become interested in the law as a subject for empirical research. Social science and law have converged

[27]George B. Vold, *Theoretical Criminology*, pp. v–vi. For recent discussions of the dual problems of behavior and definition, see David J. Bordua, "Recent Trends: Deviant Behavior and Social Control," *Annals of the American Academy of Political and Social Science*, 369 (January, 1967), pp. 149–163; Jack P. Gibbs, "Conceptions of Deviant Behavior: The Old and the New," *Pacific Sociological Review*, 9 (Spring, 1966), pp. 9–14; Ronald L. Akers, "Problems in the Sociology of Deviance: Social Definitions and Behavior," *Social Forces*, 46 (June, 1968), pp. 455–465.

[28]Austin T. Turk, "Prospects for Theories of Criminal Behavior," *Journal of Criminal Law, Criminology and Police Science*, 55 (December, 1964), pp. 454–461.

[29]Richard Quinney, "Crime in Political Perspective," *American Behavioral Scientist*, 8 (December, 1964) pp. 19–22; Richard Quinney, "Is Criminal Behavior Deviant Behavior?" *British Journal of Criminology*, 5 (April, 1965), pp. 132–142.

[30]Herman and Julia Schwendinger, "Defenders of Order or Guardians of Human Rights?" *Issues in Criminology*, 5 (Summer, 1970), pp. 123–157.

[31]Clayton A. Hartjen, "Legalism and Humanism: A Reply to the Schwendingers," *Issues in Criminology*, 7 (Winter, 1972), pp. 59–69.

in a movement that defines and combines their mutual interests.[32] To ensure the exchange of ideas among the various disciplines interested in legal matters, the Law and Society Association was formed in 1964. In the first issue of the association's journal, the editor described the new convergence of law and the social sciences:

> During the past decade, each of the social sciences has found it necessary to face legal policy issues of highest relevance to the disciplines themselves and to the society as a whole. In political science, the decision process in the courts and administrative agencies has been explored to an extent which parallels earlier and continuing work on the legislatures. Political scientists have also turned their attention to the implementation of legal decisions, especially where the institutions of government have been seen as an important determinant of the impact of law. Sociologists, too, are showing increasing interest in the legal process. Their studies have been concerned with the manner in which the population is affected by law in such areas as civil rights, poverty, and crime. Both professions have joined with the anthropologists in studying the relationship between society and culture on the one hand and the nature and operation of legal institutions on the other. In addition, other professional groups — notably economists, social workers, clinical and social psychologists, and psychiatrists — are increasingly called upon for information thought to be of value in the formulation of legal policy. Above all, the legal profession has moved from a position of reluctant consumer of such information to an active participant in the research process.[33]

The research resulting from this convergence and the recent research in criminology form the basis for the sociology of criminal law.

In a relatively short period a body of empirical research has been developed on the sociology of criminal law. Most of the research is dominated by the positivistic mode of thought and, therefore, takes for granted the necessary existence of the legal system. The research is directed, instead, toward explaining how the system operates — how laws are formulated, enforced, and administered.[34] Little attention is devoted to questions about why law exists, whether law is indeed necessary, or what a just system would look like. If the value of justice is considered at all, the concern is with the equitability of the system, rather than whether the very existence of the system is just. Suggestions may be made for changing particular laws, but the legal system itself is to remain intact.[35] Inadequacies in the administration of justice may be noted, but prescriptions for change merely call for more technical and efficient procedures.

Even the research that departs from the positivistic mode avoids a critical

---

[32]See Gilbert Geis, "Sociology, Criminology, and Criminal Law," *Social Problems*, 7 (Summer, 1959), pp. 40–47.

[33]Richard D. Schwartz, "From the Editor," *Law and Society Review*, 1 (November, 1966), p. 6.

[34]See, for example, the research contained in William J. Chambliss (ed.), *Crime and the Legal Process* (New York: McGraw-Hill, 1969); and Quinney (ed.), *Crime and Justice in Society*.

[35]Morris and Hawkins, *The Honest Politician's Guide to Crime Control*; Packer, *The Limits of the Criminal Sanction*.

analysis of the existing system. Social constructionist thought, for example, as found in the ethnomethodological studies, may suggest that the administration of criminal law involves the construction of a reality by those in positions of power.[36] But this research fails to provide a stance that would allow us to analyze the existing reality in the light of a higher ideal of human justice. A critique of the legal order of advanced capitalist society is missing in the sociology of criminal law. Without an image of what could be, the sociology of criminal law offers no possibility of understanding even the current reality.

The theoretical perspective that does exist in the sociology of criminal law is one that accepts the legal order. Law is regarded as the realization of rationality. Furthermore, it is thought that the legal order can be strengthened and made more efficient by the application of scientific methods. Philip Selznick writes, in an essay on the sociology of law, that "legal reasoning cannot but accept the authority of scientifically validated conclusions regarding the nature of man and his institutions. Therefore, inevitably, sociology and every other social science have a part in the legal order."[37] The sociology of law — narrowly construed as the scientific study of law — not only studies law but supports the legal order; the fate of the legal order and the fate of the scientific study of law are tied together.

To base a legal system on the scientific ethos is the objective of the sociologist of law. With the accumulation of empirical research and communication with legal agencies, the reasoning goes, human affairs will become rational. An editor of the *Law and Society Review* is able to write:

> As more empirical studies of the legal process emerge, we may ultimately be able to construct a scientific model of law in society which can serve to refine and supplement the traditional models. We need to learn more about the manner in which law creates, supports, and regulates the various institutions of a complex society; how its actions affect its own position in society; what leads to the acceptance of its legitimacy and to the effectiveness of its sanctions; how these effects in turn relate to the influences exerted on law by public opinion, interest groups, and agencies of government; and how these influences are in turn translated into action. Such a model is certain to differ from the models implicitly held at present by legal decision makers and explicitly by men of jurisprudence. As the models of jurisprudence and social science become more consistent and find expression in the legal process we will have made an advance in the eternal battle to increase rationality in human affairs.[38]

A sociology of criminal law as presently conceived and practiced cannot break out of the ideology of the age. It can only confirm the existing order; problems

---

[36]See, for example, Howard S. Becker, *Outsiders: Studies in the Sociology of Deviance* (New York: The Free Press, 1963); Aaron V. Cicourel, *The Social Organization of Juvenile Justice* (New York: John Wiley & Sons, 1968); Richard Quinney, *The Social Reality of Crime* (Boston: Little, Brown and Company, 1970).

[37]Philip Selznick, "The Sociology of Law," in Robert K. Merton, Leonard Broom, and Leonard S. Cottrell, Jr. (eds.), *Sociology Today* (New York: Basic Books, 1959), p. 126.

[38]Richard Schwartz, "Introduction," *Social Problems*, Supplements (Summer, 1965), p. 3.

of the age are only exacerbated by the sociological-scientific study of law. Such study of criminal law systematically ignores moral questions about the legal order, devoting attention instead to supporting the existing order.

Contemporary Criminology and Corrections

Criminology, including the theories and practices of what is to be done about crime, continues to be dominated by a single purpose: preservation of the existing order. The established system is taken for granted; departures from and threats to social order are the objects of investigation. In the name of developing knowledge about crime, most criminologists support current institutions at the expense of human freedoms and social revolution.[39]

Criminologists have traditionally asked the question, "What causes crime?" The answer has been sought in the study of the "criminal." That is, the sources of crime are believed to be located in the person who violates the law rather than in the authority that defines behavior as criminal. This emphasis has meant that criminal law and political theory have been ignored. To critically understand and question the existing legal system falls outside the scientific and ideological interests of most criminologists.

Criminologists generally serve the interests of the state by following their own unexamined assumptions about the nature of the world and the process of understanding it. By pursuing a narrow scientific model, supported by an ideology of social order, the criminologist finds his interests tied to those of the state and the ruling class. He holds fast to a scientific conception of his field. Indeed, it has been argued that the term *criminology* "should be used to designate a body of *scientific* knowledge about crime."[40] And in an attempt to show that this is not a restricted definition, Marvin E. Wolfgang adds:

> This conceptualism of criminology is neither narrow nor confining. A scientific approach to understanding the etiology of crime may include the statistical, historical, clinical, or case-study tools of analysis. Moreover, there is nothing inherently quantitative in scientific methodology, albeit the most convincing evidence, data, and presentation in general sociological replications of propositions appear to be quantitative. Probably the most fruitful source of analysis of empiric uniformity, regularity, and systems of patterned relationships can be found in the statistical studies of causation and prediction. However, interpretive analyses that may occasionally go beyond the limits of empirically correlated and organized data (but not beyond empiric reality) can be useful and enlightening. If description of the phenomena of crime is performed within a meaningful theoretical system, the methods and the goals of science are not necessarily discarded in the process but may be retained

[39]See Richard Quinney, "From Repression to Liberation: Social Theory in a Radical Age," in Robert A. Scott and Jack D. Douglas (eds.), *Theoretical Perspectives on Deviance* (New York: Basic Books, 1972), pp. 317–341.

[40]Marvin E. Wolfgang, "Criminology and the Criminologist," *Journal of Criminal Law, Criminology and Police Science*, 54 (June, 1963), p. 155. Italics in the original.

with all the vigor commonly attributed to sophisticated statistical manipulation.[41]

The scientific study of criminal behavior is closely associated with attempts to control crime. In fact, criminology is strengthened by practical applications in the field of corrections. As Stanton Wheeler writes, referring to the common interests of corrections and criminology: "The movement toward professionalism in the practicing fields should lead to an increased number of competent and skilled practitioners and the recognition of need for more systematic research on crime and its control. Increased public attention to problems of delinquency and crime, particularly as reflected in increased budgets for prevention and research efforts, may attract a larger number of social scientists to problems of delinquency and crime."[42] Moreover, crime control and scientific prediction go hand in hand. Science and politics are united: "If control and prediction in experimentation are integral goals of research and, regardless of the substantive area, if analysis proceeds by means of the scientific method, then we may include within the scope of criminology any correctional research that embraces these goals and this method."[43] Scientific criminology and the state's correctional aims are mutually supportive of one another.

We are told in criminology textbooks that not only is criminology a body of verified principles about crime but that, in addition:

Criminology is concerned with the immediate application of knowledge to programs of crime control. This concern with practical programs is justified, in part, as experimentation which may be valuable because of its immediate results but at any rate will be valuable in the long run because of the increased knowledge which results from it. If practical programs wait until theoretical knowledge is complete, they will wait for eternity, for theoretical knowledge is increased most significantly in the efforts at social control.[44]

Would a scientific criminology be possible without a state that controls citizens? At least, we are informed, theoretical knowledge is increased in the efforts at social control. A critical criminology, a radical criminology, would certainly depart significantly from the control interests of current scientific criminology.

Among the various capitalist ideologies, the liberal ideology dominates most of criminology and corrections today. The theories and practices of criminologists, accordingly, take the existing capitalist system of institutions for granted.[45] Furthermore, criminal behavior is regarded as being the result of such problems in the social environment as poverty, lack of opportunity, and improper socialization. The proposed solutions call for ameliorating the existing conditions. As the

[41]*Ibid*.

[42]Stanton Wheeler, "The Social Sources of Criminology," *Sociological Inquiry*, 32 (Spring, 1962), pp. 158–159.

[43]Wolfgang, "Criminology and the Criminologist," p. 159.

[44]Edwin H. Sutherland and Donald R. Cressey, *Criminology*, 8th edition (Philadelphia: J. B. Lippincott, 1970), p. 3.

[45]See David M. Gordon (ed.), *Problems in Political Economy: An Urban Perspective* (Lexington, Mass.: D. C. Heath, 1971), pp. 9–11, 275–276.

social science staff of the National Commission on Violence wrote regarding a solution to the crimes of violence:

> The perspective advocated here accepts the present system as the framework within which changes should be made. It does not call for total change; it does not denounce major institutions in their entirety. It argues, rather, that there are significant defects in the operating social institutions; that these defects place a disproportionate burden on the backs of certain segments of society, especially the poor and the black; that the provisions for the incorporation of young people into adult society are generally inadequate; and that, in sum, these basic inequities and burdens must be redressed substantially and promptly, lest they continue to generate increasing disrespect for our society, its institutions, and its laws. Such changes are not likely to occur overnight, but immediate movement in their direction can and must be initiated.[46]

Combined with social amelioration, of course, is the liberal belief in the rationalization of crime control. Law enforcement is to be improved, and the administration of justice is to be made more efficient. Finally there is the liberal faith that crime will be reduced by spending more money, conducting more research, and developing new technology.[47]

The contemporary criminologist, following the liberal ideology within the capitalist system, turns to the state as the ultimate agency to control crime. In contrast to the conservative approach within capitalism, which would restrict crime control to a few limited and definite crime prevention and punitive techniques, the liberal approach to crime control provides a wide range of programs and techniques. Therefore, the state, with the assistance of its "experts" (especially criminologists and correctional workers), is to intervene in the criminal process by instituting not only various forms of imprisonment, but a host of programs that involve rehabilitation and reintegration of the offender into the dominant society.[48] In the course of these efforts, the existing social and economic system is to be protected and preserved.

Criminologists today are furnishing the information and knowledge necessary for the manipulation and control of those who threaten the social system. The consequence may be the creation of a new age of crime control in America. Already we are being advised on the contributions that men of science are making to the control of domestic crime.

Crime control, being largely a social problem, may appear to be outside the realm of the scientists' skills. Indeed, many aspects of the problem do fall outside their scope. The experience of science in the military, however,

---

[46]*Crimes of Violence*, vol. 12, A Staff Report Submitted to the National Commission on the Causes and Prevention of Violence, Donald J. Mulvihill and Melvin M. Tumin, Co-Directors (Washington, D.C.: U.S. Government Printing Office, 1969), p. 727.

[47]Such are the recommendations in the President's Commission on Law Enforcement and Administration of Justice, *The Challenge of Crime in a Free Society* (Washington, D.C.: U.S. Government Printing Office, 1967).

[48]See, for example, the recommendations in National Commission on the Causes and Prevention of Violence, *Crimes of Violence*, vol. 12, pp. 753–787; and President's Commission on Law Enforcement and Administration of Justice, *The Challenge of Crime in a Free Society*, passim.

suggests that a fruitful collaboration can be established between criminal justice officials on one hand and engineers, physicists, economists, and social and behavioral scientists on the other. In military research organizations these different professions, working with military officers in interdisciplinary teams, have attacked defense problems in new ways and have provided insights that were new even to those with long military experience. Similar developments appear possible in criminal justice.[49]

The time has been reached when military operations abroad and crime control at home have become one — in objective and in technique. The purpose is to secure the capitalist system. Until criminologists become aware of what they are doing in the name of science and liberal scholarship, they will continue to make their contribution to these new and dangerous policies. What is needed now is a critical approach in criminology.

Critical Theory of Criminal Law

A critical theory is one that is *radically* critical. It is a theory that goes to the roots of our lives, to the foundations and the fundamentals, to the essentials of consciousness.[50] In the rooting out of presuppositions we are able to assess every actual and possible experience. The operation is one of demystification, the removal of the myths — the false consciousness — created by the official reality. The true meaning of current reality is thereby understood.

Without critical thought we are bound to the only form of social life we know — that which currently exists. We are unable to choose a better life; our only activity is in further support of the system in which we are enslaved. Our current cultural and social arrangements, supported as they are by a bureaucratic-technological system of production and distribution, are a threat to the fulfillment of human possibilities — including the freedom to know that this system is oppressive and may be altered. Such a system tends to preclude the possibility of an opposition emerging within it. In aspiring to the rewards that the system holds out to us, we find it difficult to consider an alternative existence.[51]

What prevents us from seeing clearly, then, is the ideology of the age. The modern institutional order finds its legitimation in an ideology that stresses the rationality of science and technology.[52] A generalized belief in the importance of controlled scientific-technical progress gives legitimacy to a particular class — the one that utilizes science and technology. The extent to which this ideology pervades the whole culture limits the possibility of emancipation, limits even the perception of the need for this liberation. Moreover, the technocratic consciousness prevents

[49]President's Commission on Law Enforcement and the Administration of Justice, *Science and Technology*, Task Force Report Prepared by the Institute for Defense Analyses (Washington, D.C.: U.S. Government Printing Office, 1967), p. 2.

[50]Richard M. Zaner, *The Way of Phenomenology: Criticism as a Philosophical Discipline* (New York: Pegasus, 1970), especially pp. 112–113, 117, 196, and 203.

[51]Herbert Marcuse, *One-Dimensional Man* (Boston: Beacon Press, 1964), p. 9.

[52]Jurgen Habermas, *Toward a Rational Society: Student Protest, Science, and Politics* (Boston: Beacon Press, 1970), pp. 81–121.

a critical theory. Our understanding about the legal order, in particular, is limited by the ideology on which the legal order itself rests. That is, the legal order is founded on the rationality of science and technology, and the dominant mode of thought in understanding that order is based on this same ideology. Little wonder that we have been unable to break out of our conventional wisdom.

It is in a critical theory that we are able to break with the ideology of the age. For built into the process of critical thinking is the ability to think negatively. This dialectical form of thought allows us to question current experience.[53] By being able to entertain an alternative, we can better understand what exists. Rather than merely looking for an objective reality, we are concerned with the negation of the established order. Through this negation we are better able to understand what we experience. Possibly only by means of this dialectic can the present be comprehended. Certainly the present cannot be surpassed until the dialectic is applied to our thought.

But more than negative thinking is required in a theory that will move us to a radical reconstruction of our lives — indeed, to revolution itself. In order to reject something we must have some idea of what things could be like. It is at this point that a critical philosophy must ultimately develop a Marxist perspective. In the Marxian notion of the authentic human being we are provided with a concrete image of the possible. Current realities are judged according to how they alienate human beings. Only in the conscious grasp of the world can we change the world. The process is a collective one, consciousness and action developed in association with others. The imagery is transcendental, to attain what is natural to us by removing that which obstructs our lives. It is in the contradiction of an oppressive existence, between what exists and what is authentically human, that we understand our reality and act to bring about a liberating existence.

To think in a Marxian fashion is to be genuinely critical, to the fullest extent of our critical resources. For most of us, however, Marxian thought has been presented in two forms: either in the liberal reactionary version, as a response to the Cold War mentality of the last twenty years, or in the orthodox realpolitik version. That we accepted these versions, and resorted to positivistic-pluralist thought, is the stark measure of our lack of critical faculties.

In contrast, what we are experiencing today is the creation of an underground Marxism.[54] In the course of developing our critical capacities, we are rediscovering and recreating a form and body of thought that finds its grounding in Marxian analysis. Marxism is the philosophy of our time that takes as its focus the oppression produced by a capitalist society. It is the one form of analysis that is historically specific and locates the problems of the age in the economic-class relations.[55]

[53]Herbert Marcuse, *Reason and Revolution* (Boston: Beacon Press, 1960), especially pp. vii–xiv and 3–29.
[54]See, for example, Karl E. Klare, "The Critique of Everyday Life, Marxism, and the New Left," *Berkeley Journal of Sociology*, 16 (1971–72), pp. 15–45.
[55]Horowitz writes in this regard: "There already exists, of course, a traditional *corpus* of Marxian theory which would logically form the starting point of any new analytical approach. But revision of the analytic tools and propositions of traditional Marxist theory is inevitable if the theory is to develop as an intellectual doctrine, and not degenerate into mere dogma. In principle, it may even

A Marxian critique provides, most importantly, a form of thought that allows us to transcend in thought and action that kind of existence.

Contrary to both liberal and orthodox interpretations, Marxism is highly creative thought, open to the interpretations of each generation. And with the changes in capitalism itself, from industrial capitalism to advanced monopoly capitalism, new and critical readings of Marx are necessary.[56] Critical thought makes possible a new understanding of Marx in each age. Which is also to say, a new understanding of Marx makes critical thought possible.

All thinking, all life, is subject to critical thought. A critical theory of criminal law, in particular, allows us to understand what has been otherwise unexamined. In a critical understanding of the true meaning of the legal order we are able to transcend the present and create an alternative existence.

Crime and the Ruling Class in America. According to liberal intelligence, the state exists to maintain order and stability in civil society. Law is regarded as a body of rules established through consensus by those who are governed, or rather by the "representatives" of the governed. Such a notion of the state and its law presents a misconception of our current reality.

An alternative position gets to the deeper meaning of the existence of the state and the legal order. Contrary to the dominant view, the state is created by that class of society that has the power to enforce its will on the rest of society; it is a political organization created out of force and coercion. It is established by those who desire to protect their material basis and have the power (because of material means) to maintain the state. The law in capitalist society gives political recognition to powerful social and economic interests.

The legal system provides the mechanism for the forceful and violent control of the rest of the population. In the course of battle, the agents of the law (police, prosecutors, judges, and so on) serve as the military force for the protection of domestic order. Hence, the state and its accompanying legal system reflect and serve the needs of the ruling class. Legal order benefits the ruling class in the course of dominating the classes that are ruled. And it may be added that the legal system prevents the dominated classes from becoming powerful. The rates of crime in any state are an indication of the extent to which the ruling class, through its machinery or criminal law, must coerce the rest of the population, thereby preventing any threats to its ability to rule and possess. The perception

---

be possible to create a theory which is Marxist in the restricted sense urged here, but which has little surface relation to the traditional Marxist categories and conclusions. Nonetheless, at this historical juncture, the traditional Marxist paradigm is the only economic paradigm which is capable of analyzing capitalism as an historically specific, class-determined social formation. As such it provides an indispensable framework for understanding the development and crisis of the present social system and, as an intellectual outlook, would occupy a prime place in any scientific institution worthy of the name." David Horowitz, "Marxism and Its Place in Economic Science," *Berkeley Journal of Sociology*, 16 (1971–72), p. 57. Also see Jean-Paul Sartre, *Search for a Method*, trans. Hazel E. Barnes (New York: Alfred A. Knopf, 1963).

[56]Paul A. Baran and Paul M. Sweezy, *Monopoly Capitalism: An Essay on the American Economic and Social Order* (New York: Monthly Review Press, 1966).

of criminal law as a coercive means in establishing domestic order for the ruling class is a basic assumption in a radical critique of crime.

The idea that American society can best be understood in terms of its class structure violates conventional knowledge. Because the liberal perspective, which benefits the ruling class, determines the prevailing view, it still comes as a surprise to many citizens that 1 percent of the population owns 40 percent of the nation's wealth. Yet the evidence now overwhelmingly supports the radical critique of American society.[57] The liberal assumption of a pluralistic American economy — with corporations as just one kind of interest group among many others — is negated by the fact that the major portion of the wealth and nearly all the power in American society are concentrated in the hands of a few large corporations. Furthermore, those who benefit from this economy make up a small cohesive group of persons related to one another in their power, wealth, and corporate connections. In addition, the pluralistic conception ignores all the manifestations of the alliance between business and government. On the evidence of radical scholarship, government and business are inseparable; government is run by and for large corporations.

A critique of the American political economy begins with the acknowledged assumption that life in the United States is determined by the capitalist mode of production. And here as in any capitalist society, a class division exists between those who rule and those who are ruled. As Ralph Miliband writes, in reference to the class structure of capitalist societies:

> The economic and political life of capitalist societies is primarily determined by the relationships, born of the capitalist mode of production, between these two classes — the class which on the one hand owns and controls, and the working class on the other. Here are still the social forces whose confrontation most powerfully shapes the social climate and the political system of advanced capitalism. In fact, the political process in these societies is mainly *about* the confrontation of these forces, and is intended to sanction the terms of the relationship between them.[58]

Although there are other classes, such as professionals, small-businessmen, office workers, and cultural workmen, some of these either within or cutting across the two major classes, it is the division between the ruling class and the subordinate class that establishes the nature of political, economic, and social life in capitalist society.

The *ruling class* in capitalist society is "that class which owns and controls the means of production and which is able, by virtue of the economic power thus conferred upon it, to use the state as its instrument for the domination of

[57]See Richard C. Edwards, Michael Reich, and Thomas E. Weisskopf, *The Capitalist System: A Radical Analysis of American Society* (Englewood Cliffs, N.J.: Prentice-Hall, 1972); Tom Christoffel, David Finkelhor, and Dan Gilbarg (eds.), *Up Against the American Myth* (New York: Holt, Rinehart and Winston, 1970).

[58]Ralph Miliband, *The State in Capitalist Society*, p. 16. This and all following excerpts from *The State in Capitalist Society* are reprinted by permission of the publishers. © 1969 by George Weidenfeld & Nicolson Ltd., London. Basic Books Inc., Publishers, New York.

society.''[59] The existence of this class in America, rooted mainly in the corporations and financial institutions of monopoly capitalism, is well documented.[60] This
is the class that makes the decisions that affect the lives of those who are subordinate to it.

It is according to the interests of the ruling class that American society is governed.
Although pluralists may suggest that there are diverse and conflicting interests
among groups in the upper class, what is ignored is that members of the ruling
class work within a common framework in the formulation of public policy. Superficially, groups within the ruling class may differ on some issues. But in general
they have common interests, and they can exclude members of the other classes
from the political process entirely.

> If powerful economic groups are geographically diffuse and often in competition
> for particular favors from the state, superficially appearing as interest groups
> rather than as a unified class, what is critical is not who wins or loses but
> what kind of socioeconomic framework they *all* wish to compete within, and
> the relationship between themselves and the rest of the society in a manner
> that defines their vital function as a class. It is this class that controls the
> major policy options and the manner in which the state applies its power.
> That they disagree on the options is less consequential than that they circumscribe
> the political universe.[61]

In contrast to pluralist theory, radical theory notes that the basic interests, in spite
of concrete differences, place the elite in a distinct ruling class.

In a radical critique of American society we are able, in addition, to get at
the objective interests that are external to the consciousness of individuals. We
are able to suggest, furthermore, normative evaluations of these interests. Pluralists,
on the other hand, are bound by the subjective interests of individuals.[62] The
critical perspective allows us to understand the actual and potential interests of
classes, of the ruling class as well as those who are ruled. What this means for
a critique of legal order is that we can break with the official, dominant ideology
which suggests the diversity of interests among numerous competing groups. We
are able to determine the interests of those who make and use law for their own
advantage.

The primary interest of the ruling class is to preserve the existing capitalist
order. In so doing, this class can protect its existential and material base. This
is accomplished ultimately by means of the legal system. Any threats to the established order can be dealt with by invoking the final weapon of the ruling class,
its legal system. Threats to American economic security abroad are dealt with
militarily; our armed forces are ready to attack any foe that attempts (as in a

---

[59]*Ibid*., p. 23. Reprinted by permission.

[60]Gabriel Kolko, *Wealth and Power in America* (New York: Frederick A. Praeger, 1962); G.
William Domhoff, *Who Rules America?* (Englewood Cliffs, N.J.: Prentice-Hall, 1967); G. William
Domhoff, *The Higher Circles: The Governing Class in America* (New York: Random House, 1970).

[61]Gabriel Kolko, *The Roots of American Foreign Policy* (Boston: Beacon Press, 1969), pp. 6–7.

[62]Isaac D. Balbus, ''The Concept of Interest in Pluralist and Marxian Analysis,'' *Politics and
Society*, 1 (February, 1970), pp. 151–177.

revolution) to upset the foreign markets of American capitalism.[63] American imperialism fosters and perpetuates the colonial status of foreign countries, securing American hegemony throughout as much of the world as possible. This has been the history of American foreign relations, dominated by the corporate interests of the ruling class.[64]

Similarly, the ruling class uses the criminal law at home to maintain domestic order; it secures its interests by preventing any challenge to its moral and economic structure. In other words, the military abroad and law enforcement at home are two sides of the same phenomenon: the preservation of the interests of the ruling class. Its response to any challenge is force and destruction. The weapons of crime control, as well as the idea and practice of law itself, are dominated by the ruling class.

From this critical perspective, then, crime is worthy of the greatest consideration. To understand crime radically is to understand the makings and workings of the American empire.

Crime Control in the Capitalist State. Awareness that the legal system does not serve society as a whole, but serves the interests of the ruling class, is the beginning of a critical understanding of law in capitalist society. The ruling class through its use of the legal system is able to preserve a domestic order that allows the dominant economic interests to be maintained and promoted. The ruling class, however, is not in direct control of the legal system but must operate through the mechanisms of the state. Therefore it is to the state that we must turn for further understanding of the nature and operation of the legal order. For the role of the state in capitalist society is to defend the interests of the ruling class, and crime control becomes a major device in this defense.

Criminologists and legal scholars generally neglect the state as a focus of inquiry. In failing to distinguish between civil society and the political organization of that society, they ignore the major fact that civil society is secured politically by the state and that a dominant economic class is able by means of the state to advance its own interests. When the state *is* admitted into a criminological or legal analysis, it is usually conceived as an impartial agency devoted to balancing and reconciling the diverse interests of competing groups in the society. This view, I am arguing, not only obscures the underlying reality of advanced capitalist society but is basically wrong in reference to the legal order, which is actually a coercive instrument.

Several basic observations must be made in a critical analysis of crime control in the capitalist state. First, we must inquire into the nature of the state, that is, into the complexity of that which we call the state. Second, we must examine the problem of how the dominant economic class relates to the state, that is, how that class becomes a ruling class and how the state governs in relation to

---

[63]David Horowitz, *Empire and Revolution: A Radical Interpretation of Contemporary History* (New York: Random House, 1969).

[64]William Appleman Williams, *The Roots of the Modern American Empire* (New York: Random House, 1969).

the ruling class. Third, we must observe the development of the state in reference to capitalist economy.

"The state," as Miliband notes, is not a thing that exists as such. "What 'the state' stands for is a number of particular institutions which, together, constitute its reality, and which interact as parts of what may be called the state system."[65] Miliband goes on to observe that the state, or state system, is made up of various elements: (1) the government, (2) the administration, (3) the military and the police, (4) the judiciary, and (5) the units of sub-central government.[66] The government of the time, and its duly empowered agents, is invested with state power and speaks in the name of the state. The administration of the state is composed of a large variety of bureaucratic bodies and departments concerned with the management of the economic, cultural, and other activities in which the state is involved. The directly coercive forces of the state, at home and abroad, are the police and the military. They form that branch of the state which is concerned with the "management of violence." The judiciary — although supposedly independent of the other branches of government — is an integral part of the state — which affects the exercise of state power. Finally, the various units of sub-central government constitute the extension of the central government. They are the administrative devices for centralized power, although some units may exercise power on their own over the lives of the populations they govern.

It is in these institutions that state power lies, and it is in these institutions that power is wielded by the persons who occupy the leading positions within each institution. Most important, these are the people who constitute the *state elite*, as distinct from those who wield power outside of state institutions.[67] Some holders of state power, members of the state elite, may also be the agents of private economic power. But when members of private economic power are not members of the state elite, how are they able to rule the state? Somehow the interests of the dominant economic class must be translated into the governing process in order for that class to be a true ruling class.

Miliband has observed the essential relation between the dominant economic class and the process of governing.

What the evidence conclusively suggests is that in terms of social origin, education and class situation, the men who have manned *all* command positions in the state system have largely, and in many cases overwhelmingly, been drawn from the world of business and property, or from the professional middle classes. Here as in every other field, men and women born into the subordinate classes, which form of course the vast majority of the population, have fared very poorly — and not only, it must be stressed, in those parts of the state system, such as administration, the military and the judiciary, which depend on appointment, but also in those parts of it which are exposed or which appear to be exposed to the vagaries of universal suffrage and the fortunes of competitive politics. In an epoch when so much is made of democ-

[65]Miliband, *The State in Capitalist Society*, p. 49. Reprinted by permission.
[66]*Ibid.*, pp. 49–55. Reprinted by permission.
[67]*Ibid.*, p. 54. Reprinted by permission.

racy, equality, social mobility, classlessness and the rest, it has remained a basic fact of life in advanced capitalist countries that the vast majority of men and women in these countries has been governed, represented, administered, judged, and commanded in war by people drawn from other, economically and socially superior and relatively distant classes.[68]

The dominant economic class is thus the ruling class in capitalist societies. Viewed historically, the capitalist state is the natural product of a society divided by economic classes. Only with the emergence of a division of labor based on the exploitation of one class by another, and with the breakup of communal society, was there a need for the state. The new ruling class created the state as a means for coercing the rest of the population into economic and political submission. That the American state was termed "democratic" does not alter its actual purpose.

Hence, the state, as Engels observed in his study of its origins, has not existed in all societies. There have been societies which have had no notion of state power. Only with a particular kind of economic development, with economic divisions, did the state become necessary. The new stage of development, Engels observes, called for the creation of the state:

Only one thing was wanting: an institution which not only secured the newly acquired riches of individuals against the communistic traditions of the gentile order, which not only sanctified the private property formerly so little valued, and declared this sanctification to be the highest purpose of all human society; but an institution which set the seal of general social recognition on each new method of acquiring property and thus amassing wealth at continually increasing speed; an institution which perpetuated, not only this growing cleavage of society into classes, but also the right of the possessing class to exploit the non-possessing, and the rule of the former over the latter.

And this institution came. The *state* was invented.[69]

And the state, rather than appearing as a third party in the conflict between classes, arose to protect and promote the interests of the dominant economic class, the class that owns and controls the means of production. The state continues as a device for holding down the exploited class, the class that labors, for the benefit of the dominant class. Modern civilization, as epitomized by capitalist societies, is founded on the exploitation of one class by another, and the state secures this arrangement.

Law became the ultimate means by which the state secures the interests of the ruling class. Laws institutionalize and legitimize the existing property relations. A legal system, a public force, is established: "This public force exists in every state; it consists not merely of armed men, but also of material appendages, prisons and coercive institutions of all kinds, of which gentile society knew nothing. It may be very insignificant, practically negligible, in societies with still undeveloped class antagonisms and living in remote areas, as at times and in

[68]*Ibid.*, pp. 66–67. Reprinted by permission.
[69]Frederick Engels, *The Origin of the Family, Private Property, and the State* (New York: International Publishers, 1942), p. 97.

places in the United States of America. But it becomes stronger in proportion as the class antagonisms within the state become sharper and as adjoining states grow larger and more populous."[70]

It is through the legal system, then, that the state explicitly and forcefully protects the interests of the capitalist ruling class. Crime control becomes the coercive means of checking threats to the existing social and economic arrangements. The state defines its welfare in terms of the general well-being of the capitalist economy.

Demystification of Crime and Justice in America. The purpose of a critical understanding of criminal law is to expose the meaning of crime and justice in America. The false reality by which we live, the one that serves the established system, must be understood. To demystify crime and justice in America is the goal of a critical theory of criminal law.

The above critical discussion of crime and justice in America can be summarized in the following statements.[71] The critical theory of criminal law states that:

1. American society is based on an advanced capitalist economy.
2. The state is organized to serve the interests of the dominant economic class, the capitalist ruling class.
3. Criminal law is an instrument of the state and ruling class to maintain and perpetuate the existing social and economic order.
4. Crime control in capitalist society is accomplished through a variety of institutions and agencies established and administered by a governmental elite, representing ruling class interests, for the purpose of establishing domestic order.
5. The contradictions of advanced capitalism — the disjunction between existence and essence — require that the subordinate classes remain oppressed by whatever means necessary, especially through the coercion and violence of the legal system.
6. Only with the collapse of capitalist society and the creation of a new society, based on socialist principles, will there be a solution to the crime problem.

As capitalist society is further threatened by its own contradictions, criminal law is increasingly used in the attempt to maintain domestic order. The underclass, the class that must remain oppressed for the triumph of the dominant economic class, will continue to be the object of criminal law as long as the dominant class seeks to perpetuate itself. To remove the oppression, to eliminate the need for further revolt, would necessarily mean the end of the ruling class and its capitalist economy. The crimes of those who profit from the capitalist system,

---

[70]*Ibid.*, p. 156.

[71]Though I am presenting the beginning of a general theory of criminal law, there remains much to be done in further theoretical development. On the problems facing American sociologists in developing Marxist theory, see Richard Flacks, "Towards a Socialist Sociology: Some Proposals for Work in the Coming Period," *The Insurgent Sociologist*, 2 (Spring, 1972), pp. 18–27.

particularly the crimes of criminal syndicates and the crimes committed by American corporations in the course of business operations, are the product of a capitalist society. Whether criminal law and law enforcement are directed against the underclass or against those who profit from the existing economy, the purpose of the capitalist legal system is to protect and strengthen capitalism.[72]

Moreover, criminal law continues to secure the colonial status of those who are oppressed in the social and economic order of the United States. The events of the last few years relating to crime, including both "disruption" and repression, can only be understood as part of the crisis of the American system. The oppression within the United States cannot be separated from American imperialism abroad. The war waged against people abroad is part of the same war waged against the oppressed at home.[73] The ruling class, through its control of the state, must resort to a worldwide counterrevolution. A counter-insurgency program is carried out — through the CIA abroad and the FBI, the Law Enforcement Assistance Administration (LEAA), and local police forces at home. A military war is being fought abroad, while a war on crime with its own weaponry is being fought within the United States. All of this to avoid changing the capitalist order, indeed to protect it and to promote its continuation.

The crisis in the American empire will inevitably result in revolutionary changes. The outcome, however, is far from certain. What we know is that crime will continue as long as people are oppressed by the capitalist system and as long as others profit from the capitalist system through their own crimes. And as counterrevolutionary forces continue, in response to the crisis, behavior that threatens the advanced capitalist system will be defined as criminal. The capitalist legal system serves the forces of repression.

The alternative to the contradictions of capitalism is a truly democratic society, a socialist society in which human beings no longer suffer the alienation inherent in capitalism. When there is no longer the need for one class to dominate another, when there is no longer the need for a legal system to secure the interests of a capitalist ruling class, then there will no longer be the need for crime.

Therefore, our task as students of crime is to consider the alternatives to the capitalist legal order.[74] Further study of crime and justice in America must be devoted to the contradictions of the existing system. At this advanced stage of capitalist development, law is little more than a repressive instrument of manipulation and control. We must make others aware of the current meaning of crime and justice in America. The objective is to move beyond the existing order. And this means ultimately that we are engaged in socialist revolution.

---

[72]On the relation of the various types of criminal behavior to the capitalist legal system, see Marshall B. Clinard and Richard Quinney, *Criminal Behavior Systems: A Typology*, 2nd edition (New York: Holt, Rinehart and Winston, 1973).

[73]Horowitz, *Empire and Revolution*, pp. 257–258.

[74]Socialist alternatives to the capitalist legal system are discussed in Jesse Berman, "The Cuban Popular Tribunals," *Columbia Law Review*, 69 (December, 1969), pp. 1317–1354; Michael E. Tigar, "Socialist Law and Legal Institutions," in Robert Lefcourt (ed.), *Law Against the People* (New York: Random House, 1971), pp. 327–347; José Antonio Viera-Gallo, "The Legal System and Socialism," *Wisconsin Law Review*, no. 3 (1972), pp. 754–763.

Chapter Two

THE LEGAL ORDER

Central to conventional wisdom is the belief in the necessity of the state and inevitability of law. These assumptions are so ingrained in us that we rarely, if ever, consciously think about them. Yet, the state and its legal order intimately shape the reality of our lives. Miliband has written: "More than ever before men now live in the shadow of the state. What they want to achieve, individually or in groups, now mainly depends on the state's sanction and support. . . . It is possible not to be interested in what the state does; but it is not possible to be unaffected by it. The point has acquired a new and ultimate dimension in the present epoch: if large parts of the planet should one day be laid waste in a nuclear war, it is because men, acting in the name of their state and invested with its power, will have so decided, or miscalculated."[1]

The failure to recognize the influence of the state on our lives has precluded an understanding of why the state (and the legal system) exists and the ways in which it continues to survive. An unquestioning belief in the state prevents an analysis that would allow us to view the state, as Marx did, as the coercive instrument of the economically dominant class.[2] Such an examination would raise critical questions about the state and the existing legal order.

The state and the legal order are inseparable; to understand one is to understand the other. In the first essay of this book, "The Rule of Law Versus the Order of Custom," anthropologist Stanley Diamond examines the popular assumption that the legal order of the state has

[1]Ralph Miliband, *The State in Capitalist Society*, p. 1. Reprinted by permission of the publishers.©George Weidenfield & Nicolson Ltd., London. Basic Books Inc., Publishers, New York.

[2]Karl Marx, *Selected Writings in Sociology and Social Psychology*, trans. T. B. Bottomore (New York: McGraw-Hill, 1964), pp. 222–223.

progressed naturally from the customary patterns of prepolitical societies. His observation is that the relation between custom and law is one of contradiction rather than continuity. Law, instead of being an embodiment of custom, is symptomatic of the emergence of the state. Diamond writes: "Law is the instrument of civilization, of political society sanctioned by organized force, presumably above society at large, and buttressing a new set of social interests. Law and custom both involve the regulation of behavior but their characters are entirely distinct; no evolutionary balance has been struck between developing law and custom, whether traditional or emergent." Law is, and continues to serve as, the device to enforce the interests of the state and its dominant class.

Law is thus a mark of "civilization." A legal order was necessary only when the state broke down communal solidarity and divided the group into conflicting factions.[3] In the early states, as Diamond notes, crimes were invented to serve the needs of the state; that is, legal sanctions were needed to protect the new interests of the emerging state. Rather than healing any breaches of custom, the laws protected the sovereign. In other words, as Diamond observes, crime and the laws which served it were possible only with the emergence of the state. The state necessarily broke up customary patterns, in the interest of economic and political dominance, and established a legal system to enforce its sovereignty.

With this understanding of the legal order, we begin to see that law is the antonym rather than the synonym of order. Law has its origins in the pathology of social relations brought about by the state itself. Diamond writes: "Law arises in the breach of a prior customary order and increases in force with the conflicts that divide political societies internally and among themselves. Law *and* order is the historical illusion; law versus order is the historical reality." Diamond concludes that modern Western civilization, with its state and legal order, is the one least likely to serve as a guide for building a human society.

The legal order of the state necessarily uses coercive and violent force. The state is based on repressive organized force, and law serves to implement this force. So that the state may control the conflicts created by its own divisiveness, the force of law must be used to prevent any threats to the established order. That repression is to be expected, that it is basic to the modern state, is the observation contained in the article by Alan Wolfe, "Political Repression and the Liberal Democratic State." In an extension of Marxist theory, Wolfe contends that "repression is one of a number of reproductive mechanisms which capitalism requires in order to maintain itself as a system." And state violence is not the only reproductive mechanism. Democratic societies, in fact, engage in a continuous process of "consciousness-manipulation," creating a belief system that indoctrinates the citizens into accepting as their own the interests of the state and its ruling

[3]This is also observed in Frederick Engels, *The Origin of the Family, Private Property, and the State* (New York: International Publishers, 1942).

class. Violent repression, nevertheless, stands ready whenever people fail to be bound by the ideology of the state. Repression is therefore an essential aspect of state rule, not something alien to it.

In the remainder of the essay, Wolfe elaborates on the use of repressive force in the modern liberal state. He concludes by noting that repression by the state is most likely a sign of its weakness, rather than its strength. "Those who are disillusioned by the amount of state violence in the United States are those who had illusions about the democratic state in the first place. If we understand that repression is used out of desperation, we are one step closer to understanding how a non-repressive society can be built."

That the modern state is responding to its own weaknesses is the message of John H. Schaar's important essay on "Legitimacy in the Modern State." In focusing on the idea of legitimate authority, Schaar examines the decline of the moral rule of the modern state. The author shows us that "law and order" is the basic political question of our day. Both the revolts of the people and the repressive measures of the state can be understood as stemming from the decline in legitimate authority.

Schaar states that "the crisis of legitimacy is a function of some of the basic, defining orientations of modernity itself; specifically, rationality, the cult of efficiency and power, ethical relativism, and equalitarianism." He argues that "the modern mind, having now reached nearly full development, is turning back upon itself and undermining the very principles that once sustained order and obedience in the modern state." Moreover, social science has "failed to appreciate the precariousness of legitimate authority in the modern states because it is largely a product of the same phenomena it seeks to describe and therefore suffers the blindness of the eye examining itself." Hence, in our popular mind as well as in scientific work, we have failed to come to grips with the problems of the age. By examining the crisis in legitimate authority, Schaar gives us a critical understanding of our contemporary experiences.

No longer can people accept the beliefs and principles that once granted authority to the state. The older epistemology of unexamined allegiance to the state no longer prevails. We now base allegiance on will rather than on blind acceptance of existing power. And on moral grounds, as well, the modern state is challenged. The social and political world has become "unfrozen"; the existing order is no longer granted authority merely because it exists.

The modern state is left with an authority that can be obtained only by means of bureaucratic coordination, manipulation, and legal control. Yet, as Schaar writes, "such mechanisms of control are inherently vulnerable and in the long run unworkable, incapable of responding to men's needs for understanding and counsel on the basic, inescapable question of human existence." He adds, "So long as men remain what we have hitherto called human, they will require of power which strives to become authority that it respond to those questions in ways that have meaning for men." "Law and order" in its various manifestations may be the response of the state. But the underlying crisis of legitimacy in the modern state remains a crisis that marks the movement toward a new age.

The legal order is seen in this chapter as a system that is fostered and perpetuated in legal scholarship and in the official reality of those who govern. Ultimately law serves the dominant economic class in capitalist society. To critically understand the existing legal order and to work toward an authentic existence are the objectives of this discussion. A future without a state and without a legal order as we know it now is a distinct possibility. An existence free of the tyranny of the modern capitalist state is emerging. Such examination of the legal order leads us to critical questions about our existence — and toward a life of which we are capable as human beings.

1. Stanley Diamond

The Rule of Law Versus the Order of Custom

Creon: Knowest thou the edict has forbidden this?
Antigone: I knew it well. Why not? It was proclaimed.
Creon: But thou didst dare to violate the law?
Antigone: It was not God above who framed that law,
Nor justice, whispering from the underworld,
Nor deemed I thy decrees were of such force
As to o'er ride the sanctities of heaven;
Which are not of today or yesterday.
From whom — whence they first issued, no one knows.
I was not like to scant their holy rites
And brave the even justice of the gods
For fear of someone's edict.

Sophocles, *Antigone*

The lowest police employee of the civilized state has more "authority" than all the organs of gentilism combined. But the mightiest prince and the greatest statesman or general of civilization may look with envy on the spontaneous

Reprinted by permission of the author from *Social Research*, 38 (Spring 1971), pp. 42–72. Copyright © 1971 by Stanley Diamond.

and undisputed esteem that was the privilege of the least gentile sachem. The one stands in the middle of society, the other is forced to assume a position outside and above it.

Frederick Engels, *Origin of the*
Family, Private Property and the State

There's too much due process of law. The electric chair is a cheap crime deterrent to show these criminal elements that law and order is going to triumph.

Detective Sergeant John Heffernan,
current vice-president of the International
Conference of Police Associations and head of
the New Jersey State Police Benevolent Association

I

We must distinguish the rule of law from the authority of custom. In a recent effort to do so (which I shall critically examine because it is so typical), Paul Bohannan, under the *imprimatur* of the *International Encyclopedia of the Social Sciences*,[1] contends that laws result from "double" institutionalization. He means by this no more than the lending of a specific force, a cutting edge, to the functioning of "customary" institutions: marriage, the family, religion. But, he tells us, the laws so emerging assume a character and dynamic of their own. They form a structured, legal dimension of society; they do not merely reflect, but interact with given institutions. Therefore, Bohannan is led to maintain that laws are typically out of phase with society and it is this process which is both a symptom and cause of social change. The laws of marriage, to illustrate Bohannan's argument with the sort of concrete example his definition lacks, are not synonymous with the institution of marriage. They reinforce certain rights and obligations while neglecting others. Moreover, they subject partners defined as truant to intervention by an external, impersonal agency whose decisions are sanctioned by the power of the police.

Bohannan's sociological construction does have the virtue of denying the primacy of the legal order, and of implying that law is generic to unstable (or progressive) societies, but it is more or less typical of abstract efforts to define the eternal essence of the law and it begs the significant questions. Law has no such essence but a definable historical nature.

Thus if we inquire into the structure of the contemporary institutions which, according to Bohannan, stand in a primary relation to the law, we find that their customary content has drastically diminished. Paul Radin made the point as follows: "A custom is, in no sense, a part of our properly functioning culture. It belongs definitely to the past. At best, it is moribund. But customs are an integral part of the life of primitive peoples. There is no compulsive submission to them. They are not followed because the weight of tradition overwhelms a man . . . a custom

---

[1]Paul Bohannan, "Law," *International Encyclopedia of the Social Sciences* (New York, 1968), pp. 73–78.

is obeyed there because it is intimately intertwined with a vast living network of interrelations, arranged in a meticulous and ordered manner.''[2] And, ''What is significant in this connection,'' as J. G. Peristiany indicates, ''is not that common values should exist, but that they should be expressed although no common political organization corresponds to them.''[3]

No contemporary institution functions with the kind of autonomy that permits us to postulate a significant dialectic between law and custom. We live in a law-ridden society; law has cannibalized the institutions which it presumably reinforces or with which it interacts.

Accordingly, morality continues to be reduced to or confused with legality. In civil society we are encouraged to assume that legal behavior is the measure of moral behavior, and it is a matter of some interest that a former Chief Justice of the Supreme Court proposed, with the best of intentions, that a federal agency be established in order to advise government employees and those doing business with the government concerning the legal propriety of their behavior. Any conflict of interest not legally enjoined would thus tend to become socially or morally acceptable; morality becomes a technical question. Efforts to legislate conscience by an external political power are the antithesis of custom: customary behavior comprises precisely those aspects of social behavior which are traditional, moral, and religious, which are, in short, conventional and non-legal. Put another way, custom *is* social morality.[4] The relation between custom and law is, basically, one of contradiction, not continuity.

The customary and the legal orders are historically, not logically related. They touch coincidentally; one does not imply the other. Custom, as most anthropologists agree, is characteristic of primitive society, and laws of civilization. Robert Redfield's dichotomy between the primitive ''moral'' order and the civilized ''legal'' or ''technical'' order remains a classic statement of the case.

''The dispute,'' writes William Seagle, ''whether primitive societies have law or custom, is not merely a dispute over words. Only confusion can result from treating them as interchangeable phenomena. If custom is spontaneous and automatic, law is the product of organized force. Reciprocity is in force in civilized communities too but at least nobody confuses social with formal legal relationships.''[5] Parenthetically, one should note that students of primitive society who use the term ''customary law'' blur the issue semantically, but nonetheless recognize the distinction.

---

[2]Paul Radin, *The World of Primitive Man*, (New York, 1953), p. 223.

[3]J. G. Peristiany, *The Institutions of Primitive Society*, Glencoe, Illinois, 1956, p. 45.

In the words of V. C. Uchendu, writing about the Ibo: ''. . . the use of force is minimal or absent; . . . there are leaders rather than rulers, and . . . cohesion is achieved by rules rather than by laws and by consensus rather than by dictation. In general, the Igbo have not achieved any political structure which can be called a federation, a confederacy, or a state.'' V. C. Uchendu, *The Igbo of Southeast Nigeria*, N.Y. 1965, p. 46.

[4]Sydney P. Simpson and Julius Stone, *Law and Society in Evolution*, Book I, Saint Paul, 1942, p. 2.

[5]William Seagle, *The History of Law, Tudor*, 1946, p. 35.

It is this overall legalization of behavior in modern society which Bohannan fails to interpret. In fascist Germany, for example, laws flourished as never before. By 1941, more edicts had been proclaimed than in all the years of the Republic and the Third Reich. At the same time, ignorance of the law inevitably increased. In a sense, the very force of the law depends upon ignorance of its specifications, which is hardly recognized as a mitigating circumstance. As Seagle states, law is not definite and certain while custom is vague and uncertain. Rather, the converse holds. Customary rules must be clearly known; they are not sanctioned by organized political force, hence serious disputes about the nature of custom would destroy the integrity of society. But laws may always be invented, and stand a good chance of being enforced: "Thus, the sanction is far more important than the rule in the legal system . . . but the tendency is to minimize the sanction and to admire the rule."[6]

In fascist Germany, customs did not become laws through a process of "double institutionalization." Rather, repressive laws, conjured up in the interests of the Nazi Party and its supporters, cannibalized the institutions of German society. Even the residual customary authority of the family was assaulted: children were encouraged to become police informers, upholding the laws against their kin. "The absolute reign of law has often been synonymous with the absolute reign of lawlessness."[7]

Certainly, Germany under Hitler was a changing society, if hardly a progressive one, but it was a special case of the general process in civilization through which the organs of the state have become increasingly irresistible. It will be recalled that Bohannan takes the domination of law over custom to be symptomatic of changing societies. But the historical inadequacy of his argument lies exactly here: he does not intimate the overall direction of that change and therefore fails to clarify the actual relation between custom and law. Accordingly, the notion that social change is a function of the law, and vice versa, implies a dialectic that is out of phase with historical reality.

Plato, it deserves note, understood this well enough when he conceived the problem of civilization as primarily one of injustice, which he did not scamp by legalistic definition. His remedy was the thorough restructuring of society. Whether we admire his utopia or not, The Republic testifies to Plato's recognition that laws follow social change and reflect prevailing social relationships, but are the cause of neither. Curiously, this view of the relationship between law and society accords with the Marxist perspective on the history of culture. Customary societies are said to precede legal societies, an idea which, semantics aside, most students of historical jurisprudence would accept. But Marxists envision the future as being without laws as we know them, as involving a return to custom, so to speak, on a higher level, since the repressive, punitive and profiteering functions of law will become superfluous. Conflicts of economic and political interest will be resolved through the equitable reordering of institutions. Law, for the Marxists

[6]Ibid., pp. 19–20.
[7]Ibid.

and most classical students of historical jurisprudence, is the cutting edge of the state — but the former, insisting on both a historical and normative view of man, define the state as the instrument of the ruling class, anticipating its dissolution with the abolition of classes and the common ownership of the basic means of production. Whatever our view of the ultimate Marxist dynamic, law is clearly inseparable from the state. Sir Henry Maine equates the history of individual property with that of civilization: "Nobody is at liberty to attack several property and to say at the same time that he values civilization. The history of the two cannot be disentangled. Civilization is nothing more than the name for the . . . order . . . dissolved but perpetually re-constituting itself under a vast variety of solvent influences, of which infinitely the most powerful have been those which have, slowly, and in some parts of the world much less perfectly than others, substituted several property for collective ownership."[8] In the words of Jeremy Bentham, "Property and law are born together and die together."

Law, thus, is symptomatic of the emergence of the state; the legal sanction is not simply the cutting edge of institutions at all times and in all places. The "double institutionalization" to which Bohannan refers needs redefinition. Where it does occur, it is an historical process of unusual complexity and cannot be defined as the simple passage of custom into law. It occurs, as we shall see, in several modes. Custom — spontaneous, traditional, personal, commonly known, corporate, relatively unchanging — is the modality of primitive society; law is the instrument of civilization, of political society sanctioned by organized force, presumably above society at large, and buttressing a new set of social interests. Law and custom both involve the regulation of behavior but their characters are entirely distinct; no evolutionary balance has been struck between developing law and custom, whether traditional or emergent.

II

The simple dichotomy between primitive society and civilization does not illustrate the passage from the customary to the legal order. The most critical and revealing period in the evolution of law is that of *archaic societies*, the local segments of which are the cultures most often studied by anthropologists. More precisely, the earlier phases of these societies, which I call proto-states, represent a transition from the primitive kinship-based communities to the class-structured polity. In such polities, law and custom exist side by side; this gives us the opportunity to examine their connections, distinctions, and differential relationship to the society at large. The customary behavior typical of the local groups — joint families, clans, villages — maintains most of its force; the Vietnamese, for example, still say: "The customs of the village are stronger than the law of the emperor." Simultaneously, the civil power, comprising bureaucracy and sovereign, the dominant emerging class, issues a series of edicts that have the double purpose of confiscating "surplus" goods and labor for the support of those not directly engaged

[8]Henry Maine, *Village Communities and Miscellanies*, New York, 1889, p. 230.

in production while attempting to deflect the loyalties of the local groups to the center.

These archaic societies are the great historical watershed; it is here that Sir Henry Maine and Paul Vinogradoff located the passage from status to contract, from the kinship to the territorial principle, from extended familial controls to public law. One need not be concerned with the important distinctions among archaic societies, or with the precise language or emphases of those scholars who have recognized their centrality for our understanding of the law. The significant point is that they are transitional. Particularly in their early phase they are the agencies that transmute customary forms of order into legal sanction. Here we find a form of "double institutionalization" functioning explicitly; we can witness, so to speak, what appears to be the *emergence* of a custom, in defense of the kinship principle against the assault of the state, and the subsequent shift of the customary function into its own opposite as a legal function. The following example from the archaic proto-state of Dahomey, prior to the French conquest in 1892, will make this process clear.

Traditionally, in Dahomey each person was said to have three "best" friends, in descending order of intimacy and importance. This transitional institution, a transfiguration of kin connections, of the same species as blood brotherhood, reinforced the extended family structure, which continued to exist in the early state, but was being thrown into question as a result of the political and economic demands made by the emerging civil power. So, for example, the best friend of a joint-family patriarch would serve as his testator, and, upon the latter's decease, name his successor to the assembled family. It seems that the ordinary convention of succession no longer sufficed to secure the family's integrity, since the central authority was mustering family heads as indirect rulers. In this instance, the institution of friendship was assimilated to the form and purpose of customary behavior. On the other hand, the best friend of a man charged with a civil "crime" could be seized by the king's police in his stead. However, these traditional friendships were so socially critical, so deeply held that the person charged, whether or not he had actually committed a civil breach, would typically turn himself in rather than implicate a friend in his punishment. The custom of friendship was thus given a legal edge and converted by the civil power into a means of enforcing its will. This example of "double institutionalization" has the virtue of explicitly revealing the contradiction between law and custom; but there are others in which law appears as a *reinforcement* of customary procedure.

In eleventh century Russia, for instance, Article 1 of the codified law states, "If a man kills a man . . . the brother is to avenge his brother; the son, his father; or the father, his son; and the son of the brother [of the murdered man] or the son of his sister, their respective uncle. If there is no avenger [the murderer] pays 40 grivna wergeld. . . ."[9]

Similarly, circa A.D. 700, the law of the Visigoths states, "Whoever shall have

---

[9]George Vernadsky, *Medieval Russian Laws*, 1947, pp. 26–27.

killed a man, whether he committed a homicide intending to or not intending to [*volens aut nolens*] . . . let him be handed over into the potestas of the parents or next of kin of the deceased. . . ."[10] In these instances, a custom has been codified by an external agency, thus assuming legal force with *its punitive character sharpened*. Such confirmation is both the *intimation* of legal control and the antecedent of institutional change beyond the wish or conception of the family. "Whatever princes do, they seem to command," or, as Sir Henry Maine put it, "What the sovereign permits, he commands."[11] Maine had specifically in mind "the Sikh despot who permitted heads of households and village elders to prescribe rules, therefore these rules became his command and true laws, which are the solvent of local and domestic usage." Simpson and Stone explain this apparent reinforcement of custom by the civil power as follows: "Turning then to the role of law in the emergent political society . . . it is true that political institutions, independent of the kin and the supernatural, had risen to power; yet these institutions were young, weak and untried. Their encroachment on the old allegiance was perforce wary and hesitating. Social cohesion still seemed based on nonpolitical elements, and these elements were therefore protected. It is this society which Pound has perceived and expressed when he says that the end of law envisaged in his period of strict law, is the maintenance of the social *status quo*. In modern terminology this means the primacy of the interest in the maintenance of antecedent social institutions." [italics added][12]

This sort of confirmation, which betrays the structural opportunism of the early civil power, inheres in the limitations of sovereignty, and is further apparent in the sovereign's relation to the communally held clan or joint-family land. In Dahomey, for example, where the king was said to "own" all property, including land, it is plain that such ownership was a legal fiction and had the effect of validating the pre-existent joint-family tradition. That is, the king "permitted" the joint families, by virtue of his fictional ownership, to expand into new lands and continue transmitting their property intact, generation after generation. The civil power could not rent, alienate or sell joint-family property, nor could any member of a joint family do so.[13] This is borne out by A. I. Richards, who informs us that "in Northern Rhodesia [Zambia] the statement that 'all the land is mine' does not mean that the ruler has the right to take any piece of land he chooses for his own use . . . I have never heard of a case where a chief took land that had already been occupied by a commoner."[14] The same point is made by Rattray on the Ashanti[15] and Mair on the Baganda,[16] among others. Civil validation, then, expresses the intention but not yet the reality of state control.

[10]Quoted by Simpson and Stone, *op. cit.*, p. 78.
[11]Henry Maine, *Early History of Institutions*, 1897, p. 383.
[12]Simpson and Stone, *op. cit.*, p. 177.
[13]Stanely Diamond, *Dahomey, a Proto-state in West Africa*, Ann Arbor, Microfilm, 1951, p. 109.
[14]Quoted by Max Gluckman, "Studies in African Land Tenure," *African Studies*, Vol. III, 1944, pp. 14–21.
[15]R. S. Rattray, *Ashanti, Law and Constitution*, London, 1929.
[16]L. P. Mair, "Baganda Land Tenure," *Africa*, Vol. VI, 1933.

We might more realistically formulate Maine's epigram as: What he cannot command, the sovereign permits.

Ultimately, local groups have maintained their autonomy when their traditional economies were indispensable to the functioning of the entire society. They could be hedged around by restrictions, harassed by law, or, as we have seen, they could be "legally" confirmed in their customary usage; but, so long as the central power depended on them for support, in the absence of any alternative mode or source of production, their integrity could be substantially preserved. This certainly seems the case during the early phases of state organization in the classic nuclear areas (e.g., Egypt, Babylonia, Northern India) before the introduction of large-scale irrigation and analogous public works, and it was true of pre-colonial Africa. But in all archaic societies, whether incipient, as in sub-Saharan Africa, florescent, as in the ancient peasant societies of the Middle East or China, or in cognate contemporary societies which probably still embrace most of the world's population, the extensive kin unit was more functional, in spite of varying degrees of autonomy, than the family in commercial and industrial civilization.

As the state develops, according to Maine, "the individual is steadily substituted for the family as the unit of which civil laws take account."[17] And in Jhering's words, "The progress of law consists in the destruction of every natural tie, in a continued process of separation and isolation."[18] That is to say, the family increasingly becomes a reflex of society at large. Hence, one might add, the legal stipulation that spouses may not testify against each other appears as one of the last formal acknowledgements of familial integrity, and the exception that proves the historical case. Clearly, the nuclear family in contemporary urban civilization, although bound by legal obligations, has minimal autonomy; obviously, the means of education, subsistence and self-defense are outside the family's competence. It is in this sense that, given the absence of mediating institutions having a clearly defined independent authority, the historical tendency of all state structures vis-à-vis the individual may be designated as totalitarian. Indeed, the state *creates* the disaffiliated individual whose bearings thus become bureaucratic or collective; the juridical "person," who may even be a corporation doing business, is merely the legal reflection of a social process. If "totalization" is *the* state process, totalitarianism cannot be confined to a particular political ideology but is, so to speak, *the* ideology, explicit or not, of political society.

This étatist tendency has its origins in archaic society; we can observe it with unusual clarity in the proto-states of sub-Saharan Africa. In East Africa, pastoralists, competing for land, and in West Africa, militaristic clans, catalyzed by the Arab, and, later, the European trade, notably in slaves, conquered horticulturalists, thereby providing the major occasions for the growth of civil power. Since the basic means of exploiting the environment in these polities remained substantially unchanged, and, to some extent, survived under colonialism, we can reconstruct through chronicles extending back for centuries and by means of contemporary field work, the

[17]Henry Maine, *Ancient Law*, p. 140.
[18]R. von Jhering, *Geist des Romischen Recht*, 1866, Vol. II, p. 31.

structure of early state controls, which evolved in the absence of writing and the systematic codification of law. The absence of writing *should* relieve the scholar from that dependence on official records that has so thoroughly shaped our sense of European history; unfortunately, rubbing shoulders with the upper class in a non-literate state creates equivalent distortions.

In such societies, Rattray tells us, referring to Ashanti, "the small state was ever confronted with the kindred organization which was always insidiously under-mining its authority by placing certain persons outside its jurisdiction. It could only hold its own, therefore, by throwing out an ever-widening circle to embrace those loyalties which were lost to it owing to the workings of the old tribal organization which has survived everywhere."[19] Further, "the old family, clan and tribal organization survived in the new regime which was ever striving to make territorial considerations, and not the incidence of kinship, the basis of state control." Rattray concludes that "corporate responsibility for every act was an established principle which survived even the advent of a powerful central public authority as the administration of public justice."[20] Nadel asserts, concerning the Islamized Nupe of the Nigerian Middle Belt, that what emerged from his analysis was "a much more subtle development and a deeper kind of antagonism [than interstate warfare], namely, the almost eternal antagonism of developed State versus that raw material of the Community which, always and everywhere, must form the nourishing soil from which alone the state can grow."[21] And Engels refers to the "irreconcilable opposition of gentile society to the state."[22]

I have documented this conflict in detail in a study of the Dahomean proto-state. There, as elsewhere, it is apparent that the contradictory transition from customs to specified laws, "double institutionalization," if you will, *is by no means the major source of law*. Whether the law arises latently in "confirmation" of previous usage, or through the transformation of some aspect of custom, which the law itself may have, in the first instance, provoked, as in the example of the "best friend," neither circumstance brings us to the heart of the matter. For we learn by studying intermediate societies that the laws so typical of them are *unprecedented*; they do not emerge through a process of "double institutionalization," however defined. They arise in opposition to the customary order of the antecedent kin or kin-equivalent groups; they represent a new set of social goals pursued by a new and unanticipated power in society. These goals can be reduced to a single complex imperative: the imposition of the inter-related census-tax-conscription system. The territorial thrust of the early state, along with its vertical social entrenchment, demanded conscription of labor, the mustering of an army, the levying of taxes and tribute, the maintenance of a bureaucracy, and the assessment of the extent, location, and numbers of the population being subject. *These were the major direct or indirect occasions for the development of civil law.*

[19]Rattray, *op. cit.*, p. 80.
[20]*Ibid.*, p. 286.
[21]S. F. Nadel, "Nupe State and Community," *Africa*, Vol. VIII, p. 303.
[22]Engels, p. 133 (see N. 58).

The primary purpose of a census is indicative. Census figures (in non-literate societies, pebbles, for example would be used as counters) provided the basis on which taxes were apportioned among the conquered districts and tribute in labor exacted from the constituent kin units. The census was also essential for conscripting men into the army. This information was considered so important in Dahomey that each new king, upon his enstoolment, was escorted by his two leading ministers to a special hut in the royal compound and there admonished as he knelt: "Young man, all your life you have heard Dahomey, Dahomey, but you have never until today seen the true Dahomey, for Dahomey is its people and here they are."[23]

With this declaration, the two elders pointed to sacks of pebbles, each pebble representing a person, each sack representing a sex or age group. The young king was then told that he must never allow the contents of the sacks to diminish and that every year the pebbles would be counted to see whether their number had increased or declined. He was then given an old gun (in earlier times a hoe handle) and advised, "Fight with this. But take care that you are not vanquished."[24]

The census figures represented the potential power of the state and were carefully guarded; perhaps they were the first state secret. The act and intent of the census turned persons into ciphers, abstractions in civil perspective; people did all they could to avoid being counted. Suspicion persists; even in the United States the authorities during the period of census taking find it necessary to assert that census information will not be used to tax or otherwise penalize the individual, and, in fact, to do so is said to be against the law.

The double meanings of certain critical terms in common English use — "custom," "duty," and "court," reveal this conflict between local usage and the census-tax-conscription system of the early state. We have been speaking of custom as traditional or conventional non-legal behavior, but custom also refers to a tax routinely payable to the state for the transportation of goods across territorial borders. All such taxes are clearly defined legal impositions, frequently honored in the breach, and they do not have the traditional command of custom. In Dahomey, the "Grand Customs" held at the unveiling of a new king, presumably in honor of his ancestors, were the occasion for the payment of taxes, the large-scale sentencing and sacrifice of criminals, and the prosecution of other state business. Camus has Caligula describe such an event in a passage that could have been extrapolated from a Dahomean chronicle: "It's only the Treasury that counts. And living is the opposite of loving . . . and I invite you to the most gorgeous of shows, a sight for gods to gloat on, a whole world called to judgment. But for that I must have a crowd — spectators, victims, criminals, hundreds and thousands of them. Let the accused come forward. I want my criminals, and they are all criminals. Bring in the condemned men. I must have my public. Judges, witnesses, accused — all sentenced to death without a hearing. Yes, Ceasonia, I'll show them something they've never seen before, the one free man in the Roman

[23]M. J. Herskowitz, *Dahomey, an Ancient West African Kingdom*, New York, 1938, p. 73.
[24]*Ibid.*

Empire."[25] Along with the annual "customs," the "Grand Customs" paralleled the form of local ceremonies, but the substance had entirely changed. Fiscal or legal coercion, political imposition were not the purpose of these ancestral ceremonies which ritually re-enacted reciprocal bonds. The "customs" of the sovereign were laws, the ceremonies of the kin groups were customs.

Similarly, the term "duty" implies a moral obligation on the one hand and a tax on the other. Naturally, we assume that it is the duty of citizens to pay taxes: the paradox inherent in the term becomes more obvious, as one might imagine, as we examine archaic civilizations.

The term "court" is analogously ambivalent. On the one hand, it refers to the residence or entourage of the sovereign; on the other, to a place where civil justice is dispensed, but at their root the functions fuse. The prototypical juridical institution was, in fact, the court of the sovereign where legislation was instituted, for which no precedent or formal analogue existed on the local level. Peristiany, speaking of the Kipsigis, sharpens the latter point: "One of the most significant differences between the . . . council of elders and a Europpean judicature is to be found in the relation between officer and office. The Council elders do not hold their office from a higher authority. They are not appointed. . . ."[26] As Seagle, among others, indicates, the court is the first, most important, and perhaps the last legal artifact. In Montaigne's words, "France takes as its rule the rule of the court."[27] Put another way, the court is a specialized legal structure and it embraces all those particular and determinate legal bodies which are peculiar to civilization.

Clearly, the function of the court was not primarily the establishment of order. In primitive societies, as in the traditional sectors of proto-states, there already existed built-in mechanisms for the resolution of conflict. Generally speaking, as Max Gluckman, among others, has shown, in such societies conflicts generated by the ordinary functioning of social institutions were resolved as part of the customary ritual cycle integral to the institutions themselves.

With regard to more specific breaches, we recall Rattray's observation on the Ashanti: "Corporate responsibility for every act was an established principle which survived even the advent of . . . the administration of public justice." That is to say the kin unit was the juridical unit, just as it was the economic and social unit. Furthermore, "Causes which give rise to the greater part of present 'civil' actions were practically nonexistent. Inheritance, ownership of moveable and non-moveable property, status of individuals, rules of behavior and morality were matters

[25]Albert Camus, *Caligula and Three Other Plays*, Stuart Gilbert (trans.), New York, 1958, p. 17.

[26]Peristiany, *op. cit.*, p. 42.
The contrast is well remarked by V. C. Uchendu: "Under a constitution like that of the Igbo, which does not provide for a specialized court, judicial matters are ad hoc affairs. The injured party takes the initiative. He may appeal to the head of the compound of the offender or to a body of arbitrators. . . . Since the arbitrators have no means of enforcing their decision, for it to be respected it must be acceptable to both parties." Uchendu, *op. cit.*, p. 43.

[27]Montaigne, (see N. 56 for full citation) p. 197.

inevitably settled by the customary law, with which everyone was familiar from childhood, and litigation regarding such matters was . . . almost inconceivable. Individual contract, moreover, from the very nature of the community with which we are concerned, was also unknown, thus removing another possible, fruitful source of litigation."[28]

The primary purpose of the historically emerging court, the sovereign's entourage and habitation, was to govern. The distinguished British jurist Sir John Salmond has observed, "Law is secondary and unessential. . . . The administration of justice is perfectly possible without law at all."[29] And Sir William Markby writes, "Tribunals can act entirely without law."[30] The perhaps unintended point here is that justice, commonly defined, is neither deducible from the law, nor was the legislation of the court a measure of justice, but of the political thrust of the early state, and that flowed from the implementation of the census-tax-conscription system.

In the census-tax-conscription system, every conceivable occasion was utilized for the creation of law in support of bureaucracy and sovereign. We observe no abstract principle, no impartial justice, no *precedent*, only the spontaneous opportunism of a new class designing the edifice of its power. It should be re-emphasized, however, that in certain instances formal analogues for civil imposition existed on the local level, but no formal or functional precedents. Civil taxation, for example, can be rationalized in the context of reciprocal gift-giving in the localities, but the latter was not confirmed by law, or specifically used by the sovereign; similarly, corvée labor is a political analogue of local cooperative work groups. But such evolutionary, and dialectical, relationships are most important for their distinctions.

Stubbs writes about the Norman kings that "it was mainly for the sake of the profits that early justice was administered at all."[31] Burton relates that at Whydah, in native Dahomey, in the event of a financial dispute the Yevogan, the leading bureaucrat in the district, sat in judgment. For his services, he appropriated half the merchandise involved, in the name of the king, and another quarter for various lesser officials. The remainder presumably went to the winning contestant in the judicial duel.[32] Among the Ashanti, the central authority relied on the proceeds of litigation as a fruitful means for replenishing a depleted treasury. Litigation, Rattray notes, came actually to be encouraged.[33]

Tolls were an important source of revenue. In Ashanti, the king had all the roads guarded; all traders were detained until inquiries were made about them, whereupon they were allowed to pass on payment of gold dust.[34] W. Bosman writes that in early eighteenth century Whydah, the king's revenue "in proportion

[28]Rattray, *op. cit.*, p. 286.
[29]Sir John Salmond, *Jurisprudence*, 1920, p. 13.
[30]Sir William Markby, *Elements of Law*, 1905, p. 21.
[31]William Stubbs, *The Constitutional History of England*, London, 1890, Vol. I, p. 48.
[32]Burton, Richard F., *A Mission to Gelele, a King of Dahomey*, London, 1864, Vol. II, p. 2l'1.
[33]Rattray, *op. cit.*, p. 292.
[34]Rattray, *op. cit.*, p. 111.

to his country is very large, of which I believe, he hath above one thousand collectors who dispose themselves throughout the whole land in all market roads and passages, in order to gather the king's toll which amounts to an incredible sum, for there is nothing so mean sold in the whole kingdom that the king hath no toll for it. . . ."[35]

The punishment for the theft of property designated as the king's was summary execution by "kangaroo courts" organized on the spot by the king's agents.[36] This is echoed in the code of Hammurabi: "if a man steals the property of a god [temple] or a palace, that man shall be put to death; and he who receives from his hands the stolen [property] shall also be put to death."[37] Where the king's property was concerned, no judicial duel was possible. In these instances, which could be endlessly multipled, we witness the extension of the king's peace, the primary form of the civil "order," actually the invention and application of sumptuary law through the subsidiary peaces of highway and market. In Maitland's words, "the king has a peace that devours all others." If, in these proto-states, the sovereign power is not yet fully effective, it nonetheless strives to that monopoly of force which characterizes the mature state.   •

The purpose and abundance of laws inevitably provoked breaches. The civil authority, in fact, continually probed for breaches and frequently manufactured them. In Dahomey, for example, a certain category of the king's women were distributed to the local villages and those men who made the mistake of having intercourse with them were accused of rape, for which the punishment, following a summary trial, was conscription into the army.[38] Thus, rape was invented as a *civil* crime. If rape had, in fact, occurred in the traditional joint-family villages — and such an occurrence would have been rare, as indicated by the necessity of civil definition — the wrong could have been dealt with by composition (the ritualized giving of goods to the injured party), ritual purification, ridicule, and, perhaps, for repeated transgressions, banishment; the customary machinery would have gone into effect automatically, probably on the initiative of the family of the aggressor. Such instances as this only sharpen the point that in early states crimes seem to have been invented to suit the laws; the latent purpose of the law was punishment in the service and profit of the state, not prevention or the protection of persons, not the *healing* of the breach. As Seagle indicates, "The criminal law springs into life in every great period of class conflict," and this is most obviously the case during the initial phases of state formation.

In its civil origins, then, a correlation existed between law and crime which partook of entrapment. One may even state that the substantial rationale for law developed *after* the fact of its emergence. For example, civil protection of the market place or highway was certainly not necessary to the degree implied in

---

[35]W. Bosman, *A New and Accurate Description of the Coast of Guinea*, London, 1705, p. 362.
[36]R. Norris, *Reise nach Abomey, der Hofstadt des Königs von Dahomey an von Guinea im Jahr 1772*, Leipzig, 1790, pp. 221 ff.
[37]*Code of Hammurabi*, Harper translation, 1904, paragraph 6, p. 13.
[38]A. Le Herisse, *L'Ancien Royaume du Dahomey*, Paris, 1911, p. 72.

the archaic edicts at the time they were issued. Joint-family markets and village trails were not ordinarily dangerous places, if we are to believe the reports of the earliest chroniclers, as well as those of more contemporary observers. Moreover, if trouble had developed, the family, clan or village was capable of dealing with it. But, in an evolving conquest state, the presence of the king's men would itself be a primary cause of disruption. Indeed, as M. Quénum, a descendant of Dahomean commoners, informs us in a remarkable work, the solders were referred to as bandits and predators who victimized many people. Sometimes their forays were confined to a single compound, where someone, whether man, woman or child, resided who had spoken badly of the sovereign or whom the king suspected.[39] In common parlance, the very names of the elite army units became insults; one meant "nasty person," another "arrogant person," and one would say of a tragic event that it was worthy of yet another military cadre. It is, therefore, understandable that the peace of the highway became an issue.[40]

As the integrity of the local groups declined, a process which, in the autochthonous state, must have taken generations or even centuries, conditions doubless developed which served as an *ex post facto* rationalization for edicts already in effect. In this sense, laws became self-fulfilling prophecies. Crime and the laws which served it were, then, co-variants of the evolving state.

Just as entrapment was characteristic of early civil law, the idea of protection, in the sense of a protection racket, also inheres in its origins. In Dahomey, we are told by Norris and others, prostitution was encouraged by the civil power and prostitutes were distributed through the villages, the price of their favors being set by civil decree. They were obliged to offer themselves to any man who could pay the moderate fee and once a year were convened at the "annual customs" where they were heavily taxed.[41] Skertchly notes that the prostitutes were licensed by the king and placed in the charge of the Mew, the second leading bureaucrat, who was entrusted with the task of "keeping up the supply."[42] Bosman observes at Whydah that "for every affair that can be thought of, the king hath appointed a captain overseer."[43] *What the king permits, he commands; what he "protects," he taxes.*

The intention of the civil power is epitomized in the sanctions against homicide and suicide, typical of early polities; indeed they were among the very first civil laws. Just as the sovereign is said to own the land, intimating the mature right of eminent domain, so the individual is ultimately conceived as the chattel of the state. In Dahomey, persons were conceived as *les choses du monarque*. Eminent domain in persons and property, even where projected as a fiction, is, of course, the cardinal prerequisite of the census-tax-conscription system. We recall that Maine designated the individual the unit of which the civil law steadily takes account. Seagle stated the matter as follows: "By undermining the kinship bond, they [the

---

[39]M. Quénum, *Au Pays des Fons*, Paris, 1938, p. 7.
[40]Quénum, pp. 21–22.
[41]Norris, *op. cit.*, p. 257.
[42]Skertchly, *Dahomey As It Is*, London, 1874, p. 283.
[43]Bosman, *op. cit.*, p. 361.

early civil authorities] made it easier to deal with individuals, and the isolation of the individual is a basic precondition for the growth of law."[44]

Homicide, then, was regarded as an offense against the state. In Rattray's words, "The blow which struck down the dead man would thus appear to have been regarded as aimed also at the . . . central authority."[45] In Ashanti homicide was punishable by death in its most horrible form; in Dahomey, by death or conscription into the army. There is a nuance here which should not be overlooked. By making homicide, along with the theft of the king's property, a capital offense, the sovereign power discouraged violent opposition to the imposition of the civil order.

Traditionally, murder in a joint-family village was a tort — a private, remediable wrong — which could stimulate a blood feud, not to be confused with the lex talionis, until redress, which did not imply equivalent injury, was achieved. But a breach was most often settled by composition. As Paul Radin put it: "The theory of an eye for an eye . . . never really held for primitive people . . . rather it was replacement for loss with damages."[46] And this is echoed by Peristiany: ". . . they claim restitution or private damages and not social retribution."[47] In any case, the family was fully involved. "The family was a corporation," said Rattray, "it is not easy to grasp what must have been the effect . . . of untold generations of thinking and acting . . . in relation to one's group. The Ashanti's idea of what we term moral responsibility for his actions must surely have been more developed than in peoples where individualism is the order of the day."[48] This more or less typical anthropological observation makes it clear that the law against homicide was not a "progressive" step, as if some abstract right were involved which the state, coming of age, finally understands and seeks to establish. "Anti-social conduct [is] exceptional in small kinship groups," writes Margery Perham of the Ibo.[49] Crimes of violence were rare, Richard Burton reported of Dahomey, and "murder virtually unknown."[50] Of course, as with

---

[44]Seagle, *op. cit.*, p. 64. Quénum had a poor opinion of the ethnographers who claimed to understand and interpret his country. They failed, he believed, because of inadequate sources of information, and (or) ignorance of social customs. "Most of our ethnographers," he wrote, "have had as collaborators princes and ex-ministers of state and have believed their tales." He adds that ignorance of the native language and deficient sympathy compounded the problem. The point to note here is that Quénum is objecting to the view from the top which is a critical issue in the writing of all political history.

[45]Rattray, *op. cit.*, p. 295.

[46]Radin, *op. cit.*, p. 252.

[47]Peristiany, *op. cit.*, p. 43.

[48]Radin, *op. cit.*, p. 62.

[49]Margery Perham, *Native Administration in Nigeria*, London, 1962, pp. 229 ff.

[50]Burton, *op. cit.*, p. 56.

Acts of violence must be distinguished from *crimes* of violence. The incidence, occasions for, and character of violence in primitive, as opposed to civilized societies, is a subject of the utmost importance, which I have discussed elsewhere (see footnote 52). But the question here has to do with crimes in which violence is used as a means for, e.g., the theft of property. In contemporary societies unpremeditated acts of personal violence which have no ulterior motive, so-called crimes of passion, may not be penalized or carry minor degrees of guilt, that is, their status as legally defined crimes is ambiguous. This would certainly seem to reflect a historically profound distinction between crime and certain types of violence. In primitive societies violence tends to be personally structured, nondissociative, and, thereby, self-limiting.

other crimes defined by civil law, they may have increased as the social autonomy, economic communalism, and reciprocity of the kin units weakened. But this is much less important than Dalzel's observation that in Dahomey "many creatures have been put to death . . . without having committed any crime at all,"[51] thus exemplifying the power of the sovereign literally to command the lives of his citizens. The threat and example of summary execution, especially but by no means exclusively evident at the mortuary celebrations of "Grand Customs" on the enstooling of a king, encouraged obedience to civil injunctions.

The law against suicide, a capital offense, was the apotheosis of political absurdity. The individual, it was assumed, had no right to take his own life; that was the sole prerogative, presumably, of the state, whose property he was conceived to be.

The fanatical nature of the civil legislature in claiming sole prerogative to the lives of its subjects is conclusively revealed among the Ashanti, where, if the suicide was a murderer, "the central authority refused to be cheated thus and the long arm of the law followed the suicide to the grave from which, if his kinsmen should have dared to bury him, he was dragged to stand trial."[52] (One recalls Antigone's defiance.) This contrasts remarkably, if logically, with the behavior of the more primitively structured Ibo, as reported by Victor Uchendu, an anthropologist who is himself an Ibo: "Homicide is an offense against ala — the earth deity. If a villager is involved, *the murderer is expected to hang himself*, after which . . . daughters of the village perform the rite of . . . sweeping away the ashes of murder. If the murderer has fled, his extended family must also flee, and the property of all is subject to raids. When the murderer is eventually caught, he is required to hang himself to enable the daughters of the village to perform their rites. It is important to realize that the village has no power to impose capital punishment. In fact, no social group or institution has this power. Everything affecting the life of the villager is regulated by custom. The life of the individual is highly respected; it is protected by the earth-goddess. The villagers can bring social pressure, but the murderer must hang himself."[53]

It can hardly be argued that the purpose of the civil sanction against suicide was to diminish its incidence or to propagate a superior moral consciousness. Dare we say, as with other crimes, that attempts at suicide increased as society became more thoroughly politicized? The law against suicide reveals, in the extreme, the whole meaning and intent of civil law at its origins. In the proto-state, the quintessential struggle was over the lives and labor of the people, who, still moving in a joint family context, were nonetheless conceived to be *les choses du monarque*.

III

If revolutions are the acute, episodic signs of civilizational discontent, the rule of law, in seven millennia of political society, from Sumer or Akkad to New

[51]A. Dalzel, *The History of Dahomey, an inland kingdom of Africa*, etc., London, 1793, p. 212.
[52]Rattray, *op. cit.*, p. 299.
[53]Uchendu, *op. cit.*, pp. 42–43.

York or Moscow, has been the chronic symptom of the disorder of institutions. E. B. Tylor stated, "A constitutional government, whether called republic or kingdom, is an arrangement by which the nation governs itself by means of the machinery of a military despotism."[54]

The generalization lacks nuance but we can accept it if we bear in mind Tylor's point of reference: "Among the lessons to be learnt from the life of rude tribes is how society can go on without the policeman to keep order."[55] When he alludes to constitutional government, Tylor was not distinguishing its ultimate sanction from that of any other form of the state: all political society is based on repressive organized force. In this he was accurate. For pharaohs and presidents alike have always made a public claim to represent the common interest, indeed to incarnate the common good. Only a Plato or a Machiavelli in search of political harmony, or a Marx in search of political truth, has been able to penetrate this myth of the identity between ruler and ruled, of equality under law. The tradition of Plato and Machiavelli commends the use of the "royal" or "noble lie," while that of Marx exposes and rejects the power structure (ultimately the state) that propagates so false a political consciousness. On this issue, I follow Marx.

Tylor distinguishes the civilized from the primitive order. Such a distinction has been made at every moment of crisis in the West but nowhere so pertinently as in Montaigne's contrast of a primitive society with Plato's ideally civilized republic: "This is a nation, I should say to Plato, in which there is no sort of traffic, no knowledge of letters, no science of numbers, no name for a magistrate or for political superiority, no custom of servitude, no riches or poverty, no contracts, no successions, no partitions . . . no care for any but common kinship. How far from this perfection would he find the Republic he imagines!"[56] The issue of law and order implicit in Montaigne's contrast between primitive and civilized societies has been a persistent underlying theme for the most reflective and acute minds of the West. The inquiry into the nature of politics probably demarcates most accurately the boundaries of our intellectual landscape. The evolution of the state toward what Max Weber called maximally politicized society, the unprecedented concentration of bureaucratic and technological power, which economically and culturally dominates the rest of the world, creates a climate in which all problems cast a political shadow. We may flee from the political dimension of our experience or we may embrace it in order to do away with it, but we are obsessed by politics. It was perhaps Plato's primary virtue that, at the very origin of the Western intellectual tradition, he understood that, in civilization, all significant human problems have a political aspect and he insisted

[54]E. B. Tylor, *Anthropology*, Vol. II, London, 1946, p. 156.
[55]*Ibid.*, p. 134.
[56]Michel de Montaigne, *The Complete Essays*, trans. Donald Frame, Stanford, 1965. In ignorance of Montaigne's contrast between primitive society and Plato's ideal republic, I published an article, "Plato and the Definition of the Primitive," *Culture in History*, New York, 1960, which explicates some of the points briefly noted above. For a more comprehensive model of primitive society see my "The Search for the Primitive" in *Man's Image in Medicine and Anthropology*, New York, 1963, edited by I. Galdston, pp. 62–115. In order to understand the functioning of custom in primitive society fully, one should have such a model in mind. Unfortunately, in this article I can only suggest its outlines.

upon the solution of the latter as a coefficient of the creative resolution of the former. *The Republic* is the first civilizational utopia, and it maintains its force both as a model of inquiry and as antithesis to all projections of the nature of primitive society. Any contrary view of the possibilities of human association must take *The Republic* into account.

The legal order, which Plato idealized, is as Tylor maintained and Marx understood, synonymous with the power of the state. "The state," writes Paul Vinogradoff, "has assumed the monopoly of political co-ordination. It is the state which rules, makes laws and eventually enforces them by coercion. Such a state did not exist in ancient times. The commonwealth was not centered in one sovereign body towering immeasurably above single individuals and meting out to everyone his portion of right."[57] And Engels, reflecting on the origins of the state, asserts: "The right of the state to existence was founded on the preservation of order in the interior and the protection against the barbarians outside, but this order was worse than the most disgusting disorder, and the barbarians against whom the state pretended to protect its citizens were hailed by them as saviors."[58] Moreover, "The state created a public power of coercion that did no longer coincide with the old self-organized and [self] armed population."[59] Finally, in a passage that epitomizes the West's awareness of itself, Engels writes: "The state, then, is by no means a power forced on society at a certain stage of evolution. It is the confession that this society has become hopelessly divided against itself, has estranged itself in irreconcilable contradictions which it is powerless to banish. In order that these contradictions, these classes with conflicting economic interests may not annihilate themselves and society in a useless struggle, a power becomes necessary that stands apparently above society and has the function of keeping down the conflicts and maintaining 'order.' And this power, the outgrowth of society, but assuming supremacy over it and becoming more and more divorced from it, is the state. . . ."[60] In a word, the state is the alienated form of society: and it is this process which has fascinated the Western intellect and which may, in fact, have led to the peculiar intensity of the reflective, analytic, and introspective consciousness in the West, to our search for origins and our inexhaustible concern with secular history. A knowledge of one's present, as Montaigne maintained, implies not only a knowledge of one's past but of one's future.

However we project, imagine, or reconstruct the past, we recognize the division, the objective correlate of the division within ourselves, between primitive and civilized society, between moral and civil order, between custom and law. Interpretation of the nature of the primitive and the civilized has, of course, not been uniform. Hobbes versus Rousseau is paradigmatic. But most theorists tend to see civilization as a kind of fall from a "natural," or at least more natural, to a legal or more repressive order. No matter how the virtues of civilization are weighted, the price

[57]Paul Vinogradoff, *Outlines of Historical Jurisprudence*, Vol. I, London, 1920, p. 93.
[58]Friedrich Engels, *Origin of the Family, Private Property and the State*, Chicago, 1902, p. 179.
[59]*Ibid*., p. 207.
[60]*Ibid*., p. 206.

exacted is inevitably noted. This is as true of Plato as of Freud or Engels. Plato, for example, notes, however inadequately, a condition of existence prior to the city-state, a type of rusticity which he views nostalgically and whose destruction he maintains was socioeconomically determined. I suspect that even the great majority of anthropologists, despite professional illusions of dissociated objectivity, sense that primitive societies are somehow closer than civilized societies to the realization of "natural" law and "natural" right. I believe this emphasis in the Western tradition to be the sounder, and it serves as the basis of my own thinking. There is, as Montaigne noted, an "amazing distance" between the primitive character and our own. In the contrast between these two sides of our historical nature, which we existentially re-enact, we come to understand law as the antonym and not the synonym of order.

IV

I agree with Nadel that in the transition from primitive to political society the means of control and integration employed were, in a wider sense, "all . . . deliberately conceived and [executed]: they are agencies of an assimilation conscious of itself and of the message which it carries."[61] Finally, we are led to ask, as did Nadel about the Nupe: "What did the tax-paying law-abiding citizen receive in return for allegiance to king and nobility? Was extortion, bribery, brutal force, the only aspect under which the state revealed itself to the populace? The people were to receive, theoretically, on the whole, one thing: security — protection against external and internal enemies, and general security for carrying out the daily work, holding markets, using the roads. We have seen what protection and security meant in reality. At their best, they represented something very unequal and very unstable. This situation must have led to much tension and change within the system and to frequent attempts to procure better safeguards for civil rights."[62]

The struggle for civil rights, then, is a response to the imposition of civil law. With the destruction of the primitive base of society, civil rights have been defined and redefined as a reaction to drastic changes in the socioeconomic structure, the rise of caste and class systems, imperialism, modern war, technology as a means of social exploitation, maldistribution and misuse of resources, racial hatred. The right to socially and economically fruitful work, for example, which did not come into question in a primitive society or in a traditional sector or an early state (and therefore was not conceived to be a stipulated right) becomes an issue under capitalism. The demand implies a need for profoundly changing the system and indicates that our sense of the appropriately human has very ancient roots indeed. However, we are reminded by the struggle for civil rights, that legislation alone has no force beyond the potential of the social system that generates it. From the study of proto-states we also learn that the citizen must be constantly alert to laws which seek to curb his rights in the name of protection or security.

[61]S. F. Nadel, *A Black Byzantium*, London, New York, Toronto, 1942, p. 144.
[62]Nadel, "Nupe State and Community," *Africa*, Vol. VIII, p. 287.

Restrictive legislation is almost always a signal of repressive institutional change, but is, of course, not the cause of it.

The major focus of the defense of the citizen as a person can only be on procedure or, as we call it in our own society, due process. Quénum reports, of the early state of Dahomey, "There was no penal code promulgated . . . punishment had no fixity . . . the Miegan [leading bureaucrat, chief judge, and executioner] would become restive if capital punishment would be too long in coming."[63] In the words of Dalzel, "There was a vast disproportion between crimes and punishments."[64] And in early states, most if not all civil breaches were what we would define as crimes, just as in primitive societies "civil crimes" were considered, where they were not unprecedented, torts or private remediable wrongs. As every intelligent lawyer knows, the substance of the law can hardly be assimilated to morality. It is clear, therefore, why Jhering insisted that "Form is the sworn enemy of unlimited discretion [of the sovereign power] and the twin sister of freedom."[65] The degrees of theft or homicide, the question of double jeopardy, habeas corpus, the right to counsel, the question of legitimate witness, trial by jury and the selection of jurors, protection against summary search and seizure, the very division between civil and criminal law — these intricacies of procedure are the primary, but far from absolute, assurance of whatever justice can be obtained under the rule of law.

For example, the only way dissidents in Russia can defend themselves against summary punishment and make their cases universally understandable is by calling attention to abuses of procedure. The spirit of the laws, mummified in the excellent constitution of 1936, is irrelevant, abstract. The tribunal that discharges the intentions of the state can discard, suspend, reinterpret, and invent laws at will. The court, not the constitution, is the primary legal reality. And the politically inspired charge of insanity, which can remove dissidents from the body politic altogether, is the ultimate étatistic definition of the person — a nonbeing incapable of autonomy. And that, I should note, is foreshadowed in the consummate anti-Socratic Platonism of the Laws, the heavenly city brought to earth, wherein the ordinary citizen is "to become, by long habit, utterly incapable of doing anything at all independently."

Procedure is the individual's last line of defense in contemporary civilization, wherein all other associations to which he may belong have become subordinate to the state. The elaboration of procedure then, is a unique, if fragile, feature of more fully evolved states, in compensation, so to speak, for the radical isolation of the individual. In the proto-states, the harshness of rudimentary procedure was countered by the role of the kinship units which, as we recall, retained a significant measure of functional socioeconomic autonomy and, therefore, of local political cohesion.

But "law has its origin in the pathology of social relations and functions only

[63]Quénum, *op. cit.*, p. 22.
[64]Dalzel, *op. cit.*, p. 212.
[65]Jhering, *op. cit.*, Vol. II, p. 471.

when there are frequent disturbances of the social equilibrium."[66] Law arises in the breach of a prior customary order and increases in force with the conflicts that divide political societies internally and among themselves. Law *and* order is the historical illusion; law versus order is the historical reality.

In the tradition of Rousseau, Lévi-Strauss, in a moment of candor, declares, "We must go beyond the evidence of the injustices and abuses to which the social order gives rise, and discover the unshakable basis of human society. . . . Anthropology shows that base cannot be found in our own civilization, ours is indeed perhaps the one furthest from it."[67]

The progressive reduction of society to a series of technical and legal signals, the consequent diminution of culture, i.e., of reciprocal, symbolic meanings, are perhaps the primary reasons why our civilization is the one least likely to serve as a guide to "the unshakable basis of human society."

2. Alan Wolfe

Political Repression and the Liberal Democratic State

Repression in a bourgeois-democratic society is not as clear-cut a phenomenon as it is under, say, a police dictatorship of a fascist order. The state seems to operate in contradictory fashion, smashing certain groups while ignoring others, the reason for the distinction not always being clear. At other times a political trial is proof of repression, while a verdict of innocence is taken as a sign that the state really is not so repressive after all. In short, the dynamics of how repression works in the liberal state are little understood, even by those who are repressed.

A full understanding of political repression would be obtained if a comprehensive theory of the state existed, because repression is a form of rule, a method of preserving capitalism.

That theory, however, does not yet exist; the political dimension of Marxism is one of the most poorly worked out.[1] Thus, for the present, we shall not be able to understand completely the nature of political repression in democratic

---

[66]Seagle, *op. cit.*, p. 36.

[67]Claude Lévi-Strauss, *A World on the Wane*, New York, 1961, p. 390.

Reprinted by permission of the publisher from *Monthly Review*, 23 (December 1971), pp. 18–38. Copyright © 1971 by Monthly Review, Inc.

[1]The most interesting attempt to work on this problem is Nicos Poulantzas, *Pouvoir Politique et Classes Sociales* (Paris: François Maspero, 1968). See also Ralph Miliband, *The State in Capitalist Society* (New York: Basic Books, 1969).

societies. But we can, at the very least, address ourselves to conceptions, shared to some extent by both liberals and radicals, which are very likely incorrect. In that spirit, I offer the following seven propositions.

(1) *Repression is one of a number of reproductive mechanisms which capitalism requires in order to maintain itself as a system.* One of the most powerful notions in all of Marxist theory is the concept of reproductive mechanisms, those aspects of capitalism which tend to perpetuate traditional forms of institutions and behavior, as well as stabilizing new ones. Consumerism is a good example. The economic system requires that a goodly amount of products be manufactured. The very existence of such quantity creates a justification for quantity. To the extent that consumers come to depend on the existence of a certain number and kind of products, to that extent has capitalism created a mechanism for its own reproduction.

Matters cannot be left to the economy alone, however. One of the functions of a government is to create the conditions under which the system will be success-fully reproduced. At certain points, there are more important ways to reproduce a society than by the ruling class acting alone in furtherance of its economic control over the society. At those times (some of which will be discussed shortly), the state is asked to play a major role in preserving the capitalist order. In doing this, the state can act in a number of ways, all of which are repressive in the sense that they are designed to stymie those forces which work for revolutionary change, but only one of which is generally called repression, i.e., the physical use of force or the threat of force by those in power to meet challenges to their legitimacy. In order that this discussion be generally understood, I will accept this distinction between repression and other reproductive mechanisms, so long as it is understood that all these tactics are dedicated to the same end — the mainte-nance of the order.

Repression can be understood by comparing it to these other non-terroristic reproductive mechanisms. One of them is clearly co-option, the blunting of a revolutionary challenge by partially accepting either some of its premises or some of its leaders, in the hopes of absorbing the threat. Similarly, political reform is a reproductive mechanism. There are times when sections of the ruling class become sponsors of reform in order to rationalize the system and make it work better. Each of these strategies has advantages and disadvantages to both the state and the revolutionary movement, but it is not my intention to go into them here. The point is that both of them are seen by rulers as conscious alternatives to repression, alternatives in the sense that they may obtain the same end at less cost.

The most important reproductive mechanism which does not involve the use of state violence is consciousness-manipulation. The liberal state has an enormous amount of violence at its disposal, but it is often reluctant to use it. Violence may breed counter-violence, leading to instability. It may be far better to manipulate consciousness to such an extent that most people would never think of engaging in the kinds of action which could be repressed. The most perfectly repressive (though not violently so) capitalist system, in other words, would not be a police state, but the complete opposite, one in which there were no police becuase there was nothing to police, everyone having accepted the legitimacy of that society and all its daily consequences.

Democratic societies, in general, stress consciousness-manipulation over violent repression to a greater degree than do other political forms of capitalism, though this may be changing at the moment, at least in the United States. This means that within liberal society a series of institutions — ranging from the family through schools, the media, the churches, athletics, etc. — will have a political function that sometimes meshes with and sometimes contradicts their other functions, be they child rearing, product-selling, knowledge-accumulating, or rest and relaxation. Those operating within these institutions often perceive the contradictions, as students did when they first began their critique of their university. In other words, there are times when attempts to manipulate consciousness fail because the contradictory nature of the institution reveals a hypocrisy which creates as many activists as it does passivists.

This discrepancy between the professed goals of a non-governmental institution and its actual reproductive consequences does not exist when the state itself becomes involved. The goal of a state propaganda apparatus is to coerce mentally, and little attempt is made to suggest anything else. The origins of a state propaganda machine in the United States can be traced back to George Creel's Committee on Public Information (CPI), designed to win support for the First World War (and the capitalist system) among the two groups whose support was least likely to be spontaneous: labor union members and immigrants. The CPI worked among Swedes, Danes, Norwegians, Finns, Italians, Czechs, Poles, Hungarians, Germans, Russians — twenty-four ethnic groups in all — utilizing secretly financed members of those groups and a variety of other covert practices. CPI functionaries sent material to all 745 foreign-language newspapers in the United States, attended conventions, published leaflets, and gave lectures.[2] Reviewing these efforts, Creel noted the systematic nature of this type of activity:

> The loyalty of "our aliens," however splendid as it was, had in it nothing of the spontaneous or the accidental. Results were obtained only by hard, driving work. The bitterness bred by years of neglect and injustice were not to be dissipated by any mere war-call, but had to be burned away by a continuous educational campaign.[3]

That campaign was continued, especially after the New Deal and the Second World War. The Harness Committee of the House of Representatives found in 1947 that the federal government spent $74,829,467 on publicity alone, while the 1950 Hoover Commission put the figure at $105 million.[4] It is impossible

---

[2]James R. Mock and Cedric Larson, *Words That Won the War: The Story of the Committee on Public Information 1917–19* (Princeton: Princeton University Press, 1939), p. 219. George Creel, *How We Advertised America* (New York: Harper, 1920), pp. 192–194.

[3]Creel, p. 184.

[4]Final Report of the Subcommittee on Publicity and Propaganda (Harness Committee), *Twenty-Third Intermediate Report of the Committee on Expenditures in the Executive Departments* (Washington:

to estimate the current rate, but that it is much higher is indicated by the fact that the printing budget of the Army Department alone in 1970 was $43 million.[5] State-directed propaganda is now a permanent feature of the liberal democratic state.

Permanent consciousness-manipulation is only one reproductive mechanism. In spite of being heavily propagated, the ideology of capitalism is not always well received. When the mechanisms of consciousness-manipulation break down and threats to the stability of the system are real, then chances are that a new reproductive mechanism will be used: state violence, commonly called repression. This does not mean that all uses of state violence indicate that the other mechanisms have failed. Repression might be used because it is cheaper, because the spirit of a group has been broken and the state wishes to wipe it out, or for essentially irrational reasons having no apparent, coherent motivation. But in most cases, the existence of political repression testifies to a struggle taking place between those in control of the system and those trying to change the system's nature. The dynamics of that relationship is what much of the rest of this essay is about.

(2) *Repression is an essential aspect of liberal rule, not something alien to it.* The theory of liberal democracy, from Locke through Mill to the corporate liberalism of the twentieth century, is a series of agreements on how repression is to be practiced. Assume for the moment that liberalism's goals could actually be reached. The result would be something like the following: (a) access to the means of repression, open only to a few, would be egalitarian; anyone would have as likely a chance as anyone else to obtain the requisite positions; (b) the practice of repression would always be done according to certain well-defined rules and would never be arbitrary; and (c) any group would be as likely as any other group to be repressed, the distribution being without regard to class. That would be the case for an ideal liberal society, but none has so far existed. Instead, access to the means of repression is closed to most of the population, due process is rarely followed when it is against the interests of the state, and a ruling class exists which benefits from repression at the expense of those who challenge their rule. But phrased in this way, it is clear that much liberal criticism of repression covers only the failure to reach the ideal. What must be understood is that the ideal itself is a rationale for repression.

There is a reason for that. By its very nature, capitalism benefits a few at the expense of the many; if it did not, as Lenin once remarked, it would not be capitalism.[6] The maldistribution of rewards in the economic sector means that the political system is faced with an enormous task, which is to convince people

---

Government Printing Office, 1949). 80th Congress, Second Session. House Report No. 2474. The figure cited is from a summary of the Report, *Congressional Record,* vol. 96, part 17, p. A6861. 81st Congress, Second Session. For a summary of the Hoover Commission, see *Congressional Record, ibid.* For a discussion of the whole problem, see Francis E. Rourke, *Secrecy and Publicity* (Baltimore: Johns Hopkins Press, 1961), p. 187.

[5] Appendix, *The Budget of the United States (Fiscal Year 1971)* (Washington: Government Printing Office, 1970), p. 274.

[6] V. I. Lenin, *Imperialism* (New York: International Publishers, 1939), p. 63.

that something which is not in their best interest *is* in their best interest. Liberal democracy, because it includes a political sphere in which access is slightly more egalitarian than it is in the corporate order, is an ideal answer. And if the historical conditions are right, it is possible for a liberal democratic society to undertake its task under conditions of relative peace, relying on non-terroristic reproductive means to make its case. But class struggle is never muted for good. The more unequal the distribution of the economic rewards of the society, the greater will be the chance that challenges will arise, which means that the use of state violence will be that much more frequent. Hence the repressive nature of capitalism and the built-in repressive quality of that liberal theory (and practice) which has been designed to serve as its ideology.

Radicals do not always act on these premises; there is a tendency to think of one's own repression as unique. In his account of his own experience with the liberal state, for example, Tom Hayden noted:

> [The Chicago] trial . . . symbolized the beginning of full-scale repression in the United States. . . . Future histories will locate the sixties as the time when America's famous democratic pragmatism began hardening into an inflexible fascist core. . . . The pursuit of imperialism created a necessity for repression, even fascism, to stabilize the home front.[7]

Hayden is wrong. While any historical event is unique, there was nothing startlingly new about the Chicago trial. Judge Hoffman was no more notoriously idiosyncratic than the man who tried the IWW in 1919 (also in Chicago and also on a conspiracy charge), Judge (later Baseball Commissioner) Kenesaw Mountain Landis.[8] Nor was he more severe; sentences for the IWW defendants were much higher. Nor was the reaction of the defendants all that different. Some fled the country (just as some of those prosecuted in the Smith Act cases did, after their experience with another egocentrically repressive judge, Harold Medina), while others went on to further radical activity. If repression is basic to the society, certain methods, once found to work, will be repeatedly used. The Chicago trial was such a method. Far from being a unique event, it was part of a show which has had a long run.

(3) *The history of repression does not necessarily reveal a linear development.* There are two positions here which need examination. One held by liberals like Milton Konvitz is that the civil liberties of Americans have been continually on the rise, implying that state repression has continually decreased. The other position, generally associated with radicals like the late Bertrand Russell, is that the United States has increasingly become a repressive society, to the point where it may emerge into fascism.[9] Neither view is necessarily correct, though Russell comes closer to the truth than Konvitz.

[7]Tom Hayden, *Trial* (New York: Holt, Rinehart, and Winston, 1970), pp. 4, 9, 11.

[8]For details, see Philip Taft, "The Federal Trials of the IWW," *Labor History*, (Winter 1962), p. 60.

[9]The argument between Konvitz and Russell is summarized in Milton Konvitz, *Expanding Liberties* (New York: The Viking Press, 1967), p. xiii.

One should avoid being abstract here, talking about repression as if it materialized out of thin air. It is not the amount of repression over time which is important, but the forms that repression takes. In fact, the amount of repression is probably a function of governmental output, i.e., the more the state is called upon to do, the more repression there will be, because that is one of the things it does. A discussion of the changing nature of repression, then, invariably implies a discussion of the changing nature of the capitalist state, of the shift from essentially private to essentially public activities.

In the latter part of the nineteenth century, while capitalism was still basically private, repression tended to be left in private hands. Corporations had their own police forces (or hired agencies like the Pinkertons) for purposes of breaking strikes. Even the non-terroristic reproductive mechanisms were private. In the town of Pullman, this was an exaggerated development in which the corporation controlled all information and nearly all private activities, including religion, a model which reveals in its clearest form the general case. However, as the entire corporate order became professionalized, with the state intervening to benefit the corporate class as a whole, the means of repression came to be centralized in the state. The crucial period, as James Weinstein has shown, was 1912–1920, when a new capitalist order emerged in which the state was to play a crucial role.[10]

In other words, it was liberalism which led to the modern repressive state and it was liberals who brought it into existence. In the search for ways of expanding state power in order to protect an emerging ruling class, it was a short step for progressive thinkers of the time to expand the repressive role of the state as well as its other aspects, especially when the force would be used against "unruly," "ill-behaved," "uncivil" elements who did not understand that politics required delicate balances among gentlemen. Only this paradox faced by liberals explains why the man who trained a whole generation of progressives to aid the state in extending its welfare privileges, Felix Frankfurter, could also be credited, as Melvyn Dubofsky so credits him, with developing the means for the destruction, through violent repression, of the Industrial Workers of the World.[11]

The modern repressive state was formed at the same time that the modern corporate state was formed — in the years of Woodrow Wilson. Consider some of the unique "firsts" of the Wilson administration. Besides the appointment of George Creel to head the first important state propaganda machine in the United States, Wilson's second administration also saw the following, more directly repressive, developments: the appointment of J. Edgar Hoover to head the Radical Division of the Justice Department;[12] the first extensive use of deportation as a political weapon;[13] the first use of systematic, nationally planned raids on the offices of local political

[10]James Weinstein, *The Corporate Ideal in the Liberal State* (Boston: Beacon Press, 1968).

[11]Melvyn Dubofsky, *We Shall Be All* (Chicago: Quadrangle, 1967), p. 916.

[12]On Hoover's appointment (from a favorable point of view), see Don Whitehead, *The FBI Story* (New York: Random House, 1956).

[13].William Preston, Jr., *Aliens and Dissenters* (New York: Harper Torchbooks, 1966), p. 83.

groups;[14] the first use of a selective service system (and the first arrests, like that of Eugene Debs, for interference with its functioning);[15] the first important racial pogroms of the twentieth century (Omaha and Chicago), and the first co-ordinated effort by police to develop a strategy for controlling them, including co-ordinated police work and the publication of riot-control manuals;[16] the first intervention into the affairs of another country for purposes of containing an explicitly socialist revolution (because it was the first country to have an explicitly socialist revolution);[17] the first attempt by the government to take over the hiring of undercover agents to report on "subversive activity" (such as Francis Morrow, who became the agent who revealed the location of the Communist Party's Bridgman, Michigan meeting, leading to one of the largest political raids in American history);[18] the first extensive recruiting of labor leaders by the state to work directly in repressing their own memberships;[19] the creation of a Militia Bureau to centralize somewhat the use of state and federal troops (the Militia Bureau later became the National Guard);[20] and the first ruling by the Supreme Court interpreting the First Amendment in such a way as to provide a justification for governmental repression.[21] In addition, the same period also saw the federal trials of the IWW and the first general strike in American history.

Clearly, elements of all these things existed before 1919. And that year, which novelists like Dos Passos saw as a turning point in the development of America, represented a culmination of all these trends. It is therefore hardly good history to date the emergence of the modern repressive state to that time.[22] The story of state repression since 1919 has been one of refinement, one which has seen the emphasis shift from one reproductive mechanism to another. But it has not differed in any fundamental degree from what emerged during the Wilson administration.

Since that time, the amount of state violence actually used has varied up and down, though the repressive potential of the state has always been large. For example, use of the National Guard for explicitly political purposes — a good indication of violent repression — has varied tremendously. In the decade of the

---

[14]Robert Murray, *Red Scare* (Minneapolis: University of Minnesota Press, 1955).

[15]On the use of the Selective Service Act as a political weapon, plus material on the Debs case, see H. C. Peterson and Gilbert C. Fite, *Opponents of War, 1917–18* (Seattle: University of Washington Press, 1968).

[16]William M. Tuttle, Jr., *Race Riot* (New York: Atheneum, 1970). Arthur Waskow, *From Race Riot to Sit-In* (Garden City: Doubleday Anchor, 1967).

[17]William Appleman Williams, *American-Russian Relations, 1781–1947* (New York: Rinehart, 1952).

[18]The story is contained in Theodore Draper, *The Roots of American Communism* (New York: Viking Press, 1957), pp. 366–375.

[19]Ronald Radosh, *American Labor and United States Foreign Policy* (New York: Random House, 1970).

[20]Martha Derthick, *The National Guard in Politics* (Cambridge: Harvard University Press, 1965).

[21]*Schenck v. United States*, 249 U.S. 47 (1919).

[22]John Dos Passos, *1919* (New York: Harcourt, Brace, 1932). Waskow, *From Race Riot to Sit-In*, p. 1, also attaches a great deal of importance to this year.

1920s, the Guard was used 78 times, while from 1940 to 1949 it was used only 22 times. By comparison, the Guard was called out 25 times in 1967 alone and 101 times in 1968.[23] Such figures suggest that the use of violent repression is a cyclical phenomenon, high in some periods, low in others. A hypothesis might be that while there is almost always some violent repression (the Wilson administration, criminal syndicalism laws in the 1920s, strike-breaking in the 1930s, "relocation camps" in the 1940s, McCarthyism in the 1950s, what we just saw so much of, in the 1960s), it will decrease when there is little active struggle taking place and increase as other reproductive mechanisms break down. The important point is that such a hypothesis is not a commentary on the role of the state, which is by its nature repressive, but a comment on the role of a dissenting consciousness.

(4) *Repression is not a policy question; conventional thinking is confused as to who supports what kinds*. No administration, whether Democratic or Republican, can ever end repression. This point needs emphasis because — even if radicals understand it intellectually — there is still the unconscious feeling that a political leader like Nixon is "worse" than someone like Kennedy on the repression "issue." This is a variation on the theme of liberals like Richard Harris, who argue that John Mitchell inaugurated a new era of repression, turning his back on the liberal tolerance of Ramsey Clark.[24] Yet it was Clark himself who began the current wave of political trials through his indictment of Spock, Coffin, and their co-defendants.[25] In other words, no matter what their attitude toward political dissent when out of office, liberals like Ramsey Clark will act repressively when in office or find the office taken away from them.

To this point one might wish to argue that while both Democrats and Republicans will be repressive, there is a real difference between them, and that — unless one wishes to follow the disastrous policy of supporting quasi-fascistic leaders in order to make things worse so that they might then get better — one should see this difference in degree as vitally important. Such an argument holds or implies that liberals will place more of their faith in consciousness-manipulation and long-term repressive strategies, while conservative Republicans are more likely to use the police and military in order to get their way. Since the latter policy involves greater threats to human life, while the former presents more contradictions which can be exploited, the Republican-type approach should be avoided if possible.

The conventional wisdom on this point is strong, but it falls apart on close examination. The presidents most inclined to use the instruments of state violence for purposes of repression in this century have been liberal Democrats, not Republi-

---

[23]These figures were compiled from a variety of sources, including: *Annual Report of the Chief of the Militia Bureau* (Washington: Government Printing Office, 1920–1932); *Annual Report of the Chief of the National Guard Bureau* (Washington: Government Printing Office, 1933–1969); *New York Times* (various issues, 1919–1969); and Philip Taft and Philip Ross, "American Labor Violence: Its Causes, Character, and Outcome," in Hugh Davis Graham and Ted Robert Gurr, *Violence in America* (New York: Signet Books, 1969), pp. 270–376.

[24]Richard Harris, *Justice* (New York: Dutton, 1969).

[25]See Jessica Mitford, *The Trial of Dr. Spock* (New York: Vintage, 1970).

cans. Why, to cite one rather typical yet good example, did Woodrow Wilson spend so much time sending Debs to jail, and why was it Harding who freed him? The usual answer sees the repressive character of the Wilson administration as irrelevant to Wilson himself, as the fault of men like his Attorney General, A. Mitchell Palmer. Yet Wilson was quite aware of what his administration was doing. A more likely explanation is the one advanced above: liberals are much more likely to use the state as an instrument of corporate rule, playing a "progressive" role in helping the economy resolve, at least temporarily, some of its contradictions. As the state takes on a more positive role in the affairs of the citizenry, it is a small step to make the repressive role of the state more positive as well.

It follows that conservatives, who tend — at least in rhetoric, but also to some extent in practice — to rely on "individual initiative" rather than the state, will be reluctant to see the means of repression centralized in a federal bureaucracy in Washington. This has by and large been true. Eisenhower, for example, did not contribute as much to the growth of the FBI as Kennedy. And even though Eisenhower's attitude toward McCarthy was characterized by inconsistencies, who among the liberal democrats at the time was an outspoken opponent of that form of repression? This general conservative reluctance to use the state as an instrument of repression has been discussed candidly by the man most responsible for repression in the Nixon Administration, Deputy Attorney-General Richard Kleindienst. Asked if he felt that the liberal government of Pierre Trudeau in Canada had overreacted to political kidnappings, Kleindienst replied:

> We conservatives would not have reacted that way. Cool-headed Wall Street types — like Nixon, Mitchell, and me — would never respond emotionally. We would be conservative in invoking extraordinary powers. You liberals, on the other hand, you don't anticipate crises; you worry about upsetting constituencies. When you finally do act, things have gotten so far out of hand that you have to overreact. That's why liberals are more likely to invoke emergency powers than conservatives.[26]

Granted that mere words do not a policy make, and that the Nixon administration may be more repressive than Eisenhower, Harding, and Coolidge, nonetheless Kleindienst's point is worth considering.

(5) *The relationship between violent repression and the tactics of dissenting groups is probably the reverse of what is most often suggested.* In the world of the daily newspaper columnist and editorial writer, repression is "caused" by groups on the Left when they choose certain tactics. Such groups are urged not to engage in disruptive and militant activities because that will bring down the full power of the state against not only them but all right-thinking people as well. In one sense this argument is correct, for if there were no obvious and visible dissent, there would be no need for violent repression. But it is not an

---

[26]Quoted in Alan Dershowitz, " 'Stretch Points' of Liberty," *The Nation* (March 15, 1971), vol. 212, p. 329.

argument based on either the empirical evidence concerning the use of repression or the logic of the situation, as a few examples might make clear.

It has most often been the case that groups have been violently repressed, not when they have made their activities more militant and terroristic, but when they have softened their rhetoric and pursued mass-organizing techniques. The IWW, for example, was put on trial and raided just at the point when it stopped talking about armed self-defense and began to stress its non-violent aspects.[27] There is a logic to this. The continued escalation of rhetoric often comes about when a group has little mass support; revolutionary rhetoric then serves as a surrogate for the lack of anything else. Since little support exists, there is no real reason to repress because there is no real danger. In those periods, the role of the state is actually the opposite of trying to repress out of existence revolutionary rhetoric; in fact, through its undercover agents, the state seeks to encourage the group to engage in more terroristic words, not, as most people hold, in order to repress it later, but to isolate it from a mass base. If a group gets through that period and does begin to organize, then its rhetoric and tactics will become decidedly less militant and terroristic, as if almost by law. But it is at that point, when the state's policy of encouraging more militance breaks down, that the use of violence by the state is substituted as a form of repression, because that is when the group is most dangerous. It is interesting that the most severe repression of the Black Panther party came, not after it carried guns into the California legislature, but after it instituted a program of free breakfasts.

It should also be pointed out that there are times when the tactics of dissenting groups have nothing to do with repression. Because of its ties to the Soviet Union, the U.S. Communist party was continually under siege by the government of the United States. After the Second World War the government moved to destroy it, and it was irrelevant whether the CP adopted a popular front line or an ultra-leftist line. Thus even in situations like this, the point holds that the state's decision to use repression is not determined by a dissenting group's choice of tactics but by the state itself.

(6) *Repressive forces are not omnipresent and impenetrable.* It is fairly easy to overestimate the potential danger of repression, if the number of people who do so is any indication. At times, for example, Herbert Marcuse can be read in such a way that there is almost no hope for those struggling to create a non-repressive society.[28] The means of repression are so subtle, so internalized, so changed from basically political phenomena to basically psychic ones, that even a struggle for liberation can actually be part of a repressive strategy. In contrast, I would argue that the strength of repression is about as great as the strength of the capitalist system it is designed to support. And since the system is rendered

---

[27]For documentation of this point, see Dubofsky, *We Shall Be All*.

[28]Herbert Marcuse, *One-Dimensional Man* (Boston: Beacon Press, 1964). However, Marcuse seems to have moderated his view in *Essay on Liberation* (Beacon Press, 1969) and *Five Lectures* (Beacon Press, 1970).

unstable and ultimately self-destructive by its internal contradictions, so the repressive apparatus is replete with paradoxes which, while not rendering it impotent, at least make it vulnerable to some forms of attack.

For example, there are times in the development of the liberal state when the very means of consciousness-manipulation create the basis for radicalization. In most urban high schools at the moment, students are either on drugs (in the case of heroin, clearly a form of repression) or are enemies of those who run the schools and, in that sense, also of the state. Originally designed to foster obedience and teach traditions, American public secondary schools currently do neither: they are vast breeding grounds for discontent, even though there are ruling-class spokesmen (like Charles Silberman) who realize this and periodically make eloquent pleas to reform the schools.[29] Perhaps this is because the schools simply cannot do what the society asks of them in the face of enormous political and cultural change. The same is true of many other institutions. It is the nuclear family which is responsible for the commune and the collective, the media which created the underground newspapers, religion which breeds agnosticism or the search for new spiritualism, work which creates alienation and discontent. The new society is being born of the old, and the attempts by the old to reinforce patterns which have become illegitimate in the eyes of many simply create further illegitimacy.

Increased use of the means of state violence — repression — is a response to those breakdowns. Often, in a short-term sense, this violence may be effective. Repression of the Black Panther party seems to have destroyed the viability of that organization. The McCarthy period clearly stifled political discussion for a long time. Yet even in spite of that effectiveness, such represstion creates its own problems. Out of the experience of the Panthers black groupings have arisen in parts of the country which are consciously trying to avoid the pattern into which the Panthers fell. And the McCarthy period, effective for a while, may just have postponed a confrontation with virulent anti-communism until the present time. But the best example of the paradoxical nature of such repression is the Chicago Eight trial. Whatever the motive of the government in prosecuting, that event contributed to massive feelings of illegitimacy toward the state on the part of young people throughout the country. It confirmed for many the idea that something is fundamentally wrong with America, for the obvious reason — but one that it is essential to continually remember — that something *is* fundamentally wrong with America. It was not "we" who thought up that trial but "they"; they acted as we expected them to act, which is all we could have asked of them.

There may well be times when repressive policies force political groups into dilemmas from which there is no easy way out. But there are also times when the rulers of the democratic state face impossible situations as well. Should Lt. Calley be found guilty? If the answer is no, then an indictment of the entire

---

[29]Charles Silberman, *Crisis in the Classroom* (New York: Random House, 1970).

army is the result. If the answer is yes, then troops will be encouraged not to shoot in Vietnam. What made this dilemma (for them) real was the massive opposition to the war on the part of most Americans and many soldiers. That consciousness forced the Army into a position from which it could not extricate itself simply. For a moment in history, it was the army, not the antiwar movement, which was up against the wall.

The state's use of repression is also hindered, particularly in liberal democracies, by a rhetorical commitment to due process. Originally an aspect of liberal thought, because it afforded protection to businessmen to accumulate capital undisturbed, due process of law has increasingly been interpreted by the courts to apply to civil liberty cases. This does not mean an end to repression; it means that repression should not be arbitrary. For example, after the May Day events of 1971 in Washington, the American Civil Liberties Union ran a full-page ad critical of the Nixon administration's handling of the arrests, suggesting that the same goal — keeping the government functioning — could have been obtained by means more in keeping with the Bill of Rights. There are, then, people who are interested in procedure to the point where ends are irrelevant, and often their voices are eloquent, sometimes even influential.

The development of a concern with civil liberty does complicate matters for the repressors. They are not free to switch back and forth in a search for the best repressive policy. Traditions and procedures do play a role, and it is perfectly natural that dissenting groups, when being repressed, will exploit these contradictions and use procedures and traditions to protect themselves whenever possible. It is also clear that to the extent that the tradition of civil liberty is near extinction, the threat comes from those who wield state power, not from those who challenge them.

(7) *It follows from this that the use of violent repression by the state could easily be a sign of its weakness, not its strength.* The ruling class is armed and dangerous; of that there is no doubt. It possesses an enormous amount of destructive weaponry, and — as the case of Fred Hampton indicates — it is not afraid to use it. It is clearly an error to take a Pollyannaish view of such a violent potential. But though tigers they may be, there is some truth in Mao's dictum that the tigers may be made of paper, and the reasons for that should be stated.

Violent repression exists because there is struggle; without a political movement, there need not be any repression. Instead of reacting with hurt surprise at the existence of such repression, and instead of simply calling for civil liberty — which means acting in a civil fashion — that repression should be understood as an opportunity to teach something about the nature of the liberal state. When a repressive society acts repressively, it is, in other words, doing what it is supposed to do. If it acted in any other way — say, by appointing members of the Black Panther Party to commissions instead of raiding their offices — it would not be what it is. This is a simple point, but it has taken a while for it to sink home. The defendants in the Spock trial, from this perspective, acted wrongly in restricting themselves to an insistence on procedure and fairness. They were found guilty anyway. On the other hand, the defendants in the Chicago trial had a remarkably sophisticated understanding of what repression meant. They used the trial in a political way, proper because it was a political trial. By their response, they put the government on trial for trying them, and they even won some sympathy from the jury in doing that. (This, plus the astounding support from the jury received by the Panther Thirteen, where an alliance was created between defendants and jury against the credibility of the state, indicates that such a strategy need not mean an automatic jail sentence.) Both groups used their trials to expand the political movement which brought them to trial, and they undoubtedly had an important effect upon the consciousness of, in the one case, young people and, in the other, black people.

Since non-terroristic reproductive mechanisms are generally preferred by the rulers of the bourgeois-democratic state, when state violence is used it is most likely an indication that affairs have not been running smoothly. In that sense, it indicates a crisis for the state, a period in which the ruling class is so unsure of its rule that it seeks the protection that only troops and police can provide, which turns out to be ambiguous protection at best. It follows that those periods which see an increase in violent repression are the same periods in which dissenting groups are most successfully building their movement. The present moment is such a time. The extraordinary number of political trials (Chicago Eight, Harlem Five, Panther Thirteen, Spock, draft resistance cases, drug frame-ups, indictments of May Day organizers, etc.), the return to raids and evidence-seizures, the drastic increase in the use of National Guard troops, and the revelations of the use of infiltrators and informers do not necessarily mean that the democratic state is turning into a fascistic-type police state, as some on the Left feel. That can only take place when there is no important progressive movement. On the contrary, the increase in violent repression is a response to a progressive movement (and its potential) and is being determined by that movement itself. If the movement went away, so would violent repression. In other words, it is not the tactics of any one group which affects repression, but the state of the movement as a whole.

If the reactionaries are paper tigers, it is because time is not on their side. Those who see fascism as inevitably coming out of the repressive potential of the democratic stage give more time to the rulers of that state than they actually have; they give them more credit than they deserve. It is true that there is a fascist potential in liberal-democratic societies, but it is just as true that socialist movements — in the United States and abroad — have the potential to prevent that from materializing. Why assume that one side will win and not the other? Those who are disillusioned by the amount of state violence in the United States are those who had illusions about the democratic state in the first place. If we understand that repression is used out of desperation, we are one step closer to understanding how a non-repressive society can be built.

3. John H. Schaar

Legitimacy in the Modern State

I

Authority is a word on everyone's lips today. The young attack it and the old demand respect for it. Parents have lost it and policemen enforce it. Experts claim it and artists spurn it, while scholars seek it and lawyers cite it. Philosophers reconcile it with liberty and theologians demonstrate its compatibility with conscience. Bureaucrats pretend they have it and politicians wish they did. Everybody agrees that there is less of it than there used to be. It seems that the matter stands now as a certain Mr. Wildman thought it stood in 1648: "Authority hath been broken into pieces."[1]

About the only people left who seem little affected by the situation are the political scientists. Authority used to be a central term in learned political discourse, perhaps the governing term in philosophical treatments of politics. Except for a few renegade Catholic philosophers, that is obviously no longer the case. You can read a dozen authoritative texts on the American political system, for example, and not find the concept seriously treated. Its use is restricted to discussions of such ritual matters as "the authority of the people" or to descriptions of the "authority" of this or that institution or office. Even the recent spate of writing on the theory of democracy contains no substantial treatment of the topic.[2]

Max Weber pretty thoroughly did our work for us here. His exposition of the three types of authority, or the three grounds upon which claims to legitimate authority can be based, has the same status in social science that an older trinity has in Christian theology. Since Weber, we have been busy putting the phenomena into one or another of his three boxes and charting the progress by which charismatic authority becomes routinized into traditional authority, which, under the impact of science and secularism, gives way in turn to rational-legal authority. It all looks pretty good to the political scientists, as more and more traditional societies enter the transitional stage and gather their resources for the hopeful journey toward the modern stage, where rational-legal authority holds sway, along with prosperity,

[1]From "The Whitehall Debates," in A.S.P. Wodehouse, ed., *Puritanism and Liberty* (London, J. M. Dent, 1938), p. 127.

[2]The only important exception is Yves R. Simon, *Philosophy of Democratic Government* (Chicago, University of Chicago Press, 1951), pp. 1–72. Simon's book lies within the Aristotelian-Thomist tradition.

moderation, and a "participant" and empathetic citizenry. It is admitted, to be sure, that there are many obstacles on the path, that some traditional folk still hold out, and that there are even one or two troublesome cases of regression. But on the whole, history is the story of the rational-legal state.[3]

But while the discipline cumulates, things outside jump. We hear of riots and rebellions, demonstrations and assassinations. Heads of state in many modern countries cannot safely go among the citizenry. Dignified ceremonies are raucously interrupted by riotous crowds chanting obscenities at the officials. Policemen have been transformed from protectors into pigs. A lot of young people are trying drugs, and a lot of older people are buying guns. A few months ago, a man entered the employment security building in Olympia, Washington, and tried to murder a computer. He failed, however, because 1401's brains were protected by a bulletproof steel plate. Some developers recently announced plans for a "maximum security subdivision" in Maryland at a minimum cost of $200,000 per house. The subdivision will be ringed by a steel fence and patrolled by armed guards, the shrubbery will hide electronic detectors, and visitors will be checked through a blockhouse. In 1968, American governmental units hired 26,000 additional policemen, an increase of 7 percent over 1967; 1968 was the second year in a row during which police employment rose more steeply than any other kind of public employment.[4]

We can feel the chill of some sentences Henry Adams wrote over sixty years ago:

The assumption of unity which was the mark of human thought in the middle-ages has yielded very slowly to the proofs of complexity. . . . Yet it is quite sure . . . that, at the accelerated rate of progression shown since 1600, it will not need another century or half century to tip thought upside down. Law, in that case, would disappear as theory or *a priori* principle, and give place to force. Morality would become police. Explosives would reach cosmic violence. Disintegration would overcome integration.[5]

It is the thesis of this essay that legitimate authority is declining in the modern states; that, in a real sense, "law and order" *is* the basic political question of our day. The seamless web of socialization described by such leading students of the subject as Easton, Greenstein, Hess, and Hyman shows rips and frays. Many of the sons are no longer sure they want the legacy of the fathers. Among young people, the peer group increasingly takes priority as the agency of socialization, and the values it sponsors are new and hostile to those of the adult world. Many people are seeking ways to live in the system without belonging to it: their hearts are elsewhere. Others, convinced that the organized system will not

[3]For a recent specimen, see the sections by Lerner in Daniel Lerner and Wilbur Schramm, eds., *Communication and Change in the Developing Countries* (Honolulu, East-West Center Press, 1967).
[4]*San Francisco Chronicle,* June 5, 1969, p. 42.
[5]Letter to Henry Osborne Taylor, January 17, 1905. In Harold Dean Cater, ed., *Henry Adams and His Friends.* Quoted here from William H. Jordy, *Henry Adams: Scientific Historian* (New Haven, Yale University Press, 1963), p. xi.

in the long run permit the escape into private liberty, or feeling that such an escape is ignoble, are acting politically to transform the system. In the eyes of large and growing numbers of men, the social and political landscape of America, the most advanced of the advanced states, is no green and gentle place, where men may long abide. That landscape is, rather, a scene of wracked shapes and desert spaces. What we mainly see are the eroded forms of once authoritative institutions and ideas. What we mainly hear are the hollow winds of once compelling ideologies, and the unnerving gusts of new moods and slogans. What we mainly feel in our hearts is the granite consolidation of the technological and bureaucratic order, which may bring physical comfort and great collective power, or sterility, but not political liberty and moral autonomy. All the modern states, with the United States in the vanguard, are well advanced along a path toward a crisis of legitimacy.[6]

The essay has two subsidiary theses. First, that the crisis of legitimacy is a function of some of the basic, defining orientations of modernity itself; specifically, rationality, the cult of efficiency and power, ethical relativism, and equalitarianism. In effect, it will be argued that the modern mind, having now reached nearly full development, is turning back upon itself and undermining the very principles that once sustained order and obedience in the modern state. Secondly, it will be argued (mainly indirectly) that contemporary social science has failed to appreciate the precariousness of legitimate authority in the modern states because it is largely a product of the same phenomena it seeks to describe and therefore suffers the blindness of the eye examining itself.

What the thesis essentially asserts, then, is that the philosophical and experiential foundations of legitimacy in the modern states are gravely weakened, leaving obedience a matter of lingering habit, or expediency, or necessity, but not a matter of reason and principle, and of deepest sentiment and conviction. We are nearing the end of an era, and it is beccoming clear that the decline of legitimate authority is the product of the ideal and material forces that have been the defining attributes of modern authority itself. This movement has been visible for a long time in most of the nonpolitical sectors of life — family, economy, education, religion — and it is now spreading rapidly into the political realm. The gigantic and seemingly impregnable control structures that surround and dominate men in the modern states are increasingly found to have at their centers, not a vital principle of authority, but something approaching a hollow space, a moral vacuum.

A preliminary word on the scope and perspective of the essay, and on its political and methodological orientations.

The major thesis and its subsidiaries can be expanded and elucidated in a number

---

[6]When I refer to a crisis of legitimacy, I mean more than an intensification of controversy about various public issues and policies — the kind of thing Dahl discusses in his analysis of the periodicity of opposition in the United States; or the kind of thing treated by the Michigan group under the category of critical or realigning elections. For a study of American voting patterns and electoral behavior that is important to an understanding of legitimacy in the United States, see Walter Dean Burnham, "The Changing Shape of the American Political Universe," *American Political Science Review*, LIX, No. 1 (March 1965), 7–28. What I mean by legitimacy will become clear as the essay proceeds.

of ways. Its critical terms can be defined with precision, and its relevance to the contemporary political scene in the United States can be shown. Empirical evidence can be brought to bear on the propositions. But these propositions cannot be made operational, tested, and verified or falsified beyond reasonable doubt by the criteria of a rigorous behavioralism. This essay will report no opinion survey, present no input-output charts, attempt no stimulus-response or cognitive-dissonance analysis of legitimacy. It will, instead, utilize a variety of materials that help illuminate the problem, including some materials of dubious scientific quality. Perhaps it really is possible to say something about the truth without first polling a sample of one's contemporaries in order to get the facts.

The recent disturbances and novelties in the modern states have taken the political science profession largely by surprise. That is due in fair part, I think, to the very methods which now enjoy favor in the discipline and to the narrow standards set by those methods concerning the materials that qualify as worthy of professional attention. Those methods are poorly designed for dealing with change. The insistence upon rigor means that very often the methods are permitted to determine the subjects studied, rather than vice versa. The erection of the logical distinction between fact and value into a metaphysical dualism has simultaneously cut the profession off from the dominant concerns of modern philosophy and rendered it vulnerable to the grossest of all logical and practical errors, the idealization of the actual. The profession has devised a whole kit of tools for dealing with the routine and predictable but is largely at a loss in the face of genuine novelty. The virtual equation of operationalism and the verifiability theory of meaning with science has meant both a narrowing of many of the most basic concepts of political life and an inability even to perceive whole ranges of empirical phenomena. But this is not the place for a discourse on method: it must suffice to say that behavioral political science has some grave debilities on subjects such as those treated in this essay.

While the essay grew out of a concern with the recent appearance of novel, radical, and sometimes violent forms of speech and action in various sectors of modern life, it does not deal directly with those matters. It is clear to nearly everybody that a limited but quite significant "de-authorization" of the dominant institutions and ideas is taking place today. The causes and consequences of this movement have been treated in a thousand books, articles, and speeches, and no literate man can be unaware of the main analyses and proposed solutions. The essay has little to say on this level of the subject. It does not discuss the generation gap or the credibility gap. It has nothing to say specifically about permissiveness and firmness. It offers no analyses of the SDS or the University of California, no judgments on Anti-Communism or Imperialism. I would like to think that the essay does, however, deal with these matters in an important way by going beneath them to the underlying sources and dimensions of the present de-authorization.

No man can pretend to full moral and political neutrality on this subject. It is easy for one of my age and vocation to be simultaneously afraid, contemptuous, and envious of much of what today goes under the labels "youth culture" and

"New Left." Their language and their manners are offensive. There are good reasons for worrying about their lack of discipline, their uncertain devotion to the practices of fair play, their instant communities of dope, music, and self-indulgent rhetoric, and their readiness for extreme actions. It is no true service to keep silent about these things, let alone to take the view that the young, the black, and the radical have a monopoly of the true, the beautiful, and the good.

On the other hand, he who veils fear and envy as patriotism, and hides contempt under the slogans of tolerance, or openly urges ferocity against the young and the radical, sins against life and the future. We are members one of another. The established, the respectable, and the frightened of this land appear on the edge of an utterly nihilistic war against the future — war against their own young, who *are* the future; and war against the black and the poor, who once were creators of wealth, but who now are seen only as expensive and dangerous nuisances. This war must be prevented, for we are members one of another. Furthermore, at their center and at their best, the youthful, black, and radical protest movements have served America well. Their criticisms of the repressiveness, unresponsiveness, bureaucratization, and hypocrisy of the dominant institutions have been incisive and courageous. Their rejection of the "technetronic society" now being built is an effort for the common redemption, without regard to differences of age, race, or station. So, too, is their call for a more democratic and humane society and their insistence that knowledge be integrated with identity, and both tied to commitment. In a basic way, this essay is an attempt to understand the ways in which certain modern definitions of knowledge and processes of control have contributed to the weakening of legitimate authority and the dehumanization of relations among men which the radicals of our day no longer ignore or endure.

II

Start by comparing the traditional and common meanings of legitimacy with the usage of leading modern social scientists. The *Oxford English Dictionary* says the following:

Legitimacy: (a) of a government or the title of a sovereign: the condition of being in accordance with law or principle. . . . (b) conformity to a rule or principle; lawfulness. In logic, conformity to sound reasoning.
Legitimate: (a) etymologically, the word expresses a status, which has been conferred or ratified by some authority. (b) conformable to law or rule. Sanctioned or authorized by law or right; lawful; proper. (c) normal, regular; conformable to a recognized standard type. (d) sanctioned by the laws of reasoning; logically admissible or inferable.

The most relevant entries from Webster's *Unabridged* are:

Legitimate: (1) lawfully begotten. . . . (2) real, genuine; not false, counterfeit, or spurious. (3) accordant with law or with established legal forms and requirements; lawful. (4) conforming to recognized principles, or accepted rules or standards.

Now, three current professional definitions:

1. Legitimacy involves the capacity of the system to engender and maintain the belief that the existing political institutions are the most appropriate ones for the society.[7]
2. In the tradition of Weber, legitimacy has been defined as "the degree to which institutions are valued for themselves and considered right and proper."[8]
3. We may define political legitimacy as the quality of "oughtness" that is perceived by the public to inhere in a political regime. That government is legitimate which is viewed as morally proper for a society.[9]

The contrast between the two sets of definitions, the traditional and lexical on the one side and the current scientific usage on the other, is basic and obvious. The older definitions all revolve around the element of law or right, and rest the force of a claim (whether it be a claim to political power or to the validity of a conclusion in an argument) upon foundations external to and independent of the mere assertion or opinion of the claimant (e.g., the laws of inheritance, the laws of logic). Thus, a claim to political power is legitimate only when the claimant can invoke some source of authority beyond or above himself. History shows a variety of such sources: immemorial custom, divine law, the law of nature, a constitution. As Arendt has pointed out, "In all these cases, legitimacy derives from something outside the range of human deeds; it is either not man-made at all . . . or has at least not been made by those who happen to be in power."[10]

The new definitions all dissolve legitimacy into belief or opinion. If a people holds the belief that existing institutions are "appropriate" or "morally proper," then those institutions are legitimate. That's all there is to it. By a surgical procedure, the older concept has been trimmed of its cumbersome "normative" and "philosophical" parts, leaving the term leaner, no doubt, but now fit for scientific duty. It might turn out that Occam's Razor has cut off a part or two that will be missed later on.

A few implications of these new formulations should be articulated.

First of all, when legitimacy is defined as consisting in belief alone, then the investigator can examine nothing outside popular opinion in order to decide whether a given regime or institution or command is legitimate or illegitimate. To borrow the language of the law, there can be no independent inquiry into the title. In effect, this analysis dissolves legitimacy into acceptance or acquiescence, thereby

---

[7]Seymour Martin Lipset, *Political Man* (Garden City, N.Y., Doubleday, 1960), p. 77.

[8]Robert Bierstedt, "Legitimacy," in *Dictionary of the Social Sciences* (New York, The Free Press, 1964), p. 386. Bierstedt is here paraphrasing Lipset, *Political Man*.

[9]Richard M. Merelman, "Learning and Legitimacy," *American Political Science Review*, LX, No. 3 (September 1966), 548.

[10]Hannah Arendt, "What Was Authority?" in Carl J. Friedrich, ed., *Authority* (Cambridge, Harvard University Press, 1958), p. 83.

rendering opaque whole classes of basic and recurrent political phenomena, e.g., a group or individual refuses consent and obedience to the orders of a regime or institution on the ground that the regime or institution is illegitimate; a regime or institution is acknowledged to be legitimate as such, but consent is withheld from a particular order on the ground that the regime had no legitimate right to make that order; one consents or acquiesces out of interest or necessity, although he regards a regime or an order as illegitimate. In short, legitimacy and acquiescence, and legitimacy and consensus, are not the same, and the relations between them are heterogeneous. The older formulations made these empirical situations comprehensible, while the newer usages obfuscate them. The phenomenon of legitimacy, far from being identical with consensus, is rather, as Friedrich says, "a very particular form of consensus, which revolves around the question of the right or title to rule."[11] Legitimacy is that aspect of authority which refers to entitlement.

Another important feature of these new formulations, which emerges clearly when the definitions are examined within the context of the larger works in which they appear, is that they see legitimacy as a function of a system's ability to persuade members of its own appropriateness. The flow is from leaders to followers. Leaders lay down rules, promulgate policies, and disseminate symbols which tell followers how and what they should do and feel. Thus, Merelman explains legitimacy within the framework of stimulus-response psychology, which he rather narrowly equates with learning theory. The regime or the leaders provide the stimuli, first in the form of policies improving citizen welfare and later in the form of symbolic materials which function as secondary reinforcements, and the followers provide the responses, in the form of favorable attitudes toward the stimulators — which, to reiterate, is what Merelman means by legitimacy. The symbols become, in the minds of the followers, condensations of the practices and intentions of the rulers. Over time, if the rulers manipulate symbols skillfully, symbolic rewards alone may suffice to maintain supportive attitudes.[12] The symbols may actually conceal rather than reveal the real nature of the regime's policies and practices, as the symbols of democracy becloud the actual processes of rule in the modern states.

We should be clear about the understanding of the relationship between "community" and control that informs such a conception of legitimacy. Merelman and others in this tradition see a polity not as a people with a culture seeking together the forms of order and action that will preserve and enhance that culture, but as a mass or collective that is made into a unit of control by propaganda.[13]

---

[11]Carl Joachim Friedrich, *Man and His Government: An Empirical Theory of Politics* (New York, McGraw-Hill Book Company, 1963), p. 233.

[12]There is evidence that in the United States symbolic rewards alone do largely suffice. See Herbert McClosky, "Consensus and Ideology in American Politics," *American Political Science Review*, LVIII, No. 2 (June 1964), 361–82. A study of the tables on cynicism and futility shows that on item after item members of the general electorate express a strong sense of their own political powerlessness. Yet, 90 percent of the respondents say that they "usually have confidence that the government will do what is right."

[13]David Easton's treatment, in *A Systems Analysis of Political Life* (New York, John Wiley & Sons, 1965), esp. Ch. 18, also remains within this perspective although his reification of "the system" and his employment of the term as a noun of agency becloud what actually goes on. But consider:

That is no doubt a fairly accurate conception of most modern systems of rule, but it is worth remembering that a politics of propaganda and ideology is not the only possible politics.[14]

Legitimacy, then, is almost entirely a matter of sentiment. Followers believe in a regime, or have faith in it, and that is what legitimacy is. The faith may be the product of conditioning, or it may be the fruit of symbolic bedazzlement, but in neither case is it in any significant degree the work of reason, judgment, or active participation in the processes of rule. In this analysis, people do not attribute legitimacy to authority because they recognize its claim to a foundation in some principle or source outside itself. This emerges clearly in Lipset's treatment of the specific institutional arrangements and procedures which are conducive to legitimacy: cross-pressures; widespread and multiple membership in voluntary associations; widespread and multiple membership in voluntary associations; the two-party system; federalism, territorial rather than proportional representation.[15] In a most confusing way, an analysis of something called legitimacy first equates legitimacy with opinion, then goes to a restatement of the standard liberal-pluralist description of the structure of power in the United States, turns next to a discussion of stability, and finally resolves stability into passivity or acquiescence caused by cognitive confusion, conflict of interest, and inability to translate one's desires into political decisions due to certain institutional arrangements. Obviously, we are no longer talking about faith or belief at all, let alone legitimacy, but about confusion and indifference, stability and efficiency. There is where the contemporary social treatment of legitimate power rests. A fuller view is needed.

No matter where we go in space, nor how far back in time, we find power. Power is ancient and ubiquitous, a universal feature of social life. But if it is a fact, it is nonetheless a complex fact:

Power exists . . . only through the concurrence of all [its] properties . . . it draws its inner strength and the material succour which it receives, both from the continuously helping hand of habit and also from the imagination; it must possess both a reasonable authority and a magical influence; it must operate like nature herself, both by visible means and by hidden influence.[16]

Force can bring political power into being but cannot maintain it. For that, something else is required: "Will, not force," said T. H. Green, "is the basis of the state." Once power is established and set on course, as it were, then obedience

---

"Under the usual conception of legitimacy as a belief in the right of authorities to rule and members to obey . . . the major stimulus for the input of diffuse support would arise from efforts to reinforce such ideological convictions among the membership" (p. 288).

[14]Lipset also sees legitimacy largely in terms of symbol manipulation. Thus, he says that "a major test of legitimacy is the extent to which given nations have developed a common 'secular political culture,' mainly national rituals and holidays." The United States has passed the test, for it possesses "a common homogeneous culture in the veneration accorded the Founding Fathers, Abraham Lincoln, Theodore Roosevelt, and their principles." (Lipset, *Political Man*, p. 80.) I refrain from comment on this pantheon.

[15]*Ibid.*, pp. 88–92.

[16]In Necker, *Du Pouvoir executif dans les Grands États*, 1792, p. 22. Quoted here from Bertrand de Jouvenel, *Power*, trans. by J. F. Huntington (London, Barchworth Press, 1948), p. 30.

is largely a matter of habit. But there are two critical points in the life of power when habit does not suffice. The first is at its birth, when habits of obedience have not formed. The other comes when the customary ways and limits of power are altered, when subjects are presented with new and disturbing uses of power and are asked to assume new burdens and accept new claims. At those two points — and most of the states of our day, old and new, are at one or the other of the two — theory must be called in to buttress and justify obedience. There is no denying a certain pragmatic or expediential element in all theories of legitimacy. Such theories are never offered idly, they never appear accidentally. Rather, they appear when the uses of power are matters of controversy, and they are weapons in the struggles of men to enjoy the benefits and escape the burdens of power. This is not to say that all theories of legitimacy are only or merely "rationalizations"; rather, it is to say that they have an element of rationalization in them.

Theory, then, by making power legitimate, turns it into authority. All theories of legitimacy take the form of establishing a principle which, while it resides outside power and is independent of it, locates or embeds power in a realm of things beyond the wills of the holders of power: the legitimacy of power stems from its *origin*. In addition, most theories of legitimacy simultaneously attempt to justify power by reference to its *ends*. As was suggested by the earlier quotation from Arendt, the originating principles have been many and diverse. So too have the ends. But in our time this great complexity has been reduced, in virtually all states, to a gratifying simplicity: for power to become authority, it must originate in "democratic consent" and aim at the "common good" or "public interest."

I shall not rehearse here in any detail the many assaults that have been made against both these concepts. They are familiar enough. Let it suffice to say that criticism and hard events have done their work: both concepts have been reduced to rubble. Democracy is the most prostituted word of our age, and any man who employs it in reference to any modern state should be suspect either of ignorance or of bad motives.[17] The public good has not fared much better. It is widely agreed among political scientists that it is more a term of political art than of political analysis, but if it has any cognitive content at all it can mean only the sum or aggregate of individual, subjective interests.[18]

---

[17]Put less polemically: the looseness of the term is indicated by the fact that virtually every new or modern political ideology or system has been identified somewhere in the literature as democratic. See, for example, C. B. Macpherson, *The Real World of Democracy* (Oxford, Oxford University Press, 1966).

[18]I think this contemporary professional understanding of the public interest is a superficial one. It fails, for example, to consider Rousseau's effort to distinguish qualitatively between aggregated private interests and genuine common concerns. It fails also to come to terms with Burke's distinction between interest and opinion — an important distinction which appears in many everyday expressions, as when we say a man is "mistaken as to his interest." It excludes J. S. Mill's attempt to make qualitative distinctions between types of subjective interests and values. It is blind to Madison's distinctions between types of groups and publics: reasonable and long-range versus passionate and temporary. Above all, the contemporary understanding restricts and debases the function of discussion in political life, reducing all speech to the lowest common denominator of "rationalization" or deception, or, at best, bargaining. American political parties and legislatures are not the whole of the political experience relevant to an understanding of the concept of public interest.

The whole question of the status and function of the notion of the public interest within the framework

That offered little trouble for a time, because it seemed perfectly compatible with popular sovereignty and majority rule, which everyone agreed were basic principles of democratic decision making. But then Arrow showed that there was no way to produce a unique social ordering of the preferences of individuals that would be compatible with the requirements of popular sovereignty and majority rule — thereby leaving both the theory of democracy and the concept of the public interest in a shambles.[19]

There the matter stands among the sophisticated. The most benighted savage of yesterday's anthropology, sacrificing to his totemic ancestor and groveling before his sacred king, is no worse off for a theory of legitimacy that will pass the tests of reason than is the most advanced "democratic" theorist among us today.

The case is not much better among ordinary men. Most of them really know that "the people" do not run things: a plethora of surveys and voting studies confirms that. Hence, the test of legitimacy for them is not power's origins but its ends. And from this point of view, the "public interest" means just about what it has always meant: security and material abundance. The sacred king once had to make the crops grow and provide victory in battle. The government must now defend national security and enlarge the GNP. But it is increasingly clear that the nation-state can no longer guarantee the first at all and that in the modern states the second has been accomplished to the point where it threatens the irreversible degradation of the environment and the species.

We have finally made the engine that can smash all engines, the power that can destroy all power. Security today, bought at the price of billions, means that We shall have fifteen minutes warning that They intend to annihilate us, during which time we can also annihilate them. The most powerful state today cannot provide security but only revenge. There is not a person among us who has not himself imagined the destruction of all things by nuclear holocaust. Not since civilization began has man been so totally reduced to the status of temporary occupant of his home, the earth. The dream of total security through total power has ended in the reality of total vulnerability.[20]

---

of democratic theory is complex and problematic. Historically, the notion has often played about the same role in domestic politics as "reason of state" or "national interest": it releases officials from restrictions imposed by the democratic principle of popular sovereignty. But if officials can claim authority, usually on grounds of superior knowledge, to determine the public good, then democracy, or democratic consent, is nothing more than a method for selecting rulers.

Richard E. Flatham, *The Public Interest* (New York, John Wiley & Sons, 1966) has tried to restore the concept to a status of philosophic dignity, with results that are, for me, murky. Brian Barry, *Political Argument* (London, Routledge and Kegan Paul, 1965), esp. Chs. 11–13, has laid solid foundations for further analytic work on the topic.

[19]Kenneth Arrow, *Social Choice and Individual Values* (New York, John Wiley & Sons, 1963). Lindblom has argued that Arrow's conditions are not the preconditions of popular sovereignty. Lindblom's formulation, however, rests upon a very special understanding of democracy. He asks what process can produce the right ordering of preferences, answers that it is "partisan mutual adjustment," and concludes that this process is "democratic" *because* it produces the public good. See Charles E. Lindblom, *The Intelligence of Democracy* (New York, The Free Press, 1965).

[20]I am aware that the typical, explicit popular response to this radical insecurity is: "Well, what can I do? Besides, we've all got to die sometime, anyway, and when you're dead, you're dead." That is now, as it has always been, the response of fools, though for ages wise men and saints

The case with abundance comes out about the same way. Inexcusable injustices of distribution still prevail in the modern states, but the "battle of production" is nearing total victory. Societies have always been, in part, organizations for the production of the nutrients of life, but modern civilizations are dominated as no others have ever been by the law of production.[21] Modern production is dedicated almost entirely to consumption; and since consumption is limitless, so too is production. But to produce something means to destroy something else; hence, destruction keeps pace with production. There is the deepest law of modern production: it must continue as long as there is anything left to destroy. That is not metaphor but the precise dynamic of modern economies.

Modern production has obscured the sun and stars toward which men once aspired. It pollutes the air and chews up great forests. It drinks whole lakes and rivers. It has already consumed many species of creatures, and it is making ready to consume the oceans. Its factories once ate children and more recently have been fed slaves. This civilization of production periodically devours men by heaps and piles in war, and it daily mangles the spirits of others in meaningless labor. The only aim of this civilization is to live, that is, to grow, and to grow it must consume. Ellul has shown, unanswerably I think, that the process must run until it consumes those who think they run it — until man is absorbed into technique and process. That will be the total victory in the battle of production; and as always with total victories, no atonement will avail.[22]

The modern state, then, insofar as it is provider and guarantor of increase, and insofar as its success in this task is a source of legitimacy, has succeeded too well: its success has become a threat to survival. The masses have not yet heard this message, though some hints have begun to penetrate the thicket of propaganda and inherited ideas. Most importantly, this understanding is growing among young people and among the cultural elites: even Galbraith has anxiously asked whether the impulse toward destruction might not be an inherent dynamic of the new order.[23] Once again we reach the same conclusion. The new state

---

had enough authority to persuade or impose upon men a belief in responsibility and immortality, so that fools were ashamed or afraid to speak their foolishness aloud. I am also aware that the typical, explicit professional response to this radical insecurity is something like, Total vulnerability is equal to security so long as the vulnerability is both mutual and really total. This is the strategy of deterrence. This theory redefines security to me, not freedom from fear, but the ability to believe that fears will not be realized. Such a notion of security requires endless and accelerating technological advance, increasing military power, and permanent inequalities of distribution. But all this is really beside the point. What matters here is that the "strongest" nation-states have failed the test of legitimacy through the provision of security. See Georges Bernanos, *Last Essays*, trans. Joan and Barry Ulanov (Chicago, Henry Regnery, 1955), esp. pp. 195–97.

[21]Some perspective is provided by Walt Whitman's assessment, made over a century ago, that America had already overdeveloped the economic sector of life and should now turn to other efforts.

[22]Jacques Ellul, *The Technological Society*, trans. John Wilkinson (New York, Vintage Books, 1967).

[23]He, of course, did not put the point as bluntly as it is put here. Rather, he argued that high and ever-increasing military expenditures are an organic feature of the new industrial state, and concluded that "modern military and related procurement and policy are, in fact, extensively adapted to the needs of the industrial system." John Kenneth Galbraith, *The New Industrial State* (New York, New American Library, 1967), p. 241. See also Chs. 20 and 29.

of production has fulfilled its promise of abundance, but only at the price of raising a new and formidable threat to freedom, and even to survival.[24]

III

I do not wish to poke about among these ruins. Rather, I shall take a backward look over the roads which have led to the modern condition, which, to say it again, is the condition of the shattering of authority. The modern condition is not "new" in the strict sense of the term. Rather it is an intensification and a fulfillment of certain tendencies which are quite old. On the axiom that in the human sciences inquiry must begin where the subject begins, I wish to look at the basic elements, the principles or starting points, of the modern condition. The question is, What are the main routes by which modern states have reached the stage where power has lost most of the attributes of legitimate authority?

In order to be as clear as possible about the subject under discussion, it will be useful to say a few words about the nature of authority. Following Bertrand de Jouvenel, authority can be defined basically as "the faculty of gaining another man's assent."[25] The word's origins and rich associations suggest the place of authority in human life. An authority is one whose counsels we seek and trust and whose deeds we strive to imitate and enlarge. He is one who, while lacking most of the specific attributes of power as force, makes recommendations which cannot safely be ignored because they are usually right: "While power resides in the people, authority rests with the Senate [of Rome]."[26] An authority is one who starts lines of action which others complete. Hence he is, metaphorically, the father of their actions. A man or an institution becomes a father and augmenter of others' actions in one of two ways. First, by example: he shows others the way by going there first himself. Secondly, he has the ability to assure others that the actions he recommends are rightful and will succeed. Here, then, are the two basic functions of authority: it provides counsel and justification, and it increases the confidence and sense of ability of those under it by assuring them that the actions it recommends will succeed and will enlarge the actors. Seen in this light, authority, far from confining and depleting men, liberates and enriches them by bringing to birth that which is potentially present. It is only under the impact of the liberal ideology that men came to formulate authority and liberty as opposites and enemies. In an older understanding, authority, while it defined and limited liberty, thereby also fulfilled and directed it. As Nietzsche understood,

---

[24]Galbraith again: "If we continue to believe that the goals of the industrial system . . . are coordinate with life, then all of our lives will be in the service of these goals. . . . What will eventuate . . . will be the benign servitude of the household retainer who is taught to love her mistress and see her interests as her own, and not the compelled service of the field hand. But it will not be freedom." *Ibid.*, p. 405.

[25]Bertrand de Jouvenal, *Sovereignty: An Inquiry into the Political Good*, trans. J. F. Huntington (Chicago, University of Chicago Press, 1957), pp. 203–4.

[26]Cicero, *De Legibus*, 3, 12, 38. Quoted here from Hannah Arendt, "What Was Authority?" p. 100.

absence of horizons is not liberty but madness and impotence. Can anyone today still believe that liberty grows stronger as authority grows weaker?

If authority is to initiate actions and vouch for their rightness and success, it must have a rationale that backs its claim to assent.[27] As Plato put it, each law must have a preamble, a statement that walks before the law, justifying and explaining it. This rationale includes an account of reality, an explanation of why some acts are preferable to others, and a vision of a worthwhile future toward which men can aspire. Put differently, the rationale consists of a more or less coherent body of shared memories, images, ideas, and ideals that gives to those who share it an orientation in and toward time and space. It links past, present, and future into a meaningful whole, and ties means and ends into a continuum that transcends a merely pragmatic or expediential calculation. Authorities at once personify or incarnate this rationale, this conception of legitimacy, and are justified by it. Without such rationales, or "stories," authority dissipates, leaving a vacuum to be filled by power. As Adams put it, morality becomes police.

This understanding of authority has concentrated so far on what R. S. Peters has called its de facto aspects or dimensions. The concept also has what might be called de jure meanings, as when Hobbes says "the right of doing any action, is called AUTHORITY. So that by authority is always understood a right of doing any act; and *done by authority*, done by commission, or license from him whose right it is."[28] Webster's clearly recognizes both usages, for while it gives "legal or rightful power; a right to command or to act," it also gives "power derived from opinion, respect, or esteem; influence of character, office, or station, or mental or moral superiority." The de jure usage welds authority with rights and connects both with office or position in a system of rules and relations. This is the usage most commonly met in traditional political philosophy and in the philosophical analysis of such subjects as institution, obligation, command, and law. The reasons for this are obvious. Men live in societies, which means they regulate their relations with each other largely by systems of rules. This specifically human form of order can be maintained only if "there is general acceptance of procedural rules which lay down who is to originate rules, who is to decide about their concrete application . . . and who is entitled to introduce changes."[29] All these are functions of authority within human society.

The de facto and de jure uses of the term, while conceptually distinct at their outer margins, also have common dimensions. Both share the common root *auctor*, or originator. Furthermore, both share the idea of originator by right, though in the de facto sense the right or entitlement rests mainly upon the personal attributes of the individual who has authority, while de jure authority comes from position

---

[27]The rest of this paragraph is drawn from my "Violence in Juvenile Gangs: Some Notes and a Few Analogies," *American Journal of Orthopsychiatry*, XXXIII, No. 1 (January 1963), 33.

[28]*Leviathan*, ed. Michael Oakeshott (Oxford, Blackwell, n.d.), p. 106. I have borrowed the de jure–de facto distinction for this discussion from R. S. Peters, "Authority," in Anthony Quinton, ed., *Political Philosophy* (Oxford, Oxford University Press, 1967), pp. 83–96, at p. 84.

[29]Peters, *ibid.*, p. 94.

or office in a system of rules and practices. Finally, both stress ways of governing conduct by means other than force, manipulation, or propaganda. Authority commands, decides, recommends, and persuades, and resorts to force only when these fail. "To follow an authority is a voluntary act. Authority ends where voluntary assent ends. There is in every state a margin of obedience which is won only by the use of force or the threat of force: it is this margin which breaches liberty and demonstrates the failure of authority."[30]

In an older vocabulary, authority has both the cross and the sword; but while the former is of its essence, the latter is not.

IV

A serious account of the contemporary problem of "law and order" would be an account of the hollowing out of the theoretical and empirical foundations upon which authority (de jure and de facto) has rested in the states of the West. Weber thought that the day of charismatic and traditional structures of legitimacy was over and that both were being displaced by rational-legal authority. But he did not see far enough into the matter, for rational-legal authority has also been undermined, leaving the great institutions it brought into being gravely weakened from within. I cannot supply anything like a full map of the routes leading to this end. What follows is a sketch of the main routes on this journey into emptiness.

1. The Epistemological Route. This route consists in charting the connections between the status of the concept of truth on the one side, and the growing feeling of disengagement or alienation from authoritative structures of order on the other. Until recently, the concept of truth rested upon certain assumptions about the relations between the knower and the known. Two of these assumptions are of greatest importance: (1) the notion that man's cognitive apparatus did not itself basically condition the quality and nature of what was known; and (2) the notion that there existed a kingdom of order outside man and independent of him (e.g., the laws of nature, God, the laws of history). Given the first assumption, truth always meant *discovery*. Given the second, truth meant discovery of a *pre-established* order. Discoveries made by the methods of science, philosophy, and theology were not fabrications of the human mind, but faithful reflections or representations of an order independent of the discoverer. For man to increase his own harmony with the pre-established harmony outside himself, he had only to increase his knowledge of the world.[31] Given the right methods and concepts, increasing

---

[30]De Jouvenel, *Sovereignty*, p. 33.

[31]Even Hume's thought reflects these patterns. Hume is, of course, famous for shattering the two-thousand-year-old concept of natural law — the idea that man could, by rational processes alone, discover universal norms of moral and political conduct. But while Hume, through his skeptical analysis of the character and functions of reason, undermined the ancient rationalist and transcendental conception of natural law, he replaced it by still another, more empirical, conception of natural law whose norms were as certain as those they replaced. He tried to show that the empirical existence of universal norms could be established by observation and that these norms were necessary products of social

knowledge brought increasing harmony between man and the world. Anthropological and mythological researches have shown that in the ages before philosophy and science, myth served this same function of bringing men into contact with the sources of order outside themselves.

Given this concept of truth, social and political life too could be seen as a harmonious association of self and society with an objective order external to man and constituted by some force independent of him. Political societies were not works of human art and will, but were embedded in and even constituted by a larger order of being. Human authority rested on bases more "solid" than individual choice and will.

That older view of knowledge and truth has now just about disappeared, and with its disappearance men have lost most of their older principles of legitimation. In the older view, a structure of order could base its claim to legitimacy on some foundation other than the choices and opinions of the members. In the newer view, order becomes dependent upon will, with no source of rewards and punishments external to the system and its members. With that, the social and political world becomes "unfrozen" as it were, movable by skill and power, for it is seen that there is no necessity in any given arrangement of things. All things could be other than they are. It is the world of Sorel, rather than the world of Plato. It is not even a world in which change or becoming follows a necessary pattern. It is the world of Sartre, rather than the world of Hegel.[32]

Furthermore, the death of the older views also spelled death for the authoritative classes of priests and nobles who claimed a right to rule on the grounds that they possessed knowledge of the true order of things and of the methods needed for gaining further knowledge of that order. The oldest and most basic justification for hierarchy has dissolved. The only class that could conceivably make that claim today is the class of scientists. But in order to occupy this role, the scientific estate would have to transform itself into something very like a priesthood, along lines which Comte understood perfectly. The foundations for that are already present. For the masses, science is largely a matter of miracle, mystery, and authority. Translated into educational terms, the slogan that through science man has gained increasing knowledge of nature really means that a few men now know a great

---

life. His logic was similar to that of the ancient theorists of the *jus gentium* and remarkably like that of modern linquistic philosophers, who argue that certain broad and necessary truths can be derived from the prerequisite conditions essential for the existence of a language. See Hume, *Treatise of Human Nature,* Book III, Part II, Sections I–VI; Part III, Section VI. See also his essay "That Politics May Be Reduced to a Science."

[32]The scientific, objective, manipulative epistemology presupposes that the knower stands outside nature and studies it by assault. Thus: "A long time ago, we developed modern science as veritable outsiders of nature. In order to become scientific observers, we had to denature ourselves. We have succeeded. When we say, now, that we are reasonable we mean that we are engaged in calculations. When we hold something to be irrational we are merely indignant that our predictions have not been borne out, or perhaps, we are amused, for we make rash distinctions between the irrational and the stupid. When we say 'naturally,' we are hardly ever right." Hans Speier, "Shakespeare's 'The Tempest,' " reprinted in Speier, *Social Order and the Risks of War* (Cambridge, M.I.T. Press, 1969), p. 132.

deal about how nature "works," while the rest of us are about as ignorant as we have always been. Translated into political terms, the slogan that through knowledge man has gained the means of unprecedented power over a great many other men. On the other hand, there are good reasons for thinking that the scientists and experts may not be able to perform the priestly role with enduring success. I shall indicate some of these reasons later.

When the secret that nature is no guide is finally known to all — the secret exposed by the Sophists and in our age by Nietzsche — the whole question of legitimacy will have to be reopened. Order will be seen as artificial, the result of will and choice alone, as vulnerable to change and challenge as will itself is. Structures of authority will not be able to invoke the ancient and once ubiquitous idea that each thing under the sun has its own right nature and place in the constitution of the whole. For centuries, this sense of the fitness and rightness of things set boundaries to men's pretensions to control and shaped their moral attitudes concerning the permissible limits within which they might legitimately impose their desires on the world around them. A basic piety toward the world and toward the processes that sustain it will disappear, and all things, including polities and men themselves, will come to appear artificial and malleable.[33] Whole new sets of arguments and images imposing limits on man's urge to satisfy his desires will have to be found. And until they are found, the idea and the very experience of legitimate authority cannot have anyting like the bedrock importance they have heretofore had in political life.

2. The Moral Route. The knowledge that civilization begins when men understand that any shared custom at all is better than none is as old as Homer and as new as the researches of Lévi-Strauss. All morality is in the beginning group morality. Each tribe believes that there is no morality outside the tribe and that the tribe without its morality is no longer a tribe. Morality is, then, both a means and the basic means for preserving a community — holding it together, marking pathways through the landscape of social relations, defending it against threats from strangers and the gods. Men everywhere are taught to fear those who violate morality and to revere its authors and upholders.

Furthermore, as Nietzsche understood, and as scientific research increasingly confirms, nations and communities are "born."[34] And birth requires a father or author, the one who, whether mythologically or actually, brought the original laws and customs, thereby making a people a people.[35] The founder of a people

---

[33]For the impact of this upon the scope and nature of violence in the modern world, see Sheldon S. Wolin, "Violence and the Western Political Tradition," *American Journal of Orthopsychiatry*, XXXIII, No. 1 (January 1963), 15–29.

[34]The words *nature* and *nation* come from the same root, the word for birth. Etymologically, a nation is a birth, hence a group of persons made kindred by common origin. Nations are also continually reborn, through the death of old customs and institutions and the generation of new ones. A nation has a unique birth and is also a continuous rebirth.

[35]Law means limit or boundary. In Greek, the words for law, boundary line, and shepherd had the same root.

is usually either a god or a messenger and mediator between gods and men: the creative moment in the birth of a nation is the birth of a religion.[36] Even the Enlightened American Founding Fathers saw the Constitution as a partial embodiment of that higher order called the Laws of Nature and of Nature's God. Prophets and messengers appear not only at the original birth, but also at times after the founding when the boundaries have been altered or obscured and need to be rectified. In addition, through actions based on myth and ritual, the people themselves also reenact and reaffirm the harmony between the ontological order and their own human realm. In sum, founders and prophets create and correct, and myth and ritual recreate and restore, a community identity set within a cosmology. Identity and legitimacy are thus inseparable.[37]

No one needs to be told that these ancient patterns of thought no longer prevail. The old moralities of custom and religion are husks and shells. With the growth of the special modern form of individual self-consciousness as consciousness of separation, men lose sight of the dependence of the group upon morality and of the dependence of morality upon the group. These paths run parallel to the one, discussed earlier, by which men have journeyed toward epistemological emptiness. Individual withdrawal from the group consciousness and individual rejection of received knowledge proceed concurrently. There is an intimate connection between the decline of custom and "nature" as the setter of boundaries in the social realm, and the Cartesian and Hobbesian rejection of received opinion as the starting man becomes his own author and oracle, his own boundary setter and truth maker. The ego recognizes no source of truth and morality external to itself.

Bacon, Descartes, and Hobbes first decisively stated this modern perspective, and Rousseau formulated the basic political problem stemming from it. He was the first to understand fully, I think, that ours is the task of developing the theory and institutions of a community in which men can be *both* conscious and individual *and* share the moral bonds and limits of the group. Rousseau thought, and much modern experience suggests he was right, that until such a polity was built, modern men would often be, and would even more often feel like, slaves, and that no modern state would be truly legitimate.

Hobbes and just about all later writers in the liberal line — T. H. Green nearly escaped — left this problem on shaky foundations. Hobbes never conceived the possibility of a selfhood which transcended the purely individual. Hence, for him, there is no trouble so long as one self does not impinge upon another. When that happens, Leviathan puts curbs on all. In this perpsective, order is a question of power, and legitimacy is reduced to prudent calculations of self-interest. That

---

[36]Vico expressed the point perfectly in his assertion that there were as many Joves, with as many names, as there are nations. *The New Science of Giambattista Vico*, trans. Thomas Goddard Bergin and Max Harold Fisch (Garden City, N.Y., Doubleday Anchor Books, 1961), pp. xxix, 31.

[37]Machiavelli, obviously not under the spell of mythological thought, gave great attention to this problem of how to keep alive and intact the guiding spirit of a polity and in the end saw it as almost synonymous with popular remembrance of the founding premises: order and action perpetually re-created and renewed through remembrance of origins.

line of thought remains dominant in Sartre, though the vocabulary has shifted to "seriality," and in much contemporary behavioral science, though the Hobbesian vocabulary of "prudence" has shifted to "satisficing" and "maximizing utility."

All this might be made a little more concrete by bringing it closer to home. The United States can be seen as a great experiment in the working out of these ideas. As Lipset has pointed out, the United States is in a very real sense the "first new nation." Our founding took place at an advanced stage of the progress toward epistemological and moral individualism which was sketched above. At the time of the founding, the doctrine and sentiment were already widespread that each individual comes into this world morally complete and self-sufficient, clothed with natural rights which are his by birth, and not in need of fellowship for moral growth and fulfillment. The human material of this new republic consisted of a gathering of men each of whom sought self-sufficiency and the satisfaction of his own desires. Wave after wave of immigrants replenished those urges, for to the immigrant, America largely meant freedom from inherited authorities and freedom to get rich. Community and society meant little more than the ground upon which each challenged or used others for his own gain. Others were accepted insofar as they were useful to one in his search for self-sufficiency. But once that goal was reached, the less one had to put up with the others the better. Millions upon millions of Americans strive for that goal, and what is more important, base their political views upon it. The state is a convenience in a private search; and when that search seems to succed, it is no wonder that men tend to deny the desirability of political bonds, of acting together with others for the life that is just for all. We have no political or moral teaching that tells men they must remain bound to each other even one step beyond the point where those bonds are a drag and a burden on one's personal desires. Americans have always been dedicated to "getting ahead"; and getting ahead has always meant leaving others behind. Surely a large part of the zealous repression of radical protest in America yesterday and today has its roots in the fact that millions of men who are apparently "insiders" know how vulnerable the system is because they know how ambiguous their own attachments to it are. The slightest moral challenge exposes the fragile foundations of legitimacy in the modern state.

I am aware that my argument and conclusions here stand in opposition to the standard liberal-pluralist view of American politics. In that view, Americans are enthusiastic joiners. They seek goals through associational means more readily than do citizens in other lands.[38] In addition, Americans have been found to be less cynical about politics than the citizens of some other states. And Americans early learn attitudes of trust and respect for their regime and its authority figures.

---

[38]Tocqueville is frequently cited at this point in the standard exposition. But Tocqueville has been abused. He hoped and thought that, through voluntary associations, Americans could break out of the cell of individualism and learn the art of politics. But for this to happen, the associations themselves would have to be democratic and political in their internal character. That is rarely the case; but in its absence, Tocqueville's argument simply does not support the uses to which it has been put by contemporary pluralists.

But this literature is largely beside the point; and to the degree that it has been expressed doctrinally — as evidence for the democratic and participatory character of political decision making in the United States — it is misleading.[39] What matter here are questions of quality, not quantity. The professional literature glorifies the sheer, gross quantity of associational life — though it has never quite known what to say about the majority of adults who are members of no association except a religious one. Little is said about the quality and meaning of associational life, the narrowness of the constituencies, or the intentions that bring men together.[40] The associational life praised in the literature originates in and is pervaded by the kinds of liberal intentions and feelings described above. The individual takes little part in "group life," apart from lending his quantum of power to the whole. Membership is instrumental: the association is an efficient means for the achievement of individual goals, not an expression of a way of life valued in and for itself.

Affective life centers almost exclusively in the family, and other associations are more or less useful in the pursuit of private goals. Once the goal of self-sufficiency is reached, the individual retreats from group life. Or individuals are held in formal association by the subtle arts of managerial psychology, the not-so-subtle arts of bureaucratic control, the revision upwards of personal desires and demands, and the redefinition of material goals in symbolic terms. It is, then, a question not of how many associations there are, but of what being together means.[41]

This point, however, is a minor one, even though discussion of it occupies a large place in the professional literature. The main point remains: modern man has determined to live without collective ideals and disciplines, and thus without obedience to and reliance upon the authorities that embody, defend, and replenish those ideals. The work of dissolution is almost complete, and modern man now appears ready to attempt a life built upon no other ideal than happiness: comfort and self-expression. But if this is nihilism, it is nihilism with a change of accent that makes all the difference. Gone is the terror, and gone too the dedication to self-overcoming of the greatest nihilist. All ideals are suspect, all renunciations and disciplines seen as snares and stupidities, all corporate commitments nothing but self-imprisonments. Modern prophets rise to pronounce sublimation and self-

---

[39]Hopefully, Grant McConnell's work, *Private Power and American Democracy* (New York, Alfred A. Knopf, 1966) will put an end to the idealization of the interest-group system as a process of partisan mutual adjustment which assures rationality and secures the public interest, thereby meeting the criteria of democracy. McConnell shows that "to a very considerable degree [the system of private power] makes a mockery of the vision by which one interest opposes another and ambition checks ambition. The large element of autonomy accorded to various fragments of government has gone far to isolate important matters of public policy from supposedly countervailing influences" (*ibid.*, p. 164).

[40]I am, of course, speaking here of American writers, not of the European pluralist tradition of Von Gierke, Maitland, Duguit, Figgis, *et al*. Mary Parker Follett's *The New State: Group Organization, the Solution of Popular Government* escapes these strictures.

[41]At the least, it is a question of authorities here. Against the professional view of the seamless web of political socialization stand Malcolm X's *Autobiography* and, say, the two major studies by Kenneth Keniston. Against the voluminous professional accounts of the American as joiner stands the literature of the great American novels, which, from Melville to Faulkner, is an exploration of metaphysical and social isolation, a literature which sees the American as the wanderer, the one who does not belong.

mutilation the same. We, especially the young among us, presume that an individual can live fully and freely, with no counsel or authority other than his desires, engaged completely in the development of all his capacities save two — the capacity for memory and the capacity for faith.

No one can say where this will lead, for the attempt is without illuminating precedent. But it is clear that for our time, as Rieff has written, "the question is no longer as Dostoevski put it: 'Can civilized men believe?' Rather: Can unbelieving men be civilized?''[42] Perhaps new prophets will appear; perhaps tribalism will reappear; perhaps the old faiths will be reborn; perhaps Weber's "specialists without spirit, sensualists without heart" will stalk the land; or perhaps we really shall see the new technological Garden tilled by children — simple, kind, sincere innocents, barbarians with good hearts. But however it comes out, we must be clear that already the development of the postmoral mentality places the question of authority and legitimacy on a wholly new footing.[43]

3. Rationality and Bureaucratic Coordination. At least one portion of the liberal impulse has reached near completion in the modern state: the urge to replace the visible with the unseen hand.[44] Personal and visible power and leadership decline, supplanted by impersonal, anonymous, and automatic mechanisms of control and coordination. Overall, we are confronted not with a situation of "power without authority," as Berle, Drucker, and others have described it, though that is part of it, but with a situation of the "autonomy of process," as Ellul and Arendt have described it. The results, as they bear on the meaning of authority and legitimacy, are mainly two: a reduction in the scope for human freedom and responsibility; and the dehumanization — in concrete ways — of leadership. We

---

[42]Philip Rieff, *The Triumph of the Therapeutic: Uses of Faith After Freud* (New York, Harper & Row, Publishers, 1966), p. 4. Rieff's book is an important attempt to come to an understanding of the meanings of "postcommunal culture."

[43]The spread of this new, postmoral mentality is bound to have corrosive consequences for the liberal doctrine of contract — the doctrine which bases government on consent of the governed and postulates an original contract by which the people who voluntarily set themselves under authority reserve the right to resist government when it abuses the agreement. The doctrine has always been a quicksand for logicians, a despair for sociologists and historians, and an invitation to resistance for men of conscience and just plain egotists. Historically, obedience has rarely been founded on contract; and as Hume said, "in the few cases where consent may seem to have taken place, it was commonly so irregular, so confined, or so much intermixed either with fraud or violence, that it cannot have any great authority." ("Of the Original Contract," in Frederick Watkins, ed., *Hume: Theory of Politics* [Edinburgh, Nelson, 1951], p. 201). Few men really consent to government, whether openly or tacitly. And as Jefferson understood, the logic of contract is incapable of binding men to the promises made by their predecessors. These logical shortcomings all become otiose in the face of the simple sociological fact that "obedience or subjugation becomes so familiar that most men never make any enquiry about its origin or cause, more than about the principle of gravity" (*ibid.*, p. 197). But all such habits are weakening in the modern states. As they weaken, the doctrine of consent becomes explosive. Every society rests upon a fiction, which usually encompasses both the society's origins and its ends, thereby helping make life and the world intelligible and endurable. Most of these fictions have failed. The fiction of contract and consent was never one of the best (strongest). To take it seriously now would mean the dissolution of the modern state.

[44]Ironic evidence is provided by the "Who Governs" literature. After prodigious professional labors we still have no authoritative answer. Apparently, everybody governs. Or nobody.

are beginning to gather the bitter harvest of these triumphs of rationality in the seemingly irrational, nihilistic, and self-indulgent violent outbursts of our day.

It was mentioned before that modern civilizations seem committed to no ideal beyond their own reproduction and growth. A man from another era might say that collectively we have sunk into mere life; the men of our era prefer to call it a celebration of life. Setting that matter of judgment aside, the point which must be understood is that this condition, combined with some of the basic characteristics of modern social systems and some of the basic components of the modern climate of opinion, decisively alters most of our inherited conceptions of authority and leadership.

Our familiar ways of thinking prepare us to imagine that a society must have ''someone'' in charge, that there must be somewhere a center of power and authority. Things just would not work unless someone, somewhere, knew how they worked and was responsible for their working right. That image and experience of authority has almost no meaning today — as the people in power are the first to say. Modern societies have become increasingly like self-regulating machines, whose human tenders are needed only to make the minor adjustments demanded by the machine itself. As the whole system grows more and more complex, each individual is able to understand and control less and less of it. In area after area of both public and private life, no single identifiable office or individual commands either the knowledge or the authority to make decisions. A search for the responsible party leads through an endless maze of committees, bureaus, offices, and anonymous bodies.[45]

The functions of planning and control, and ultimately of decision making, are increasingly taken away from men and given over to machines and routine processes. Human participation in planning and control tends to be limited to supplying the machines with inputs of data and materials. And still the complexity grows. Modern

---

[45]Admittedly, there are more sanguine vocabularies for describing the situation: "The fundamental axiom in the theory and practice of American pluralism is, I believe, this: Instead of a single center of sovereign power there must be multiple centers of power, none of which is or can be wholly sovereign. . . . Why this axiom? The theory and practice of American pluralism tends to assume, as I see it, that the existence of multiple centers of power, none of which is wholly sovereign, will help (may indeed be necessary) to tame power, to secure the consent of all, and to settle conflicts peacefully." Robert Dahl, *Pluralist Democracy in the United States* (Chicago, Rand McNally & Co., 1967), p. 24.

This description, I believe, misses three central features of the situation: (1) it fails to point out that with all this dispersion there is still a powerful central tendency of policy, a pattern of movement; (2) it fails to point out that some persons and groups in the right positions and possessed of the right resources benefit much more from the system than do others — "noncumulative inequalities" is a dangerous euphemism; and (3) it fails to point out both the real nature of what is lost by the losers — identity, self-respect, and faith in others, as well as wealth and power — and the reparations those losers might someday demand. Thus: The chief of an Indian tribe, seeking redress for a grievance felt by his people, was advised to present his case to the government. He went from this office to that, was sent from one official to another and back again and again. He met no one who looked like himself, though everybody seemed to listen politely enough in the special way that bureaucrats listen. But much time passed, and nothing happened. The chief sadly concluded that the fault was his, because, despite his many interviews and diligent searchings, he had apparently failed to find the "government." Here indeed power was tamed, consent obtained, and conflict settled, but that Indian may not always conclude that the fault was his.

man is haunted by the vision of a system grown so complex and so huge that it baffles human control. Perhaps the final solution to the problem of human governance will be to make a machine king. That is surely the immanent end toward which the efforts of all the linear programmers and systems analysts are headed.[46]

This is what I mean to suggest by the autonomy of process. The system works, not because recognizable human authority is in charge, but because its basic ends and its procedural assumptions are taken for granted and programmed into men and machines. Given the basic assumptions of growth as the main goal, and efficiency as the criterion of performance, human intervention is largely limited to making incremental adjustments, fundamentally of an equilibrating kind. The system is glacially resistant to genuine innovation, for it proceeds by its own momentum, imposes its own demands, and systematically screens out information of all kinds but one. The basic law of the whole is: Because we already have machines and processes and things of certain kinds, we shall get more machines and processes and things of closely related kinds, and this by the most efficient means. Ortega was profoundly right when a generation ago he described this situation as one of drift, though at that time men still thought they were in command. That delusion is no longer so widespread.[47]

The organization of the human resources needed to serve this process is done in the bureaucratic mode. It would be superfluous here to describe the essential characteristics of bureaucracy: that has been done capably by a number of writers. What I want to do instead is describe briefly what can best be called the bureaucratic epistemology, the operative definition of knowledge or information which is characteristic of all highly developed modern bureaucracies, for this is the screen through which information must pass before it becomes useful knowledge. This screen is one of the basic agencies by which the autonomy of process is assured.[48]

We are taught that the three great planning and control processes of modern society — bureaucracy, technology, and science — are all value-free means or instruments, just tools, which men must decide how to use by standards drawn from some other source than the realms of science, technology, and bureaucracy. This fairy tale is widely believed among the sophisticated and the naïve alike.

---

[46]See Robert Boguslaw, *The New Utopians* (Englewood Cliffs, N.J., Prentice-Hall, 1965).

[47]The description is not limited to control processes in the nongovernmental sector. In fact, any distinction between public and private, in both process and substance (except for the military power) would be very hard to draw in the United States. In 1908, Henry Adams wrote: "The assimilation of our forms of government to the form of an industrial corporation . . . seems to me steady though slow." (W. C. Ford, ed., *Letters of Henry Adams* [Boston, Houghton Mifflin Company, 1930], Vol. II, p. 482). Public, governmental bureaucracy grows apace: In 1947, there were about 5.8 million people in government civilian employment, and in 1963 there were 9.7 million; government expeditures, exclusive of "defense," space, veteran, and debt outlays, grew eightfold between 1938 and 1963. The main impulse of large organizations, as most students of the subject agree, is toward the maintenance and growth of the organization itself, which requires increasing control over all aspects of the organizational environment.

[48]The following draws heavily on Weber's classic analysis and on the equally incisive work of Kenneth Keniston, *The Uncommitted: Alienated Youth in American Society* (New York, Dell Publishing Co., 1967), esp. pp. 253–72.

Many things could be said about it, but here one thing is most important.[49] It is misleading to say that bureaucracy, for example — to focus on the force that matters most in a discussion of legitimacy — is a neutral means that can be used to achieve any end. Here, as in all human affairs, the means profoundly shape the ends. Bureaucracy may have no ultimate values, but it has a host of instrumental values, and among these is a conception of what counts as knowledge or useful information. This bureaucratic epistemology decisively shapes the outcomes — so decisively, in fact, that if you assign a certain task to a bureaucratic agency, you can largely say beforehand how the bureaucratic epistemology will constitute and alter the task itself. To put what follows in a phrase, if you were to assign the task of devising a religion to a bureaucracy, you could say beforehand that the product would be all law and no prophecy, all rule and no revelation.

More and more of men's energies are channeled through bureaucratic forms. Bureaucracy had advanced, as Weber pointed out, by virtue of its superiorities over other modes of directing human energy toward the ends of mastery over nature and other men. It is superior in speed, precision, economy, and clarity over alternative modes of controlling men and coordinating their energies. Hence, one can say, again with Weber, that modern bureaucracy is one of the supreme achievements of modern Western man. It is simultaneously an expression of the drive for rationality and predictability and one of the chief agencies in making the world ever more rational and predictable, for the bureaucratic mode of knowing becomes constitutive of the things known. In a way Hegel might barely recognize, the Rational does become the Real, and the Real the Rational.

Bureaucracy is rational in certain specific ways. First, it is in principle objective and impersonal, treating all cases without regard to their personal idiosyncrasies: all must stand in line. The objects of bureaucratic management are depersonalized. (Though, typically, each bureaucracy has a favored clientele group: all others must stand in line.) Secondly, bureaucracy is objective in the sense that the official is expected to detach his feelings from the conduct of his office. Subjectivity is for the private life. Thirdly, since bureaucracy proceeds by fixed rules and techniques, the incumbent of an office is in principle replaceable by any other individual who knows the rules and procedures governing that office and commands the skills appropriate to it.

This form of organizing human effort has a conception of knowledge which is also rational in specifiable senses. In the bureaucratic epistemology, the only legitimate instrument of knowledge is objective, technically trained intellect, and

---

[49]Though I cannot resist adding a brief appeal to those who still believe that science — especially social science — acquires "objective" knowledge and that any such knowledge that can be acquired is worthy of being acquired. Nietzsche exposed the fallacies here. The number of things one might want to know is, in principle, infinite. Therefore, every act of knowing requires a prior act of choosing and desiring. The knowledge sought and gained necessarily reflects, in many ways, the impulses (values, intentions, urges) which launched the search. Since it is a manifestation of desire and choice, knowledge is subject to moral judgment; and its "worth" is partly a function of the motives that led to its acquisition. Our age, for example, has *chosen* to know how to command *power* over nature and other men. Since Nietzsche, we must recognize both the psychology and the morality of knowledge.

the only acceptable mode of discourse is the cognitive mode. The quest for knowledge must follow specified rules and procedures. Thus, many other paths to knowledge are blocked. Specifically, everything thought of as "subjective" and tainted by "feeling" must be suppressed. Any bureaucrat who based his decisions upon conscience, trained prudence, intuition, dreams, empathy, or even common sense and personal experience would be ipso facto guilty of malfeasance. The bureaucrat must define whatever is to be done as a problem, which implies that there is a solution and that finding the right solution is a matter of finding the right technique. In order to solve a problem, it must be broken down into its component parts. Wholes can appear as nothing more than clusters of parts, as a whole car or watch is an ensemble of parts. In order for wholes to be broken into parts, things that are in appearance dissimilar must be made similar. This is done by extracting one or a few aspects which all the objects dealt with have in common and then treating those aspects as though they were the whole. Thus, there is in this conception of knowledge an urge toward abstraction and toward comparison and grouping by common attributes. Abstraction and comparison in turn require measuring tools that will yield comparable units: among the favored ones are units of money, time, weight, distance, and power. All such measurements and comparisons subordinate qualitative dimensions, contextual meanings, and unique and variable properties to the common, external, and quantifiable.[50]

This conception of knowledge also entails a whole conception of reality. Reality is that which is tangible, discrete, external, quantifiable, and capable of being precisely conveyed to others. Everything that is left over — and some might think that this is half of life — becomes curiously unreal or epiphenomenal. If it persists in its intrusions on the "real" world, then it must be treated as trouble; and those who act from motives embedded in the unreal world are treated as deviant cases, in need of repair or reproof. Bureaucrats still cannot quite believe that the human objects of "urban renewal" see themselves as victims.

All that remains to be added is the obvious point that he who would gain this kind of knowledge of this kind of reality must himself be a certain kind of man. The model is the knowledge seeker who is perfectly "objective" and dispassionate, detached from the objects of knowledge and manipulation, and blind to those aspects of the world that lie outside his immediate problem.

Now, when men treat themselves and their world this way, they and it increasingly become this way.[51] And somehow, this way includes consequences that an older vocabulary would have called horrible or evil. But if this is evil, it is evil of a special quality, the quality that Arendt calls banality. Bureaucracies staffed by "perfectly normal men" somehow perform horrors, but not out of ideology or

[50] As a measure of the bureaucratization of American higher education, consider Clark Kerr's incisive definition of the multiversity as "a mechanism held together by administrative rules and powered by money." *The Uses of the University* (Cambridge, Harvard University Press, 1963), p. 20. He is talking about what used to be called the community of scholars.

[51] Reread W. H. Auden's "The Unknown Citizen," dedicated to JS/07/M/378, in *Another Time* (New York, Random House, 1940). Or C. Virgil Gheorghiu, *The Twenty-Fifth Hour* (New York, Alfred A. Knopf, 1950).

love of evil. In 1576 the Duke of Alba marched into the Low Countries at the head of a uniform and thoroughly disciplined army of soldiers wholly devoted to the True Faith. When those soldiers, contrary to their disciplined and predictable appearance, began furiously burning and pillaging, the people called them "machines with devils inside." Today when we see bureaucracies perform their work of classifying, herding, expediting, and exterminating when necessary, we know they are machines without devils inside. What is inside is merely a certain conception of knowledge and the self, which has been long growing and which is widely distributed. It is a conception which means by thought only a process of rational and efficient calculation of the most efficient way to handle materials, a conception which trains men how to behave efficiently, but not how to act responsibly. When thought is so defined, the roles once filled by human leaders wither and computers can perform them better than men. Computer 1401 is worth much more to the State of Washington than the man who tried to kill it. In some remarkable way, Eichmann was no more responsible than a computer. Bureaucratic behavior is the most nearly perfect example (along with certain areas of scientific and technical experimentation) of that mode of conduct which denies responsibility for the consequences of action on the grounds that it lacks full knowledge of the reasons for action. All bureaucrats are innocent.

V

Weber's account of charismatic authority leaves one with a divided impression. On the one hand, he understood the strong bonds and powerful currents of feeling that are possible between leaders and followers, and sensed that in some way these relations were distinctively human. On the other, Weber's tone suggests that charismatic authority is for the childhood of the race and that the spread of rational-legal authority, even though it too comes at a price, is somehow progressive, more fitted to mature and independent adulthood. He frequently argues that we cannot return to that earlier condition of ignorance and innocence, for "disenchantment" has gone too far, and he recommends the Church with its music and incense for those who are too "weak" to bear the burdens of the present. "Science as a Vocation" concludes on a note of warning to those "who today tarry for new prophets and saviors" and urges all to "set to work and meet the demands of the day." Modern life is disenchanged and hollowed of meaning, but we must manfully live it anyway and not yearn for the gifts of faith and charisma. Each of us must, like Weber himself, see how much he can bear.

But Weber's formulation puts this whole question on the wrong footing. First of all, Weber "romanticized" charismatic authority, making it seem much more mysterious than it really is. He also dealt mainly with very "strong" figures, thereby skewing perception away from charismalike phenomena on a smaller scale and even in everyday life. He emphasized its dark aspects and saw it nearly always as the ravishing of the weak and gullible by the strong and hypnotic, almost as Mann described it in "Mario and the Magician." But more importantly, the basic opposition is not between charismatic and rational authority, but between what can only be called personal and human authority on the one side and bureaucratic-rational manipulation and coordination on the other. It is obviously not charismatic leadership that has been driven out by rational-legal authority, for our age abounds in charismatic figures and putative prophets: Rome of the second century of the Christian Era was no richer. Such men have set the destinies of states, and they may be met on every street corner and in every rock band. The proliferation of these figures is plainly the dialectical fruit of technological and bureaucratic coordination.

Rather, what is missing is humanly meaningful authority and leadership. For this, the age shows a total incapacity. Establishment officials and hippies alike share the conviction that the only alternatives to the present system of coordination are repression or the riot of passion and anarchy. Both groups, the high and the low, are unable to escape the crushing opposites that the world presents to us and that Weber taught us to believe are the only possible choices. Both groups conceive of authority almost exclusively in terms of repression and denial and can hardly imagine obedience based on mutal respect and affection. Confronted with the structures of bureaucratic and technological coordination, the young fear all authority and flee into the unreason of drugs, music, astrology, and the *Book of Changes*, justifying the flight by the doctrine of "do your own thing" — something that has never appeared on a large scale among any populace outside Bedlam and the nursery, where it can be indulged because there is a keeper who holds ultimate power over the inmates. No doctrine was ever better designed to provide its holders with the illusion of autonomy while delivering real power to the custodians. When those in high positions are confronted with challenges, their first response is to isolate themselves from the challengers by tightening the old rules and imposing tougher new rules. When the managers do attempt reforms in a "humanistic" direction, the result is nearly always a deformity: to humanize leadership, institute coffee hours, fabricate human-interest stories to show that the powerful one is human after all, and bring in the makeup aritists when he has to go on television; to humanize bureaucracy, appoint T-groups and ombudsmen; to humanize the law, introduce the indeterminate sentence, special procedures and officials for juvenile offenders, and psychiatrists who will put a technical name on any state of mind for a fee. It is always an alliance between "democratic" ideology and expert manipulation, in a hopeless attempt to reconstruct something now almost forgotten — the idea and the experience of genuine authority.

To escape this trap, we must reject Weber's false opposites, and with it his test of manliness. It is not a question of either retreating to charisma or advancing bravely to the rational-legal destiny, but of developing something different from both. It is perfectly possible that the march toward the rationally integrated world is not progressive at all, but a wrong turning, a mistake, whose baneful consequences need not be supinely accepted as inevitable or slavishly rationalized as developmental.[52]

It is certainly necessary to understand that natural human authority has been overwhelmed by the combined impact of the very forces, structures, and intellectual and moral orientations that we identify with modernity. A mere partial listing must suffice. Huge populations have made men strangers to each other and have made it necessary to develop efficient means of mass measurement and control. Centrally controlled communications systems can reach into all corners of the society, encroaching upon small human units of unique experience and outlook. Furthermore, the communications revolution makes possible the elaborate feedback circuitry necessary to the processes of automatic control. Intricate division of labor reduces common experience, producing both pluralistic ignorance and fragmentation of the process of work. The data explosion has produced microspecialization of the mind and the narrowing of perspectives on human problems. The relativization, materialization, and secularization of values makes it impossible for men to relate to one another on the basis of shared commitments to transcendent and demanding purposes and values. The sheer quantity and variety of artifacts and material needs and desires requires a vast system of administrative regulation and control, and thoroughly blurs the distinction between public and private, with the result that authorities cannot pretend to speak for public and objective goods but must accept the popular equation of private desire with public right.[53] The decline of tradition removes another rich source of shared meanings and limits, while rapid technological change proceeds by its own imperatives and enslaves its human attendants. All these add up to a scope and complexity so vast that humanly meaningful authority and leadership are baffled. Control must be accomplished either by bureaucratic coordination and self-regulating devices that govern the technical system by standards generated by the system itself, or by deliberately fabricated ideologies and images.

All these structures and processes will have to be confronted — and radically revised, in ways that no man can clearly foresee — before humanly meaningful authority and leadership can reappear.[54] But before that confrontation can

[52]I wish to make it explicit here that while I have often treated Weber critically, the "real" Weber was a far more powerful man than the Weber canonized by social science. Social scientists have borrowed Weber's discussion of the ideal-typical characteristics of bureaucracy, but without his passionate concern to defend politics against bureaucracy. They have enthroned his fact-value distinction but have not even begun to come to terms with his profound criticism of the social science model of cumulative knowledge. They cite his dedication to science and rationality, but they ignore his acceptance of Nietzsche's view of contemporary conceptions of science and rationality as potentially dehumanizing forces. What was not "operational" in Weber has been largely ignored.

[53]Perhaps this is excessive. Perhaps it is not yet a "popular equation." Most adult Americans do limit private desire by public right. But among the young the equation is surely growing: either private desire is equated with public right, or the existence of anything like public right is simply denied, leaving only private desire.

[54]In the earlier ages of man, leaders were made by art to appear as more than human: as divine or semidivine personages. Today the ones who stand at the command posts and switching points are made by art to appear as more than mechanical: as human beings.

begin — or begin in ways that offer some prospect of a worthy and merciful outcome — there must be an even more basic shift in our understanding of the kind of knowledge that can properly be accepted as constituting a claim to authority in the human realm. I presented the administrative and scientific conception of knowledge as a specimen of what such knowledge must not be. It remains to sketch what it must be.

All leaders perform the same functions. They interpret events, explore possible responses to problematic situations, recommend courses of action, and vouch for the rightness and success of actions taken. They advise, recommend, warn, reprove, and command.[55] All this is so manifest in common experience that the large social science literature which attempted to "explain" leadership by distinguishing between "functional" and "trait" theories should have been seen from the outset as superficial and unimportant, doomed to trivial answers because it asked trivial questions. The fact that it has been taken seriously supports the suggestion made earlier that certain experiences of leadership and authority really have become rare among men in the modern states. The question is not whether leaders hold their positions by performing certain functions or possessing certain traits. The question is, rather, precisely how those functions are construed and what kind of knowledge is understood to be appropriate to their performance.

Each man is born, lives among others, and dies. Hence, each man's life has three great underpinnings, which no matter how far he travels must always be returned to and can never be escaped for long. The three underpinnings present themselves to each man as problems and as mysteries: the problem and mystery of becoming a unique self: but still a self living among and sharing much with others in family and society: and finally a unique self among some significant others, but still sharing with all humanity the condition of being human and mortal. Who am I as an individual? Who am I as a member of this society? Who am I as a man, a member of humanity? Each of the three questions contains within itself a host of questions, and the way a man formulates and responds to them composes the center and the structure of his life.

Given this, it can be said quite simply that humanly significant authorities are those who help men answer these questions in terms that men themselves implicitly understand. The leader offers interpretations and recommendations which set off resonances in the minds and spirits of other men. When leaders and followers interact on levels of mutual, subjective comprehension and sharing of meaning, then we can say that there exists humanly significant leadership. The relationship is one of mutuality, identification, and co-performance. The leader finds himself in the followers, and they find themselves in the leader. I am aware that to the rational and objective men of our day, this is mysticism. But it is those same rational men who cannot understand why the rational, objective, and expert administrators are losing authority, if not yet power, in all the modern states. The answer

---

[55]This formulation cuts across Jourvenel's distinction between *dux* and *rex*, though that distinction is very useful for locating the performance of leadership roles within a social setting. Jouvenel, *Sovereignty*, esp. pp. 40–70.

is mysteriously simple: to the degree that the rational, expert administrative leader achieves the objectivity and expertise which are the badges of his competence, he loses the ability to enter a relationship of mutual understanding with those who rely on him for counsel and encouragement.

Humanly significant leadership bases its claim to authority on a kind of knowledge which includes intuition, insight, and vision as indispensable elements. The leader strives to grasp and to communicate the essence of a situation in one organic and comprehensive conception. He conjoins elements which the analytic mind keeps tidily separate. He units the normative with the empirical, and promiscuously mixes both with the moral and the aesthetic. The radical distinction between subjective and objective is unknown in this kind of knowledge, for everything is personal and comes from within the prepared consciousness of the knower, who is simultaneously believer and actor. When it is about men, this kind of knowledge is again personal. It strives to see within the self, and along with other selves. It is knowledge of character and destiny. Most of the facts which social scientists collect about men are in this epistemology superficial: information about a man's external attributes, rather than knowledge of who he is and what his possibilities are.

One who possesses and values this kind of knowledge bases his claims to its validity on grounds which are quicksand to the objective and rational man. One of the foundations is strength of conviction. A belief is true, or can be made true, when it is believed in strongly enough to base action on it, in precisely the way James described in his essay on "The Will To Believe." The other ground is the resonance set going between leader and followers when communications "make sense." When leader and followers begin to understand and respond to each other on a profound, personal level, each gains confidence that what is being communicated is true. All authority must believe that its knowledge is true. Rational, scientific authorities enjoy this confidence when they have followed the prescribed methods of inquiry and when their professional colleagues also share the belief. Personal authorities mean by verification the sympathetic vibrations set going by communications between leaders and followers who share a common background and outlook.

The language in which the knowledge appropriate to humanly significant leadership is expressed is also very different from the language of rational and objective discourse. It is a language profuse in illustration and anecdote, and rich in metaphor whose sources are the human body and the dramas of action and responsibility. This language is suggestive and alluring, pregnant, evocative. It is in all ways the opposite of the linear, constricted, jargonized discourse which is the ideal of objective communication. Decisions and recommendations are often expressed in parables and visions whose meanings are hidden to outsiders but translucent to those who have eyes to see. Teaching in this language is done mainly by story, example, and metaphor — modes of discourse which can probe depths of personal being inaccessible to objective and managerial discourse. Compare the Sermon on the Mount with the last communiqué from the Office of Economic Opportunity in the War on Povery; or Lincoln's Second Inaugural with Nixon's first.

The final distinctive characteristic of the knowledge appropriate to humanly meaningful authority is that it is dynamic and transactional. Currents of meaning and influence flow back and forth during the process of transmission, so that both the content of the message and the parties to the transaction are caught up and transformed in the flow. The contrast between this and objective discourse is decisive, for the goal of the latter is to send information economically from transmitter to receiver, altering neither the instruments nor the message in the process. Most of what modern information theory calls noise is of the essence of human communication between human authorities and their followers.

VI

Very little of this — especially the material on leadership and authority — is new; and up until a short time ago it would have been unnecessary to say it. The tradition of political theory has always included leadership and authority among its central themes, and in that tradition the languages of discursive reason and of metaphor and myth were not permitted to fall apart and oppose each other either in the analysis of action or in the education of actors. As examples, consider Plato's theory of learning as remembrance, his emphasis on the right music and poetry in the education of statesmen, and his dialogues on justice and power. Aristotle said in the *Politics* that "the same education and the same habits will be found to make a good man and a good statesman and king." In the *Rhetoric* he tried to construct the enthymeme as a tool specifically appropriate to practical discourse just as the syllogism was appropriate to theoretical discourse. Logic and rhetoric were important subjects in the education of citizens because both taught ways of thinking and speaking which would make actors intelligible to each other. Or consider the incomparable treatment of prudence, which is excellence in action, formulated by Aristotle and perfected by Aquinas.[56] This treatment ascends from custom and circumstance, through the pyschology of motivation, to ethics and philosophy organized for the sake of action. Or take the literature of counsel, ranging from the profound and subtle works of More and Machiavelli through the more limited works of Bacon and the "Mirror for Princes" literature. All these branches of the tradition are rich in precise observation of men and manners, historical allusion, story, myth, and metaphor, and also in scientific and philosophical argument and analysis. The tradition starts with men where it finds them — located in a comunity, tied by custom and memory, full of prejudices, vices, and fears, but also possessed of natural virtues — and strives by a language appropriate to the subject to refine and enlarge character and knowledge so that men will be fit for action and the exercise of authority.

In the modern world, and in the social science spawned by that world, the "two sides" of this language have fallen apart. We take it to be almost natural that the political world, and the language and methods appropriate both to understanding and to acting in that world, should be divided, as it were, between Sorel

---

[56]Aristotle, *Ethics* 6; Aquinas, *Summa Theologia*, i–ii 57.4–6; 58.4, 5; ii–ii 47–56.

and McNamara. While I have concentrated on the ideal and material conditions producing the crisis of legitimate authority, it should be clear that the crisis also extends to our dominant ways of studying these matters, which in turn conditions our ways of transmitting a political culture and preparing men to participate in it. Political Science has become a political problem.

In conclusion, there are senses, which I have tried to specify, in which de facto, humanly meaningful leadership *does* carry its own principle of legitimacy. But there are other senses in which it does not, or may not. There obviously can be illegitimate, albeit humanly meaningful authority. Without the setting and limits imposed by tradition, shared values and experience, institutions, and philosophical reason, humanly meaningful leadership can be as pathological and dangerous, and as illegitimate, as the processes of power-without-authority characteristic of modern states. Hence, one way to describe the crisis of legitimacy is to say that the basic features and tendencies of modernity have produced a situation in which the established processes and formal structures of control are at war with the conditions necessary for authority. In this battle, legitimacy is destroyed.

Events, institutions, and moral and epistemological ideas which, taken together, constitute modernity have virtually driven humanly meaningful authority and leadership from the field, replacing it with bureaucratic coordination and automatic control processes, supplemented when necessary by ideology and phony charisma. Furthermore, our methods of study have blocked us from seeing that such mechanisms of control are inherently vulnerable and in the long run unworkable, incapable of responding to men's needs for understanding and counsel on the basic, inescapable questions of human existence. So long as men remain what we have hitherto called human, they will require of power which strives to become authority that it respond to those questions in ways that have meaning for men. The current epidemic of revolts and uprisings, the current challenging of established institutions and processes, the thickening atmosphere of resentment and hostility, the dropout cultures of the young — these are something other than the romantic, reactionary, or nihilistic spasms which they are seen as in some quarters of the academy and the state. They are the cries of people who feel that the processes and powers which control their lives are inhuman and destructive. They are the desperate questionings of people who fear that their institutions and officials have no answers. They are overt signs of the underlying crisis of legitimacy in the modern state.

Chapter Three

CRIMINAL LAW IN AMERICA

Criminal law emerged simultaneously with the creation of the political state. In early societies custom prevailed, and injuries to wronged persons were handled by the family and the community. The concept of criminal law developed only when the custom of private or community redress of wrong was replaced by the principle that the state is injured when one of its subjects is harmed. Thus, the right of the community to deal with wrongdoing was taken over by the state as the "representative" of the people. What this meant was that the state could now act by means of the criminal law to protect its own interests and those of the dominant economic class.

Criminal law, therefore, could develop only with the achievement of political domination by the state — allowing law to be established and administered in the name of a centralized governmental authority. For Anglo-American law, this occurred in England during the latter part of the eleventh century and continued throughout the twelfth.[1] With the Norman invasion of 1066 and the strong rule of the Norman kings, the old tribal-feudal system of law was replaced by a criminal law held in the hands of a central authority, the King. In order to place law under the jurisdiction of the Crown, several types of courts were created, writs were devised to carry cases out of baronial courts and into the King's courts, and eventually a "common law" was established for governing all people within the country. This new system of law determined the offenses that violated the peace of the King and his nation.

Gradually, with the consolidation of power in the hands of the domi-

---

[1]C. Ray Jeffery, "The Development of Crime in Early English Society," *Journal of Criminal Law, Criminology and Police Science*, 47 (March–April, 1957), pp. 647–666.

nant economic class, laws for the protection of private property were established. The rise of mercantilism — that is, the movement from an agricultural economy to a new order based on industry and trade — required a legal structure to protect the interests of the new economic class. These interests were secured through such laws as the theft law. By the judicial ruling in the Carrier's Case of 1473, the products of industry (in this case those of the textile industry) were protected from theft.[2] The decision in the Carrier's Case, a decision that necessarily broke precedent, provided the framework for the further development of the theft law. Eventually, with the growth of banking and the use of paper currency, the law was expanded to include embezzlement and similar acts that threatened the interests of the class that owned and managed the means of production.

At the same time, laws were being made to control the labor supply for the benefit of the propertied classes. Particularly with the enactment of the vagrancy law of 1349 in England, and the formulation of supplementary statutes, an important purpose was accomplished: "to force laborers (whether personally free or unfree) to accept employment at a low wage in order to insure the landowner an adequate supply of labor at a price he could afford to pay."[3] By the sixteenth century, with the increased emphasis on commerce and industry, the vagrancy laws were used to control those persons who might endanger the property of the new classes. A conviction for being "idle," or a "vagabond," or for "refusing to labor" could result in a criminal sanction. The ruling class was protected from those "undesirable elements" of the state that might threaten the existing order. With only minor variations the vagrancy statutes were adopted by the American colonies and states to serve the same purposes.

The laws of the American colonies continued to develop within the tradition of the English common law.[4] Yet local conditions shaped some of the colonial laws. The Massachusetts Bay Colony was faced with the critical problem of finding the proper place for law in a religious community. Although the colony had been chartered as a commercial enterprise in 1630, the principal objectives of the settlers clearly were religious and social. The difficulty of relating law to such objectives was resolved by constructing a legal system based on biblical authority.[5] The Scriptures served as the most appropriate source for establishing a government in accordance with God's word. Most provisions in the Puritans' legal code were annotated by chapter and verse from the Old Testament, and many incorporated biblical phraseology. In such a fashion, the state's authority was condoned and supported by religion.

---

[2]Jerome Hall, *Theft, Law and Society*, 2nd edition (Indianapolis: Bobbs-Merrill, 1952).

[3]William J. Chambliss, "A Sociological Analysis of the Law of Vagrancy," *Social Problems*, 12 (Summer, 1964), p. 69.

[4]See Roscoe Pound, "The Development of American Law and Its Deviation from English Law," *Law Quarterly Review*, 67 (January, 1951), pp. 49–66.

[5]George Lee Haskins, *Law and Authority in Early Massachusetts* (New York: Macmillan Company, 1960). pp. 141–162.

Ultimately this meant that the welfare of the state, rather than that of the person and his group, was the state's chief concern.

Hence, the early criminal codes in America were primarily religious, equating sin with crime. The laws punished religious offenses, such as idolatry, blasphemy, and witchcraft; and infractions against persons or property were declared to be offenses against God. In the first selection presented here, William E. Nelson, in "Emerging Notions of Modern Criminal Law in the Revolutionary Era: An Historical Perspective," finds that most criminal cases in early Massachusetts were for moral offenses against God and religion. However, prosecutions for morality practically disappeared in Massachusetts after the Revolution, while prosecutions for economic and disorderly offenses increased.

Nelson shows that there was a dramatic shift from the pre-Revolutionary notion that the function of criminal law was to enforce the morals and religion of the community to the post-Revolutionary view that the purpose of criminal law was to protect property and ensure physical security. The state had become actively involved, through its use of the criminal law, in promoting stability of the social order. Moreover, political acts against the state and its economy were controlled by the criminal law. Rather than being worried about sinners, Nelson observes, the new state elite "feared organized groups of malcontents bent upon reconstruction of society. . . . In short, their fear was that the economically underprivileged would seek material gain by banding together to deprive more privileged persons of their wealth and standing."

With the increasing use of criminal law to protect the interests of the state, concerns developed about protecting the rights of the citizen from the abuses of government. This libertarian response sought restriction on the state's prosecution of offenders. Given the legal order, individuals had to have some procedural protections from the government.

Though civil liberties are necessary once the state establishes a legal system, it is a liberal illusion to think that justice is achieved with the granting of a few procedural safeguards.[6] The larger question is whether the state should have the right in the first place to control the population according to its own interests. Nevertheless, notions regarding criminal law and civil liberties have changed little since the American Revolution. The interests of the state and the ruling class still dominate the law and the legal ideology.

To understand criminal law in America we must also examine the emergence of law outside of the eastern colonial states; we must observe the development of a legal tradition in the expansion of the western frontier. The legal history of the American west is yet to be written.

[6]For a critique of the civil liberties issue, see Richard Quinney, "The Ideology of Law: Notes for a Radical Alternative to Legal Oppression," *Issues in Criminology*, 7 (Winter, 1972), pp. 1–35.

We do know, from an early study, that the fast-growing settlements developed their own codes to promote local order. For example, local rules were established to regulate the disputes that arose over land and mining rights in the western mining camps.[7] Since there were as yet no territorial or state governments to formulate and administer law, there emerged a "local law" among the miners to regulate their own social and economic interests. These laws spread throughout the western territories, and eventually, when states were formed, many of the local laws were enacted into statute law or were incorporated into court decisions.

Troops of the United States Infantry brought "law" to the Indian territory, carrying out the treaties and the government policies of moving the Indians from their land. Courts were then established to settle disputes that arose between the white men and the Indians. With the establishment of the United States Court at Fort Smith for the Western District of Arkansas, and the appointment of Judge Isaac C. Parker, a new phase of law and order arrived on the western frontier. From that time, Judge Parker, as one writer contends, "took the fate of civilization's outpost in brave and willing hands."[8]

In his twenty-one years on the bench at Fort Smith, Judge Parker heard 13,490 cases and convicted 9,454 persons, of whom 344 were tried for offenses punishable by death. Of the 344 cases, 165 were convicted, and 160 of these were sentenced to the gallows. Seventy-nine persons were eventually hanged, two others were killed in attempting to escape, and two more died in jail awaiting execution. The Judge saw his mission in the following terms: "During the twenty years that I have engaged in administering the law here, the contest has been one between civilization and savagery, the savagery being represented by the intruding criminal class. . . . I have this much satisfaction, after my twenty years of labor; the court at Fort Smith, Arkansas, stands as a monument to the strong arm of the laws of the United States, and has resulted in bringing to the Indian Territory civilization and protection."[9]

With the eventual closing of the frontier, new problems emerged which required new laws for the preservation of domestic order. Once again, as in a former time, a host of laws was enacted for the regulation of morality, although this time more than religion was at stake. Morality, or control of the moral order, became an excuse for the control of the more material aspects of society. Laws bearing on private and public morality reflected the desire to preserve all aspects of life. If the moral base of social and economic life should be threatened, then the social and economic order itself might give way. Thus laws regulating

[7]Charles Howard Shinn, *Mining Camps: A Study in American Frontier Government* (New York: Harper & Row, 1965). Originally published in 1884.

[8]Glenn Shirley, *Law West of Fort Smith: A History of Frontier Justice in the Indian Territory, 1834–1896* (Lincoln: University of Nebraska Press, 1968).

[9]Quoted in *ibid*., p. 157.

sexual activities, drinking, drug use, and the like were enacted to control the total environment, even the most intimate aspects of one's life, so that the existing order would be secured and perpetuated — according to the interests of the established order.

For example, with the passage of the Harrison Act by Congress in 1914, the users of certain drugs became defined as criminal.[10] Technically, the Harrison Act simply required that all drug-handlers be registered and that the fact of securing drugs be made a matter of record. But through the interpretation of the act, the court rulings in specific cases, and the enactment of supplementary laws, criminal sanctions were provided for the unauthorized possession, sale, or transfer of drugs. Moreover, the state, in defining drug use and addiction as a moral problem, has conditioned the public to think of drugs in moral terms and to respond by condemning the drug user rather than by questioning the kind of social order that makes drug use a viable alternative to the everyday reality. If we can be taught to believe that the problem is in the morality of the drug user, rather than in the pathology of the existing social order, then those who rule can have their order maintained without changing the existing system. The capitalist order is secured by the legislation of morality. The moral order (as determined by the dominant class) and the social-economic order are inseparable; they serve each other.

During the last decade the control of crime has entered a new stage. The rapid increase in criminal legislation, law enforcement programs, and judicial activity marks the attempt by the government and the ruling class to respond to the crisis in the capitalist system. Instead of responding by changing the social and economic system to relieve or eliminate the oppressive conditions of advanced captialism, the state has reacted by protecting the existing order. In waging a "war on crime," the state has sought to preserve domestic order by means of the criminal law.

Beginning in the early 1960s the nation's problems began to be focused simply and conveniently on a domestic enemy — crime. Crime and the fear of crime played a crucial role in the political campaigns of the decade. The Johnson administration finally assumed the task of launching the war on crime. In a presidential message to the 89th Congress in 1965, Lyndon Johnson declared that "we must arrest and reverse the trend toward lawlessness."[11] Suggesting that "crime has become a malignant enemy in America's midst," the President charted a course of action based on legal control and law enforcement: "This active combat against crime calls for a fair and efficient system of law enforcement to deal with those who break the law. It means giving

---

[10]See Alfred R. Lindesmith, *The Addict and the Law* (Bloomington: Indiana University Press, 1965).

[11]"Crime, Its Prevalence, and Measures of Prevention," Message from the President of the United States, House of Representatives, 89th Congress, March 8, 1965, Document No. 103.

new priority to the methods and institutions of law enforcement.'' The problem was conceived to be a national one, with crime prevention and crime fighting to be intensified at all levels of government. The federal effort, Johnson continued, would consist of ''(1) increased federal law enforcement efforts, (2) assistance to local enforcement efforts, and (3) a comprehensive, penetrating analysis of the origins and nature of crime in modern America.''

The President appointed a commission — the President's Commission on Law Enforcement and Administration of Justice — to study the crime problem and to make recommendations for action. Hearings were held by the Senate Judiciary Committee (Subcommittee on Criminal Laws and Procedures) and by the House Judiciary Committee. The hearings provided the framework for defining the crime problem in modern terms, suggesting new criminal laws, stricter law enforcement, denial of basic rights for defendants, and the use of modern technology in the war on crime. The Senate committee's chairman, John McClellan, opened the hearings on March 7, 1967, by stating that ''It is quite probable that these hearings and the bills we will be considering will mark the turning point in the struggle against lawlessness in this nation.''[12] The survival of the state and the current social and economic order (the ''society'') were at stake: ''The rate of increase in crime cannot continue if our society is to remain safe and secure and our people protected against the ravages of crime.''

The result of these efforts was the enactment of the Omnibus Crime Control and Safe Streets Act of 1968. The new crime legislation initially assisted state and local governments in increasing the effectiveness of law enforcement and criminal administration — in trying more effectively to secure domestic order. By the time the bill was passed several amendments were added that deliberately attempted to overturn previous Supreme Court decisions which supposedly ''coddled criminals'' and ''handcuffed the police.'' For example, one amendment provided that all voluntary confessions and eyewitness identifications — regardless of whether a defendant had been informed of his rights to counsel — could be admitted in federal trials. In another provision, state and local law enforcement agencies were given broad license to tap telephones and engage in other forms of eavesdropping without obtaining a court order. Another amendment provided that any persons convicted of ''inciting a riot or civil disorder,'' ''organizing, promoting, encouraging, or participating in a riot or disorder,'' or ''aiding and abetting any person in committing'' such offenses, would be disqualified from employment by the federal government for five years. The legislation was a clear attempt to control by means of the criminal law any behavior that would threaten the established order.

---

[12]''Controlling Crime Through More Effective Law Enforcement,'' *Hearings* Before the Subcommittee on Criminal Laws and Procedures of the Committee on the Judiciary, United States Senate, 90th Congress (Washington, D.C.: U.S. Government Printing Office, 1967), p. 1.

The government has continued its course of enacting crime control legislation. The administration and several congressional committees have worked to construct a comprehensive program of crime control, including a crime bill for the District of Columbia, drug control legislation, an organized crime bill, and a series of proposals for future legislation.

As in the Omnibus crime bill, the recent crime control laws contain many repressive measures. Fundamental procedural policies are instituted covering such matters as preventive detention, "no-knock" searches, extension of grand jury powers, long-term sentencing, and reversals in the due process of law. Upon passage of this legislation, the Senate majority leader could state: "After the passage of these bills, we may then direct ourselves to the more difficult tasks of identifying and addressing ourselves to the task of eradicating the causes of criminal behavior."[13] Even if the government were to turn its attention to the conditions that underlie criminally defined behavior, it is unlikely that there would be a critical examination of capitalism. The new crime control laws are simply a reaction to the crisis of our age, a reaction that attempts to promote the established order.

What is the future of criminal law in America? In the last essay in this chapter, "The 1970s: A Decade of Repression?," Harvey A. Silverglate observes how the legal institutions are continually being used to repress the far-reaching changes occurring in American society. What characterizes modern repression is the coalition of the federal government (including the President, the Attorney General, and other agencies of the Justice Department) with local law enforcement and judicial agencies. Legal repression in the 1970s is the state's reaction to the threat of an indigenous revolution. Silverglate discusses some of the many cases in which the state has punished revolutionary thought and action. He sees the immediate future as a battle between the indigenous revolutionary movement and the repressive reaction by the government. As long as the crisis in American institutions lasts, Silverglate concludes, legal repression will continue.

According to our critique, then, only with an examination of the American social and economic system can we understand the meaning of criminal law, including the recent crime control programs. The conclusion is that crime control serves the existing order, the economically dominant class and the state. And as long as that order is oppressive, criminal law will be used to further the oppression. A critical understanding of criminal law leads to proposals and actions that will foster a new existence.

[13]*Congressional Record*, Vol. 16, Part 2, 91st Congress, January 28, 1970 (Washington, D.C.: U.S. Government Printing Office, 1960), p. 1690.

4. William E. Nelson

Emerging Notions of Modern Criminal Law in the Revolutionary Era: An Historical Perspective

Historians have devoted a great deal of attention to studying the law of the early American colonies, especially the criminal law,[1] and no jurisdiction has commanded as much attention as the Puritan colony of Massachusetts Bay.[2] One reason for this interest, perhaps, is that Puritan criminal law was vastly different from the criminal law of today. Religion "was a way of life"[3] for the early settlers of Massachusetts, and all of the Bay Colony's institutions reflected its religious values. Thus, the early settlers "adopt[ed] the Judicial Laws of Moses which were given to the Israelites of Old . . . [and] punished Adultery . . . [and] Blasphemy, with Death. . . . ."[4] They equated crime with sin and thought of the state as the arm of God on earth. Modern law, on the other hand, rarely seeks to enforce morality and has thrown up a "wall of separation"[5] between religion and the state. Only incidentally is today's criminal considered a sinner; first and foremost, he is regarded as a threat to the peace and order of society.

The purpose of this article is to study the forces which have altered criminal law since early colonial times — a subject much neglected in our legal history. Such a study requires close attention to trial court records, and the large number of these records necessitates limitation to one locality. Middlesex County, Massachusetts,[6] was chosen largely for convenience, but also because it seems to have been more typical of Massachusetts and perhaps of the United States during the period under study than, for example, urban Boston or frontier Berkshire.

Reprinted by permission of the publisher and the author from *New York University Law Review*, 42 (May 1967), pp. 450–482.

[1]See, e.g., Law and Authority in Colonial America (G. A. Billias ed. 1965); J. Goebel & T. R. Naughton, Law Enforcement in Colonial New York (1944); A. P. Scott, Criminal Law in Colonial Virginia (1930); R. Semmes, Crime and Punishment in Early Maryland (1938).

[2]See, e.g., G. L. Haskins, Law and Authority in Early Massachusetts (1960); E. Powers, Crime and Punishment in Early Massachusetts 1620–1692 (1966). Seven of the ten articles in Law and Authorty in Colonial America (G. A. Billias ed. 1965) concern Massachusetts.

[3]Haskins, supra note 2, at 16.

[4]Grand Jury Charge by Hutchinson, C.J., Suffolk Super. Ct., March 1768, in J. Quincy, Reports of Cases Argued and Adjudged in the Superior Court of Judicature of the Province of Massachusetts Bay, Between 1761 and 1772, at 258, 259 (S. Quincy ed. 1865).

[5]Engel v. Vitale, 370 U.S. 421, 425 (1962).

[6]The chief towns of Middlesex in the late 1700s were Charlestown, Cambridge, Concord, Lexington, Newton, Watertown, and Framingham.

The court records indicate that most of the developments which transformed Puritan criminal law into the criminal law of today occurred during the three decades following the American Revolution. This article will concentrate upon that period. Of course changes, sometimes important ones, had occurred earlier, but nonetheless, the criminal law of pre-Revolutionary Massachusetts was remarkably similar to that of the Puritan era. The old Puritan ethic remained strong enough in the 1750s so that crime was still looked upon as sin; the criminal, as a sinner; and criminal law, as the earthly arm of God. Criminal law surely was not the tool of the royal government in Boston, which was unconcerned with the outcome of most cases and, in any event, had little real power to influence that outcome. As a result, the chief function of the courts, the primary law-enforcement agencies, remained, as in the early colonial era, the identification and punishment of sinners.

By 1810, some thirty years after the Revolution, a system of law enforcement similar to today's had emerged. This article will trace the development of the new system. Part I will discuss the shift in the law's basic function between 1760 and 1810, from the preservation of morality to the protection of property. Part II will consider the process by which, as an unintended consequence of Revolutionary events, defendants in criminal cases found themselves engaged in unequal struggles with government, and will trace the libertarian response to these struggles — new procedures for the protection of individuals against abuses of government law-enforcement power.[7]

I. The Substance of the Law: From Preservation of Morality to Protection of Property

A. Criminal Law at the Close of the Colonial Period: 1760–1774. Describing the criminal law of pre-Revolutionary Massachusetts in terms that will have meaning for the reader and that also would have been meaningful to the Revolutionary generation is a matter of some difficulty. A scheme for the classification of crimes must be adopted for today's reader; but, unfortunately, no such scheme was ever developed in colonial Massachusetts. Blackstone did develop a classification scheme in England, however, and, by the Revolution, lawyers in Massachusetts knew

---

[7]A brief word must be said about the immediate impact of the Revolution upon the law-enforcement process. In September 1774, a mob, similar to mobs elsewhere in Massachusetts, gathered at Concord and prevented the Court of General Sessions, which had jurisdiction over the trial of all criminal offenses other than those very serious ones tried before the Superior Court of Judicature and the petty ones tried before individual justices of the peace, from holding its scheduled sitting. See Middlesex General Sessions, Sept. 1774, at 133–34 [hereinafter Msex Gen. Sess.]. Middlesex then remained completely without courts until February 1776, when the old courts met again. See Msex Gen. Sess. Feb. 1776, at 143; Middlesex Superior Court, Oct. 1776, Minute Book, f. 36 [hereinafter Msex Super. Ct.]. Although they were no longer under royal control, they were staffed by many of the same judges, used the same procedure, and applied the same law as before the Revolution. This continuity in judicial structure and practice even during the Revolution is of much importance. At no time during the period under study in this article was there any radical change in judicial structure or personnel in Middlesex County.

of it.[8] It included offenses against God and religion, offenses against government, offenses against public justice, offenses against public trade and health, homicide, offenses against the person, and offenses against habitations and other private property.[9]

Most cases were within the category of offenses against God and religion. Between 1760 and 1774 there were 370 prosecutions in Middlesex in the Superior and General Sessions Courts. Of these, 210 were for fornication. Since only mothers of illegitimate children were brought into court, one might think that fornication was punished not because it offended God but because it burdened towns with the support of the children.[10] Such a conclusion would be premature. Although the economic interests of the towns cannot be denied,[11] the fact is that prosecutions were brought even when no economic interests were at stake,[12] and the same penalties were imposed in those prosecutions as in cases where economic interests may have played a part.[13] That the offense, when committed by a woman who did not marry, happened to burden her town was of little import; her offense against God was the essential evil for which she, like the woman who did marry, was punished.

Also within Blackstone's category of offenses against God and religion were 27 prosecutions for violation of the Sabbath,[14] 2 for cohabitation,[15] and 1 for adultery.[16] These 240 cases accounted for 65 per cent of all prosecutions.

Statistically the next most significant category was that of offenses against habitations and other private property. Between 1760 and 1775, there were 32 larceny prosecutions and 15 prosecutions for burglary and breaking and entering — which, together with 6 miscellaneous cases within this category,[17] amounted to 53 prosecutions, or 14 per cent of the total.[18] The fact that Blackstone placed offenses against

[8] 2 Diary and Autobiography of John Adams 27 (Butterfield, Faber & Garrett eds. 1961).

[9] 4 Blackstone, Commentaries, Table of Contents.

[10] See A. P. Scott, supra note 1, at 280–81.

[11] This interest is indicated by the requirement that a man found guilty of fornication give a bond to the town as a guarantee of his undertaking to support the child. See The King v. Mallet, Msex. Gen. Sess., May 1760, at 582.

[12] Ten women were prosecuted even though at the time of their prosecution they had married their partners. See, e.g., The King v. Paterson, Msex Gen. Sess., March 1761, at 618.

[13] Compare, e.g., The King v. Munro, Msex Gen. Sess., Nov. 1770, at 521 (5s. fine), with The King v. Paterson, supra note 12, at 618 (5s. fine).

[14] The offense of Sabbath breaking was of several sorts. See, e.g., The King v. Hayward, Msex Gen. Sess., March 1773, at 76 (not attending worship on Sunday); The King v. Cutler, Msex Gen. Sess., Nov. 1769, at 473 (traveling on Sunday); The King v. Osborne, Msex Gen. Sess., Dec. 1762, at 79 (working on Sunday).

[15] The King v. Goodenow, Msex Super. Ct., April 1768, f. 164, affirming Msex Gen. Sess., Nov. 1767, at 381; The King v. Lawrence, Msex Super. Ct., Jan. 1763, f. 11.

[16] Rex v. Eaton, Msex Super. Ct., Oct. 1770, f. 223.

[17] Two were prosecutions for forgery. The King v. Garfield, Msex Super. Ct., April 1770, f. 58; The King v. Garfield, Msex Super. Ct., Oct. 1767, f. 76. The others were for fraud, arson, and malicious mischief. The King v. Temple, Msex Super. Ct., Oct. 1767, f. 77 (fraud); The King v. Bacon, Msex Super. Ct., Jan. 1763, f. 11 (fraud); The King v. Brunowitz (or Bruscowitz, text illegible), Msex Super. Ct., Jan. 1761, f. 165 (arson); The King v. Ingersoll, Msex Gen. Sess., Nov. 1771, at 16 (malicious mischief).

[18] Between 1760 and 1775, there were 31 prosecutions for offenses against the persons of individuals, 16 for offenses against public trade and health, 14 for offenses against public justice, 11 for offenses against government, and 4 for homicide.

property in a separate category should not be taken to mean, however, that in pre-Revolutionary Massachusetts, these crimes were prosecuted solely because their commission interfered with the enjoyment of property. Blackstone's classification scheme is useful primarily as an analytical tool for giving the modern reader a statistical picture of pre-Revolutionary law. While lawyers were aware of the scheme, it does not represent the mainstream of thought in mid-eighteenth century Massachusetts, which still adhered to the traditional view of crime as synonymous with sin. For example, grand jurors were urged by a judge to present wrongdoers so "that they may Receive the Just Demerit of their Crimes [and so that] all vice prophaness & Imorality may be Suppressed & man-kind Reformed and Brought to act with a Due Regard to God. . . ."[19] Several years later the same judge, disturbed that despite efforts made by the government to create "a Civil and Christian State," the people "remain[ed] a Savage & Barba[ric] People, Lead by their Lusts, Gove[rned] by their Passions . . . ," charged another grand jury to make "Inquiry into all Capital Offenses . . . , More Especially as to ye Sin of Murder."[20] Theft, like fornication and murder, was a sin against God, which government was obligated to suppress.[21]

Related to men's view of crime was their view of the criminal. The typical criminal was not, as today, an outcast from society, but only an ordinary member who had sinned. Like sin, crime could strike in any man's family or among any man's neighbors. As Sir Michael Foster, with whose work Massachusetts lawyers of 1760 were especially familiar,[22] observed:

For no Rank, no Elevation in Life, and let me add, no Conduct how circumspect soever, ought to tempt a reasonable Man to conclude that these Inquiries [into criminal law] do not, nor possibly can, concern Him. A Moment's cool Reflection on the utter Instability of Human Affairs, and the numberless unforeseen Events which a Day may bring forth, will be sufficient to guard any Man conscious of his own Infirmities against a Delusion of this Kind.[23]

Blackstone concurred,[24] and contemporaries in Massachusetts, aware of no contrary authority and constantly reminded by their clergymen of the omnipresence of sin,[25] probably would have too.

[19]Grand Jury Charge by Cushing, J., Nantucket Super. Ct., Aug. 1742, in William Cushing Papers (mss. at Massachusetts Historical Society, Boston, Mass.).
[20]See Grand Jury Charge by Cushing, J., Nantucket Super. Ct., Aug. 1746, in William Cushing Papers.
[21]See S. Howard, A Sermon Preached Before the Honorable Council and the Honorable House of Representatives of the State of Massachusetts-Bay, in New-England, May 31, 1780, in J. W. Thornton, The Pulpit of the American Revolution 355, 382–83, 393–94 (1860).
[22]See the jury charge of Trowbridge, J., in Rex v. Wemms, Suffolk Super. Ct., Dec. 1770, in 3 Legal Papers of John Adams 282 (Wroth & Zobel eds. 1965). Foster is cited in 23 of Trowbridge's 59 footnotes.
[23]M. Foster, A Report on Some Proceedings on the Commission of Oyer and Terminer and Goal Delivery for the Trial of Rebels in the Year 1746 in the County of Surry, and of other Crown Cases at v–vi (1767).
[24]4 Blackstone, Commentaries *2.
[25]See, e.g., S. Langdon, Government Corrupted by Vice, and Recovered by Righteousness, Sermon to the Congress of the Massachusetts Bay Colony, May 31, 1775, in J. W. Thornton, supra note 21, at 227, 247–48.

The court records of the 1760s and 1770s indicate that all elements of society committed crimes. Of 47 men accused between 1770 and 1774 of being fathers of illegitimate children, 18 were laborers, 15 were farmers, 12 were artisans, and 2 were gentlemen.[26] Moreover, unlike today, a convicted criminal was not placed in a prison and segregated from the rest of society; in the fiteen-year period before the Revolution, there was only one instance of a person being imprisoned for more than one year.[27] Colonial penalties usually did not sever a criminal's ties with society; fines and mild corporal punishments which left no permanent mark were the usual chastisements. Nor did the only punishment that was commonly of a long duration — the sale into servitude of a convicted thief unable to pay treble damages — result in the thief's segregation from society; rather, its probable effect was to integrate him more fully into society by reorienting him toward normal social contacts.

The years after the Revolution brought forth vast changes in attitudes toward crime and the criminal. Prosecutions for various sorts of immorality nearly ceased, while economically motivated crimes and prosecutions therefor greatly increased. During the same period, old punishments were being discarded and new sanctions imposed.

B. The Decline in Prosecutions for Offenses Against God and Religion. During the last fifteen years before the Revolution, there had been an average of fourteen prosecutions for fornication each year. The first ten years after the Revolution produced no change. However, in 1786, the General Court enacted a new statute for the punishment of fornication,[28] permitting a woman guilty of the crime to confess her guilt before a justice of the peace, pay an appropriate fine, and thereby avoid prosecution by way of indictment in the Court of General Sessions. Although the new law did not immediately produce any significant decline in prosecutions,[29] by 1789 only five convictions were recorded. The last indictment was returned in 1790,[30] and, after 1791, women stopped confessing their guilt,[31] apparently aware that even though they did not confess, they would not be indicted.[32]

---

[26]Of 16 accused between 1760 and 1774 of Sabbath breaking, 8 were farmers; 4, artisans; 2, laborers; and 2, gentlemen. The statistics given are not for total prosecutions, but only for cases in which the court records give defendants' occupations.

[27]The King v. How, Msex Super. Ct., Jan. 1762, f. 285 (20 years of hard labor for counterfeiting).

[28]An Act for the Punishment of Fornication, and for the Maintenance of Bastard Children, Mass. Acts and Laws 1785, ch. 66 (enacted March 15, 1786) [hereinafter Fornication Act].

[29]In 1786, there were at least 8 cases, the same number as in 1785, one more than in 1780, and only one less than in 1764, while in 1787, there were at least 12 convictions.

[30]Commonwealth v. Wright, Msex Gen. Sess., March 1790, at 480.

[31]The last two confessions were in 1791. See Examination of Susanna Denn, Aug. 22, 1791, in Denn v. Tay, Msex Gen. Sess., 1791, Middlesex Court Files for 1791; Examination of Rebecca Lane, Jan. 11, 1791, in Lane v. Kelly [also appears as Calle, Calley, and Kalley], Msex Gen. Sess. 1791, Middlesex Court Files for 1791.

[32]Although 1791 is probably the date of the last conviction, it is possible that subsequent convictions, the records of which have been lost, occurred. After the Fornication Act, convictions before individual justices were not recorded in the General Sessions judgment books, but only on small scraps of paper sent by the justices to the court clerk and preserved by him with other loose papers in the court's

Prosecutions for Sabbath breaking also continued at the pre-war rate of about two per year until the mid-1780s, after which, except for a brief interval in 1800–1802,[33] only three cases appear.[34] As a publication issued in 1816 stated, "[F]or many years previous to 1814, the Laws of this State against profanations of the Sabbath, had fallen into general neglect. . . . [T]housands of violations occurred every year, with scarcely a single instance of punishment."[35]

The law's attitude toward adultery was also changing, although the number of prosecutions remained relatively constant.[36] In 1793, three divorces were granted by the Supreme Judicial Court for the commission of adultery,[37] but the guilty spouses were never criminally punished. After 1793, divorces for adultery were regular occurrences,[38] yet only one prosecution was commenced.[39] This increase in divorce indicates not a rise in the incidence of adultery, but rather, the development of an attitude of legal hypocrisy which made it possible, at least in divorce proceedings, for a court to acknowledge publicly the existence of sin without prosecuting it.

A parallel development occurred in paternity litigation. As prosecutions for fornication ceased, it appears that a question arose whether an unwed mother not convicted of the crime could bring a paternity action against the putative father. One woman instituted such a suit in 1790[40] and gave bond to appear at the next term of court to prosecute it. At that term, however, a new condition was added to her bond — namely, that she also appear to answer a criminal charge of fornication.[41] Thus, the first attempt by a woman to sue without first suffering the consequences of her own misdeed failed. Yet, within five years,

---

files. Perhaps the justices after 1791 stopped sending the scraps to the clerk, although this seems unlikely since the Fornication Act, by implication, required that the scraps be filed. See Fornication Act, Mass. Acts and Laws 1785, ch. 66, §2. It seems equally unlikely that the filing system was changed in 1791, since the same man was clerk of the sessions throughout the 1780s and 1790s. A real decline in the number of convictions must have occurred around 1790, and although records of a small number occurring after 1791 may have been lost, it is accurate for general purposes to say that convictions ceased in the latter year.

[33]There were 12 prosecutions during these three years. No reason for this sudden increase is apparent, although it is possible that it was related to the "Second Awakening" then occurring in New England. See P. Miller, The Life of the Mind in America from the Revolution to the Civil War 6–7 (1965).

[34]Commonwealth v. Walker, Msex C. P., June 1806, at 692; Commonwealth v. Clafflin, Msex Gen. Sess., Sept. 1789, at 457; Commonwealth v. Clafflin, Msex Gen. Sess., Sept. 1789, at 456.

[35]Remarks on the Existing State of the Laws of Massachusetts Respecting Violations of the Sabbath 3 (1816).

[36]There had been one case in the fifteen years before the Revolution, see note 16 supra, while there were two in the thirty years after. Commonwealth v. Priest, Msex Sup. Jud. Ct., Oct. 1797, at 61; Commonwealth v. Pollard, Msex Sup. Jud. Ct., Oct. 1781, f. 117 (nolle prosequi entered by Attorney General).

[37]Lawrence v. Lawrence, Msex Sup. Jud. Ct., Oct. 1793, f. 301; Bemis v. Bemis, Msex Sup. Jud. Ct., Oct. 1793, f. 300; Blanchard v. Blanchard, Msex Sup. Jud. Ct., April 1793, f. 55.

[38]See, e.g., Remmie v. Remmie, Msex Sup. Jud. Ct., Nov. 1808, Minute Book (not paginated); Brown v. Brown, Msex Sup. Jud. Ct., Oct. 1795, f. 316.

[39]Commonwealth v. Priest, Msex Sup. Jud. Ct., Oct. 1797, at 61.

[40]Hiley v. Farmer, Msex Gen. Sess., Sept. 1790, at 4.

[41]Hiley v. Farmer, Msex Gen. Sess., Nov. 1790, at 16.

a new attempt had succeeded,[42] and thereafter paternity suits by women not punished for their own sin succeeded regularly.[43] Allowing such suits was a step even more radical than granting divorce for adultery without prosecuting the adulterer. In the divorce cases, the courts took merely a neutral attitude toward the sinner. In paternity cases, on the other hand, the courts not only ignored the plaintiff's "sinner" status, but also rendered the sinner affirmative help in obtaining relief from the consequences of her sin.

The de-emphasis of prosecution for sin appears to have been related to what the Congregational ministry condemned as "a declension in morals."[44] President Timothy Dwight of Yale traced the decline to the French and Indian War, and especially to the Revolution, which, he said, added "to the depravation still remaining [from the French War] . . . a long train of immoral doctrines and practices, which spread into every corner of the country. The profanation of the Sabbath, before unusual, profaneness of language, drunkenness, gambling, and lewdness were exceedingly increased. . . ."[45] Others also alluded to habits of card playing and gambling, and to instances of social vice and illegitimacy.[46] Chief Justice William Cushing, for example, feared that "some men have been so liberal in thinking as to religion as to shake off all religion, & while they have labored to set up heathen above Christian morals, have shown themselves destitute of all morality. . . ."[47]

Notwithstanding these complaints, a modern author has concluded that there was no "deepseated coarseness or general immorality"[48] during the closing years of the eighteenth century. What seems to have occurred after the Revolution was a relaxation not of private, personal morality but of what contemporaries referred to as public morality.[49] What occurred was "a general relaxing of social customs"[50] — an emergence not of significantly more immorality but of a new social and legal attitude toward the immorality that had always existed.

C. The Increase in Prosecutions for Offenses Against Habitations and Private Property.

In the late eighteenth and early nineteenth centuries, prosecutions for offenses against habitations and private property greatly increased; but the increase did not commence immediately after the Revolution. From 1776 to 1783, there

---

[42]Brooks v. Frost, Msex Gen. Sess., Nov. 1795, at 247.

[43]See, e.g., Ramsdell v. Woods, Msex Gen. Sess., May 1799, at 448; Tunnicliff v. Brown, Msex Gen. Sess., March 1796, at 262.

[44]See P. Goodman, The Democratic Republicans of Massachusetts 89 (1964).

[45]T. Dwight, A discourse on Some Events of the Last Century, delivered Jan. 7, 1801, quoted in V. Stauffer, New England and he Bavarian Illuminati, 82 Colum. U. Studies in Hist., Econ. & Pub. L. 25 (1918).

[46]V. Stauffer, supra note 45, at 24.

[47]W. Cushing, Notes on Biennial Elections and Other Subjects Under Debate in Massachusetts Ratifying Convention, Jan. 1788, in William Cushing Papers.

[48]V. Stauffer, supra note 45, at 26.

[49]See, e.g., Remarks on the Existing State of the Laws in Massachusetts Respecting Violations of the Sabbath 5, 12 (1816), for examples of the use of such terminology.

[50]V. Stauffer, supra note 45, at 26.

was an average of 3 cases per year, the same as before the Revolution. But in 1784, the number of prosecutions quadrupled,[51] and then averaged 11 per year for the remainder of the decade, a period of economic difficulty.[52] With the return of prosperity in the 1790s,[53] the average dropped to 7 per year,[54] and, apart from an unexplained rise in 1800–1801,[55] remained constant until 1806. Then came the embargo of 1807, depression, [56] and an increase in the average of theft prosecutions during the remainder of the decade to 21 per year.[57]

Apart from the correspondence in time of the periods of economic distress and two of the periods of increasing prosecutions, there are other reasons for believing that the increases were results of the distress. As indicated by Josiah Quincy, Jr., in a speech on the relationship of "Poverty, Vice and Crime," larceny was a crime committed almost entirely by the urban poor.[58] Court records support this view. Of the 38 theft prosecutions in the Supreme Judicial Court between 1807 and 1809, 27 were against the urban poor,[59] and urban poor were defendants in 53 of 71 cases in all courts between 1784 and 1790.[60] It is also significant that many thought of crime as a product of idleness. Governor Strong, for example, told the legislature in 1802 that "a great proportion of crimes are the effects of idleness. . . ."[61] such a view indicates that crime was often committed by the unemployed, such as poor laborers unable to find work during periods of economic dislocation.

Both the statistical and the impressionistic evidence suggests, then, that most theft was to some extent a consequence of poverty. Economic distress was apparently causing increasing numbers of the poor to turn to crimes against property during the post-Revolutionary years.

D. The Use of Hard Labor as a Punishment. The third development occurring during the years between 1776 and 1810 was the gradual emergence of hard labor as a punishment in place of the wide variety of penalties used before the Revolu-

---

[51]While there had been only 2 cases each in 1782 and 1783, there were 11 each in 1784 and 1785.

[52]O. Handlin & M. F. Handlin, Commonwealth; a Study of the Role of Government in the American Economy: Massachusetts, 1774–1861, at 35–36, 59–64 (1947); S. E. Morison, The Maritime History of Massachusetts 1783–1860, at 30–32, 35–36 (Sentry ed. 1961); W. B. Weeden, 2 Economic & Social History of New England 1620–1789, at 843 (1890).

[53]See S. E. Morison, supra note 52, at 166–67.

[54]The drop between 1790 and 1791 was dramatic. There were 12 cases in 1789, 19 in 1790, 3 in 1791, and 5 in 1792.

[55]There were 17 cases in 1800 and 20 in 1801.

[56]See S. E. Morison, supra note 52, at 191.

[57]There were 22 cases in 1807, 24 in 1808, and 18 in 1809.

[58]J. Quincy, Remarks on Some of the Provisions of the Laws of Massachusetts Affecting Poverty, Vice and Crime (1822).

[59]The 27 were laborers. Six of the remaining cases were against artisans and 5 against farmers.

[60]Of the 53, 46 were laborers and 7 were "transient persons." The remaining defendants were 15 farmers, 2 artisans, and 2 gentlemen.

[61]Speech by His Excellency Caleb Strong, Esq., Before the Senate and House of Representatives of the Commonwealth of Massachusetts, Jan. 15, 1802, in Patriotism and Piety: the Speeches of His Excellency Caleb Strong, Esq. 48, 50 (1808).

tion. Hard labor was first imposed with frequency in theft cases. Although there is no direct evidence of why the punishment was first used, the reason can be surmised by tracing the gradual evolution in the penalties imposed for theft during the Revolutionary era.

The basic penalty for theft in pre-Revolutionary Massachusetts was twofold: first, a fine or some sort of mild corporal punishment was imposed on behalf of the government; second, the convicted thief was required to pay treble damages to the owner of the stolen goods. Enforcement of the second part of the penalty was apparently difficult, for many thieves simply could not pay. In such circumstances, the owner of the stolen goods was usually authorized to sell the defendant in service for a specified period varying according to the amount of the treble damages.[62] The market for convict-servants must have been depressed, however, for judgments as early as 1772 contain provisions that, if an owner could not sell a defendant within thirty days of his conviction, the defendant was to be released, unless the owner compensated the government for the costs of keeping the defendant in jail.[63] The government, it seems, did not want to be charged with the burden of supporting thieves. Its dilemma, though, was that setting convicted thieves free excused them from "that grievous . . . [penalty] of being sold in servitude"[64] — the most severe of the penalties imposed upon them.

The dilemma was resolved in 1785, when the legislature provided for the imprisonment of thieves at hard labor,[65] for the state expected that the proceeds of such labor would pay the costs of imprisoning those so punished.[66] Originally hard labor was to be imposed only in cases where the old penalty of treble damages was not workable,[67] but the Supreme Judicial Court soon began to impose it even in cases where the old punishments could be used,[68] apparently because the judges thought it a more efficacious penalty. At the same time, though, they continued to impose the old penalties in some cases.[69] As a result, a defendant convicted of larceny could, by the early 1800s, look forward to almost any penalty.[70]

[62]See, e.g., The King v. Smith, Msex Super. Ct., April 1773, f. 29 (sale for fourteen years); The King v. Polydore, Msex Super. Ct., Oct. 1772, f. 186 (sale for six months); The King v. Powell, Msex Super. Ct., Oct. 1769, f. 202 (sale for four years).

[63]See, e.g., The King v. Manhall [or Marshall], Msex Gen. Sess., Nov. 1772, at 63.

[64]Commonwealth v. Andrews, 2 Mass. 14, 31 (1806).

[65]Act for the Punishing and the Preventing of Larcenies, Mass. Acts and Laws 1784, ch. 66 (enacted March 15, 1785); Act Providing a Place of Confinement for Thieves and Others to Hard Labor, Mass. Acts and Laws 1784, ch. 63 (enacted March 14, 1785).

[66]G. Bradford, Description and Historical Sketch of the Massachusetts State Prison 10 (1816).

[67]The act authorizing the penalty in larceny cases so provided. Mass. Acts and Laws 1784, ch. 66, §3.

[68]See, e.g., Commonwealth v. Foster, Msex Sup. Jud. Ct., Oct. 1792, f. 274; Commonwealth v. Blood, Msex Sup. Jud. Ct., April 1790, f. 65; Commonwealth v. Moor, Msex Sup. Jud. Ct., Oct. 1785, f. 296.

[69]See, e.g., Commonwealth v. Hall, Msex Sup. Jud. Ct., April 1796, f. 64.

[70]In 3 cases in the Supreme Judicial Court's November Term of 1804, for example, the following penalties were imposed: (1) one hour on the gallows plus a whipping of 30 stripes plus six years hard labor, Commonwealth v. Tuttle, Msex Sup. Jud. Ct., Nov. 1804, at 78; (2) payment of treble

Meanwhile, a movement for general penology reform had begun. Having had its origin in Philadelphia in 1776,[71] this movement may have been partly responsible for the legislation of 1785. Any influence it may have had in 1785, however, was slight for the legislature in that year explicitly decided to retain the old punishments for certain crimes.[72] This was directly contrary to the reform movement's aims, which are best stated in a message from Governor Hancock to the General Court in 1793:

> It may well be worthy of your attention to investigate the question whether the infamous punishments of cropping [ears] and branding, as well as that of the public whipping post, so frequently administered in this Government, are the best means to prevent the commission of crimes, or absolutely necessary to the good order of Government or to the security of the people. It is an indignity to human nature, and can have but little tendency to reclaim the sufferer. Crimes have generally idleness for their source, and where offences are not prevented by education, a sentence to hard labor will perhaps have a more salutary effect than mutilating or lacerating the human body. . . .[73]

The movement reached fruition in 1805, when the state prison was reopened,[74] and corporal punishment and treble damages were imposed for the last time in a Middlesex case.[75]

E. The New Attitude Toward Crime and the Criminal. Each of the three developments discussed thus far was, of course, important in itself. Moreover, in combination with an ideological outgrowth of the Revolution, they transformed the legal and social attitudes toward crime and the criminal. Before the Revolution, two-thirds of all prosecutions were for immorality, and crime was pictured as sin. By 1810, on the other hand, crime was prosecuted to "insure the peace and safety of society"[76] and to relieve the public from the "depradations" of "notorious offenders"[77] and the "tax levied on the community by . . . privateering"[78] of thieves. More than fifty per cent of all prosecutions were for theft, and only one-half of one per cent for conduct offensive to morality. The criminal

---

damages plus seven years of hard labor, Commonwealth v. Moore, Msex Sup. Jud. Ct., Nov. 1804, at 79; and (3) a whipping of 30 stripes plus either payment of treble damages or sale in service for three years, Commonwealth v. Moore, Msex Sup. Jud. Ct., Nov. 1804, at 80.

[71]See H. E. Barnes, The Evolution of Penology in Pennsylvania, a Study in American Social History 80–81 (1927).

[72]See Act to Prevent Forgery, and for the Punishment of Those Who Are Guilty of the Same, Mass. Acts and Laws 1784, ch. 67.

[73]Address by Governor John Hancock to a Joint Session of the Massachusetts Legislature, Jan. 31, 1793, quoted in Powers, Crime and Punishment in Early Massachusetts 192–93 (1966).

[74]Powers, supra note 73, at 193.

[75]Commonwealth v. Sykeston, Msex C. P., Dec. 1805, at 379.

[76]G. Bradford, State Prisons and the Penitentiary System Vindicated 5 (1821).

[77]G. Bradford, Description and Historical Sketch of the Massachusetts State Prison 15 (1816).

[78]G. Bradford, supra note 76, at 12.

in 1810 was no longer envisioned as a sinner against God, but rather as one who preyed upon his fellow citizens.

The transition from the attitude of 1760 to that of 1810 seems to have occurred largely during the decade following the conclusion of peace with Britain in 1783. But the first step in the change began earlier, in the 1760s. During that decade and the first half of the following one, Massachusetts Tories carefully cultivated a fear that rebellion against British authority would lead ultimately to the destruction of all authority. The consequence of rebellion, they maintained, would be that "the bands of society would be dissolved, the harmony of the world confounded, and the order of nature subverted. . . ."[79] In a series of grand jury charges given during the 1760s, Chief Justice Thomas Hutchinson suggested how law should be used to prevent the destruction of authority. Expressing his concern that "Disorders are seldom confined to one Point" and that "people who begin with one View, seldom end there,"[80] Hutchinson urged the jurors "to point out and bring forward all Crimes and Offenses against the Tranquillity and Order of the Society. . . ."[81] Hutchinson's argument essentially was that in order for society to protect itself, its better elements had to be watchful of attacks by mean, lawless, and ignorant men upon order — that is, upon authority and wealth. Proper watchfulness included reliance upon law to punish and hence deter such attacks.

Many Whigs had similar apprehensions. John Adams was as concerned as Hutchinson when, in 1765, a mob of rioters broke into a royal official's home. "[T]o have his Garden torn in Pieces, his House broken open, his furniture destroyed and his whole family thrown into Confusion and Terror, is a very atrocious Violation of the Peace and of dangerous Tendency and Consequence."[82] By the outbreak of hostilities between the British and Americans in 1774–1775, apprehension of the danger of possible lawlessness and mob rule had grown into an obsession common to all. An example is the conduct of the people of Groton in sending supplies in 1774 for the relief of residents of Boston. With the supplies, the town clerk of Groton sent a letter: "The inhabitants of this Town have . . . this day sent forty bushels of grain . . . and we earnestly desire you will use your utmost endeavor to prevent and avoid all mobs, riots, and tumults, and the insulting of private persons and property."[83]

This emerging fear of the mob seems to have been primarily of a political nature. Adams and Hutchinson were not worried that *sinners* would break into

---

[79]T. B. Chandler, A Friendly Address to All Reasonable Americans on the Subject of Our Political Confusions 5 (1774), quoted in 1 Pamphlets of the American Revolution, 1750–1776, at 198–99 (B. Bailyn, ed. 1965).

[80]Grand Jury Charge by Hutchinson, C.J., Suffolk Super. Ct., Aug. 1766, in J. Quincy, Reports of Cases Argued and Adjudged in the Superior Court of Judicature of the Province of Massachusetts Bay, Between 1761 and 1772, at 218–220 (S. Quincy ed. 1865).

[81]Grand Jury Charge by Hutchinson, C.J., Suffolk Super. Ct., March 1765, in J. Quincy, supra note 80, at 110.

[82]1 Diary and Autobiography of John Adams 260 (Butterfield, Faber & Garrett eds. 1961).

[83]Letter From Oliver Prescott, Town Clerk of Groton, Mass., to Town of Boston, Mass., 1774, quoted in 12 C. K. Shipton, Sibley's Harvard Graduates 1746–1750, at 570 (1962).

their homes and take away their property; nor did they fear an individual thief motivated by a longing for personal material gain. Rather, they feared organized groups of malcontents bent upon the reconstruction of society. Yet they feared such political activity because they expected that it would be economically motivated. They were concerned that debtors would grow insolvent[84] and that mobs would "invade private rights."[85] In short, their fear was that the economically under-privileged would seek material gain by banding together to deprive more privileged persons of their wealth and standing.

Despite these new concerns, however, the old conception of the purpose of criminal law still persisted at the outset of the Revolution. Thus, the General Court in 1776 urged the people to

lead sober, Religious and peaceable Lives, avoiding all Blasphemies, contempt of the holy Scriptures, and of the Lord's day and all other Crimes and Misdemeanors, all Debauchery, Prophaneness, Corruption, Venality, all riotous and tumultuous Proceedings, and all Immoralities whatsoever. . . .[86]

In this statement, though, one can also see the emergence of a new concern with political and economic disorder. Although the new concern was at first peripheral, by the early 1780s it was becoming a central one, as men came to view criminal law as having a dual function, "to discourage [both] vice . . . and disorders in society. . . ."[87]

Although quite real, the new concern had little support in the events of the time. During the 1760s and early 1770s, Middlesex experienced relatively few violent attacks on property; indeed during the two decades, only four instances of such violence were prosecuted.[88] Although there were undoubtedly additional cases, historians of the Revolution are nonetheless agreed that very little violence of the sort Adams and Hutchinson feared did take place during the course of struggle with Britain.[89]

In the 1780s, however, fears previously ungrounded were confirmed by a number of attacks upon authority and property. Between 1781 and 1786, there were four prosecutions for rioting[90] and five for assaults on tax collectors,[91] in one of which

---

[84]See 1 Diary, supra note 82, at 264.

[85]Grand Jury Charge by Hutchinson, C.J., Suffolk Super. Ct., Aug. 1776, in J. Quincy, supra note 80, at 218, 219.

[86]Proclamation of the General Court, Jan. 23, 1776, in O. Handlin & M. F. Handlin, The Popular Sources of Political Authority 68 (1966).

[87]Draft of Grand Jury Charge by Cushing, C.J., 1783, in William Cushing Papers 21.

[88]See notes 119–121 infra and accompanying text.

[89]Bailyn, Introduction, in 1 Pamphlets of the American Revolution, 1750–1776, at 190 (Bailyn ed. 1965); G. S. Wood, Rhetoric and Reality in the American Revolution, 23 William & Mary Q.3d 3, 5–6, 11 (1966).

[90]Commonwealth v. White, Msex Gen. Sess., Sept. 1785, at 367; Commonwealth v. Orr, Msex Gen. Sess., Sept. 1785, at 366; Commonwealth v. Frost, Msex Gen. Sess., Sept. 1781, at 259; Commonwealth v. Russell, Msex Sup. Jud. Ct., Dec. 1782, f. 387.

[91]Commonwealth v. Richardson, Msex Sup. Jud. Ct., Oct. 1784, f. 340; Commonwealth v. Shattuck, Msex Sup. Jud. Ct., April 1782, f. 160; Commonwealth v. Parker, Msex Sup. Jud. Ct., April 1781, f. 15; Government v. Parker, Msex Super. Ct., Nov. 1780, f. 251.

eighteen codefendants had participated.[92] Then a most noteworthy attack occurred when, on September 12, 1786, the Court of General Sessions was scheduled by law to meet at Concord. "But a large armed Force, under the Command of one Job Shattuck of Groton (as it was said) being previously collected had taken Possession of the Court House to prevent their sitting. The Justices of the said Court did not attempt to open the Court."[93] Thus did Shay's Rebellion, which sought to close the courts to prevent the collection of debts, extend eastward into Middlesex. It led to several prosecutions.[94]

Culminating in open rebellion, these five years of violence undoubtedly strengthened the fear which society's well-to-do had of the designs of the lower classes upon their wealth and standing. The simultaneous increase in the incidence of theft appears to have contributed to both a strengthening and a modification of the fear. Adams and Hutchinson, it will be recalled, did not worry about individual thieves. A man living in 1786, however, must have viewed all attacks upon property, on the one hand by poverty-stricken mobs and, on the other, by poverty-stricken individuals, as part of a single phenomenon. What was at stake, ultimately, was his security of person and property, which members of the lower classes were seeking to disrupt. They used a variety of techniques: they rioted; they attacked courts and tax collectors; they refused to pay debts; they entered men's homes and carried away their possessions. Logically, though, their various techniques could be reduced to two. Some men — the thieves and recalcitrant debtors — broke the law and infringed property rights directly; others — the rioters and those who attacked the courts and tax collectors — worked indirectly by destroying the institutions of government upon which enforcement of law, and thus security of property rights, rested. Thus, when Governor Hancock, in an address to the legislature in 1793, suggested that the primary function of criminal law was to insure "the good order of Government . . . [and] the security of the people,"[95] he was saying in effect that it must perform two functions: first, it must punish and deter direct attacks on property, and second, it must preserve the power of government to perform that first function.

Hancock's address, which said nothing about the preservation of religion and morality, further shows that the old theocratic view of crime was rapidly dying. A "liberalizing of the older New England religious tradition" was occurring, especially among the upper classes of eastern Massachusetts.[96] As Chief Justice Cushing explained, when men rejected the old religious traditions, they also rejected many of the old moral ones,[97] among them the theretofore unquestioned assumption

---

[92]Commonwealth v. Shattuck, Msex Sup. Jud. Ct., April 1782, f. 160.

[93]Msex Gen. Sess., Sept. 1786, at 396–97.

[94]In one, a jury found Shattuck guilty of conspiring to levy war against the state. He was sentenced to death, Commonwealth v. Shattuck, Msex Sup. Jud. Ct., May 1787, f. 122, but was later pardoned. See O. Handlin & M. F. Handlin, supra note 52, at 50. A jury found two other defendants guilty of rioting. Commonwealth v. Page, Msex Sup. Jud. Ct., May 1787, f. 125; Commonwealth v. Shattuck, Msex Sup. Jud. Ct., May 1787, f. 125.

[95]Message from Governor Hancock to the General Court, 1793, quoted in Powers, supra note 73, at 193.

[96]G. A. Koch, Republican Religion: The American Revolution and the Cult of Reason 295 (1933).

[97]See note 47 supra and accompanying text.

that government should enforce morality. Such men, it would seem, were taking a step toward a modern view of criminal law — a view that its purpose is to protect men from unwanted invasions of their rights. At the same time, churchmen and others faithful to the old tradition were abandoning "the dream of theocracy,"[98] as it became "evident that the salvation of the nation . . . had to be won . . . with no assistance from any civil authority."[99] The end result was that criminal law became secularized; its purpose came to be seen not as the preservation of morality, but rather as the protection of social order and property.

With the cessation in the 1790s of anti-governmental violence and prosecutions for immorality, criminal law in fact as well as in theory became concerned primarily with the punishment of theft. During the two decades after 1790, prosecutions for various sorts of theft amounted to forty-seven per cent of all cases. This in turn produced a further modification of the theory of criminal law; by 1810 the obsession with mob violence was declining, and the law's purpose was coming to be seen almost entirely as the relief of the public from the "depredations"[100] of thieves.

Meanwhile, the criminal was becoming an outcast of society. Prior to the Revolution, all sorts of men became involved in crime. By 1810, though, the well-to-do rarely became involved with the criminal law, and it was greatly to be regretted "when the offender has some rank in society, with respectable connections who may suffer with him."[101] Such connections were rare, though, for the poverty of most criminals isolated them from the better elements of society on whom they preyed. Criminals in 1810, unlike the mere sinners of old, were different from other men. Nor were their differences and their consequent isolation from society ameliorated by the increasing use of hard labor as a punishment. As some began to observe soon after 1810, long terms of imprisonment did not reform men and enable them to take their place in society, but instead confirmed them in their criminal ways by giving them an opportunity "for corrupting one another."[102] Whereas God could forgive the sinner of old, the villain of 1810 kept returning to crime and was forever condemned to segregation from the society whose peace and prosperity he challenged.

II. Government Versus Individual in the Criminal Process: From Regulation of Power to Prohibition of Its Use

A. Colonial Safeguards in the Criminal Process. Like most legal thinkers over the course of Anglo-American history, those of Massachusetts in the mid-eighteenth century were concerned with the problem of insuring fairness in the criminal process.

---

[98]P. Miller, From the Covenant to the Revival, in 1 Religion in American Life 322, 354 (Smith & Jamison eds. 1961).

[99]Id. at 356.

[100]See note 77 supra and accompanying text.

[101]Commonwealth v. Waite, 5 Mass. 261, 264 (1809).

[102]G. Bradford, supra note 76, at 51.

But for them this was only one part of a broader problem of insuring liberty. The pre-Revolutionary generation feared that all agencies of power, including the courts, posed a potential threat to liberty.[103] They recognized, however, that the exercise of power was an essential attribute of effective government;[104] hence, they sought not to prevent power from being exercised, but only to establish safeguards to prevent it from being arbitrarily used.

As long as established safeguards were unimpaired, the pre-Revolutionary generation felt secure. It did not fear the courts because, as the judicial system was then constituted, three trusted safeguards were provided — the jury system, an independent judiciary, and law itself. The pre-Revolutionary generation concentrated its efforts on the preservation of these safeguards. As the Middlesex County Convention explained in 1774, "no state can long exist free and happy . . . when trials by juries . . . are destroyed or weakened . . .,"[105] for the jury system introduces into the "executive branch . . . a mixture of popular power," whereby "the subject is guarded in the execution of the laws."[106] Also crucial was the independence of the judiciary. "It was taken as a maxim by all . . . that it was the function of the judges 'to settle the contests between prerogative and liberty' . . . and that in order for them to perform this duty properly they must be 'perfectly free from the influence of either.' "[107] To have judges "dependent on the Crown" would result in "natural evil consequences . . . obvious and truly alarming,"[108] for it would subvert "a free administration of justice. . . . "[109] An independent judiciary in turn guaranteed an independent administration of the law, which was itself viewed as a safeguard of liberties because it "preserved . . . every possible Case . . . in Writing, and settled in a Precedent, leav[ing] nothing, or but little to the arbitrary Will or uninformed Reason of Prince or Judge."[110]

This protective framework was well grounded in reality, for two factors neutralized the power of the state. One was the absence of any direct state interest in the outcome of most criminal cases. Although prosecutions were formally instituted by a governmental agency — either the grand jury or the crown prosecutor — many criminal trials were in reality contests between subjects rather than contests between government and subject. For example, the colonial government was not the real party in interest in theft cases, since it had neither control over the imposition of nor a right to receive the treble damages. These damages were paid to the

---

[103]See Bailyn, supra note 89, at 38–39.

[104]Id. at 40.

[105]Resolves of Middlesex County Convention of August, 1774, printed in L. Shattuck, A History of the Town of Concord 84 (1835).

[106]3 Works of John Adams 481 (C. F. Adams ed. 1850–1856), quoted in Bailyn, supra note 89, at 48.

[107]Bailyn, supra note 89, at 48–49.

[108]Letter From Selectmen of Newton, Mass., to Selectmen of Boston, Mass., in Samuel F. Smith, History of Newton, Massachusetts 325, 326 (1880).

[109]Resolves of the Middlesex County Convention of August, 1774, printed in Shattuck, supra note 105, at 82, 85.

[110]1 Diary and Autobiography of John Adams 167 (Butterfield, Faber & Garrett eds. 1961).

complaining individual, who could release his right to them,[111] thereby virtually ending prosecution. Government was also disinterested in the outcome of cases involving offenses against God and religion. One gets the impression that the royal governor and his associates did not care whether fornicators and Sabbath breakers were punished, and that prosecutions for these offenses were simply contests between citizens. These two categories of cases accounted for almost eighty per cent of all prosecutions in pre-Revolutionary times. The second factor neutralizing the power of government was the real inability of the courts to influence the outcome of most cases. The important issue in every case — whether the defendant committed the well-defined criminal act charged — was decided by the jury of his neighborhood. Even if the government could have controlled the judiciary, it could not have controlled the juries.[112] Courts do not seem to have had many opportunities to influence the outcome of cases by deciding nice questions of law. Substantive motions were made in only eleven cases, all of them petty offenses tried before justices of the peace. On appeal, the judgments were set aside for legal insufficiencies, but the insufficiencies were apparently of a technical nature.[113]

Even if serious issues had arisen, the approach of the bench and bar to the process of decision was such that the court would have had little freedom in reaching a result. When a legal question arose, the task for the colonial lawyer was to find the applicable British precedent. For example, Adams' argument on behalf of William Wemms, a defendant in the Boston massacre trial, cited, with one exception, only British cases and texts, frequently quoting or paraphrasing them to the jury.[114] Judge Trowbridge's charge to the jury in *Wemms* was similar, consisting, apart from a discussion of the evidence, of statements of rules of law supported by fifty-nine footnotes to British authority.[115] Such unquestioning acceptance of British precedent meant that, as long as counsel were assiduous, there would rarely be any issue left to the court.

[111]The King v. Dun, Msex Gen. Sess., March 1764, at 149.

[112]See notes 123–124 infra and accompanying text.

[113]In 7 of the 11 cases, it is possible to determine what the insufficiency was. In the first case, in 1760, a defendant was required to find sureties for his good behavior for an indeterminate period — an improper requirement. The King v. Bent, Msex Gen. Sess., Dec. 1760, at 609. See Commonwealth v. Ward, 3 Mass. 497 (1808). In the second case, the justice's argument did not sufficiently describe the defendant's offense. The King v. Brown, Msex Gen. Sess., Dec. 1763, at 130. The third error was the same: the judgment merely described the offense as "a breach of the peace but not so aggravated as is set forth in the complaint. . . . ." The King v. Taylor, Msex Gen. Sess., Sept. 1764, at 171. The error in the fourth case was the total absence of a complaint; the charge against the defendant was made only in the warrant for his arrest. The King v. Goodenow, Msex Gen. Sess., Sept. 1764, at 171. In the fifth case, the justice of the peace failed to indicate the date on which the defendant had been tried. The King v. Moor, Msex Gen. Sess., Sept. 1764, at 171. In the sixth, the justice's proceeding was quashed because his warrant was insufficient: it was addressed only to the county sheriff or his deputy, and not, as it should have been, to the constables of the defendant's home town as well. The King v. Fenton, Msex Gen. Sess., March 1767, at 336. The seventh was quashed for an error in the judgment: it stated that the defendant had committed his offense on September 25, 1769, while the complaint accused him of committing it on September 20. The King v. Stimson, Msex Gen. Sess., Nov. 1769, at 472.

[114]3 Legal Papers of John Adams 242–60 (Wroth & Zobel eds. 1965).

[115]Id. at 282–302.

As a result of the courts' lack of power, men in pre-Revolutionary Massachusetts were content to give them relatively free rein in the suppression of criminal conduct. The courts and their procedures were attuned to finding the truth — who in fact had sinned. Upon arrest, defendants were interrogated thoroughly by a judge,[116] and search warrants were broadly drawn lest they impede the search for physical evidence of the truth. In the early 1760s, for example, royal customs officers could obtain "general standing warrants, good from the date of issue until six months after the death of the issuing sovereign, which permitted the holder to enter any house by day . . . and there search for smuggled goods without special application to a court."[117] Even in the regular criminal proceedings, search warrants gave officers broad powers. A warrant issued in 1769, for example, authorized a search of an entire farm, and the arrest of any person in whose possession certain stolen property was found.[118]

The protective scheme of 1760 proved, however, to be inadequate. Men began to apprehend the possibility that, despite the safeguards of the jury, the independent judiciary, and the settled law, abuses of government law enforcement power might well occur. They perceived that even an independent judiciary could and would twist the law to suit the government's ends, and that, as a result, criminal law enforcement posed a potential threat to civil liberty, calling for new devices to safeguard it.

B. The Government as Antagonist of the Individual. During and after the Revolution, government showed an interest in the outcome of many criminal cases. A series of prosecutions, beginning in the last years of the colonial era and continuing thereafter, had stimulated that official interest. In the closing years of the colonial era, the British administration brought four prosecutions against its Whig rivals in Middlesex — all four of them for rioting. Two, in 1764 and 1770, were for riotously assembling and breaking into private homes.[119] The other two arose from related incidents. One involved a group of students who broke into a Tory dwelling and attacked an occupant; this group was later tried by a jury, perhaps of Whig leanings, and acquitted.[120] Before trial, however, a second incident took place — another group of students assaulted a deputy sheriff while he had the first group in custody. The second group was tried and convicted but appealed to the superior court, which held the case for six years. Finally, at the first session of the court of the independent state of Massachusetts, the case was dismissed.[121]

---

[116]See, e.g., The King v. Bradish, Msex Super. Ct., Jan. 1762, 1003 Suffolk Court Files No. 147139.

[117]2 Legal Papers of John Adams 108 (Wroth & Zobel eds. 1965).

[118]The King v. Smith, Msex Gen. Sess., March 1769, Middlesex Court Files for 1769.

[119]The King v. Henshaw, Msex Super. Ct., April 1770, f. 66; The King v. Scott, Msex Super. Ct., April 1764, f. 228.

[120]The King v. Langdon, Msex Gen. Sess., May 1770, at 497.

[121]The King v. Murray, Msex Gen. Sess., May 1770, at 495, dismissed on appeal, Msex Super. Ct., Oct. 1776, 17 Minute Book f. 37.

Political prosecutions under the British were not of serious consequence for two reasons. The first was British leniency — in all four rioting cases, the only punishments imposed were fines, the largest being five pounds.[122] The second was the jury system — the government could rarely get grand jurors to consent to political prosecution of their fellow subjects. During much of his tenure on the bench, Chief Justice Hutchinson, for example, urged Suffolk County grand jurors to return indictments against libelers and rioters, but the jurors refused.[123] There is no reason to suppose that he did not do the same in Middlesex. Hutchinson himself said that he had charged grand juries in other counties as to libel, and that they too had refused to return indictments.[124] This inability of the administration to use the courts as it wished probably confirmed the Whigs in their view that, as long as the three safeguards against oppression — juries, independent judges, and the law — were not impaired, at least one of them could always be trusted to thwart any attempt by government to abuse its power in the criminal process.

Political prosecutions under the rebel government were far more numerous than under the old regime, and the stakes were higher. The only prosecutions in Middlesex of a strictly criminal nature were tried at several special meetings of the Court of General Sessions, and the only record preserved is an incomplete and tattered file of loose papers. Hence it is impossible to give a complete picture of these prosecutions, and one example must suffice to indicate their nature. Samuel Teagers was prosecuted in 1777 for two crimes — being "inimical to the Liberties of America" and "counteract[ing] the united struggles of this and the united States for the Preservation of their Rights & Priviledges."[125] Teagers' offense had been to "say that he would travel Fifty Miles to blow out the Brains of Samuel Adams & John Hancock. . . . [He also said] that he hoped to see the Hills covered with the Dead Bodies of the Rebels, & many other such like Expressions."[126] Both prosecutions against Teagers were commenced when the selectmen of Cambridge presented his name to a town meeting as a possible defendant. A majority of the voters present favored making him one, and so it was done. He was then tried by a jury, convicted of the charge of being "inimical," and exiled.[127]

[122]The King v. Scott, Msex Super. Ct., April 1764, f. 228.

[123]Grand Jury Charge by Hutchinson, C.J., Suffolk Super. Ct., March 1768, in J. Quincy, supra note 80, at 258; Grand Jury Charge by Hutchinson, C.J., Suffolk Super. Ct., Aug. 1765, in J. Quincy, supra note 80, at 175.

[124]Grand Jury Charge by Hutchinson, C.J., Suffolk Super. Ct., March 1769, in J. Quincy, supra note 80, at 306, 309.

[125]Government v. Teagers, Msex Gen. Sess., Special Term 1777, Middlesex Court Files for 1777.

[126]Deposition of Joana Carnes, Government v. Teagers, Msex Gen. Sess., Special Term 1777, Middlesex Court Files for 1777. Another deponent said that when he asked Teagers' advice about whether he should re-enlist in the Continental Army, Teagers "told me I was a fool if I did, for I must be Sensible that General Howe would Counter us, in a short time, and then what hanging work their would be amoungst the Damn'd [word illegible]." Deposition of Captain T. J. Carnes, Government v. Teagers, supra.

[127]Exile was authorized by Mass. Province Laws of 1776–1777, ch. 48, §§4–7. In addition to Teagers' case, there were sixteen similar prosecutions in Middlesex. In Government v. Littlefield, Msex Gen. Sess., Special Term 1777, Middlesex Court Files for 1777, the defendant had "even

The various prosecutions growing out of Shays' rebellion and similar violence[128] were, of course, of great concern to the government. The stakes in these cases also were high; one defendant was sentenced to death, [129] and fines, as high as 100 pounds,[130] were imposed on others. Prosecutions for counterfeiting, although not of a political nature, were also of major governmental concern. While there had been only seven prosecutions between 1760 and 1774, twenty-five cases were brought during the first fifteen years of independence. As before the Revolution, punishments were often severe, including fines as high as 100 pounds,[131] treble damages,[132] severe corporal punishment,[133] and hard labor.[134]

In short, a comparison of the fifteen-year periods before and after the Revolution shows a large increase in the number of cases in which the government had a direct interest. During the colonial period, there were eleven such cases. In the latter half of the 1770s alone there were at least thirty-seven and, in the next decade, another twenty-one.

The above increase appears to have been a direct — and undesired — consequence of the Revolution. The increase in prosecutions for counterfeiting almost surely resulted from the increase in the incidence of the crime; the Revolution produced a large array of new paper currencies, many of which were poorly manufactured and, as a result, easily copied or altered.[135] Likewise, the prosecutions against Tories were obvious outgrowths of the Revolution. The closing of the court at Groton was also an outgrowth; it was an attempt to employ a technique developed for use against the British for largely the same purpose for which it had been developed — to obtain concessions from the government or to bring it down.

---

been So Daring as in Public Town Meeting to oppose; when matters have been Transacting for Supporting the Cause; Declareing the meeting to be a Mobb, & that he would have no hand in the Rebellion. . . .'' For a similar prosecution in Boston, see Government v. Williams, Suffolk Super. Ct., Aug. 1777, f. 146. See also Government v. Wallace, Msex Gen. Sess., March 1777, at 168, where a defendant was ''indicted for not marching, when duly drafted.''

In addition to criminal cases, the government brought a number of civil condemnation actions having political overtones. Most notable were the proceedings brought to condemn the property of loyalists who had fled from Massachusetts. See R. D. Brown, The Confiscation and Disposition of Loyalists' Estates in Suffolk County, Massachusetts, 21 William & Mary Q.3d 534 (1964). There were also four cases brought against cargoes of sugar and rum being transported in violation of a price control statute. Mass. Province Laws of 1776–1777, ch. 14, at 583–89, as amended, Mass. Province Laws of 1776–1777, ch. 46, at 642–47. Government v. One Barrel of Sugar, Msex Gen. Sess., Sept. 1777, at 183; Government v. Mitchell, Msex Gen. Sess., May 1777, at 180; Government v. Ward, Msex Gen. Sess., May 1777, at 179–80; Government v. Jones, Msex Gen. Sess., May 1777, at 179.

[128]See notes 90–94 supra and accompanying text.

[129]Commonwealth v. Shattuck, Msex Sup. Jud. Ct., May 1787, f. 122.

[130]Commonwealth v. Page, Msex Sup. Jud. Ct., May 1787, f. 125.

[131]Government v. Williams, Msex Super. Ct., Nov. 1780, f. 252.

[132]Ibid.

[133]Commonwealth v. Smith, Msex Sup. Jud. Ct., April 1788, f. 367 (lower part of ear amputated).

[134]Commonwealth v. Frost, Msex Sup. Jud. Ct., Oct. 1787, f. 290 (one hour in pillory and two years at hard labor).

[135]See Government v. Danforth, Msex Super. Ct., April 1777, f. 86 (involving alteration of a handwritten government bill).

In fact, the various attacks on governmental authority throughout the 1780s were part of a struggle between the new Commonwealth government and anti-authoritarian forces unleashed by the Revolution, to determine whether the new government could effectively consolidate its authority.[136]

Although political disorder and hence political prosecutions declined after 1790, the government's interest in the outcome of many criminal cases continued to emerge. For with the imposition of hard labor instead of treble damages as the usual punishment in theft cases, the victim of the theft ceased to be the real party in interest in a theft prosecution. Instead, government, as representative of the propertied elements of society, became the truly interested party. Since prosecutions for theft accounted for a majority of all cases by the early 1790s, the state's interest in the entire criminal process was surely significant. When, after 1805, fines and prison terms became the modes of punishment in all cases, the government's interest became even greater. The true magnitude of that interest, as compared with the interest of private individuals, is perhaps best illustrated by the practice developed by 1810 of the state's paying private individuals the expenses they incurred in assisting in the prosecution of cases.[137] A social expectation had developed that, without a promise of recompense, no one but the government would have any interest in participating in the criminal process.

The increased interest of government in the outcome of criminal cases was not something which men sought intentionally to bring about. Until 1790, the increase was due largely to the increase in violence against the government; after that date, it was due to the increase in the incidence of theft. Neither of these causative developments was desired by the Revolutionary generation, obsessed as it was with the evils of violence and crime against property.

C. Legal Confusion and the Changed Function of the Court. At the same time that government was developing an interest in the outcome of prosecutions, the courts were developing an ability to influence that outcome. Within a year after the reorganization of the courts in 1776, the first in a series of hitherto unused challenges — challenges to the substance of the law — was made. During the years which followed, substantive legal challenges became commonplace. Since the court was often free to decide these challenges as it wished, it gained a new power to affect the outcome of a criminal case.

Most of the substantive challenges are traceable to the new political and constitutional background of the law growing out of the Revolution. *Government v. Ward*, decided in 1777, is an example. A proceeding in rem was instituted against a hogshead of sugar being transported in violation of price control legislation.[138]

---

[136]See O. Handlin & M. F. Handlin, Commonwealth; a Study of the Role of Government in the American Economy: Massachusetts, 1774–1861, at 44–46 (1947); 2 Weeden, Economic & Social History of New England, 1620–1789, at 842–44 (1890).

[137]See, e.g., Cutler's Pet'n, Msex Sup. Jud. Ct., Oct. 1809, at 445.

[138]Mass. Province Laws of 1776–1777, ch. 14, as amended, Mass Province Laws of 1776–1777, ch. 46.

The legal issue arose when Ward, the owner of the sugar, moved to quash the information. The motion was granted because of the information's "informality."[139] A new information was then brought against the same sugar, a jury found that the facts contained therein were true, and the sugar was condemned. Ward then moved to arrest the judgment, but this second motion was denied.[140]

The issue for decision upon the first motion was whether the name of the owner of goods could appear in an information instituting the condemnation proceeding.[141] The court held that it could not. The issue was not solely one of form. The price control law which authorized the condemnation was a new piece of legislation authorizing an unusual remedy — a remedy not against an individual but against property. It was an effort at trade regulation growing out of the economic chaos resulting from the war and the demise of British authority. The issue raised by the *Ward* case was whether the new legislation would be enforced by an action solely against illegally transported property, or by an action against both the property and its owner. The court decided in favor of an action solely against the property.

Ward's second motion, made after the jury found the second information true, alleged that the information had been brought forward and the verdict returned without his knowledge, after he had left the courtroom. Phrased in modern terms, his argument was that his property had been confiscated without his having had an opportunity to defend it, and that such action by the government was improper. Despite the apparent weight of such an argument, the court, confronted with an unprecedented issue resulting from an unprecedented economic and political situation, denied the motion.

Other cases, like Ward's, grew directly out of the upheaval caused by the Revolution. One involved the issue whether the new Commonwealth government acceded to the old rights of the king in treasure trove, or whether the finder of a treasure, who was being prosecuted for not turning it over to the government, could keep it.[142] Another involved redefining who was an alien incapable of serving upon a criminal jury.[143] A number of cases raised the question of when the law of one state could take cognizance of a crime committed in another.[144] Finally, sev-

---

[139]Government v. Ward, Msex Gen. Sess., May 1777, at 179.

[140]Id. at 180.

[141]Although the ground of the motion in the first Ward case is not stated, it can be determined by comparing the two informations. The only difference between them is that one names Ward, who in fact was the owner of the sugar, as the owner, whereas the other does not. Unfortunately, the informations are not numbered, but textual evidence indicates that the one containing Ward's name was the first and hence the invalid one. As a rule, the court's recorded judgment in a case accurately paraphrased the charge against a defendant, as that charge was contained in an indictment or information. The first entry in the court records dealing with Ward's matter contains his name in the portion of the judgment paraphrasing the information, whereas the second entry does not. Further textual evidence is the case of Government v. One Barrel of Sugar, Msex Gen. Sess., Sept. 1777, at 183, the first case arising under the price control legislation at a term of court subsequent to the decision of the Ward case. It too does not name any person as the owner of the condemned goods.

[142]See Commonwealth v. Baisto, Msex Gen. Sess., Sept. 1784, at 343, and March 1785, at 357.

[143]Commonwealth v. Hager, Msex Gen. Sess., Sept. 1785, at 365.

[144]Commonwealth v. Cone, 2 Mass. 132 (1806); Commonwealth v. Andrews, 2 Mass. 14 (1806); Commonwealth v. Cullins, 1 Mass. 115 (1804).

eral cases after 1790 raised issues of federal-state relations.[145] When these issues arose, the courts, because of lack of precedent, were generally free to decide them as they wished. This new freedom greatly increased judicial power to influence the outcome of a case.

In addition to creating new issues for court decision, the Revolution gave the courts new freedom in dealing with British precedent by bringing about a change in the earlier unquestioning acceptance of British authority. While some post-Revolutionary judges believed they were "bound to go upon authority,"[146] others argued that "whatever usages formerly prevailed or slid in upon us by the example of others on the subject" need not be followed since "sentiments more favorable to the natural rights of mankind, and to that innate desire of liberty . . . have prevailed since the glorious struggle for our rights began."[147] The former colonies were now free to make their own law. Thus, if a British rule were repugnant to the Constitution, it would not be followed.[148] In general, the courts after the Revolution seemed to depart from British authority if "reasons . . . [of] necessity, convenience, or public policy, required it."[149]

Examination of legal papers indicates that after the break with Britain, the bar did in fact feel less dependent upon and more free of British precedent. Although lawyers in Massachusetts retained a wide knowledge of British authorities and frequently cited not only Blackstone but other precedents as well,[150] one no longer finds lawyers gathering long lists of British authorities as did Adams and Trowbridge. Lawyers preferred to rely more upon the logical strength of their arguments than upon the weight of the authority behind them.[151]

D. The Danger of a Prejudicial Tribunal. The new willingness to ignore British precedents, plus the presence in many cases of legal issues for which no precedents existed, combined to put an end to Adams' expectation "that every possible Case . . . [would be] settled in a Precedent, leav[ing] nothing, or but little to . . . [the] Judge."[152] A significant number of cases now existed in which, once a jury had found the facts, the court was relatively free to find a defendant guilty or not guilty according to its own views of law and justice. The court no longer had a merely passive role in the criminal process.

The increased interest of the government in many cases and the increased power of the courts to affect the outcome of those cases created a danger that courts

---

[145]Commonwealth v. Knox, 6 Mass. 76 (1809); Commonwealth v. Smith, 1 Mass. 245 (1804).
[146]Commonwealth v. Brown, 4 Mass. 580, 585 (1808).
[147]W. Cushing, Notes of cases decided in the Superior and Supreme Judicial Courts of Massachusetts from 1772 to 1789, f. 34 (mss. in Harvard Law School Library).
[148]Letter from William Cushing to John Adams, Feb. 18, 1789, in William Cushing Papers at 5–7.
[149]Commonwealth v. Hutchinson, 1 Mass. 7, 8 (1804).
[150]See, e.g., the authorities cited by Selfridge in his argument for the defendant in Commonwealth v. Clap, 4 Mass. 163 (1808), none of which are in Blackstone.
[151]See, e.g., the arguments recorded in W. Cushing, supra note 147, at f. 17, in the case of Commonwealth v. McGregory, Suffolk Super. Ct., Aug. 1780, f. 210.
[152]1 Diary and John Adams 167 (Butterfield, Faber & Garrett eds. 1961).

might abandon their role as arbiter between government and subject, and become an oppressor of the latter. This seems in fact to have happened in at least two instances. The *Ward*[153] decision violated a maxim of justice, held then[154] as now, that property cannot be taken by government without giving its owner a chance to defend his right to it. In another case, there was a possibility of prejudice where one judge admitted he felt no such tenderness for thieves, as to desire that they should not be punished wherever guilty.''[155] He also predicted that an acquittal of the defendant Andrews would lead to mischiefs which private citizens would be unable to combat. In effect, the judge was stating that since a jury had found the defendant morally blameworthy and since mischiefs would result from his acquittal, the legal merits of the claim should be ignored and he should be convicted.

Contemporaries were not blind to the possible existence of judicial prejudice. Thus, during the prosecutions of the Tories, the courts were aware that their judgments might be deemed irregular and, accordingly, did not record them in the usual judgment books. Another example may be seen in James Sullivan's question during one of the cases growing out of Shays' Rebellion: "Can there be an impartial Tryal in a tryal for Treason?"[156]

Fear of prejudice also existed with regard to juries. In 1788, during the Massachusetts State Convention debates on the proposed federal constitution, a delegate remarked about the "maxim universally admitted, that the safety of the subject consists in having a right to a trial as free and impartial as the lot of humanity will admit of" and expressed his fear that under the new constitution a defendant might be tried by "a jury who may be interested in his conviction. . . ."[157] And finally, in 1809, in a case in which a defendant moved to set aside a verdict on the ground of the jury's prejudice, the Supreme Judicial Court observed "that great care should be taken to provide judges and jurors as [unprejudiced as possible] . . . . It is not only a maxim of law, but a sound principle of natural justice."[158]

E. The Libertarian Response — Concern for Procedural Rights of the Accused.
By the late 1780s, Massachusetts men had come to believe that the safeguards of a jury trial and an independent judiciary applying settled rules of law were alone no longer adequate to protect their liberty. The defendant in a criminal case was seen as being engaged in an unequal struggle with the government. The most perceptive American student of criminal law in the early nineteenth century described how "a criminal in his trial — squalid in his appearance, his

---

[153]The case is discussed at notes 139–141 supra and accompanying text.

[154]See 3 Blackstone, Commentaries 357.

[155]Commonwealth v. Andrews, 2 Mass. 14, 22–23 (1806).

[156]R. T. Paine, Minutes of Trials & Law Cases, 1760–1788, case of Commonwealth v. Chamberlain, Worcester Sup. Jud. Ct., April 1787 (mss. in Massachusetts Historical Society).

[157]Debates and Proceedings in the [Constitutional] Convention of the Commonwealth of Mass., held in the year 1788, at 211 (1856).

[158]Commonwealth v. Ryan, 5 Mass. 90, 92 (1809).

body debilitated by confinement, his mind weakened by misery or conscious guilt, abandoned by all the world, . . . stands alone, to contend with the fearful odds that are arrayed against him." Even if he had counsel assigned him, "this counsel is generally the youngest counsellor at the bar, who is thus made to enter the lists with one of the highest abilities and standing, with a reputation so well established as to have made him the choice of government as the depository of its interests."[159]

In an apparent response to the defendant's unequal position, the bar sought to bolster that position by strengthening the defendant's procedural rights. Early evidence of the interest in such rights is a notation in the Attorney General's trial minutes that a defense counsel in 1787 had advanced an argument concerning "the legal rights of the subject."[160] This interest continued. Some years later, a eulogizer of Chief Justice Parsons noted that "in the administration of criminal law . . . [Parsons] required of the public prosecutors the most scrupulous exactness, believing it to be the right, even of the guilty, to be tried according to known and practiced rules; and that it were a less evil for a criminal to escape, than that the barriers established for the security of innocence should be overthrown."[161]

The concern for procedural rights was evident in a number of libertarian reforms and practices. One was the establishment of strict rules for obtaining and executing search warrants. By the early nineteenth century, warrants of the type common before the Revolution had become illegal "because of the danger and inconvenience of leaving it to the discretion of a common officer to arrest such persons, and search such houses as he thinks fit."[162] A search warrant could be granted only upon an oath stating that a felony had been committed, and, in theft cases, that the party complaining thereof had probable cause to suspect that stolen property was in a particular place. The reasons for the suspicion also had to be stated, and any warrant issued had to state the specific places to be searched and persons to be seized.[163]

In a second reform, the practice of having justices of the peace interrogate defendants was ended. It had been prevalent before the Revolution and had continued during the years immediately following the reorganization of the courts.[164] But in the 1790s, signs of its impending demise appeared. Although one defendant acknowledged his guilt before a justice as late as 1793,[165] three other abstracts

[159]E. Livingston, Introductory Report to the Code of Procedure, in 1 The Complete Works of Edward Livingston on Criminal Jurisprudence 331, 387 (1873).

[160]R. T. Paine, Criminal Trials: Minutes of the Attorney General, 1780 to 1789, case of Commonwealth v. White, Falmouth Super. Ct., 1787 (mss. in Massachusetts Historical Society).

[161]Grand Jury Address by Parker, J., Nov. 1813, in T. Parsons, Memoir of Theophilus Parsons 403, 413 (1861).

[162]Davis, A Practical Treatise upon the Authority and Duty of Justices of the Peace in Criminal Prosecutions 47 (1824).

[163]Id. at 45–47.

[164]See, e.g., Government v. Potamy, Msex Super. Ct., April 1777, 1021 Suffolk Court Files No. 148285.

[165]Commonwealth v. Tarbell, Msex Sup. Jud. Ct., April 1793, 1053 Suffolk Court Files No. 150465.

of preliminary hearings in the 1790s indicate that the only question asked a defendant was whether he was guilty or not guilty of the crime charged.[166] In 1797, printed forms came into use for recording preliminary hearings, and the forms left space for an answer by an accused to only one question — whether he was guilty or not guilty[167] — indicating that the standard practice was for justices to ask only this one question. In the early nineteenth century, it was even doubted whether this question was permissible.[168]

Two more libertarian practices were introduced by the Supreme Judicial Court between 1800 and 1810. In *Commonwealth v. Andrews*,[169] the court announced a doctrine of waiver strikingly similar to the modern doctrine of *Johnson v. Zerbst*.[170] The case involved the question whether a defendant charged with receiving stolen property, who had a right not to be tried until the thief had been convicted, had waived that right by submitting to trial. The court held that "in criminal cases, an express relinquishment of a right should appear, before the party can be deprived of it. Here is no such relinquishment, but merely a silent submission, which probably arose from ignorance at the time that such right existed."[171]

The second libertarian development involved the acceptance of guilty pleas. In *Commonwealth v. Battis*,[172] a defendant sought to plead guilty to charges of rape and murder. The court informed him of the consequence of such a plea, and that he did not have to plead but could "put the government to the proof of" the charges. It then refused to accept the plea until the next day, after it had "allow[ed] him a reasonable time to consider what had been said to him," and after it had "examined, under oath, the sheriff, the jailer, and the justice . . . as to the *sanity* of the prisoner; and whether there had not been tampering with him. . . ."[173] Only then did it accept the plea.

Finally, it must be noted that assignment of counsel in capital cases, a practice usually adhered to before the Revolution,[174] was continued thereafter.[175]

Unfortunately, because of the absence of contemporary commentary, it is impossible to prove a direct causal relationship between the perception of the accused's

[166]Commonwealth v. Waite, Msex Sup. Jud. Ct., April 1793, 1053 Suffolk Court Files No. 150471; Commonwealth v. Chadwick, Msex Sup. Jud. Ct., April 1793, 1053 Suffolk Court Files No. 150460; Commonwealth v. Baker, Msex Sup. Jud. Ct., Oct. 1792, 1052 Suffolk Court Files No. 150363.

[167]Commonwealth v. Lepear, Msex Sup. Jud. Ct., April 1797, 1066 Suffolk Court Files No. 151077.

[168]Davis, supra note 162, at 106–07.

[169]3 Mass. 126 (1807).

[170]304 U.S. 458 (1938).

[171]3 Mass. 126, 133 (1807).

[172]1 Mass. 94 (1804).

[173]Id. at 95.

[174]Although the pre-Revolutionary court records do not indicate the existence of this practice, John Adams has left a record of a case in which he received such an appointment. See 1 Diary and Autobiography of John Adams 353 (Butterfield, Faber & Garrett eds. 1961). Modern writers agree that the practice existed at least in capital cases. See Papers of John Adams at li–lii (Wroth & Zobel eds. 1965); 2 Legal Papers of John Adams 402 (Worth & Zobel eds. 1965).

[175]See, e.g., Commonwealth v. McGregor, Suffolk Super. Ct., Aug. 1780, f. 210, 211; Commonwealth v. Green, Msex Super. Ct., Nov. 1779, f. 135.

unequal position and the growing concern for his procedural rights. Both developments, however, commenced at about the same time, and the latter posed an
answer to the problem created by the former. Moreover, it is difficult to establish
any other causal relationship. The concern for procedural liberties does not seem
to have been a direct consequence of the Revolution; none of the specific libertarian
practices which manifested the concern developed before the 1790s, and, except
for search warrants, none of them was at issue in the Revolutionary struggle.
Perhaps Massachusetts lawyers were merely copying legal developments in other
states.[176] Such developments may have contributed to the growth of a concern
for procedure in Massachusetts, but it is unlikely that they were the sole impetus.
The concern of Massachusetts lawyers seems to have been too strong and genuine
to have been mere mimicry.

It seems instead that their solicitude reflected a broader concern that personal
liberty not be arbitrarily infringed by the state, either in the criminal process
or elsewhere. This concern was present in Massachusetts from at least 1760. In
the years immediately before the Revolution, men believed that they had developed
a program to protect personal liberty. Safeguards within the structure of the judicial
system were thought sufficient to prevent the arbitrary use of law enforcement
power. When, during the war years and immediately thereafter, events proved
that their safeguards might not alone be adequate, the Revolutionary generation
did not abandon its quest for liberty, but set out, consistently with that quest,
to develop additional protections. Some of the new protections however, such as
the restrictions on searches and on pretrial interrogation of defendants, were of
a nature fundamentally different from that of the old safeguards. The latter had
never prohibited the exercise of governmental power; realizing the social value
inherent in the exercise of power, the pre-Revolutionary generation had sought
only to insure that power was exercised fairly and impartially. The post-
Revolutionary generation, on the other hand, concluded that the fair and impartial
exercise of power could not always be assured. This generation went a step further
and totally prohibited the exercise of power in those instances where fair and
impartial exercise could not be guaranteed.

It does not appear that lawyers in the early nineteenth century recognized that
their restrictions on governmental power could ultimately hamper government in
achieving the now primary aim of the criminal law — the protection of property.
Theophilus Parsons, the Chief Justice of Massachusetts during the first decade
of the century, is an example. A thorough conservative,[177] he observed that it
was more unfortunate for a rich man than a poor one to become involved in
crime.[178] He believed strongly in the preservation of order, authority, and property. Yet, at the same time, he was concerned about safeguarding liberty, believing

---

[176]See Rutland, The Birth of the Bill of Rights: 1776–1791, at 94–100 (1955), for a discussion
of developments in other states.
[177]See T. Parson, Memoir of Theophilus Parsons 36 (1861).
[178]See note 101 supra and accompanying text.

"that it were a less evil for a criminal to escape, than that the barriers established for the security of innocence should be overthrown."[179] Parsons and his contemporaries believed fervently in both order and liberty, and tried to achieve both without giving inordinate emphasis to either.

III. Conclusion

The various libertarian procedural reforms following the Revolution are for the modern lawyer undoubtedly the most interesting and significant because of the their relevance to the solution of modern legal issues. Let us consider, for example, the prohibition of pretrial interrogation of defendants. If actual practice in American trial courts in 1790, or the trend of that practice, was to prohibit all pretrial interrogation of potential defendants out of fear that they might be compelled to incriminate themselves, one may cogently argue that the fifth amendment, adopted against the background of such practice, codified it. Similarly, one can develop modern legal arguments on the basis of other post-Revolutionary libertarian reforms. A word of caution must be inserted here, however. This study, of necessity, rests upon a very narrow geographical sample, and broader study may disclose that the trends occurring in Middlesex were rarely duplicated elsewhere.

Thus, further study of legal developments during the post-Revolutionary period is needed. Such study would, in fact, be valuable not only on the criminal but also on the civil side of the law. It was during the years after the Revolution that law and lawyers attained a central position in American society.[180] It was during these years that American legal methodology was developed and that some of our greatest judges — Marshall, Story, Kent, and Shaw — began their careers. The neglected years between the Revolution and the War of 1812 are pregnant with opportunity for legal scholarship, for it was then that the essentially British law of the late colonial period was transformed into what emerged after 1820 as the law of an American "golden age."[181]

[179]Grand Jury Address by Parker, J., *supra* note 161, at 413.

[180]2 Chroust, The Rise of the Legal Profession in America 30 (1965); P. Miller, The Legal Mind in America from Independence to the Civil War 41 (1962).

[181]C. M. Haar, The Golden Age of American Law at v (1965).

5. Harvey A. Silverglate

The 1970s: A Decade of Repression?

The signs are strong that the stage is now being set for an upswell of political and intellectual repression in the 1970s. As society accelerates its war against crime, drugs, freaks, civil disorder, and "dangerous" political doctrines and organizations, the higher ranks of government join the lower echelons, such as the police, to wage the battle. Thus, "law enforcement" tactics which only recently were officially condemned and used only by undisciplined lower level law enforcement officers, are now being given a veneer of respectability and even legality. What is perhaps more frightening is that the judiciary is being recruited in this effort, affirming questionable practices in the name of necessity and law and order. Consequently, the forces of repression in the 1970s may well be led not by local police, but by a coalition headed by the President of the United States, the Attorney General, the Director of the Federal Bureau of Investigation, and the Chief Justice of the United States.

Historically, the American constitutional system, with its long list of personal liberties preserved in writing and in court decisions for the benefit of the American people, has been the chief protector of the right of citizens to say and do things which others may dislike. Various public opinion polls and other studies have consistently shown that large numbers of Americans — perhaps even a majority — do not approve of certain of the liberties embodied in the Bill of Rights, particularly as interpreted and broadened by the Supreme Court; yet the system has achieved sufficient durability and rigidity by virtue of its being based upon a written document, drawn up by the eminent "Founding Fathers," and interpreted by a Court composed of men with life tenure.

At crucial times in the history of the nation, however, we have seen that no amount of rigidity or historical respectability can withstand pressures of society's demand that individual liberties be curbed. At such times, any general agreement that the Bill of Rights should be kept intact has fallen apart at the seams, and our codified written system has been worse than ignored — it has been turned around and used as an instrument of repression against the free individual. It is this remarkable ability of the American constitutional system to act as both the rigid bulwark of our liberties and as the resourceful and diligent persecutor of our unpopular fellow citizens in time of national fear or stress that has led

Reprinted by permission of Beacon Press from *With Justice for Some*, edited by Bruce Wasserstein and Mark J. Green, pp. 353–379, 399–400. Copyright © 1970 by Bruce Wasserstein and Mark J. Green.

analysts to talk of citizens receiving "due process of law" during good times and of their being "due processed to death" in bad times. We have witnessed within the last few years events which indicate that the decade of the seventies may bear witness to more of the latter than the former. When a citizen is "due processed to death," he finds himself receiving all of the trappings of fair treatment and fair trial according to law; but he soon notices that the law has become sufficiently distorted that it cannot function as a wall between the dissenting individual and the demanding society.

The danger is not only that during the onset of legal repression many individuals will suffer; there is also the possibility that by embodying the concept of repression too deeply into the legal system and by making actual substantive and procedural changes in our laws, we may inflict irreparable injury upon the Bill of Rights, making it impossible for the nation to return to traditional libertarianism even after the current crisis of fear and disorder has passed.

Lower Level Repression

Repression by police and lower court authorities is endemic in our society; yet, it must be distinguished from deliberate attempts by the policy-making organs of government to stifle dissent, which can be termed "legal repression." In the absence of higher level "legal repression," intimidation and abuse of authority by the lower officials is not condoned. To carry it out, members of the lower law enforcement echelons are forced to resort to secrecy, truth-stretching, outright lying, or even perjury. As a result of this type of harassment numerous victims have won jury verdicts under one or more of the federal Civil Rights Acts. For example, one such statute enables an aggrieved citizen to file suit against persons who acting "under color of law" deprive them of their civil rights.[1] Another statute provides for redress against those who conspire to violate a person's civil rights, including persons other than officers acting in the name of or "under color of" the law.[2] These are the statutes most commonly used in "police brutality" cases, where an officer of the law abuses his position and illegally acts as the tormenter of the citizen rather than as his protector. Such statutes are necessary to deter unlawful official conduct. It is not sufficient that an illegally arrested and unlawfully charged defendant merely obtain an acquittal of the criminal charges brought against him. The law gives aggrieved citizens access to the courts to punish officials who act illegally, which is important since public prosecutors may be slow to move against police and other officials who abuse citizens' rights.

Yet it would take a flight of fancy to believe that the Civil Rights Acts or any other remedies available to a citizen, as well as the protections given a defendant at a criminal trial, are sufficient to protect the average citizen who incites the wrath of his would-be protectors. Most victims of repressive and discriminatory

[1] Civil Rights Act, 26 U.S.C. §1983.
[2] Civil Rights Act, 26 U.S.C. §1985.

police and judicial behavior do not have the knowledge or resources to invoke the proper remedies and to lay the foundations at the early stages for such action. Furthermore, even the sophisticated victim must run the gauntlet of official prevarication in taking his case to the courts. Even if those obstacles are met and overcome, it is a general practice for municipalities to soften the blow against policemen who have civil rights suits brought against them or money judgments returned against them by providing the officers with legal counsel at no personal cost and by assuming the payment of any damages.

Some degree of disrespect for constitutional rights has long been evident in the police and lower court establishments. Defense attorneys handling routine, nonpolitical criminal cases have always known about these problems. For example, one trial court judge in Massachusetts was reported several years ago to have reminded a Boston criminal attorney arguing for the federal constitutional rights of his client that, "This is Massachusetts, and the federal constitution does not apply." Other municipal and police court judges as a matter of course penalize a defendant for choosing to exercise his Fifth Amendment privilege against self-incrimination. Lawyers and citizens alike, particularly black citizens, have long been aware of the propensity of some policemen to routinely engage in technically unlawful conduct in the area of "stop and frisk" and "search and seizure." Such illegal conduct is often encouraged by the inability of minority group citizens to protest effectively the invasion of their rights, and by the willingness of some lower court judges to look the other way in the face of often obvious police perjury on the witness stand. Thus, the judge or jury might believe the arresting officer as he testifies that when he approached, the defendant dropped a marihuana cigarette onto the sidewalk; therefore, the arrest of the defendant was lawful, since no search of the defendant's person preceded the circumstances which gave the officer probable cause to believe that the defendant was committing a felony. It often does the defendant little good to claim that he was stopped for no reason (other than the color of his skin or his style of dress) and subjected to an illegal search on the street. Many attorneys suffer a feeling of dismay and anger (not to mention embarrassment as the client wants to know "how can they get away with that?") as some lower court judges hear and believe, the marihuana-cigarette-on-the-sidewalk story as it is repeated verbatim by police officers on the witness stand day after day.

Legal procedures make it difficult for a defendant to obtain justice on an appeal once the factual record is established in the trial court. The judge or jury in the trial court determines what transpired factually, and it is at that stage that the police version of events often becomes accepted. An appellate court, in reviewing the validity of a conviction by a lower court, is often bound by the lower court's determination of the facts and limits itself to reviewing the correctness of the legal principles applied to the facts found by the court or jury. By the time a case reaches the appellate court, what actually was a blatantly illegal street search of a long-haired "hippy-type" might be determined because of fact findings by a judge or jury, to be a perfectly legal search and arrest.

The legal system is further structured to make police perjury easy. Many crimes in the statute books make it unlawful to engage in conduct which does no injury to persons or property, but which goes contrary to prevailing standards of acceptable morality. Such crimes are often called "crimes without victims" — the kind of behavior termed by John Stuart Mill as "self-regarding conduct," indicating that such behavior affects and concerns only the individuals who voluntarily engage in it. Such "crimes" include, among others, obscenity, fornication, adultery, blasphemy, drug use, gambling, and public drunkenness. Since there are no victims of such crimes and no concrete evidence of their commission in most cases, courts are faced with a credibility contest between defendant and arresting officer.

Perjury is also encouraged by the vague wording of a great number of criminal laws, such as those against "disturbers of the peace," "loitering," and being "idle and disorderly." An arresting officer often can make a conviction stick if he can convince a court that what the defendant says was merely loud talking on a street corner was actually shouting, which disturbed the orderly passage of pedestrians and disturbed the surrounding area and people there. Usually the only victims of such "crimes" are the defendants persecuted for committing them.

Criminal laws against "self-regarding conduct," which is often engaged in by large numbers of people, combined with the vague language of many criminal laws, serve to allow police and prosecutors to engage in discriminatory, selective law enforcement. Thus, even if no police perjury is involved in a particular case, and the defendant committed some crime of a "moral" nature, the police often choose to arrest, and prosecutors often decide to charge such persons for reasons other than the "enormity" of their infractions. Persons who are unpopular or who harbor thoughts and philosophies at odds with those of local officials are most often the persons charged with such crimes. A tremendous amount of prosecutorial discretion is placed in the hands of law enforcement personnel very low on the echelon.

Society would doubtless benefit if the criminal law were reserved for those antisocial acts which do injury to persons and property. Even those policemen least concerned with the truthfulness of their testimony in court would hesitate to lie in a case involving a crime the commission and existence of which would have to be proven by evidence other than the officer's own testimony standing alone. Thus, a policeman could not easily charge a defendant with murder if no body were found; nor could he charge a man with armed robbery if the victim could not identify the "suspect" as the man who committed the crime. Persons are not so easily framed for the commission of crimes which do indeed have victims other than the sensibilities of a police officer or prosecutor.

It is because of these elements in our legal system that it has been possible for our courts to convict innocent citizens with all of the trappings of due process of law. The system has thus allowed its lower level members, including the police and the police courts and municipal courts, to punish unpopular citizens, while the upper echelons of the system in the executive, judicial, and legislative departments can earnestly believe, or at least lead others to believe, that the system affords liberty and justice for all.

Yet even under such circumstances, society as a whole seems to disapprove of illegal conduct aimed against any particular group of citizens. There is some comfort in the fact that violations of the citizen's liberties are officially condemned, and periodic efforts to correct blatant abuses often surface to public scrutiny. In the wake of a series of murders of white and black civil rights workers in the South in the early sixties, when local and state prosecutors refused to bring charges against, or when juries refused to convict, the alleged murderers, federal authorities brought prosecutions under the Civil Rights Acts. Juries still did not always return a favorable verdict, but the point was made that higher authorities disapproved of such conduct. An atmosphere was maintained in which violators of individual liberties at least had to act in secret.

The serious problem which America will be facing in the decade of the seventies is the transition from repression emanating almost exclusively from lower echelon levels, officially condemned from above, to a more subtle, but probably more effective form of official, legal repression aimed against those engaged in radical challenges to the system. At such times the upper echelons set the tone and rallying cry and spearhead the drive by using the courts against prominent radicals, while the reins on the police are loosened to make lower level repression more effective, less fraught with risks for the police, and more respectable. In such an atmosphere, the usual lower echelon repression is not supplanted; it is supplemented and nourished.

Official Crackdowns: Past and Present

Today is not, to be sure, the first time that the phenomenon of official repression has appeared on the American scene. Indeed, periods of repression alternating with periods of relative freedom have been part of our national cycles since the Sedition Acts of 1798 were created to "protect" the infant republic. As has already been pointed out, lower echelon repression, not officially recognized or sanctioned, has long been with us. But many times before the current decade higher echelon levels within the administrative, executive, or legislative branches have added hysterical voices to the outcries for law and order.

During times of real or imagined "emergency" facing the nation, the courts have offered varying degrees of resistance to another branch of government which has overstepped its bounds. During the Civil War, President Lincoln suspended the writ of *habeas corpus* by executive order, thereby purporting to deprive courts of their jurisdiction to review the legality of arrests, and the judiciary found itself hard pressed to make its weight felt. When, in 1861, a petition for *habeas corpus* was presented to Chief Justice Taney of the Supreme Court on behalf of one John Merryman,[3] who it was claimed was arrested at night and illegally confined at Fort McHenry near Baltimore, the Chief Justice issued the writ to be served upon Brevet Major General Cadwalader, who commanded Fort McHenry. The writ ordered Cadwalader to bring the prisoner before Taney the next day. However,

[3]Ex parte Merryman, 17 Fed. Cas. 144, No. 9, 487 (C.C.D. Md. 1861).

when the United States marshal attempted to serve the writ, he was unable to get past the outer gate. Cadwalader claimed that he was duly authorized by the President to disregard the writ of *habeas corpus*. The Chief Justice, obviously a bit piqued, excused the marshal from making service because "The power refusing obedience was so notoriously superior to any the marshal could command." Taney then proceeded to commit his opinion to writing, ordered that the prisoner be turned over to the civil authorities and that his opinion should be filed and "laid down before the president, in order that he might perform his constitutional duty, to enforce the law, by securing obedience to the process of the United States." Shortly thereafter, Merryman was released from Fort McHenry, turned over to civilian custody, and indicted for treason.[4]

The Civil War period was notorious for such incursions of personal liberty and the refusal of the executive to be fully cooperative with the judiciary. Only after the conclusion of the war did the Supreme Court become bolder, striking out on behalf of the civil liberties of citizens. Justice Davis commented why in 1866: "Congress was obliged to enact severe laws to meet the crisis; and as our highest civil duty is to serve our country when in danger, the late war has proved that rigorous laws, when necessary, will be cheerfully obeyed by a patriotic people, struggling to preserve the rich blessings of a free government."[5]

During the First World War, First Amendment rights fell under heavy attack. There was great difficulty in knowing what speech was protected and what was not. In one case decided March 3, 1919,[6] Justice Holmes wrote a majority opinion upholding a conviction under the Espionage Act[7] based upon circulation of an antidraft pamphlet urging citizens to oppose conscription. Mr. Justice Holmes here formulated his classic analysis:

The most stringent protection of free speech would not protect a man in falsely shouting fire in a theatre and causing a panic. It does not even protect a man from an injunction against uttering words that may have all the effect of force. The question in every case is whether the words used are used in such circumstances and are of such a nature as to create a clear and present danger that they will bring about the substantive evils that Congress has a right to prevent.

Using this new "clear and present danger test," the Court and Holmes found that the defendant fell within its ambit.

A couple of months later in another Espionage Act case,[8] the majority again upheld the conviction of a defendant who had circulated printed pamphlets designed "to excite, at the supreme crisis of the war, disaffection, sedition, riots, and,

---

[4]Details of the case are set forth and discussed in Randall, *Constitutional Problems under Lincoln*, 162 (rev. ed. 1951).

[5]Ex parte Milligan, 4 Wall 2, 18 L. Ed. 281 (1866).

[6]Schenck v. United States 249 U.S. 47 (1919).

[7]Espionage Act of June 15, 1917, Comp. St. 1918, §10212C, Title 1, Sec. 3.

[8]Abrams v. United States, 250 U.S. 616 (1919).

as they hoped, revolution in this country for the purpose of embarrassing and if possible defeating the military plans of the government in Europe.'' This time Justice Holmes dissented, blasting the majority with the admonition that ''We should be eternally vigilant against attempts to check the expression of opinions that we loathe. . . .'' His own First Amendment loophole of ''clear and present danger'' had been used against him, now being enlarged to suppress nondangerous speech. The best minds on the highest bench of the land were thus wrangling over so basic an issue as the First Amendment. One had Justice Holmes' own wavering and his frank statement that ''The character of every act depends upon the circumstances in which it is done'' and that ''when a nation is at war many things that might be said in time of peace are such a hindrance to its effort that their utterance will not be endured so long as men fight and that no Court could regard them as protected by any constitutional right.''[9] How, then, was the average citizen to feel secure in deciding what he might, or might not lawfully do?

It was around this period, just after the First World War, that American concern for internal subversion reached the point of frenzy. Under the leadership of A. Mitchell Palmer, the then Attorney General of the United States, radical organizations were subjected to a series of blitzkrieg-like raids. Alien radicals were ordered deported from the country. The President, Woodrow Wilson, was gravely ill during these episodes, and he was in no condition to exercise the restraint over his Attorney General which one might have expected from this source of moral rectitude. This was not to be the last time in American history that a ''law and order'' Attorney General was to acquire substantial sway over official treatment of civil liberties without a salutary restraining hand reaching out from the White House. A similar problem was to spring up in the 1970s, only this time presidential restraint was to be absent not because of incapacitation or illness of the President, but because the rooting out of dissidents and extremists was to become an official national policy.

The Second World War had its own brand of court-sanctioned incursions against the civil liberties of citizens. Perhaps most notorious was the relocation and segregation of citizens of Japanese descent who lived on the West Coast.

In 1943, when the war was at its height, Chief Justice Stone, in an opinion for the Court,[10] upheld the conviction of a Japanese-American for violating an act of Congress and an accompanying order making it a misdemeanor knowingly to disregard restrictions placed upon all persons of Japanese ancestry residing in areas of the West Coast. The restrictions consisted of a curfew placed upon Japanese-Americans by the military commander. Chief Justice Stone pointed out that the Constitution ''does not demand the impossible or the impractical,'' and, while claiming the Court would not review in detail the factual basis of the government's finding that these citizens posed a danger, he went on to note that there were facts and circumstances ''which support the judgment of the war-waging branches

---

[9]Schenck v. United States, 249 U.S. at 52.
[10]Hirabayashi v. United States, 320 U.S. 81 (1943).

of the Government that some restrictive measure was urgent." Even Justice Douglas professed not to have as much knowledge of the facts of the situation as was in the possession of the military authorities. "The point is that we cannot sit in judgment on the military requirements of that hour."[11]

It was not until nearer the end of the war, after the tide had turned in favor of the Allies, that Mitsuye Endo,[12] another American of Japanese ancestry, received a ruling from the Supreme Court declaring that the government had no right to detain her in a relocation camp under the auspices of the War Relocation Authority. True, Justice Douglas, in the opinion for the Court, managed to distinguish the Hirabayashi situation from the Endo situation by resorting to interpretation of the Executive Order involved; but one might make an educated guess as to what the outcome of that case might have been had it reached the Supreme Court when the national emergency was at its height.

Thus, during times of national emergency or danger the executive and legislative branches have assumed extraordinary powers to curtail liberties which at other times were relatively freely accorded to individuals. These incursions came from the very top echelons of government, and they were often validated by the highest Court in the land, which sometimes did and sometimes did not admit in all frankness that it was only because of the presence of an emergency that the incursions were being upheld. Justice Holmes is to be congratulated for his frankness in making it clear that the dangers of the times affect the breadth of individual liberty, but it also must be admitted that it is precisely that doctrine which opens up a Pandora's box, particularly when less Olympian judges than Holmes sit on the bench. It is quite simple to detect when a crowded movie theatre is or is not burning, and when a false alarm would or would not cause a riot. But simplicity ends there. We pay a heavy price for resorting to the "balancing process" whereby the state's interests are purportedly weighed against the individual's.

Perhaps the most memorable example of official repression that comes to the contemporary mind is the McCarthy era in the early 1950s. Individual citizens found themselves helpless and stifled in the face of often wild accusations of Communist or left-wing taint made by the senator from Wisconsin. Even the United States Government was hard put to fend off the charge that 215 Communists inhabited the ranks of the State Department. It is well to remember that the Communist witch hunts of the fifties were not technically illegal. They resulted from a mass hysteria, promoted by a powerful senator, and nurtured by official silence. President Eisenhower did not enter the battle against McCarthy until the senator attacked his army.

The McCarthy era was not an aberration, or if it was, then we have seen other such aberrations appearing periodically. Just a few years after the demise of Joe McCarthy, the United States Supreme Court[13] upheld the validity of the

---

[11]*Id.*, at 26.

[12]Ex parte Endo, 323 U.S. 283 (1944).

[13]Communist Party of the United States v. Subversive Activities Control Board, 367 U.S. 1 (1961); Scales v. United States, 367 U.S. 203 (1961).

McCarran and Smith Acts,[14] which require that the American Communist Party register as a foreign agent, and which also provide penalties for belonging to an organization knowing that the organization advocates the violent overthrow of the government. A member of the four-man minority dissent, Justice Hugo L. Black, declared that the majority was condoning governmental action which banned "an association because it advocates hated ideas." Joe McCarthy might have been dead, but his immortal soul was still lingering.

Indeed, Justice Black correctly understood what the majority of the Court was allowing the government to do. The majority condoned such practices at the highest levels of government. Repression had taken a legal form, and the law not only failed to protect dissidents, but it was also turned directly into an instrument to control the growth of dissent. America began to get a taste of why it was worse to have repression by bad laws rather than repression despite good laws.

Good laws might be ignored at the lower echelons; but bad laws handed down from the highest levels are even more dangerous. When a repressive law is passed and then enforced under Supreme Court imprimatur, only a fool could mistake the message that all stops have been pulled out in the battle against liberty in its own name.

The Supreme Court is thrown into a position of extreme pressure and tension during periods of governmental and popular outrage over "crime in the streets" or "subversion and anarchy." The Supreme Court has often stood up to such pressures, at least for a time. In a 1967 opinion,[15] for example, the same Supreme Court which upheld the Smith and McCarran Acts struck down the Subversive Activities Control Act of 1950,[16] which forbade Communists from working in defense plants. Perhaps the Court felt that the witchhunts had gone far enough. Then — Chief Justice Earl Warren observed in the Court's opinion that in the course of promoting and protecting the national defense we must take care in maintaining and defending "those liberties . . . which make the defense of the nation worthwile."

The Current Crisis

The current problem — call it "emergency" if you will — facing the American Republic seems for the first time to involve less of a threat of attack from without than it does revolution from within. Of course, most of this nation's prior bouts with legal repression have revolved around the friends or supposed friends of the nation's enemies. Japanese-Americans on the West Coast were suspected of being at least emotionally sympathetic to the enemy Japanese Empire. And the victims of the McCarthy era were thought to be the internal allies of Soviet Russia, a fifth column.[17]

---

[14]Internal Security Act of 1950, 64 Stat. 987, 50 U.S.C. 781 et seq. Title I of the Act is the Subversive Activities Control Act. The Smith Act is found at 18 U.S.C. §2385.

[15]United States v. Robel, 389 U.S. 258, 88 S. Ct. 419 (1967).

[16]64 Stat. 992, section 5(a) (1)'(D), 50 U.S.C. §784(a) (1) (D).

[17]*See* E. Goldman, *Rendezvous With Destiny* (1952).

But the current threat is apparently seen by the government as involving something more sinister — an internal threat not tied to any particular foreign power, but tied rather to an indigenous revolutionary doctrine, promulgated by militant blacks and by white radicals. Historians and political analysts up until quite recently felt that development of a revolutionary movement in America was impossible in view of the "consensus" whereby nobody really wanted to destroy the pie-making apparatus, but rather everyone wanted a larger slice of it. In the demonology of no less an "authority" than J. Edgar Hoover, the Black Panthers have replaced the Communist Party as the most serious threat to the internal security of the United States. And the FBI Director, in making this analysis, added that "despite its record of hate, violence, and subversion, the Black Panther Party continues to receive substantial monetary contributions from prominent donors."[18] And the enemy will be thwarted, not merely by the classic devices used for years by police against "undesirables." Law and order will be protected by resort to respectable and lawful legislation — respectable because it is created by Congress in the name of preserving law and order, and lawful because much of it will probably survive Supreme Court scrutiny, if indeed the High Court chooses to scrutinize much of this legislation. The Court might instead refuse to exercise discretionary Supreme Court review, and thus allow the lower courts to be "hatchet men." Thus, not only can the Party be destroyed, but its respectable donors and supporters can be frightened away.

"Only emergency can justify repression," said Justice Brandeis during the First World War. The emergencies in our nation's past have almost always been war emergencies, or threats from without supported by collaborators from within. Yet the non-war, internally generated revolution of today, and the reaction that has begun to set in, encompass the creation of a substantial body of statutes and law enforcement practices which may be with us far longer than the "Red raids" of Attorney General Palmer, or the ravings, rantings, and witch hunts of the McCarthy era. Repression of Communists in the State Department or at defense plants was a mere game compared to the repression of elements of contemporary society whose revolutionary doctrines are rubbed into the public consciousness daily by means of mass demonstrations, inflammatory rhetoric, threats of violence, and periodic violence.

To combat this threat, Congress endeavors to punish more than revolutionary action. It threatens to punish revolutionary thought, and it threatens to discover the presence of such revolutionary thought in an individual's head by eavesdropping as those thoughts pour out of his mouth in private conversation. A celebrated example of the government's preference to punish "thoughtcrime" rather than substantive criminal acts is the draft conspiracy trial of baby doctor Benjamin Spock, the Reverend William Sloane Coffin, Jr., and three other draft and Vietnam War opponents in a showcase trial held in Boston in 1968. The defendants were accused of conspiring to interfere with the operation of the Selective Service System

[18]New York Times, July 14, 1970, page 21.

by organizing public rallies, writing and circulating dissident manifestoes, encouraging draft-age young men to resist the draft, and similar actions.

Four of the "Boston Five" were convicted; but, largely because the government chose to prosecute under the conspiracy theory, the convictions were reversed on appeal.[19] Most legal scholars seemed to believe that the government could have more easily obtained convictions and had them upheld if it prosecuted each defendant for a substantive crime. It is likely that the government chose the conspiracy route because to have done otherwise would have allowed a reviewing court to rule on the legality or illegality of many specific acts of dissent against the war and the draft. Such an appellate opinion could have read like a manual and guide to lawful, protected dissent. But conspiracy law is sufficiently broad and vague so that a conviction for conspiracy would have the effect of threatening any citizen who at any time expressed his views on the war or the draft to other persons, or who participated in any group or mass action program to protest the war. Even a Supreme Court decision would probably not be decisive enough to dissipate the vague, general fears that such an indictment might be expected to generate among many ordinary citizens.[20]

Similarly, the government invoked an even more vague, more ominous statute in prosecuting the "Chicago Eight" for conspiring to cross state lines with the intent of inciting riot, and in also accusing each defendant of crossing state lines with intent to commit some illegal act. The government tried to make out a case of a substantive violation against each defendant, presumably as a backstop to the general conspiracy charge against all of them, just in case the conspiracy statute did not hold up under constitutional scrutiny by a reviewing court. The jury acquitted all of the defendants on the conspiracy charge, and convicted five of them for crossing state lines with intent to incite riot. The specific acts committed by each defendant might in and of themselves have been lawful and protected by the First Amendment, but taken together along with the act of crossing a state line, the acts were enough to warrant jury conviction. Never before in our jurisprudence has a state of mind been such a crucial element in a criminal statute.

The extreme dangers of statutes passed as part of a program of legal repression are exemplified by the rare view of the jury decision-making process given to us when one of the "Chicago Seven" jurors wrote a series of newspaper articles on the jury's deliberations. The articles pointed out that while some jurors raised the question of the constitutionality of such a statute, they decided that it would be best to leave that question to the judges.[21] Apparently the jurors were not made aware of the high odds against any appellant convincing four justices of

[19]*See* United States v. Spock, 416 F. 2d (1969). The Court of Appeals for the First Circuit indicated that two defendant-appellants, namely Coffin and Michell Goodman, could be re-tried for conspiracy, but the government chose not to re-try them. Hence the indictments were dismissed.

[20]The views of the author regarding the *Spock* case are set forth in more detail in a book review appearing the Book Section of the Boston Sunday Herald-Traveler, Oct. 19, 1969, at 1.

[21]The series of articles by the juror, Kay S. Richards, appeared in several major newspapers. E.g., the Boston Sunday Globe, Feb. 22, 1970, at 28.

the Supreme Court to vote to review a case. Besides, the interviews with the jurors made it painfully clear that while they did not convict on the conspiracy charge, they did not do so partly because they compromised and convicted on the substantive charges. Thus, the presence of the broad conspiracy charge, despite the verdict of not guilty, had its effect on the jury's decision.

Juries, even though they are composed of ordinary members of the community who are assumed to possess all of the prejudices of "average" Americans or members of the "silent majority," often do return verdicts of not guilty in cases where evidence is exaggerated, fabricated, or where an earnest defendant, long hair and all, has convinced them of his credibility. This is possible even in the face of grossly unfair methods of jury selection, which virtually preclude certain elements of the population from obtaining juries composed of their peers. In Massachusetts, for example, persons under 25 years of age have long been exempted and for practical purposes excluded from jury duty.[22] A major complaint by observers of the Spock conspiracy trial in Boston was that the jury that tried the famed baby doctor had a conspicuous lack of women, and of course, mothers. Few blacks serve, and many of the best educated members of the community evade jury duty.

The composition of the jury is of crucial importance in the modern day conspiracy and political trials, since the government in such cases often charges, in broad, catchall, vague indictments, acts the commission of which are hardly in dispute. All that is in dispute is the conclusion that the conduct charged is either illegal or unwarranted. This is one of the hallmarks of the "politcal trials" which are becoming familiar spectacles. Thus, when the prosecutor of Alameda County, California, charged that the "Oakland Seven," who organized the militant "Stop the Draft Week" demonstration at the Oakland Armed Forces Induction Center in 1967, were guilty of conspiracy to commit the misdemeanors of trespass and resisting arrest, the jury was presented with unrebuttable evidence as to the actions of the defendants. The defense did not try to deny the role of the defendants in the antiwar movement; rather, it tried to justify this role to the jury. The jury was allowed by the judge to take into consideration, in trying to determine whether or not the defendants had criminal intent, the defendant's belief as to the illegality of the Vietnam War and the defendants' right to resist unlawful, excessive police violence. An acquittal resulted.

Thus, the trial of a "political" case is not altogether hopeless. The Spock case was won on appeal. The "Oakland Seven" case was won at the trial level. But the government is not interested only, or perhaps even primarily, in winning cases and in putting dissidents behind bars. In fact, the appellate court in *Spock* would have allowed the government to re-try two of the defendants, but the government turned down the invitation and the indictments were dismissed. The point had been made — the government would follow, investigate, film, photograph,

---

[22]General Laws of Massachusetts, Chapter 234, Section 1.

and prosecute selected enemies of the Republic who would serve as warnings and examples to others.

Furthermore, the government has weapons other than political trials, perhaps more potent weapons. The government can take steps to encourage lower echelon "law enforcement" officials and to signal an end to high level condemnation of uncivilized police tactics. The lower echelons are quick to take up the lead in restricting the exercise of civil liberties.

A recent example of the officially sanctioned encroachments on our liberties has been the growth of wiretapping. In 1967, the very same year the Supreme Court was appearing at its libertarian best, President Johnson took cognizance of a growing national uneasiness over the issue of privacy, electronic surveillance, and wiretapping, telling the nation:

> We should protect what Justice Brandeis called "the right most valued by civilized men" — the right to privacy. We should outlaw all wiretapping, public and private, wherever and whenever it occurs, except when the security of the nation itself is at stake — and only then with the strictest safeguards. We should exercise the full reach of our constitutional powers to outlaw electronic "bugging" and "snooping."[23]

The careful observer would have noted that the President's proclamation was not as sweepingly libertarian as it might have seemed at first glance. The ominous phrase "except when the security of the nation itself is at stake" springs out at the reader. Such language supplies the government and courts with the same opportunity to justify invasions of privacy as Chief Justice Holmes' famous dictum about not being allowed to yell "Fire!" in a crowded movie theatre has given the opponents of free speech to make serious incursions into the First Amendment. It is similar to the vague and broad "disturbing the peace" statutes which say very little as to the kind of conduct proscribed or the types of dangers to be guarded against.

Few men doubt the good faith of Justice Holmes when he sought to protect theatregoers, and perhaps it is too early in the historical record to judge the good faith of Lyndon Johnson in the privacy area. The fact is, however, that shortly after the 1967 State of the Union address, the Congress passed the most sweeping invasion-of-privacy legislation ever to be placed on the books. While prior law tended to circumscribe to a large extent the right of governmental agents or private citizens to utilize wiretapping devices, including both federal[24] and state[25] enactments, and while the courts seemed to be becoming ever more solicitous of the rights of the citizen,[26] in 1968 the whole privacy framework was dramatically torn asunder by the Omnibus Crime Control Act.[27] Wiretapping and eavesdrop-

---

[23]State of the Union Address, 1967.
[24]Communications Act of 1934, 48 Stat. 1064, 47 U.S.C. §151, particularly 47 U.S.C. §605.
[25]General Laws of Massachusetts, Chapter 272, Sections 99–101; Commonwealth v. Spindel, 351 Mass. 673 (1968).
[26]*See,* e.g., Berger v. New York, 388 U.S. 41 (1967); Katz v. United States, 389 U.S. 347 (1967).
[27]Pub. L. 90–351, 18 U.S.C. §251 et seq.

ping by state, federal, and local law enforcement officers and agents were suddenly not only no longer forbidden, but these practices were actively encouraged under a procedure which offers little protection to the individual. Eavesdropping is permitted in cases involving the national security, but the Congress interpreted the area of national security so broadly that the act allows eavesdropping for such "national security" crimes as robbery, marihuana and narcotics traffic, and other assorted offenses posing a threat to "life, limb, and property." It would appear, then, that almost any crime will justify official snooping.

One can only guess how long it will take the "new" Supreme Court to come around to upholding the position of the President, Attorney General, and the Congress in this and other areas. The Omnibus Crime Control Act was apparently a successful attempt to short-circuit federal case law in the privacy area, law which had likened unauthorized invasions of privacy to warrantless searches and seizures which violate the Fourth Amendment. Federal court case decisions[28] had predicated the right to privacy on the Constitution, but the Congress nevertheless virtually repealed that case law by passing a statute. One must assume that the Congress knows that no statute can supersede the Constitution, but until the Supreme Court would act, the statute was to provide a facade of legitimacy to governmental wiretapping. Of course, there was always the chance that the Court might abdicate its prior position and join the other high echelons of government aboard the repression bandwagon, thereby fully legitimating the statute in the process.

Under the Omnibus Crime Control Act, broad as it is, court orders are required for eavesdropping. However, in security cases eavesdropping can begin in advance of an order. Out of this narrowly carved exception, the Attorney General of the United States, John Mitchell, created a huge, yawning canyon in which no law or constitution was seen as a hindrance to governmental snooping. In 1969, Mitchell stated that the Federal Bureau of Investigation had eavesdropped into the affairs and lives of the "Chicago Eight" who were indicted for, among other things, conspiring to cross state lines with the intent to promote riot at the 1968 Democratic National Convention. Said the chief law enforcement official of the nation:

While it may be appropriate for Congress to establish rules limiting the investigative techniques which the Executive may employ in enforcing the laws that Congress has enacted, a serious question exists as to the power to restrict the President's power to gather information which he deems necessary to the proper exercise of powers which the Constitution confers on him alone. . . .

The President . . . has the constitutional power to authorize electronic surveillance to gather intelligence information concerning domestic organizations which seek to attack and subvert the Government by unlawful means.[29]

After all of the years of wiretapping and electronic surveillance by the FBI done in violation of state and federal statutes and court decisions, now at least

---

[28]Refer to footnote 26.

[29]Quoted in Mayer, *On Liberty: Man v. the State*, 112–113 (1969). *See also* The New York Times, June 14, 1969, at 1, col. 5, reporting on a brief filed in the United States District Court for the Northern District of Illinois by United States Attorney Foran in the case of United States v. Rubin, one of the "Chicago Eight" conspiracy cases.

the problem is out in the open. But faced with Attorney General Mitchell's bold admission of the practice, and his defense of its probity and legality, civil libertarians are hard pressed to devise an appropriate response. The government cannot now be embarrassed on account of its position and its actions, because the government has turned the sinner into a saint, the sin into a virtue. The government has legitimated its own activities by exercising its legislative prerogative.

As has already been pointed out, this legislation is as much symbolic as it is real. Thus, the inclusion in a recent Washington, D.C., crime control bill of the "no-knock" search rule does not really change the police practice very much. Attorneys and others involved in criminal cases report generally that police rarely knock on the door prior to entry onto a premises which is the subject of a search warrant. The no-knock law merely legitimizes a long-standing lower echelon law enforcement tactic. Similarly, few people are naive enough to believe that wiretapping begins with the Omnibus Crime Control Act. All that the act does is allow the fruits of this kind of surveillance to be used as evidence: it thus legitimates the prior practice. As criminal law expert Professor Yale Kamisar points out, this kind of legislation is a warning that the era of the Warren Supreme Court is over. "It's very symbolic," he states. "The political movement is now in favor of the no-nonsense, get-tough boys."[30]

These highly symbolic higher echelon steps have not been lost on the law enforcement officials below. At the current time all of the forces of legal repression, and illegal repression, are being turned against the Black Panther Party and its members. The Party's top leadership, including Eldridge Cleaver, Huey Newton, and Bobby Seale, are either fugitives from justice or are under indictment or sentence. But on a lower level, Panther leaders and members have been harassed and arrested under vague and broad statutes while they have been passing out political literature. They have been attacked while gathered in the privacy of their homes and headquarters. They have been shot by policemen who later charged that the Panthers opened fire on a small army of policemen who came with peaceful, lawful intentions. Panthers on the streets are subjected to continual illegal stops, frisks, and searches. Many have been indicted and tried on seemingly nonpolitical charges such as robbery and even murder, but great doubts and questions have overhung the propriety of some of the evidence in these cases. The Panthers apparently pose too big a threat at times to give the state the luxury of "due processing them to death." Some Panthers have suffered more summary dispositions at the hands of police.

If and when the Panther "threat" subsides, it is quite probable that the official wrath will focus even more intently upon white radicals and students, whose revolutionary chants pose a more generalized challenge and promise more thoroughgoing and radical change to America than do the Panthers. The current practice of beating student demonstrators into bloody submission will probably give way to more permanent forms of punishment, including long prison sentences meted out by the upper echelons of the law enforcement establishment, and perhaps

[30]*New York Times*, July 26, 1970, p. 7.

summary executions performed by the lower echelons without substantial interference from their superiors. Grave dangers face America, and one fears that the current collision course may already have too much momentum to be stopped. The lines are being drawn ever more clearly, and many fair-minded citizens who abhor violence and persecution may be forced to choose sides in a battle that they wish was not theirs.

If a man has broken a criminal law, that is one thing. If a dissident is charged with breaking a criminal law on the basis of fabricated evidence, that is bad. But when that same dissident is convicted because he has in fact broken a law which is so broad as to encompass a whole range of activity — in which the right to engage had, until then, been thought to belong to every American citizen — then legal repression has set in. Thus, the "Oakland Seven" jury had to be reminded by the judge that much of the evidence presented by the prosecution consisted of acts, such as making public antiwar speeches, which are protected by the First Amendment. The Spock jury was not so clearly informed, which perhaps helped account for the verdict of guilty in that case. The powers-that-be on the highest levels of the administrative and legislative branches have stepped into the act of repressing the unpopular, the dissident, the nonconformists, the troublemakers. They leave in their wake a record, a history, and a plethora of legislation which it will be difficult to repeal even after the passage of the nadir of the Dark Ages of the seventies.

But the forces of repression have gone well beyond mere indictments and legislation. Perhaps recognizing that zealous and talented civil liberties and radical lawyers have managed to win significant jury verdicts and overturn repressive legislation in the appellate courts, these forces have begun an attack upon members of the bar who are "too zealous" in the defense of their unpopular clients. The judge in the Spock trial treated defense lawyers with a disdain which was not lost on the jury. Judge Julius Hoffman in the trial of the "Chicago Seven" conspiracy case treated defendants' attorneys without respect, refused to allow the defense attorneys to speak uninterrupted, and then sentenced them to jail terms of up to four years and thirteen days. Perhaps the most outrageous and frightening recent case was the decision by the Grievance Committee of the United States District Court in Washington, D.C., finding Attorney Philip J. Hirschkop guilty of professional misconduct and recommending that he be suspended or disbarred.

The Hirschkop case a a large segment of the liberal and radical legal profession up in arms. In the first place, while the behavior of the judge in the Spock trial did not go beyond unpleasantness for the attorneys personally, and while some feel that the behavior of the attorneys in the "Chicago Seven" case, while provoked by the judge, was nevertheless not justified, there is little or no support among reasonable men for the action of the Grievance Committee judges. Even the Ethics Committee of the District of Columbia Bar Association voted 21–3 that Hirschkop's court conduct in defense of the "D.C.9" did not violate the canons of legal ethics. Hirschkop, one of the eminent civil liberties attorneys in the country, a member of the National Board of the American Civil Liberties Union, took on

the defense in February, 1970, of a group of antiwar protestors. In the course
of the trial, Hirschkop asked Judge John H. Pratt to disqualify himself from trying
the case. "I will be brief, Judge," he said, out of the hearing of the jury, "because
I firmly believe that I am just wasting my time. I think you have made up your
mind before you have heard anything this morning. I am very discouraged about
the proceedings this morning." The attorney protested that the judge was not allowing him sufficient latitude to defend his clients. "I am afraid of making this
system rotten by not being able to do my job. . . ." He protested the judge's assumption, an assumption held by many judges and even attorneys, that an attorney
should not put up a fight which makes life unpleasant in the courtroom. "I am
not here to expedite [the case]. I will do it with all the dignity of a lawyer,
and all the sanctions of a bar in mind, but I will not take part in greasing the
wheels, not of justice, but of expeditiously packing these nine people off to jail
as quickly as we can."

The American Civil Liberties Union termed the actions of the Grievance Committee "outrageous." "By recommending disbarment, the Grievance Committee is,
in effect, serving notice on all attorneys who handle the defense of political dissidents — in the best spirit of the Bill of Rights — that their effectiveness in behalf
of their clients is enough to bring them under attack," stated the ACLU. The
Washington Post editorialized that "it is essential to the fair administration of
justice that impecunious and unpopular defendants have able representation when
they come to trial. The effect of the suspension or disbarment of Mr. Hirschkop
would be to discourage such representation."[31] In addition to filing the complaint
against Hirschkop, Judge Pratt sentenced him to thirty days in jail for contempt.
And the Grievance Committee agreed with the trial judge that the attorney's statements were "prejudicial to the administration of justice." One wonders what kind
of justice cannot bear an attorney attempting to dislodge a rigid judicial mind
or expressing dismay at his failure to obtain a fair trial for his unpopular clients.

The campaign against attorneys who are either too successful or too vigorous
has spread quickly and widely. Thus, even a nonpolitical attorney such as famed
criminal trial counsel F. Lee Bailey was censured by a Justice of the Massachusetts
Supreme Judicial Court for using the news media to "generate a climate of opinion
among the public" which would be "favorable to his clients and hostile to the
prosecution."[32] And perhaps not so coincidentally the American Bar Association
Special Committee on Evaluation of Disciplinary Enforcement chose this period
of time to issue a new report entitled "Problems and Recommendations in Disciplinary Enforcement,"[33] which concentrates on creating more efficient machinery
for processing complaints of misconduct lodged against attorneys.

[31]American Civil Liberties Union, "Civil Liberties," No. 271 (Sept., 1970), p. 8, discusses the
case.
[32]The Boston Globe, September 17, 1970, p. 7.
[33]American Bar Association, *Problems and Recommendations in Disciplinary Enforcement*
(Preliminary Draft, Jan. 15, 1970).

This trend became crystal clear in the recent testimony of Nixon-appointed director of Selective Service, Curtis Tarr, at the hearings on the military draft held by the Special Subcommittee on the Draft of the House Armed Services Committee, which hearings were held in late summer and fall of 1970. "The spread of draft counseling is certainly one of the most alarming changes in America as it relates to the draft right now," reported Director Tarr to the Subcommittee. He attacked attorneys and draft counselors for aiding draft-age men "to avoid a legal obligation." "I am alarmed," said Tarr, "that in a nation like ours there is such a blatant open attempt to make it difficult for us to carry out the law." Tarr thus brands attorneys and draft counselors with a tinge of disloyalty, perhaps even a tinge of antidraft conspiracy, despite the testimony of a Justice Department official at those same hearings, who reported that the "procedural errors committed by local [draft] boards in classifying registrants are the greatest factor contributing to the high incidence of our prosecutive problems." Tarr thus castigated attorneys for trying to have the law enforced, rather than castigating draft boards for frequent and blatant violation of the rights of draft registrants. One wonders if the government will ever launch an attack on tax lawyers for helping their clients "avoid" taxes.

The prospects for an effective repression are enhanced, of course, by the contribution to efficiency that the computer has been making. With the FBI checking up on such activities of activists as their banking practices,[34] their reading habits,[35] their police and court records, and other personal details, and feeding such information into central data banks, one cannot hope for much longer to find or preserve privacy because of the proverbial inefficiency of governmental bureaucracy.[36] Technology will be no small aid to the repression of the 1970s.

As reported by Ben A. Franklin in the *New York Times* of December 27, 1970, the Justice Department's "civil disturbance group" has since its organization in 1969 collected 13,200 names in its computerized records of persons connected with riots or reported to have urged violence. The national computer file in the Transportation Department contains for police or governmental use the names and offense records of 2.6 million people who have had a driver's license suspended or revoked. The Civil Service Commission has more than 15 million names and index files and personnel dossiers, 10.2 million of them in a "security file" designed to provide "lead information relating to possible question of suitability involving loyalty and subversive activity." The hearings before Senator Sam J. Ervin Jr.'s Subcommittee on Constitutional Rights in the winter of 1971 revealed a shocking buildup of a domestic surveillance program of the Army. Thousands of citizens have been investigated, including leading political figures. As former military intelligence Captain Christopher H. Pyle testified at the Ervin hearings, "The

---

[34]"F.B.I. Accused of Checking War Foes' Bank Files," New York Times, July 7, 1970, p. 5.
[35]"Whaddya Read?," New York Post, July 11, 1970, p. 24.
[36]Tom Wicker, "A Right Not to Be Data-Banked?," New York Times, July 7, 1970, editorial page.

United States today possesses the intelligence buildup of a police state.'' It turns out that the Army was able to beef up its spying system on the strength of evidence such as its February 1969 directive which warned of a "true insurgency, should external subversive forces develop successful control" of the racial and antiwar dissidents. As Tom Wicker noted in a March 2, 1971, column in the *New York Times*, "Now available are some almost unbelievable documents couched in Pentagon jargon, which show the kind of thinking that went into the surveillance program — if thinking is the word.'' Wicker goes on to point out that although government officials at first expressed a lack of knowledge about the whole area, "it is clear that Senator Ervin ought really to be looking into the highest levels of the Johnson Administration; for it was there that the Army got what authority it had, and there that the Army's blundering, blunderbuss plans got their approval.'' And now federal money is financing a merger of all state and federally gathered information into a single central data bank. It appears quite likely that within a couple of years the government will have secret files and computerized memory banks on perhaps 30 or 40 million citizens. One doubts that even then the government will possess sufficient integrity and introspective powers to ask itself why it has to doubt the loyalty of such a large number of its citizens. If government surveillance activities at least led to the asking of this crucial question, then one would not be entirely dismayed at the situation. But the king is going among his subjects incognito not to gather their true opinions as to how the defects of the government might be remedied, but rather to learn whom to watch and perhaps punish.

Many think that all of these problems will subside if and when the war in Vietnam ends. This, however, appears unlikely, since the American radical movement seems to have gone well beyond the single issue of the war. Fundamental changes in American society are being called for in perhaps the first indigenous American revolutionary movement since 1776. Our society and governmental institutions appear to be reacting by hardening their stance. Suddenly even small reforms aimed at refining the American political and judicial systems and bringing them closer to the democratic ideal, the classic "New Deal" and "liberal" programs, are running into heated opposition. The Vice President of the United States, Spiro T. Agnew, has coined the phrase, "RadicLibs" for what he considers those "radical Liberals" in and out of Congress and the Senate. The end of the war might quiet the liberals, but it is not essentially at the liberals that the machinery of legal repression is aimed.

Furthermore, if America's withdrawal from the Vietnam War comes on terms seen as dishonorable, that very withdrawal may provoke a reaction of its own, just as our less-than-victory conclusion of the Korean conflict immediately preceded the McCarthy era. When the richest and most powerful nation in the world cannot subdue a relatively primitive country, the search for a scapegoat might be expected to commence.

The longer our tensions last, the firmer will the machinery of legal repression become entrenched. The personnel of the Supreme Court may change entirely, and numerous oppressive statutes may fill the lawbooks. Analogies to the past, when liberty has emerged at least somewhat vigorous after periods of repression, may become inapposite, for we may soon experience a repression different not in degree but rather in kind. As Supreme Court Justice William O. Douglas has written, "A black silence of fear possesses the nation and is causing us to jettison some of our libertarian traditions."[37] Once jettisoned, some of them may never return. We may be in the process of creating new traditions.

[37]W. O. Douglas, *Points of Rebellion*, at p. 6 (1970).

Chapter Four

LAW ENFORCEMENT

The substantive criminal law is but one aspect of the legal order. The state, in addition, creates a complex of bureaucracies to enforce and administer the law. These agencies protect and secure the interests of the state and its ruling class. Law enforcement, in particular, plays a crucial role in maintaining the social and economic order of capitalist society. Law enforcement agencies, including local police departments, are coercive bureaucracies that serve the state and its material interests.

The role of the police in capitalist society has always been to preserve the existing order. In fact, the rise of the police in the nineteenth century was a response to attacks that were being made on domestic order. The creation of the police as an attempt to preserve domestic order is discussed in the first selection in this chapter. Allan Silver, in his essay on "The Demand for Order in Civil Society: A Review of Some Themes in the History of Urban Crime, Police, and Riot," argues that the attitude toward urban crime and violence in the London and Paris of the late eighteenth and the early nineteenth centuries reflected a fear of the "dangerous classes." The social order appeared to be threatened by an "agglomeration of the criminal, vicious, and violent — the rapidly multiplying poor of cities whose size had no precedent in Western history." Silver suggests, moreover, that the current fear of crime draws on this earlier conception of crime in the city.

The propertied classes responded to threats to their social order by creating the modern institution of the police. This institution relieved the propertied classes of the need to coerce the population by themselves and provided a domestic force outside of the military for the purpose of maintaining domestic order. Mobs and riots, as reactions to oppressive conditions, could be contained by a separate police force, performing for the propertied classes.

The newly created police bureaucracy could penetrate society in a way impossible for military forces. Furthermore, being diffused throughout society, the police could engage in crime prevention by detecting and apprehending criminals. This was more than a technical convenience. Silver argues: "The replacement of intermittent military intervention in largely unpoliced society by continuous professional bureaucratic policing meant that the benefits of police organization — continual pervasive moral display and lower long-term costs of official coercion for the state and propertied classes — absolutely required the moral cooperation of civil society." The police, in other words, had become an integral part of society, to be morally accepted by everyone.

Little wonder, then, that today the public looks to the police for the protection of "law and order." Other possibilities for a civil society have been excluded by the adoption of the police as the primary domestic peace-keeping agency of the state. Police forces have come, as Silver concludes, "to be seen as they were in the time of their creation — as a sophisticated and convenient form of garrison force against an internal enemy." The solutions to the problems of the age, however, lie beyond Silver's call for the development of a language that the oppressed may share with the propertied classes. Instead, radical changes in the class structure and economy of the country are required.

Once the policed society was constructed, local police departments were established throughout the country to carry out the interests of the state. These local agencies have been the subject of considerable sociological research. In their empirical investigations, sociologists have described the workings of police departments and the occupational activity of the police.[1] The second selection in this chapter presents and interprets much of the research on the sociology of the police. Peter K. Manning, in his essay on "The Police: Mandate, Strategies, and Appearances," observes that the police have "trouble." That is: "They have been assigned the task of crime prevention, crime detection, and the apprehension of criminals. Based on their legal monopoly of violence, they have staked out a mandate that claims to include the efficient, apolitical, and professional enforcement of the law. It is the contention of this essay that the police have staked out a vast and unmanageable social domain. And what has happened as a result of their inability to accomplish their self-proclaimed mandate is that the police have resorted to the manipulation of appearances."

[1]See, for example, Egon Bittner, "The Police on Skid-Row: A Study of Peace Keeping," *American Sociological Review*, 32 (October, 1967), pp. 699–715; David J. Bordua and Albert J. Reiss, Jr., "Command, Control and Charisma: Reflections on Police Bureaucracy," *American Journal of Sociology*, 72 (July, 1966), pp. 68–76; Arthur Niederhoffer, *Behind the Shield: The Police in Urban Society* (Garden City, New York: Doubleday, 1967); Irving Piliavin and Scott Briar, "Police Encounters with Juveniles," *American Journal of Sociology*, 70 (September, 1964), pp. 206–214; Jerome H. Skolnick, *Justice Without Trial: Law Enforcement in Democratic Society* (New York: John Wiley & Sons, 1966).

In coping with an unworkable mandate, the police have developed an "occupational culture" that contains its own assumptions about everyday life and serves as the basis for organizational strategies and tactics. In the course of his discussion, Manning provides us with an understanding of the police, including the ethic of professionalism, police bureaucracy, technology, styles of patrol, and secrecy and corruption. The author concludes by making suggestions for modifying the present structure of police work. The most important recommendation is for community control of the police. But we should add that given the purpose of the police in capitalist society — to protect the existing order — reforms must be viewed critically. Anything that would deter the police from their ultimate goal will not likely be allowed by the state. And reforms that are acceptable to the power structure are those that will further the cause of the established social and economic system. There is the remote possibility, however, that changes made by the people will, in the long run, alter the total system.

In the meantime, the police continue to carry out their mandate, resorting to violence and brutality as part of their occupational activity. That police engage in brutality should come as no surprise, since their mandate is one of coercing the population; the police are engaged in the management of violence for the state. The essay by Paul Chevigny, "Police Power," presents a discussion of some of the abuses by the police, viewed in the larger context of society and the nature of police work. Chevigny's observations come from a study he conducted for the New York Civil Liberties Union of cases of police abuse in New York City. The selection in this chapter pertains to "street abuses," that is, brutality by the police in relation to arrest and criminal charges.

Chevigny begins by stating that "the one truly iron and inflexible rule we can adduce from the cases is that any person who defies the police risks the imposition of legal sanctions, commencing with a summons, on up to the use of firearms." Furthermore, he continues, "The police may arrest *anyone* who challenges them (as they define the challenge), but they are more likely to further abuse anyone who is poor, or who belongs to an outcast group." But the real problem, according to Chevigny, is that the police often provoke citizens to violence or disorderly conduct in order that an arrest may be made. And through such provocation the police can continue to abuse the citizen.[2]

However, the worst abuse, Chevigny notes, is the abuse of power — the fact that the police not only assault persons but arrest them also. "If the police simply hit a man and let him go, there would be an abuse of the authority conferred by the uniform and the stick, but not the compound abuse of hitting a man and then dragging him

[2]Further documentation of police misconduct and illegal behavior is found in Albert J. Reiss, Jr., *The Police and the Public* (New Haven: Yale University Press, 1971): and William A. Westley, *Violence and the Police: A Sociological Study of Law, Custom, and Morality* (Cambridge: MIT Press, 1970).

to court on criminal charges, really a more serious injury than a blow. One's head heals up, after all, but a criminal record never goes away. There is no more embittering experience in the legal system than to be abused by the police and then to be tried and convicted on false evidence." Since the policeman is likely to get in trouble if he lets an abused person go free, an arrest is made to cover the abuse. The police can conceal their own violence by arresting and charging the citizen with some offense.

Thus, through a private code of police conduct, and the complicity of the courts in accepting the criminal charges, the police continue their practice of violence, arrest, and cover charges. And as long as the public accepts this situation, Chevigny argues, the abuses will go on. But since the institution of the police is generally accepted by the public, with law enforcement being regarded as the most appropriate way to handle problems, these abuses are likely to continue until a new consciousness develops.

Law enforcement involves more than police activity, however. The modern form of law enforcement is much more sophisticated than the older system of enforcement by local police departments. By the mid-1960s a rationalized, coordinated, and scientifically advanced system of law enforcement was developing to meet the increasing challenges to the existing order. Since crime could not be reduced without drastically altering the capitalist system, the only alternative open to the state was the modernization of law enforcement. Therefore, in the middle 1960s the federal government responded, in its "war on crime," by creating law enforcement apparatus unparalleled in the history of any nation.

It was in 1965 that the federal government began to increase its role in crime control. Although the first attempt was rather low-keyed in comparison with what was soon to follow, the federal government made a commitment to a new form of crime control. The government had previously shied away from interfering in local police activities, but the time was now ripe for a program that would give national direction to law enforcement. Congress responded by creating the office of Law Enforcement Assistance, within the Department of Justice. The new agency, operating from 1965 to 1968, supported nearly 400 projects aimed at "helping local governments improve their overall criminal justice systems" These projects included "training, research and demonstration efforts to prevent and control crime; to improve law enforcement, corrections, courts and other criminal justice agencies; and to assist these agencies in recruiting and upgrading personnel."[3]

But this was only the beginning. By 1968 Congress had passed the Omnibus Crime Control and Safe Streets Act which contained a major provision (Title I) for the creation of the Law Enforcement Assistance Administration (LEAA). As an agency within the Depart-

[3]Law Enforcement Assistance Administration, *Grants and Contracts Awarded Under the Law Enforcement Assistance Act of 1965*, Fiscal 1966–1968 (Washington, D.C.. U.S. Government Printing Office, 1968), p. 1.

ment of Justice, to replace and supersede the Office of Law Enforcement Assistance, LEAA assumed a broader and more pervasive plan of federal involvement in law enforcement and crime control.

LEAA has grown steadily since its creation in 1968. During its first year of operation, LEAA received a congressional appropriation of $63 million. The budget increased sharply to $268 million in 1970 and was further increased to $529 million in 1971. The Senate authorized $1.15 billion for 1972 and $1.75 billion for 1973. In preparing the annual report, the Administrator of LEAA, after citing the generous appropriations, advised the President and the Congress on the mission and impact of his agency: "The mission of LEAA is to reduce crime and delinquency by channeling Federal financial aid to state and local governments, to conduct research in methods of improving law enforcement and criminal justice, to fund efforts to upgrade the educational level of law enforcement personnel, to develop applications of statistical research and applied systems analysis in law enforcement, and to develop broad policy guidelines for both the short and long-range improvement of the nation's Criminal Justice System as a whole."[4]

In addition to encouraging, or forcing, state governments to develop law enforcement plans, LEAA awards federal funds to state and local governments for the development of programs to improve and strengthen law enforcement, gives funds for the training of law enforcement agents, and supports research and the development of methods for improvement of law enforcement and the reduction of crime. Furthermore, local police are being armed with sophisticated "crime prevention" techniques and equipment. As one critical investigator writes: "The purpose is to curb robberies, burglaries and violent street crimes. The result, however, enables police to keep citizens — the innocent and the guilty alike — under electronic and photographic surveillance while they are shopping, walking public streets, driving automobiles, and visiting both private and public buildings."[5] Massive computerized "intelligence systems" are being developed to predict disorder and to contain information on "dangerous" persons. Great amounts of money are being given for the development of techniques for the control of the population, for the prevention of disorder, for the preservation of domestic order.

It is this new system of law enforcement that Jeff Gerth critically examines in the last selection in this chapter. In "The Americanization of 1984," Gerth documents the modern form of crime control in this country. Involved in this crime control program are various agencies in the Department of Justice, the FBI, LEAA, state crime agencies,

[4]LEAA, *Third Annual Report of the Law Enforcement Assistance Administration,* Fiscal Year 1971 (Washington, D.C.: U.S. Government Printing Office, 1972), p. ii.

[5]Joseph C. Goulden, "Tooling Up for Repression: The Cops Hit the Jackpot," *The Nation,* 211 (November 23, 1970), p. 520. Also see National Action/Research on the Military-Industrial Complex, *Police on the HomeFront* (Philadelphia: American Friends Service Committee, 1971).

and local police departments. Gerth discusses how the federal government is developing and supporting programs in civil disorder assistance, weapons stockpiling, surveillance, and data gathering. The modern system of crime control employs the latest methods and devices of science and technology. The legal order is reaching its highest form of rationality.

Gerth's conclusion is that American society is well on the way to becoming a police state. "The enactment of this police state — less conspicuous yet far more threatening than one dominated by the military — is a scientific enterprise. Its low-profiled selective repression is based on surveillance, fear, intimidation, and information control, rather than on the massive deployment of police."

More insidious and pervasive than the older form of law enforcement, the new crime control system seeks to provide the ultimate means of preserving the existing social and economic order.

6. Allan Silver

The Demand for Order in Civil Society: A Review of Some Themes in the History of Urban Crime, Police, and Riot

Criminals and the "Dangerous Classes"

Crime and violence in the life of city dwellers have long evoked complaints which have a quite contemporary tone. Peaceful and propertied people in eighteenth-century London, for example, confronted a level of daily danger to which they and their spokesmen reacted indignantly. It was in such terms that Daniel Defoe dedicated a pamphlet on crime to the Lord Mayor of London:

The Whole City, My Lord, is alarm'd and uneasy; Wickedness has got such a Head, and the Robbers and Insolence of the Night are such, that the Citizens are no longer secure within their own Walls, or safe even in passing their Streets, but are robbed, insulted and abused, even at their own Doors. . . . The Citizens . . . are oppressed by Rapin and Violence; Hell seems to have let loose Troops of human D——ls upon them; and such Mischiefs are done within the Bounds of your Government as never were practised here before

Reprinted by permission of the publisher from *The Police: Six Sociological Essays*, edited by D. J. Bordua, pp. 1–24. Copyright © 1967 by John Wiley & Sons, Inc.

(at least not to such a degree) and which, if suffered to go on, will call for Armies, not Magistrates, to suppress.[1]

In the body of his pamphlet, Defoe describes a situation of pervasive insecurity, stressing the mounting and unprecedented extent of criminal attack. The idea of crime is already quite explicit:

> Violence and Plunder is no longer confin'd to the Highways. . . . The Streets of the City are now the Places of Danger; men are knock'd down and robb'd, nay, sometimes murther'd at their own Doors, and in passing and repassing but from House to House, or from Shop to Shop. Stagecoaches are robb'd in High-Holbourn, White-Chappel, Pall-Mall, Soho and at almost all the Avenues of the City. Hackney-Coaches and Gentlemen's Coaches are stopt in Cheapside, St. Paul's Church-yard, the Strand, and other the most crowded streets, and that even while the People in Throngs are passing and repassing . . . Tis hard that in a well-govern'd City . . . it should be said that her Inhabitants are not now safe. . . .[2]

We may note in passing that equally contemporary themes richly abound in magazines that urban Americans read six decades ago. To cite but two examples:

> Individual crimes have increased in number and malignity. In addition to this . . . a wave of general criminality has spread over the whole nation. . . . The times are far from hard, and prosperity for several years has been wide-spread in all classes. Large sums are in unaccustomed hands, bar-rooms are swarming, pool-rooms, policy shops and gambling houses are full, the races are played, licentiousness increases, the classes who "roll in wealth" set intoxicating examples of luxury and recklessness, and crime has become rampant.[3]

In that period, it was, of course, commonplace also to ascribe the fundamental causes of mass criminality to large-scale immigration:

> In the poorer quarters of our great cities may be found huddled together the Italian bandit and the bloodthirsty Spaniard, the bad man from Sicily, the Hungarian, the Croatian and the Pole, the Chinaman and the Negro, the cockney Englishman, the Russian and the Jew, with all the centuries of hereditary hate back of them. They continually cross each others' path. It is no wonder that altercations occur and blood is shed. . . . We claim to be a rich and prosperous city and yet we cannot afford to employ enough policemen to keep thieves and burglars out of our houses and thugs and robbers from knocking us on the head as we walk along our own streets. . . . The bald, bare, horrible

---

[1]*An Effectual Scheme for the Immediate Prevention of Street Robberies and Suppressing of all other Disorders of the Night; with a Brief History of the Night-houses and an Appendix relating to those Sons of Hell call'd Incendiaries* (London, 1730).

[2]*Ibid.*, pp. 10–11.

[3]James M. Buckley, "The Present Epidemic of Crime," *The Century Magazine,* (November 1903), p. 150.

fact is that the conditions existing in Chicago today are the most criminal and damnable of any large city on the face of the earth.[4]

Thus the current rhetoric of concern about crime and violence draws on established motifs of both older and newer vintage: an indignant sense of pervasive insecurity; a mounting current of crime and violence as a result of both unaccustomed prosperity and prolonged poverty; the bad example of the self-indulgent wealthy; the violent proclivities of immigrants and other newcomers; and the ironic contrast between the greatness of the metropolis and the continued spread of crime.

But at times there was a somewhat different attitude toward urban crime and violence. In the London and Paris of the late eighteenth and the early nineteenth centuries, people often saw themselves as threatened by agglomerations of the criminal, vicious, and violent — the rapidly multiplying poor of cities whose size had no precedent in Western history. It was much more than a question of annoyance, indignation, or personal insecurity; the social order itself was threatened by an entity whose characteristic name reflects the fears of the time — the "dangerous classes." The phrase occurs repeatedly. Thus, an anonymous essayist of 1844 writes of the situation in urban England, where "destitution, profligacy, sensuality and crime, advance with unheard-of-rapidity in the manufacturing districts, and the dangerous classes there massed together combine every three or four years in some general strike or alarming insurrection which, while it lasts, excites universal terrors. . . ."[5] But even where the term is not explicitly invoked, the image persists — one of an unmanageable, volatile, and convulsively criminal class at the base of society.[6]

This imagery is only in part the product of class antagonisms in early industrial society; rather, the working classes were included in an older and continuing concern with criminality.[7] Urban administrators regarded the swelling numbers of the poor as unmanageable. Indeed, the image of the "dangerous classes," as distinct from that of pervasive criminality, seems to have flourished especially during periods of very rapid population growth, reflecting the migration of the numerous poor,

---

[4]James Edgar Brown, "The Increase of Crime in the United States," *The Independent* (April 11, 1907), pp. 832–33.

[5]"Causes of the Increase of Crime," *Blackwood's Magazine* (July 1844), p. 2. The phrase appears in another work published four years later, *The Communist Manifesto* — where, however, *it is instantly interpreted in terms of the "lumpen-proletariat" idea.*

[6]Honoré Antoine Frégier, *Les Classes Dangereuses de la Population dans les Grandes Villes* (Paris, 1840) is a work often cited by contemporaries. A relevant modern work on Paris is Louis Chevalier's *Classes Laborieuses et Classes Dangereuses à Paris pendant la Première Moitié du XIX Siècle* (Paris, 1958). In the Paris of that time, he writes, "le proliferation des classes dangereuses était . . . l'un des faits majeurs de l'existence quotiene de la capitale, l'un des grands problèmes de l'administration urbaine, l'une dès principales préoccupations des tous, l'une des formes les plus incontestables de l'angoisse sociale." The city was one "où le crime a une importance et une signification que nous ne comprenons guère . . ." (pp. iii–iv).

[7]Influential books expressing this concern were Henry Fielding's *Enquiry into the Causes of the Late Increase of Robbers* (1751) and Patrick Colquhoun's *Treatise on the Police of the Metropolis* (1796). According to Chevalier *(op. cit.,* pp. 451–68), the Parisian bourgeoisie made little distinction between the "industrious" and the "dangerous" poor.

without employment skills or a history of urban life. During this period, the labor force of the metropolis was still not primarily industrial.[8] Thus, the events and antagonisms of early industrialism inflamed but did not create the image of the "dangerous classes." It referred primarily to the unattached and unemployed. An advocate of police reform in London, writing in 1821, defined the problem in these terms:

> The most superficial observer of the external and visible appearance of this town, must soon be convinced, that there is a large mass of unproductive population living upon it, without occupation or ostensible means of subsistence; and, it is notorious that hundreds and thousands go forth from day to day trusting alone to charity or rapine; and differing little from the barbarous hordes which traverse an uncivilized land. . . . The principle of [their] action is the same; their life is predatory; it is equally a war against society, and the object is alike to gratify desire by strategem or force.[9]

As class tensions involving the threat of riot and revolutionary violence subsided in London, the older concern with diffuse criminality rather than the "dangerous classes" reemerged. Thus, Henry Mayhew's immense reportage on London's criminals, vagabonds, and casually employed, published in 1861, was suffused variously by moralism, indignation, pity, compassion, horror, and mere curiosity — but not by the sense of dread that had earlier afflicted those confronted by the dangerous classes.[10] Indeed, contemporary writing in midcentury London exhibits a sense of relief and victory over the forces of mass violence. Contrasting the present with the past, a writer in 1856 observed that "the only quarter in which any formidable riot could take place would be eastward, in the neighborhood of the docks, where there are at least twelve thousand sailors in the river or on shore, ready for a spree, fearless and powerful, and acting with an undoubted esprit de corps. These, if associated with the seven or eight thousand dock labourers and lightermen, would certainly produce a force difficult to cope with."[11] Such a prospect clearly was judged as a great improvement.

---

[8] According to the census, the population of London tripled in the first half of the nineteenth century. On its occupational composition, see the *Census of Great Britain in 1851* (London, 1854), p. 182, *passim.*

[9] George Mainwaring, *Observations on the Present State of the Police of the Metropolis* (London, 1821), pp. 4–5. The anonymous essayist of 1844, quoted above on the connection between the dangerous classes and the "manufacturing districts," went on to write: "In examining the classes of society from which the greater part of the crime comes, it will be found that at least three-fourths, probably nine-tenths, comes from the very lowest and most destitute. . . . If we examine who it is that compose this dismal substratum, this hideous *black band of society*, we shall find that it is not made up of any one class more than another — not of factory workers more than labourers, carters or miners — but it is formed by an aggregate of the most unfortunate or improvident of *all classes. . . .*" *Blackwood's Magazine* (July 1844), p. 12 (italics in original).

[10] This was the fourth and final volume of *London Labour and the London Poor,* separately titled *Those That Will Not Work.*

[11] *London Quarterly Review* (July 1856), p. 94. Many observers, though still concerned with criminality, acknowledge a change for the better at this time. Remarking that accounts of the earlier situation in London "seem like tales of another country," a writer in 1852 went on to detail improvements: "No member of Paliament would now venture to say that it was dangerous to walk in the streets of London by day or night. . . . Bad as the dens of infamy in London still are they are not to

To judge from contemporary accounts, New York did not experience a comparable sense of relief or improvement. Indeed, it appears that by 1872 New York was already being compared unfavorably to London with respect to crime and violence:

> . . . If the vice and pauperism of New York are not so steeped in the blood of the populace [as in London and other European cities] they are even more dangerous. . . . They rob a bank, when English thieves pick pockets; they murder, where European prolétaires cudgel or fight with fists; in a riot they begin what seems about to be the sacking of a city, where English rioters merely batter policemen or smash lamps. . . .[12]

For this observer, whose book is largely concerned with relief and other remedial programs among New York's poor, the dangerous classes are very much a part of the city — which, after all, had only a decade earlier suffered the great Draft Riot of 1863:

> There are thousands upon thousands in New York who have no assignable home, and "flit" from attic to attic, and cellar to cellar; there are other thousands more or less connected with criminal enterprises; and still other tens of thousands, poor, hard-pressed. . . . Let but Law lift its hand from them for a season, or let the civilizing influences of American life fail to reach them, and, if the opportunity afforded, we should see an explosion from this class which might leave the city in ashes and blood.[13]

Such rhetoric is not, as we have seen, an inevitable expression of concern with criminality, riot, and violence — even when these were of an order unthinkable in daily urban life today.[14]

What are some of the factors that underlie relationships between urban criminality and disorder and the significance ascribed to them by the peaceful and propertied classes? An adequate answer to this question would need to consider important aspects of economic, political, and urban history, the labor movement, and demography. For our purposes, however, we will focus on two aspects of the situation that until recently have been neglected: the significance of the police and the culture of riotous protest.

The Policed Society

Some modern nations have been police states; all, however, are policed societies. Practical men have never underestimated, though they have often distorted, the importance of the police. Sociological theory in the "social control" tradition,

---

be compared with those older places of hideous profligacy. . . . In the most disorderly part of the town, such as St. Giles, Covent Garden, and Holborn, the streets every Sunday morning exhibited the most outrageous scenes of fighting, drunkenness and depravity. . . . Crimes, too, are greatly diminished in atrocity. The large gangs of desperate robbers, thirteen or fourteen in number, now no longer exist. . . ." *Edinburgh Review* (July 1858), p. 12–3.

[12]Charles L. Brace, *The Dangerous Classes of New York* (New York, 1872), p. 26.

[13]*Ibid.*, p. 29.

[14]Thus, Defoe saw the intolerable conditions of his time as a result of the arrogance and bad influence of a rapidly increasing group of prostitutes and their "bullies"; and his solution was to disperse them by raids (*op. cit.*, pp. 26–32).

however, has usually slighted the police in favor of normative or voluntary proces-ses.[15] The significance of the police, for our purposes, can best be understood as they appeared to a generation for whom modern police were an unprecedented innovation — Englishmen in the middle third of the nineteenth century.

The London police, created in 1829, were from the beginning a bureaucratic organization of professionals.[16] One of their tasks was to prevent crime by regularly patrolling beats, operating under strict rules which permitted individual discretion. The police also had a mission against the "dangerous classes" and political agitation in the form of mobs or riots. On all fronts they were so successful that initial and strong objections to them rapidly diminished; from being a considerable novelty, they quickly became a part of "British tradition."

The policed society is unique in that central power exercises potentially violent supervision over the population by bureaucratic means widely diffused throughout civil society in small and discretionary operations that are capable of rapid concentration. All of these characteristics struck contemporary observers as remarkable. Fear of mob or riot diminished when early police showed that fluid organization can overcome numbers:

> There seems to be no fear a London mob will ever prove a serious thing in the face of our present corps of policemen. A repetition of the Lord George Gordon riots would be an impossibility. Those who shudder at the idea of an outbreak in the metropolis containing two millions and a half of people and at least fifty thousand of the "dangerous classes" forget that the capital is so wide that its different sections are totally unknown to each other. A mob in London is wholly without cohesion, and the individuals composing

[15]In the book which more than six decades ago named and founded this tradition, E. A. Ross was crisply aware of the expanding role of police: "In the field of physical coercion, there is an increase in the number of lictors, bailiffs, police, and soldiers told off to catch, prod, beat, and hold fast recalcitrants, and they are brought under a stricter discipline. They are more specialized for their work, and an *esprit de corps* is carefully cultivated among them." *Social Control* (New York, 1901), pp. 398–9. Furthermore, Ross was quite tough-minded about the cause of this development: "All this does not happen by simple fiat of the social will. Certain groups of persons — the executive, cabinet, the central government, the party machine, the higher clergy, the educational hierarchy, 'authorities' of every kind in short — are always striving for more power. When the need of a more stringent control makes itself felt, they find the barriers to their self-aggrandizement unexpectedly giving way before them. Formerly they were held in check, while now they find encroachment strangely easy" (*Ibid.*). Neither kind of emphasis survived the subsequent failure of works in social control to treat the characteristics of the policed society in a comprehensive way or to see organized and legitimate coercion as intrinsic to social control. (Representative treatises are L. L. Bernard, *Social Control,* New York, 1939, and Richard T. LaPiere, *A Theory of Social Control,* New York, 1954.) Ross himself distinguished between the normative processes of "public opinion" — uniquely flexible, preventive, and ubiquitous—and the coercive effects of "law"—which were clumsy, retrospective, and remote *(op. cit.,* pp. 89–105). Important and influential as this distinction is, it tends to obscure — as we shall see — some of the distinctive features of policed society. Recent attempts to incorporate civil violence in the framework of social theory are included in *Internal War,* Harry Eckstein, ed. (New York, 1964), especially the essays by Eckstein, Parsons, and Feldman.

[16]Useful accounts of British police history are the writings of Charles Reith, especially *The Police Idea* (1938), *British Police and the Democratic Ideal* (1943), *The Blind Eye of History* (1952), and *A New Study of Police History* (1956). See also F. C. Mather, *Public Order in the Age of the Chartists* (Manchester, 1959). Like most contributors to the English literature on "public order," these writers — especially Reith — work from palpably conservative assumptions.

it have but few feelings, thoughts or pursuits in common. They would immediately break up before the determined attack of a band of well-trained men who know and have confidence in each other.[17]

Another writer put the same point in more impersonal terms:

As each police constable being alone might easily be overpowered, and as the men of each section, or even division, might be inferior in numbers to some aggregation of roughs or criminals collected in a given spot, it is arranged that . . . reserves of force can be gathered . . . and concentrated upon the disquieted area, and as the commissioners command the whole district, and the force is organized and united, while roughs act in small areas, and have diverse and selfish interests, the peace of London may be held secure against violence.[18]

The peaceful and propertied classes appreciated two other advantages of the modern police: they relieved ordinary respectable citizens of the obligation or necessity to discharge police functions, especially during emergencies; and they also made less likely a resort to the military for the purposes of internal peace-keeping. Both involved changes in the relationship of these classes to the criminal or disorderly.

In unpoliced society, police functions were often carried out — if at all — by citizens rotating in local offices (sheriffs, constables, magistrates) or acting as members of militia, posses, Yeomanry corps, or watch and ward committees.[19] Not only was this system inefficient but it also directly exposed the propertied classes to attack. Agrarian men of property were frequently willing to undertake these tasks. Thus the Yeomanry, a cavalry force whose characteristic tactic was the sabre charge, was largely composed of small landowners[20] who were especially zealous in police duty against mobs and riots and especially disliked by working people.[21] For these reasons, the Yeomanry were particularly popular among the landowning classes as a means of defense. Praising them in the course of a parliamentary debate in 1817, for example, a member observed that the people would in many instances be debarred from violence by seeing those arrayed against them to whom they were accustomed to look up to as their masters."[22]

[17]"The Police and the Thieves," *London Quarterly Review* (July 1856), p. 93.

[18]"The Metropolitan Police System," *Westminster Review* (January 1873), p. 16. An early historian of the New York Draft Riot of 1863 was similarly impressed by the decisive contribution of the telegraphic system in linking police stations within the city to each other and to those in Brooklyn. He devoted considerable space to the mob's attacks on the telegraphic system, citing the defense of its equipment and personnel as a key phase in the struggle for control of the streets. See J. T. Headley, *The Great Riots of New York* (New York, 1873).

[19]A good summary is in F. C. Mather, *Public Order in the Age of the Chartists,* pp. 75–95.

[20]John Fortesque, *A History of the British Army* (London, 1923) Vol. XI, p. 43. Since the yeomanry were required to supply their own horses and equipment, their status as agrarian men of property was largely assured. See K. Chorley, *Armies and the Art of Revolution* (London, 1943), p. 167.

[21]J. L. and B. Hammond, *The Town Labourer* (London, 1928), p. 89. Also, F. C. Mather, *op. cit.,* p. 148. Yeomanry, for example, precipitated the "Peterloo" massacre.

[22]Quoted in Reith, *The Police Idea*, p. 191.

But this machinery exposed the Yeomanry, once an emergency had passed, to direct attack in the course of daily life.[23] It also enabled private persons sometimes to modify police missions to suit their own proclivities and convenience. Thus, during the extensive agricultural uprisings of 1830 in southern England, fifty men of the village of Holt enrolled as special constables and "declared their willingness to turn out to protect all property except threshing machines; they did not wish to show disrespect to their poorer neighbors."[24] Yet threshing machines were the very form of property then under attack.

The urban and industrial propertied classes, however, were much less eager to take up the tasks of self-defense as volunteer or co-opted police. Landowning military officers attempting to encourage self-defense among commercial or industrial capitalists met with much reluctance. Replying in 1819 to advice from Wellington, the army commander in the newly industrializing north of England replied in exasperated terms:

> I have always fought against the dispersal of my force in trivial detachments; it is quite impossible to defeat the disaffected if they rise, and at the same time to protect any town from plunder; that resistance should be made by the inhabitants. . . . But I am sorry to say the general remark from the manufacturers is that government is bound to protect them and their property.[25]

We are dealing here not merely with the classic confrontation of an agrarian military tradition and a pacific commercial and industrial one; what also emerges is a specific demand for the bureaucratization of police functions. Not only did the manufacturing classes wish to avoid personal danger and inconvenience while protecting their property, but they also saw that — contrary to the social rationale underlying the yeomanry — the use of social and economic superiors as police exacerbated rather than mollified class violence.[26] This emerges clearly in the testimony of one Thomas Ashton, "the owner of considerable property in manufactures, and the employer of about 1500 persons," before the Royal Commission of 1839 concerned with extending the professional police from London to the provinces.[27] Among other reforms, Ashton favored the use of personnel from outside a locality affected by violence and for a reason other than the reluctance of local personnel to act against their neighbors:

> On such urgent occasions, I think it extremely desirable that a stipendiary magistrate should be sent into the district and entrusted with the administration of the law. A great majority of the more serious disturbances originate in disputes between master and servant. The local magistracy is chiefly com-

---

[23]For example, many resigned when they received threatening letters after Peterloo. See Ione Leigh, *Castlereagh* (London, 1951), p. 127.

[24]J. R. M. Butler, *The Passing of the Great Reform Bill* (London, 1914), p. 132.

[25]Despatch of General Byng quoted in Reith, *The Police Idea*, p. 202.

[26]"Respectable tradesmen cannot, without detriment to themselves, be so engaged as constables . . ." (George Mainwaring, *Observations on the Police . . .*, p. 46).

[27]*First Report of the Commissioners Appointed as to the Best Means of Establishing an Efficient Constabulary Force in the Counties of England and Wales* (London, 1839), pp. 158–9.

posed of the resident landowners and manufacturers, and the irritation of the workmen against their employers is greatly increased when they find the person, with whom the disputes have arisen openly supported by, and giving directions to, the military, and subsequently punishing them for breaches of the peace, which would never have been committed unless such disputes had occurred. Ought the employer to be placed in such a situation? Is it likely that animosities would be allayed or peace maintained by it? What safety has the proprietor of machinery?

This reasoning was accepted by the commissioners in their report, which was largely written by the Benthamite reformer Edwin Chadwick:

> In several instances where there was an effective resistance given to the rioters, we have been informed that the animosities created or increased, and rendered permanent by arming master against servant, neighbour against neighbour, by triumph on one side and failure on the other, were even more deplorable than the outrages actually committed. . . . The necessity for such painful and demoralizing conflicts between connected persons should be avoided by providing a trained and independent force for action in such emergencies. . . . The constitutional authority of the supreme executive is then emphatically asserted. In reply to recent inquiries made of local authorities in the manufacturing districts, why so long a career of criminal incitements was permitted, the prevalent answer has been, that such proceedings were understood to be exclusively within the province of government.[28]

Thus, at a time when the agrarian rich often sought to multiply and reconstruct the traditional means of self-defense against violent uprising and attack, those who sprang from the newer sources of wealth turned toward a bureaucratic police system that insulated them from popular violence, drew attack and animosity upon itself, and seemed to separate the assertion of "constitutional" authority from that of social and economic dominance.[29]

Other means than a bureaucratic police — especially the army itself — were available for this purpose. But although the army played a crucial role during crises or situations with revolutionary potential, it was ill-equipped to meet the enduring needs of a policed society.[30] It was largely officered by an agrarian class which sometimes did not distinguish itself for zeal in protecting the property of manufacturers.[31] More fundamentally, however, it was difficult for the army to act continuously in small dispersed units in civilian society, although it might do so on an emergency basis. More characteristic of the army was an alternation

[28]*Ibid.*, p. 205.

[29]"I hope to get up a troop of Yeomanry at Cheltenham," wrote Lord Ellenborough during the critical year of 1832, "but this requires delicate management. . . . Yeomanry however we must have, or we shall be beaten." A. Aspinall, *Three Early Nineteenth Century Diaries* (London, 1952), p. 275.

[30]See the accounts in F. C. Mather, *Puiblic Order in the Age of the Chartists*, pp. 153–81, and Joseph Hamburger, *James Mill and the Art of Revolution* (New Haven, 1963), pp. 203–14.

[31]See, for example, Frank Darvell, *Popular Disturbances and Public Order in Regency England* (Oxford, 1934), pp. 80–1, 267–8.

between no intervention and the most drastic procedures — the latter representing
a declaration of internal war with lingering consequences of hate and resentment.[32]
The police were designed to penetrate civil society in a way impossible for military
formations and by doing so to prevent crime and violence and to detect and apprehend
criminals.[33] Early descriptions by contemporaries describe both sorts of police-
action, taken today as routine, as novel and startling.[34]

The police penetration of civil society, however, lay not only in its narrow
application to crime and violence. In a broader sense, it represented the penetration
and continual presence of central political authority throughout daily life. In an
important defense of characteristically modern social arrangements, Edward Shils
has argued that close integration of the social and geographic periphery is a unique
achievement of "mass society." In his view

mass society is not the most peaceful or "orderly" society that has ever.
existed; but it is the most consensual. The maintenance of public peace through
apathy and coercion in a structure of extremely discontinuous interaction is
a rather different thing from its maintenance through consensus in a structure
of more continuous interaction between center and periphery. . . .[35]

But in Shils' account the integration of the periphery emerges entirely as a
moral or normative process:

The mass of the population is no longer merely an object which the elite
takes into account as a reservoir of military and labor power or as a possible
or actual source of public disorder. . . . Most of the population . . . stand
in closer moral affinity and in a more frequent, even though mediated, interaction
with the center than has ever been the case. . . . The greater proximity to
the center — to the institutions which constitute it and the views which are
embodied in it. There is, accordingly, a greater feeling within the mass of
being a part of the same substance of which one is oneself formed.

That the modern nation represents an unprecedented extension of the organizational and moral community is undoubted. But the wholly normative language
in which this account is cast risks eliding the simultaneous extension of the police
throughout the "periphery" both as the agent of legitimate coercion and a personi-
fication of the values of the "center." Far from being a latter-day consequence
of organizing the police for purely coercive tasks, this was explicit in early police

[32]All these points of superiority of police over army were explicit among those who advocated
or created the early professional police. See for example, the *First Report of the Commissioners*
. . ., *op. cit.*, pp. 159–61; George Mainwaring, *Observations on the Present State of the Police*
. . ., p. 69; Charles Reith, *British Police and the Democratic Ideal*, pp. 9–30; and *Edinburgh
Review* (July 1852), p. 6.

[33]Great stress was initially laid on the "preventive principle," at the time a new principle in internal
peace-keeping. See Reith. *ibid.*, pp. 18–23, and the same author's *A New Study of Police History*,
pp. 221–4. For the view of a contemporary advocate of police, see Mainwaring, *op. cit.*, pp. 9–10.

[34]Note, for example, the obvious astonishment that underlies an account of the tracing of a burglar,
who had robbed a house in central London, to an obscure hiding place in the East End ("The Police
System of London," *Edinburgh Review*, July 1852, pp. 8–10).

[35]"The Theory of Mass Society," *Diogenes* (1962) pp. 53–4 (for this and succeeding quotations).

doctrine and much remarked upon by early observers. Their accounts stress the capacity of bureaucratic organization to make the values of the "center" palpable in daily life by means of detached persons operating on organizationally defined missions.

> Amid the bustle of Piccadilly or the roar of Oxford Street, P.C.X. 59 stalks along, an institution rather than a man. We seem to have no more hold of his personality than we could possibly get of his coat buttoned up to the throttling-point. Go, however, to the section-house . . . and you no longer see policemen, but men. . . . They are positively laughing with each other![36]

And they also stress the power of the police over mass disorder, which stems not only from superior organization and the rational application of force but also from its presence as the official representative of the moral order in daily life:

> The baton may be a very ineffective weapon of offence, but it is backed by the combined power of the Crown, the Government, and the Constituencies. Armed with it alone, the constable will usually be found ready, in obedience to orders, to face any mob, or brave any danger. The mob quails before the simple baton of the police officer, and flies before it, well knowing the moral as well as physical force of the Nation whose will, as embodied in law, it represents. And take any man from that mob, place a baton in his hand and a blue coat on his back, put him forward as the representative of the law, and he too will be found equally ready to face the mob from which he was taken, and exhibit the same steadfastness and courage in defense of constituted order.[37]

In this setting, early police doctrine and observers agreed from the beginning that it was necessary to rely on the moral assent of the general population; even the earliest policemen were elaborately instructed in the demeanor and behavior required to evoke, establish, and sustain that assent.[38] This was more than a mere technical convenience. The replacement of intermittent military intervention in a largely unpoliced society by continuous professional bureaucratic policing meant that the benefits of police organization — continual pervasive moral display and lower long-term costs of official coercion for the state and propertied classes — absolutely required the moral cooperation of civil society.

Thus, the extension of moral consensus and of the police as an instrument of legitimate coercion go hand in hand. Along with other ramifying bureaucratic agencies of the center, the police link daily life to central authority. The police, however, rely not only on a technique of graduated, discretionary, and ubiquitous coercion but also on a new and unprecedentedly extensive form of moral consensus. The center is able to supervise daily life more closely and continuously than ever before; but police organization also requires pervasive moral assent if it is

---

[36]"The Police and the Thieves," *London Quarterly Review* (July 1856), p. 93.

[37]"The Police of London," *London Quarterly Review* (July 1870), p. 48.

[38]Charles Reith, *A New Study of Police History*, pp. 140–2.

to achieve the goals peculiar to its technique. In earlier times, as we have seen, voluntaristic and nonbureaucratic police permitted the sabotage of official coercion by allowing participating classes to make their services conditional. In a policed society (as distinct from a police state), a hostage is also given to fortune: the fundamental assent, not of the classes who comprise volunteer or nonprofessional quasi-police, but of the general population. Without at least a minimal level of such assent, coercive functions become costly in exactly the ways that those who created the policed society in England sought to avoid. In this sense, then, the extension of the moral community and of the police are aspects of the same historical development.

Cultures of Riotous Protest

The themes of mass criminality and of political riot and mob protest have long been intertwined. In a notable and recent contribution George Rudé has been especially concerned to refute the classic view — associated with such nineteenth-century conservatives as Burke, Taine, and Le Bon — that political crowds, mobs, and riots are essentially criminal in character.[39] According to Rudé's analysis, demonstrating crowds and mobs in the latter half of the eighteenth and the first half of the nineteenth century were characteristically composed not of pauperized, unemployed and disorganized "rabble" but of locally resident, respectable, and employed people.[40] It is not surprising that privileged classes attempt to define popular protest as criminal — that is, fundamentally and unconditionally illegitimate. But this rhetoric and the very real fears of privileged and propertied people facing recurrent popular agitation in an unpoliced age, must not lead us to overlook the evidence for another aspect of this older relationship between elite and agitational population: riots and mobs, however much they were feared and detested, were also often means of protest that articulately communicated the desires of the population to a responsive, if not sympathetic, elite.[41]

[39]*The Crowd in History, 1730–1848* (New York, 1964), pp. 7–8, 199–204.
[40]*Ibid.*, p. 47–65.
[41]Expressions of this fear are vivid and aboundingly frequent. "At this time wrote the Tory poet Southey in 1812, "nothing but the Army preserves us from the most dreadful of all calamities, an insurrection of the poor against the rich, and how long the Army may be depended upon is a question which I scarcely dare ask myself" (Elie Halevy, *A History of the English People,* New York, 1912, Vol. I. p. 292). Seven years later a peer discussing the political situation observed: "We are daily assailed with undisguised menace, and are little removed from the expectation of open violence . . ." *(Substance of the speech of the Rt. Hon. Lord Grenville in the House of Lords, November 19, 1820,* London, p. 23). A year later in a memorandum to Liverpool, Wellington, then Prime Minister — urging the creation of a police force — wrote: "I feel the greatest anxiety respecting the state of the military in London. . . . Very recently strong symptoms of discontent appeared in one battalion of the guards. . . . There are reports without number in circulation respecting all the Guards. . . . Thus, in one of the most critical moments that ever occurred in this country, we and the public have reason to doubt the fidelity of the troops, the only security we have, not only against revolution but for the lives and property of every individual in this country who has anything to lose . . ." (Quoted in Reith, *The Police Idea,* p. 213). Robert Peel, fearing for his family's safety at their country estate, left London during the crisis of 1831 and asked a friend to send weapons. "I have this day got you fourteen carbines, bayonets, and accoutrements," the friend replied. "How will

This is a major feature of Eric Hobsbawm's analysis of the pre-industrial "city mob."[42] While stressing that such mobs were a "pre-political phenomenon" and often reacted directly to fluctuations in wages and food prices, Hobsbawm also emphasizes, in effect, the normative character of such riots:

> . . . There was the claim to be considered. The classical mob did not merely riot as a protest, but because it expected to achieve something by its riot. It assumed that the authorities would be sensitive to its movements, and probably also that they would make some immediate concession; for the "mob" was not simply a casual collection of people united for some *ad hoc* purpose, but in a recognized sense, a permanent entity, even though rarely permanently organized as such.[43]

Insisting with Rudé on the essentially noncriminal character of such riotous protests, Hobsbawm summarizes the system as a whole:

> Provided that the ruler did his duty, the populace was prepared to defend him with enthusiasm. But if he did not, it rioted until he did. This mechanism was perfectly understood by both sides, and caused no political problems beyond a little occasional destruction of property. . . . The threat of perennial rioting kept rulers ready to control prices and distribute work or largesses, or indeed to listen to their faithful commons on other matters. Since the riots were not directed against the social system, public order could remain surprisingly lax by modern standards.[44]

We will briefly illustrate the system as described by Hobsbawm and Rudé with an example from rather late in this period — London in 1831.[45] "Illuminations" were occasions on which those favoring a given cause or person placed lights in their windows; and it often happened that demonstrating crowds went from house to house demanding that those within "illuminate" and smashing their windows or sacking their houses if they did not. The residences thus besieged were usually selected with precision — the ruling class in eighteenth- and early nineteenth-century cities was not anonymous, physically inaccessible, or effectively insulated by a professional and preventive police force. Such a crowd, pressing for electoral reform of the Commons, gathered in April 1831. The fol-

---

you have them sent to you? I have only desired a cask of ball cartridges to be put in the case" (Tresham Lever, *The Life and Times of Sir Robert Peel*, New York, 1942, p. 144). A general description of the situation is given in Reith, *Police Principles and the Problem of War*, pp. 46–8. In his revisionist account, *James Mill and the Art of Revolution*, Joseph Hamburger maintains that this standard portrait of elite mentality is exaggerated and that it does not apply to the Whig reformers in the period before 1832, who were more concerned with long-range than with imminent crises (see pp. 33–47).

[42]*Primitive Rebels: Studies in Archaic Forms of Social Movements* (Manchester, 1959).

[43]*Ibid.*, p. 111.

[44]*Ibid.*, p. 116.

[45]See the summary of this theme in *The Crowd in History*, pp. 254–7. See also the interesting article by R. B. Rose, "Eighteenth Century Price Riots and Public Policy in England," *International Review of Social History* (1961), pp. 277–92, and the more general remarks in this connection by Joseph Hamburger, *op. cit.*, pp. 199–202.

lowing is a contemporary account of its doings, clearly written from an unfriendly point of view:

> . . . The reformers of London endeavoured to get up an illumination on Monday, the 25th; but that having been a failure, they prevailed on the Lord Mayor to announce another for the evening of Wednesday the 27th. On that evening, the illumination was pretty general. . . . The mobs did a great deal of mischief. A numerous rabble proceeded along the Strand, destroying all windows that were not lighted. . . . In St. James' Square they broke the windows in the houses of the Bishop of London, the Marquis of Cleveland and Lord Grantham. The Bishop of Winchester and Mr. W. W. Wynn, seeing the mob approach, placed candles in their windows, which thus escaped. The mob then proceeded to St. James' street where they broke the windows of Crockford's, Jordan's, the Guards, and other Club houses. They next went to the Duke of Wellington's residence in Piccadilly, and discharged a shower of stones which broke several windows. The Duke's servants fired out of the windows over their heads to frighten them, but without effect. The police-men then informed the mob that the corpse of the Duchess of Wellington was on the premises, which arrested further violence against Apsley House. . . .[46] After the action just described the mob marched off to attack other residences, including that of Robert Peel, the political founder of the police.

At every point the normative character of the mob is clear. In this case their cause was generally popular, and they had the support of the Lord Mayor and many other worthies favoring reform, whereas many mob actions, of course, lacked such sanctions. But "antagonistic cooperation" between the mob and parts of the elite had a long history.[47] Indeed, even prereform electoral politics some-times required parts of the elite not only to compete for the favor of the people but to expose themselves to rough treatment by electors and nonelectors alike. Thus, a French observer of 1819, watching the customary postelection procession of successful parliamentary candidates, described a scene which Halevy calls "one long familiar to the English public":

> [They] were immediately pelted with filth, greeted with a shower of black mud. . . . I saw Lord Nugent with one side all black. . . . Lord John Rus-

---

[46]*Annual Register*, 1831, p. 68. Quoted by Reith in *British Police and the Democratic Ideal*, pp. 90–1. Hamburger places this incident squarely in the "tradition of riot" (see *James Mill. . . .*, pp. 139–42).

[47]It is Hamburger's thesis that in the case of the Reform Crisis of 1830–1832, proreform leaders manipulated the threat of the mob, rather than wielding a substantial revolutionary threat. But this sort of manipulation was itself a tradition — for a case that succeeded before the mob ever took to the streets, see Thomas Perry, *Public Opinion, Propaganda and Politics in Eighteenth Century England: a study of the Jew Bill of 1753* (Cambridge, Massachusetts, 1962). So strong was this tradition that Lady Holland, the wife of the great Whig aristocrat prominent in the struggle for reform, could remark disapprovingly on Wellington's reaction to the prospect of mob attack on his house: "Is it not strange that the Duke of Wellington has boarded with very thick planks *all* his windows upstairs to Piccadilly and the Park? . . . The work of *darkness* began on Coronation Day and is now completed. He says, I hear, that it is to protect his plate glass windows from the mob, who will assail him on the Reform Bill! As it cannot be for thrift, it looks like defiance; and the mob will be irritated when they discover his intentions." Earl of Ilchester, ed., *Elizabeth, Lady Holland to Her Son,* (London, 1946), p. 118. (Italics in original.)

sell attempted with difficulty to wipe off the stinking patches of dirt which continually bespattered his cheeks. . . . Some had their windows broken and their furniture damaged. The houses of Lord Castlereagh and several others met with the same fate. The constables were insufficient to restore order, and the troops had to be called out.[48]

The English elite, then, sometimes lived on rather casual terms with popular volatility so long as the latter did not — as for a time the "dangerous classes" and early working class movements seemed to — challenge the fundamentals of the current system. They did not do so willingly, to be sure, but in a kind of symbiosis in which "consideration" was exchanged for "support." Thus, to see everyday, nonrevolutionary violence or unruliness solely or even largely as an impediment to the emergence of stable democracy is to blur important distinctions between kinds of popular violence and ways in which it may be integrated into a political system. Popular violence which forms part of an articulate system of demands and responses, in which needs and obligations are reasonably clear to each party, may not be at all necessarily "irrational," "criminal," or "point-less" — to use words often applied to riotous protest in contemporary democ-racies. Indeed, the English case suggests that — granted the many other condi-tions that lie outside our present scope — such a system may well conduce to the establishment of stable democracy. For although Hobsbawm calls the system "pre-political," it is one in which ordinary people express their will and elites have learned to listen.[49] The existence of the normative culture of mob and riot in many places other than England is enough to show — if the disclaimer need be made at all — that the mere existence of normative riot and violence is not a sufficient condition for the emergence of institutionalized democracy.[50] Yet in an age when institutions did not organize, represent, or press the claims of ordi-nary people, and in which the streets were therefore a political arena, it is impor-tant to distinguish between kinds of popular violence, rather than consider it wholly as an anachronism.

The Demand for Order in Contemporary Democracy

Such a protodemocratic system of riotous demand and elite response, however, is confined to unpoliced, hierarchical, pre-industrial society. It is not found where

[48]Halevy, *op. cit.*, p. 118.

[49]It is suggestive to compare Hobsbawm's perceptive comment on the situation in parts of Europe which did not experience a comparably gradual development of democratic institutions. Speaking of popular riot and enthusiasm in support of the *status quo*, he remarks: "Legitimate monarchs or institu-tions like churches may not welcome this. The Emperor Francis I of Austria took a poor view of the revolutionary legitism of his people, observing correctly: 'Now they are patriots for me; but one day they may be patriots against me!' From the point of view of the genuinely conservative institution, the ideal is obedience, not enthusiasm, whatever the nature of the enthusiasm. Not for nothing was 'Ruhe ist die Erste Bürgerpflicht' (Tranquility is the first duty of every citizen) the slogan of every German princeling" (*Primitive Rebels . . . .*, p. 119).

[50]See Hobsbawm, *passim*. See also the comprehensive discussion by Charles Tilly, "Reflections on the Revolution of Paris," *Social Problems* (Summer 1964), pp. 99–121, which, among other matters, deals with the literature on these themes in the case of France.

entrepreneurs or managers, career bureaucrats, or professional politicians have displaced former ruling groups; where popular volatility may disrupt tightly woven political and market ecologies; and where the state makes its presence felt ubiquitously in the form of police. In the latter situation, the demand for "law and order" becomes what it was not before — a constitutional imperative stemming from an unprecedentedly pervasive consensus and personified and enforced by police. Simultaneously, the standards of daily decorum increasingly restrict occasions for normative violence; thus Georg Sorel observed at the start of this century how marked had been the decline of daily and casual violence during the last, and how crucial a role these new standards played in the emerging policy of the liberal democratic state toward both the working and dangerous classes.[51]

With rising standards of public order has come an increasing intolerance of criminality, violence, and riotous protest. Daniel Bell has suggested that a breakdown of spatial barriers between the daily round of urban propertied classes and the criminal or unruly poor has made the former more aware of violence in daily life.[52] We may perhaps envisage three stages in such a sequence: one in which the prosperous or respectable often lived in unimagineable closeness to crime and the threat of riot or mob; a second in which these groups succeeded in insulating themselves — spatially, by regroupment in and outside the centers of cities and organizationally, by the police;[53] and a third in which penetrations of these barriers evoke a response which would be considered exorbitant by the standards of earlier years.

The character of the police as a public bureaucracy may also raise expectations about the level of public peace it is possible to attain. As the instrument of public policy they are easily seen in terms of a naive social instrumentalism — as technicians applying efficient means that are in principle capable of fully realizing their ends. Have not public bureaucracies eliminated plague, solved the enduring problems of urban sanitation, and prevented gross impurities in purchased foods? Why cannot the police similarly "clean up" crime and control violence?[54] In

---

[51]See Chapter 6 of *Reflections on Violence*. On the special sensitivity of modern society to public disorder, see Karl Polyani, *The Great Transformation* (New York, 1944), pp. 186–7: "The market system was more allergic to rioting than any other economic system we know. . . . In the nineteenth century breaches of the peace, if committed by armed crowds, were deemed an incipient rebellion and an acute danger to the state; stocks collapsed and there was no bottom to prices. A shooting affray in the streets of the metropolis might destroy a substantial part of the nominal national capital."

[52]"The Myth of Crime Waves: the actual decline of crime in the United States," in *The End of Ideology* (New York, 1962), pp. 151–74.

[53]"The beats vary considerably in size; in those parts of the town which are open and inhabited by the wealthier classes, an occasional visit from a policeman is sufficient, and he traverses a wide district. But the limits of the beat are diminished, and of course the frequency of the visits increased, in proportion to the character and the density of the population, the throng and pressure of traffic, and concentration of property, and the intricacy of the streets. . . . Nor must it be supposed that this system places the wealthier localities at a disadvantage, for it is an axiom in police that you guard St. James' by watching St. Giles' " ("The Police System of London," *Edinburgh Review*, July 1852, p. 5). St. Giles was one of the most notorious of London's "rookeries."

[54]It is more than accidental that Edwin Chadwick (see p. 26, above) was also a prime mover in the reform of urban sanitation. See his report, *Sanitary Conditions of the Labouring Population in England, 1842* (London, 1843).

short, the historic and strategic success of the police raises expectations and exposes them to pressures engendered by the idea of a uniformly peaceful civil society.[55]

Not only are expectations of public order higher than before, but the arena to which these expectations refer has expanded. It has done so not only because of the continuing, though obviously very incomplete, extension of a single moral order throughout the national community — a process which takes territoriality rather than the divisions of class, locality, or group as its ideal boundaries. The arena of expectation widens as smaller formations — regions, states, local communities — find it harder to control or influence the moral climate in which they live. The "nationalization" of civil rights, federal involvement in municipal programs like housing, the erosion of the power of localities to control the content of mass media, pressure from judiciaries on informal and quasilegal police practices — all mean that smaller formations come to see themselves as less able to control or influence their moral destiny.[56] Thinking themselves more vulnerable to incursion from the larger society, they extend moral demand and expectations to a wider environment than in the past was thought relevant to daily life.

These trends mesh with others. The imagery of the "dangerous classes" is being reborn in contemporary America. The nascent demand for a pervasively benign environment arises as the urban poor, disorganized, and unemployed — especially Negroes — bear more heavily upon the awareness and daily life of an urban society in which proportionately more people are "respectable" than ever before.[57] Violence, criminality, and riot become defined not only as undesirable but as threatening the very fabric of social life. Police forces come to be seen as they were in the time of their creation — as a sophisticated and convenient form of garrison force against an internal enemy.[58] Lacking a strong tradition of urban violence as a form of articulate protest, it is all the easier to

[55]See Bell, *op. cit.*, p. 152 on the relationship between better policing and a "higher" crime rate. The artifactual character of this relationship, sometimes hard for contemporaries for whom the police are taken for granted to grasp, was obvious to an observer witnessing the transition to a policed society. See "Causes of the Increase of Crime," *Blackwood's Magazine* (July 1844), p. 5.

[56]Attempting to account for respectable people's greater awareness of violence in daily life, Bell has also suggested that the emergence of heterogeneous audiences for the mass media, which include groups previously less exposed to violent themes, has heightened awareness of violence even as its occurrence in daily life has declined (*ibid.*, pp. 170–4). Simultaneously, local communities and states are losing their formal powers to control such materials and are relying more often on informal control. (See Richard Randall, *Some Political Theories in Motion Picture Censorship Decisions: Prior Restraint Reconsidered.* Paper delivered at the Midwest Conference of Political Science, Bloomington, Indiana, April 1965.)

[57]Here we follow Shils' argument, *op. cit.*, p. 56.

[58]For the American police this situation may render a chronic problem acute. At the time when the police are more urgently charged than ever before to do society's "dirty work" but also are more stringently supervised by the public, various interest groups and the judiciary, their morale and operating problems are further exacerbated by their failure to embody moral consensus in the eyes of the general community, their "clientele," and themselves as thoroughly as do the British police. For detailed observations about some of these matters, especially the last, see Michael Banton, *The Policeman in the Community* (London, 1964), a comparative account of Scottish and American police forces.

define such events as merely criminal.[59] Such definitions work not only on the respectable but also on the riotous poor. Like American society as a whole, the American poor lack a traditional past: on neither side of the boundaries of class and race do the conditions for "articulate riot" exist in generous measure. "Criminal" acts like looting and violent assault are likely to dominate riotous protest, rather than explicitly political gestures. Similarly, the propertied and respectable are ill-prepared to react in terms other than a confrontation with uncontained and shapeless criminality. Articulate riot, however, requires that both rioters and their target or audience jointly define the meaning of riotous acts. The frequency with which recent riots by Negroes in American cities are interpreted officially as "meaningless"[60] contrasts with the ability of the English elite, especially before it was severely threatened from the late eighteenth century on, to interpret the meaning of riotous behavior.

Current concern over violence and riot, then, involves a problem of the political language in which these events are described and interpreted. The problem is likely to sharpen as the official stance, relying in part upon the rhetoric of diagnostic sociology, becomes strained by the urgent pressure of events. The gap between the official diagnostic style and a cultural response that makes little provision for "normative riot" is likely to widen as the urban situation grows even more aggravated. It therefore remains to be seen whether American elites — creative, professional, and political — can or will sustain a diagnostic posture that seeks and interprets the meaning of these events.

It is not to idealize even the optimal "traditional" political society — that of England — with its brutalities, squalidness, and hardness of soul, to point out that it often provided the unorganized poor with a language by which, in the absence of representative institutions or the ability to participate in them, they might articulately address the propertied classes through riot and disorder. And it is not to derogate the American adventure in modernity to suggest that, however richly endowed with representative and responsive institutions, it has not provided such a language for those in its cities who have long been outside their compass — a language whose grammar is shared by speaker and listener, rioter and pillaged, violent and frightened.

---

[59]Obviously, the rural South would require special treatment. See W. J. Cash, *The Mind of the South* (New York, 1941), *passim,* and H. C. Brearly, "The Pattern of Violence", in W. T. Couch, ed., *Culture in the South* (Chapel Hill, 1934). Our focus, however, is on urban situations. Thus, for example, there is a suggestion in that the few food riots of nineteenth-century New York, in 1837 and 1857, were carried out largely by foreign-born, rather than native, poor. See the chapters on these episodes in J. T. Headley, *The Great Riots of New York* (New York, 1873).

[60]I am indebted to Robert Fogelson's analysis (as yet unpublished) of these riots and of the official responses to them — notably the McCone Commission's report on the Watts riot of August 1965.

7. Peter K. Manning

The Police: Mandate, Strategies, and Appearances

I. Introduction

All societies have their share of persistent, chronic problems — problems of life, of death, problems of property and security, problems of man's relationship to what he consecrates. And because societies have their quota of troubles, they have developed ways in which to distribute responsibility for dealing with them. The division of labor that results is not only an allocation of functions and rewards, it is a moral division as well. In exchange for money, goods, or services, these groups — such as lawyers or barbers or clergymen or pharmacists — have a *license* to carry out certain activities that others may not. This license is a legally defined right, and no other group or groups may encroach upon it.[1]

The right to perform an occupation may entail the permission to pick up garbage or to cut open human bodies and transfer organs from one to another. What it always involves, however, is a series of tasks and associated attitudes and values that set apart a specialized occupational group from all the others. Further, the licensed right to perform an occupation may include a claim to the right to define the proper conduct of others toward matters concerned with the work. The claim, if granted, is the occupation's *mandate*. The mandate may vary from a right to live dangerously to the right to define the conditions of work and functions of related personnel.

The professional mandate is not easily won, of course, for clients are often unwilling to accept the professional definition of their problem. Professions claim a body of theory and practice to justify their right to discover, define, and deal with problems. The medical profession, for example, is usually considered the model of a vocation with a secure license and mandate. Yet even in medicine the client may refuse to accept the diagnosis; he may change physicians or fail to follow doctor's orders or insist upon defining his troubles as the product of a malady best cured by hot lemonade or prayer. The contraction and expansion of an occupation's mandate reflects the concerns society has with the services

Reprinted by permission of the author from *Crime and Justice in American Society*, edited by Jack D. Douglas (Bobbs-Merril Company, 1971), pp. 149–193.

[1]See Everett C. Hughes, *Men and Their Work* (New York: The Free Press, 1958), chap. 6; idem, "The Study of Occupations," in *Sociology Today*, ed. R. K. Merton, Leonard Broom, and L. S. Cottrell (New York: Basic Books, 1959), pp. 442–458.

it provides, with its organization, and with its effectiveness. In times of crisis, it is the professions that are questioned first.[2]

Some occupations are not as fortunate as others in their ability to delimit a societal "trouble" and deal with it systematically. The more power and authority a profession has, the better able it is to gain and maintain control over the symbolic meanings with which it is associated in the public's mind. As we have become less concerned with devils and witches as causes of mental illness, clergymen have lost ground to psychiatrists who have laid claim to a secular cure for madness; in this sense, mental illness is a product of the definitions supplied by psychiatry. A profession, therefore, must not only compete with its clientele's definitions, it must also defend itself against the definitions of competing groups. Is a backache better treated by a Christian Scientist, an osteopath, a chiropractor, a masseuse, or an M.D.? Professional groups whose tools are less well-developed, whose theory is jerry-built or unproved, and who are unable to produce results in our consumer-oriented society will be beset with public doubt, concern, and agitation. In other words, these are the groups that have been unable to define their mandate for solving social "troubles" in such a way that it can be accomplished with ease and to the satisfaction of those they intend to serve.

The police have trouble. Among the many occupations now in crisis, they best symbolize the shifts and strains in our changing socio-political order. They have been assigned the task of crime prevention, crime detection, and the apprehension of criminals. Based on their legal monopoly of violence, they have staked out a mandate that claims to include the efficient, apolitical, and professional enforcement of the law. It is the contention of this essay that the police have staked out a vast and unmanageable social domain. And what has happened as a result of their inability to accomplish their self-proclaimed mandate is that the police have resorted to the manipulation of *appearances*.

We shall attempt to outline the nature of the police mandate, or their definiton of social trouble, their methods of coping with this trouble, and the consequences of their efforts. After developing a sociological analysis of the paradoxes of police work and discussing the heroic attempts — *strategies* – by police to untangle these paradoxes, we shall also consider the recommendations of the President's crime commission[3] and assess their value as a means of altering and improving the practical art of managing public order.

To turn for the moment to "practical matters," the same matters to which we shall return before concluding, the troubles of the police, the problems and paradoxes of their mandate in modern society, have become more and more intense. Police today may be more efficient in handling their problems than were the first bobbies who began to patrol London in 1829. Or they may not be. There may

[2]Hughes, *Men and Their Work.*
[3]The President's Commission on Law Enforcement and Administration of Justice (hereafter cited as President's Commission), *The Challenge of Crime in a Free Society* (Washington, D.C.: United States Government Printing Office, 1967); and idem, *Task Force Report: The Police* (Washington, D.C.: United States Government Printing Office, 1967).

or may not be more crime. Individual rights may or may not be greatly threatened by crime or crime-fighters, and the enforcement of law in view of recent Supreme Court decisions may or may not be a critical issue in crime control. The police may or may not have enough resources to do their job, and they may or may not be allocating them properly. Peace-keeping rather than law enforcement may or may not be the prime need in black communities, and the police may or may not need greater discretionary powers in making an arrest. But however these troubles are regarded, they exist. They are rooted deeply in the mandate of the police.

Some Sociological Assumptions. This essay makes several assumptions about occupations, about people as they execute occupational roles, about organizations as loci or structures for occupational activities, and about the nature of society. Not all activity taking place "on the job" can be construed as "work"; goldbricking is not unknown in American society and some professionals have even been known to use their places of work to conduct business somewhat outside the mandate of their organization. An individual's "organizational" behavior varies with what the organization is said to require or permit, with his particular place in the organizational hierarchy, and with the degree of congruence between the individual's personal definition of his role and the organization's definition of his role. In a given situation, then, organizational rules and regulations may be important sources of meanings ("He's working hard"), or other criteria may provide more relevant meanings of behavior ("He can't be expected to work. His wife just had a baby"). The ways in which people explain or account for their own organizational activities and those of others are problematic. How do people refer to their organizational roles and activities? How do they construct their moral obligations to the organization? What do they think they owe the organization? How does this sense of obligation and commitment pattern or constrain them in another role — the role of golfer or father or politician?

People as they perform their roles are actors. They are alert to the small cues that indicate meaning and intention — the wink, the scowl, the raised eyebrow. Those who attend to these behavioral clues are the audience. All actors try to maximize the positive impression they make on others, and both experience and socialization provide them with a repertoire of devices to manage their appearance.

People as actors in roles must also make assumptions about their audience. The politician, for example must make certain assumptions about his constituency, the lawyer certain assumptions about clients. Assumptions are an important part of urban life. Some actors with white faces, for instance, may make certain assumptions about others with black faces, that they will be ill-mannered or badly educated and that any request for directions is a prelude to a holdup. Assumptions are not simply individual in nature; they are shared, patterned, and passed on from one social group to the next.

One of the most important aspects of assumptions, however, is that they are the basis for strategies.[4] Strategies arise from the need of organizations and individuals to cope with persistent social problems about which assumptions have been made. Strategies are often a means of survival in a competitive environment; they can be inferred from the allocation of resources or from the behavior and pronouncements of an organization. In short, strategies assist any organization within the society in managing its appearance and in controlling the behavior of its audience.

All organizations and individuals, we assume, are bent on maximizing their impressions in order to gain control over an audience.[5] The audience for the police is diverse; it should be considered many audiences. For the police must convince the politicians that they have used their allocated resources efficiently; they must persuade the criminals that they are effective crime-fighters; they must assure the broader public that they are controlling crime. Rather than a single rhetoric — the "use of words to form attitudes or induce actions in other human agents"[6] — directed toward convincing one audience, the police must develop many rhetorics. Linguistic strategies to control audiences are only one of many ploys used by the police organization to manage its impression. Not all the results of the use of rhetorics are intended; the consequence of the rhetorical "war on crime" in Detroit in the fall of 1969, to cite one example, was a continued advance in the city's downtown crime rate. Moreover, rhetoric can take on different meanings even within the organizational hierarchy. To patrolmen, the term "professionalism" means control over hours and salary and protection from arbitrary punishment from "upstairs"; to the chief and the higher administrators, it relates to the public-administration notions of efficiency, technological expertise, and standards of excellence in recruitment and training.

Tactics are the means by which a strategy is implemented. If the strategy is to mount a war on crime, then one tactic might be to flood the downtown area with scooter-mounted patrolmen. Tactics, in other words, are the ways in which one group of people deals with others in face-to-face encounters. How does the policeman handle a family quarrel in which the wife has the butcher knife and the husband already knows how sharp it is? Strategies pertain to general forms of action or rhetoric while tactics refer to the specific action or the specific words used to best meet a specific, problematic situation.[7] The tactic of flattery may be far more effective — and safer — in wresting the butcher knife than a leap over the kitchen table.

---

[4]The important, sociological notions of "strategy" and "tactics" come from military theory and game theory. See, for example, Erving Goffman, *The Presentation of Self in Everyday Life* (Garden City, N.Y.: Doubleday, 1956).

[5]Ibid.

[6]Kenneth Burke, *A Grammar of Motives and a Rhetoric of Motives* (New York: Meridian Books, 1962), p. 565.

[7]D. W. Ball makes this distinction between rhetoric and what he terms "situated vocabularies" in "The Problematics of Respectability" in *Deviance and Respectability*, ed. Jack D. Douglas (New York: Basic Books, 1970).

All occupations possess strategies and tactics, by means of which they attempt to control their most significant audiences. However, our analysis must do more than describe the existence of such means of creating impressions. So far as the police are concerned, impression management, or the construction of appearances, cannot substitute for significant control of crime. To maintain the dramaturgic metaphor, we suggest that there are significant flaws and contradictions in the performance of the police that cast a serious doubt on the credibility of their occupational mandate.

The mandate of the police is fraught with difficulties, many of them, we shall argue, self-created. They have defined their task in such a way that they cannot, because of the nature of American social organization, hope to honor it to the satisfaction of the public. We will argue that the appearances that the police create — that they control crime and that they attain a high level of efficiency — are transparent on close examination, that they may, in fact, be created as a sop to satisfy the public's impossible expectations for police performance. By utilizing the rhetoric of crime control, the police claim the responsibility for the social processes that beget the illegal acts. They cannot control these social processes that are embedded in American values, norms, and cultural traditions. Creating the appearance of controlling them is only a temporizing policy; it is not the basis for a sound, honorable mandate.

The police mandate and the problems it creates in American society are our central concern. We will rely on the concepts of actor, organization, and audience, of mandate, and of strategy and appearances. We will show that the police mandate, as presently defined, is full of contradictions. We will further demonstrate that the strategies and tactics of the American police are failing in a serious way to meet the need of controlling crime.

The Occupational Culture of the Police. Before beginning an analysis of the police mandate, a brief comment is necessary about the occupational culture of our law enforcers. The American police act in accord with their assumptions about the nature of social life, and their most important assumptions originate with their need to maintain control over both their mandate and their self-esteem. The policeman's self is an amalgam of evaluations made by the many audiences before whom he, as social actor, must perform: his peers, his family, his immediate superiors and the higher administrators, his friends on and off duty. His most meaningful standards of performance are the ideals of his *occupational culture*. The policeman judges himself against the ideal policeman as described in police occupational lore and imagery. What a "good policeman" does is an omnipresent standard. The occupational culture, however, contains more than the definition of a good policeman. It contains the typical values, norms, attitudes, and material paraphernalia of an occupational group.

An occupational culture also prompts the *assumptions* about everyday life that become the basis for organizational strategies and tactics. Recent studies of the occupational culture of the police allow the formulation of the following postulates or assumptions, all of which are the basis for police strategies to be discussed later:

1. People cannot be trusted; they are dangerous.
2. Experience is better than abstract rules.
3. You must make people respect you.
4. Everyone hates a cop.
5. The legal system is untrustworthy; policemen make the best decisions about guilt or innocence.
6. People who are not controlled will break laws.
7. Policemen must appear respectable and be efficient.
8. Policemen can most accurately identify crime and criminals.
9. The major jobs of the policeman are to prevent crime and to enforce the laws.
10. Stronger punishment will deter criminals from repeating their errors.[8]

Some qualifications about these postulates are in order. They apply primarily to the American noncollege-educated patrolman. They are less applicable to administrators of urban police departments and to members of minority groups within these departments. Nor do they apply accurately to nonurban, state, and federal policemen.

We shall now describe the paradoxes of the police mandate, the strategies of the police in dealing with their troubles, and some of the findings and recommendations of the President's crime commission as they bear on the current attempt by the police to make a running adjustment to their problems.

II. The "Impossible" Mandate

The police in modern society are in agreement with their audiences — which include their professional interpreters, the American family, criminals, and politicians — in at least one respect: they have an "impossible" task. Certainly, all professionals have impossible tasks insofar as they try to surmount the problems of collective life that resist easy solutions. The most "successful" occupations, however, have managed to construct a mandate in terms of their own vision of the world. The

---

[8]These postulates have been drawn from the work of Michael Banton, *The Policeman in the Community* (New York: Basic Books, 1965); the articles in *The Police: Six Sociological Essays*, ed. David Bordua (New York: John Wiley & Sons, 1967), esp. those by Albert J. Reiss and David Bordua, and John H. McNamara; Arthur Niederhoffer, *Behind the Shield* (Garden City, N.Y.: Doubleday, 1967); Jerome Skolnick, *Justice Without Trial* (New York: John Wiley & Sons, 1966); and William A. Westley, "Violence and the Police," *American Journal of Sociology* 59 (July 1953), pp. 34–41; idem, "Secrecy and the Police," *Social Forces* 34 (March 1956), pp. 254–257; idem, "The Police: Law, Custom and Morality," in *The Study of Society*, ed. Peter I. Rose (New York: Random House, 1967). See also James Q. Wilson, *Varieties of Police Behavior: The Management of Law and Order in Eight Communities* (Cambridge: Harvard University Press, 1968); idem, "The Police and Their Problems: A Theory," *Public Policy* 12 (1963), pp. 189–216; idem, "Generational and Ethnic Differences Among Police Officers," *American Journal of Sociology* 69 (March 1964), pp. 522–528.

policeman's mandate, on the other hand, is defined largely by his publics — not, at least at the forma! level, in his own terms.

Several rather serious consequences result from the public's image of the police. The public is aware of the dramatic nature of a small portion of police work, but it ascribes the element of excitement to all police activities. To much of the public, the police are seen as alertly ready to respond to citizen demands, as crime-fighters, as an efficient, bureaucratic, highly organized force that keeps society from falling into chaos. The policeman himself considers the essence of his role to be the dangerous and heroic enterprise of crook-catching and the watchful prevention of crimes.[9] The system of positive and negative sanctions from the public and within the department encourages this heroic conception. The public wants crime prevented and controlled; that is, it wants criminals caught. Headlines herald the accomplishments of G-Men and F.B.I. agents who often do catch dangerous men, and the reputation of these federal authorities not infrequently rubs off on local policemen who are much less adept at catching criminals.

In an effort to gain the public's confidence in their ability, and to insure thereby the solidity of their mandate, the police have encouraged the public to continue thinking of them and their work in idealized terms, terms, that is, which grossly exaggerate the actual work done by police. They do engage in chases, in gunfights, in careful sleuthing. But these are rare events. Most police work resembles any other kind of work: it is boring, tiresome, sometimes dirty, sometimes technically demanding, but it is rarely dangerous. Yet the occasional chase, the occasional shoot-out, the occasional triumph of some extraordinary detective work have been seized upon by the police and played up to the public. The public's response has been to demand even more dramatic crook-catching and crime prevention, and this demand for arrests has been converted into an index for measuring how well the police accomplish their mandate. The public's definitions have been converted by the police organization into distorted criteria for promotion, success, and security. Most police departments promote men from patrol to detective work, a generally more desirable duty, for ''good pinches'' — arrests that are most likely to result in convictions.[10] The protection of the public welfare, however, including personal and property safety, the prevention of crime, and the preservation of individual civil rights, is hardly achieved by a high pinch rate. On the contrary, it might well be argued that protection of the public welfare could best be indexed by a low arrest rate. Because their mandate automatically entails mutually contradictory ends — protecting both public order and individual rights — the police resort

[9]Although the imagery of the police and their own self-definition coincide on the dangers of being a policeman, at least one study has found that many other occupations are more dangerous. Policemen kill six times as many people as policemen are killed in the line of duty. In 1955, Robin found that the rate of police fatalities on duty, including accidents, was 33 per 100,000, less than the rate for mining (94), agriculture (55), construction (76), and transportation (44). Between 1950 and 1960, an average of 240 persons were killed each year by policemen — approximately six times the number of policemen killed by criminals. Gerald D. Robin, ''Justifiable Homicide by Police Officers,'' *Journal of Criminal Law, Criminology and Police Science* 54 (1963), pp. 225–231.

[10]Niederhoffer, *Behind the Shield*, p. 221.

to managing their public image and the indexes of their accomplishment. And the ways in which the police manage their appearance are consistent with the assumptions of their occupational culture, with the public's view of the police as a social-control agency, and with the ambiguous nature of our criminal law.

The Problematic Nature of Law and Order. The criminal law is one among many instrumentalities of social control. It is an explicit set of rules created by political authority; it contains provisions for punishment by officials designated with the responsibility to interpret and enforce the rules which should be uniformly applied to all persons within a politically defined territory.[11] This section discusses the relationships between the laws and the mores of a society, the effect of the growth of civilized society on law enforcement, and the problematic nature of crime in an advanced society. The differential nature of enforcement will be considered as an aspect of peace-keeping, and will lead to the discussion of the police in the larger political system.

A society's laws, it is often said, reflect its customs; it can also be said that the growth of the criminal law is proportionate to the decline in the consistency and binding nature of these mores. In simpler societies, where the codes and rules of behavior were well known and homogeneous, sanctions were enforced with much greater uniformity and predictability. Social control was isomorphic with one's obligations to family, clan, and age group, and the political system of the tribe. In a modern, differentiated society, a minimal number of values and norms are shared. And because the fundamental, taken-for-granted consensus on what is proper and respectable has been blurred or shattered, or, indeed, never existed, criminal law becomes a basis of social control. As Quinney writes, "Where correct conduct cannot be agreed upon, the criminal law serves to control the behavior of all persons within a political jurisdiction."[12]

Social control through the criminal law predominates in a society only when other means of control have failed. When it does predominate, it no longer reflects the mores of the society. It more accurately reflects the interests of shifting power groups within the society. As a result, the police, as the designated enforcers of a system of criminal laws, are undercut by circumstances that accentuate the growing differences between the moral order and the legal order.

One of these complicating circumstances is simply the matter of social changes, which further stretch the bond between the moral and the legal. The law frequently lags behind the changes in what society deems acceptable and unacceptable practice. At other times, it induces changes, such as those pertaining to civil rights, thereby anticipating acceptable practice. The definition of crime, then, is a pro-

[11]See Richard Quinney, "Is Criminal Behavior Deviant Behavior?" *British Journal of Criminology* 5 (April 1965), p. 133. The following two pages draw heavily from Quinney. See also R. C. Fuller, "Morals and the Criminal Law," *Journal of Criminal Law, Criminology and Police Science* 32 (March–April 1942), pp. 624–630.

[12]Quinney, "Criminal Behavior," p. 133.

duct of the relationship between social structure and the law. Crime, to put it another way, is not a homogeneous entity.

The perspective of the patrolman as he goes about his daily rounds is a legalistic one. The law and the administrative actions of his department provide him with a frame of reference for exercising the mandate of the police. The citizen, on the other hand, does not live his life in accordance with a legalistic framework; he defines his acts in accordance with a moral or ethical code provided him by his family, his religion, his social class. For the most part, he sees law enforcement as an intervention in his private affairs.

No matter what the basis for actions of private citizens may be, however, the patrolman's job is one of practical decision-making within a legalistic pattern. His decisions are expected to include an understanding of the law as a system of formal rules, the enforcement practices emphasized by his department, and a knowledge of the specific facts of an allegedly illegal situation. The law includes little formal recognition of the variation in the private arrangement of lives. Even so, the policeman is expected to take these into account also. No policeman can ever be provided with a handbook that could tell him, at a moment's notice, just what standards to apply in enforcing the law and in maintaining order. Wilson summarizes the difficulty inherent in law enforcement as follows:

> Most criminal laws define *acts* (murder, rape, speeding, possessing narcotics), which are held to be illegal; people may disagree as to whether the act should be illegal, as they do with respect to narcotics, for example, but there is little disagreement as to what the behavior in question consists of. Laws regarding disorderly conduct and the like assert, usually by implication, that there is a condition ("public order") that can be diminished by various actions. The difficulty, of course, is that public order is nowhere defined and can never be defined unambiguously because what constitutes order is a matter of opinion and convention, not a state of nature. (An unmurdered person, an unraped woman, and an unpossessed narcotic can be defined so as to be recognizable to any reasonable person.) An additional difficulty, a corollary of the first, is the impossibility of specifying, except in the extreme case, what degree of disorder is intolerable and who is to be held culpable for that degree. A suburban street is quiet and pleasant; a big city street is noisy and (to some) offensive; what degree of noise and offense, and produced by whom, constitutes "disorderly conduct"?[13]

The complexity of law enforcement stems from both the problem of police "discretion" and the inherent tensions between the maintenance of order and individual rights. The law contains rules on how to maintain order; it contains substantive definitions of crime, penalties for violations, and the conditions under which the commission of a crime is said to have been intended.[14] Further, the law contains procedures for the administration of justice and for the protection

[13]Wilson, *Varieties of Police Behavior,* pp. 21–22.
[14]Skolnick, *Justice Without Trial,* pp. 7–8, 9.

of the individual. The complexities of law enforcement notwithstanding, however, the modern policeman is frequently faced with the instant problem of defining an action as either legal or illegal, of deciding, in other words, whether to intervene and, if so, what tactic to use. He moves in a dense web of social action and social meanings, burdened by a problematic, complex array of ever-changing laws. Sometimes the policeman must quickly decide very abstract matters. Though a practitioner of the legal arts, his tools at hand are largely obscure, ill-developed, and crude. With little formal training, the rookie must learn his role by absorbing the theories, traditions, and personal whims of experienced patrolmen.

Police Work as Peace-Keeping.[15] The thesis of two recent major works on the police, Wilson's *The Varieties of Police Behavior* and Skolnick's *Justice Without Trial,* can be paraphrased as follows: the policeman must exercise discretion in matters involving life and death, honor and dishonor, and he must do so in an environment that he perceives as threatening, dangerous, hostile, and volatile. He sees his efficiency constrained by the law and by the police organization. Yet, he must effectively manage "disorder" in a variety of unspecified ways, through methods usually learned and practiced on the job. As a result of these conditions, the policeman, in enforcing his conception of order often violates the rights of citizens.

Many observers of police work regard the primary function of a policeman as that of a *peace-keeper,* not a *law enforcer.* According to this view, police spend most of their time attending to order-maintaining functions, such as finding lost children, substituting as ambulance drivers, or interceding in quarrels of one sort or another. To these observers, the police spend as little as 10 to 15 per cent of their time on law enforcement — responding to burglary calls or trying to find stolen cars. The large-scale riots and disorders of recent years accounted for few police man-hours. Wilson illustrates the peace-keeping (order maintenance) and law-enforcement distinction this way:

> The difference between order maintenance and law enforcement is not simply the difference between "little stuff" and "real crime" or between misdemeanors and felonies. The distinction is fundamental to the police role, for the two functions involve quite dissimilar police actions and judgments. Order maintenance arises out of a dispute among citizens who accuse each other of being at fault; law enforcement arises out of the victimization of an innocent party by a person whose guilt must be proved. Handling a disor-

---

[15]This perspective on police work is emphasized by Wilson, *Varieties of Police Behavior;* Banton, *The Policeman in the Community;* and Skolnick, *Justice Without Trial.* In addition, see the more legalistically oriented work of Wayne R. LaFave, *Arrest,* ed. F. J. Remington (Boston: Little Brown, 1965); Joseph Goldstein, "Police Discretion Not to Invoke the Legal Process: Low-Visibility Decisions in the Administration of Justice," *Yale Law Journal* 69 (1960), pp. 543–594; and Herman Goldstein, "Police Discretion: The Ideal Versus the Real," *Public Administration Review* 23 (September 1963), pp. 140–148.

derly situation requires the officer to make a judgment about what constitutes an appropriate standard of behavior; law enforcement requires him only to compare a person's behavior with a clear legal standard. Murder or theft is defined, unambiguously, by statutes; public peace is not. Order maintenance rarely leads to an arrest; law enforcement (if the suspect can be found) typically does. Citizens quarreling usually want the officer to "do something," but they rarely want him to make an arrest (after all, the disputants are usually known or related to each other). Furthermore, whatever law is broken in a quarrel is usually a misdemeanor, and in most states, an officer cannot make a misdemeanor arrest unless one party or the other will swear out a formal complaint (which is even rarer).[16]

The complexity of the law and the difficulty in obtaining a complainant combine to tend to make the policeman underenforce the law — to overlook, ignore, dismiss, or otherwise erase the existence of many enforceable breaches of the law.

Some researchers and legalists have begun to piece together a pattern of the conditions under which policemen have a tendency not to enforce the law. From a study of police in three Midwestern states, LaFave has concluded that two considerations characterize a decision not to arrest. The first is that the crime is unlikely to reach public attention — for example, that it is of a private nature or of low visibility — and the second is that underenforcement is unlikely to be detected or challenged.[17] Generally, the conditions under which policemen are less likely to enforce the law are those in which they perceive little public consensus on the law, or in which the law is ambiguous. LaFave found that policemen are not apt to enforce rigorously laws that are viewed by the public as dated, or that are used on the rare occasions when the public order is being threatened.

There is a certain Benthamic calculus involved in all arrests, a calculus that is based on pragmatic considerations such as those enumerated by LaFave. Sex, age, class, and race might also enter into the calculus of whether the law should be enforced. In a case study of the policeman assigned to skid row, Bittner illustrates the great degree of discretion exercised by the policeman. Yet the law, often reified by the policeman, is rarely a clear guide to action — despite the number of routine actions that might be termed "typical situations that policemen perceive as *demand conditions* for action without arrest."[18]

In the exercise of discretion, in the decision to enforce the law or to underenforce, the protection of individual rights is often at stake. But individual rights are frequently in opposition to the preservation of order, as a totalitarian state exemplifies in the extreme. The police try to manage these two contradictory demands by emphasizing their peace-keeping functions. This emphasis succeeds only when a consensus exists on the nature of the order (peace) to be preserved.

---

[16]James Q. Wilson, "What Makes a Better Policeman?" *Atlantic* 223 (March 1969), p. 131.

[17]LaFave, *Arrest*.

[18]Egon Bittner, "The Police on Skid-Row: A Study of Peace-Keeping," *American Sociological Review* 32 (October 1967), pp. 699–715.

The greater the difference in viewpoint between the police and the public on the degree and kind of order to be preserved, the greater will be antagonism between the two; the inevitable result of this hostility will be "law breaking."

The resolution of the contradictions and complexities inherent in the police mandate, including the problems of police discretion, of individual rights, of law enforcement and peace-keeping, is not helped, however, by the involvement of police in politics. Politics only further complicates the police mandate. The law itself is a political phenomenon, and at the practical level of enforcing it, the local political system is yet another source of confusion.

The Police in the Political System. In theory, the American police are apolitical. Their own political values and political aims are supposed to be secondary to the institutional objective of law enforcement. In practice, however, police organizations function in a political context; they operate in a public political arena and their mandate is defined politically. They may develop strategies to create and maintain the appearance of being apolitical in order to protect their organizational autonomy, but they are nonetheless a component of American political machinery. There are three reasons why the police are inextricably involved in the political system, the first and most obvious being that the vast majority of the police in this nation are locally controlled.

[Among the 40,000 law-enforcement agencies in the United States], there are only 50 . . . on the federal level . . . 200 on the state level. The remaining 39,750 agencies are dispersed throughout the many counties, cities, towns, and villages that form our local governments. . . . Only 3,050 agencies are located in counties and 3,700 in cities. The great majority of the police forces — 33,000 — are distributed throughout boroughs, towns, and villages.[19]

In 1966 there were 420,000 full- and part-time law-enforcement officers and civilians employed by police agencies in the United States. Most of them — 371,000 — were full-time employees; about 11 per cent — 46,000 — were civilians. Of the full-timers, 23,000 served at the federal level of government, 40,000 at the state level, and the remaining 308,000, or 83 per cent of the total, were divided between county and local political jurisdictions. Of the 308,000, somewhat more than 197,000 were employees of counties, cities under 250,000, townships, boroughs, and villages; the balance of 110,500 served in the 55 American cities with populations of more than 250,000. The number of police personnel in any one type of political division varied widely, of course. For example, on the county level of government, the roster of the 3,050 sheriff's offices in the United States ranged from a one-man force in Putnam County, Georgia, to a 5,515-man force in Los Angeles County.

What all these figures indicate is the massive dispersal of police authority — and political authority — throughout the nation. What these figures also indicate is the existence of overlapping laws governing law enforcement.

[19]President's Commission, *Task Force Report: The Police,* pp. 7, 8–9.

Further, they show that the responsibility for maintaining public order in America is decentralized, and that law-enforcement officers are largely under the immediate control of local political authorities.

The second reason why the police are an integral part of the political system is this: law is a political entity, and the administration of criminal law unavoidably encompasses political values and political ends. The police are directly related to a political system that develops and defines the law, itself a product of interpretations of what is right and proper from the perspective of different politically powerful segments within the community.

The third reason why the police are tied to the political system emanates from the second: the police must administer the law. Many factors pattern this enforcement, but they all reflect the political organization of society. The distribution of power and authority, for example, rather than the striving for justice, or equal treatment under the law, can have a direct bearing on enforcement.

Because law enforcement is for the most part locally controlled, sensitivity to local political trends remains an important element in police practice. Since the police are legally prohibited from being publicly political, they often appeal to different community groups, and participate sub rosa in others, in order to influence the determination of public policy. Community policy, whether made by the town council or the mayor or the city manager, affects pay scales, operating budgets, personnel, administrative decisions, and, to some extent, organizational structure. The police administrator must, therefore, be responsive to these controls, and and he must deal with them in an understanding way. He must be sensitive to the demands of the local politicians — even while maintaining the loyalty of the lower ranks through a defense of their interests.

There are several direct effects of the political nature of the police mandate. One is that many policemen become alienated; they lose interest in their role as enforcers and in the law as a believable criterion. The pressures of politics also erode loyalty to the police organization and not infrequently lead to collusion with criminals and organized crime.

The policeman's exposure to danger, his social background, low pay, low morale, his vulnerability in a repressive bureaucracy all conspire to make him susceptible to the lures of the underhanded and the appeals of the political. Studies summarized by Skolnick[20] reveal a political profile of the policeman as a conservative, perhaps reactionary, person of lower-class or lower-middle-class origin, often a supporter of radical right causes, often prejudiced and repressive, often extremely ambivalent about the rights of others. The posutlates or assumptions of the police culture, the suspiciousness, fear, low self-esteem, and distrust of others are almost diametrically opposed to the usual conception of the desirable democratic man.

Thus, the enforcement of some laws is personally distasteful. Civil-rights legislation, for example, can be anathema. Or truculence can be the reaction to an

---

[20]Jerome Skolnick, ed., *The Politics of Protest* (New York: Simon & Schuster, 1969), pp. 252–253.

order relaxing controls in ghettos during the summer months. It is the ambivalence of policemen toward certain laws and toward certain local policies that fragments loyalty within a department and causes alienation.

There is another consequence of the political nature of the police mandate: the police are tempted. They are tempted not to enforce the law by organized crime, by the operators of illegal businesses such as prostitution, and by fine "law-abiding," illegally parked citizens. All too frequently, the police submit to temptations, becoming in the process exemplars of the corruption typical of modern society, where the demand for "criminal services" goes on at the station house.[21]

Police and politics within the community are tightly interlocked. The sensitivity of the police to their political audiences, their operation within the political system of criminal justice, and their own personal political attitudes undermine their efforts to fulfill their contradictory mandate and to appear politically neutral.

The Efficient, Symptom-Oriented Organization. The Wickersham report, the Hoover administration's report on crime and law enforcement in the United States, was published in 1931. This precursor of the Johnson administration's *The Challenge of Crime in a Free Society* became a rallying point for advocates of police reform. One of its central themes was the lack of "professionalism" among the police of the time — their lack of special training, their corruption, their brutality, and their use of illegal procedures in law enforcement. And one of its results was that the police, partly in order to demonstrate their concern with scientific data gathering on crime and partly to indicate their capacity to "control" crime itself, began to stress crime statistics as a major component of professional police work.

Crime statistics, therefore — and let this point be emphasized — became a police construction. The actual amount of crime committed in a society is unknown — and probably unknowable, given the private nature of most crime. The *crime rate,* consequently, is simply a construction of police activities. That is, the crime rate pertains only to "crimes known to the police," crimes that have been reported to or observed by the police and for which adequate grounds exist for assuming that a violation of the law has, in fact, taken place. (The difference between the *actual* and *known crimes* is often called the "dark figure of crime.") Of course, the construction of a crime rate placed the police in a logically weak position in which they still find themselves. If the crime rate is rising, they argue that more police support is needed to fight the war against crime; if the crime rate is stable or declining, they argue that they have successfully combated the crime menace — a heads-I-win-tails-you-lose proposition.

In spite of their inability to control the commission of illegal acts (roughly, the actual rate), since they do not know about all crime, the police have claimed

---

[21]There are several popular treatments of police corruption, none of them very good. Ralph L. Smith, *The Tarnished Badge* (New York: Thomas Y. Crowell, 1965); Ed Cray, *The Big Blue Line* (New York: Coward-McCann, 1967).

responsibility for crime control, using the crime rate as an index of their success. This use of the crime rate to measure success is somewhat analogous to their use of a patrolman's arrest rate as an indication of his personal success in law enforcement. Questions about the actual amount of crime and the degree of control exercised are thus bypassed in favor of an index that offers great potential for organizational or bureaucratic control. Instead of grappling with the difficult issue of defining the ends of police work and an operational means for accomplishing them, the police have opted for "efficient" law-enforcement defined in terms of fluctuations of the crime rate. They have transformed concern with undefined ends into concern with available means. Their inability to cope with the causes of crime — which might offer them a basis for defining their ends — shifts their "organizational focus" into symptomatic concerns, that is, into a preoccupation with the rate of crime, not its reasons.

This preoccupation with the symptoms of a problem rather than with the problem itself is typical of all bureaucracies. For one characteristic of a bureaucracy is goal-displacement. Bureaucratic organizations tend to lose track of their goals and engage in ritual behavior, substituting means for ends. As a whole, bureaucracies become so engrossed in pursuing, defending, reacting to, and, even, in creating immediate problems that their objective is forgotten. This tendency to displace goals is accelerated by the one value dear to all bureaucracies — efficiency. Efficiency is the be-all and end-all of bureaucratic organizations. Thus, they can expend great effort without any genuine accomplishment.

The police are burdened with the "efficiency problem." They claim to be an efficient bureaucratic organization, but they are unable to define for themselves and others precisely what it is they are being efficient about. In this respect, they do not differ from other paper-shuffling organizations. The police's problem is that the nature of their work is uncertain and negatively defined. It is uncertain in the absence of a consensus not only between the police and the public but also among themselves as to what the goals of a police department should be. It is defined in the negative because the organization punishes its members — patrolmen — for violating departmental procedures but offers no specifications on what they should do or how they should do it.

What do the police do about the problematic nature of law, about the problems arising from their involvement with politics, about their preoccupation with the symptoms of crime rather than the causes? Do they selectively adopt some strategies at the expense of others? Do they vacillate? Are the roles of the organization's members blurred? Before answering these questions, let us examine how the police, through various strategies, manage their appearance before the public. The questions will then be easier to answer.

III. Major Strategies of the Police

The responsibilities of the police lead them to pursue contradictory and unattainable ends. They share with all organizations and occupations, however, the ability to avoid solving their problems. Instead, they concentrate on managing them through strategies. Rather than resolving their dilemmas, the police have manipulated them with a professional eye on just how well the public accepts their dexterity. Thus, law enforcement becomes a self-justifying system. It becomes more responsive to its own needs, goals, and procedures than to serving society. In this section, we will show the ways in which the police have followed the course of most other bureaucratic institutions in society, responding to their problems by merely giving the appearance of facing them while simultaneously promoting the trained incapacity to do otherwise.

The two primary aims of most bureaucracies, the police included, are the maintenance of their organizational autonomy and the security of their members. To accomplish these aims, they adopt a pattern of institutional action that can best be described as "professionalism." This word, with its many connotations and definitions, cloaks all the many kinds of actions carried out by the police.

The guise of professionalism embodied in a bureaucratic organization is the most important strategy employed by the police to defend their mandate and thereby to build self-esteem, organizational autonomy, and occupational solidarity or cohesiveness. The professionalization drives of the police are no more suspect than the campaigns of other striving, upwardly mobile occupational groups. However, since the police have a monopoly on legal violence, since they are the active enforcers of the public will, serving theoretically in the best interests of the public, the consequences of their yearnings for prestige and power are imbued with far greater social ramifications than the relatively harmless attempts of florists, funeral directors, and accountants to attain public stature. Disinterested law enforcement through bureaucratic means is an essential in our society and in any democracy, and the American police are certainly closer to attaining this ideal than they were in 1931 at the time of the Wickersham report. Professionalism qua professionalism is unquestionably desirable in the police. But if in striving for the heights of prestige they fail to serve the altruistic values of professionalism, if their professionalism means that a faulty portrait of the social reality of crime is being painted, if their professionalism conceals more than it reveals about the true nature of their operations, then a close analysis of police professionalism is in order.

Police professionalism cannot be easily separated in practice from the bureaucratic ideal epitomized in modern police practice. The bureaucratic ideal is established as a means of obtaining a commitment from personnel to organizational and occupational norms. This bureaucratic commitment is designed to supersede commitments to competing norms, such as obligations to friends or kin or members of the same racial or ethnic group. Unlike medicine and law, professions that developed outside the context of bureaucracies, policing has always been carried out, if done on a full-time basis, as a bureaucratic function.

Modern police bureaucracy and modern police professionalism are highly articulated, although they contain some inherent stresses that are not our present concern. The strategies employed by the police to manage their public appearance develop from their adaptation of the bureaucratic ideal. These strategies incorporate the utilization of *technology* and *official statistics* in law enforcement, of *styles of patrol* that attempt to accommodate the community's desire for public order with the police department's preoccupation with bureaucratic procedures, of *secrecy* as a means of controlling the public's response to their operations, of *collaboration* with criminal elements to foster the appearance of a smoothly run, law-abiding community, and of a *symbiotic relationship* with the criminal justice system that minimizes public knowledge of the flaws within this largely privately system.

Professionalism. To say that a type of work can only be carried out by professionals is to make both it and them immediately acceptable. The need of the police to proclaim themselves professionals arises out of their need to control both the public and their own organization. Externally, professionalism functions to define the nature of the client, to maintain social distance with the clientele, and to define the purposes, the conventions, and the motivations of the practitioners; internally, it functions to unify the diverse interests and elements that exist within any occupational or organizational group. This view sees professionalism as an ideology. Habenstein has described it as follows:

> Certain groups, claiming special functions, have been able to arrogate to themselves, or command increased power over, the conditions of members' livelihood. . . . "Profession" is, basically, an ideology, a set of rationalizations about the worth and necessity of certain areas of work, which, when internalized, gives the practitioners a moral justification for privilege, if not license. . . .[22]

Efforts toward the professionalization of any occupation are, above all, efforts to achieve power and authority. In police work, professionalization serves the self-esteem of all practitioners, from patrolman to commissioner, by gilding the entire enterprise with the symbols, prerequisites, tradition, power, and authority of the most respected occupations in American society.

The Bureaucratic Ideal. The organizational *ideal* of the "professional" police department is a rational, efficient, scientifically organized, technologically sophisticated bureaucracy. This is the way Niederhoffer depicts a modern police organization:

> Large urban police departments are bureaucracies. Members of the force sometimes lose their bearings in the labyrinth of hierarchy, specialization, competitive examinations, red tape, promotion based on seniority, impersonality, rationality, rules and regulations, channels of communication, and massive files.[23]

They are bureaucracies because the bureaucratic organization is perceived by the police as the best way to solve their problems. To them, a bureaucracy is the best device for managing appearances and the best method of working out a running

---

[22]Robert W. Habenstein, "Critique of 'Profession' as a Sociological Category," *Sociological Quarterly* 4 (November 1963), p. 297. This notion follows H. S. Becker's in "The Nature of a Profession," in *Yearbook of the National Society for the Study of Education* (Chicago: National Society for the Study of Education, 1961).

[23]Niederhoffer, *Behind the Shield,* p. 11.

adjustment to the pressing nature of their problems. And bureaucratic rhetoric, with its reverence for science and professionalism, is accurately assessed as the most powerful source of legitimation in American society. All modern bureaucratic organizations claim to be efficient and all strive in varying degrees to become more efficient. Understandably, they inevitably fail because the organizational rules under which the bureaucrats work are never able to cover all contingencies.

Technology. One of the strategies employed by the police to appear professional and bureaucratically efficient is the use of technology. Again quoting from Niederhoffer:

> The modern police specialist requires a wide range of technical and scientific skills. Experts are needed to operate radar, photographic equipment, electronic listening devices, instruments for analysis of evidence, computers, complex office machines, radio, television, airplanes, and helicopters. The scientific devices used in detective investigations have created a corps of specialists, quasi-scientists, [and] technicians. . . .[24]

All these devices illustrate the technological strategy and are related to the police assumptions that if they have more information more quickly, more visibility, more policemen, more firepower, and better allocation of resources, all organized around technology, they will be able to efficiently prevent and deter crime. These assumptions are also manifested in the President's crime commission report. The police have brought a scientific perspective to crime prevention, elaborating on the means of obtaining more information more quickly, and on methods of more efficiently allocating men, material, and more potent weapons. Technology, of course, does not deal with the great difficulties in obtaining information.

Official Statistics. Another strategy used by police to convey the appearance of efficiency is their pursuit of "official statistics." Nothing sells easier than a statistic, no matter what it says, and the police use them not only for self-justification and organizational survival but for enhancement of community relations. All bureaucracies ply the official-statistics strategy, and insofar as the police are concerned, they "very often corrupt the statistics," as Jack Douglas has pointed out.[25]

The police construct and utilize official statistics, such as the clearance rate and the crime index, to manage the impression of efficiency. The clearance rate so popular among professionalized police departments, is a measure of a patrolman's or a detective's efficiency. Offenses categorized as "solved" become part of the clearance rate. The police ignore all unreported crimes and all crimes without victims where no complainant is required; these crimes, therefore, are never "cleared" — they never become part of the clearance rate. As for the index of

[24]Ibid., pp. 17–18.
[25]Jack D. Douglas, "Deviance and Order in a Pluralistic Society," in *Theoretical Sociology: Perspectives and Development,* ed. Edward A. Tiryakian and John C. McKinney (New York: Appleton-Century-Crofts, 1970).

crime being an index of efficiency, no mandatory, centralized crime-reporting system exists, although many police departments have adopted and report on the basis of the F.B.I. index of crimes: murder, aggravated assault, rape, burglary, robbery, larceny over $50, and auto theft. Needless to say, the more the police enforce the laws, the higher the crime rate. Because there has been very little in the way of standard reporting and investigation practices, the police have been able to control the crime rate to a large degree by controlling aspects of enforcement.

The use of technology and offical statistics as strategies, in the context of professionalism, is related to patrol strategies adapted by departments in their efforts to resolve the "problematic nature of the law." Styles of patrol, or modes of law enforcement by patrolmen, characterize departments as a whole. They represent a means of integrating community norms and expectations with the legal and procedural rules of the community and the police department.

Styles of Patrol. Patrol strategies, to the police at least, are an aspect of bureaucratic efficiency. They are closely related to the differential enforcement of the law. Enforcement must be differential because if it were not, "we would all," in Dodson's often quoted remark, "be in jail before the end of the first day. The laws which are selected for enforcement are those which the power structure of the community wants enforced."[26]

The tasks absorbed by the police have burgeoned in recent years — along with the demands for their services. The police have tried to answer these demands of their environment by three distinct types of patrol — what Wilson describes as the *watchman, legalistic,* and *service* styles.[27] The watchman style is the classic mode of policing urban areas and is still used in some degree in most cities. It is a style of patrol that emphasizes maintenance of public order rather than enforcement of the law. The policeman is instructed to be sensitive to the interests of groups within his beat and to overlook many of the minor offenses connected with juvenile infractions, traffic violations, vice, and gambling. A legalistic style, on the other hand, rests heavily upon enforcement of the law to control the routing situations encountered by the patrolman. The police using this style of patrol are instructed to act as if a single level of order was desirable in all settings and for all groups, and to enforce the law to that end. The service style, Wilson's third type of patrol, is "market-oriented," that is, it is designed to meet the fairly well-articulated demand of "homogeneous middle-class communities." The police respond to and take seriously all calls for police action (unlike the watchman style which ignores certain kinds of demands for intervention), but (unlike the legalistic style which it more closely resembles) the police seldom use the law to control the situation. They prefer informal action to law enforcement.

The value of these varied styles to the police is the survival potential they provide. They allow the police administrator a certain leeway in trying to control

---

[26]Daniel Dodson, as quoted in Niederhoffer, *Behind the Shield,* p. 12.
[27]Wilson, *Varieties of Police Behavior,* pp. 140–141.

his men in line with the demands of the most powerful interests in the community and to mitigate the strain between preserving individual liberty and protecting the collective social enterprise.

Secrecy and Public Complaints. No matter what the level of operation of a police force, it will generate citizen complaints. It will generate complaints because the role of the policeman is to restrain and control, not to advise and remedy. While advice and solutions are usually welcome, restraint is not. For a substantial proportion of the population, the policeman is an adversary; he issues summonses, makes arrests, conducts inquiries, searches homes and people, stops cars, testifies in court, and keeps a jail. For the police, threats from outside, such as citizens' complaints and political moves to control police policy, are efforts to destroy their organization. One strategy used by police to withstand these threats is to keep all information they obtain secret.

The shared secrets possessed by the police assist them in creating internal cohesion. Information is concealed for the additional reason that the police fear and dislike their clients — the various segments of the public. Westley, one of the first and most profound sociological analysts of the police culture, here describes the occupational perspective of the policeman and the centrality of secrecy:

> The policeman finds his most pressing problems in his relationships to the public. His is a service occupation but of an incongruous kind, since he must discipline those whom he serves. He is regarded as corrupt and inefficient by, and meets with hostility and criticism from, the public. He regards the public as his enemy, feels his occupation to be in conflict with the community, and regards himself to be a pariah. The experience and the feeling give rise to a collective emphasis on secrecy, an attempt to coerce respect from the public, and a belief that almost any means are legitimate in completing an important arrest. These are for the policeman basic occupational values. They arise from his experience, take precedence over his legal responsibilities, [and] are central to an understanding of his conduct. . . .[28]

Most observers of the police have noted their penchant for secrecy as a strategy used for their own protection. Secrecy helps keep the public at arm's length; further, it helps the police to maintain their power. Indeed, its very existence suggests power. One aspect of the strategy of secrecy is that it deliberately mystifies, and mystification has always been a means of sustaining respect and awe. As a strategy, then, secrecy is one of the most effective sources of power that the police have over their audiences.

One aspect of the secrecy strategy is that it constrains many citizens from making complaints about police misconduct. No adequate records are kept on police malfeasance. While the misconduct of the citizen — his law-breaking activities — are closely monitored and recorded, little attempt is made by most departments to maintain publicly available records of police wrongdoing. Cer-

---

[28]Westley, "Violence and the Police," p. 35.

tainly, few cities have bureaus that make systematic examinations of police activities for public assessment. Many efforts by citizens to set up public files on police services or to create civilian review boards have failed. The police have in every instance opposed moves to establish evaluational mechanisms; they have continued to prefer losing most citizens' complaints in an endless tangle of red tape. The battle with crime thus goes on largely unmonitored by the public at large.

Collaboration, the Strategy of Corruption. In dealing with the demands of certain segments of their criminal audience, some police departments find that the most expedient policy is simply to acquiesce. This is a strategy adopted by corrupt departments. It is a strategy that reduces the pressures of organized crime against the department and that minimizes the chances of organized crime deliberately and publicly embarrassing the police in order to control police activities. As a strategy, it is the least common used by police to manage their appearance of efficient crime-fighters. What it amounts to is that the police collaborate with the criminal element by taking the line of least resistance: they enter into the vice, gambling, and protection rackets themselves or in concert with organized crime. Because the police have resorted to secrecy and the fractionalization of public demands, they have at times been free enough from the constraints of justice to engage in full-scale lawlessness. This strategy, although relatively infrequent for entire departments, involves selective enforcement of the law together with the encouragement of a lack of consensus on enforcing certain laws, particularly those pertaining to gambling, prostitution, homosexuality, and abortion. Of course, an alliance with organized crime for the purpose of receiving payoffs is involved, too. Complicity with the criminal element is sometimes also necessary in order to obtain information that can be used against those who are not in league with the police and their allies. The corruption strategy is ultimately a self-defeating strategy, but to those in our police forces who are corrupt, this is a relatively unimportant matter.

Symbiosis and Justice. The relationship between the police and our system of criminal justice is symbiotic — each is dependent upon the other for support. One of the reasons why the professionalized police department is so concerned with its public image originates with its inability to control the conviction process. Because the courts control the process, the police are eager to make the "good pinch," the one that will result in a conviction. To the police, failure to obtain a conviction is a failure of their mandate.

The symbiotic relationship between law enforcement and our system of criminal justice is largely sustained through the abrogation of the right of due process. This is accomplished through the simple expedient of what has been termed "bargain justice." Under the bargain-justice system, accused persons are persuaded to plead guilty to a lesser offense than the one with which they are charged, thereby forgoing their right to a trial by jury. But the complicity of the police in this system allows them to maintain their rate of good pinches. At the same time, it permits the prosecutor's office to preserve its conviction rates and it allows the courts to meet production quotas.

The system works on the assumption that all accused persons are guilty and that almost all of them, whether they are or not, will plead guilty. As Skolnick and Blumberg have shown, the assumption of guilt is the oil that lubricates an otherwise outdated, overworked, inadequate system of justice.[29]

Complicity in bargain justice is one more strategy employed by our police departments in their efforts to manage a troublesome mandate. In the second part of this essay the major problems of the police were outlined under the general themes of the problematic nature of the law and law enforcement, the political context of police work, and the symptomatic quality of their occupational tasks. In the preceding section, we focused on the major strategies the police have used to manage their troublesome mandate. In the following section, we will assess the relative efficacy of police strategies in battling crime in American society.

IV. The Effectiveness of Police Strategies

The police have developed and utilized the strategies outlined above for the purpose of creating, as we have said, the appearance of managing their troublesome mandate. To a large extent, they are facilitated in the use of these strategies, in being able to project a favorable impression, by a public that has always been apathetic about police activity. Moreover, what activity the public does observe is filtered through the media with its own special devices for creating a version of reality. The public's meaning of police action is rarely gathered from firsthand experience, but from the constructed imagery of the media — which, in turn, rely upon official police sources for their presentation of the news. The police for their part, understandably, manipulate public appearances as much as they possibly can in order to gain and maintain public support.

The specific strategies used by the police to create a publicly suitable image were described in Section III: the guise of professionalism; the implementation of the bureaucratic ideal of organization; the use of technology, official statistics, and various styles of patrol; secrecy; collaboration with corrupt elements; and the establishment of a symbiotic relationship with the courts. This section will present evidence by which to evaluate these strategies. The term "effectiveness" is used only in the context of how well these devices accomplish the ends which the public and the police themselves publicly espouse; the recommendations and evaluations of the President's crime commission will be central in making judgments of police effectiveness. This appraisal of how well the police manipulate their appearance will also be a guideline for evaluating the recommendations of the commission's task force report on the police.

---

[29]Skolnick, *Justice Without Trial,* and Abraham Blumberg, *Criminal Justice* (Chicago: Quadrangle Press, 1967).

Professionalism and the Bureaucratic Ideal. The assumptions of professionalism and of a bureaucratic organization include a devotion to rational principles and ends that may then be translated into specific work routines having predictable outcomes. The police are organized in a military command fashion, with rigid rules and a hierarchy governing operations. However, the patrolman, the lowest man in the hierarchy — and usually the least well-trained and educated — is in the key position of exercising the greatest amount of discretion on criminal or possibly criminal activities. Especially in his peace-keeping role and in dealing with minor infractions (misdemeanors), the patrolman has wide discretionary power concerning if, when, why, and how to intervene in private affairs.

Police work must both rely on discretion and control it. Excessive inattention and excessive attention to infractions of the law are equally damaging to a community. However, the complexity of the law, its dynamic and changing properties, the extensiveness of police department regulations, policies, and procedures, and the equivocal, relativistic nature of crime in regard to certain situations, settings, persons, and groups make it impossible to create a job description that would eliminate the almost boundless uncertainty in police patrol.

Neither professionals nor bureaucrats, however, have yet found an effective means of controlling discretion. If an organization cannot control those of its members with the greatest opportunity to exercise discretion, it flounders in its attempts to accomplish its stated purposes. Two general principles suggest why the police have not been able to control discretion. The first has to do with the general problem of control and the second with the specific nature of police work.

Men are unwilling to submit completely to the will of their organizational superiors. Men will always attempt to define and control their own work. Control means the right to set the pace, to define mistakes, to develop standards of "good" production and efficiency. But as surely as superiors seek to control the quality and the extent of work performed by their subordinates in a hierarchy, just as surely will they meet with attempts to reshape and subvert these controls.

In the specific instance of police bureaucracies, the patrolman conceives of himself as a man able to make on-the-spot decisions of guilt or innocence. He does not think of himself as a bureaucratic functionary nor as a professional. Further, since the police oranization itself has become far more interested in efficiency than in purpose, since it is unable to specify its overall objectives, the patrolman finds it difficult, if not impossible, to demonstrate that necessary devotion to rational ends required of professionalism and bureaucratic organizations. Until police departments are able to control the amount and kind of discretion exercised by their members, and until the police are able, with the help of lawyers and other citizens, to develop positive means of motivation and reward in line with clear, overall policy directives, the failure of what we have called the professionalism-bureaucracy strategy is an absolute certainty.

Technology, Statistics, and the Crime Rate. This section will evaluate the strategy of technology in the control and prevention of crime, the use of statistics, and the significance of the so-called crime rate. Given the sociological nature of crime, let it be said immediately that present technology deals with unimportant crime and that the F.B.I. index of crimes, by which we base judgments of police effectiveness, is biased and an unrealistic reflection of the actual crime rate.

One of the striking aspects of the President's crime commission report is the thoroughly sociological nature of the document. The discussion of the causes of crime in the first two chapters points to the growth of urbanism, anonymity, the breakdown in social control, and the increasing numbers of frustrated and dissatisfied youth who have always constituted the majority of known lawbreakers. There are no labels such as "evil people," "emotionally disturbed," "mentally ill," or "criminally insane." The first set of recommendations under prevention in the summary pages of the report are "sociological": strengthen the family, improve slum schools, provide employment, reduce segregation, construct housing. All these matters are patently and by definition out of the control of the police.

There is every evidence that the police themselves subscribe to a thoroughly social, if not sociological, definition of the causes of crime — that is, that crime is the manifestation of long-established social patterns and structures which ensnare and implicate the police and the criminals as well as the general public. And they are doubtless correct.

Surveys done by the President's crime commission revealed that there are always contingencies in the information police receive about a crime even before they are able to investigate it. These contingencies involve such matters as the nature of the relationship between the victim and the offender and whether or not the victim believes the police are competent to investigate and solve the crime. Computer technology depends on informational "input." On that point, the police seem both unable to define what sort of information would be useful and unable to obtain, and probably never can obtain in a democratic society, information that would make them better able to enforce the law.

The facts in the problem of "crime prevention" overwhelmingly doom the present professionally based notion that the application of science and technology will begin to ease the distress the police feel as they face the escalating demands of their audiences. Also, it would be easier to assess the value of the technology strategy if we were able to define exactly to what end the technology would be applied and in what ways it could be expected to work.

Styles of Patrol. Police strategy is subject to many contingencies. It is a basic principle of public administration that policy made at the higher echelons of an organization will be effective only if each successively lower level of the organization complies with that policy and is capable of carrying it out. It is also a truism that participants at the lowest level in the hierarchy are the most "difficult" to mobilize and integrate into the organization. A style of patrol is basically the manner in which an administrative police policy is executed. The policy may prescribe that the patrolman overlook certain types of illegal acts; it may order that he minimally enforce particular laws or be sensitive to and strictly enforce others. If the administrative order setting a patrol style does not win the cooperation of the patrolman it is certain to fail. Thus, the success of any high-echelon policy that involves the performance of the patrolman is contingent upon his compliance with that policy. If the administrator's orders are not binding on the patrolman, no distinctive style of patrol will result; all that will be demonstrated will be the responses of the patrolman to other aspects of his social environment, especially, how his fellow patrolmen perform.

The success of this strategy is dependent upon the capacity of the administrator to create loyalty to his internal policies. With the rise of police unions, the discontent of the black patrolman, low pay, and relatively less security for the policeman, organizational control is a major problem in all the large police departments of the country — with Los Angeles possibly the single exception.

The effectiveness of the watchman, legalistic, and service styles of patrol will also depend on the degree of political consensus among the community groups patrolled, the clarity of the boundaries of community neighborhoods, competition between the police and self-help or vigilante groups, and the relative importance of nonoccupational norms in enforcement practices — that is, the importance of racial or ethnic similarities between the patrolman and the people in his neighborhood. If a clear social consensus on the meaning of the law and what is expected of the police can be established within a community, a well-directed policy of control over police patrol is the most logical and rational approach to police work. In some communities, largely suburban and middle-class, the police can carry out what their public demands and a degree of harmony exists. This consensus is absent in our inner cities.

Secrecy and Collaboration. The use of secrecy by the police is, as we have pointed out, a strategy employed not only to assist them in maintaining the appearance of political neutrality but to protect themselves against public complaints. Secrecy also helps to forestall public efforts to achieve better police service and to secure political accountability for police policy. Police collaboration with criminal elements — corruption, in other words — has much the same effect since it decreases the pressure to enforce "unenforceable" laws against certain segments of the police's clientele.

These two strategies were among the major concerns of the President's crime commission task force on police. The task force's report devoted major attention to the fact that political forces influence police actions and policies. The report affirmed the political nature of police work; what concerned the writers of the report was the nature and type of political influence on police actions. Their recommendations, furthermore, were based on their recognition of the fact that the police have been fairly successful in managing the appearance of being apolitical.

There are several reasons why the police strategies of secrecy and collaboration will continue in force: (1) as long as the client — the public — is seen as the enemy, the police will treasure their secrecy and use it to engineer public consent to their policies and practices; (2) as long as a new political consensus is not formed on the nature and type of police control necessary in society as a whole, the organized, self-serving survival aims of police organizations will emerge victorious. Any well-organized consensual, secretive organization can resist the efforts of an unorganized public, managed by rhetoric and appearances, to reform it; (3) as long as there remains a lack of consensus on the enforcement of many of our "moralistic" laws, police corruption and selective law enforcement will continue. Collaboration to reduce adversary relationships with the criminal segment of society will always be an effective strategy — providing a sudden upsurge in public morality doesn't temporarily subject the police to a full-scale "house-cleaning." Replacements would, of course, be subject to the same pressures and would, in all likelihood, eventually take the same line of least resistance.

One solution to corruption is said to be better educated, more professional policemen. By recruiting better educated men, the more professionalized police departments also seek to diminish the expression of political attitudes on the job and the tendency of policemen to form political power groups based on their occupation. These are also assumptions made by the crime commission's task force on police. There is, however, no evidence that college-educated or better-paid policemen are "better policemen"; nor is there any evidence that "better men" alone will solve the essentially structural problems of the occupation.

We can tentatively conclude from this review that corruption will remain with us as long as laws remain which stipulate punishments for actions on which a low public consensus exists. It will remain when there is likely to be a low visibility of police performance, and it will remain while there is a high public demand for illegal services — gambling, prostitution, abortion — and the concomitant need of the police for information on these services from the practitioners themselves.

Symbiosis and Justice. Although the police have the principal discretion in the field with reference to the detection, surveillance, and appraisal of alleged offenders, the final disposition of a criminal case must be made in the courts. The police are thus dependent on the courts in a very special way for their successes. The ideal model of the criminal-justice system makes the police essentially the fact gatherers and apprehenders, while the courts are to be the decision-makers.

The police attempt to appear efficient has led them, as we have noted before, to seek the good pinch, the arrest that will stand up in court. With victimless crimes, such as those involving gambling or drugs or prostitution, the police control the situation since they alone decide whether an offense has been committed and whether they have a legal case against the offender. To control the success rate in these cases, the police create a gaggle of informants, many of whom are compelled to give the police evidence in order to stay free of a potential charge against themselves for a violation similar to the one they are providing information about. In the case of more serious crimes, the problems are more complex; in these cases the police must rely on other informants, and their discretion on arrests and charges are more often exercised by administrators and prosecuting attorneys.

In the prosecution stage, the bureaucratic demands of the court system are paramount. Abraham Blumberg describes these demands and the tension between efficiency and "due process":

> The dilemma is frequently resolved through bureaucratically ordained short-cuts, deviations and outright rule violations by the members of the courts, from judges to stenographers, in order to meet production norms. Because they fear criticism on ethical as well as legal grounds, all the significant participants in the court's social structure are bound into an organized system of complicity. Patterned, covet, informal breaches, and evasions of "due process" are accepted as routine — they are institutionalized — but are nevertheless denied to exist.[30]

The net effect of this strain within the court system is to produce a higher rate of convictions by means of encouraging a plea of guilty to a lesser charge. As far as the police are concerned, then, the strategy of symbiosis is sound.

There are several undesirable effects of this symbiosis. First, it encourages corruption by permitting the police to make decisions about the freedom of their informants; it gives them an illegal hold and power over them, and thus it undercuts the rule of law. Second, many offenders with long criminal records are either granted their freedom as informants or allowed to plead guilty to lesser charges in return for the dismissal of a more serious charge. Skolnick calls this the "reversal of the hierarchy of penalties," because the more serious crimes of habitual criminals are prosecuted less zealously than the minor violations of first offenders. Third, it helps blur the distinction between the apprehension and prosecution aspects of our criminal-justice system.

V. Conclusions and Proposed Reforms

The allocation of rewards in a society represents both its division of labor and its configuration of problems. Ironically, the allocation of rewards is also the allocation of societal trouble. Societal trouble in a differentiated society is occupational trouble. The ebb and flow of rewards emanating from the division of labor becomes structured into persistent patterns that are sustained by continuous transactions among organizations and occupational groups. Occupational structures reflect societal structures, but they reflect them in ways that have been negotiated over time. The negotiation is based upon the universal human proclivity to differentiate roles, organizations, and occupations. The more dependent an organization is upon its environment for rewards, the more likely it is to rely on the management and presentation of strategies to establish the appearance of autonomy.

Organizations without a high degree of autonomy in the environments in which they operate are greatly constrained by the internal pressure of competing aims and roles of members. The agreement on problems, goals, values, and self-

---

[30]Blumberg, *Criminal Justice,* p. 69.

concepts that emerges from occupational socialization and functioning is a strong basis for influencing organizational direction. The occupational standards in this case subvert the rule of law as a system of norms outside the informal norms of the occupation. The policeman's view of his role and his occupational culture are very influential in determining the nature of policing. The basic source of police trouble is the inability of the police to define a mandate that will minimize the inconsistent nature of their self-expectations and the expectations of those they serve.

The problems derived from a contradictory mandate remain unaffected by the efforts of the institution to solve them; they do, however, take the shape into which they have been cast by institutional functionaries. Cooley long ago discussed the process of institutional ossification, the process by which institutions stray from serving the needs of their members and their publics, thereby losing the loyalty of those within and the support of those without. The consequences of institutional ossification as related to the police are twofold. First, the police begin to search for a so-called higher order of legitimacy; they make appeals to morality, to patriotism, to "Americanism," and to "law and order" to shore up eroded institutional charters and to accelerate their attempts to control and manipulate their members and clients. Second, the police, as they develop a far greater potential for controlling those they serve through their presentational strategies, come to serve themselves better than ever before.

The problem of the police is, essentially, the problem of the democratic society, and until the central values and social structures of our society are modified (and I think we are seeing such a modification), there can be no real change in the operation of social control. The needed changes are, by and large, not those dealt with in the crime commission report. And this is telling. For an eminently sociological document, it did not focus on the heart of the problem: our anachronistic, moralistic laws, with which the police are burdened, and our dated political system, which is unable to bring political units into a state of civil accountability. The focus of the report and recommendations was predictably on symptoms of crime, not oncauses of crime. The "managerial focus" of the report, or its public-administration bias, outlined needed reforms, but not ways in which to implement them, and the problem of efficiency was never really faced.

Not surprisingly for a political document having a variety of public functions, the report has little to say about the nature of the present criminal laws. It dwells, like the police themselves, on means, not ends. As Isidore Silver points out in a critique of the report, more than one-half the crimes committed do not harm anyone: more than one-third are for drunkenness, and a small but important portion are for other "crimes without victims." Most crimes are committed by juveniles who inexplicably "grow out" of their criminality. In 1965, 50 per cent of the known burglaries and larcenies were committed by youths under 18.[31] The report

---

[31]Isidore Silver, "Introduction" to *The Challenge of Crime in a Free Society* (New York: Avon Books, 1968), p. 25. The President's Commission, *Task Force Report: The Courts*, discusses substantive criminal law, however, and does make some suggestions for legal change.

does note what was a central point of our discussion of the political nature of crime, that police corruption is, in almost every instance, a consequence of trying to enforce admittedly unenforceable laws. The demand for services provided by homosexuals, by gamblers, prostitutes, and abortionists is high, and the supply is legally made unavailable to anyone who wants to remain in the so-called "law-abiding" category. The laws, in effect, create the crime and the criminals.

Changes in laws to reduce their absolutistic element and to free people who deviate with little harm to others from the onus of criminalization cannot be accomplished without a parallel change in the nature of police accountability. As we have seen, the strategies of secrecy and rhetoric used by the police play on the fears of society and provide a basis for police control. The managerial reforms contained in the task force report — more public debate on and greater internal and external control over police actions — are needed. Even more urgently required are specific ways in which the cities can control the police and make them strictly accountable for their actions — methods, that is, which go a good deal further than merely disposing of the chief or convening a judicial review board. To give city governments this kind of control over the police, however, entails the reorganization of police departments themselves so that their goals are clear and defined and so that the occupational rewards within the police organization are aligned with public goals.

Three interrelated organizational changes must be made to insure that police attend to the job of maintaining public order. One is to reorganize police departments along functional lines aimed at peace-keeping rather than law enforcement; the second is to allocate rewards for keeping the peace rather than for enforcing the law; the third is to decentralize police functions to reflect community control without the diffusion of responsibility and accountability to a central headquarters.

Present police departments are organized in a military fashion; orders move down the line from the chief to departmental sections assigned law-enforcement functions. These sections usually include such divisions as traffic, patrol, records, detective, juvenile, intelligence, crime-lab, and communications. The principal basis for the assignment of functions, however, is law enforcement;[32] what is needed is a new set of organizational premises so that the basis for the assignment of functions is not law enforcement but the maintenance of order. As Wilson explains:

> If order were the central mission of the department, there might be a "family disturbance squad," a "drunk and derelict squad," a "riot control squad," and a "juvenile squad"; law enforcement matters would be left to a "felony squad." Instead there is a detective division organized, in the larger departments, into units specializing in homicide, burglary, auto theft, narcotics, vice, robbery, and the like. The undifferentiated patrol division gets everything else. Only juveniles tend to be treated by specialized units under both schemes, partly because the law requires or encourages such specializa-

[32]President's Commission, *Task Force Report: The Police,* charts on pp. 46–47.

tion. The law enforcement orientation of most departments means that new specialized units are created for every offense about which the public expresses concern or for which some special technology is required.[33]

What is called for, then, is a new organizational pattern that will provide a domestic unit (as is now being tried in New York City), a juvenile unit, and a drunk unit with a detoxification center, all with a peace-keeping orientation and peace-keeping functions. Only a felony squad and perhaps a riot squad should be used to enforce the law.

One of the obvious ways in which to improve the morale of the patrolman is to let him do a greater amount of investigative work and to take on the responsibility for "solving" some of the crimes originating with his patrol. Rewards could then be allocated in accord with the more limited ends of peace-keeping — for instance, in rewarding a patrolman for a decline in the number of drunks who reappear in court. Since no comprehensive policy can be imagined to guide order maintenance, limited ends for various departments must be developed and subjected to public review. The key is to allow the policeman to develop judgment about the motives and future intentions of people with whom he comes in contact, and to reward him for peace-keeping, not "good pinches" alone.

This reappraisal of the allocation of rewards means, of course, that there must be greater coordination of police and other agencies within the criminal-justice system in order to increase the benefits to the client (the offender or the criminal) and break down the isolation of the police.[34] To allow the policeman to assume greater peace-keeping responsibilities would allow him to play a functional role parallel to that of the better general practitioner of medicine: the referral specialist, the coordinator of family health, the source of records and information, and the family friend and counselor. Such an organizational change in the policeman's function would, naturally enough, make community control of the police a greater possibility. It would begin to bridge the chasm between the police and many hostile segments within the public, a process that could be facilitated by the creation of a community relations division within police departments.

The third needed modification of the present structure of police work is the development of decentralized operations. One of the major social trends of the last ten years has been the increase in the lack of attachment people have for their major institutions. Police today suffer from a crisis of legitimacy, and this crisis is heightened by their failure to promote a sense of commitment to their operations by the citizens they serve. One way in which to introduce commitment and a sense of control over the police by members of a community is to make the police more accessible. St. Louis, for example, has experimented with "store-

[33]Wilson, *Varieties of Police Behavior*, p. 69.
[34]See John P. Clark, "The Isolation of the Police: A Comparison of the British and American Situations," in *Readings in Social Problems*, ed. John Scanzoni (Boston: Allyn and Bacon, 1967), pp. 384–410. See also David Bordua, "Comments on Police-Community Relations," mimeographed (Urbana: University of Illinois, n.d.).

front'' police stations, staffed by a few men who are available as advisers, counselors, protectors, and friends of the people in the immediate neighborhood. If the police should begin to differentiate the role of the patrolman to include the functions of a peace-keeping community agent, the control of these agents should reside in the community. Thus, public participation in the decision making processes of the police would begin at the precinct or neighborhood level; it would not be simply in the form of a punitive civilian review board or a token citizen board at headquarters.

We began with the notion of trouble, police trouble, the troublesome mandate of the policeman. There will be little succor for him as long as our social structure remains fraught with contradictory value premises, with fragmented political power and the consequent inadequate control of the police, with the transformation of public trusts into institutional rights. There will be little succor for him as long as our political agencies resist moving to de-moralize our criminal laws. As it is, we can expect that the management of crime through police strategies and appearances will continue to be a disruptive element in American society.

9. Paul Chevigny

Police Power

Force, Arrest, and Cover Charges

Arbitrary arrest and summary punishment have been recurring themes . . . and we are ready now to draw up an Anatomy of Street-corner Abuses.

The one truly iron and inflexible rule we can adduce from the cases is that any person who defies the police risks the imposition of legal sanctions, commencing with a summons, on up to the use of firearms. The sanction that is imposed depends on at least three factors: the character of the officer, the place where the encounter occurs, and the character of the person with whom the encounter is had. The police may arrest *anyone* who challenges them (as they define the challenge), but they are more likely to further abuse anyone who is poor, or who belongs to an outcast group.

Members of outcast groups, by their mere presence, seem to offer an affront to order such that the police will themselves initiate action against them by ordering them to move along, breaking into a party, or some similar action. To the

Reprinted by permission of Pantheon Books, a Division of Random House, Inc., from *Police Power*, by Paul Chevigny, pp. 136–146, 276–283. Copyright © 1969 by Paul Chevigny.

police, the ordinary citizen begins to assume the status of a pariah only when he actively defies the police, whereas a member of an outcast group need take no such action.

John McNamara, reviewing "critical incidents" involving police and citizens, in his work with New York City police recruits was "struck by the extent to which the handling of relatively minor incidents such as traffic violations or disorderly disputes between husbands and wives seemed to create a more serious situation than existed prior to the police attempt to control the situation."[1] In many of our cases, the police have gone further and caused a situation to degenerate into an argument when it was scarcely a dispute at all to begin with. McNamara attributes the phenomenon to mistaken assumptions on the part of the police about how they ought to behave toward the public. For example, he found that 39 to 40 percent of policemen agree with the proposition that "a patrolman can be pretty sure he will gain compliance from a person who appears to be somewhat frightened of the patrolman," as well as with the proposition that "when patrolmen indicate they will use the force necessary to gain compliance from a citizen, they are helped considerably if the citizen thinks they are getting angry."[2] These police opinions are so potentially dangerous, and in many cases so catastrophically applied, that it is not enough to think of them only as mistaken assumptions. The reason why policemen act so aggressively as to exacerbate street situations is, of course, that they seek to establish their authority by such transactions. The answers to McNamara's questions indicate that a large percentage of policemen will usually try to obtain compliance by an unconditional demand or the use of force. Many people wonder whether police work attracts young men who already have such attitudes, or whether the police role develops those attitudes in them. Most authorities who have studied the problem intensively seem to agree that the second alternative is the correct one. Police recruits are much like other young men of a similar background; it is police mores and the police role that make them adopt police attitudes.[3]

In the paradigmatic street encounter there are three steps:

1. Police perception of a challenge to authority. In the case of a member of an outcast group this step is eliminated, or at least minimized.

2. Police demand for submission. This is most commonly enshrined in the question, "So, you're a wise guy, eh?" In my office we sat through many lengthy and excited complaints listening only for the words "wise guy," knowing well that an arrest would have occurred shortly after they were uttered.*

---

[1]John H. McNamara, "Uncertainties in Police Work," in David Joseph Bordua, ed., *The Police: Six Sociological Essays* (New York, John Wiley & Sons, Inc., 1967), p. 168.

[2]*Ibid.*, pp. 226, 228.

[3]*Ibid.*, p. 194; Arthur Niederhoffer, *Behind the Shield: The Police in Urban Society* (New York, Doubleday & Company, Inc., 1967), Ch. 5.

*Paul Chevigny gathered this information while working on the Police Practices Project of the Civil Liberties Defense and Education Fund, New York Civil Liberties Union. — Editor's note.

3. Response to the demand. The citizen in effect either admits that he is a wise guy, or denies it by complying with the police demand, if it involves an action like moving along, or by apologizing to the policeman if no action is demanded.

People in minority and outcast groups, who are the most likely to be subjected to a police demand for submission, at the same time find it hardest to comply with it. The middle-class man thinks nothing of saying, "Sorry, officer," but to the oppressed and downtrodden those words are galling. It is especially hard for a Negro, for whom such an act seems just one more token of submission. The combination of being an outcast (step one) and refusing to comply in step three is explosive; thereby hangs the tale of many police brutality cases.

The police rationale for this three-step process is that people who present a challenge to them are troublemakers, as the police might put it, or symbolic assailants, as Skolnick calls them. They are, quite literally, potential offenders, and so to arrest one of them is at least the ethical (if not the legal) equivalent of arresting a criminal. The policeman will go on to say that he must maintain his authority against those who challenge it, in order to enforce the laws effectively. In short, his authority over others will be lost if he backs down with one person. It inevitably follows that his authority as a policeman is asserted in situations which are personal disputes, or at least have a personal dimension, like nearly all of the cases recounted in previous chapters. In some of those cases, the provocation comes principally from the citizen, and in others, principally from the police. The point is that they are street arguments, not so very different from those which arise every day between private citizens when one insults another or tries to get him to do something he does not want to do. Although it is true that policemen take umbrage very easily, and that they sometimes see a threat where there is none . . . it is equally clear that in many instances . . . some sort of retaliation was almost inevitable. The chief difference is that one of the parties is a policeman, and for him no dispute is purely personal. It is no accident that in old-fashioned journalistic parlance the officer was personified as "John Law" or the "long arm of the law." Policemen apparently do see themselves as personifying authority, and a challenge to one of them (or to all of them, as in the case of civilian review) is a challenge to the Law. Everybody knows that when you defy the Law, you go to jail.

The apparently irrational and sometimes provocative behavior of the police in street conflicts has often raised the question whether the police deliberately encourage violence or at least disorderly behavior from a troublemaker, in order to show that he really is an offender and to provide grounds for removing him from the street by arrest. This is one of the unresolved questions about police behavior, and one that is central to an understanding of police abuses. If the police react in a rough manner to provocation from citizens, if they in fact themselves behave in a rude and ham-handed fashion, that is one problem, but it is quite another if the police deliberately provoke to violence people they believe to be troublemakers. Westley, in his research on a Midwestern police department, felt that there was a tendency for the police to provoke anyone who was disrespectful until there was an assault, and then to retaliate with violence.[4] Werthman and Piliavin detected the same thing in their work on police treatment of juveniles,[5] and at least one writer in the professional journal *Police* has criticized the practice, while carefully labeling it "unusual."[6] . . .

The consensus among the authorities who have studied the problem is that the police do sometimes try to provoke violence in order to make an arrest. It is logical to think that policemen will try such things on with outcasts, whom they fear and dislike and would prefer to see in jail. One young Negro in a ghetto neighborhood in Brooklyn, who had the reputation of being a "cop fighter," complained that the police would not let him alone. Whenever they saw him on the street they slowed down their cars and asked him if he wanted to fight. In New York City in 1967, however, I think that the challenge by a policeman to physical combat, or even to a public disturbance, is the exception. In my office we did not receive more than a handful of complaints of such deliberate provocation, and it cannot be a widespread problem if there are so few complaints. In most cases, even if a policeman wanted to use such crude tactics, they would not be necessary. The New York police are sophisticated enough in drawing charges and making them stick not to need an actual act of physical violence to arrest anyone. If they feel that a man is a troublemaker, they can, unfortunately, charge him with resisting arrest, without the necessity of risking injury to an officer.

The worst problem in street-corner incidents is not that of police quarreling with citizens. Most such quarrels, while never admirable, are at least understandable; they are much like quarrels between private citizens. The worst abuse is not even the police hitting people in such quarrels; pugnacious citizens hit others in private disputes every day. The root problem is the abuse of power, the fact that the police not only hit a man but arrest him. Once they have arrested him, of course, lying becomes an inevitable part of the procedure of making the quarrel look like a crime, and thus the lie is the chief abuse with which we must come to grips. If the police simply hit a man and let him go, there would be an abuse of the authority conferred by the uniform and the stick, but not the compound abuse of hitting a man and then dragging him to court on criminal charges, really a more serious injury than a blow. One's head heals up, after all, but a criminal record never goes away. There is no more embittering experience in the legal system than to be abused by the police and then to be tried and convicted on false evidence.

---

[4]William A. Westley, "Violence and the Police," *American Journal of Sociology*, LIX (August 1953), p. 39.

[5]Carl Werthman and Irving M. Piliavin, "Gang Members and the Police," in David Joseph Bordua, ed., *The Police: Six Sociological Essays* (New York, John Wiley & Sons, Inc., 1966), p. 93.

[6]Richard H. Blum, "The Problems of Being a Police Officer," *Police*, January 1961, p. 12.

Police abuse and consequent conviction on false evidence are a combination which feeds the impulse to riot; once respect for the legal process is gone, grievances can be expressed only by force. Despite these obvious repercussions upon community relations, it is rarely that anyone is abused without being criminally charged, not only because of the rationale for such abuses ("he was guilty anyhow") but because the policeman is likely to get into trouble if he lets an abused person go free. There is nothing to cover a later accusation of abuse if an arrest has not been made.

There can be no doubt that police lying is the most pervasive of all abuses. In most of the cases reported . . . there was a lie whenever there was a criminal trial. If the charge was disorderly conduct, officers lied to create a breach of the peace where none existed. If the charge was assault or obstructing an officer, they supplied blows by the defendant when none had been struck. In the police canon of ethics, the lie is justified in the same way as the arrest: as a vindication of police authority, by proving that defiance of the police is a crime in fact if not in law. A member of a pariah group, or anyone who defies the police, being guilty at heart and sometimes potentially guilty in fact, deserves to be punished out of hand. Besides, the police dislike such people so much that they consider them unworthy of the protection of the law. By lying, the police enforce these folkways of their own, while preserving the shell of due process of law.

Not surprisingly, police lying is a problem about which little reliable research has been done. William Westley, after breaking ground upon the police use of violence in his first article, went on to open the problem of lying in "Secrecy and the Police."[7] He found that 11 out of 15 men said they would not report a brother officer for taking money from a prisoner, and 10 out of 13 said they would not testify against the officer if he were accused by the prisoner. Comments on police honesty since the publication of Westley's article have often taken the form of avuncular warnings in the professional journals. Richard H. Blum wrote in *Police*: "The conflict of loyalty versus lawfulness is always with the officer, as he is faced with wanting trust, friendship and reliability on the one hand, while wanting to be lawful on the other."[8] Both Blum and Westley deal with honesty about the conduct of a fellow officer; obviously the temptation is even stronger for an officer to cover up when he himself is in trouble, as he usually is when he has abused a citizen.

Once an arrest is made, the police begin to consider what testimony is necessary for a conviction, and what charges are necessary to create pressure on the defendant for a plea of guilty. The Criminal Court is not viewed as a tribunal for the determination of fact, but as a sort of administrative adjunct to the police station for the purpose of obtaining desirable results. Lying is a litigation tool much like, say, investigation. Once the police have arrested a man, particularly

---

[7]William A. Westley, "Secrecy and the Police," *Social Forces*, XXXIV (March 1956), 254.
[8]Blum, "Problems of Being a Police Officer," p. 10.

under circumstances when charges have been made against an officer, the only real objective is conviction, and the police feel that they have made a mistake if they fail to obtain the conviction, not if they lied to obtain it. The arresting officer who has abused a citizen makes it his business to get out of trouble, as does any other accused party, and his original aim of "preserving police authority" becomes little more than a rationalization. The lie serves the double purpose of preserving his authority and his job.

It seems that there is some sort of folklore or underground standard circulating in the Department, according to which charges are drawn to cover abuses. Lying to cover a mistake and the use of a criminal charge to buttress the lie are such a natural development that it would hardly seem necessary to do more than give a patrolman a hint. Charges are so invariably preferred, however, and the charges are so much alike from one case to the next, that I am constrained to believe that something a little more definite than a hint is at work. At some level in the Department, something close to this standard has been accepted: when a citizen is injured by a policeman, he must be charged with resisting arrest, together with the underlying crime for which he was arrested. If there was no crime, but rather a personal dispute with the policeman, then the defendant must be charged with disorderly conduct and resisting arrest. Other, more serious charges become something of a matter of taste. Experienced men tend to add other charges, in order to increase the pressure for a plea of guilty to one of the charges. I once heard two transit policemen arguing in the hallway outside the courtroom after one of my clients had refused to plead guilty to disorderly conduct in exchange for a dismissal of the charge of resisting arrest. The more experienced of the two was saying, "You see? He wouldn't take it. I *told* you you should have charged him with felonious assault." These charges — disorderly conduct, resisting arrest, and felonious assault, or all three — together with a story to establish them, constitute the system for covering street abuses. According to a task force of the President's Commission on Law Enforcement, the system exists in many other cities with conditions similar to those of New York, notably in Philadelphia.[9]

It is my guess that the system is perpetuated at the middle level, among the sergeants and possibly the lieutenants. I cannot, of course, be sure, because I rarely hear a reliable account of what is being said at the precinct. However, investigators for a field survey of the President's Commission, covering police departments in major cities outside New York, were able to gain access to the precincts, and their direct observation supports the theory that it is the officers at the middle level who tend to cover for the abuses of the men working under them.[10] This cover may take the form of advice about criminal charges, the sys-

[9]*The Task Force Report on the Police* (Washington, Government Printing Office, 1967), p. 195. (This report is hereafter referred to as TFRP.)
[10]President's Commission on Law Enforcement and the Administration of Justice, *Field Survey V*, pp. 189 ff.

tem I describe here, or simply of keeping quiet about abuses; in any case, it is characteristic of the extreme solidarity and secrecy of policemen in every city. No doubt the solidarity is as tight as it is because every ranking officer in the typical urban police department has come up through the ranks and shares the mores of the men below him. By the same token, it follows that the introduction of new men at the middle level, specially trained for their jobs rather than drawn from the ranks, would be the most effective way of breaking through the police secrecy. Under present civil service laws, in New York as well as most other communities, it is difficult to alter the system of seniority, but any limitation on the protection of underlings by superiors may be impossible without it.

The Review Board and other institutions in the New York City Police Department do little to discourage the system of cover charges. The Review Board does not hold a hearing until after criminal charges against the complainant have been disposed of, and the charges at a departmental trial are always artfully drawn to avoid any conflict with criminal charges made by the officer involved, even when they have been disposed of. . . . These practices encourage officers to believe that if they can cover themselves by a criminal charge, they will escape censure. If the Department were vitally concerned about seeing justice done, it would make sure that criminal charges were dropped against citizens when a departmental investigation showed that they were unwarranted. Instead, the Department sits back to see whether the officer can make his criminal case stick before proceeding against him.

It is worth mentioning here that the ironclad system of cover charges exists in New York City partly because certain other abuses do not. For example, the New York City Police Department does not permit arrests on "suspicion," a practice allowed by departments in other cities such as Detroit, where 13 percent of the arrests in 1964 were for "detention."[11] Dragnet arrests for suspicious persons do occasionally occur after serious crimes in New York, but in general, if a city policeman has a defendant in custody, he must try to show probable cause for arresting him, and if he is to account for a defendant's injuries by resistance to arrest, he must commence his explanation with a lawful arrest. Hence the elaborate lies about disorderly conduct. It is because the men at the top of the Department are trying to maintain a façade of probable cause for arrest that the men in the middle and at the bottom go to such lengths to cover their mistakes. To be an oppressor is a tricky business in New York, this most liberal of all possible worlds. In jurisdictions where no attempt is made to maintain the requirements of probable cause, the system of cover charges is correspondingly less deeply entrenched.

Furthermore, in other jurisdictions a policeman can afford to be a little lax in covering himself because he can rely on the district attorney to help him out if he makes a mistake. In the District of Columbia, for example, the authorities

[11]TFRP, p. 186.

have in the past preferred charges of filing a false report against people who made complaints about policemen.[12] In one case from that jurisdiction the District Attorney started a prosecution upon minor traffic charges three months after the events were supposed to have occurred, and solely because the defendant had complained against the police officer involved in the incident.[13] If there is an instance of equal skulduggery perpetrated by any of the five New York City district attorneys, I have not heard of it. The only incident in my experience which approaches these in depravity was a threat by the prosecutor in one of my cases, after he had consented to a dismissal of the charges against two out of three codefendants, to reinstate the charges against them if they testified in defense of the third. That is an exceptional incident, however, and it is generally up to the New York City policeman to provide his own cover for his mistakes. If he does not make his accusation at the time of the occurrence, the prosecutor is not likely to look upon the case with favor. The system is the policeman's only solution.

If officials outside the Police Department in New York do not participate directly in protecting police officers, they do so by their silence. The judges, the prosecutors, even the commissioner himself, cannot appear to condone slipshod police work or police abuses. On the other hand, they know that there is such poor police work, and although they would not participate in it, they do not expect to do very much to improve it. The district attorneys go right on taking waivers of damage claims in return for the dismissal of criminal charges, the remedies for abuses continue to be inadequate, and all in all, with some exceptions, the system works nearly as effectively as if all the other officials participated in it. They become parties to the system in the sense that they know, or should know, that the policeman is covering his mistakes by lying and are content to let him go on doing it. They maintain the rigid standards of due process required in a modern liberal society by letting the patrolman vary the facts to fit the case. They have helped to make the policeman the target for much of the hostility in the city by making him do all the dirty work.

Ironically, the vigilance and sophistication of citizens in pursuing what few poor remedies are open to them have probably helped to make the system as rigid as it is. In rural communities and small towns, where abused citizens are satisfied to forget the whole thing if the police will forget it, criminal charges may not be used by the police as a cover, but in New York, where many abused citizens are very likely to complain to the Department and perhaps even bring a lawsuit, criminal charges are almost invariably preferred. One thoroughly puzzled woman who complained of being manhandled in a welfare center by a policeman told me that the officer had later bought her lunch and said that he would like to drop the charges, but he dared not because she might sue the city. She tried to convince him that she would not sue, but he felt that he could not

---

[12]*Ibid.*,p. 195.
[13]Miller Dixon v. District of Columbia, D.C. Cir. Dkt. No. 21084/67.

trust her; regardless of the promises she made while she was under arrest, she might change her mind later. The system was too ironclad for him to let her go.

• • •

The Police and Society

. . . The policeman on the beat sees his job to be one of maintaining tranquillity and perpetuating the established routine. Any person out of the ordinary is suspicious; if he is recognizably deviant, then he is potentially criminal. Potentially criminal also, and a severe threat to good order, is any challenge to the policeman's authority. A challenge may come either from the deviant, simply by his failure to respond to an officer's order, or from the ordinary citizen who is openly defiant. In either case, the challenge will be met by anger and one or more weapons out of the arsenal of legal sanctions, from a summons up through summary corporal punishment. Criminal charges, beginning with disorderly conduct and ranging up to felonious assault, are commonly laid to cover the actions of the policeman and to punish the offender. In the eyes of the police, arrest is practically tantamount to guilt, and the police will supply the allegations necessary for conviction; the courts are treated as a mere adjunct to their purpose. Distortion of the facts becomes the most pervasive and the most significant of abuses. The police ethic justifies any action which is intended to maintain order or to convict any wrongdoer (i.e., anyone actually or potentially guilty of crime). In studying search and seizure, for example, we found that the police tend to justify a search made "in good faith" — really looking for a crime — regardless of whether it is a lawful search or not. Once again, the facts are distorted so as to justify the search in the eyes of the courts, although there is less distortion in connection with house searches than with searches of persons on the street.

We have seen that some abuses do not precisely fit our conception of the tendencies in police behavior that give rise to abuses — those, for example, which are committed for personal reasons like family revenge or professional advancement. Although it is significant that these are the abuses which are generally condemned by policemen themselves, it is important to observe that such actions shade off subtly into duty-oriented abuses, because the Department encourages the man to identify himself with his authority. Other abuses, such as those that occur during mass police action, seem to be similar in origin to ordinary street abuses, but are distorted out of all recognition by mass frenzy. Finally, a few abuses are chronic because they are systematically encouraged by the Department. In condoning systematic abuses, the Department itself acts upon much the same rationale that the individual policeman uses to justify isolated street abuses. When the Department authorizes an action in violation of due process, such as a roundup of prostitutes, it does so to preserve order ("a clean city") and to harass a group of people who are considered undesirable. The chief difference between isolated and systematic abuses is that there is less distortion of the facts about the latter, because the individual officers find it unnecessary and thus make no attempt to cover their own actions. Except in the case of systematic harassment, then, distortion of fact is the thread than runs through all abuses, however different they may seem. The distortion of fact, and indeed every abuse, is rationalized by the need to maintain authority and catch wrongdoers.

The tendencies in police behavior which give rise to abuses do form a sort of "police character": a man, suspicious of outsiders, who is concerned with order, reacts aggressively to threats to his authority, and regards every attempt to control that authority with cynicism. Other authors have attempted to mold this character, or a similar one, into a sociological or psychological framework Neiderhoffer, for example, has analyzed the policeman according to the characteristics of an "authoritarian personality."[14] For our purposes terms like this are tautological; the word "authoritarian" either reiterates what we know already about policemen, or else it is irrelevant. To get at the roots of police behavior, I should have to go to a deeper psychological level, and the fragmentary nature of the evidence collected here, together with the fragmentary nature of the available psychological studies, prevents me from performing the task adequately. It is enough here for us to know that the characteristic police reactions are a logical product of the police role (e.g. maintaining order) and the traditions of the Department (e.g. secrecy).

The important point for us here is that police abuses *do* form a pattern, and that they reveal one aspect of police character. Police abuses are a set of consistent responses in similar situations, and not very surprising responses at that. The policeman identifies with the office with which he is vested, and considers a threat to that office the most serious of threats to good order. It is misleading to say that his views are unlawful or unethical. They may participate in a different ethic, and perhaps even in a somewhat different law from the criminal law of the modern, liberal state, but unquestionably there are ethics and law at work here. It is a "good guys versus bad guys" ethic, free of the strictures of procedure: the person who is "wise to a cop" has no respect for authority and deserves to be punished. Deviants are undesirable, and the police should ride herd on them to keep them from intruding on the rest of society. A criminal ought to be caught and put in jail the quickest way that one can get him there.

Is this really such an unfamiliar canon of ethics? Doesn't it rather ring of the opinion reflected in most of our newspaper editorials and shared by thousands of citizens? We should realize that the appeals courts ask an extraordinary act of will from the policeman. They ask him to be concerned solely with "enforcing law," not with simply catching wrongdoers. It is an abstract distinction that most of us treat with the same suspicion as does the policeman, and the policeman continues to ignore it partly because we encourage him to do so.

Max Weber distinguished between the substantive rationality and the formal rationality of legal systems.[15] A substantively rational system obeys generally

---

[14]Niederhoffer, *Behind the Shield*, p. 107.

[15]Max Rheinstein, ed. *Max Weber on Law and Economy in Society*, trans. Edward Shils (Cambridge, Mass., Harvard University Press, 1954), Chs. 7 and 8.

consistent, if poorly articulated, norms of ethics and law. The formally rational legal system is more coherent and logically consistent. It is the typical system of a society governed by an impersonal bureaucracy dealing at arm's length with citizens. Our criminal law is becoming increasingly rational in the formal sense, as economic and political relations become more abstract, while the police continue to adhere to a kind of substantive rationality. Formal rationality is increasing partly because the rough rules of the police are simply inadequate to the social changes taking place in our society, and to the ideal of equal justice. The conflict in which the police are placed — between their own code and the formal code — is the conflict of modern city administration, and indeed, of the people who live in the cities. The question which the citizens of New York, and of every city which pretends to a liberal administration, must ask themselves is whether they would rather have the police follow their old-fashioned rules, or whether they really want the police to adhere to the formally rational (and substantively different) rules of due process of law. It is clear that there is something in most of us that does not want the police to change; the landslide vote against a civilian review board demonstrated that, if nothing else. We want efficiency, quick work, order above all, though we claim to want due process and equal justice as well. Without basic changes to eliminate the obvious injustices in our society, we cannot expect to have all these, but if all else fails, we think we would like to preserve at least the appearance of order ("peace and quiet"). It is for the police to play the tough, no-nonsense half of this conflict. The enlightened feel a little guilty about their own impulse to coerce respect by force, and it is easier for them to turn the police into a whipping boy than to admit to such instincts themselves. The police do all the "wrong" things — club people who are outcasts or defiant of authority — but the unfortunate truth is that much public disapproval of their actions is sheer hypocrisy. Many, perhaps most, citizens feel that it is desirable for a policeman to coerce adherence to his code by punching a "wise kid" or ransacking an apartment without a warrant. They hide from themselves the fact that every act which coerces obedience from a man by unlawful means is by definition an act of oppression. . . .

For legislators and judges the police are a godsend, because all the acts of oppression that must be performed in this society to keep it running smoothly are pushed upon the police. The police get the blame, and the officials stay free of the stigma of approving their highhanded acts. The police have become the repository of all the illiberal impulses in this liberal society; they are under heavy fire because most of us no longer admit so readily to our illiberal impulses as we once did.

The welter of statutes intended to control morality by penalizing the possession of some contraband, or the act of vagrancy or loitering, pointedly reveals the hypocrisy in the administration of our laws. The legislature passes such statutes, knowing quite well that their enforcement encourages a host of police abuses, including unlawful searches, dragnet arrests, and systematic harassment. The links between these abuses and morals legislation is no accident; the impulse in each is the same. It is the drive to legislate the lives of others and to force them to adhere to an accepted mode of life; that impulse cannot be enforced without abusing the rights of citizens.

Viewed in this light, the distortions of fact by policemen, which we have pronounced at once the most dangerous and the most pervasive of abuses, do not seem quite so shocking or unnatural. Lying is a bridge between the substantively rational rules of the police and the formally rational ones of the criminal law, by which the first are made to appear to conform to the second.

The actions of the police probably embody a natural tendency of any group of bureaucrats, working out in the field where their decisions have low visibility, to avoid the effect of restrictive regulations that conflict with existing practices. . . . The effects of the conflict between rule and practice are more dramatic in the case of the police than of other bureaucrats because the victims of their practices wind up in jail, and more prolonged and exaggerated because of the traditional solidarity and secrecy of the police. Like many other minor bureaucrats before them, however, the police continue to adhere to their old customs because they know that their superiors and much of the rest of society approves. They have no motive to change.

Up to this point, I have made little effort to choose between the substantively rational rules of the police and the formally rational rules of the courts. Even without a choice between the two, the distortion of facts by the police is an inherently dangerous practice. In our society, law enforcement officers are expected to respond to civilian legal directives, and if they fail to do so, then the power of society to change its laws is significantly decreased, and the police in effect control the criminal law. But the covert adherence to another set of laws is not nearly so serious if in fact those laws are superior to, or just as good as, the stated laws. If the formally rational rules are unworkable or unnecessary, to avoid them is a relatively minor failing, because in the long run the laws themselves will probably change. It is not the function of this [essay] to make value judgments about hhe effectiveness of the formal rules, but the problem cannot be ignored entirely if we are to understand the effect of police abuses. We must at least look a little more deeply into the formal rules.

Let us consider, as an example, the requirements of "probable cause" for an arrest and search. The limitations of probable cause are established to make sure that the police arrest only people whom a neutral and rational observer would suppose to be guilty. A system of dragnet arrest and search would probably catch more persons carrying contraband than the application of probable cause, but the courts attempt to make a prior judgment so that those who are obviously or probably innocent will not be harassed. Any rule that relaxes the requirements of probable cause necessarily lowers the standards of suspicion and tends to include more innocent persons. As we have seen, police methods, when they depart from probable cause, do tend to punish innocent people together with the guilty. The point for use here is that the courts have made a policy judgment to exclude as many arrests of the innocent as possible, consistent with catching the obvious criminal. The rule of the courts, apart from being formally rational, also embodies a substantively rational rule *different* from that of the police, and the formal nature of the rule is intended to control police action and enforce the underlying substantive principle. The substantively rational police rule favors investigation so long as it is done in good faith, a policy judgment which is properly for the courts rather than the police to make because the courts are better equipped to strike the balance between investigation and freedom. The police rule inevitably favors investigation — favors the authorities, in short. It is apparent, then, that the rule of the courts is not dryly logical or lacking in practical effectiveness, but is simply based on a judgment different from that of the police about the needs of society.

There are two principles underlying such procedural rules: first, that the elaboration of legal rules is properly a matter for the courts, and second, that the balance is properly struck on the side of personal liberty. Our society is suspicious of both these principles; it finds the police rules easier to grasp than the court rules. Though the incidence of police abuses may be reduced by institutional reforms, the police rules cannot change finally until society decides to disapprove of them. More citizens must come to accept the principle that the term "law enforcement" refers to enforcement of the laws and not to the arrest or harassment of defiant or deviant citizens. More citizens must come to accept the principle that all police abuses constitute the enforcement of a private code by unlawful means and that, as such, they are inherently oppressive. Too many people, in fact, understand this already and yet secretly (or openly) approve the acts of the police because they fear the defiance of others as much as do the police. They recognize that nearly every form of defiance of an authority, whether it be from a "wise" teen-ager, from the hippie way of life, or finally, from an open revolt by students or black people, is a demand for a new way of life both social and economic. They fear that demand for change enough to use force to oppose it, and unless that fear disappears, they will continue to condone police acts of oppression, and police rules willl not change.

The saddest aspect of police abuses is that they defeat their avowed purposes. The rationalization for street abuses is that they create or at least maintain respect for authority. Punishment for the wise guy is supposed to "teach him a lesson," but the system of police abuses creates only contempt for authority. A man, and especially the already defiant black man in this country, does not feel respect when he is clubbed, when he is charged with a crime, and when he loses his only job because he has been convicted. Words cannot convey the despair, the hatred, induced by a system which injures a man and then brands him as a criminal. It is not enough to say that the behavior of all the administrators involved — the officer, his superiors, the prosecutor, the judge — is understandable. The system within which the police work is evil, for the simplest of reasons: because it injures people and destroys their respect for the legal process. It is not for nothing that ghetto people have chosen police abuses as the symbol of oppression; it is because they actually *are* acts of oppression.

This brings us back to the importance of police abuses and the urgency of the problem they present. They are hardly the only acts of oppression in our cities, but they are the easiest to recognize. The anger they instill is part of the fuel for the violent uprisings in our cities during the past five years. As an indispensable condition for ending those uprisings, the police must change their allegiance from a private code to a publicly recognized rule of law, and it is only when society itself demands this change that it will take place.

9. Jeff Gerth

The Americanization of 1984

Every Sunday night, without fail, special agent Lew Erskine "gets his man." Occasionally, at the end of another thrilling episode of the TV show, "The FBI," Efrem Zimbalist, Jr., who portrays Erskine, comes on the screen to enlist the public's aid in the FBI's search for Bernardine Dohrn or some other "dangerous fugitive" on the "Ten Most Wanted" list.

But Zimbalist has not been making very many post-show pep talks lately. Perhaps this is because they are tired of showing the same old faces. After all, Bernardine has been on the "most wanted" list for over six hundred days now. And other New Left fugitives such as Katherine Power, Susan Saxe, and Dwight Armstrong have proved similarly elusive. In fact, there have been so few dropouts, the list has become more of a "Top Sixteen." This is all pretty embarassing to the FBI, especially considering that in the past "Top Ten" fugitives were nailed within an average of 132 days.

The change in "most wanted" types to political activists from "public enemies" like John Dillinger and Baby Face Nelson indicates that a major shift has taken place within the FBI in particular, and the Justice Department in general. This shift in focus is partly a reaction to the mass uprisings of the last six years — Watts, Newark, Detroit, the post-Cambodian/Kent State riots — and the threat they present to those in power.

In response to this threat, John Mitchell, Richard Kleindienst and their associates at Justice have quietly implemented a broad strategy against "domestic subversion," despite the ex-Attorney General's private claim that "there is no such thing as the 'New Left.' "

Reprinted from *Sundance Magazine*, 1 (April/May 1972), pp. 58–65, by permission of the publisher, 1913 Filmore Street, San Francisco, California 94115.

The FBI's difficulty in tracking down the New Left fugitives has only led to an intensification of this strategy. The ten thousand files pilfered from the Media, Pennsylvania FBI office in March 1971 show the Bureau's preoccupation with domestic subversion: over half of the files deal with political investigation and surveillance. A distinct minority of the files involve crimes such as murder, rape, burglary; only *one percent* deal with organized crime. Instead, private citizens, college professors, Quakers, and minority group members engaged in neighborhood projects are the subject of FBI investigative and surveillance activities. All, apparently, are included in the government's loose definition of "dangerous radicals."

Over the past three years, Mitchell and Kleindienst have effected a tremendous consolidation of political, legal and police power within the Justice Department; operating at the top through the appointments to the Supreme Court and on the bottom through the education, training, and deployment of the nation's 420,000 policemen. America's criminal justice system, its main bulwark against development of a police state, is becoming increasingly vulnerable to an ideological use of power by top Justice officials. Acting Attorney General Kleindienst and his former boss Mitchell leave no doubt where their politics are. "This country is going so far to the right you are not even going to recognize it," Mitchell bragged at a cocktail party (though he later denied it when it appeared in print). And Kleindienst has branded radicals as "ideological criminals" who should be incarcerated in "detention camps."

Through a number of little-known Justice Department agencies and the FBI, Mitchell, Kleindienst, Assistant Attorney General Robert Mardian, J. Edgar Hoover, and others, have quietly broadened the scope of clandestine surveillance and intelligence-gathering in the U.S. One crucial aspect of their effort is that the military plays only a marginal role — that of supplying weapons and intelligence-gathering techniques. The "science" of counter-insurgency perfected in Vietnam has been transplanted back on the home front in the form of an extensive domestic intelligence system. But by operating through the criminal justice system — the police, the courts and the prisons — and with the technical advice of police "scientists," Justice officials have put forth a civilian facade.

But the essence of the emerging state is clear. Robert Gallatti, head of the New York State Intelligence and Information System (NYSIIS), remarked in 1970 that "the public is concerned, and rightfully so, about such things as 1984. It is getting awfully close — 1984 is obviously only fourteen years away, and some of the predictions of George Orwell are holding up pretty well. We had better be concerned about this because people are beginning to get mighty nervous."

The two on-going stages in the construction of a police state in America are first, the collection and evaluation of data; and second, political or police action based on this data. The first stage involves the use of huge computerized data banks, infrared and TV cameras, neighborhood spy networks and a staggering variety of other intelligence-gathering devices. Technology has accelerated the development of stage one considerably. Computers alone have offered an exponential leap forward. (Consider, for instance, how many twelve-digit numbers an average person can add in twenty seconds — two, compared with an adding machine — twenty, or a computer — 160 million.) Other technological advances are equally important. It is now possible to simultaneously tap a phone and bug the room where the phone is located without tampering with the phone itself or even going near the premises. And new domestic surveillance techniques first developed in Vietnam include robot televisions and cameras that "see" in the dark. All of this new technology is placed in the hands of a burgeoning U.S. intelligence community that now numbers over 200,000.

Stage two — political or police action based on intelligence data — includes the use of provocateurs to infiltrate radical organizations, the black-listing of individuals by federal or other intelligence organizations, and the release of information leading to the virtual conviction through the media of the Harrisburg Seven and alleged bank bomber Ronald Kaufman.

Some of the biggest but subtlest steps toward 1984 have been taken through the Law Enforcement Assistance Administration (LEAA) — a Justice Department agency which obtained its original legislative mandate in the 1968 Safe Streets Act, a law passed hastily in the wake of wide-spread unrest triggered by the assassination of Martin Luther King. Under Mitchell and Kleindienst, LEAA has become the fastest growing agency of government, its budget increasing twenty-five fold from $63 million in fiscal year 1968 to the latest authorization of $1.75 *billion* for fiscal year 1973. The majority of LEAA's money goes to the purchase of weapons and electronic hardware for police departments around the country.

Since last summer, the man heading LEAA has been Jerris Leonard, a close friend of Mitchell's for the past fifteen years. Leonard was formerly the chief of the Justice Department's civil rights division, where he was responsible for the decision not to press charges against the National Guard in the Kent State killings, or against the Chicago police in the Fred Hampton case. Earlier, in the fall of 1969, over half of the lawyers in Leonard's civil rights division publicly protested his blocking of a Mississippi school desegregation case.

Some of the programs LEAA has funded are:

Civil Disorder Assistance
—The sweeping arrest of 894 students (out of a total enrollment of 2500) at all-black Mississippi Valley State College, thereby breaking a peaceful campus-wide strike. The *Washington Post* noted that LEAA's action "marked the beginning of one of the Nixon Administration's potentially most volatile policies — federal 'technical assistance' in local suppression of 'campus disorders.' " The crime in this "disorder" was "obstructing a public road on a campus." Police action was made possible by a LEAA grant of $288,405 to the Mississippi State Commission for "developing plans and procedures for coping with civil disorders (riot control and natural disaster) and organized crime."

— The deaths of four people in the disorders in Baton Rouge, Louisiana were underwritten in part by LEAA grants, one of which was for $48,708 on June 25, 1970, and called for the creation of a "special trouble shooting squad." Another was for $31,942 on November 30, 1970 for "police technical assistance for prevention and control of civil disorders." A special squad made up of city police, sheriffs, and parish county police, equipped with submachine guns and M-16's with bayonets, sealed off the streets where a Black Muslim rally was being held. Soon afterward the shooting began.

— LEAA has to date supplied $750,000 to the cities of San Diego and Miami to develop joint defenses against potential demonstrations at the conventions this summer. Some equipment will be transferred to San Diego when the Miami convention is finished.

Weapon Stockpiling

— LEAA is arming the police to the teeth. For $16,464 LEAA bought the tank used by Louisiana police to storm a New Orleans Black Panther headquarters September 10, 1970. The same tank, classified by LEAA bureaucrats as a "command and control vehicle," had been used earlier against demonstrating black students.

Clandestine Surveillance

— A LEAA grant in Delaware financed mobile surveillance units hidden in civilian rental trucks. The grant provided for operators dressed in the uniforms of dry-cleaner delivery men, salesmen, public utilities workers, and others, "making it possible to be in a neighborhood without being obvious." The trucks are to be equipped with infrared cameras and video equipment for taking pictures night or day of "suspicious pesons."

— In Tampa, Florida a LEAA-sponsored surveillance system costing $150,000 will use computers to control a network of videotape cameras and alarms placed in "convenient" grocery stores and overlooking shopping center parking lots. Operators will monitor the cameras constantly, using their zoom lenses for close-ups of any "suspicious activity."

— In San Jose, California; Hoboken, New Jersey; and Mount Vernon, New York; TV cameras are placed throughout the cities' business areas, flashing their images back to the local police headquarters where they are monitored for "suspicious" goings on. The Mt. Vernon equipment, which cost LEAA $47,000, is capable of discerning a man-sized object in extreme darkness from more than a half-mile away.

Data Gathering

— LEAA has sponsored the construction of statewide data banks on "actual or *potential* troublemakers." (Italics added.) In Oklahoma, for example, a $29,453 grant enabled the National Guard to compile dossiers on six thousand individuals, only one-third of them Oklahomans. The ACLU and Oklahoma Civil Liberties Union have filed suit in federal court maintaining the dossiers are used to "harass and intimidate." One of the lawyers, Stephen Jones, has evidence that some Oklahomans have been blacklisted as a result of the dossiers. "A number of Negroes and whites who have taken part in peace rallies or racial demonstrations," he told the *New York Times*, began "having trouble finding jobs or getting into college."

— A $46,000 appropriation has been made to the New Haven, Connecticut Police Department for an "exploration of law enforcement utilization of the 1970 Census Bureau Data." The police can use the census data, which will be stored in IBM computers, during "civil disorders" to obtain vital background information (age, schooling, occupation) on the residents of the area. (The New Haven project has caused considerable public outcry.)

All of the aforementioned projects have been implemented under a cloak of secrecy. Some LEAA schemes have aroused enough public anger, however, that they had to be shelved at the last moment. But indications are that many of them will be reactivated at a later date. Some examples:

— A psychiatric prison center at Vacaville, California which would administer "advance therapy" to inmates considered the "most violent." Electric brain implants and lobotomies, insulin and electric shock treatment, and the use of a death-simulating drug called Anectine were some of the techniques being considered. Some parts of this proposal were dropped but only after a loud public outcry. According to Walter Barkdull, director of prison planning for the California Department of Corrections, however, the brain surgery plan "hasn't been abandoned."

— A plan for black-suited "night riders" in Alabama. This group would operate only at night, keeping a constant check on the whereabouts of suspects. The proposal, developed by Alabama's LEAA-backed Law Enforcement Planning Agency, stated, that "for practical and psychological reasons, officers . . . will drive only black, unmarked patrol cars. They will be attired in black uniforms, shoes and caps with no bright or reflective buttons, badges or buckles visible.

"The primary impact of this detail on the criminal community will be psychological — and to this purpose officers will make maximum use of the opportunity to question suspects during the hours of darkness.

"In addition, officers will range as far as possible during each night's operation to create the impression that the detail's numbers are much greater than is actually the case."

— A plan for a neighborhood spy network in Indiana. This proposal, drafted by the LEAA-funded Indiana Criminal Justice Planning Agency, called for the hiring of "rumor monitors" or "individuals who know their neighborhoods well" and who "will report to city officials possible dangerous situations."

Agency director William Greenman was asked in a TV interview whether the plan would lead to a spy network. "That's what it could amount to," he replied. "We might not be able to trust our neighbors after a while. But as long as we're not doing anything wrong, we shouldn't have to worry, I don't suppose."

Greenman blamed "unfortunate publicity" for the LEAA decision to shelve his plans for the informer network.

These LEAA projects are part of a larger Justice Department strategy to use the criminal justice system for political purposes. Another key part of this strategy is the development of a comprehensive intelligence network. In the short run, such a network enables the government to prevent as well as quell civil disorders. In the long run, it aids the government in establishing more total control.

Without fanfare, and conveniently couched in the Newspeak of "police scientists" and bureaucrats, America moved a long way down the road toward 1984 on November 29, 1971. On that date, the FBI opened the first national computerized "criminal justice information center" — a system which superseded a $45 million LEAA pilot project, started in 1969, called Project SEARCH (System for Electronic Analysis and Retrieval of Criminal Histories).

Public demands on the Justice Department and the FBI to create a centralized intelligence system date back to 1951 and the Kefauver Hearings on organized crime. At that time, however, the demands fell on a deaf ear. In 1956, after being turned down by the FBI, a number of local police intelligence officals formed the Law Enforcement Intelligence Unit, independent of the Bureau, to coordinate organized crime intelligence data. Then, in 1960, at its annual convention, the International Association of Chiefs of Police formulated a resolution calling for the creation of a federal nerve center on organized crime. FBI Director Hoover lobbied strongly against the measure, saying it would lead to a "Gestapo," and it was defeated.

Finally, in the late Sixties the government reacted to the threat, not of organized crime, but of Watts, with the introduction of its computerized SEARCH system.

The FBI did not publicly name its successor to SEARCH: in fact, it has been extremely secretive about all the details of the system. But the key concept behind it is the instantaneous input/output of massive intelligence information. While former FBI data banks were extensive, access to the files was hindered by lags in computer technology. The Bureau has fingerprints of over eighty-six million people, or data on more than one-third of the population of the U.S., in its files. In addition, the federal investigators have access to overlapping, occasionally outdated information recorded in 264 million police records, 323 million medical case histories, 279 million psychiatric dossiers, and 100 million credit files.

Traditionally, all data has had to be sent and received through the regular U.S. postal system, causing as much as a seven to ten day lag between the time a person is arrested and fingerprinted, and the time local police receive a verification of the suspect's identity and his criminal record from the FBI. But by the time the new computer system is in full operation (sometime in 1975) law enforcement officials and many others will have instant access to information on any person they deem "suspicious."

The prototype intelligence system, SEARCH, grew out of recommendations by a number of Presidential commission reports in the late Sixties and the two major pieces of crime legislation of the last four years. Most important among the reports were those written by the Kerner Commission and the RAND and IDA (Institute for Defense Analysis) task forces. All three recommended steps aimed at correcting the root causes of crime: poverty, discrimination, lack of education and employment. The government, while virtually ignoring these recommendations, concentrated instead on developing measures to combat crime itself. The three reports also contained recommendations for more effective crime-fighting: namely, get as much information on as many people as possible and make it quickly and easily accessible to the law enforcement officers; or, in other words, data-ize the people.

The Safe Streets Act of 1968 and the Organized Crime Control Act of 1970 (pushed through Congress after the rash of west coast Weatherman bombings in October of that year), authorized improved intelligence-gathering techniques, thereby providing the legislative mandate for development of the centralized computer system.

Beginning with LEAA's Project SEARCH in 1969, six pilot states developed a prototype for comptuer integration ("interfacing") of all state and local computer networks with a central coordinating computer bank in Washington. Information flow in the system was multi-directional; not only was there a two-way flow with the big Washington computer, but any one local terminal could transmit information to any other local terminal. The big coordinating computer interfaced not only with local police "criminal" networks, but with all law enforcement data banks relating to "civil disorders" and "organized crime."

The most obvious use of a SEARCH-like system would be by a policeman in a patrol car stopping a "suspect" and wanting to determine whether he has a "criminal history." Instantly available would be a complete record of any arrest the suspect has ever had anywhere, *regardless* of the eventual disposition of the case. In other words, it would make no difference whether he had been found guilty of the crime, his "criminal history" contains the fact of his arrest. This "criminal history" was (under the pilot project) to include only matters of the "public record." These facts would consist of the suspect's name, age, sex, description, arrests, and court dispositions. Information compiled from informers, tips, wiretaps, or other potentially inaccurate sources was *not* to be included.

Under the FBI, however, the new intelligence system has access to a considerably wider range of information. Hoover's insistence that none of the "raw material" in FBI dossiers be "evaluated" for accuracy or substance means that data gathered from informers and wiretaps now *will* be included in a person's "criminal history." A good deal of damaging information, much of it of questionable reliability or legality, is therefore made readily available by this new system.

Probably the most frequent source of unreliable information is the paid informer. In a paper submitted to the Princeton FBI conference October 29–30, 1971, sponsored by the Committee on Public Justice, Frank Donner of the American Civil Liberties Union notes that "of all the techniques of collecting political information about a subject or target, the use of informers is by far the most intensive; it is also the most widespread and pervasive."

The informer, while he is the chief contributor of raw, unevaluated data to FBI dossiers, remains the most unreliable element of the intelligence system. As the FBI has stepped up its recruitment campaign for informers, it has, according to Donner, "increased the risk of hoaxes."

A case in point is a twenty-year-old Baltimore high school dropout named Robert Savage, Jr., whom the FBI payrolled as an informer for fourteen months.

Savage, reportedly while on LSD, concocted an imaginary plot to bomb a federal building in Chicago. He then selected names and addresses of the "plotters" at random from a telephone book. Finally, in late 1969, he approached agents with a letter, written as a joke by his girlfriend, detailing plans to dynamite the building. The Bureau sent Savage on expense-paid trips to Philadelphia and Chicago to meet with the fictional plotters.

The critical point is that this type of unreliable data gets placed in FBI files without any evaluation for accuracy.

Recognizing the threat to the individual's right of privacy, a special SEARCH privacy committee had submitted a report on May 25, 1970 calling for the exclusion of all "unverified data." But Jerome Daunt, FBI Information Director, denounced and ignored the committee's recommendations, which included one providing for the right of any citizen to inspect his own file. This public discussion of the privacy controversy was conducted during the time SEARCH was still under LEAA's direction. Then on December 19, 1970, shortly before the pilot project expired, Attorney General Mitchell, in an internal directive that was not released publicly, transferred prime responsibility for any future development of a "nationwide system for exchanging criminal histories" from LEAA to the FBI. This was the green light for the new SEARCH. According to Senator Charles Mathias (D) of Maryland, the directive "made no reference to privacy issues or the fate of the standards so carefully shaped by the SEARCH Project Group."

Even the policy recommendation mentioned by Mathias and approved by the SEARCH Project Group would have been inadequate. It simply read: "Users of SEARCH should be cautioned that reliance upon unverified data is hazardous." This would have done nothing to prevent dissemination of derogatory information.

The FBI's current practices are serious infringements of any reasonable standards for "criminal histories." The Bureau does not require its arrest records to be updated with the disposition of a case. Whether an individual is innocent or guilty is irrelevant; if he has been arrested, he is branded a "criminal." This lack of differentiation between the innocent and the guilty adds to the FBI's files considerably. Every year, 3.5 million (or almost fifty percent) of the 7.5 million people arrested are either acquitted or never prosecuted.

The FBI also makes no distinction between adult and juvenile arrest records, thereby adding approximately two million "criminal histories" to the system every year. Many of these arrests are for truancy or violation of a curfew.

The Justice Department, too, has devised new methods for building bigger and better data banks. On March 10, 1970 Mitchell asked Congress to pass a law enabling federal law enforcement officers to obtain court orders that would require "suspects" in criminal cases to submit to identification by "fingerprints, palm prints, foot prints, measurements, blood specimens, urine specimens, saliva samples, photographs, and line-ups." Failure to comply would mean contempt of court and a subsequent jail sentence.

Maybe you have never been arrested. Maybe you do not have any "associates." Well, you are probably a "suspect" for something or other, and if you do not agree that you are a "suspect," you are arrested! The Attorney General will get your name in his computer one way or another. Congress so far has not approved the Justice Department's request, but they are still trying.

Because respect for privacy is not built into the massive computer network, and the data flow between any two cities or states cannot be controlled, the privacy of the entire system is only as strong as its weakest link. If the present practices of law enforcement agencies at all levels of government are any indication, future access to and dissemination of inaccurate dossiers will be virtually unrestricted.

One example is the Leneka, Kansas Police Department, which has used its terminals (which connect with Washington via the Kansas City Police Department) to inquire, upon request by Leneka apartment owners, into the arrest records of prospective tenants. A spokesman for the Leneka Police Department justified this free service to city businessmen by pointing out that several "undesirables" had thus been kept out of the city.

Another example of abuse is the New York State Intelligence and Information System (NYSIIS). Operated by the state police, this huge network has sold its information to American Airlines, Pinkerton's, Burns Detective Agency, and Retail Credit Co., the nation's largest insurance investigative agency which itself has forty-five million dossiers. Under a 1969 New York state law, member firms of the New York Stock Exchange have access to NYSIIS information on any of their employees.

But the FBI itself is the most flagrant abuser of police intelligence data. The Bureau collects four million fingerprints a year from banks, insurance companies, school boards, and other sources not in any way connected with law enforcement. According to Aryeh Nein, executive director of ACLU, (in a paper entitled "The Dissemination of Derogatory Data by the FBI" and submitted to the Princeton FBI Conference), "The standard operating procedure followed by the FBI on receiving these (non-criminal) prints was to report to the submitting agency the material in the FBI files on the subject of the fingerprints.''

According to a bill (S-2546) introduced at the Justice Department's request by Senator Roman Hruska (R) of Nebraska, ''Access to criminal justice information systems shall be available only to law enforcement agencies. Criminal justice information may be used only for law enforcement purposes.''

But this is only Justice Department Newspeak. The bill also states: '' 'law enforcement' means any activity pertaining to crime prevention, control, or reduction, or the enforcement of the criminal law, including but not limited to police efforts to prevent, control, or reduce crime or to apprehend criminals, activities of correction, probation, or parole authorities.''

Since barring persons with arrest records from employment or licenses has previously been construed by the FBI as an effort at ''crime prevention, control, or reduction,'' the Attorney General's bill is a smokescreen for the institutionalization of blacklisting by the FBI.

The FBI, in fact, already has a regular practice of making confidential information available to various friendly public and private sources.

Rep. John Rooney of Brooklyn (D), chairman of the House appropriations subcommittee, the man who guides Hoover's budget requests through Congress, has admitted on TV that the Director told him ''confidential information'' about the activities and associations of Martin Luther King, Jr.

The Bureau also makes a regular practice of passing unverified data on to friendly media like the *Chicago Tribune* and the *San Francisco Examiner*. *Examiner* reporter Ed Montgomery serves as an outlet for FBI news.

This practice of planned leaks is a dangerous abrogation of the Bureau's responsibilities as a national agency of justice. Take, for example, the case of the alleged bank bomber Ronald Kaufman, who suddenly found a version of his life story splashed all over the nation's front pages in mid-January. A good portion of that story presumably was gathered from ''reliable'' informers, and now Mr. Kaufman has been practically convicted through the media. With no chance to challenge his character assassination, Mr. Kaufman's only comfort comes from the FBI's difficulty in capturing him — a factor, no doubt, in the decision to release damning information on him in the first place.

The FBI's computerized intelligence system, laced with unreliable data and abuse of that data, has the ultimate ability to incarcerate those it brands serious threats to domestic security.

According to the *Washington Post,* the FBI maintains a 'super-secret'' listing of so-called ''potential subversives'' — a file ''that would be the basis for federal arrests in the event of war or an 'internal security emergency.' '' The file, called the ''security'' or ''agitator index,'' is reported to contain at least ten thousand names. The FBI's new intelligence system will give law enforcement officials the capability to determine instantaneously whether a person stopped on the street during an ''internal security emergency'' would be eligible for ''detainment.''

On November 30 last year, when the FBI phased out project SEARCH and put the massive new intelligence system into operation, it refused to release to the press a copy of the criminal data bank regulations. In fact, it refused to answer any questions whatsoever regarding the project. What the American people do not know *will* hurt them. And the FBI does not want them to find that out.

Furthermore, the Justice Department has not released *any* news about the biggest, most secret plan of all — a mammoth "computerized National Law Enforcement Communications System" (NLECS) to be fully operative by the early 1980's. At the Symposium on Law Enforcement Science and Technology sponsored by LEAA from March 31 to April 2, 1970, Claude T. Smith, of UNIVAC Division Sperry Rand, outlined a super computer network designed to tap all "federal information systems currently planned or under development." Included would be all the computer systems in the Census Bureau, the Internal Revenue Service, the Social Security Administration and the Veteran's Administration. While this idea exists only on paper right now, it should be remembered that the formulation of Project SEARCH evolved out of papers submitted to a similar symposium in 1967. There is no reason to believe that anything will stop development of NLECS early in the next decade.

Who funds Big Brother? A look at the appeals by Nixon, Mitchell and Hoover to Congress over the last three years, and the actual use of the grants they have succeeded in getting reveals a masterful deception by the Administration, not just of the public, but of Congress itself. Under the guise of fighting "organized crime," the Administration has channeled appropriations into the LEAA and SEARCH projects, and through the promise of cracking down on the flow of narcotics, the Nixon team has eroded such civil liberties as the right to bail and protection from unlawful search and seizure. Organized crime and narcotics, meanwhile, flourish unabated.

Every year since the ghetto insurrections of 1965, Congress has appropriated more and more money to fight crime. And the Nixon Administration has been more than adroit at manipulating the issues and emotions which govern the purse strings, acquiring money on one pretense and using it on another.

On April 24, 1969, three months after taking office, Nixon began his "fight" against organized crime with the first of the four major "crime" speeches he has made to Congress. Nixon asked Congress to approve approximately $300 million for LEAA, promising that "a substantial portion of this assistance money will be utilized to fight organized crime."

Four days later, Mitchell addressed the U.S. Chamber of Commerce, reiterating the same line: "We are asking for a $300 million appropriation for the Law Enforcement Assistance Administration, which supplies funding to state and local anti-crime programs. We hope that a substantial portion of these funds will be used by state and local law enforcement to attack organized crime." Congress approved the requested appropriation.

But Nixon also wanted a specific crime legislation package. Introduced in January 1969, it was finally passed in October 1970 as the Organized Crime

Control Act. This important piece of legislation contained new provisions in the areas of grand jury powers, electronic surveillance and self-incrimination.

A careful analysis of the bill, created by law and order zealot Sen. John McClellan (D) of Arkansas, shows that it provides a legislative framework for the police state apparatus now under construction. Even the staid Association of the Bar of New York City called the bill "almost Kafkaesque" and concluded in an exhaustive fifty-two page analysis that the bill not only contains "the seeds of repression," but "frequently hits targets which were not intended and misses those that were."

Most of those who have suffered under the Organized Crime Control Act are political activists. Leslie Bacon, Sister Jocques Egan (friend of the Berrigans), and Anthony Russo (colleague of Daniel Ellsberg) — all have spent time in jail as a direct result of the expanded grand jury powers granted government prosecutors. In all, more than 150 activists were subpoenaed by investigative grand juries around the country in 1971 alone.

Government prosecutors, led by Guy Goodwin of the Justice Department's Internal Securities Division, turned federal grand juries into rubber stamps in this new method of radical witch-hunting. Meanwhile, organized crime cases were shunted aside and ignored. Assistant Attorney General Robert Mardian was appointed head of the ISD within three weeks of the act's passage, and his staff of investigative lawyers was doubled.

The administration also used the threat of organized crime to justify its plea for expanded funds for intelligence-gathering. LEAA official Clarence Coster, in a speech on organized crime February 10, 1970, noted that "a major grant awarded by LEAA in fiscal 1969 will help build the prototype of a Criminal Justice Information System which will collect and store in one place all recorded data about criminals, including members of the syndicate." He was talking, in Newspeak, about the SEARCH project.

Until the late Sixties, as noted above, Hoover consistently rejected the idea of a national intelligence apparatus to attack organized crime. This was in keeping with his adamant refusal to admit even the existence of criminal syndicates in this country. As author and organized-crime expert Hank Messick has written: "In the Twenties, when city gangs were transformed into regional crime syndicates, Hoover rounded up alleged Reds. In the Thirties, when gangsters began bankrolling businessmen and politicians, Hoover chased 'Ma' Barker and 'Pretty Boy' Floyd. In the Forties, when the National Crime Syndicate operated black markets and established regional gambling centers, Hoover hunted Nazi spies. In the Fifties, as the crime syndicate expanded to Havana and London, Hoover helped (Joe) McCarthy create a national hysteria (against Communism). In the Sixties, as the syndicate began its crucial transition to respectability. Hoover turned back the clock thirty years and 'discovered' La Cosa Nostra."

Though he was late to join the battle with "La Cosa Nostra," Hoover has made the most of it in his requests for larger appropriations. In 1969 he asked for and received 535 additional agents to "strengthen the fight against organized crime." Then, in 1970, the Organized Crime Control Act authorized an additional thousand special agents. The overall increase, both in percentage and numbers of agents during the Nixon Administration, is the largest for any comparable time period in the history of the FBI.

Over the same period, the Bureau of Narcotics and Dangerous Drugs (located in the Justice Department since 1968) has seen its corps of agents increased from eight hundred to two thousand. As in his appeals for funds to fight organized crime, Nixon has used deception in his narcotics legislation program. The Federal Narcotics Law, a one-hundred page document passed by Congress, contained a one-paragraph provision allowing federal agents to break into a home without warning or court order in order to prevent the destruction of narcotics.

The tactic used to pass this "no-knock" provision was repeated later in the enactment of "pre-trial detention" in the District of Columbia Crime Bill. The bill legalized detention of narcotics addicts and sellers, and various other "dangerous criminals." Sen. Sam Ervin (D), a strict constructionist from North Carolina, noted that "the Justice Department has chosen to hide its preventive detention legislation in the deepest recesses of the House version of the D.C. crime bill." Ervin said the bill was "unconstitutional and smacks of a police state rather than a democracy under law."

This tremendous intensification of effort would seem to indicate a crusade against organized crime and narcotics, but in fact, as the *New York Times* has noted, most of the new FBI agents have been assigned to campus, bombing or hi-jacking cases. The Justice Department's report of a three-hundred percent increase in narcotics seizures for 1971 is a result, not of tougher enforcement, but of the increased flow of drugs into the country. ABC-TV newsman Tom Brannigan reported January 26, 1972 on the availability of heroin, citing the negligible effects of a recent $40 million smack seizure in New York City: "This used to cause panic among the addicts on the streets of Harlem, causing the prices to skyrocket. Now the supply is so great, it barely causes a ripple."

The FBI record in dealing with organized crime, conspicuously blank for forty years, remains virtually blank to the present. According to a column written by Jack Anderson in September, 1971, the FBI had assigned only four agents to a federally coordinated task force against organized crime, whereas other federal agencies had provided 224 detectives. As already noted, only one percent of the Media files related to syndicate activity — and this is at a time when there is almost unanimous agreement that the Mafia is more powerful than ever before.

The Justice Department as a whole has been no more energetic than the FBI in its "fight" against organized crime. According to its own figures, only 3.5 percent of the nearly $300 million LEAA received in 1970 after Mitchell promised a "substantial portion" of it would go to fight organized crime actually was used for that purpose. And of that small amount, over two-thirds was spent building intelligence systems which were "interfaceable with civil disorder computer systems.'' This means most of the already miniscule organized crime allocation was used to build better data banks against non-organized ''criminals.''

One Justice Department step "against" organized crime was the establishment in April 1969 of a special New York task force, the primary purpose of which, editorialized the *New York Times*, was to "bypass" U.S. Attorney for New York City, Robert Morgenthau. Morgenthau is recognized by almost every expert in the field as the country's leading prosecutor of organized crime. His regional jurisdiction allowed him to move against the penetration of Wall Street by the most powerful and sophisticated elements of the syndicate, particularly the financial manipulations of Mafia kingpin Meyer Lansky. Before the end of 1969, Mitchell wrote Morgenthau flatly telling him to resign.

In infiltrating Wall Street, the Mafia had begun the last step in its ''crucial transition to respectability'', its tentacles already reaching into such legitimate businesses as banking, insurance, real estate, transportation, hotels, restaurants and the entertainment industry. With this penetration of legitimate businesses in mind, Mitchell spoke before the anti-trust section of the American Bar Association March 28, 1969 and suggested that anti-trust action be used against the Mafia as a means to crack organized crime finances. Many lawyers present at the meeting went home marvelling at this new technique, but Mitchell's proposal turned out to be an empty gesture. FBI statistics show that convictions in anti-trust cases have dropped steadily from 139 in fiscal year 1969, to 55 in fiscal 1970, to only 34 in fiscal 1971!

Furthermore, Kleindienst, Mitchell and Richard McLaren, former head of the Justice Department's anti-trust division, have all been implicated in the International Telephone & Telegraph scandal. The Justice Department dropped anti-trust charges against IT&T in return for a $400,000 contribution to the fund-raising efforts for this summer's Republican convention in San Diego.

Overall, the Justice Department's record in the fight against organized crime and narcotics appears to be at best a carefully executed strategy of "benign neglect" — and at worst a scandalous case of systematic deception.

The Americanization of 1984 is well under way. Through LEAA and the FBI's new version of SEARCH, the legal and technological groundwork has been furtively laid. But the creators of Big American Brother — an apparatus designed to keep track of people's thoughts and actions — have carefully avoided a military image. For His brain, they have chosen the "criminal justice information center," rather than the more ominous-sounding "national data bank" — an idea shelved by the government in 1966. Whereas in the Orwellian nightmare Big Brother helped the Ministry of Love maintain "law and order," in 1972 He is aiding the Department of "Justice" in its fight against "crime."

The enactment of this police state — less conspicuous yet far more threatening than one dominated by the military — is a scientific enterprise. Its low-profiled selective repression is based on surveillance, fear, intimidation, and information control, rather than on the massive deployment of police.

An underlying drive facilitating development of a police state is the historical governmental trend toward centralization. Information-gathering is merely one more example of the federal government's tendency to centralize and coordinate state and local activities. The implications of information concentrated in Washington are clear: Senator Charles Mathias, commenting in 1967 on the government's 3.1 billion records about individual citizens, suggested that "if knowledge is power, this encyclopedic knowledge gives government the raw materials of tyranny."

Technological advances have facilitated the drive to increased concentration of information and power. Computers and Vietnam-perfected hardware applied on the home front are shortening the road to 1984.

To obtain Congressional funding for its activities, the Administration has used secrecy, false promises and outright deception. And a government predicated on deception is inevitably threatened by the truth. Therefore, the public's growing appeals for truth in government have only resulted in more closed doors.

Police vulnerability in the last few years has contributed to this paranoia. FBI agents have failed to apprehend bank bombers as easily as bank robbers. Government prosecutors have been unable to convince jurors of alleged conspiratorial plots. While pretending to have "an FBI agent behind every mailbox" (as one Media document suggests), the Bureau remains baffled as to the whereabouts of such publicized figures as fly-by-night parachuter D. B. Cooper or the Capitol bombers. The police state mentality, already shrouded in secrecy, is forced to cover up or downplay its failures.

Secrecy is vital to the success of the Administration's effort. Clandestine political intelligence-gathering, surveillance, the suppression and manipulation of information — all are central to the smooth operation of a police state. LEAA's plans for television sets on street corners, in unmarked rental trucks and in shopping center parking lots are *secret* projects. The government releases only sketchy details of these projects to the press, because publicity usually leads to widespread outrage in the community.

Thought control in America will not come easily. Consciousness is shaped by a myriad of media whose constant bombardment create an information overload. But while the dissemination of information may be fragmented, the origin of that information is dangerously concentrated. The primary sources of "crime news" in this society — the police, district attorneys, and government officials — selectively choose which facts to release, when to release them, and whom to release them to. A select few facts may get dissected by commentators a thousand times over, while other relevant information remains suppressed and undiscussed.

Periodic revelations like the Pentagon Papers or the Anderson Papers merely expose the tip of an informational iceberg which remains hidden from the public eye. The role of the press as an investigative counter-force is limited. After all, who in the society has the money and power to gather large amounts of information, subpoena witnesses, and compel testimony? Not the press. Nobody, in fact, except the police and the government.

What if the FBI files were open to inspection by non-FBI personnel? What if the minutes of the Attorney General's meetings with the FBI Director were part of the public record?

What is actually in those files and what is talked about at those meetings remains unknown. We can speculate, but those we would expose are secure in their ability to dismiss our speculation as lacking in "documentation" — something only they themselves could supply.

Adolph Hitler implemented the "big lie": the more you have to cover up, the bigger the lie you tell the people. Because the American people have always distrusted politicians, government officials have been forced to perfect the "big lie" even further. After all, who would believe the government would lie that much? One of the most blatant lies by a government official in recent months was Assistant Attorney General Mardian's barefaced assertion to ABC-TV's Frank Reynolds during an interview January 8: "There is no surveillance of political activists as such."

The Americanization of 1984, the creation of an invisible police state, is just what Mitchell ominously promised — that the country will go "so far to the right," that its citizens will not "recognize" it. Because if the people recognize what is happening, they will never accept it.

Chapter Five

THE ADMINISTRATION
OF CRIMINAL LAW

According to the legal ideology, administration of criminal law is also
the "administration of justice." Whether justice is indeed attained in
such administration is a vital question, but what this ideology ignores
is the prior question of the "justice of the law." That is, if the legal
order itself is not just, no amount of just administration can correct
this basic injustice. The development of a critical understanding of
the justice of the legal system has been our concern in the previous
chapters.

In turning our attention to the administration of criminal law, we
begin to examine how the law is practiced after persons have been
arrested. The fate of the accused is now in the hands of the judicial
system and its related bureaucracies. Decisions are made at various
stages of the judicial process. The stages consist of the first judicial
appearance (including the preliminary hearing), the formal charge (including indictment and filing of information), the arraignment (including pretrial motions and applications), the trial or nontrial adjudication, the sentence, and the final release from the legal system. At
each stage the decision reached by certain officials limits the alternatives for decisions in the subsequent stages.

Judicial decision-making has been investigated by social scientists
in recent years. Such research is removing the "purple curtain" of
justice from the activities of the judicial system. The criminal court,
we know from observation, has an organization and an operation of
its own outside of public scrutiny and beyond legal considerations:
"The court, unlike most other formal organizations, functions as a
genuinely 'closed community' in that it successfully conceals the true
nature of its routine operations from the view of outsiders — and

sometimes even from some of the participants themselves. It socializes its members and participants toward compliance with specific objectives which are not part of the official goals of justice and due process."[1]

The first selection in this chapter, "Prosecution: Law, Order, and Power," documents the actual operations of the judicial system, including the scope and degree of discretion in judicial decision-making. The authors, William J. Chambliss and Robert B. Seidman, note earlier in their work that they are extending the study of "law in action" begun by the American legal realists. As legal realists, their purpose is to examine the factors that determine how the law is administered. The result of their work is the destruction of myths about legal order in America. Not only do they destroy the myth that "the normative structures of the written law represent the actual operation of the legal order," but they attack the corollary myth that "despite the existence of sharp conflicts between interest groups in the society, the State itself, as represented by the courts and the police, as well as other elements, provides a value-neutral framework within which struggle can take place."[2] The authors add that "this myth of the operation of the law is given the lie daily," and that the legal order "is in fact a self-serving system to maintain power and privilege."

In the selection in this chapter, Chambliss and Seidman proceed to destroy the myths of the legal order in the course of discussing prosecution. They observe that the decision to prosecute is affected by bureaucratic features of the judicial system. The prosecutor will "bargain" with defendants whenever possible in order to achieve a high proportion of convictions. And important as the trial is as an ideal in the administration of criminal law, the fact remains that the most commonly used method of settling cases is adjudication without a trial. Roughly 90 percent of criminal convictions are made on the basis of guilty pleas which are adjudicated without a trial.[3] Because of a tremendous case load, the judicial system depends upon the use of the practice known as "plea bargaining." Furthermore, the interests and interactions of the prosecutor and the defense attorney are crucial in arriving at a charge.[4] In the course of repeated negotiations, the prosecution and defense develop unstated guides, outside of the penal

---

[1]Abraham S Blumberg, *Criminal Justice* (Chicago: Quadrangle Books, 1967), p. 70. For other observations on the social organization of the administration of criminal justice, see Jerome H. Skolnick, "Social Control in the Adversary System," *Journal of Conflict Resolution*, 11 (March, 1967), pp. 52–70. On the juvenile court, see Aaron V. Cicourel, *The Social Organization of Juvenile Justice*, (New York: John Wiley & Sons, 1968).

[2]William J. Chambliss and Robert B. Seidman, *Law, Order, and Power* (Reading, Mass.: Addison-Wesley, 1971), p. 3.

[3]Donald J. Newman, *Conviction: The Determination of Guilt or Innocence Without Trial* (Boston: Little, Brown and Company, 1966).

[4]David Sudnow, "Normal Crimes: Sociological Features of the Penal Code in a Public Defender Office," *Social Problems*, 12 (Winter, 1965), pp. 255–276.

code, for the conviction of the defendant, usually reducing the original charges to lesser charges for the certainty of a conviction.

When negotiation between legal representatives has failed to result in the defendant's plea of guilty, or when the defendant pleads not guilty without any attempt at bargaining, a criminal trial provides the setting for adjudication. The criminal trial is a process of constructing a reality of the case at hand. Social and subjective factors enter into the arguments of the attorneys, the testimony of witnesses, the deliberations of jurors, and the prejudices and actions of the judge. The criminal trial is not strictly an exercise in fact-finding and logical deduction but is a product of politics and discretions, ultimately for the benefit of the state.

Regarding the jury, the assumption is that defendants are tried by a representative body of the citizenry. However, research has shown that social and economic biases operate in the methods by which jurors are selected and in the ways in which they deliberate. Lower occupational groups tend to be excluded from juries systematically, and foremen are often selected on the basis of their social position in the community.[5] Furthermore, the social status and sex of an individual juror are related to his participation and influence in jury deliberations.

Following conviction of the defendant, a decision is made regarding the sentence that will be attached to the conviction. Sentencing involves manipulation and use of discretion by a number of persons. Even when sentencing is the province of the judge, other persons participate in making the decision. In many jurisdictions a presentence investigation is made by personnel of the probation department attached to the court. The report, which covers the defendant's personal and social background, his criminal record, and his mental and physical condition, includes the probation department's recommendations for sentencing. With the report and recommendations in hand, the judge then imposes a sentence.[6] Though the final sentencing decision may belong to the judge, the decisions of others are important in the actual disposition of the sentence.

Sentencing statistics and studies indicate that criminal court judges differ in their use of discretion in sentencing. For example, a study of sentences assigned in nearly 7,500 criminal cases, handled by six judges over ten years in a county in New Jersey, reported that the judges differed considerably in the frequency, length, and type of sentence they assigned to convicted offenders.[7] Other studies have shown

[5]W. S. Robinson, "Bias, Probability, and Trial by Jury," *American Sociological Review*, 15 (February, 1950), pp. 73–78; Fred L. Strodtbeck, Rita M. James, and Charles Hawkins, "Social Status and Jury Deliberations," *American Sociological Review*, 22 (December, 1957), pp. 713–719.

[6]Robert M. Carter and Leslie T. Wilkins, "Some Factors in Sentencing Policy," *Journal of Criminal Law, Criminology and Police Science*, 58 (December, 1967), pp. 503–514.

[7]Frederick J. Gaudet, "The Difference Between Judges in Granting Sentences of Probation," *Temple Law Quarterly*, 19 (April, 1946), pp. 471–484.

that sentences differ according to such characteristics of the defendants as race.[8] Even when nonracial characteristics are controlled in the analysis, blacks are found to receive longer prison sentences than whites.

Chambliss and Seidman, in their review and analysis of the judicial process, conclude that given the bureaucratic complexity of the judicial system it is difficult for the citizen to discern the operation of bias and institutionalized discrimination. In fact, it is the complexity of the system that allows the myth of justice to prevail. The myth continues to serve those who profit from it — the state and the ruling class.

The next selection, Robert Lefcourt's "Law Against the People," begins by recognizing the discriminatory practices of the judicial system and goes on to make a critique of the system. In a vivid portrayal of the American legal system, Lefcourt argues that the existing law cannot resolve the contradictions that have developed within American society. The judicial system cannot meet the challenges of today because its purpose is to protect existing economic, political, and social relations. Lefcourt writes that the legal system is bankrupt, beyond technical solutions and reform.

Lefcourt's examination of the American legal system adds to our critical understanding of criminal law. His account of the operation of the judicial process is to the point: "The class and racist practices inherent in the bail system and plea bargaining contradict democratic principles at the same time as they uphold the economic relationship of a capitalist society. The legal superstructure is not designed to dispense justice to a whole community nor to allow changes in property relations. It legitimizes the power of the few and punishes those who have been defeated by or who challenge this power." And his view of the future, based on a critical understanding of the administration of criminal law, is plausible: "But as the Establishment uses its law to cut off resistance, people will begin to see legal relationships as they actually are, coexisting with the economic and political system. Law will be demystified. People will no longer tolerate a system in which large corporations, wealthy individuals, and property owners receive the greatest benefits. They will no longer accept the pluralist mask behind which the law pretends to be an impartial voice among conflicting groups or individuals. The people themselves will then assume authority and become their own lawmakers."

Haywood Burns, in "Racism and American Law," deals specifically with the racist character of the American judicial system. He states, in fact, that "in this country law has been the handmaiden of racism." That is, not only is law discriminatory, but it perpetuates

[8]Henry Allen Bullock, "Significance of the Racial Factor in the Length of Prison Sentences," *Journal of Criminal Law, Criminology and Police Science*, 52 (November–December, 1961), pp. 411–417.

the racism in American society. Burns examines from a historical perspective the racism in the law (both criminal and civil) regarding the Indian, the Oriental, and the black experiences in America. In the last part of the essay he analyzes the manner in which racism continues to play a role in the judicial system.

The law has been used against minorities "to make sure that these inferior beings stayed in their place — whatever that might be at the moment." Laws have thus excluded Indians, Orientals, and blacks from their lands, from participation in the political process, and from basic human rights. And in spite of Supreme Court decisions and civil rights legislation, racism continues to operate in the American legal system, maintaining the subordinate position of Third World people. Justice for blacks is still different from that for whites, as witnessed in disparities in sentencing and in the granting of probation and parole. Racism in the law is institutionalized as a product of caste and class subordination in capitalist society. Burns concludes by observing that law cannot transcend racism but can only confirm it, as long as the social order is racist and class determined.

The political quality of justice is most obvious in the criminal trial. Though there have always been political trials in the United States, the response of the capitalist order to the challenges of the last decade has exposed the political nature of the criminal trial.[9]

The last selection in this chapter applies an understanding of the criminal trial and the judicial system to the political events of recent years. In "The New Radical-Criminal Trials: A Step Toward a Class-For-Itself in the American Proletariat?" David Sternberg contrasts the traditional trial model with the more recent trials that involve a challenge to the legitimacy of the court. Sternberg describes the character of these trials, ranging from the conspiracy trial of the Chicago Eight (following the demonstrations at the 1968 Democratic National Convention) to the trials of the Black Panthers. Finally he considers the possible impact of these trials on the future of the administration of justice in the United States.

Sternberg concludes that these trials will have a significant effect on the administration of criminal justice in the 1970s. He writes:

I believe that these trials, interacting with rebellions in the houses of detentions and prisons during the same period, have permanently affected the political consciousness of large numbers of present (and future) "clients" in various stages of the administration of justice. Although it is blurred by the complicating variable of race consciousness in our society, it seems to me that the political element is substantial enough to allow one to refer, in Marxist-Leninist terms, to an acceleration of *class* consciousness among these clients, and to some progress toward a "class-for-itself." The emerging solidarity

[9]See Leon Friedman, "Political Power and Legal Legitimacy: A Short History of Political Trials," *The Antioch Review*, 30 (Summer, 1970), pp. 157–170.

and power of that class-for-itself, catalyzed by the radical-criminal trials, may drastically reshape the ground rules and outcomes of criminal procedures during the 1970s.

The major impact of these trials will be that accused persons will demand a trial instead of subjecting themselves to the plea-copping strategy of the state. The result may be a considerable alteration in the administration of criminal justice in America.

In recent years, however, the state has created a judicial structure to handle the challenges to the existing order. The modern form of criminal justice consists of a complex of judicial weapons to secure domestic order, including the use of conspiracy charges, preventive detention, grand jury proceedings, mass prosecutions, and the like.[10] Though these tactics do not usually result in a successful prosecution and often are judged to be unconstitutional, they enable the government to repress threatening thoughts and actions. Again, the legal system serves the purposes of the state. The legal order and political order are one; and the economic order is ultimately secured by both law and politics.

The judiciary, in other words, is playing a vital role in the new program of crime control. Crime, as the new enemy of the state, is replacing internal communism as the threat to domestic security. Not only conventional attacks on private property (such as robbery and burglary), or crimes against the person (murder and assault), but also those acts that appear to threaten domestic order are now being handled by the government as crime — civil disobedience, verbal expression of political dissent, and organized protest of various forms.

From a radically critical perspective, the new era in crime control is more than a matter of government officials imposing their will on the people. What is occurring is the logical extension of an innately oppressive system. The only way the capitalist system can survive when the people begin to question its legitimacy is by applying the law. The judicial system has long been a tool of repression, but in the last few years we have experienced the true nature of criminal justice in capitalist society. The state is using its ultimate weapon — the administration of "justice" — to protect the established order.

[10]See, for example, Richard Harris, *Justice: The Crisis of Law Order, and Freedom in America* (New York: E. P. Dutton, 1970); *Trials of the Resistance* (New York: Vintage Books, 1970); Frank J. Donner and Eugene Cerruti, "The Grand Jury Network: How the Nixon Administration Has Secretly Perverted a Traditional Safeguard of Individual Rights," *The Nation*, 214 (January 3, 1972), pp. 5–20.

10. William J. Chambliss
Robert B. Seidman

Prosecution: Law, Order, and Power

The typical situation surrounding criminal prosecution is characterized by Wayne LaFave as

one in which the police make an arrest without a warrant and then bring the suspect to the prosecutor with a request that he approve the issuance of a warrant. The decision to arrest is clearly made by the police. The decision as to whether to charge the suspect and the selection of the charge are the responsibility of the prosecutor. The prosecutor's charging decision is manifested by his approval or refusal of the issuance of the warrant.[1]

For an offense to move from arrest to consideration by a court it must pass through intermediary processing by the prosecutor's office. At this stage of the legal process it is determined in which of essentially three possible ways the case is to move from arrest to court proceedings: indictment, information, and complaint.

In general, all three possibilities hinge on prosecutorial willingness to proceed. An indictment is a finding by a grand jury that there is probable cause to believe that the accused committed the crime charged. Since there is no defense before a grand jury, the grand jury considers only the evidence presented by the prosecutor. It is a rare grand jury that defies the prosecutor. An information is a charge of criminal offense filed by the prosecutor on the basis of his own determination of probable cause. A complaint by a citizen charging a man of criminal offense in most states cannot be heard in court, but must be made to the prosecutor. The prosecutor stands astride the criminal process, controlling the gates that lead to the trial court.

. . . . The articulated norms for police conduct require the police to enforce every violation of the law. Judges, too, formally are not in the position to dismiss a charge or, if the accused is proven guilty, to find the accused not guilty, although they are given vast powers of discretion in the choice of sentence. Of the three principal actors in a criminal prosecution, the prosecutor alone is formally to decide whether or not to enforce the law, and the degree of crime with which to charge the offender.

Reprinted by permission of Addison-Wesley Publishing Company, Reading, Mass., from *Law, Order, and Power,* by William J. Chambliss and Robert B. Seidman, 1971, pp. 395–414.
    [1]Wayne R. LaFave, *Arrest: The Decision to Take a Suspect into Custody*, Little, Brown, Boston, 1965, p. 53. . . .

What is the scope of the discretion lodged in the prosecutor's office? How in fact is this discretion used? What are the consequences of the prosecutor's having discretion and his use of it in particular ways? It is to these questions that we now turn.

The Scope of the Prosecutor's Discretion

In England, the power of prosecuting criminal cases was originally, and remains in theory today, largely lodged in the hands of private persons, who are not compelled by law to initiate such prosecutions.[2] When initiated, the action still resembles a private lawsuit between private parties rather than a prosecution initiated and carried on by the sovereign power.

In the United States, the office of the public prosecutor was grafted on the traditional system of private criminal litigation.[3] The public prosecutor thus assimilated the functions of the private prosecutor, and just as the private prosecutor had discretion whether or not to prosecute, so the public prosecutor was endowed with the same discretion.

In actuality, the prosecutor's discretion is almost unlimited. As the court said in *Brack v. Wells*,[4] a Maryland case,

As a general rule, whether the State's Attorney does or does not institute
a particular prosecution is a matter which rests in his discretion. Unless the
discretion is grossly abused or such duty is compelled by statute or there is
a clear showing that such duty exists, mandamus will not lie.

That is, a court will not issue a writ compelling the prosecutor to prosecute. It is true that if the power to prosecute is used in a discriminatory manner, its use may be enjoined,[5] but that is nearly the only grounds for interference with the prosecutor's discretion. Occasionally, a court has removed a prosecutor from office for failing to prosecute manifest and flagrant violations of crime within the court's jurisdiction.[6] However, such occasions have been rare. In practice, the prosecutor's decision to initiate a prosecution, and the degree of crime to be charged, lie entirely in his discretion. That discretion is, for all practical purposes, unreviewable.

His discretion is almost as broad if he wants to decline to prosecute a charge already laid. In some states, there are no limits placed upon the prosecutor's discretion to stop a prosecution *in media res*. In most states, however, a small element of judicial control is inserted into the process by permitting the prosecutor to initiate prosecution, but requiring judicial approval for a withdrawal of the

---

[2]Pendleton Howard, *Criminal Justice in England: A Study in Law Administration*, Macmillan, New York, 1931, p. 3.

[3]*Ibid.*, p. 5.

[4]184 Md. 86, 40 A 2d 319 (1944).

[5]LaFave, *op. cit.*, p. 8.

[6]*State ex rel McKittrick v. Graves*, 346 Mo. 990, 144 S.W. 2d 91 (1940); see also *State v. Winnem*, 12 N.J. 152, 96 A 2d 63 (1953); *Wilbur v. Howard*, 70 F. Supp. 930 (E.D. Ky 1947).

charges.[7] In fact, however, as in the case of the decision to prosecute, "the prosecutor's discretion in the use of nol pros (*nolle prosequi*, or decision not to prosecute) is an enormous power in the hands of one public official. Its use is generally not subject to publicity and public scrutiny. . . ."[8]

The scope of the prosecutor's discretion to prosecute or not to do so can be justified in terms of the due-process model. Even within the framework of full enforcement, somebody must make preliminary decisions concerning the probability of success of a prosecution — to decide whether the evidence is sufficient for conviction or whether the facts as claimed fall within or without a rule of law. Moreover, there are numerous cases in which considerations individual to a defendant suggest that invocation of the awful machinery of the criminal law is unnecessary or undesirable:

There are many legitimate reasons for a prosecutor's failure to prosecute: where the alleged criminal act may be the result of some quarrel between neighbours and all parties are equally at fault; where the alleged criminal act may be the result of some minor domestic dispute; where an overzealous creditor may be attempting to pervert the criminal process for the purpose of collecting a civil debt; where the expense of extradition might not justify the spending of public funds to bring back a person accused of a petty crime; where a person may have committed a technical violation of the law, and a warning may be sufficient to prevent further infractions; where the evidence is so slim that it would be unfair to subject a person to the ordeal and notoriety of a prosecution — these are some of the considerations that a prosecutor must weigh before proceeding in any particular case.[9]

In fact, as might be predicted, the decision to prosecute at all tends to be a function of the sorts of pressure to which the prosecutor is subject. That white-collar crime is treated with exceptional leniency by prosecutors has been often documented. They are crimes that frequently do not carry deep social stigmas, and hence the prosecutor rarely feels much animus toward the criminals. His values not being involved, it is easy for him to agree not to prosecute, and to leave to civil action or to the noncriminal action of a regulatory agency the sanctioning of the individuals involved. Ferdinand Lundberg writes:

In the case of white-collar crimes of corporations, if any individual is punished (usually none is) it is only one or very few. The authorities do not dig pertinaciously with a view to ferreting out every last person who had anything to do with the case. But . . . it is different with crimes of the lower classes. In kidnapping, for example, the FBI, in addition to seizing the kidnappers, flushes to the surface anyone who (1) rented them quarters to conceal the kidnapped person or to hide in; (2) acted as unwitting agents for them in conveying messages or collecting ransom; (3) transported them; (4) in any way innocently gave aid and assistance; or (5) was a witness to any of these

[7]See Note, "Prosecutor's discretion," *U. Pa. Law Rev.*, **103**, 1955, p. 1057.
[8]*Ibid.*, p. 1071.
[9]Douglas B. Wright, "Duties of a prosecutor," *Conn. Bar J.*, **33**, 1959, p. 293. . . .

separate acts. The government men do such a splendid job that almost everyone except the obstetricians who brought the various parties into the world are brought to bar, where the aroused judge "breaks the book over their heads" in the course of sentencing.[10]

Prosecutorial discretion is notoriously gentle with the moneyed rich. Cleveland Amory says that in at least seven notorious "society" murders since 1920, the investigations were dropped "for the sake of the families."[11] Lundberg writes:

The mechanics of these affairs are, in general, as follows: After the crime, with the police beginning to set up their lines of investigation, prominent individuals in the same social set, with at least the consent of the family . . . get in touch with the leading politician or politicians upon whom the police are dependent for their jobs. The right politician, responsive to the halo of money, tells the chief of police, "Drop this investigation, for the sake of the grief-ridden family. The guy got what he deserved anyhow, and the family knows it."[12]

It is a rare community in which it is not common knowledge that there is strong evidence that a member of the local elite once committed manslaughter while driving in a drunken state, or something even worse, and escaped prosecution.

In practice, of course, the prosecutor's discretion is not so frequently invoked for the determination of whether or not to prosecute as for the determination of the degree of crime with which the accused is to be charged. According to the due-process model, the considerations to be taken into account in determining the degree of crime to be charged are not different from those to be taken into account in determining whether to prosecute at all. One would expect, therefore, that prosecutors would usually charge less than the maximum conceivable crime, which logically should be reserved only for the most heinous offender. *In fact, however, prosecutors invariably initiate prosecutions for the highest degree of crime that the evidence can sustain.* Before this phenomenon can be explained, however, we must first explain the significance of the negotiated plea of guilty in American criminal procedure.

The Use of Guilty Pleas in the Legal Process

If due process is to be followed, criminal proceedings must clothe the accused with the presumption of innocence until he is proved guilty in an adversary proceeding. . . . the adversary proceeding is supposed to be the sovereign remedy for earlier ills. It is in the courtroom, at the trial itself, that the majestic rights enshrined in the Constitution are upheld; it is there that evidence illegitimately obtained will be suppressed; it is there that the prosecution will be required to keep the high standards to which it is held; and it is there that the presence of

---

[10]Ferdinand Lundberg, *The Rich and the Super-Rich: A Study in the Power of Money Today*, Lyle Stuart, New York, 1968, p. 135. . . .

[11]Cleveland Amory, *Who Killed Society?*, Harper, New York, 1960, pp. 544–551.

[12]Lundberg, *op. cit.*, p. 376. . . .

counsel and judge will prevent oppression or overreaching by police or prosecutor, however weak, humble, or lowly the accused may be.

In fact, these things do happen in many, probably most, cases that actually reach adversary, public hearings. But in the United States, it is an abnormal criminal proceeding that ends up in public hearings. *At least ninety percent of all criminal prosecutions result in guilty pleas*, most of them after negotiations between the accused (or his counsel) and the prosecuting attorney. To understand the nature of criminal prosecution, therefore, it is essential to understand the process by which guilty pleas are reached in so high a proportion of the cases, and to see the consequences.

The norms which formally control the processes by which guilty pleas are reached are consistent with due process. The adversary system allows that there must be some cases in which the proof of guilt is so overwhelming that it is a waste of time for a defendant to insist on a trial when the result is obvious. In such cases, a plea of guilty is not an abridgement of due process.

The principal requirement is that there be some guarantee that the plea is reached not as a result of improper coercion, trickery, promise of lenient treatment, but is the genuine expression of the defendant's free will.

A plea of guilty is of course, frequently the result of a "bargain," but there is no bargain if the defendant is told that, if he does not plead guilty, he will suffer consequences that would otherwise not be visited upon him. To capitulate and enter a plea under a threat of an "or else" can hardly be regarded as the result of the voluntary bargaining process between the defendant and the people sanctioned by propriety and practice.[13]

Hence in most states there is a formal ceremony when a plea of guilty is accepted. Donald Newman reports a typical case, in which a defendant was originally charged with armed robbery. The charge was reduced, after negotiation, to unarmed robbery, a much less serious offense. The following dialogue occurred in open court:

Judge: You want to plead guilty to robbery unarmed?
Defendant: Yes, Sir.
Judge: Your plea is free and voluntary?
Defendant: Yes, Sir.
Judge: No one has promised you anything?
Defendant: No.
Judge: You're pleading guilty because you are guilty?
Defendant: Yes.
Judge: I'll accept your plea of guilty to robbery unarmed and refer it to the probation department for a report and for sentencing December 28.[14]

Indeed, the formal rules frequently require the judge to make such an inquiry. Rule 11 of the Federal Rules of Criminal Procedure provides: "A defendant may

[13]*People v. Picciotti*, 4 N.Y. 2d 340, 151 N.E. 2d 191 (1958).
[14]Donald J. Newman, *Conviction: The Determination of Guilt or Innocence Without Trial*, Little, Brown, Boston, 1966, p. 83. . . .

plead not guilty, guilty, or, with the consent of the court, *nolo contendere*. The court may refuse to accept a plea of guilty, and shall not accept a plea of guilty without first determining that the plea is made voluntarily with understanding of the nature of the charge. If the defendant refuses to plead or if the court refuses to accept a plea of guilty or if a defendant corporation fails to appear, the court shall enter a plea of not guilty.'' Under a federal statute[15] a conviction based on a plea of guilty may be set aside after sentencing if the plea proved to have been involuntary, obtained through promises of leniency, or entered without knowledge of the defendant's rights.

Apart from these grounds, however, a plea of guilty is beyond review. Whatever may have preceded the plea is forever painted out. No court will ever have an opportunity, save in the most extraordinary and unusual cases, to examine the conduct of officials which led to the arrest, the charge, or the plea itself. Thus the guilty plea is at once an admission of guilt by the accused and a cover of obscurity for prior police and prosecutorial activities.

The seemingly mindless ritual by which a defendant assures the court that what everyone present knows is not the case, is the case, is, therefore, not a meaningless little ceremony that does not differ from a host of other seemingly mindless ceremonials in the law. It is the significant act by which the accused surrenders himself voluntarily to the forces of the State; he signifies his cooperation and acquiescence. Those acts of cooperation and acquiescence are the very contrary of the adversary posture which lies at the heart of the due-process proceedings. The assurance that the plea is the genuine expression of the accused man's free will, which is the necessary validation of the plea under the due-process requirements, becomes the instrument by which the defendant voluntarily and finally abandons claims for protection under the due-process guarantees.

As might be expected, a plea of guilty is a source of considerable psychological satisfaction to many of the participants in the law-enforcement agencies. To the police, it is an assurance that their suspicions were accurate.[16] To the prosecutor, it is another case expeditiously handled. To the judge, it places his conduct beyond any possibility of appeal (for sentences are not ordinarily appealable). To the correctional authorities, it suggests that the accused can be rehabilitated, for without recognition of wrongdoing, it is believed, rehabilitation cannot succeed.[17]

The defense counsel, under the due-process model, has a significant role to play in the process of negotiating with the prosecutor for a guilty plea. A federal court has commented:

In a sense, it can be said that most guilty pleas are the result of a "bargain" with the prosecutor. But this standing alone, does not vitiate such pleas. A guilty defendant must always weigh the possibility of his conviction on all

---

[15]28 U.S.C. §2255.
[16]Jerome H. Skolnick, *Justice Without Trial*, Wiley, New York, 1966.
[17]Newman, *op. cit.*, p. 96.

counts, and the possibility of his getting the maximum sentence, against the possibility that he can plead guilty to fewer, or lesser, offenses, and perhaps receive a lighter sentence. The latter possibility exists if he pleads guilty . . . to the whole charge against him.

No competent lawyer, discussing a possible guilty plea with a client, could fail to canvass these possible alternatives with him. Nor would he fail to ascertain the willingness of the prosecutor to "go along." Moreover, if a codefendant is involved, and if the client is anxious to help that codefendant, a competent lawyer would be derelict in his duty if he did not assist in that regard. At the same time, the lawyer is bound to advise his client fully as to his rights, and to the alternatives available to him, and of the fact that neither the lawyer nor the prosecutor nor anyone else can bargain for the court. There is nothing wrong, however, with a lawyer's giving the client the benefit of his judgment as to what the court is likely to do, always making it clear that he is giving advice, not making a promise.

The important thing is that there shall be no "deal" or "bargain" but that the plea shall be a genuine one, by a defendant who is guilty; one who understands his situation, his rights, and the consequences of the plea, and is neither deceived nor coerced.[18]

It can be argued that even the negotiated guilty plea is consistent with due process. It is said to be an essential safety valve to permit the softening of the impersonal general commands of the law.

The negotiated plea is a way in which prosecutors can make value judgments. They can take some of the inhumanity out of the law in certain situations. The law, for example, might in a given case require the death penalty and yet the prosecutor may believe that the death penalty would be unfair, because of the defendant's age, lack of education, drunkenness, or other factors. Our sentencing laws are exceedingly severe and, if they were strictly applied, they would be great breeders of disrespect for the law.[19]

Newman reports a variety of other reasons for charge-reduction in order to humanize criminal justice. The personal characteristics of the accused may suggest the desirability of a reduction — for example, the youth and inexperience of the violator; the "respectability" of the defendant; the disrepute of the victim, complainant, or witnesses; the low mentality of the accused; and the fact that the conduct in question is viewed as normal within the subculture of the defendant (probably the most frequently invoked reason to reduce the charges in cases of blacks involved in violence within the ghetto). Charges are frequently reduced because of mitigating circumstances: violence arising out of a mutual affray; the prior illegal relationship of victim and defendant (it is difficult to press a charge of theft against a prostitute who takes the customer's money without accomplishing the promised act), and the like.

---

[18]*Cortez v. United States*, 337 F. 2d 699, 701 C.A. 9 (1964).

[19]Harris B. Steinberg and Monrad G. Paulsen, "A conversation with defense counsel on problems of a criminal defense," *The Practical Lawyer*, 7, No. 5, 1961, pp. 25–43. . . .

In practice, there are heavy institutional pressures on the prosecutor to obtain guilty pleas. His own office is, at least in urban centers, invariably overworked. Trials are arduous. They require that witnesses be interviewed and their statements taken, the law researched, motions drawn and filed, and perhaps an appeal briefed and argued. To the overworked prosecutor, a short hearing on plea and sentence is a welcome respite.

The police reward the prosecutor when he succeeds in obtaining a guilty plea by praise and good will. Courtroom time for many police is not paid; even when it is paid, it frequently comes in the policeman's off hours. Trials call for putting in extra time by the police, not only in court but in the preparation of testimony as well. If there was police misconduct in the gathering of evidence, a trial risks its exposure.

Judges, too, place enormous pressure on prosecutors to process the criminal docket expeditiously. In every State, there is a chronic shortage of trial judges. Dockets, both civil and criminal, get longer every year as society becomes more complex and more sophisticated, and as the number of automobile accidents continues to mount. Criminal actions take precedence over civil actions. In every civil action, however, there is a hungry lawyer with channels for placing heavy pressure on trial courts through professional associations and personal contact. Moreover courts are always under heavy political and public pressure simply to reduce costs. Perhaps the single most frequent reason given for imposing a relatively light sentence on a guilty plea is that the accused should be rewarded for saving the State the expenses of a trial. Pressures to save money, and to expedite the criminal docket so that lawyers can get their much more lucrative civil cases tried, combine. The higher judiciary (which in most states are responsible for judicial administration) constantly place enormous pressure on lower courts to speed up the docket.

This pressure can be extremely heavy on occasion. The lawyer author remembers a young and relatively inexperienced Public Defender who took his position seriously. Instead of pleading practically everybody guilty (as his predecessor had done), he began to try a relatively high proportion of his cases. The docket in the local trial court immediately slowed up. Out of three judges assigned to that particular bench, one began to spend all his time on criminal trials instead of a third of that time. Since there are a variety of matters — not only criminal cases, but injunctions, receivership matters, cases with elderly defendants, etc. — which have priority, every bit of the delay tended to operate to the detriment of the ordinary civil docket, especially the jury docket. After some six months, this young Public Defender received a peremptory order to come to the state capitol to see the Chief Justice. The Chief Justice read him the riot act in terms of the need to avoid "frivolous" trials and the like, warning him of the necessity of "cooperating" with the prosecution and the judges. The Chief Justice was successful; the Public Defender resigned in disgust.

The trial judge feels very sharply the pressure of the higher judiciary to expedite the docket. This pressure comes in the form of constant judicial pressure to settle civil lawsuits without trial. In criminal cases, there is constant pressure on both the prosecutors and the defense counsel to negotiate guilty pleas. So strong is this interest of the trial judge to expedite the cases that not infrequently either the defense counsel or the prosecutor will find a way to include the judge directly in the plea-bargaining session, knowing that almost invariably the judge will put pressure on whichever party seems most willing to go to trial.

Finally, there are political incentives working on the prosecutor to obtain guilty pleas. A conviction is a conviction. In the election wars, the only measure of a prosecutor's efficiency that the public seems to understand is the gross number of convictions he has obtained. Whether the convictions are for very minor offenses or for major felonies, whether they are obtained by way of guilty pleas or trials, whether they are of the highest or lowest possible charge — no matter; the essential figure is the gross number of convictions. The more trials there are, the lower will be the number of convictions.

There are, therefore, heavy institutional and bureaucratic pressures on the prosecutor to obtain guilty pleas and avert a trial. How widespread bargaining with defendants for guilty pleas has become is indicated in a *University of Pennsylvania Law Review* survey which disclosed that eighty-six percent of the prosecutors responding to the questionnaire had answered "yes" to the question: "Is it the practice of your office to make arrangements with criminal defendants (or their counsel) when appropriate, in order to obtain a plea of guilty?"[20] The same survey revealed that these guilty pleas were obtained through bargaining with the accused. Three types of bargains most often used were promise of sentence-reduction made by the prosecutor, acceptance of pleas to lesser offenses which were included in the charge, and dismissal of some counts or of other indictments. The most prevalent practice was the use of less serious charges by the prosecutors.

Donald Newman investigated the use of bargaining to obtain guilty pleas in one medium-size county in the midwest. His investigation disclosed that of the felons convicted by one particular court ninety-three percent were disposed of by guilty pleas. Newman's findings from this one court in a midwestern community are generally confirmed by Blumberg's study of the use of guilty pleas in a large metropolitan court. Blumberg concludes:

The overwhelming majority of convictions in criminal cases (usually over 90%) are not the product of a combative trial-by-jury process at all, but instead merely involve the sentencing of the individual after a negotiated, bargained-for plea of guilty has been entered.[21]

For the most part, then, the day-to-day activities of a prosecuting attorney in processing criminal cases is to use his office to obtain guilty pleas. The evidence indicates that in a sizeable proportion of the cases processed plea-bargaining is

[20]Dominick R. Vetri, "Guilty plea bargaining: compromise by prosecutors to secure guilty pleas," *U. Pa. Law Rev.*, **112**, 1964, pp. 896–908.

[21]Abraham S. Blumberg, "The practice of law as a confidence game: organizational co-optation of a profession," *Law and Society Rev.*, Vol. 1, No. 2, 1967, p. 18. . . .

completed between the prosecutor and the defendant without a lawyer or public defender intervening on the part of the defendant. Newman found, for example, that fifty percent of the defendants who pleaded guilty did so without the advice of or consultation with counsel.[22]

Judges, too, recognize that without a high proportion of guilty pleas, the whole court administration of criminal law would break down. Newman quotes a judge:[23] "The truth is, that a criminal court can operate only by inducing the great mass of actually guilty defendants to plead guilty, paying in leniency the price for the pleas."[24] In fact, however, as we have seen, the excessive case loads of the courts are themselves a function of decisions within the legal system.

If there is so much pressure to expedite the docket, why do law-enforcement agencies expend so much of their resources in the repeated arrest of drunkards, only to release them after a short confinement in jail and return them to their old habits?[25] There is, it would seem, no particular public pressure on the police or the courts to persist in this mockery of the legal system. The explanation for its continuance seems to be in the bureaucratic structure of the legal system. The arrest of "drunken," "disorderly," and "suspicious" persons provides a source of continuing evidence for the necessity to increase the size of the law-enforcement agencies. It also serves as a constant reminder to "the public" indirectly and the resource allocators directly of the "crime problem" and of the law-enforcement agencies' efforts to "do something" about it. The fact that, by their own admission, what they are doing is not really solving the problem — it is in all likelihood aggravating it — seems to be of little consequence. In the absence of any other solution — and no acceptable alternative has been found — the resource allocators must choose between supporting the present policies, with all their shortcomings, or doing nothing. Doing nothing may well be able. The politicians support the law-enforcement agencies' requests for bigger and presumably better bureaucracies to cope with the problem, by arresting more drunks.

The Consequences of the Guilty Plea System

As a result of these pressures on the prosecutors and the courts, the negotiated plea becomes, not the exception, but the rule. Negotiations between prosecutors and defense counsel become institutionalized. In Detroit, for example, there is one assistant prosecutor whose only job is to screen cases just prior to arraignment with the express purpose of singling out those cases in which guilty pleas are to be obtained for reduced charges.[26] In a typical trial court in Connecticut, the prosecutor has regular office hours in which to confer with defense counsel for plea-bargaining.

[22]Donald J. Newman, "Pleading guilty for considerations: a study of bargain justice," *J. Criminal Law, Criminology, and Police Science*, **46**, 1956, p. 780 at 782.
[23]Justice Henry T. Lummus.
[24]Newman, *Conviction*, p. 76.
[25]LaFave, *op. cit.*, pp. 439–440.
[26]Newman, *Conviction*, p. 80.

All the legal roles involved change radically as plea-negotiation becomes institutionalized. The police, knowing that a negotiation will take place and in order to enhance the prosecution's bargaining position, will tack on numerous charges where one charge might have sufficed as the cause of an arrest. For example, a man arrested for disorderly conduct will be charged with public intoxication, disorderly conduct, resisting arrest, and assaulting a police officer. While there may be some evidence that the additional charges can be sustained, the primary purpose of adding them to the information is to increase the pressure on the defendant to plead guilty to a "lesser" charge — namely, one of the alleged crimes, rather than standing trial for all four.

The prosecutor's discretion is no longer used primarily for independent determination of the appropriate charges. Instead, aware that a bargaining session with a defense counsel is ahead, prosecutors invariably bring the highest charge that the facts will permit. In Detroit, an assistant prosecutor whose job is to file the original charges explained to Newman:

The other day the bargaining prosecutor came in and told us: "For God's sake, give me something to work with over there. Don't reduce these cases over here; let me do it over there or many of these guys will be tried on a misdemeanor." What he was referring to is, if we had graded a case at the lowest charge in the class of offenses in which it logically belonged, a defense attorney could conceivably get his man to plead to even a lower crime, a misdemeanor, for example. We will limit to the highest possible charge because we expect a reduction in court for a plea.[27]

It is, of course, the pervasive vagueness of the substantive criminal law that makes such flexibility possible. As we saw, that vagueness is an important source of prosecutorial discretion. This discretion is supposed to be used, on the due-process model, to humanize the application of the rules so as to achieve "substantial justice." In fact, however, the charges as originally brought are not shaped by these considerations, but by the expectation of bargaining before trial.

The judge's role becomes warped as well. Despite the strictures of the due-process rules, the judges are completely aware that the pleas which are solemnly asserted by defendants to be free and voluntary, made without coercion or promise of benefit, are almost invariably the result of a bargain struck in the hallways. In fact, sometimes one sees a judge solemnly approving a defendant's statement that his plea was not induced by threat or promise, when the plea bargain was actually struck in the judge's chambers!

That plea-bargaining warps the judicial process from its ostensible functions is evident in those cases in which the judges approve a change in plea to a charge which the accused could not possibly have committed. For example, one of the authors . . . represented a defendant on a speeding charge in Connecticut many years ago. A conviction of speeding then resulted in an automatic loss of license for thirty days, which the defendant was loath to incur. There was considerable

[27]*Ibid.*, p. 81. . . .

doubt that the prosecution could prove the speeding charge. The prosecutor offered to reduce the charge to the very minor offense of crossing a white line, usually subject to a $5 fine. The charge was appropriately reduced, and the plea solemnly recorded, although on the street in question there was no white line.

Appellate courts have condoned the practices of plea-bargaining even to the point of refusing to overturn decisions where there was no logical connection between the defendant's acts, and the crime to which he pleaded guilty. A defendant in a New York court who had been charged with manslaughter was permitted to plead guilty to "attempted manslaughter in the second degree."[28] (An attempt at a crime is usually subject to more lenient punishment than the crime itself.) The New York penal code defines manslaughter as a homicide committed "without a design to effect death"; i.e., it is an accident. In his appeal the defendant insisted that one could not be guilty of "attempted manslaughter." One could not "attempt" an accident. The appellate court was well aware that the reduction in charge from "manslaughter" to "attempted manslaughter" which had been made in a lower court was a result of bargaining for a guilty plea between the defendant and the prosecutor. The court upheld the plea, despite the patently illogical nature of the reduced charge:

The question on this appeal is whether this definition which includes an "intent to commit a crime" renders the plea taken by the defendant inoperative, illogical or repugnant and, therefore, invalid. We hold that it does not when a defendant knowingly accepts a plea to attempted manslaughter as was done in this case in satisfaction of an indictment charging a crime carrying a heavier penalty. In such a case, there is no violation of defendant's right to due process. The defendant declined to risk his chances with a jury. He induced the proceeding of which he now complains. He made no objection or complaint when asked in the presence of his counsel whether he had any legal cause to show why judgment should not be pronounced against him, and judgment was thereafter pronounced. As a result, the range of sentence which the court could impose was cut in half — a substantial benefit to the defendant . . . While there may be question whether a plea to attempted manslaughter is technically and logically consistent, such a plea should be sustained on the ground that it was sought by the defendant and freely taken as part of a bargain which was struck for the defendant's benefit.[29]

Of all the roles involved in the criminal process, it is defense counsel's which is most deeply affected by the plea-bargaining system. The guilty plea represents the final submission of the accused to the crime-control model. In the very process of striking it, the defense counsel is ensnared in that model. He is transformed from an adversary upholding the values of due process to a cooperator in crime control. This transformation can be seen by examining the roles of the public defenders and the "courthouse regulars" who handle the bulk of criminal matters.

---

[28]Cited in Donald R. Cressey, "Negotiated justice," *Criminologica*, February 1968.
[29]*Ibid.*

A few states have established public defender's offices. Ordinarily, a public defender is to assist only indigent defendants. The theory on which the role is built is that due process requires an adversary system, the operations of which become a sham when a defendant is without the benefit of counsel. The formal role of the public defender thus places him in perpetual and uncompromising opposition to the public prosecutor.

In fact, it does not work that way, however. Gresham Sykes has shown that even in a maximum-security penitentiary, in which guards and inmates are nominally in completely antagonistic positions, in fact the "society of captives" functions by way of successive bargains struck between guards and prisoners.[30] The bargaining process itself demands that the guards adopt, to a degree, the values of the convicts. In the same way, the bargaining process that is the daily business of the public defender and prosecutor ensnares the defender in the prosecutorial and police culture, the culture upholding the crime-control model of legal system. David Sudnow writes from his study of a public defender's office in California:

> In the course of routinely encountering persons charged with "petty theft," "burglary," "assault with a deadly weapon," "rape," "possession of marijuana," etc., the Public Defender gains knowledge of the typical manner in which offenses of given classes are committed, the social characteristics of the persons who regularly commit them, the features of the settings in which they occur, the types of victims often involved, and the like. He learns to speak knowledgeably of "burglars," "petty thieves," "drunks," "rapists," "narcos," etc., and to attribute to them personal biographies, modes of usual criminal activity, criminal histories, psychological characteristics, and social backgrounds.[31]

As the public defender learns the faces of crime, the personal characteristics and typical behavior patterns of criminals, he comes to adopt the perspective of the prosecutor's office. He adopts this perspective in part because the public defender is dependent on the prosecutor for defining the situation for him. More significantly, the public defender's office must in fact accept the view of the defendant adopted by the prosecutor's office if it is to operate with maximum efficiency as an organization. There will be essentially no rewards (save perhaps the vague and intangible one of serving the clients) for the public defender who too vigorously opposes the view of the prosecuting attorney. Indeed, such a stance would so effectively interrupt the "normal processes" of the organizations concerned to such a degree, that it would simply not be tolerated, as the young public-defender friend of Seidman discovered. On the other hand, a public defender who cooperates with the prosecuting attorney's office in securing guilty pleas from defendants will find that everything, including his superior's assessment of the quality of his work, runs in his favor.

[30]Gresham M'Cready Sykes, *The Society of Captives: A Study of a Maximum Security Prison*, Princeton University Press, Princeton, N.J., 1958, pp. 56–57.
[31]David D. Sudnow, "Normal crimes: sociological features of the penal code in a public defender office," *Social Problems*, **12**, 1965, pp. 255–276. . . .

Blumberg, on the basis of an investigation of criminal lawyers practicing in criminal courts, argues that a similar process corrupts criminal lawyers generally:

The institutional setting of the court defines a role for the defense counsel in a criminal case radically different from the one traditionally depicted. Sociologists and others have focused their attention on the deprivations and social disabilities of such variables as race, ethnicity, and social class as being the source of an accused person's defeat in a criminal court. Largely over-looked is the variable of the court organization itself, which possesses a thrust, purpose and direction of its own. It is grounded in pragmatic values, bureau-cratic priorities, and administrative instruments. These exalt maximum pro-duction and the particularistic career designs of organizational incumbents, whose occupational and career commitments tend to generate a set of pri-orities. These priorities exert a higher claim than the stated ideological goals of "due process of law," and are often inconsistent with them.[32]

The defense attorney, even when he is a private attorney with no formal organi-zational ties to the court (such as those of the public defender or court appointed lawyer, for example) is nonetheless dependent on the organization of the court and the prosecutor's office if he is to be in any way effective. Frequently the defense attorney is maximally rewarded when his case is quickly disposed of. If there is only a limited source of pay for the defense, then the attorney will not receive adequate compensation for his efforts unless he manages to obtain a plea of guilty from his client and a "deal" with the prosecutor. Indeed, the pressure to obtain a plea of guilty from the defendant or to arrange a deal rather than go to trial is omnipresent, even when the defendant has moderate financial resources. The expense of an extended trial is sufficiently great so that only the most affluent defendants can really adequately compensate a lawyer who tries his case rather than obtaining from him a plea of guilty.

In addition to this very lowly economic factor is the fact that most private attor-neys who handle criminal cases become court "regulars." They appear repeatedly before the same judges, and work with the same prosecuting attorneys and the same court staff on a large number of cases. As a consequence, the attorney must operate in each case in ways that increase the likelihood of cooperation from the court and the prosecuting personnel on future cases. The court can confer many favors: low bail, easy sentences, generous continuances to permit the client to find the lawyer's fee. Judges are well aware of the importance of these favors to the private attorneys. Not infrequently, after striking a plea bargain in the judge's presence and with his approval, a judge will say, in effect, "Well, let's go out and put on the show. We must allow the defense counsel to show his client that he is earning his fee." A lawyer who can acquire the reputation that he has "the hex" on a particular judge will attract more clients than one against whom it is believed the judge constantly exercises his discretion adversely.

---

[32]Blumberg, *op. cit.*, p. 19. . . .

Prosecutors, too, can give favors to defense counsel. A reputation of having close and favorable relationships with a prosecutor more than any other single factor can build the practice, and hence the income and prestige, of a criminal lawyer. To reach such a position, the lawyer cannot cause difficulties for the prosecutor. Most important of all, he must be "reasonable" in his plea-bargaining — that is to say, he must keep his demands within the accepted range within which prosecutors exercise their discretion.

Because of the prospective continuing relationship between the prosecutor and the "courthouse regular," the personal interests of the attorney intrude into the plea-bargaining process. A continuing relationship requires good-natured compromise. What the attorney has to compromise, however, is not his personal interests but those of his client. Frequently in a plea-bargaining session in which the same defense counsel represents several clients in different and unrelated cases, at some point one or the other party will try to bargain one case against another: "You give me that one, and I'll give you this other one." The process of bargaining itself corrupts the defense counsel and lures him into the system.

The criminal defense of a client is especially amenable to this type of corruptive influence largely because once the sentence has been imposed, there are rarely any objective criteria by which the defense attorney's performance can be judged. If a man accused of grand larceny is sentenced to only three years in prison, the sentence may represent something of a victory for the defense. Indeed, if the defense attorney can convince the defendant and his relatives that things would have been much worse if they did not enter into a bargain with the prosecutor, then such a turn of events will be viewed as a successful defense. The issue of guilt or innocence takes second place to the fact that it is almost always possible for the defense attorney, trading on his claimed professional expertise, to convince the defendant that things could have been much worse. Since the maximum punishment is rarely imposed, in fact things could generally have been worse. The plea-bargain is well adapted to clothing in an appearance of client-protection a transaction that in fact protects the interests of the defense counsel, and through him the organizational interests of the prosecutor and trial court.

The consequences of the plea-negotiation system of criminal justice is in many, probably most, cases to warp the due-process model of legal system into its very opposite. Any system that depends primarily on pleas of guilty for so high a proportion of the ultimate convictions is hardly an adversary system. Equally important, however, is the effect that the guilty-plea procedures have on the preceding activities in the criminal process.

. . . The principal sanction that has been devised to control police activities is the exclusionary rule. This rule, however, can control police illegality in collecting evidence only if the police fear that the evidence so collected will not be admissible in a later trial. On the other hand, if, as is the case, ninety percent of all criminal charges end in pleas of guilty, then the police need not abstain from illegal methods for fear of a trial. The guilty plea effectively validates all that has gone before.

Indeed, the possibility of the plea-bargaining actually creates an incentive for the police to act illegally. Faced with an illegally extracted confession or evidence obtained in an illegal search, and with the prosecutor bringing the highest degree of charges which the evidence (including the illegal evidence) might sustain, it is a bold and self-confident defendant or defense counsel who will hazard a maximum penalty against the chances of having a judge or jury find that the evidence was in fact illegally obtained. Instead, when a prosecutor asserts that he will insist on trying the accused for the highest possible degree of the crime and that he will seek to validate the evidence obtained, most accused persons will accept a reduced charge in exchange for a plea of guilty. Under such circumstances, the police are acting rationally when they act illegally in obtaining evidence.

In sum, the plea-bargaining system inevitably leads the legal system down the road of crime control and makes a mockery of due process. The intriguing fact, however, is that this result is the consequence of the inherent contradictions in the due-process model itself.

The aim of the due process model is that the criminal process be governed by rules rather than by the discretion of the police, the prosecutors, or the judges. The realization of this aim demands sharply defined substantive norms, and the dogma of a full enforcement of the laws. It demands that the police be inhibited from acting merely on their own suspicion.

The government of men by rules, and not by discretion, however, is inevitably an impossible dream. Rules are necessarily vague; discretion in fact must exist at all legal stages — those of creation, application, and adjudication of rules. Moreover, if indeed it were possible to have a world of crystal-clear norms, it would be an intolerable world. Every legal system must have some flexibility to provide for the manifold differences between the persons who are subject to the rules.

The rules even in an ideal due-process system, therefore, must be flexible somewhere; and that is where the prosecutor's discretion comes in. Even in the best of all possible worlds where due process is observed, there is a place for lawyers to engage in plea-bargaining.

This is not the best of all possible worlds, and there are a variety of forces ready to sanction a lawyer at the expense of his client if he does not plead guilty. The pressures on judges and prosecutors to dispose of criminal matters expeditiously, the vagueness of the criminal law generally and hence its unpredictability, the general unpredictability of trial results, and the practice of increasing the seriousness of charges and sentence if a case came to trial — all these combine to make it rational for the lawyer who wants to play the adversary role and represent the best interests of his client to engage in plea-bargaining. By so doing, however, he puts himself into a position where all the pressures we discussed earlier tend to convert his aims into crime control.

In a way, the juvenile-court system is the limiting case of the crime-control model. It had (until *Gault*) formally abandoned due process in the belief that a system benevolently motivated "to do what's good for Johnny" would serve an offender's interests better than the adversary system and due process. Decisions to prosecute were made, not by lawyers presumably interested in convictions, but by social workers interested in the offender's well-being. What patterns can be discerned in their processing decisions?

The Prosecution of Juveniles

It is rare for prosecutions of juveniles to be determined by the prosecuting attorney's office. Since the early part of the twentieth century the juvenile-court movement has come into full flower. Juveniles are handled in specialized courts by "professionally trained" personnel (frequently social workers), whose professed aim is "to help the child." Not infrequently the juvenile court in fact operates very much like an adult court, save that the juvenile is deprived of his civil liberties. From the perspective of the prosecution, however, the important feature of juvenile justice is that the decision to prosecute is made by the police and court personnel rather than the prosecuting attorney.

In one of the few systematic studies of the selection of juveniles for court appearance, Nathan Goldman investigated the selection process in four Pennsylvania communities.[33] Goldman concentrated on juvenile offenders. He discovered that of all the persons arrested, sixty-four percent were released without charge and thirty-six percent were referred to the court by the police. There were some significant differences in the types of offenses for which the offenders were typically released and those for which the offenders were generally referred to the court. Of juveniles arrested for robbery, larceny, riding in a stolen car, committing sex offenses, and being "incorrigible," the rate of referral to the court exceeded eighty percent. By contrast, fewer than fifteen percent of the arrests made for drunkenness, violating a borough ordinance, disorderly conduct, violating a motor vehicle code, mischief, and property damage culminated in referral to the juvenile court.

On first glance these differences in percentage appear to follow quite reasonably from the "common-sense" interpretation of the relative seriousness of the offenses. Closer scrutiny, however, calls this common-sense interpretation into question. Chambliss' investigation into the activities of two delinquent gangs (a lower-class and a middle-class gang) disclosed different types of behavior.[34] Typically the middle-class gang engaged in drinking, truancy (albeit with some semblance of legitimate excuse), gambling, and the destruction of property (vandalism). The lower-class gang typically engaged in sexual offenses (mostly heterosexual intercourse), fighting (incorrigibility), and theft. As in the case of Goldman's data, the response of the police to these different patterns of delinquency was quite different. The police were generally unaware of the middle-class

---

[33]Nathan Goldman, *The Differential Selection of Juveniles for Court Appearance*, National Research and Information Center, National Council on Crime and Delinquency, 1963.

[34]William J. Chambliss, *Two Gangs*, unpublished manuscript.

gang's delinquency but quite aware of the delinquency of the lower-class gang. Even when aware of the delinquency of both gangs, the police responded with much more severity against the activities of the lower-class gang.

From Chambliss' description of the activities of these two gangs it is quite clear that the common-sense interpretation of the differential response of the authorities as a reflection of the difference in the seriousness of the two types of offenses is erroneous. Indeed, on balance, the activities of the middle-class gang were in some ways more serious than those of the lower-class gang in terms of either economic costs or threat to personal safety.

The differential response to different types of delinquency on the part of the police in fact is best understood as reflecting essentially the same kind of organizational decision-making that characterizes so many other decisions in the legal system. The police refer to court those offenders whose referral to court will bring rewards to the police organization. Concomitantly, the police will refrain from referring to court those persons whose referral is likely to bring forth the wrath of citizens capable of making "trouble" for the organization. It is essentially in this way that the police come to see those offenses of lower-class minority-group juveniles as more serious than the offenses of middle-class juveniles.

The above interpretation is quite consistent with other findings from the Goldman study. Blacks generally have low social status, and by virtue of the additional stigma of being black, are doubtless one of the "best" (i.e., organizationally safest) groups of persons to treat with severe punishment. It follows, therefore, that if the police are making the decision as to whom to send to court primarily on organizational grounds, then the blacks who are arrested should have a higher incidence of court referral than the whites. This is precisely what Goldman found. In his sample, thirty-four percent of the whites arrested were sent to court as contrasted with sixty-five percent of the blacks.

Conclusion

The decision to prosecute and whom to prosecute for alleged offenses, whether made by the prosecuting attorney's office or, in the case of juveniles, by the police, is one which takes its distinctive character from the bureaucratic features of this phase of law-enforcement. The prosecutor will engage in bargaining with defendants whenever possible in order to make certain that he is able to achieve a high proportion of convictions without jeopardizing the efficient operations of the office by prosecuting problematic cases (i.e., politically powerful persons). When the decision to prosecute rests in the hands of the police, their decisions will reflect essentially the same perspective.

As a consequence, given the social organization of most complex societies, it is the politically powerless who are most likely to be prosecuted for alleged crimes. How favorable a "bargain" one can strike with the prosecutor in the pretrial confrontations is a direct function of how politically and economically powerful the defendant is. In terms of day-to-day prosecutorial activities, what this comes down to is that the lower-class, indigent, and minority-group member is most likely to be prosecuted for his offenses, while the more well-to-do members of the society retain considerable immunity. The crime-control model of the legal system in fact described how the prosecutors exercise their discretion. The character of law-enforcement is thus shaped more by the organizational features of the legal system than by the rules and procedures which comprise the "written" though not the "real" law.

11. Robert Lefcourt

Law Against the People

To the person who waits all day to pay a traffic fine, the young man who spends a few months in jail for possessing marijuana, the woman who finds no remedy in court for an exorbitant rent hike, the Black who still cries for implementation of "civil rights" legislation, and the student who resists serving in an illegal war, the judicial process appears to worsen pressing problems rather than solve them.

It is not only that the legal apparatus is time-consuming and expensive; that unjust laws remain unchanged; that the Supreme Court has long refused to consider such "political" questions as the continuing wars in Southeast Asia and the exclusion of nonwhites, young and poor people from most juries; and that the legal system has failed to meet the expectations of certain segments of society. The legal system is bankrupt, and cannot resolve the contradictions which, like air pollution, have grown visibly more threatening to society but whose resolution still is not given high priority.[1]

This bankruptcy is clearest in the priorities of law enforcement and in the criminal courts. Criminal courts protect existing economic, political, and social relations. Historically this role has created a pattern of selective law enforcement practices of which the white upper and middle classes are the beneficiaries. Bail requirements and plea bargaining victimize propertyless defendants who are, in effect, prejudged. The roles of the judge, the prosecuting attorney, and even the defense lawyer for the poor and near-poor reinforce the bias, because they are geared only to the efficient administration of overcrowded, understaffed, and

Reprinted by permission of the author from *Law Against the People*, edited by Robert Lefcourt (Random House, 1971), pp. 21–37.

[1]See *The New York Times*, April 3, 1970, p. 48. "The Ford Foundation has appropriated $1,000,000-plus for grants to study what it feels is a growing lack of faith in this country's judicial process."

dehumanized court bureaucracies. The proposed solutions of many court officials concentrate on material rather than human problems — automating court procedures, expanding facilities, allocating more funds. But the crisis in the legal system is more fundamental and cannot be cured by technical reform: it lies in the class-based and racist character of social relationships and in the court structures which maintain these relationships.

Who Does the Law Protect?

"Jail the Real Criminals"

— A poster seen at various demonstrations in the 1960s

The myth of "equality under law" would have us believe that everyone is subject to society's laws and those who violate the laws are subject to prosecution. Yet in criminal courts across the country it can be easily observed that law enforcement affects almost exclusively the workingman and the poor, and, in recent years, the political activist. In the big cities nonwhites predominate in regular court appearances. The other criminals, the extremely wealthy, the corporations, the landlords, and the middle class white-collar workers are rarely prosecuted and almost never suffer the criminal court process as defendants.

It is impossible to enforce all laws against all lawbreakers. One survey by the President's Crime Commission reports that ninety-one percent of all Americans have violated laws that could subject them to a term in prison.[2] Choices are made as to which laws will be enforced against which people, and law enforcement officials necessarily use guidelines to make these choices.

One of the most important guiding principles behind law enforcement decisions can be inferred from the Crime Commission report. On the one hand it is stated that

Each single crime is a response to a specific situation by a person with an infinitely complicated psychological makeup who is subject to infinitely complicated external pressures. Crime as a whole is millions of such responses.[3]

Accordingly, a corporate executive who arranges to fix prices for the sale of his company's milk product is just as much a "criminal" as a man who steals food from a vegetable market. On the other hand, it is argued that the individual perpetrator of a crime must be seen in the context of his or her environment.

. . . crime flourishes, and has always flourished, in city slums; those neighborhoods where overcrowding, economic deprivation, social disruption, and racial discrimination are endemic.[4]

---

[2]*The Challenge of Crime in a Free Society*, A Report by the President's Commission on Law Enforcement and the Administration of Justice. New York: Avon Books, 1968. Hereafter, the *Crime Commission Report*.
[3]Ibid., p. 87.
[4]Ibid., p. 88.

. . . so long as the social conditions that produce poverty remain, no reforms in the criminal process will eliminate the imbalance. . . . The poor are arrested more often, convicted more frequently, sentenced more harshly, rehabilitated less successfully than the rest of society.[5]

Despite the fact that "individual responsibility" is the stated basis of our criminal law enforcement, just as "social conditions" explain the why of selected law enforcement, it is still the individual's economic and social class and the color of his skin that determine his relationship to the legal system.

Just as power in a capitalist society is not concentrated in the capitalist as an individual, the law's protection of the middle and upper classes is not exercised directly by individuals. The enforcement of criminal sanctions is dictated by the necessities of the economic and political system in which the profit motive is central. For example, it is not surprising that no law prevents industrial managers from laying off thousands of workers, or from moving plants to new locations in order to maximize profits. The people whose lives and communities may be shattered have no recourse in the legal system. No law requires institutions which control and profit from the materials and means of production to share their wealth equally among the people who produce it and need it. Despite the lip service, it is not a priority of any elected official to urge a district attorney's office to arrest the property owners and corporate managers who violate air and water pollution laws, antitrust laws, housing codes, and the health and safety laws of the drug and auto industries. The pollution, sickness, and death resulting from such illegalities have had little effect on law enforcement agencies; in fact, the corporate class exercises such control over Congress and law enforcement agencies that there are few statistics documenting abuses. The public continues to drink polluted water, breathe poisoned air, and ride unsafe automobiles.

The protection of lesser economic interests, such as those of the middle class, serves to camouflage the abuses of those higher up the ladder. The broker who sells phony stocks, the builder who deliberately uses defective materials, the diary company executive who fixes prices, the embezzler and the tax evader are the white collar criminals. As the Crime Commission report states, "These criminals are only rarely dealt with through the full force of criminal sanctions."[6] Through a multitude of regulatory statutes, the law regulates the food and drug and other industries; but the law is not enforced. "The crucial fact is that these laws are violated on a vast scale, sometimes in deliberate disregard of the law, sometimes because businessmen, in their effort to come as close to the line between legality and illegality as possible, overstep it."[7]

Avoiding taxes is the common practice for many middle class business people. Of the more than forty billion dollars collected on personal income each year, eighty-six percent comes from people in the lower brackets. These figures reflect

[5]Patricia Wald, "Poverty and Criminal Justice," in the *Crime Commission Report*, p. 151.
[6]The *Crime Commission Report*, p. 156.
[7]Ibid., p. 157.

not only the vast scale of tax evasion, but the fact that the tax law rewards a capitalist's skillful shuffling of paper. Inheritance stipends and stock dividends are subject in practice to fewer taxes than the $10,000 or less in salary earned by carpenters or secretaries.[8]

Middle class "interest groups" also are favored in law enforcement practice. White New York City high school teachers are employed in a school system that is mostly nonwhite. Teachers who closed down schools in January 1969 were not arrested, although they clearly broke the law against strikes by public employees; but a headline the next month announced a legal crackdown on students who protested the conditions in those same schools. While the antistrike law is aimed at crushing worker demands, it will not be used against white, or for Black, interests. In the teachers' strike, the law defended a white middle class constituency against Blacks who were making inroads in the white-controlled school system.

White racism is rarely prosecuted, especially when property interests are involved. For example, real estate interests continue to profit from the age-old practice of "blockbusting" (although the courts may soon be forced to face the problem). This is a tactic used by speculators involving the sale of one or two homes in a white neighborhood to Blacks to persuade the remaining white home owners to leave the neighborhood, selling at low prices. The realtors then resell the homes to middle class Blacks at high prices. In spite of Supreme Court rulings upholding the civil rights of Blacks, the law has not been enforced against Southern politicians and landowners who discriminate in schools, public facilities, housing, and jobs. In 1970 a public park in one Southern town was returned by the Supreme Court to its original white owners. A will had turned the park over to the city with the restriction that only whites could enjoy the facilities, and the Court, rather than ordering the integration of the public park, chose to respect the interest of the dead property owner by returning the land to his estate.

Legal Oppression of the Innocent

"Much better hang wrong feller than hang no feller."

— Charles Dickens, *Bleak House*

No matter how willingly or unwillingly a criminal defendant cooperates with the rules of the legal game, he is forced to submit to his own undesirability, and in effect, his prejudged guilt under the law. The prejudgment is finalized by two traditional court practices: the requirements of monetary bail and the pressure to "cop a plea," whereby a defendant pleads guilty instead of going to trial. Less blatant than these techniques is the cooperation among officials — the judge, the prosecuting attorney, and the poor person's defense lawyer — who use the legal techniques to isolate the prejudged defendants. Common class and racial bonds

[8]Gabriel Kolko, *Wealth and Power in America*. New York: Frederick A. Praeger, 1962, pp. 30–45.

unite court officials and set apart the defendant, more or less according to the particular crime he or she is alleged to have committed. In one study of arrests in Washington, D.C., ninety percent of the people taken into custody had incomes of less than $5,000; Blacks have a significantly higher rate of arrests nationally than whites in almost every offense category; nearly forty-five percent of all arrests are for crimes without victims, such as drunkenness, gambling, vagrancy, and prostitution.[9]

The poor and nonwhite, arrested at a proportionally higher rate than the rest of the population, are more likely to be jailed after arrest because of the court practice of imposing monetary bail. If the defendant cannot post the amount set by a judge or give a bail bondsman security to post it for him, he remains in jail. One study of New York bail practices indicates the extent to which the courts tend to incarcerate the innocent prior to trial: twenty-five percent of all defendants in this study failed to make bail at $500, forty-five percent failed at $1,500, and sixty-three percent at $2,500.[10]

The Eighth Amendment guarantees against excessive bail and the Supreme Court has ruled that the only function of bail is to help guarantee the appearance of the defendant in court. But bail is most often used against a defendant to "teach him a lesson" or to "protect the community."[11] A poor or nonwhite defendant languishes in jail weeks, months, and even years before trial. Nor does this preventive detention count toward whatever sentence may be imposed if the defendant is convicted; thus more pressure is placed on the accused to plead guilty quickly.

It may surprise most people that there are almost no criminal trials in the United States; but since seventy percent (over ninety percent in many states) of all defendants plead guilty, the need for most trials is eliminated.[12] In 1966, there were 9,895 felonies recorded in New York City; 9,501 of these ended in convictions by a plea of guilty. The pressures on lower class, poor, or nonwhite defendants to plead guilty has received little attention, perhaps because those who are arrested and detained illegally are generally thought to be guilty anyway.

This huge number of guilty pleas is produced by the practice known as plea copping, in which the accused pleads guilty to an offense lesser than the one originally charged, or in exchange for a promise of leniency from the judge. Frequently, the accused will be charged with more crimes than actually took place in order to persuade him to plead guilty to lesser charges. A man may be charged with armed robbery on five counts: robbery first degree, assault second degree, assault third degree, carrying a dangerous weapon, and petit larceny. If the defen-

[9]The *Crime Commission Report*, pp. 149–50, 195.

[10]Caleb Foote, "A Study of the Administration of Bail in New York City," *University of Pennsylvania Law Review*, Vol. 106 (1958), p. 633.

[11]Ibid.

[12]The percentage of trials in all states varies from none (South Dakota) to forty-five percent (Texas). The median is twelve percent. Lee Silverstein, *Defense of the Poor: The National Report*. Chicago: American Bar Foundation, 1965, Vol. I.

dant goes to trial and is convicted on every count he faces many years in prison. Instead, if he has no previous record, he is offered a lesser charge — simple assault or petit larceny — to which he can plead guilty on the spot. Regardless of whether he committed the crimes, he will plead guilty to the misdemeanor because the risk of conviction at trial, especially for a Black man or woman, is great. Meanwhile the court saves the time and expense of a trial. In many states defendants in capital cases can avoid convictions carrying a mandatory death sentence only by pleading guilty. In such cases defendants who wish to exercise their right to trial by jury risk death.

In the practice of plea copping more than in any other court ritual the common class interest of all the participants in the "adversary system" of law is apparent. It is generally thought that the defense lawyer and prosecuting attorney are opponents whose struggle will bring out the true guilt or innocence of the accused. In reality, it is through the cooperation of the judge and the prosecuting and defense attorneys that bail requirements are established or a guilty plea obtained. Because there is no conflict in the class interest of judge, defense, and prosecuting attorneys, there is no reality to their apparent opposition in court. Their task is the disposition of cases, not the trial of people. Their function is to keep the guilty guilty.

The aim of the prosecutor is to "get" people. Obtaining the guilty plea is as necessary to his personal image as it is to the smooth functioning of the system. Election campaigns play up his conviction rate like a batting average. Whether a district attorney is elected or appointed, he must have the support — financial and otherwise — of the Democratic or Republican Party, and many prosecutors use their offices as political stepping stones or to build future careers in the business world. The prosecutor must therefore avoid disrupting the traditional court practices. His stake in the status quo leads him to view defendants as criminals who should be punished if they are even slightly implicated. The prosecutor's influence is great, as he determines whom the police arrest, the volume of cases in the courts, and whether convicted offenders are imprisoned.

The judge exerts a powerful influence on all stages of the criminal process. His enforcement of class distinctions in rulings, sentencing practices, and in the speed with which he disposes of cases determines many decisions by police, prosecutors, and defense counsel. Like the prosecutors, the judges have a stake in the status quo. They are chosen by professional politicians, after nomination by the Democratic and/or Republican Parties, or appointed according to the patronage of local, state, or federal executives. It is therefore not unusual for judges to work hand in hand with prosecutors. A rebel Black judge from Michigan, George W. Crockett, Jr., states the relationship clearly: "I personally think that it's unfortunate that, for the most part, our judges are made up of members of the former ranks of the prosecutors' offices, or the U.S. District Attorney's office. I think they come to the bench conditioned to believe everything the policeman says and everything the prosecutor says."[13] Because a defendant can expect little

---

[13]George W. Crockett, "Racism in American Law," *The National Lawyers Guild Practitioner*, Fall 1968, p. 178.

from a court controlled by an Establishment judge, he is the more influenced to plead guilty.

Although the judge only acts as a rubber stamp in this process, his powers of setting bail and of sentencing, and the psychological effect of the aura of power that surrounds him, all serve to force the guilty plea. The great symbol of justice in the criminal courts, he in fact uses the prestige of traditional courtroom respect to cloak the procedure that takes place behind closed doors or before the bench itself. All must rise when the judge enters. U.S. District Court Judge Marvin E. Frankel writes, "Sitting on raised platforms, all draped in black, judges (even of lower courts) sometimes have ludicrously inflated images of themselves and of the supposed Olympian qualities of their decisions."[14] Because his role is the least questioned and the most respected of all the participants, the judge's decisions seem to confirm the guilt of the undesirables who plead guilty.

In a recent experiment in one Western county the prosecutor exchanged places in the courtroom with the defense attorney, supposedly so that each could learn the difficulties of the other's position. That the experiment could take place at all demonstrates the overt cooperation between supposedly opposing forces. The defense lawyer's role is that of a friend who leads the unsuspecting to the slaughterhouse. Of course the defense attorney is supposed to try to prove the innocence or defend the interests of his client; this is what he does when hired by a wealthy influential client. It is also true when a Movement attorney volunteers to defend a political activist. But a defense attorney for the poor or working-man, whether the state or a private agency reimburses him or whether the client pays directly, does not identify above all with the interests of the client. He is more interested in seeing the court process function smoothly — which means that his client should plead guilty.

Each year about sixty percent of all defendants in federal and state courts are financially unable to afford counsel. Most states provide lawyers by one or both of two methods. In the assigned counsel system, which covers about two-thirds of all indigent defendants, the county clerk uses a list of available lawyers to appoint an attorney for the indigent on a case-by-case basis. In large cities the "defender" system is in greater use. Here lawyers are mostly full-time salaried government employees. Since the 1963 *Gideon* decision, in which the U.S. Supreme Court decided that any person alleged to have committed a felony must have access to an attorney, the defender system has grown enormously.

Recent studies comparing both the defender and assigned counsel to the traditional private lawyer have shown that lawyers for the poor advise their clients to plead guilty somewhat more often than privately retained attorneys.[15] However, the experts do not begin to explain the relationship between the guilty plea and its class and race basis. The private "lawyer regulars," as one criminal lawyer

---

[14]Marvin E. Frankel, "Remarks on Law and Revolution," *Bar Bulletin:* New York County Lawyers' Association, Vol. 26, No. 2, 1968–1969, p. 51.

[15]See Silverstein, *Defense of the Poor*, for a comparison of legal aid systems.

calls them, use their professional role as attorneys to exploit moderate income and working class clients. These lawyers are

highly visible in the major urban centers of the nation; their offices — at times shared with bondsmen — line the back streets near courthouses. They are also visible politically, with clubhouse ties reaching into judicial chambers and the prosecutor's office. The regulars make no effort to conceal their dependence upon police, bondsmen, jail personnel, as well as bailiffs, stenographers, prosecutors, and judges.[16]

The private "lawyer regular" is not concerned with guilt or innocence — nine out of ten times he will lose in court — so he collects his fee in advance, then convinces his client that pleading guilty will be best because the charges or the sentence will be lessened. The trusting client agrees, forgetting that in so doing he is forfeiting his right to a trial by jury and, as in many states, getting a presentence hearing before a judge over facts that might mitigate the offense.

"As members of a bureaucratic system, defense attorneys become committed to rational, impersonal goals based on saving time, labor, and expense and on attaining maximum output for the system."[17] The assigned counsel or public defender has a close working relationship with the "impartial" judge and the "enemy" prosecutor. They appear again and again in the same courtroom, whereas clients come and go. One who has observed the casual offstage and onstage relations among the defense and prosecuting lawyers and the judge understands that the ties among these individuals override the interests of a particular defendant. This is not corruption in the traditional sense, although that also exists; this is the normal way that guilt is determined for the undesirables in our society. As a judge who sits on a higher court described the reality of the lower courts,

Despite the presumption of innocence, the defendant in these police and magistrate courts is, prima facie, guilty. He is almost always uncounseled and sometimes he is not even informed of the charges against him until after the so-called trial. Often no records are kept of the proceedings, and in the overwhelming majority of cases, these courts are, in practice, courts of last resort.[18]

Law and Power in a "Pluralistic" Society

Karl Marx noted that "judicial relations, like state forms, can be explained neither as things in themselves, nor by the progress of the human mind; they are rooted in the material conditions of life." As the economic organization of our society is grounded in property relations, so the law serves the most powerful property interests. The masses of people who have little or no connection to the centers

[16]Abraham S. Blumberg, "Lawyers With Convictions," *Transaction*, July 1967, p. 18.
[17]Ibid.
[18]J. Skelly Wright, "The Courts Have Failed the Poor," *New York Times Magazine*, March 9, 1969, p. 26.

of economic power are governed by rules intended to maintain existing power relationships. Criminal law enforcement controls the activities of those who are powerless because of their material conditions. While the lower classes and nonwhites dominate the court calendars, the court officers represent the interests of the power structure. The class and racist practices inherent in the bail system and plea bargaining contradict democratic principles at the same time as they uphold the economic relationships of a capitalist society. The legal superstructure is not designed to dispense justice to a whole community nor to allow changes in property relations. It legitimizes the power of the few and punishes those who have been defeated by or who challenge this power.

American social scientists use the term "pluralism" to describe American "representative democracy." They depict a society in which widely varied groups compete with each other, in which decision-making rests on give-and-take among various groups. Groups compromise, make deals, and pressure each other; public officials and lawmakers respond to these various group pressures so that no one political, economic, social, religious, regional, or racial group will dominate. This creates the "natural" system of checks and balances which maintains a democracy. People become part of the decision-making process as soon as they organize: as big labor checks big business, Catholics check Protestants, farmers check urbanites, students check school administrators.

The plausibility of this description is such that today many people are claiming that the answer to poverty is community control and that racism can be ended by supporting Black power as a check on white power. Yet the poor cannot check the rich and the Blacks will never balance whites; pluralism masks the fact that some groups and individuals hold power in capitalist society while certain classes and races are excluded. It cannot be denied that important changes occur when pressures are exerted. High-level interest groups struggle for control in the top brackets of industry; the passage of civil rights legislation in 1964 and after came as a result of the nonviolent demands of the early 1960s. What can be denied is that property relations can be changed by the pluralist process. Economic guidelines and laws give the major corporations in this free enterprise system ownership of the means of production, while the populations underlying the upper class are divided (into income, religious, ethnic, and racial groups) so that they are prevented from determining the material conditions of their lives or the policies of their government. It is now a well-established (though not so well-known) fact that economic inequality within the United States has remained generally constant throughout this century,[19] showing that the "potential for unity"[20] of the upper class is much greater than that of the middle and lower classes. Sociologists have shown that a cohesive white upper class, consisting of approximately one-half of one percent of the people in this country, controls every major

---

[19]Kolko, pp. 13–14.
[20]William Domhoff, *Who Rules America?* Englewood Cliffs, New Jersey: Prentice-Hall, 1967, pp. 151–52.

bank and corporation and personally owns over one-quarter of the country's wealth, while eighty percent of all stock value is owned by less than two percent of all familes.[21]

The wealthy exercise their power through corporations.

. . . great corporations are the important units of wealth, to which individuals of property are variously attached. The corporation is the source of the basis of continued power and privilege. All the men and the families of great wealth are identified with large corporations in which their property is seated.[22]

John Kenneth Galbraith and other apologists for monopoly capitalism argue that the increased need for technical knowledge and management expertise has come between large industrial enterprises and their owners and has democratized the corporations. Yet the profits of the top fifty corporations represent about forty percent of all industrial earnings, and the corporations are now struggling for still greater control of the economy by means of a new phenomenon, the conglomerate. It is estimated that by 1975 three hundred corporations will own two-thirds of the industrial assets of the world.[23]

Occasionally laws are passed which challenge ruling class interests, e.g., New Deal legislation resulting from workers' struggles strengthened unions and, to some extent, redistributed income. These changes, however, did not substantially diminish corporate wealth and control. The workers were diverted from the struggle to gain control over economic forces by the creation of a legal administrative bargaining structure in which the perpetuation of the power structure was assumed. Other examples of laws which challenge corporate control are consumer safety regulations concerning food and drugs and, recently, air and water pollution. The laws restrict those capitalists whose activities are so obviously harmful that public anger at them is a potential threat to corporate power. They have clearly been forced to respond in some measure to popular outcries; but the corporate elite, through its influence over law enforcement, insures that these new laws are not used to impair basic operations.

"Legality" depends not only on who is powerful but also on the intensity of the struggle by the people, which can transform legal relationships. A labor union in the early nineteenth century was defined as an illegal conspiracy to interfere with employees' freedom of contact. Courts enjoined organizing activity and jailed organizers. Company thugs were praised as protectors of law and order — that is, company property — while workers out on strike were criminals. By the late 1930s union organizing and the right to strike were protected (except among weak groups like agricultural workers and public employees) and bosses were required to bargain. Union contracts became enforceable in court. What had been criminal became legal and previously legal activity was now illegal.

---

[21]Ibid., p. 11.

[22]C. Wright Mills, *The Power Elite*. New York: Oxford University Press, 1957, Chapter 7.

[23]See *Fortune*, May 15, 1969, for the Establishment's listing of the top corporations in the U.S., and some crude justifications for the growth of conglomerates.

The changing law reflected the new power of the movement, but it also coopted it. Property relations had been slightly modified by the struggles of the people; nevertheless, the right of ownership was safe.

Because the legal superstructure is largely powerless against the pervasive abuses of the corporate world and its oppression of the large segment of the population, it opens the way for popular attacks directed at its most valued assumption, its impartiality. Resistance to the legal oppression of the lower classes and non-white peoples has in recent years resulted in the arrests, jailing, and even murders of many who are aware that the system will not change itself. This resistance, especially among the Black population — supported by a growing number of white youth — has focused attention on the role the courts play in maintaining an illegitimate order. Those who are captured in the criminal court process experience its oppressiveness concretely and are radicalized by their experience; this process leads radicals to argue that all "criminals," as defined by the Establishment, are political prisoners.

For the majority, however, the legal superstructure does not seem to impose on daily life. The separation of the law from the people obscures the true class and racist nature of the entire economic and political system. People are now focusing their resistance on the institutions which directly affect them — at their schools, on their jobs, in their neighborhoods. But as the Establishment uses its law to cut off resistance, people will begin to see legal relationships as they actually are, coexisting with the economic and political system. Law will be demystified. People will no longer tolerate a system in which large corporations, wealthy individuals, and property owners receive the greatest benefits. They will no longer accept the pluralist mask behind which the law pretends to be an impartial voice among conflicting groups or individuals. The people themselves will then assume authority and become their own lawmakers.

12. Haywood Burns

Racism and American Law

The Kerner Commission told the nation something that most Black folk have known for a long time — America is a racist country.

Race prejudice has shaped our history decisively; it now threatens to affect our future. White racism is essentially responsible for the explosive mixture which has been accumulating in our cities since the end of World War II.

Reprinted by permission of the author from *Amistad 2*, edited by Charles Harris and John Williams (Random House, 1971), pp. 43–64.

Many white Americans recoiled from the charge of racism as it applied to them, and summarily dismissed the conclusions of the report. This all-too-easy evasion of some difficult and ugly truths was made more possible by the nature of the Kerner Commission Report. Despite its many valuable contributions, the report did not delve deeply into just how decisively racial animus has shaped our past and the extent to which it puts any future in doubt. The "explosive mixture" has been accumulating not just in our cities and not just since the end of World War II. The presence of white racism has been a constant in the American past. It has defined the American past.

We must move beyond the Kerner Commission Report to understand the exact way in which our institutions, group, and personal relationships were and are determined by the fact that this has been and continues to be a country permeated by racism. A look at the interaction of American attitudes toward race with the legal system provides one of the best avenues for this inquiry; for though it is often proclaimed that ours is a "government of laws, not men," the law does not exist as a "brooding omnipresence" somewhere off in the ether. It is made by men and, in America's case, by men in a racist society. In this country law has been the handmaiden of racism. It has been the way in which the generalized racism in the society is made specific and converted into particular policies and standards of social control which mirror the racism of the dominant society.

Inquiry into the racism-law interaction can perhaps best be made by first examining from an historical perspective the Indian, the Oriental, and the Black experiences with American law, and then by analyzing the manner in which racism continues to play a role in the structural apparatus of the American judicial system.

The social pathology of American white racism is not limited in its manifestations to negative attitudes towards and hostile treatment of Blacks. The Red brother has felt the brunt of the superiority complex of the white European and his descendants here in the new world. In the beginning, at least, some of the white newcomers felt the need to deal with the indigenous Indian population in an equitable manner. William Penn and Lord Baltimore both advocated and followed a policy attempting to acquire title to Indian land through mutual agreement and fair compensation. However, their approach proved to be the exception rather than the rule. As early as the seventeenth century, English settlers were setting up reservations for Indians in the environs. As early as the eighteenth century, legislative bodies were offering bounties for Indian scalps. On the question of Indian lands, the U.S. Supreme Court in *Johnson v. M'intosh* (1823) took the position that "discovery gave exclusive title to those who made it" — upholding the land claim of whites who "discovered" certain lands occupied by Indians, and denying the Indians right and power to dispose of the land.

A treaty, once ratified by the Senate, is entered in the U.S. Statutes at Large and becomes part of the law of the land. Some of the greatest instances of official lawlessness chronicled in our nation's past are found in the pattern of treaty making followed by treaty breaking in dealing with Indians. It is the story of one continuous forked tongue. In 1830 Congress passed the Indian Removal Act, which was designed to effect the transfer of the so-called "civilized tribes" from their homeland in the East to lands west of the Mississippi. In exchange for their homeland the Indians were to receive perpetual title to the Western lands. "Perpetuity" lasted only until white Americans decided that the vast territory west of the Mississippi was too valuable to remain in Indian hands and to wrench it from them. It was illegal white encroachments which generated most of the Indian wars of the nineteenth century. Western lands taken away from the Indians and made available to white settlers under federal land grant law formed the basis for many white Americans' growth to economic independence and well-being. Many of today's middle Americans who are the staunchest advocates of law and order and free enterprise are where they are because of a land base that was provided for their forebears through theft of Indian land and the largesse of a big government benefit program.

One of the more striking examples of the perversion of the legal process in dealing with Indian land is the ruse used against the California Indians. The Indians gave up more than half the state of California in exchange for perpetual ownership of 7,500,000 acres. Because of pressure from white politicians, the Senate never ratified the treaties under which the Indians gave up their land in exchange for the 7,500,000 acres. The Indian Bureau, which had negotiated the treaties in 1851 with 119 California tribes, never told the Indians about the failure to ratify. The treaties stayed in the files of the Senate until 1905 when the 7,500,000 acres the Indians thought were theirs were sold to white settlers and land speculators.

As with Blacks, the law was used against Indians to make sure that these inferior beings stayed in their place — whatever that might be at the moment. In some parts of the country, Indians were not allowed to testify in court or become members of the bar. A special set of laws governed their social conduct in such matters as drinking and intermarriage. Custom and usage barred them from many public facilities. Governmental suggestions for dealing with "the Indian problem" ranged from penning them up on reservations to genocide. Ample efforts were made at both.

The record of the interaction of American racism and the legal system is far from unblemished in the area of this country's dealings with persons of Oriental descent. In the mid-nineteenth century Chinese were imported in droves to do the hard, dirty, and dangerous work of building the West. In particular, they were employed in the perilous tasks of cutting the first national railroad through the Western mountains. It was due to the number of Oriental workers who were injured or killed in this hazardous work that the expression "he doesn't have a Chinaman's chance" originated. As the need for Chinese labor decreased, and racial antagonism and fear of the Asiatic hordes grew, the Congress took under consideration and eventually passed a series of laws which barred the Chinese from immigrating to this country altogether. Such a legal move was unprecedented and was clearly based on race. The concern of domestic workers over foreign cheap labor is insufficient to explain this legislative action. Native American workers were worried about competition from the new immigrants of Southern and Central Europe as well, but Congress passed no comparable legislation to keep them out. The tired, the poor, the huddled masses yearning to breathe free, apparently did not include the Chinese.

In some areas, Chinese were not allowed to testify in Court. A California court upheld this rule even though there was no statutory exclusion of Chinese testimony. The reasoning of the court was that California law barred Indians from testifying, and since it was a well-known fact that Indians originally came to this continent from Asia and are racially related to Orientals, the intent of the statute was to bar Chinese testimony as well.

In the late nineteenth and into the twentieth century some Western states passed laws putting restrictions upon Orientals owning or leasing land or engaging in certain occupations. These statutes did not necessarily speak in terms of a bar to Orientals, but rather were phrased so that the exclusion from the "privilege" was based upon the person's status as an alien ineligible for citizenship. By this device the states were able to use the racist federal naturalization laws as a "neutral" cover — however transparent — for their discriminatory ends.

The Naturalization Act of 1790 limited naturalization to any alien who was a "free white person." It was not until after the Civil War that the "white only" naturalization law was altered. In 1870 it was amended to permit persons of African descent to become citizens, a change necessary to make citizenship for many former slaves possible. A racial bar to naturalization in one form or another existed throughout almost the entire history of the nation. In the 1920s, when faced with the question "who is white," the U.S. Supreme Court held (after looking to the intent of the framers) that "white" was not synonymous with Caucasian, and barred a Hindu from citizenship. It was not until 1943 that Chinese were allowed to be naturalized. This only came about because of the role of the Chinese as America's ally in World War II and because of pressure from groups and individuals on the home front — not the least of which was the resignation of the Director of the U.S. Immigration Service on this issue, who, in resigning, pointed out that the only other nation in the world at that time which had a legal barrier to naturalization based on race was Nazi Germany. When the last racial restrictions were removed by the Immigration and Nationality Act of 1952, Burmese, Japanese, Koreans, Maoris, Polynesians, and Samoans were still excluded.

The experience of the Japanese in America during World War II is another recent example of the workings of racism and American law. One hundred and ten thousand persons of Japanese ancestry, 70,000 of them citizens — men, women, and children — were involuntarily removed from their homes, jobs and communities and placed in detention camps for periods ranging up to several years — all without benefit of a trial or any fair opportunity to be heard. This policy was initiated by General John L. DeWitt, the military officer in charge of Western states, an officer who made no secret of his racist sentiments. When questioned on his wholesale abridgement of the rights of tens of thousands of persons without any efforts to distinguish among them, General DeWitt is said to have replied simply, ''A Jap is a Jap.'' The policy of internment of Japanese was followed nowhere in the Americas except General DeWitt's Western states region — not even in Hawaii where there was a much higher percentage of Japanese and Japanese-Americans in the population. It certainly was not applied to other enemy aliens as a group or persons with those nationality backgrounds. No one even suggested locking up persons of Italian and German descent for no other reason than their descent. Such a policy would have required the internment of Joe DiMaggio and Dwight David Eisenhower during World War II.

This unprecedented move by the government was in direct response to the virulent West Coast anti-Japanese feeling. The barbed-wire policy was authorized by the President, implemented by Congress, and ultimately approved by the Supreme Court, on the ground of national security. It was this last action that called forth special criticism from Professor E. V. Rostow of the Yale Law School. In a leading law journal article, written shortly after the Supreme Court's action, Professor Rostow saw reason for special concern over the action of the Court in Sanctioning the Japanese Relocation scheme in that it ''converts a piece of wartime folly into a permanent part of the law.'' The legal sanction for such a gross invasion of the personal liberties of a group of persons on the grounds of ''national security'' remains even now a potent threat to all those whom some administration may some day deem dangerous.

A close look at the work of the ''founding fathers'' in adopting the U.S. Constitution provides an excellent index of how they regarded the question of Black freedom. Though many professed an abhorrence of slavery, and moves were made toward its abolition, attempts to do away with it floundered and failed. Even among delegates of a liberal persuasion who opposed slavery there was great reluctance to tamper with so much property. Further, even in the most enlightened quarters there was a decided inability to view Blacks as men and as equals. This racism severely limited the boundaries of action of the slavery opponents, who were themselves racists. Black freedom was not a fundamental item as was white freedom, but rather a negotiable item, part of the barter and exchange system of trade-offs and accommodations by which white men conducted their affairs. Out of the welter of compromise of the Constitutional Convention came the document which constitutes our fundamental law. There enshrined, along with the guaranteed continuation of the slave trade and the obligation for the return of fugitive slaves, is the Black slave as three-fifths of a man.

It was through the law that the lives of slaves were governed in oppressive detail. The slave codes passed throughout the states of the South denied the legal personality of Blacks. Blacks could not bring lawsuits, no matter how grievously they had been wronged or how substantial their interest. They could not testify in a court of law when a white man's interests were involved. Apart from closely regulating the mobility of Blacks and their opportunities for social contact and interaction, the slave codes often made it a crime to teach slaves to read and write, and ruled out certain kinds of occupations for slave and free Blacks alike — especially occupations which involved work with drugs and explosives. Legal recognition of and protection for the family relationship was withheld by the slave codes and rejected by judicial decision. The criminal sanctions for slaves were governed by different rules or by no rules. This is partly a result of a system where men are held in bondage for life — for them the threat of jail has little or no meaning.

A special statutory penalty reserved for Blacks, and in some cases Indians, was sexual mutilation for sex crimes. Laws providing for emasculation of Black or Red offenders were passed in several jurisdictions. As late as 1857 white men sat in the Kansas Territory legislature and passed a bill which provided that a Black man convicted of having been involved in any of several different types of interracial liaisons should be castrated "by a person of suitable skill" and that the offender should be taxed with the costs of such a procedure.

As white racism was not an exclusively Southern phenomenon, neither were the laws reflecting it. While Northern politicians often attacked slavery in the South, many states above the Mason-Dixon line developed their own sets of laws for the so-called "free" Blacks. In many Northern states Blacks were banned by law from the ballot box and forced to attend segregated schools. Some areas even forbade Blacks to come within their geographical boundaries. The federal government barred Blacks from employment in the post office and vacillated greatly on the issue of granting passports to Blacks because of federal uncertainty as to the citizenship status of a Black man in America. Chief Justice Taney and the U.S. Supreme Court resolved the dilemma in *Dred Scott v Sanford*, making it quite clear that the slave Scott was not a citizen and, further (in effect, summing up the corpus of law on Blacks as it had developed to this time), Blacks "had no rights which the white man was bound to respect."

After emancipation and after Appomattox, the white South, relying on its tried and tested tool, the law, tried, insofar as was possible, to reestablish the previously existing superior position of whites. The notorious Black Codes were designed to assure a working relationship between whites and Blacks that would not offend the racist sentiments of the white South, one that would as closely as possible approximate the freedman's position to slavery. State legislatures passed bills which made it virtually impossible for freedmen to go into commercial fields or to work as artisans. Detailed, expensive licensing requirements and the necessity of serving an apprenticeship with someone already in the trade made it virtually impossible for Blacks to establish themselves in various areas of skilled labor and commercial enterprise. Service on the land was guaranteed, however. Black Codes set out in detail the obligations in the master-servant relationship, giving the master enormous control over the comings and goings of their workers, down to the most intimate details of their lives. Black Codes prohibited intermarriage, and permitted corporal punishment and convict labor. The latter was an especially useful legal device. Blacks could be arrested in numbers under exceedingly vague vagrancy and idleness statutes, and then farmed out to local landowners to work off their sentences of hard labor. Without the benefit of a date it is often difficult to tell a post–Civil War Black Code from a pre–Civil War Slave Code.

Reconstruction provided only a brief interlude in which the primary thrust of the law was turned away from suppression and denial of Blacks to progressive efforts in their favor; but even during this period the bold promises of sweeping, legal changes to create an economically viable Black community went unfulfilled. Forty acres and a mule remained in the realm of dream stuff — a dream that began to fade the more rapidly as the white South snatched back power from the hands of a North grown tired of "the Negro question" and all too willing to let the former slave masters work their will with the former slaves in the interest of "national unity" — white national unity.

In the period following Reconstruction, the law was called into play to give definition and formal structure to the Southern practices, customs, and usages of apartheid. Jim Crow hospitals, schools, transportation, public accommodations, prisons, and cemeteries, one by one were required on a statewide basis as a matter of law. Whereas previously custom and usage allowed for some variance and local deviation, state legislatures in this period dictated a uniform standard of conduct with the full force of criminal sanctions behind it. Courtrooms were segregated as a matter of law, as were even the Bibles upon which witnesses took their oaths.

On a national level the Supreme Court in the post-Reconstruction era beat a retreat from the liberal directions of the postwar Congress. From the Civil Rights cases in 1883 invalidating post–civil War public accommodations law to and beyond *Plessy v Ferguson* in 1896, upholding the doctrine of "separate but equal," the Supreme Court engaged in a systematic evisceration of the Civil War amendments and federal civil rights legislation that had been passed pursuant to those amendments. The Court imposed an increasingly restrictive view upon the scope of the Fourteenth Amendment, limiting its application to abridgments of rights by state officials or institutions, while exempting the acts of private citizens from its reach. This unwarrantedly narrow reading of the Fourteenth Amendment partially disarmed one of the most valuable weapons in the Blacks' legal arsenal for fighting racism.

The law was a major ally in aiding those who sought to strip the Black man of any vestige of political power that he had gained and exercised during Reconstruction. The attack on the Black franchise was made through creative legal stratagems that decimated the Black representation on the voting rolls in the late nineteenth and early twentieth centuries. Beginning with Mississippi in 1890, states in the Deep South revised their constitutions to erect difficult barriers to Black voting. Through a series of state constitutional conventions and legislative enactments, voter lists were purged of Blacks. The grandfather clause, property requirements, the poll tax, and the literacy test were all pressed into service as new legal apparatus designed to obliterate Black vote power.

This disenfranchisement effort was carried out in close connection with a campaign of violence, terror, intimidation, and lynching. At one period in the 1890s Blacks were lynched on the average of two a week. Though the violent terror tactics were extralegal in the sense that they did not represent the carrying out of any authoritative prescription, they were so widespread and enjoyed such a high level of community sanction that in another sense lynch law was in fact law — the imposition of community-approved sanctions for the violation of community mores. Lynch law and statutory law accomplished their purpose. By 1910 most Blacks in the South were no longer voting. In Louisiana alone, Black registration dropped from 130,334 in 1876 to 1,342 in 1904.

The edifice of *de jure* segregation remained largely intact from the late nineteenth century to modern times. *Brown v Board of Education* in 1954 represented the first major assault upon the 1896 *Plessy* "separate but equal" doctrine. Congress passed no major civil rights bill from 1875 to the Civil Rights Act of 1957.

There are serious questions about the amount of true change the series of modern civil rights court victories and legislation since *Brown* and the Civil Rights Act of 1957 have been able to effect in the real-life situations of nonwhite people in America. Court triumphs and new laws often take a long time to filter down and make a difference in peoples' lives, and the process here has been further retarded by the lack of executive will in the area of enforcement, and by the racist intransigence of the majority white society in protecting its dominance — the two being not unrelated. The problem has become particularly egregious because of the retreat of the Nixon administration in the area of minority rights. The so-called "Southern Strategy" is an assault upon all the poor and nonwhite it chooses to ignore. The newly made "discovery" of racism as a *national* problem has been an occasion for the white South to attempt to escape some of the force of remedial federal power by pointing a finger northward. White racism is a *national* disease, but that should not evade the fact that the South has its own peculiar virulent forms, nor should it be permitted to support the conclusion that there should be less vigorous action against white Southern racists, only that there should be more against white Nortern racists.

Throughout the past the racism of American society has been reflected in its legal system. Today, however, most explicit racial distinctions are gone from the statute books. Courts have struck down such statutes or new legislation has superseded them. Significantly, among the last to go were the miscegenation statutes. Almost all judges have ceased to articulate the rationale of their decisions in ways that explicitly involve the race of the parties before the bar. Legislatures, if they are not all passing civil rights bills, at least are no longer writing explicit racial distinctions into law. These are encouraging tendencies, but they should not lead to the false conclusion that in a racist society the law has somehow managed finally to escape that racism. The interaction between American racism and the legal system continues today in less visible but not necessarily less pernicious forms.

Blacks, Indians, and Orientals are no longer barred from testifying in court in matters involving white men, but many judges and juries accord much greater weight to the testimony of white witnesses than they do to nonwhite. When the issue is one of credibility, one white witness is often worth several nonwhite ones. Statutes no longer bar nonwhites from juries, and the courts have made it clear that systematic exclusion of nonwhite persons from juries is constitutionally unacceptable. Yet through prosecutors' use of the peremptory challenge of prospective jurors, legions of Black men and women have their fates decided by all-white juries from which members of their own race have been systematically exluded. The peremptory challenge allows the prosecutor in selecting the jury to remove a given number of members from the panel without giving a reason. Throughout the country this device is used by prosecutors to remove Black prospective jurors from jury panels in cases involving Black defendants. While invalidating explcit exclusion, the Supreme Court has upheld this use of the peremptory strike. There is also often a wide differential between what juries will allow white plaintiffs by way of damages in a tort suit and what they will allow Black plaintiffs similarly situated. In several parts of the country, for example, a white leg may be worth $150,000, while a Black leg only $50,000.

The areas of judicial and administrative discretion also provide opportunities for covert racism. This is particularly true in sentencing, parole, and probation. Unexpressed racial bias can creep in to pollute the process without fear of being exposed or proven. An examination of the racial pattern of sentencing in a particular area, however, can reveal racism at work. Disparity in sentences given whites and nonwhites for similar offenses is often a good indicator. In this connection, the pattern of the imposition of the death sentence in this country — especially for interracial rape — shows a clear racist bias against nonwhites.

There is much about the law today that may not be racist on its face but is racist in its impact. This racism is the result of the context in which our legal system must function — a society infected by racism — and the legacy of overt societal and explicit legal racism. Failure to take this legacy into account will often cause apparently ''neutral'' or ''objective'' systems to have an untoward racial dimension. Their impact may be intended or coincidental. However, the very failure to take this legacy into account must itself be regarded as racist, for to act as if the overt racism of the past never occurred, and to design systems of law without taking it into account, is to perpetuate the historical effect of racism.

The ''neutrality'' of such systems is entirely false. There is a structural inequality built into our law which works to the detriment of the poor and the nonwhite (often they are the same persons, but not always) because this structural inequality represents a confluence of caste and class bias in the law. It is racist in its impact because of the disproportionate number of nonwhites who are among the poor and because of the perpetuation it represents of the historical racism which is largely responsible for their impoverishment. Systems which place or keep nonwhites in positions of inferiority or disadvantage, using not race itself as the subordinating mechanism, but instead other mechanisms indirectly related to race, are properly designated "institutionally racist." This species of racism abounds in our law.

The operation of the money bail system is an example of the institutional subordination of the nonwhite. There is a constitutional right to bail in noncapital offenses, and its only legitimate purpose is to assure the appearance of the defendant at trial. However, high bail is used by a vast number of our courts as a method of pretrial punishment — ignoring nonfinancial release conditions that are available for impecunious defendants with roots in the community or for those for whom there is little likelihood of flight. This fact has been most spectacularly revealed in the exorbitant ransom courts have required for the pretrial release of Black political prisoners, but at lesser amounts and with less well-known defendants the practice is also common.

A similar structural inequality exists in the civil law. Access to the courts is restricted along economic lines. Whereas the legal system has at least reached the point of providing an accused defendant in most criminal cases with counsel, there is no such right in noncriminal cases. Poor persons seeking to use the law as a remedy in noncriminal matters may be able to obtain legal counsel (especially if they are in an area covered by a legal services program for the poor) or they may not — there is no guarantee. In some places there is a financial roadblock to the courts in the form of the requirement of a bond before eviction proceedings can be challenged. The person without funds who is being evicted cannot post a money bond and is without legal redress. He will find his goods on the sidewalk no matter how valid his claim might have been in court, had he been able to get there.

Not only does owner-biased landlord/tenant law operate to the detriment of the poor nonwhite underclass, but the structure of our creditor-biased consumer law institutionally subordinates that class as well. The "holder in due course" doctrine in the consumer area is an excellent example of the way in which unscrupulous merchants use their legal advantage to prey upon the ghetto dweller. Typically, a purchaser will be sold some goods on an installment basis. Soon after the rug or the refrigerator or the furniture arrives, it turns out to be defective. When the buyer goes back to the store to have the seller make good, the seller disclaims all knowledge of or responsibility for the defect and tells the buyer that the matter is now out of his hands, as the installment contract has been sold to a collection agency. When the poor benighted buyer goes to the collection agency, he is told that the agency knows nothing of the defect and that the agency has no legal responsibility for it. He is informed, however, that the agency as "the holder in due course" of the installment contract does own the right to collect the $31.85 a month due and owing for the next thirty-six months, and that his regular remittance will be expected.

Blacks are no longer excluded from geographical areas of the country by law, but large-acre zoning laws in the suburbs accomplish the same purpose, spreading a white noose around the inner city. Blacks are no longer formally excluded from participation in the political process, but laws which govern the political units in which nonwhites vote, through design or otherwise, often have the effect of cancelling out their vote. At-large voting systems often fall into this category. In Boston, Massachusetts, for example, the five-person School Committee is elected at large. Over the years this has resulted in the systematic cancelling out of the votes of Roxbury, the Black section of Boston. Statistically, it is as if Black residents of the city had not voted at all. Entrenched white political power has resisted all efforts to district the city to assure Blacks of effective participation in the political process. Under the current system Blacks are close to politically powerless on education issues. The Thirteenth, Fourteenth and Fifteenth Amendments were designed to make Blacks part of the polity. The mere right of an individual Black physically to place his vote in the ballot box does not accomplish that purpose. The Fifteen Amendment contemplated *effective* participation in the political process. Boston is not unique in having laws which create political units which operate to dilute or cancel out Black voting strength. The special importance of that city stems from the legal challenge to that system, based on its alleged institutionally racist effects, that has been mounted by the Boston Black community.

Further evidence of institutional subordination is found in the administrative process. Governmental officials who are entrusted with the obligation of carrying out the law often do so in a discriminatory fashion. One of the most egregious examples of this is the conduct of many policemen in minority communities. Some of the most lawless elements in our society can be found among law officials in our minority communities who daily inflict summary punishment upon minority citizens without benefit of a trial, and in other ways blatantly ignore their legal rights. The rules of the agencies themselves often reflect a societal bias. Welfare workers in the area of public assistance are permitted to assault the privacy and the dignity of recipients in ways which would never be countenanced if the public officials concerned were dealing with middle or upper class persons.

This bias is further exemplified by standards of procedural due process in administrative law. The measure of due process protection is considerably lower when what is at stake is the right to public assistance benefits, the right to a public education or of entry into public housing than it is when government is acting to substantially affect some business or commercial interest. Governmental agencies are required to follow a much more rigorous standard of fairness when they act to affect a corporate interest than they are when they wish to cut off welfare payments, expel a child from public school, or evict a family from public housing. It is only very recently that a divided U.S. Supreme Court held that a public assistance recipient was entitled to notice and an opportunity to be heard before welfare payments were cut off. Though nowhere in the scheme of administrative law and regulations is there a statement that there is a felt need for fewer safeguards to protect a poor Black mother's right to feed, clothe, house, and educate her child than there is to protect propertied interests, the institutional arrangement is such as to make it clear that this is plainly the case.

The Kerner Commission's discussion of this society's racism should have raised the critical question of whether the law, or any institution in this society, can transcend that racism. Clearly, the law has not. Rather it carries the scars of a racist national past, while assuming present-day postures which can only promise a racist future. The law cannot be viewed in a vacuum, however, It must be seen in the context of a society of inverted priorities, misallocated resources, and inhumane values, run by men and women who have drunk deeply of the heady myths of Western superiority, and now, imbued with their own sense of white worth, seek to impose their wills and their visions upon weaker nations abroad, and the darker brother and sister here at home. The law will change when men who make the law change — or when we make new men. Until such a time, if indeed there is still reason to hope for such a time, those who examine the question of racism and American law will continue to find racism in American law.

13. David Sternberg

The New Radical-Criminal Trials: A Step Toward a Class-For-Itself in the American Proletariat?

This essay consists of three parts, all bearing on the emergence of "radical-criminal trials" in the United States in the past few years. The first section analyzes more or less abstractly the crucial distinctions between the model of the traditional criminal trial in the United States and its very recent variant, the model of the radical-criminal trial. It then attempts briefly to connect the surfacing of the radical-criminal trial with the current state of political protest in the United States. Next is presented an "anatomy" of the radical-criminal trial, in which an effort is made to extract out of the great amount of available material on major trials the basic themes of these proceedings. Even though greatly condensed, this section contains a hard core of substantive and illustrative detail essential for a roughly accurate sociological picture of the trials. The final section attempts to

Reprinted by permission of the publisher from *Science & Society*, 36 (Fall 1972), pp. 274–301.

gauge the possible impact of these trials on the immediate future of the administration of justice in the United States.

Many (but certainly not all) of the structural circumstances of these trials are strikingly similar to the conspiracy trials of Leon Trotsky and his co-defendants in St. Petersburg, 1906.[1] We know that those trials portended a vast social revolution in Russia some 10 years later. Without contending that the appearance of similar trials today in the United States is an omen of general revolution, it is suggested in the final section that the radical trials may be forerunners of important gains for working-class accused persons (who constitute the vast majority of *all* accused persons) under the present bourgeois system of criminal "justice."

This is not a "value-free" sociological essay any more than are those papers that masquerade as such. The basic orientation is Marxist; the basic sympathies are with the "clients" rather than with the administrators of criminal justice.

I. The Traditional Criminal Trial

Until very recently the prevailing and largely uncontested model of criminal trials and their related pretrial hearings[2] in the United States has comprised exclusively the following six categories of active participants: the judge, and his auxiliary staff of clerks, bailiffs, and marshals; the defendant(s); the public prosecutor(s); the defense attorney(s); witnesses for the prosecution and defense; and the jury.

Not only have these groups been the exclusive legitimate actors in the criminal trial, but the patterns of interaction between and among them have been highly formalized and regularized. Thus, the judge "polices" the trial; the defense attorney speaks on behalf of his client, who does not speak out for himself; prosecutor and defense lawyer each get to question a witness in a particular style and order; witnesses answer only those questions put to them by court officials and do not "volunteer" information.

The assumption behind these trial norms is that the parties in the system and their relative power *vis à vis* each other will remain constant. One would expect, then, that the introduction of a new active party into the trial, or a shift in the relative power of one or more groups in this system, would force a restructuring of the current prevailing model of the criminal trial.

In addition to these six active groups, a seventh *passive* group, the spectators, rounds out the contemporary picture of the United States trial. Spectators consist of varying percentages of relatives and friends of defendants, members of the press and other media, and an assortment of persons from the community who bear no particular kinship, friendship, or professional relation to the defendant,

[1]For a description of the Trotsky trial see Isaac Deutscher, *The Prophet Armed, Trotsky: 1879–1921* (New York, 1965), pp. 163–169.

[2]The model of the conventional United States trial presented in the following paragraphs could be derived from virtually any text or treatise in the area. As examples, see Hans Toch (ed.), *Legal and Criminal Psychology* (New York, 1961), pp. 1–138; Paul Tappan, *Crime, Justice and Correction* (New York, 1960), pp. 326–359; and Ernest Puttkammer, *Administration of Criminal Law* (Chicago, 1953), pp. 174–208.

but who have variously motivated interests and curiosities about the administration of justice and its "clients." Statistically, the size of this spectator group has been small at usually routine criminal trials. In any event, the permitted presence of spectators at the trial has assured the "public" quality of criminal proceedings guaranteed the defendant by the Sixth and Fourteenth Amendments of the federal Constitution, as well as by the majority of state constitutions. For the most part, excepting certain "isolated incidents," the role of spectatorship in the past has been clear enough: passive, silent, and respectful observation of the trial/hearing process as performed by the six active groups of participants.

Criminal Trials of Radicals Versus Radical-Criminal Trials. It must be stressed that the traditional trial model briefly sketched above prevailed in essentials until nearly the end of the 1960s *even when radical defendants were involved.* That is to say, *criminal trials of political radicals*, whether they were specifically indicted for illegal political activity (e.g., the Wobblies, 1918), or whether they were accused of "conventional" crimes which at least superficially were unrelated to their political activities (e.g., Sacco and Vanzetti, 1920s), *rarely constituted radical-criminal trials.* That was so because up until the very end of the past decade dissenters, radicals, or revolutionaries, on trial under one indictment or another, generally accepted the traditional structure and process of the criminal procedure without challenging its fundamental political legitimacy.

Dwight Macdonald stresses the conventional courtroom deportment of radical defendants throughout American judicial history:

> In old-style political trials, from the pre-revolutionary trial in which Peter Zenger was successfully defended against His Majesty's presecutors on a charge of publishing seditious matter, to the recent trial of Dr. Spock, *et al.*, in Boston, both sides, in dress and behavior, accepted the conventions of the ruling establishment. . . . The defense behaved as if they shared the values and life style of the Court, even when they didn't, as in the big IWW trial in 1918 under the Espionage Act. There were over a hundred defendants, the entire leadership plus the Wobblies. . . . *But although the defendants were anarchists to a man . . . bold and ingenious in anti-establishment disruption outside the courtroom . . . they behaved themselves inside it.* (Italics mine)[3]

Nowhere, perhaps, was this continued acceptance of the old courtroom ground rules by radical defendants right into the late 1960s better illustrated than in the 1968–69 trial of Dr. Benjamin Spock for conspiracy to violate the federal draft laws. In her book, *The Trial of Dr. Spock*,[4] Jessica Mitford demonstrates that the traditional defense offered by Spock's old-style and conforming lawyers — which did in fact yield a not-guilty verdict on appeal — ironically succeeded in obscuring all the social and moral issues about U.S. involvement in Vietnam

---

[3]Dwight Macdonald, "Introduction," in Levine *et al.* (eds.), *The Tales of Hoffman* (New York, 1970), pp. xviii–xix.

[4]Jessica Mitford, *The Trial of Dr. Spock* (New York, 1969).

which Spock had hoped to expose in the trial. As Spock himself commented, "We sat like good little boys called into the principal's office. I'm afraid we didn't prove very much."[5] Whether the verdict was innocent or guilty, the same "good little boy" atmosphere characterized the 1960s trials of militant integrationists, draft resisters, draft-file burners,[6] criminal trespassers involved in takeovers of university buildings, and so on. In short, the militancy of the defendants almost always stopped short of the courtroom itself.[7]

Now, quite suddenly (although, as will be shown below, not unexpectedly, given the present political conditions and drastic tensions in the United States) a number of criminal trials in which radical defendants are involved have drastically challenged the kinds of "boundary-maintenance" mechanisms heretofore operating in criminal trials. The most widely publicized of these new-model trials were the Chicago Conspiracy Trial, the New York Panther 21 Trial, the New Haven Panther 14 Trial, and the Soledad Brothers and Angela Davis/Ruchell Magee trials (the last two in progress at this writing). In most of these trials the traditionally active parties have not all accepted their customary roles relative to one another, and the traditionally passive audience has assumed an active and unprecedented role in the proceedings. Consider Dwight Macdonald's evocation of the Chicago trial:

In the new-style radical courtroom tactics, either the lawyers share the alienation and often the hair style of their clients, or there are no lawyers. Also, as in the Living Theatre and other avant-garde dramatic presentations, the audience gets into the act; the spectators raise their voices, or, worse, their laughter, at crucial moments, despite all those beefy marshals. And the defendants, hitherto passive except when they had their meager moment on the witness stand — "Please answer the question, yes or no" — feel free to make critical comments on the drama when the spirit moves them.[8]

---

[5]Macdonald, *op. cit.*, p. xix.

[6]The Rev. Daniel Berrigan, the most prominent of the "Catonsville Nine" who were tried and convicted in 1969 for destroying draft-board files in Maryland, went underground in April, 1970, refusing to surrender to federal authorities and serve a three-year prison sentence. From April through part of August, 1970 when he was apprehended by the FBI, he repeatedly made the point — similar to Dr. Spock's — in speeches and articles, that his conformist behavior at his trial lent legitimacy to the system he opposed; in fact, his fugitive actions were prompted, he stated, by a recognition that to surrender to the authorities would acknowledge their legitimacy. His radical tactics, then, stopped short of the trial, but were resumed after the trial had finished.

[7]In a paper apparently largely completed just before the onset of the Chicago Conspiracy and Panther hearings, entitled "Old and New Left Activity in the Legal Order: An Interpretation," *The Journal of Social Issues*, (vol. 27, no. 1, 1971), pp. 105–121, Nathan Hakman, a political scientist, includes a section on "Radical Litigation Strategies" (pp. 116–118). It is highly instructive that no in-court radical tactics and innovations as I construe them are discussed whatsoever. Hakman sees "radical litigation strategies" in, for example, "Movement" lawyers employing perfectly legal and traditional devices, such as raising money for unpopular causes and bringing counter-law suits against public prosecutors. Hakman is not essentially "wrong" in his depiction of "radical strategies" up to the point in time when he ends his paper. Radical-criminal trials postdate his analysis. In fact his entire paper confirms the present claim about how new and unprecedented radical-criminal trials of *even radicals* are in the United States.

[8]Macdonald, "Introduction," in Levine *et al.*, *op. cit.*, p. xx.

The Current State of Political Protest in the United States. Prior to a more extended discussion of changing trial styles in America, let us consider their immediate antecedents in the contemporary political setting. There is no denying that in the United States the 1960s has been a decade of unusual protest and dissent against institutions of government. In an escalatingly militant manner various alienated minority groups — particularly black people, poor people, young people, and antiwar protesters — have picketed, confronted, and challenged various departments and agencies of federal and state governments. Yet curiously, while challenges to the executive branches had become regular and frequent by the mid-1960s, the *judicial* arm of the government had remained nearly immune to direct confrontation and accounting until nearly 1970.

Throughout the 1960s people marched (or tried to march) on the White House, on national conventions of the major parties, on the Congress and sessions of state legislatures, on the Pentagon and military recruiting stations throughout the nation, but rarely, if ever, did one hear or read of a march on the Supreme Court, indeed any court.

Why were the courts relatively isolated from protest throughout the 1960s? One factor may have been the persisting image of "majesty," indeed "sacredness," that the court seems to have held for the citizenry. The fact that judges wear priestlike black robes is evidence of and sustenance for the judiciary's religious image. If the legislature and executive have been defined pretty much within the "secular" realm of society, the courts have possessed a religious aura not to be tampered with or challenged except in the most extreme of situations.

Another factor insulating the courts has been a persistent ideology that they are disassociated from and somehow "above" the political process and arena, that the judiciary is not an independent variable in the creation of law and legal policy — and thus not a proper target for those who seek a redistribution of political power in the country. That judges are often appointed (e.g., in the federal judiciary) rather than elected, in contradistinction to major legislative and executive officials, and that their terms of office are often longer than terms in the other branches of government, are sometimes given as evidence that the courts are somehow aloof and detached from the action centers of political power. Any first-year law student knows that in fact the courts "make" as much law as they "interpret," and that their "dependent" or "agent" position in the American political structure and process is largely a myth. But the point is that until very recently even vocal protest groups seem to have accepted this high-school-textbook version of the courts' role.

One important common denominator to the numerous group protests against the executive and legislative branches of government in the past decade was the idea that, in a geometrically progressive fashion, power had been removed from the hands of the vast majority of the population and consolidated in the hands of a very few "elected" officials who were generally neither respondent nor responsible to the will of the people. Of course this complaint has been echoed from the earliest days of the Republic, but it had a peculiar urgency, and was particularly well articulated by many intelligent protesters, in the multiple crises of the 1960s.

Another common denominator of the many protests, rebellions, and revolutionary movements directed at government institutions in the last decade is that in the main they have very largely failed to achieve their purposes. To take the three most prominent examples of failure of continued protest to affect government policy: the war in Vietnam continues unabated, and now has openly spread to other parts of Indochina; black people remain essentially a colonial and oppressed people within the United States; a substantial minority of the United States citizens (black and white) continue to live in a state of poverty or near-poverty with no sign of real improvement of their lot.

The specific way in which protesters have experienced failure and frustration led them to discover the relatively untouched judicial chink in the institutional armor. That is, the types of dissent activities carried out against legislative and executive institutions — e.g., liberation of neighborhoods and parks, takeover of buildings, large-scale protest meetings and marches, burning of draft records — are defined by the criminal law in terms of statutes such as criminal trespass, riot, conspiracy to riot, disturbing the peace, and destruction of government property. Protesters, then, had been moving toward an eventual direct confrontation with the courts in an oblique way when they initially challenged the other arms of government and found themselves indicted under certain criminal laws implemented in their particular cases to protect the "garrison society." Eventually it dawned upon these defendants that far from being mere "agents" of the other institutions of power, the courts themselves were another creator and center of the very status quo they were determined to change. It is at this point that the legitimacy of the judiciary is finally brought into fundamental question, and the old cry, heard earlier concerning the executive and legislative branches, that the people have been robbed of their power, is heard in a new forum of protest. That protesters would pick the *trial level* of criminal courts to mount their challenge makes sense not only in terms of their own involvement as defendants at that level, but because it is the least "majestic" and most public and accessible one in the hierarchy of the American judicial system.

That dissenter defendants would stop playing "good little boys," that their in-court challenges to the judiciary's legitimacy would tend to be highly boisterous and dramatic follows from the protesters' growing sophistication and awareness of the previously effective role of American criminal trials in keeping radicals "out of circulation" through protracted judicial proceedings, often including long-term pre-verdict detention. The defendants in the Chicago and Black Panther trials were determined that their revolutionary voices would not be buried in a judicial morass. To that end they performed in the courtroom in such a way that their actions would be consistent headline news.[9]

---

[9]Paul Goodman has suggested that the *real* purpose of the Chicago and various Panther trials was to tie up the political activity of the defendants, and, if this were the case, they had every *right*

The astonishment and outrage of the judges, bailiffs, and prosecuting attorneys, when suddenly and vociferously confronted with across-the-board challenges to their authority, were predictable. The massive contempt sentences handed out to all defendants and lawyers in the Chicago trial, the summary contempt sentences given by Justice John Murtagh to several spectators at the pretrial hearings for the New York Panther 21; the gagging and shackling of defendant Bobby Seale in Chicago, followed a year later (March, 1970) by Supreme Court approval of such treatment of "obstreperous" defendants in *Illinois* v. *Allen*,[10] current research being conducted at the University of Michigan Law School, under a Ford Foundation grant, on the viability of various methods (plastic soundproof bubbles, separate rooms at the side of the courtroom) to control the outbursts of defendants in court[11] — all reflect the depth and breadth of a culture shock experienced by officers of the criminal court. Judges and their staffs, so long accustomed to nearly absolute deference on the part of both the general citizenry and defendants (radical or more conventional ones), so long cloistered from real public scrutiny, so secure in their tenure, could hardly have been expected to react in other than a harshly repressive way when the established roles of the customary judicial actors were drastically altered and new actors as well clamored to get on stage and take part.

II.   Emergent Features of the Radical-Criminal Trial

There already exists a massive amount of descriptive material about the above-mentioned trials — particularly about the trial of the Chicago Eight — in newspaper reports and articles, magazine pieces, a book-long excerpt of sections of the Chicago Eight trial transcript, and three histories of the Chicago trial.[12] The purpose of this presentation is not to render a history of any of these proceedings but to extract those features in the trials that appear to be most clearly innovative and hostile to the existing model of the American criminal trial. The actual occurrences that exemplify some particular feature of radical-criminal trials will not be cited individually in the text, to avoid excessive annotation, but each incident mentioned below is derived from one or more published sources. These examples are intended to present a useful and strategic new "angle" on these trials, and to provide background for the third section of this essay, which indicates possible

to disrupt the trials. Goodman, "The Disrupted Trials: A Question of Allegiance," *The Village Voice*, March 9, 1970, pp. 5, 9.

[10]*The New York Times*, April 1, 1970, pp. 1, 19.

[11]*Ibid.*, February 13, 1970, pp. 1, 42.

[12]The book-long excerpt of significant sections of the Eight Trial transcript is Levine *et al., op. cit.* The three histories of the trial are: Tom Hayden, *The Trial*, (comprising the July, 1970, issue of *Ramparts* magazine); Bobby Seale, *Seize the Time* (New York, 1970); Jason Epstein, *The Great Conspiracy Trial* (New York, 1970).

future implications for the ideology and practice of criminal justice in the United States.

Role of Defendants. Perhaps the most fundamental innovation in the radical-criminal trial is the open, incessant, and vociferous challenge made by single or multiple defendants to the very *legitimacy* of the criminal court. In fact, the resistance of the *defendants* to the court's authority is so aggressive and *offense*-like that it is almost paradoxical to refer seriously to the "role of the defendant" in a sense consistent with the meaning of that term in the proceedings of a traditional trial.

The argument that the court is illegitimate rests on the defendants' analysis and condemnation of the existing situation in the United States. They see themselves as political prisoners trapped by a power structure of laws created by societal groups hostile to their interests. The court is both an agent for these groups and institutions — most significantly, monopoly capitalism, racism, colonialism, the military-industrial complex, and incipient fascism — and also an oppressive power group in its own right. Although defendants may vary somewhat in the rank or order of their targets, all are in agreement that the criminal court's allegiances are squarely with the oppressor groups and directly hostile to the powerless classes in American society.[13] That fundamental consensus was perhaps most dramatically symbolized by the innumerable times during these trials that defendants shouted out the slogan "Power to the People."

Assuming this basic political rationale for denying legitimacy to the criminal court, what kinds of actual courtroom tactics and conduct do defendants employ in a radical-criminal trial to express their challenge and discredit the proceedings? The general procedure, implemented in many specific ways, is to flaunt the traditional rules and roles of the previously taken-for-granted norms of the courtroom social system.[14] Numerous confrontation tactics are practiced, with the aim of throwing the traditional judicial model completely out-of-whack by bewildering the entrenched courtroom personnel. Here are some of the prominent tactics, with actual examples from the major trials:

(a) Defendants frequently burst out in direct verbal (and occasionally physical) attacks on judge, prosecutor, unfriendly witnesses, or the judicial process in

---

[13]Powerless classes in the eyes of many radical critics and protesters are not confined to so-called "working classes." In the view of C. Wright Mills (*White Collar; The Power Elite*) and Herbert Marcuse (*One Dimensional Man*), the United States middle classes are also politically impotent, whether they know it or not.

[14]Many of the tactics practiced by defendants have a distinct affinity with the kinds of ethnomethodological challenges to taken-for-granted assumptions exercised in the "demonstrations" of Harold Garfinkel and his associates. See Harold Garfinkel, *Studies in Ethnomethodology* (Englewood Cliffs, N.J., 1967), pp. 35–75. As did Garfinkel's "victims" the court personnel reacted with disbelief, rage, and bewilderment. Of course ethnomethodologists would be scandalized to have their "value-free" apolitical methodology linked to disruptions in radical-criminal trials.

general, shouting down their own attorneys and insisting that they be allowed to speak out for themselves about the injustice of their prosecution. During the first 12 days of the New York Panther 21 hearings, defendants interrupted the court proceedings in this manner on 665 separate occasions; the nearly five-month-long Chicago trial was interrupted innumerable times. Pleas and threats by the judges directed to the defense attorneys to control their clients were largely ineffective. Threats to hold the defendants in contempt of court and send them to jail were answered with statements such as "We're *already* in jail" (Panther 21), or "I'd rather go to jail than let you get away with the lies you're telling in this courtroom" (defendant Dellinger to Judge Hoffman in Chicago).

(b) Defendants rejected the legitimacy and dignity of the court by pointedly ignoring its proceedings. For example, defendants on many occasions, individually and collectively, refused to stand when Judges Murtagh (in New York) and Hoffman (in Chicago) began or terminated courtroom sessions. In some cases this led to physical altercations between defendants and marshals. During the Chicago trial defendants would frequently pay no attention to the examination of witnesses, even their own; they would appear deeply absorbed in books or newspapers instead. On several occasions certain of the Chicago defendants would casually get up and walk out on the proceedings, or fail to appear in the courtroom for a particular session.

(c) Defendants mocked and parodied the ordinary legal practices and procedures of the court in a variety of ways. In Chicago, Abbie Hoffman and Jerry Rubin once appeared in court wearing black judicial robes, in obvious parody of Judge Hoffman. Sometimes surrealistic and deliberately unresponsive answers were given to "straightforward" questions, such as those of the federal attorney to Abbie Hoffman about his age, residence, name, and occupation. Or they engaged the court in ludicrous disputes and colloquies — for example, the "Bobby Seale Birthday Cake Incident" and the "Great Bathroom Debate," both of which took place in the Chicago trial. Or defendants made legal motions for adjournment of court on bases that the bench considered "outrageous" or "unheard of." For example, during the Chicago trial the defendants moved for adjournment to celebrate the mid-October, 1969, Vietnam Moratorium, and in the New York Panther hearings defendants moved for adjournment to celebrate Black Panther founder Huey Newton's birthday in mid-February, 1970.

(d) Defendants refused to confine their interactions with other role members in the trial system to the area of the courtroom. On a number of occasions defendants in the Chicago proceedings, their aides, and lawyers clashed in verbal and physical conflict with members of the prosecution staff in the halls outside the courtroom. On one occasion defendants Hoffman, Rubin, and Dellinger — in the company of author Norman Mailer, a defense witness — confronted Judge Hoffman in the elegant Standard Club's Men's Grill. "Hoffman, lunching with another federal judge, cast one horrified look at them, rose, and took another seat behind a huge pillar."

Throughout the four and one-half months of the Chicago trial many of the defendants, all free on bail and permitted to travel throughout the United States on weekends, gave many speeches attacking the progress of the trial and its specific personnel in detailed *ad hominem* terms. Those few defendants free on bail during the New York Panther pretrial hearings also made speeches attacking Judge Murtagh and the prosecuting attorneys.

(e) Defendants attempted to restructure and reverse the roles of judge, prosecutor, and defendant, so that the judge, prosecutors, and even certain witnesses for the prosecution, would be defined as the people who should really be on trial. Bobby Seale's statement, "Judge Hoffman, it's *you* who are in contempt of the American people"; the Chicago Seven's "indictment" of Mayor Richard Daley, on the eve of his testimony at the trial, as "Chicago's leading public criminal"; the New York Panther Memorandum about Judge Murtagh stating what happened to be factually true: "We are confronted with a judge who has admitted, in fact been indicted and arrested for, ignoring police graft and corruption" — these are only rather spectacular examples of countless and everyday "condemnation of the condemners"[15] tactics practiced by defendants at the trials under review.

(f) Defendants planned with and solidly supported each other in challenges to the legitimacy of the trial. Whereas multiple radical defendants in earlier American trials sat in physical proximity to one another but usually remained verbally and emotionally isolated, in the recent trials they supported each others' outbursts with verbal encouragement by shouting out slogans such as "Right On!" or even came to the physical aid of each other if the court attempted to silence one of them.

Dellinger attempted to defend Seale from the assault of federal marshals when Judge Hoffman ordered Seale to sit down. Another time, when Judge Hoffman revoked Dellinger's bail for stating a "barnyard epithet," a melée broke out among the defendants and marshals, and Rubin shouted, "You're not going to separate us! Take all of us! Take me too!"

[15]The phrase, of course, is taken from Sykes and Matza's now well-known "Techniques of Neutralization." "Techniques of Neutralization: A Theory of Delinquency," *ASR*. 22 (December, 1957). pp. 664–670. But the meaning in the present context is theoretically and ideologically far different from the attitudinal tactics of these authors' delinquent boys. For the delinquent boys use "condemnation of the condemners" and other techniques in a guilty, defensive fashion, sensing deep down in their internalized consciences that their delinquency is "wrong," whereas the radical defendants are quite confident of the rightness and righteousness of their behavior and very genuinely believe in the wrongness of the court.

Black students in the United States view these "Techniques of Neutralization," originally designed to account for working-class delinquency, as a useful social-psychological model in explaining police brutality and sometimes homicide in black ghettos, for example, with the technique known as "denial of the victim." In the same vein, a number of my black students have pointed out to me how the emerging field of "victimology" — where the argument of Wolfgang and others is that in many crimes, particularly crimes against the person, the behavior of the victim facilitates or elicits the criminal behavior of the offender — can be used ideologically to excuse murders by the police in the ghettos as "justifiable homicides."

The techniques used by defendants to illegitimate the criminal trial often indicated a "conspiratorial" element. At least two defendants, David Dellinger and Tom Hayden, have admitted that the Chicago Eight discussed delegitimating trial tactics (although with less than complete agreement among the members) before their trial began.[16] But the essential, as well as ironic, point is that the conspiracies these radical defendants engaged in were *not at all the ones for which the courts had indicted them*, i.e., conspiracy to commit riot (Chicago) and conspiracy to commit arson (New York).[17] One of the hallmarks of the radical-criminal trials is that the defendants, *after* being indicted for one criminal offense or another (the specific offense itself makes little difference), "conspired" or agreed collectively to discredit the proceedings of hearings and trial. Conspiracy, in short, viewed from the perspective of the radical-criminal trial, is the *result, not the cause*, of the indictment and criminal trial.

Role of Spectators. The role of the spectators underwent at least as drastic a transformation in the radical-criminal trial as that of the defendants. If defendants changed their style of participation from abiding by the rules to constantly challenging the court's legitimacy, spectators made an equally radical leap at the end of the 1960s from a virtual abstention from overt participation in the criminal trial or hearing to wide-scale vocal and sometimes physical participation. Such uninvited intervention has lent a new and unforeseen dimension to the Sixth Amendment's provision for a "public trial."

Certainly the history of criminal trials in this country contains earlier instances in which spectators have vigorously intervened — either for or against defendants and other court personnel — and in which defendants have been obstreperous. Indeed, Roscoe Pound comments upon the often rowdy quality of the 19th-century American criminal trials, although he notes that this rowdiness had much diminished by the early decades of the 20th century;[18] and evidence of occasional audience and defendant intervention can be found throughout this century, especially if the defendant was accused of a bizarre or heinous "conventional" crime or was a political radical. But the *pattern and quality* of audience participation in current radical trials is unprecedented; it may be designated *radical participation*, and thus set off from superficially or partially similar audience conduct in earlier judicial eras. The most general reason why the current intervention of court audiences is new and distinctive is that it is *conditioned by the radical performance of the defendants*, another event of very recent vintage. Keeping this relationship in mind, the following prominent features of radical trial spectator activism emerge from a reading of the court reports:

---

[16]David Gelber, "The Conspiracy in Jail: Transcending Differences," *The Village Voice*, March 12, 1970, pp. 11–12; Hayden, *op. cit.*, p. 10.

[17]Juries ultimately found all defendants in both the Chicago and New York trials not guilty on all of the conspiracy charges.

[18]Roscoe Pound, *Criminal Justice in America* (New York, 1930), pp. 117–166.

(a) Whether outbursts were directed to defendants, judges, prosecutors, witnesses, other members of the audience, or to "everybody in the courtroom," the participation of the audience was very frequent and continuous, day in and day out, rather than sporadic, as were most earlier spectator interventions and disruptions. For example, in the New York Panther hearings, defendants' family members and spectator Black Panthers from the first day frequently joined the chorus of comments kept up by the defendants, repeatedly called out encouragement, and echoed "Black Power to the People!" when the defendants shouted out the slogan. As that hearing proceeded, young white spectators began to displace the black audience, but the harassment of the court continued unabated. Scarcely more than three weeks after the pretrial hearings had begun, Judge Murtagh suspended the hearings indefintely, following constant interruptions by the spectators as well as by the defendants. The Chicago trial was likewise marked by incessant interventions on the part of spectators. Audience participation was also evident at the New Haven Panther hearing and trial.

(b) Attempts by judges and their staffs to control or discontinue such interruptions were largely unsuccessful. To be sure, particular offenders in the audience were spotted and removed by marshals (Judge Hoffman's approach in Chicago) or summarily sentenced and imprisoned for contempt of court (Judge Murtagh's preferred technique in New York), but they were so numerous and so easily replaced that such measures could not be more than temporarily effective. Moreover, many of the audience activists, like many of the defendants, simply did not "care" about possible sanctions, and this attitude made control of the courtroom problematic on a minute-to-minute basis.

(c) Most of the participating spectators shared class interests with the defendants; conversely they tended to have few ideological, economic, or communal "interests" in common with the institutionalized personnel of the court. In an earlier era, participating audiences had been at least as likely to share identification with the court's "reference groups" as with the defendant's. The Chicago trial courtroom, however, was packed for nearly five months with hippies, Yippies, and representatives of various radical and revolutionary organizations, whose interests in and attitudes about current politics and power organization were close to those of the radical defendants. The New York courtroom was populated mainly by Black Panthers and poor black people. In both courtrooms, conventional, white middle-class citizens — the kind of people who looked, dressed, and felt like the judges and prosecutors — were conspicuously absent, outside of the press corps. In general, then, defendants were inclined to perceive the audience at their trials as "the people," and to interpret interventions of the audience as "the will of the people."

(d) It follows that the intervening audience in the radical trial was invariably on the side of the defendants and hostile to the institutionalized judiciary. In the progressive and interactive dialogue among and between defendants and members of the audience in the radical-criminal trial, an increasingly strengthened structure of "resonating sentiments" emerged. At the same time, the dissonance of sentiments between the court on the one hand and the defendants and the audience became magnified. Examples were the massive support the audience gave to Bobby Seale in the courtroom, time after time answering his defiant raised and clenched fist with cries of "Right On!"; the solidarity the New York Panther defendants displayed with a spectator whom Judge Murtagh ordered removed for interrupting the proceedings, one defendant saying, "If she goes out, we go out!"; the concerted outrage of the entire audience when Judge Hoffman bound and gagged Seale; the continuous open as well as *sub rosa* exchanges between defendants and audience in New York and Chicago, as if the official court personnel were either absent or simply did not count. In all these instances, audience and defendants constructed a mutually supportive and subversive social reality under the very gavel and noses of the judge, prosecutors and marshals.

It was just this extra-individual build-up and persistence of shared values between defendants and audience that made it such an enveloping and formidable force for judges and even dozens of marshals to contain continually. Then too, the extensive length of the radical trials increased the resonances of shared sentiments between defendants and spectators; it reaffirmed and intensified the commitment of at least one sector of the "public" — the specialized one represented by the audience — to the defendants' cause; and it ironically perverted the state's purpose to keep some radicals "out of circulation" through drawn-out judicial proceedings.

(e) The participating audience in radical criminal trials was not *primarily* interested in (although certainly not indifferent to) the eventual "guilt" or "innocence" of the charged persons, insofar as these statuses are determined by a body which they perceive to be illegitimate. In this respect their attitudes parallel those of the defendants themselves. The primary thrust of spectator activism, then, is the radical one of discrediting the entire judicial process rather than winning a "not guilty" victory for the defendants — especially if obtaining an acquittal means "playing along" with conventional judicial assumptions of what is "right" and "just," and so on.

(f) Inasmuch as the activist audience was participating along with the defendants in the construction of a radical-criminal trial, they would tend to use — within the limitations of their somewhat more peripheral position in the courtroom (both spatially and socially) — discrediting techniques similar to those discussed in detail for defendants: open defiance of officials, pointed ignoring of the proceedings, "condemning the condemners," mockery of judicial procedures. Because of their resonant relation to the defendants, spectators would often "conspire" — like the defendants — to implement these disrupting tactics.

The Proselytizing Process. Even while attempting to discredit the criminal trial in its current condition, defendants and active spectators were simultaneously trying to re-educate those groups in the trial who support the system as it is to a more radical vision of both criminal justice and American institutions. These are some of the directions taken by such conversion attempts:

(a) Defendants and spectators have attempted to convert the "grass-roots" personnel of the court to a radical definition of the situation. In direct confrontations, they have argued with bailiffs and marshals that their real interests lie with "the people" and the defendants, not with the judge and state prosecutor. In the Chicago trial, for example, Dellinger stated that the trial proceedings demonstrated the corruption in the political system; when Judge Hoffman ordered a federal marshal to seat him, Dellinger turned to the man and said, "You don't really think this is a fair trial, do you? You're allowed to think for yourself even though you're paid by the same company." During the New York Panther hearings, a black woman sympathetic to the Panthers accosted a black bailiff in the hall and asked, "Whose side are you on, brother?" When he answered, "I'm on nobody's side, sister. I'm just trying to keep order," she snapped, "You're a pig, too."

(b) When defendants took the stand to "testify" in their own behalf, their statements were often proselytical, although both judge and prosecutor attempted to cut off these remarks as "irrelevant." Thus, in the Chicago trial, defendant Abbie Hoffman, over numerous objections from the prosecution, tried to explain on the witness stand his views of youth culture, the generation gap, hippies, Yippies, guerrilla theater, the exorcism of the Pentagon, and the "politics of ecstasy." In the New York Panther hearings, defendant Tabor employed his time on the witness stand to tell his life story in a manner that vividly brought out the oppressiveness of current American institutions toward poor people, particularly poor black people.

In the Chicago trial, defendants also tried to use many of their witnesses as proselytizers. Among these were famous, charismatic and colorful authors, poets, singers, and civil rights leaders, who shared in a general way the political attitudes, if not always the life-style, of the defendants. In every case, however, their convertive dialogues, poems, chants, or songs, were forbidden or severely circumscribed by their prospective converts, the prosecutors and judge, on the grounds of irrelevancy.

(c) In earlier "conventional" criminal trials of radicals, the defense attorneys were rarely radicals themselves; rather they were and remained "liberals" during and after their defense of radical defendants.[19] In the recent radical-criminal trials, however, defense attorneys tended to become (and stay) radicalized because of the tactical strategies of the defendants and the emergent radical structure of resonant sentiments between and among their clients and the audience, in which the attorneys also became engulfed. Tom Hayden penetratingly depicted the stage-by-stage painful radicalization of the Chicago Eight's attorneys, William Kunstler and Leonard Weinglass, through the course of the trial.[20] It was painful because, prior to the Chicago trial, both attorneys had firmly believed in the legitimacy of the traditional ground-rules. How far Kunstler, for example, moved from his

---

[19]Hakman, 1971, *op. cit.*
[20]Hayden, *op. cit.*, p. 34.

pretrial position on this point is evidenced by his statement in court near the end of the trial: "I am going to turn back to my seat with the realization that everything I have learned throughout my life has come to naught, that there is no meaning in this Court, and there is no law in this Court. . . ." The ultimate rejection of the court's legitimacy by the defense attorney was supported, as were earlier more limited, more cautious ones, by the audience shouting "Right On!"

Thus defendants in radical-criminal trials were no longer satisfied, as earlier radical defendants in conventional trials usually had been, that their attorneys should be legally competent; or even possess the further desideratum that they believe all accused persons should be afforded a spirited defense no matter how unpopular their cause; or even possess the more committed requisite that they passionately believe in their client's "innocence" — for all these forensic virtues operate within the assumptions and structure of the existing judicial system, which is precisely what the defendants will not accept. Instead, what the current defendants require, and get, at an earlier or later stage in the proceedings, are men who themselves *believe* in the defendants' political causes. They require attorneys who are themselves radical so that they will "aid and abet" the defendants in staging a radical-criminal trial. In such a staging, defense attorneys have not only identified with their clients' interests to an unprecedented extent, but in very real senses they actually became defendants themselves, as the staggeringly long contempt sentences against both Kunstler and Weinglass in Chicago demonstrated. Such heavy demands, entailing such possibly heavy punitive consequences, suggest that full-bloom radical-criminal trials cannot long persist under present conditions; the small core of "Movement" attorneys would very shortly be removed from forensic circulation by long contempt-of-court sentences.

Reaction of the Proselytized. The reaction of the institutional criminal court personnel to the radical tactics of defendants and audience constitutes the final major feature of the radical trials. Allusion has already been made to the growing dissonance of sentiments between court officials on the one hand and defendants and audience on the other as the latter groups interactively stepped up their attacks on the court's legitimacy and courtroom procedures. If the verbal prototypes for resonance between defendants and spectators have been slogans such as "Right On!" and "Power to the People," the verbal symbol best expressing the judge's dissonance with radical tactics is some variant of the expression, "Never in my many years on the bench have I ever seen . . ." — which the judge then follows with a comment on one or another innovation introduced by defendants and/or the audience, depicted above.

In all the trials under discussion the dissonance between the court and the "people" has created a "garrison" or "armed-camp" atmosphere, with the court having to protect itself not only from assaults within the courtroom, but from large protesting crowds in the surrounding corridors, streets, and plazas, who have clamored to break in and simply terminate the proceedings. In none of these trials has the court been able to maintain order without "outside" help; in none of the trials have there not been days or weeks when the trials' continued existence was problematic.

These challenges to the viability of criminal trials from the defendants, on the one hand, and the audience and citizens in the streets on the other, have urgently raised questions bearing on two related, but distinct, constitutional rights of defendants. The Sixth Amendment guarantees a criminal defendant the right to confront directly witnesses against him; and the Sixth and Fourteenth Amendments (through the "due process" clause) guarantee him the right to a "public" trial. In March, 1970, the Supreme Court held unanimously that a defendant "waived" his right to confront his accusers by disorderly behavior, and could thus be gagged and bound, or even expelled and kept isolated from the courtroom while the proceedings against him continued. In the case of isolation from the courtroom, the defendant would be allowed limited and indirect confrontation with witnesses testifying agiinst him through devices such as closed-circuit television.[21]

But this Court decision did not discuss the "public trial" guarantee to the defendant. If the defendant is isolated in a room away from the courtroom while the trial continues against him, can he be said to be getting a public trial, from *his* point of view, even if an audience sits in the courtroom? The public trial guarantee may soon emerge as an urgent decision for the higher courts, but the focus will be on the disruptive behavior of the *audience* rather than the *defendant.* The courts have always ruled that defendants must be tried in the presence of some spectators other than officials of the court, while *at the same time* ruling that the judge has the discretion to bar unruly spectators.[22] But what if *all* the spectators are unruly, as radical audiences in some trials tend to be? Surely unlike the situation in which the defendant himself is disruptive (*Illinois* v. *Allen*), unruly spectators cannot be construed to waive the *defendant's* right to a public trial.

But all indicators point to the courts protecting themselves against radical courtroom tactics at the expense of the defendant's right to a public trial. An educated guess would be that the Supreme Court — more heavily conservative and oriented toward "law and order" than it was under former Chief Justice Warren — will soon rule, employing technical legal jargon and rationale, that in cases where audience intervention is acute the judge may completely clear the courtroom and continue with a closed or secret criminal trial. The Orwellian ultimate image is one where the excluded *audience* watches via television a courtroom wherein the

---

[21]*Illinois* v. *Allen.* This case actually concerned an accused robber who continually interrupted the proceedings against him. Justice William Douglas, in a concurring separate opinion, stated that the Court should have specifically limited the implications of its decision in *Allen* to non-political trials and waited for a trial like the Chicago Conspiracy proceedings, where defendant Seale was shackled, or the Panther hearings in New York or New Haven, to make a special ruling on these special kinds of trials. He was implying that there might be different rules of the game for radical-political trials, and considering his stand on these issues (see his *Points of Rebellion*, New York, 1970), he would probably prefer more plastic and "liberal" rules for such trials. Douglas is the only man on the present Court who is remotely sympathetic to (even modified) radical-criminal trials being allowed in the federal or state court systems of the United States.

[22]David Fellman, *The Defendant's Rights* (New York, 1958), pp. 55–57; Francis H. Heller, *The Sixth Amendment* (Lawrence, Kansas, 1951), pp. 61–62.

television image of the excluded *defendant* appears. The penultimate image is one where the court recruits a "scab" audience of "law-and-orderly" citizens to preserve formally the defendant's Sixth and Fourteenth Amendments' right to a public trial.

III. The Projected Radicalization
of the Administration of Justice

The full-blown radical-criminal trial described here has perhaps already peaked within three years since its origin at the Chicago conspiracy trial. Partial elements of this kind of trial persist. But future interruptions by radical defendants have already been anticipated or curbed by *Illinois* v. *Allen*, and the likelihood is high that radical spectator intervention will soon be stopped by the court as well. For example, in the 1972 trial of the surviving Soledad Brothers, John Clutchette and Fleeta Drumgo (George Jackson had been killed in the summer of 1971), a bullet-proof structure was erected in the San Francisco courtroom to separate the spectators from the principals in the trial. Inasmuch as the radical-criminal trial requires continuous interaction between defendants and spectators — which the courts are determined to stop, and with the aid of the police and military can stop — it appears that such trials are "off" for at least the near future.

Have these trials, then, been merely an ephemeral episode, or may they have a significant effect on the administration of criminal justice in the 1970s? I believe that these trials, interacting with rebellions in the houses of detentions and prisons during the same period, have permanently affected the political consciousness of large numbers of present (and future) "clients" in various stages of the administration of justice. Although it is blurred by the complicating variable of race consciousness in our society, it seems to me that the political element is substantial enough to allow one to refer, in Marxist-Leninist terms, to an acceleration of *class* consciousness among these clients, and to some progress toward a "class-for-itself." The emerging solidarity and power of that class-for-itself, catalyzed by the radical-criminal trials, may drastically reshape the ground rules and outcomes of criminal proceedings during the 1970s. There is already fragmentary but suggestive and significant evidence to support its contention.

Plea-Copping: The Achilles' Heel of the Criminal Court System. This essay has been about criminal trials, but trials actually comprise a very small part of the total criminal cases processed in the United States. In 1967, for example, about 88 percent of indicted persons in federal and state criminal proceedings pleaded guilty before a trial;[23] the great majority of these persons "copped pleas"

[23]Edwin H. Sutherland and Donald R. Cressey, *Principles of Criminology*, 3rd ed. (Philadelphia, 1970), p. 430.

in negotiations with prosecuting attorneys.[24] Even if radical-criminal *trials* are about to be successfully repressed, it appears that many of their major themes, adapted to their new "forums," will be shifted onto the pre-arraignment, pretrial bargaining process, and challenge this taken-for-granted, bureaucratic, and largely sub rosa justice by negotiation that has affected many more people than those who actually have gone to trial. My line of reasoning is this:

Working-class poor people (black and white — although blacks are more numerous victims of the administration of justice than poor whites) comprise the great bulk of persons indicted in criminal proceedings in the United States.[25] Indeed, there is great political truth in Mark Kennedy's serious pun that "Crime is what poor people are in jail for."[26] One of Blumberg's central contentions is that the prosecutor has been so successful in obtaining guilty pleas because he had divided and conquered these isolated and powerless people. (They could in fact be additionally characterized as "class-unconscious," a condition *causing* both their isolation and powerlessness in judicial institutions.) Blumberg paints an (heretofore!) accurate picture of the typical working-class indicted felon — assaulter, thief, burglar, or robber — often in pre-arraignment detention because he cannot raise bail. He is threatened, if he does not cooperate, by the prosecutor's discretion to try him on the most serious counts of an often frighteningly long list of separate crimes itemized in a multiple-count indictment. His attorney (who is often in collusion with the prosecutor, in contradiction to the official myth that the system is basically "adversary"), his relatives and friends, and other inmates all urge him to plead guilty in return for conviction on a lesser charge with a reduced penalty. In the face of these "odds" against him, the accused confronts almost irresistible pressures to capitulate, even if he is innocent or has a "good case." It might be noted that the negotiating process so prominent in the administration of justice meshes tidily with current "social exchange" theories ("You give me something; I'll give you something") about how men interact with each other.[27] But what they do is to describe historically specific economic-social-political norms as if they were absolutes. But what would happen to the "fit" between such theories and social reality in the judicial institutions if tens of thousands of accused persons were suddenly to become aware that they did not in fact stand alone, that there were numerous brothers and sisters concerned

---

[24]Plea-copping is vividly described in depth and detailed by Abraham Blumberg, *Criminal Justice* (Chicago, 1967), pp. 39–71. From a Marxist perspective of law as superstructural to economic organization, it cannot be an accident that the most highly developed acquisitive capitalist system in the world today should also have a system of criminal justice with the greatest emphasis on individual "deals" and negotiations.

[25]Paul B. Horton and Gerald R. Leslie, *The Sociology of Social Problems* (New York, 1965), pp. 125–127.

[26]Mark C. Kennedy, "Beyond Incrimination," in *Catalyst*, Summer 1970, p. 18.

[27]In the United States the works of George Homans and Peter Blau on theories of social exchange are examples of capitalist economy lying behind supposedly "timeless" theories of how men deal socially with each other. Homans, *Social Behavior: Its Elementary Forms* (New York, 1961); Blau, *Exchange and Power in Social Life* (New York, 1964).

and ready to support them? Would not such persons be prepared to resist the blandishments of the presecutor and chance a trial?

I expect a movement in the United States, originating in the radical-criminal trials of 1969–71, particularly the Panther trials, in which the habit of black, poor, and other oppressed groups, attending en masse and monitoring the arraignments, detention, and trials of people from their own class, will seep down from these spectacular trials to thousands of everyday cases. The lesson of the radical trials is: "Don't look to who's on trial for *what* (particular charged offense); just look to *who's* on trial." Since the answer is "poor and oppressed people" most of the time, the political nature of almost all criminal proceedings should be clear — and so starkly clear that great masses of working-class people in the United States should be able to grasp it.[28]

An indicated political tactic on the part of powerless groups in American society would be to show solidarity with their "politically imprisoned" brothers and sisters by keeping a constant vigil at all stages of criminal proceedings against them, and by refusing to cooperate any longer with the prosecutor in the "betrayal" system of plea-copping which has so successfully divided indicted persons and suffocated class consciousness. If this is done, accused persons will increasingly gain courage to chance — indeed *demand* — a trial, and as accused persons find that masses of working-class people are attending very carefully to all proceedings

---

[28]For ideological reasons, criminology texts have either ignored completely the relationship(s) between political factors and definitions of crime, or have given it most superficial treatment, introducing a few pages in the first chapter and then forgetting the analysis for the rest of the book. When political crime is mentioned, it is usually totally identified with popular definitions, so that offenses like treason are the only ones seen as embraced. The notion that *all* crime might be economically-politically derived through historical development is rarely mentioned, let alone systematically analyzed.

Although he was not entirely alone among United States criminologists in the 1960s, Richard Quinney in particular developed the idea that if one sees political process as the manner in which power is fought for and distributed in society, then all crime is in an important sense politically derived. This view construes the criminal law and its enforcement as the outcome of struggles among different interest groups, often social classes, for power. The groups which win the struggle get to decide *what is* and *who commits* crime. Thus it is not surprising that in a complex class-stratified society, criminality, at least as evinced by official statistics and processes of the administration of justice, is found overwhelmingly among the powerless working classes. Quinney's work was important; see his "Crime in Political Perspective," in *American Behavioral Scientist*, 8 (December, 1964), pp. 19–22, and "Is Criminal Behavior Deviant Behaviour?" in *The British Journal of Criminology*, April, 1965, pp. 132–142.

It remained, however, for Mark C. Kennedy to place Quinney's more general points into the specific historical development of capitalism and crime in the West since feudal times, and to show the particulars of the relationship of capitalist economic power in determining what behaviors would be labeled criminal. Kennedy's article is perhaps the most important piece, from the standpoint of socialist-oriented young criminologists in the United States, to be published in United States criminology in decades. In his rigorous demonstration of the identical behavioral criteria for both crime and "punishment," excepting the sole criterion of political power, he shows once and for all the bedrock foundation of crime, at least in our society, is in sheer power. Kennedy's essay, "Beyond Incrimination," in *Catalyst*, Summer, 1970, pp. 1–37, does to traditional criminology in the United States what André Frank's "The Sociology of Development and Underdevelopment of Sociology," in *Catalyst*, Summer 1967, pp. 20–73, did to the validity of establishment sociological models for attempts of re-underdeveloped nations to develop.

against them, including trials and hearings, the odds of the Blumberg model against the defendant will be considerably reduced. And the resolution to stand trial will not only be supported by an anticipation of *audiences* of similar class, but through the intensive process of politicization that is now pervading even the working-class inmates themselves throughout the spectrum of the administration of justice, from houses of detention to trial to places of penal servitude. Proof of this tendency has already appeared in The Tombs and the Queens House of Detention in New York City, in the radical-criminal trials, and at Attica and Soledad.

Two cases before New York State criminal courts in 1972 vividly bear witness to the new inmate and detainee solidarity massing for a strike against the Achilles' heel of plea-copping. Both are "nonpolitical" trials in that the defendants were all accused of the nonpolitical criminal charge of murder; both are cases far antedating the radical trials of 1969–72.

Robert Clayton, a 42-year-old migrant farm worker, was convicted of murder in 1953 and has served 19 years in Attica prison. The Harlem Four (they were originally six — the case's history is very complicated), all black young men, were convicted of murder in 1965 and served three years until their conviction was overturned by a higher court; since that time they have undergone two more mistrials. Until released on bail in 1972 after their third trial ended in a hung jury, they had served more than seven years either as convicted felons or in detention; judges either refused to set bail or set bail so high that these poor people could not possibly raise it. In both cases there is much glaring and embarrassing evidence that key testimony against the defendants was suborned.

Prosecutors in both cases pursued plea-copping strategies. The defendants were told that if they would plead guilty to the lesser offense of manslaughter their "time served" already would be accepted as a completion of sentence and they would be released. Yet Clayton remained in prison and continued his appeal; the Harlem Four remained resolute, and finally were freed on bail. Is it unreasonable to suggest that this defiance of the plea-copping device, this refusal to "play along" with their "own best (false) interests," is bolstered, partially caused, by the wave of political radicalization among working-class accused and near-accused? These prominent "nonpolitical" criminal cases may well be the forerunners of thousand sof less publicized refusals by defendants to make plea deals.

If one is willing to acknowledge that large-scale reductions in plea-copping may be the wave of the 1970s, what will follow? First, proceeding upon the findings of a number of sociological studies that people are less apt to act offensively or oppressively toward those whom they must confront face-to-face, the court personnel may be more reluctant to proceed unjustly, sternly, and punitively against proletarian defendants under the constant and contemptuous stares of proletarian courtroom audiences. A trial and hearing situation under these circumstances would probably lead to both lower conviction rates and less severe sentences if convictions were obtained. Second, the administration of justice in metropolitan courts would surely break down under a large-scale rejection of plea-copping. The system, as Tappan and Blumberg (among others) have indicated, is already understaffed in terms of court and detention house personnel, and would rapidly be overwhelmed by this new influx of pending trial cases. Such a state of affairs would necessarily force the administrators of justice back toward a plea-copping model, but the old pattern would have to be updated in favor of defendants, whose bargaining power would be increased. So one could expect to see in the "new" bargaining a drastic selection/reduction in indictments, much more lenient bail procedures, and much better "deals" for indicted persons.

It remains finally to be stated why this limited type of attack on the administration of criminal justice has a better chance of success at present than the more total and dramatic attempts at revolt currently taking place in many prisons.

(1) Although criminally indicted persons and their class allies, by acting according to the procedure indicated, would certainly conflict with the interests of the ruling class as much as did the Attica inmates, the former would be proceeding nonviolently and even legally. The projected strategies on the part of large numbers of accused persons would ultimately disrupt the functioning of the bureaucratic structure of the courts, and yet they could more or less operate within that structure as they sow the seeds of its destruction. No "revolutionary" changes are being projected; but Marx himself always urged support for any change, even within the bourgeois capitalist system, which led to some alleviation of the workers' oppression and some enlargement of their democratic rights. Some undeniable amount of significant class consciousness has developed among oppressed persons in the last few years. Perhaps concerted action against the old plea-copping system is a response commensurate to this degree of heightened consciousness.

(2) Widespread class action at the pretrial and trial stages of criminal proceedings can statistically embrace enough persons (millions are arrested each year in the United States) to constitute a substantial social movement, whereas the number of persons engaged in disruptive activities in United States prisons must be very much smaller. Moreover, the legal and physical freedom of convicts is usually much more restricted than accused but not-yet-convicted people (with the important exception of detainees without bail). Lenin was often quoted as saying that revolution was where the millions — not hundreds of thousands — were. However, if the more limited but substantial judicial "reform" discussed above is to succeed, with vast eventual benefit to millions of working-class accused and detained persons, its attainment will have been achieved in part because of the more extreme and violent examples and sacrifices[29] set by other working-class persons in the unsuccessful, often fatal, prison rebellions currently sweeping the United States.

[29]See Paul Cowan, "Encounter with George Jackson: 'I'm willing to do the dying'," *The Village Voice*, October 7, 1971, pp. 5, 6, 47.

Chapter Six

CUSTODY AND CORRECTIONS

How does the state deal with those it convicts of criminal offenses? Once persons have been arrested and convicted for threatening the existing order, they must serve a sentence. The possibility of a criminal sentence exists in fact for every citizen in the state. Indeed, the primary purpose of the sentence is to warn the citizenry that a violation of the criminal law will lead to deprivation and punishment of some kind. In addition, the imposition of a sentence for an adjudicated offense is the state's retaliation against those who fail to abide by its dictates. A criminal sentence is the state's last attempt to preserve the established order and to punish those who have transgressed the rules of order.

The state has devised various schemes to punish the offender. Not only have there been the concrete forms of capital and corporal punishment, but the state has created punishments that supposedly "rehabilitate" ("treat" or "correct") the offender as well. To bring the deviant back into the established order is the objective of such schemes. The complete program requires both a punishment for threatening the established system and a form of treatment that will readapt the offender to the existing social and economic order. Like all the other aspects of the legal system, custody and corrections exist in America to preserve the existing capitalist system.

Confinement of offenders to an institution, as a means of dealing with crime, developed within a particular historical context in the United States. In the first selection in this chapter, "The Invention of the Penitentiary," David J. Rothman documents the emergence of the penitentiary as a solution to the crime problem. Following the American Revolution, governments became greatly concerned about the protection of the new social order, including the eradication of any conduct that threatened that order. At the beginning of his study, Rothman asserts that the development of the asylum, including the penitentiary, was an attempt by leaders in the Jacksonian period to promote stability in the new nation. "Legislators, philanthropists, and local officials, as well as students of poverty, crime, and insanity were convinced that the nation faced unprecedented dangers and unprecedented opportunities. The asylum, they believed, could restore a necessary social balance to the new republic, and at the same time eliminate long-standing problems. At once nervous and enthusiastic, distressed and optimistic, they set about constructing and arranging institutions."[1] The penitentiary would rehabilitate offenders and at the same time set an example of right action for the rest of society. "The well-ordered asylum would exemplify the proper principles of social organization and thus insure the safety of the republic and promote its glory."

In "The Invention of the Penitentiary" Rothman traces the movement as it spread in the early 1820s from New York and Pennsylvania throughout the rest of the country. Two systems of prison organization, the "congregate" system at Auburn and the "separate" system at Pittsburg and Philadelphia, provided competing models. The controversy between the two models represented differing concepts of crime and punishment. Prison architecture and social arrangements within the prison became the central concern of reformers of the period.

Regimentation, reflecting adoption of the Auburn system, became the standard mode of prison life in the United States. The convict's daily life was strictly controlled. The military style of command pervaded all aspects of prison life. In organization as well as in architecture, the prison symbolized obedience and order. The prison, Rothman concludes, provided a model for the whole society: "The functioning of the penitentiary — convicts passing their sentences in physically imposing and highly regimented settings, moving in lockstep from bare and solitary cells to workshops, clothed in common dress, and forced into standard routines — was designed to carry a message to the community. . . . By demonstrating how regularity and discipline transformed the most corrupt persons, it would reawaken the public to these virtues. The penitentiary would promote a new respect for order and authority."

Custody in the prison today is essentially the same as it was at an earlier time. Though there may be more programs in rehabilitation or treatment, the daily life of the inmate is one of routine and regimentation. Moreover, the personal costs of confinement are overwhelming. There is a vast literature on imprisonment, containing research on the social organization of the prison and the deprivations of imprisonment.[2]

[1]David J. Rothman, *The Discovery of the Asylum: Social Order and Disorder in the New Republic* (Boston: Little, Brown and Company, 1971), p. xviii.
[2]See Lawrence E. Hazelrigg (ed.), *Prison Within Society* (New York: Doubleday, 1968).

At first glance there appears to be a contradiction between the goals of custody and those of corrections.[3] But on closer examination we realize that the two are tied to the single purpose of the state: to control and manipulate the inhabitants of the state. That custody and corrections serve the same objective, and are often administered within the same setting, becomes evident in a critical understanding of the custody-treatment reaction to crime.

Robert Martinson provides us with such an understanding of modern corrections in his article "The Age of Treatment: Some Implications of the Custody-Treatment Dimension." He begins by noting that there has been a movement from custody and prison reform (in which prisons are to be made more liveable) to treatment (within the prison as well as outside of it). The aim today of professionals engaged in correctional work is that of "transforming man." We live in an age, according to Martinson, in which "people-changing" has become a skill and a profession, as well as a moral injunction. In the new applications of corrections, dangerous techniques are being practiced and undemocratic procedures are being instituted.[4]

What is emerging is a new authoritarianism, concealed under the terminology of treatment and professionalism. The consequence may be a "correctional therapeutic community" where any deviant will be treated and readjusted to the prevailing order. Through indoctrination and coercion the new professional worker (the "expert") aids the state in preserving the established arrangements. Dangerous practices are emerging, as Martinson observes, fostered "by many well-intentioned persons with little thought to the consequences."

Hence, rather than dealing with the chronic alienation of the age, representatives of the state are designing and promoting schemes that attack the victims of oppression. Criminology aids the efforts of those who would change the victims instead of altering the oppression. Only with a sensitivity to such an ethical question as "What kind of correctional system is fitting for a democratic society?" can the criminologist be on the side of liberation, against the forces of oppression. The result of such a sensitivity would be a much different criminology, one that served the people rather than the state.

Meanwhile, those who are the object of custody and corrections are themselves revolting against the oppression and exploitation of their condition. In the essay "From Riot to Revolution," John Pallas and Bob Barber document the struggle within the prison, as related to the wider struggle in American society. They trace three types of

---

[3]Donald R. Cressey, "Limitations on Organization of Treatment in the Modern Prison," in Richard A. Cloward, et al., *Theoretical Studies in Social Organization of the Prison* (New York: Social Science Research Council, 1960), pp. 78–110.

[4]Also see American Friends Service Committee, *Struggle for Justice: A Report on Crime and Punishment in America* (New York: Hill and Wang, 1971); Francis A. Allen, "Criminal Justice, Legal Values and the Rehabilitative Ideal," *Journal of Criminal Law, Criminology and Police Science*, 50 (September–October, 1959), pp. 226–232.

prison struggle occurring in the last twenty years: the traditional prison riot, the black movement within prisons, and the more recent revolutionary prison movement. The recent events, the authors suggest, represent "a radically new dimension in the prison struggle, a dimension which has implications for the wider revolutionary movement and for state repression."

Pallas and Barber observe that as prisoners have moved from riot toward revolution the state has responded with an intensification of repression. As we note in recent prison revolts, prison officials and state authorities resort to a range of repressive measures, including political transfers, torture, assassination, and authorized violence. Moreover, new techniques are being developed and applied to deal with the revolutionary movement. Tranquilizing drugs, an electronic technology, surveillance, and the like are being used on rebellious prisoners, just as these same devices are being used on those who threaten the larger social order outside of the prison. At the same time, the growth of a political consciousness among prisoners and the rest of the people is making it more difficult for the state to maintain its control. The authors thus conclude that "the rise of the revolutionary movement among prisoners is inseparable from the rise of a larger revolutionary movement in America and around the world."

We close this chapter with an essay by Anthony Platt that ties together many of the ideas developed in this book. In the first part of "The Triumph of Benevolence: The Origins of the Juvenile Justice System in the United States," Platt describes and attacks the prevailing liberal ideology that underlies most research and theory in criminology. That ideology, he notes, has supported "the extension of welfare state capitalism and gradualist programs of amelioration, while rejecting radical and violent forms of social and political change." He attributes this ideology and practice to several structural conditions of criminology, including the scholar-technician tradition, agency-determined research, the acquiescence and vulnerability of academics, and the resistance of criminal justice agencies to critical research.

In his own demystification of history, Platt provides us with an alterative understanding of the juvenile justice system in America. He writes: "The child-saving movement was not simply a humanistic enterprise on behalf of the lower classes against the established order. On the contrary, its impetus came primarily from the middle and upper classes who were instrumental in devising new forms of social control to protect their privileged positions in American society." The juvenile justice system was thus a liberal reform, bringing about a new and more extensive form of social control, instituted for the purpose of preserving the existing order. The juvenile justice system was created in order to rescue capitalism and to avert radical change.

This chapter concludes with Platt's observation that the role of the critical student is not to help legitimize the interests of the state and the ruling class. Our purpose, rather, is to critically understand and attack the oppression of the existing capitalist system. "The old models need to be completely controlled by the people. While undertaking this task, we must also discard false ideologies and break free from the myths which distort our views of the past and limit our vision of the future."

14. David J. Rothman

The Invention of the Penitentiary

Americans' understanding of the causes of deviant behavior led directly to the invention of the penitentiary as a solution. It was an ambitious program. Its design — external appearance, internal arrangement, and daily routine — attempted to eliminate the specific influences that were breeding crime in the community, and to demonstrate the fundamentals of proper social organization. Rather than stand as places of last resort, hidden and ignored, these institutions became the pride of the nation. A structure designed to join practicality to humanitarianism, reform the criminal, stabilize American society, and demonstrate how to improve the condition of mankind, deserved full publicity and close study.

In the 1820's New York and Pennsylvania began a movement that soon spread through the Northeast, and then over the next decades to many midwestern states. New York devised the Auburn or congregate system of penitentiary organization, establishing it first at the Auburn state prison between 1819 and 1823, and then in 1825 at the Ossining institution, familiarly known as Sing-Sing. Pennsylvania officials worked out the details of a rival plan, the separate system, applying it to the penitentiary at Pittsburgh in 1826 and to the prison at Philadelphia in 1829. In short order, the Connecticut legislature stopped using an abandoned copper mine to incarcerate offenders, and in 1827 built a new structure at Wethersfield. Massachusetts reorganized its state prison at Charlestown in 1829; that same year, Maryland erected a penitentiary, and one year later New Jersey followed suit. Ohio and Michigan built penitentiaries in the 1830's, and so did Indiana, Wisconsin, and Minnesota in the 1840's.[1]

Reprinted by permission of Little, Brown and Company from *The Discovery of the Asylum: Social Order and Disorder in the New Republic*, by David J. Rothman, pp. 79–108. Copyright © 1971 by David J. Rothman.

[1]Orlando Lewis, *The Development of American Prisons and Prison Customs, 1776–1845* (Albany, N. Y., 1922), surveys this material. On the origins of the Auburn plan, see W. David Lewis, *From Newgate to Dannemora*, (Ithaca, N.Y., 1965), chs. 3–4; for Pennsylvania, Negley K. Teeters and John D. Shearer, *The Prison at Philadelphia, Cherry Hill: The Separate System of Prison Discipline, 1829–1913* (New York, 1957). Some source material illustrating the lines of influence may be found

The results of all this activity deeply concerned Americans, so that annual reports to state legislators and popular journals as well contained long and detailed discussions and arguments on the merits of various enterprises. Europeans came to evaluate the experiment and the major powers appointed official investigators. France in 1831 dispatched the most famous pair, Alexis de Tocqueville and Gustave Auguste de Beaumont; in 1832 England sent William Crawford, and in 1834, Prussia dispatched Nicholas Julius. Tourists with no special interest in penology made sure to visit the institutions. Harriet Martineau, Frederick Marryat, and Basil Hall would no more have omitted this stop from their itinerary than they would have a southern plantation, a Lowell textile mill, or a frontier town. By the 1830's, the American penitentiary had become world famous.[2]

The focus of attention was not simply on whether the penitentiary accomplished its goals, but on the merits of the two competing modes of organization. The debate raged with an incredible intensity during these decades, and the fact that most prisons in the United States were modeled after the Auburn system did not diminish it. Even more startling, neither did the basic similarity of the two programs. In retrospect they seem very much alike, but nevertheless an extraordinary amount of intellectual and emotional energy entered the argument. The fervor brought many of the leading reformers of the period to frequently bitter recriminations, and often set one benevolent society against another. Periodicals regularly polled foreign visitors for their judgment or printed a vigorous defense by one school and then a critical rejoinder by the other. The roster of participants in this contest was impressive, pitting Samuel Gridley Howe (a Pennsylvania advocate) against Matthew Carey (for Auburn), Dorothea Dix against Louis Dwight, Francis Lieber against Francis Wayland. Every report from the New York and Pennsylvania penitentiaries was an explicit apology for its procedures and an implicit attack on its opponents. And as soon as a state committed its prison organization to one side or the other then it too entered the controversy with the zeal of a recent convert.

The content of the debate between the Auburn and Pennsylvania camps points to the significance of the ideas on the causes of crime to the creation of the

---

in *State Prisons and the Penitentiary System Vindicated . . . by an Officer of the Massachusetts State Prison at Charlestown* (Charlestown, Mass., 1821), 41–42, 51; see too the 1830 report of a New Jersey investigatory committee reprinted in Harry E. Barnes, *A History of the Penal, Reformatory and Correctional Institutions of the State of New Jersey* (Trenton, 1918), 402–419. A good summary of attitudes and events is found in the New York Society for the Prevention of Pauperism, *Report of the Penitentiary System,* of 1822. Here, as with the spread of other institutions, the South, while not untouched by the movement, certainly did not participate in it to the extent that other sections did. The ideology and social realities, promoting the program had less appeal and relevance to the South, given its particular problems and conditions. Indeed, one indication of the differentiation of the South from the rest of the nation is the pace of institutionalization. In the 1820's the differences were not so great by this measurement; in the 1850's, they were.

[2]Many of these visitors published full accounts which, where valuable, are cited below. For a less well-known visitor, who helped to change the penal system of Hungary, see Alfred Reich, *The Contribution of Sandor Boloni Farkas. . . .* (unpublished doctoral dissertation, Columbia University, 1970).

penitentiary, and the zeal reflects the expectations held about the innovation. To understand why men became so passionate about internal questions of design is to begin to comprehend the origins and popularity of institutionalization in this era. Under the Auburn scheme, prisoners were to sleep alone in a cell at night and labor together in a workshop during the day for the course of their fixed sentences in the penitentiary. They were forbidden to converse with fellow inmates or even exchange glances while on the job, at meals, or in their cells. The Pennsylvania system, on the other hand, isolated each prisoner for the entire period of his confinement. According to its blueprint, convicts were to eat, work, and sleep in individual cells, seeing and talking with only a handful of responsible guards and selected visitors. They were to leave the institution as ignorant of the identity of other convicts as on the day they entered. As both schemes placed maximum emphasis on preventing the prisoners from communicating with anyone else, the point of dispute was whether convicts should work silently in large groups or individually within solitary cells.[3]

To both the advocates of the congregate and the separate systems, the promise of institutionalization depended upon the isolation of the prisoner and the establishment of a disciplined routine. Convinced that deviancy was primarily the result of the corruptions pervading the community, and that organizations like the family and the church were not counterbalancing them, they believed that a setting which removed the offender from all temptations and substituted a steady and regular regimen would reform him. Since the convict was not inherently depraved, but the victim of an upbringing that had failed to provide protection against the vices at loose in society, a well-ordered institution could successfully reeducate and rehabilitate him. The penitentiary, free of corruptions and dedicated to the proper training of the inmate, would inculcate the discipline that negligent parents, evil companions, taverns, houses of prostitution, theaters, and gambling halls had destroyed. Just as the criminal's environment had led him into crime, the institutional environment would lead him out of it.

The duty of the penitentiary was to separate the offender from *all* contact with corruption, both within and without its walls. There was obviously no sense to removing a criminal from the depravity of his surroundings only to have him mix freely with other convicts within the prison. Or, as Samuel Gridley Howe put it when composing a prisoner prayer: "In the name of justice, do not surround me with bad associates and with evil influences, do not subject me to unnecessary

---

[3]The literature below provides ample sources for discussing the two systems. Probably the best introduction to the debate, and the rival plans, remains Beaumont and Tocqueville, *On the Penitentiary System in the United States,* (Carbondale, Ill., 1964). Almost all of what follows below focuses on the state institutions, for they were most affected by the changes in penitentiary design. The ideas filtered down to the county and city level, but, given intricacy and expense, they were rarely acted upon. See Orlando Lewis, *The Development of American Prisons,* ch. 22. For the condition of the county jails, and the state of thinking, see *Report on Gaols and Houses of Correction in the Commonwealth of Massachusetts* (Boston, 1834), carried out by John Lincoln and Louis Dwight; *Report of the Secretary of the [Pennsylvania] Commonwealth, Relative to County Prisons* (Harrisburg, Pa. 1839).

temptation, do not expose me to further degradation. . . . Remove me from my old companions, and surround me with virtuous associates."[4] Sharing this perspective, officials in the 1830's argued that the great mistake of the prisons of the 1790's had been their failure to separate inmates. Lacking an understanding of the forces of the environment and still caught up with the idea that humane and certain punishment would eradicate deviancy, they had neglected to organize or supervise the prisoners' immediate surroundings. Consequently their institutions became seminaries of vice. Now, however, reformers understood the need to guard the criminal against corruption and teach him the habits of order and regularity. Isolation and steady habits, the right organization and routine, would yield unprecedented benefits.[5]

As a result of this thinking, prison architecture and arrangements became the central concern of reformers of the period. Unlike their predecessors, they turned all their attention inward, to the divisions of time and space within the institution. The layout of cells, the methods of labor, and the manner of eating and sleeping within the penitentiary were the crucial issues. The most influential benevolent organization devoted to criminal reform, the Boston Prison Discipline Society, appropriately considered architecture one of the most important of the *moral* sciences. "There are," the society announced, "principles in architecture, by the observance of which great moral changes can be more easily produced among the most abandoned of our race. . . . There is such a thing as architecture adapted to morals; that other things being equal, the prospect of improvement, in morals, depends, in some degree, upon the construction of buildings." Those who would rehabilitate the deviant had better cultivate this science.[6]

As with any other science, the advocates of moral architecture anticipated that the principles which emerged from the penitentiary experiment would have clear and important applications to the wider society. An arrangement which helped to reform vicious and depraved men would also be effective in regulating the behavior of ordinary citizens in other situations.[7] The penitentiary, by its example, by its discovery and verification of proper principles of social organization, would serve as a model for the entire society. Reformers fully anticipated that their work behind prison walls would have a critical significance beyond them. Since crime was symptomatic of a breakdown in traditional community practices, the

[4]Samuel Gridley Howe, *An Essay on Separate and Congregate Systems of Prison Discipline* (Boston, 1846), 40–41; see too Beaumont and Tocqueville, *On Penitentiary System*, 55.

[5]Gershom Powers, *A Brief Account of the Construction, Management, and Discipline . . . of the New York State Prison at Auburn* (Auburn, N.Y., 1826), 34; Stephan Allen, Samuel Hopkins, and George Tibbitts, "Report from the Committee Appointed to Visit the State Prison," *Journal of the Assembly of the State of New York*, January 15, 1825, Doc. 14, p. 5.

[6]Boston Prison Discipline Society (B.P.D.S.), *Fourth Annual Report* (Boston, 1829), 54–55. For a rare criticism, made by a onetime inmate of a penitentiary, see John Reynolds, *Recollections of Windsor Prison* (Boston, 1834), 209: "The science of architecture," he declared, "has been exhausted in experiments to construct a reformatory prison, as if the form of a cell could regenerate a vicious heart into virtue."

[7]Franklin Bache, *Observations and Reflections on the Penitentiary System* (Philadelphia, 1829), 5.

penitentiary solution would point the way to a reconstitution of the social structure.

Tocqueville and Beaumont appreciated how significant both of these purposes were to the first penologists. The institutions, Americans believed, would radically reform the criminal and the society. "Philanthropy has become for them," observed the two visitors, "a kind of profession, and they have caught the *monomanie* of the penitentiary system, which to them seems the remedy for all the evils of society." Proponents described the penitentiary as "a grand theatre, for the trial of all new plans in hygiene and education, in physical and moral reform." The convict "surrendered body and soul, to be experimented upon," and the results, as the Boston Prison Discipline Society insisted would benefit not only other custodial institutions like almshouses and houses of refuge, but also "would greatly promote order, seriousness, and purity in large families, male and female boarding schools, and colleges."[8] Perhaps the most dramatic and unabashed statement of these views appeared in a memoir by the Reverend James B. Finley, chaplain at the Ohio penitentiary. "Never, no never shall we see the triumph of peace, of right, of Christianity, until the daily habits of mankind shall undergo a thorough revolution," declared Finley. And in what ways were we to achieve such a reform? "Could we all be put on prison fare, for the space of two or three generations, the world would ultimately be the better for it. Indeed, should society change places with the prisoners, so far as habits are concerned, taking to itself the regularity, and temperance, and sobriety of a good prison," then the grandiose goals of peace, right, and Christianity would be furthered. "As it is," concluded Finley, "taking this world and the next together . . . the prisoner has the advantage."[9]

It is no wonder, then that Auburn and Pennsylvania supporters held their positions staunchly, eager to defend every detail. With the stakes so high and the results almost entirely dependent upon physical design, every element in penitentiary organization assumed overwhelming importance. Nothing less than the safety and future stability of the republic was at issue, the triumph of good over evil, of order over chaos. Intense partisanship was natural where the right program would reform the criminal and reorder the society, and the wrong one would encourage vice and crime.

The Pennsylvania camp had no doubt of its superiority, defining in countless pamphlets, articles, and reports its conception of the model institution. It aggressively insisted that the separate design carried the doctrine of isolation to a logical and appropriate conclusion. The arrangements at the Philadelphia prison, as partisans described them, guaranteed that convicts would avoid all contamination and

[8]Beaumont and Tocqueville, *On the Penitentiary System*, 80. Francis Bowen, "Review of Francis Gray's *Prison Discipline in America*," *North American Review*, 66 (1848), 152; B.P.D.S., *Fourth Annual Report*, 55–61. On the prison visits of Tocqueville and Beaumont, see J. P. Mayer, ed., *Alexis de Tocqueville: Journey to America* (New Haven, Conn., 1959) and George W. Pierson, *Tocqueville and Beaumont in America* (New York, 1938). Of interest too is Seymour Drescher, *Tocqueville and Beaumont on Social Reform* (New York, 1968).

[9]James B. Finley, *Memorials of Prison Life* (Cincinnati, Ohio, 1851), 41–42.

follow a path to reform. Inmates remained in solitary cells for eating, sleeping, and working, and entered private yards for exercise; they saw and spoke with only carefully selected visitors, and read only morally uplifting literature — the Bible. No precaution against contamination was excessive. Officials placed hoods over the head of a new prisoner when marching him to his cell so he would not see or be seen by other inmates.[10]

Once isolated, the prisoner began the process of reform. "Each individual," explained Pennsylvania's supporters, "will necessarily be made the instrument of his own punishment; his conscience will be the avenger of society." Left in total solitude, separated from "evil society . . . the progress of corruption is arrested; no additional contamination can be received or communicated." At the same time the convict "will be compelled to reflect on the error of his ways, to listen to the reproaches of conscience, to the expostulations of religion."[11] Thrown upon his own innate sentiments, with no evil example to lead him astray, and with kindness and proper instruction at hand to bolster his resolutions, the criminal would start his rehabilitation. Then, after a period of total isolation, without companions, books, or tools, officials would allow the inmate to work in his cell. Introduced at this moment, labor would become not an oppressive task for punishment, but a welcome diversion, a delight rather than a burden. The convict would sit in his cell and work with his tools daily, so that over the course of his sentence regularity and discipline would become habitual. He would return to the community cured of vice and idleness, to take his place as a responsible citizen.[12]

The separate system of penitentiary organization promised to accomplish these ends with a minimum of distraction and complication. The ordinary guards would not have to be well-trained, for their contact with the inmates would be slight and superficial; prisoners continuously confined to their cells would not have to be herded to meals or supervised in workshops and common exercise yards. Security would be easily maintained, since escape plans would be difficult to plot and to fulfill. There would be little recourse to the whip — cruel punishment would be rare, since men in isolation would have little occasion to violate regulations. Finally, these arrangements would permit officials to treat prisoners as individuals, rewarding some with more frequent visitors and books for good behavior, depriving recalcitrant others of these privileges. The Pennsylvania penitentiary

---

[10]Samuel Gridley Howe, *Prison Discipline*, 88–89; Edward Livingston, *Introductory Report to the Code of Prison Discipline* . . . (Philadelphia, 1827), 51. See too Inspectors of the Eastern State Penitentiary, *First and Second Annual Report*, 9–10, 19. Almost every report contained a defense of solitary.

[11]George W. Smith, *A Defense of the System of Solitary Confinement of Prisoners* (Philadelphia, 1833), 71, 75. See too Roberts Vaux, *Letter on the Penitentiary System of Pennsylvania* (Philadelphia, 1827), 10.

[12]*Ibid.,* 24, for Smith arguing that labor would produce "relief and pleasure." See too Edward Livingston, *Code of Prison Discipline*, 52–54; Anon., "Prison Discipline: The Auburn and Pennsylvania Systems Compared," *New York Review* 1840 15.

promised to be a secure, quiet, efficient, humane, well-ordered, and ultimately reformatory institution.[13]

Advocates of the separate system dismissed the competing congregate program as an incomplete and inconsistent version of the Pennsylvania scheme. The basic imperfection of Auburn, insisted critics like Samuel Gridley Howe, was a failure to maintain a thorough isolation of inmates. New York knew enough to separate prisoners at night, but for misguided motives allowed them to work together during the day. One result was that convicts came to recognize the other inmates, making it that much more likely that they would meet after release to resume a life in crime. They would also influence one another while still within the penitentiary walls. So many possibilities for conversation occurred during work and meals and exercise that guards could not eliminate all communication.[14] Auburn's procedures diabolically tempted the convicts. They were to sit together at mess tables and workbenches, and yet abstain from talking — an unnecessarily painful situation. Officials, compelled to enforce rules that were too easily broken, inevitably meted out frequent and harsh punishments without solving the problem. These basic defects, Pennsylvania's partisans concluded, made cruelty and corruption endemic to the congregate plan.[15]

For its part, the Auburn school vigorously defended the principle of separation and the reformatory promise of the penitentiary, fully sharing the axioms and optimism of its rival. But in reply to criticism, Auburn was necessarily on the defensive, for its arrangements did not so totally isolate the inmates or so studiously aim to prevent all chance of contamination. Auburn's supporters, therefore, spent more time picking fault with their opponents than advancing the superiority of their own procedures. Wherever possible they moved the debate from the ideal to the real, insisting that New York had the more practical scheme, a balanced combination of commitment and flexibility. They argued that Pennsylvania did not carry out its program perfectly, and then went on to contend that the very consistency of the separate design was itself a grave fault. Auburn's partisans answered complaints of frequent inmate communication in congregate prisons by contending that the walls of the Philadelphia prison were not thick enough and its sewer pipes not arranged well enough to prevent convict conversations.

[13]Frederick Packard, *An Inquiry into the Alleged Tendency of the Separation of Convicts . . . to Produce Disease and Degeneration* (Philadelphia, 1849), 42; and his *A Vindication of the Separate System of Prison Discipline* (Philadelphia, 1839), 32. See too Edward Livingston, *Code of Prison Discipline*, 19, and Samuel Gridley Howe, *Prison Discipline*, 54–55.

[14]Samuel Gridley Howe, *Prison Discipline*, 25, 28–29, 38–39, 48; Richard Vaux, *The Convict, His Punishment; What It Should Be; And How Applied* (Philadelphia, 1884), 31. See also Edward Everett, "Review of the Tocqueville-Beaumont Report on American Penitentiary Systems," *North American Review*, 37 (1833), 133; Thomas McElwee, *A Concise History of the Eastern Penitentiary of Pennsylvania* (Philadelphia, 1835), 15; George Smith, *A Defense of Solitary Confinement*, 63.

[15]Dorothea Dix, *Remarks on Prisons*, 77; Howe, *Prison Discipline*, 31. Edward Livingston, *Letter . . . on the Advantages of the Pennsylvania System of Prison Discipline* (Philadelphia, 1828), 8–12, as well as *Code of Prison Discipline*, 13, 19.

Charge, of course, prompted countercharge and before long intricate measurements of institutional walls and elaborate diagrams of the layout of pipes filled much of the penitentiary pamphlet literature.[16]

One main thrust, however, of the congregate school came on the issue of the effects of constant and unrelieved isolation of prisoners. It was unnatural, the New York camp insisted, to leave men in solitary, day after day, year after year; indeed, it was so unnatural that it bred insanity. The organization of the Philadelphia institution, argued Francis Wayland, was "at variance with the human constitution," and his supporters tried to marshall appropriate statistics. The comparative mental health of prisoners under the two arrangements, the causes and rates of death, the physical health of the convicts entered the debate. No accurate data allowed precise calculations of these phenomena and partisans did little more than set down subjective judgments in the guise of absolute numbers. But the Auburn attack did manage to cast some doubt on the wisdom of Pennsylvania's routine.[17]

After asserting that the separate system was no more effective or perfect than the congregate one, the New York school presented what proved to be its most persuasive point: the added expenses of establishing the Pennsylvania program were unnecessary. Auburn-type institutions, their defenders flatly, and accurately, declared, cost less to construct and brought in greater returns from convict labor. Since the two systems were more or less equal, with faults and advantages fairly evenly distributed, states ought not to incur the greater costs of the separate plan. By having prisoners work together in shops, Auburn's cells did not have to be as large as those at Philadelphia; also, a greater variety of goods could be efficiently manufactured in congregate prisons. The New York program provided the best of both worlds, economy and reform.[18]

The pamphlet warfare between the two camps dominated practically all thinking and writing about the problem of crime and correction. The advantages and disadvantages of Pennsylvania as against Auburn blocked out any other consideration. No one thought to venture beyond the bounds of defining the best possible prison arrangements, and this narrowness of focus was clear testimony to the widespread faith in institutionalization. People argued whether solitary should be continuous

[16]Anon., *Thoughts on Prison Discipline* (Boston, 1839), 13; this work was issued by a supporter of the B.P.D.S. See also Francis Wayland, "Prison Discipline," *North American Review*, 49 (1839), 31–38; Beaumont and Tocqueville, *On the Penitentiary System*, 199.

[17]Francis Wayland, "Prison Discipline," 38; Francis C. Gray, *Prison Discipline in America* (Boston, 1847), 181–182. B.P.D.S., *Second Annual Report* (Boston, 1827), 66; almost every report of the society defended the Auburn system. For the response of the Pennsylvania school, see, in addition to the above, *Report of the Committee Appointed to Visit and Inquire into the Condition and Circumstances of the Eastern Penitentiary* (Harrisburg, Pa., 1837), 4; and, Franklin Bache, *Observations of the Penitentiary System*, 9.

[18]Anon., *Thoughts on Prison Discipline* (Boston, 1839), 11; Matthew Carey, *Thoughts on Penitentiaries and Prison Discipline* (Philadelphia, 1831), 35. See too Francis Wayland, "Prison Discipline," 32, 39–40. European legislators also made this calculation, at least when first comparing the two systems; later, as in the case of the French, they went over to the Pennsylvania camp. See Seymour Drescher, *Dilemmas of Democracy: Tocqueville and Modernization* (Pittsburgh, Pa., 1968), 136.

and how ducts ought to be arranged, but no one questioned the shared premise of both systems, that incarceration was the only proper social response to criminal behavior. To ponder alternatives was unnecessary when the promise of the penitentiary seemed unlimited.

The ideas on the origins of deviant behavior led directly to the formulation of the Auburn and Pennsylvania programs, and these in turn became the blueprints for constructing and arranging new prisons. The pamphlet literature exerted a critical influence on legislators' resolves to erect penitentiaries and officials' decisions on how to administer them. As the inspectors of the Auburn penitentiary aptly concluded in 1835: "The founders of this system relied almost entirely upon theory for the groundwork on the plan."[19]

There was a clear value and import to a program of incarceration that removed the deviant from one town without sending him to another. In a physically mobile society, the prison was a useful form of control. And undoubtedly some supporters were drawn to the program only because they believed that the terrors of isolation and silence would decrease crime. But the appeal of institutionalization was still broader. Its functionalism was part of the story of its origins but not all of it. If incarceration had been nothing more than a practical alternative to expulsion or to whippings, then a minimum of effort and expenditure would have been made on these institutions. The penitentiaries, however, in first appearance were elaborate and expensive structures, with peculiar and idiosyncratic routines that had no obvious functional quality. To understand why thick walls and individual cells and the isolation of convicts became standard one must look beyond the immediate needs of the community to broader considerations, to reform, to model-building, to an almost utopian program.

Earlier structures, erected soon after the Revolution, had operated in a very ad hoc fashion, providing few lessons worth following. By the 1820's there had hardly been any advances in prison design in the United States, and only scattered ones in Europe. In the 1790's reformers anticipating the benefits of statutory revisions had devoted little energy to internal prison arrangements. Since laws, and not blueprints, captured their attention, the prisons erected at the end of the eighteenth century usually made only minor or confused departures from colonial arrangements. As a result, they did not provide the next generation with tested principles. "Reform in prison discipline," declared one participant, "was an experiment. They had no model prison to visit; no pioneers in the march of reform, to warn them of errors or guide them to truth."[20] The first encounter

---

[19]"Annual Report of Auburn Prison," *N.Y. Senate Docs.*, 1835, I, no. 13, p. 3.

[20]On early prison history in Europe, see Max Grünhut, *Penal Reform, A Comparative Study* (Oxford, 1948). Americans certainly knew of Bentham's plans and were familiar with the English structures, as witness Haviland in Pennsylvania. But borrowing was not the heart of the story; they had to work out for themselves the administration and organization of the penitentiary, and they did so in novel ways. See New York Prison Association (N.Y.P.A.), *Second Annual Report* (New York, 1846), 15.

with institutions was so disappointing, in fact, that many observers considered them positively harmful and dangerous.

Officials in the 1790's avoided the problems critical to making a prison the basic form of criminal correction, and the consequences, to judge by frequency of riots, escapes, and statements of public displeasure, were disastrous. The architecture of the institutions still commonly followed the model of the household. The Walnut Street jail in Philadelphia, built in 1790 and quickly copied in such cities as New York, resembled an ordinary, if somewhat large, frame house, indistinguishable from other sizable dwellings. The New Jersey prison at Trenton, opened in 1798, was a typical two-storied home complete with a columned doorway, and set apart only by a low wall enclosing a courtyard.[21] One departure from this pattern occurred in Massachusetts, where architects in 1800 carefully constructed a building to provide maximum security. The Board of Visitors to the Charlestown prison was pleased with the results, especially with the high wall of hard flint stone that surrounded the structure and an arrangement that fronted two sides of the building on water. "Competent judges," it happily reported, "pronounce this to be among the strongest and best built prisons in the world. . . . It can neither be set on fire by prisoners, nor be undermined." But for all this confidence, sixteen inmates soon escaped. In fact, sensitivity to prison structures was so blunted during this period that the Connecticut legislature in 1790 decided to use an abandoned copper mine for a state prison. Prisoners served their sentences in slime-covered caverns with water dripping from the ceilings. Fortunately, no other state took over this model.[22]

The first prisons also failed to devise an alternative design to the household for their internal organization. Prisoners still lived together in large rooms and took their meals in one common dining area; they mingled freely, without restrictions. Institutional life remained casual, undisciplined, and irregular. Occasionally, prison officers instituted a new procedure intending to buttress the security of the institution. Thus in the 1790's, convicts for the first time began to wear uniforms in order to render it more difficult for an escaped inmate to disappear into a town. Maryland and New Jersey prisons relied upon a coarse brown suit; Massachusetts, among the more security conscious of systems, devised a more bizarre one, half red and half blue. New York compromised with coarse brown for the first offender, red and blue for the second. The focus on recapture pointed to the expectation as well as reality of frequent escapes. The uniform did not signal the routinization of prison life but an effort to keep the convicts from leaving the institution at will.[23]

---

[21]Negley Teeters, *The Cradle of the Penitentiary: The Walnut Street Jail at Philadelphia, 1773–1835* (Philadelphia, 1935), describes the structure and operation of this institution; for its influence on New York, see W. David Lewis, *From Newgate to Dannemora,* 29–30. For New Jersey, Harry E. Barnes, *Penal Institutions of New Jersey,* 60.

[22]Board of Visitors, *An Account of the Massachusetts State Prison* (Charlestown, Mass., 1806), 4; *Report of the Committee Appointed by the Legislature of Connecticut, to Inspect the Condition of New-Gate Prison* (Hartford, 1825), 4–18.

[23]For the chaotic conditions in the first prisons, see Harry E. Barnes, *Penal Institutions of New Jersey,* 402–419, and Negley Teeters, *The Cradle of the Penitentiary,* 105–106. See also Orlando Lewis, *The Development of American Prisons,* 48, 58, 71–73, which includes a description of the

In the same spirit, wardens confronted the problem of coping with a refractory prisoner. The dilemma had not been acute when jails confined offenders only temporarily; but once convicts became more or less permanent residents, keepers had to search for additional powers of coercion. Most of them reverted to eighteenth-century practices, whipping or chaining an unruly inmate, as they once had the violent insane. Some officials, however, tried to devise solutions more in accord with republican ideals, seeking to avoid corporal punishment within as well as without the institution. Pennsylvania, New York, and Massachusetts corrected disobedient convicts by placing them alone in single rooms on a limited diet. This punishment was to strike terror in the heart of inmates, compel them to abide by the rules, yet not require bloodletting or a basic rearrangement of the style of penitentiary life. The confinement of a prisoner to a cell was convenient. Wardens did not intend for it to reform or elevate the criminal, or to have general applicability among all convicts.[24]

Prison officials in the post-Revolution period met other difficulties. By its very nature, a lengthy sentence entailed unprecedented expenses; feeding and clothing convicts for a period of years would swell costs. Then, some kind of daily activity was necessary, for otherwise inmates might come to suffer physical or perhaps emotional disability. The common solution in the 1790's was the most obvious one, as well as the least disruptive to the structure of the institution: to set aside several rooms and a garden for convicts to labor in. This tactic appeared to be an apt way to keep prisoners busy while reimbursing the state for the growing costs of confinement. And it would help to differentiate the prison from the almshouse, making it something else than a rest home between arrests. Some students of crime declared that the routine of labor might serve to rehabilitate the offender, transforming him into a hard-working citizen. Quaker reformers in Pennsylvania especially held out this prospect. But most officials were simply trying to save the state some money, to occupy the inmates, and to make clear that incarceration was a punishment.[25]

The results were not impressive. Officials made some of the adjustments necessary to carry out the logic of the decision, ending, for example, the colonial practice of having prisoners pay the jailer for their board, and deciding that even inmates with property would have to work while serving their sentences. But

uniforms; Thomas Eddy, *An Account of the State Prison,* 39; *Rules and Regulations for the Government of the Massachusetts State Prison* (Boston, 1823), esp. p. 39; *The Acts of Assembly . . . and the Rules and Regulations Respecting the Penitentiary of Maryland* (Baltimore, 1819), 24–25. There was to be an element of shame in the donning of uniforms, but no sense of discipline or order.

[24]Caleb Lownes, *An Account of the Alteration and Present State of the Penal Law of Pennsylvania* (Philadelphia, 1793), 81–88; Robert Turnbull, *A Visit to the Philadelphia Prison* (Philadelphia, 1796), 53–56; Negley Teeters, *The Cradle of the Penitentiary,* 41. For Massachusetts, see Board of Visitors, *The Massachusetts State Prison* (1806), 13; Samuel Sewall and Nathan Dane, *A Communication . . . for the Regulation of the [Massachusetts] State Prison* (Boston, 1805), 10–11. See also Thomas Eddy, *An Account of the State Prison,* 14, 19; Harry E. Barnes, *Penal Institutions of New Jersey,* 66, 395; and W. David Lewis, *From Newgate to Dannemora,* 32, 46.

[25]Thomas Eddy, *An Account of the State Prison,* 35, 53, 56–58; Caleb Lownes, *The Penal Law of Pennsylvania,* 92–96, and his *Description and Historical Sketch of the Massachusetts State Prison* (Charlestown, Mass., 1816), 10–13.

still they came up against unanticipated difficulties not easily resolved. The houshold model was not as appropriate to the organization of labor as they had believed. Prisoners were not kinfolk, and the institution was unable to order their actions effectively. Convicts worked slowly and sloppily, shirking whatever tasks they could. Lacking incentive and close supervision, they were neither reliable nor efficient.

Officials were ill-prepared to manage their side of the enterprise. They lacked experience in bulk purchasing of raw materials and in marketing procedures; they were uncertain as to whether the state should provide all the necessary goods or lease the entire operation to private contractors. Their ignorance together with prisoners' ill will made almost every prison ledger show a loss. Most institutions, rather than abandon convict labor, increasingly used it as a method of punishment. New Jersey legislators, concerned more with correction than with profit, instructed prison officials to institute "labor of the hardest and most servile kind, in which the work is least liable to be spoiled by ignorance, neglect or obstinacy." New York experimented with a treadmill, the prisoners turning it to exhaust and discipline themselves. But no one considered the introduction of labor a success.[26]

By 1820, the viability of the entire prison system was in doubt, and its most dedicated supporters conceded a near total failure. Institutionalization had not only failed to pay its own way, but had also encouraged and educated the criminal to a life in crime. "Our favorite scheme of substituting a state prison for the gallows," concluded one New York lawyer, "is a prolific mother of crime. . . . Our state prisons, as at present constituted, are grand demoralizers of our people."[27] Other critics issued harsh verdicts. A Massachusetts investigatory body and a group of Philadelphia reformers both labeled the prison "a school for vice," while a New York philanthropic society declared that it "operates with alarming efficacy to increase, diffuse, and extend the love of vice, and a knowledge of the arts and practices of criminality." Practically no one would have estimated that within fifteen years American penitentiaries would become the object of national acclaim and international study.[28]

The key to this transformation was the Auburn and Pennsylvania programs.

---

[26]In addition to the above, see Harry E. Barnes, *Penal Institutions of New Jersey,* 62–63, 414–416; New Jersey, *Revised Statutes,* 1821, code of 1798, p. 272. See also the 1819 compilation of *Rules and Regulations Respecting the Penitentiary of Maryland,* 24–25, and Board of Directors, *Rules and Regulations for the Government of the Massachusetts State Prison* (Boston, 1811), 12, 19. The New York treadmill experiment is recounted in James Hardie, *The History of the Tread-Mill* (New York, 1824), 16, 21–22, 181.

[27]John Bristed, *The Resources of the United States of America* (New York, 1818), 436, as quoted in W. David Lewis, *From Newgate to Dannemora,* 62. See also Matthew Carey, *Thoughts on Penitentiaries,* Compare *Minutes of the Philadelphia Society for Alleviating the Miseries of Public Prisons,* entries of February 9, 1819; November 8, 1820, manuscript record at the Pennsylvania Prison Society.

[28]R. Sullivan, *et al., Report of [Massachusetts] Committee, "To Inquire into the Mode of Governing the Penitentiary of Pennsylvania"* (Boston, 1817), 2; Philadelphia Society for Alleviating the Miseries of Public Prisons, *Penal Code of Pennsylvania,* 5. The New York Society for the Prevention of Pauperism, *Report on the Penitentiary System,* 96. See also *The Committee to Inspect the Condition of New-Gate,* 12.

Their concepts restructured the penitentiary, changing the popular verdict from failure to success. Little distance separated the ideas and the reality of the new penitentiaries; construction and organization to a considerable degree followed reformers' blueprints. The match, to be sure, was by no means perfect, and by the 1850's, abuses were undermining the system. But the states made an energetic and not unsuccessful attempt to put the programs into effect. These latest institutions were not the logical end of a development that began with the seventeenth-century house of correction, continued in the eighteenth-century workhouse, and improved in the post-Revolution prison. Of course various components in the system had roots in older ideas and practices, but the sum of the penitentiary was qualitatively different from its several parts. Europeans traveled to the new world to examine an American creation, not to see a minor variant on an old world theme. The antebellum generation could rightly claim to have made a major innovation in criminal punishment.

The new principle of separation was as central to penitentiary practices as it was to reformers' pamphlets. Officials repeatedly looked to it to solve specific problems (the rules governing letter-writing, how visitors should be treated), as well as to shape general policies (the inmates' daily routine, the overall design of the structure). It was never the only guideline — wardens and agents had financial obligations to fulfill, since state legislators anticipated that prisons would contribute substantially to their own upkeep. But the ledgers alone were not determinative.

The institutions rigorously attempted to isolate the prisoner both from the general community and from his fellow inmates. To fulfill the first charge, they severed almost every tie between the prisoner and his family and friends, and even attempted with some degree of success to block out reports of outside events. Pennsylvania went to the furthest extremes. The prison at Philadelphia prohibited any relative or friend from visiting the inmate and allowed only a handful of carefully screened persons, of whose virtue there could be no doubt, to see the convict in his cell. It banned all exchanges of correspondence and excluded newspapers to insure convicts' ignorance of external affairs. Partisans accurately boasted that a Pennsylvania inmate was "perfectly secluded from the world . . . hopelessly separated from one's family, and from all communication with and knowledge of them for the whole term of imprisonment." Throughout the pre-Civil War period, penitentiaries organized on the separate system made almost no compromises with these regulations.[29]

New York's practices were hardly less rigid. The state penitentiary rules in the 1830's declared that convicts were to "receive no letters or intelligence from or concerning their friends, or any information on any subject out of prison." Relatives were not permitted to visit with an inmate and he, in turn, was not allowed to correspond with them. "The prisoner," a Sing-Sing chaplain of this

[29]Inspectors of the Eastern State Penitentiary, *Twenty-First Annual Report* (Philadelphia, 1850), 27, *Fourth Annual Report* (Philadelphia, 1833), 9–10: Anon., "Prison Discipline," 9. Also, Negley Teeters and John Shearer, *The Prison at Philadelphia*, 169.

period recalled, "was taught to consider himself dead to all without the prison walls." And the warden himself repeated this analogy when instructing new convicts on their situation. "It is true," he told them in 1826, "that while confined here you can have no intelligence concerning relatives or friends. . . . You are to be literally buried from the world."[30] Officials somewhat relaxed these regulations in the 1840's, but the concessions were minimal. At Sing-Sing convicts were then allowed to send one letter every six months, and at the new prison at Clinton, one every four months — subject of course to the chaplain writing and the warden censoring it. They could also receive a single visit from relatives, in the presence of guards, during the course of their sentence. Throughout these decades the penitentiaries prohibited newspapers and books. The results were mixed, but if convicts often managed to smuggle these materials in, periodic cell inspections ferreted them out.[31]

Institutions in other states adhered to similar standards, all attempting, with varying degrees of success, to isolate the convict from society. New Jersey officials, for example, complained bitterly in 1830 that prisoners knew too much about public events. Convinced that "discipline is interrupted by a knowledge in the prison, among the convicts, of almost everything that is done abroad," they unhappily reported that inmates were learning through newspapers and conversations what was happening at the state capital, especially in regard to prison matters. The administrative reaction was predictable: more stringent isolation of the inmates from each other, from the guards, and from the community. Indeed, New Jersey soon decided to follow the more stringent procedures of the Pennsylvania system rather than the Auburn plan.[32] Maine's prison commissioner in this period, future presidential candidate James Blaine, was also certain that "information upon events of current interest, and glimpses of the outer world, have a tendency to unsettle the convict's mind and render him restless and uneasy." Distressed to find magazines and newspapers circulating in the state's congregate prison, Blaine charged officials to work still harder at "separating the convict from all association with the world at large," at banishing external influences from the penitentiary.[33] The thick walls that surrounded the penitentiary were not only to keep the inmates in, but the rest of the world out.

---

[30]Gershom Powers, *A Brief Account of Auburn,* 1–2, 16; Inspectors of the State Prisons of New York, *Eighth Annual Report* (Albany, 1856), 339, where Chaplain John Luckey recounts his early service at Sing-Sing. The warden's quote is found in *Letter of Gershom Powers, Esq. . . . in relation to Auburn State Prison* (Albany, 1829), 14.

[31]N.Y.P.A., *Fifth Annual Report* (Albany, 1850), 186–187, surveys the prevailing practices of many penitentiaries on this matter. See too "Annual Report of Mt. Pleasant Prison," *N.Y. Senate Docs.,* 1842, II, no. 39, pp. 25–26; Inspectors of the State Prisons of New York, *First Annual Report* (New York, 1848), 144–145, 253, 348. For confiscations, see "Annual Report of Mt. Pleasant Prison," *N.Y. Senate Docs.,* 1844, I, no. 20, pp. 21–22.

[32]Harry E. Barnes, *Penal Institutions of New Jersey,* 408.

[33]James Blaine, *Report of the System of Disbursements, Labor, and Discipline in the Maine State Prison* (Augusta, Me., 1859), 36. And see, *Laws of he Commonwealth for the Government of the Massachusetts State Prison* (Charlestown, Mass., 1830), 24.

Just as critical to the organization of the penitentiary was the isolation of inmates from each other. The program was formidable, far more difficult than excluding visitors; still, wardens and keepers, especially before 1840, enjoyed a fair measure of success. The obstacles were greater in congregate than in separate institutions and the congregate system swept the states. But the popularity of Auburn was no less a triumph for the principle of separation. The prestigious Boston Prison Discipline Society announced that since congregate systems operated just as effectively as separate ones, it was senseless and wasteful to appropriate the extra funds. An influential pamphleteer like Matthew Carey also urged officials to adopt the New York plan, convinced that the separate system had no monopoly on proper discipline. Pennsylvania's defenders in rebuttal argued that no one ought to prescribe a particular medicine for the patient simply because it was cheaper. But their contentions carried little weight against the voluminous literature that legitimated the Auburn plan as a reform enterprise. Legislators deeply concerned with the issues of social control and rehabilitation, and yet tax-conscouus, could honestly conclude that the New York plan promised success equal to that of its rival.[34]

In practice, Pennsylvania's institutions effectively prevented communication between convicts. The Philadelphia prison, for example, despite charges of faulty ducts and thin walls, did eliminate almost all inmate contact. Visitors' impressions, wardens' reports, and state investigations commonly testified to its success. "It is incontestable," wrote Tocqueville and Beaumont, "that this perfect isolation [at Philadelphia] secures the prisoner from all fatal contamination."[35]

The performance of Auburn-type institutions varied, more dependent than its competitor on skillful administration. Some prisons kept communication between convicts to an absolute minimum, with a single cell for every inmate at night and effective policing of workshops and exercise yards during the day. Others were more lax, understaffed, and overcrowded, operating with too small a budget or incompetent administrators. Prisoners lived two, three, or more to a cell, mingled freely in exercise yards, conversed openly at work. Still others enforced a silence but with such repressive and cruel tactics that even the most ardent defenders of the system had their doubts. Discipline also changed over time. The penitentiaries organized in the 1820's and 1830's largely satisfied the criterion of separation, particularly in New York, Massachusetts, and Connecticut. But in later decades control weakened. Older prisons became less rigorous while newer institutions in midwestern states frequently relaxed standards.

The early years at Auburn, the model for congregate prisons everywhere, were its most disciplined. The stillness that pervaded this prison was hardly less com-

---

[34]B.P.D.S., *Eleventh Annual Report* (Boston, 1836), 80; Matthew Carey, *Thoughts on Penitentiaries*, 41–42, 46–47. The medical analogy is made by Samuel Gridley Howe, *Prison Discipline*, 79; see also Franklin Bache, *Observations of the Penitentiary System*, 39, and the 1823 *Rules for the Government of the Massachusetts State Prison*, 8–10.

[35]Beaumont and Tocqueville, *On the Penitentiary System*, 57. See also the defenses of the Pennsylvania system cited above.

plete than that at Philadelphia. "Everything passes," Tocqueville and Beaumont noted after their 1831 visit, "in the most profound silence, and nothing is heard in the whole prison but the steps of those who march, or sounds proceeding from the workshops." After the convicts returned to their cells, "the silence within these vast walls . . . is that of death. . . . We felt as if we traversed catacombs; there were a thousand living beings, and yet it was a desert solitude."

Officials were able to maintain this silence by preventing overcrowding. As soon as swelling numbers imperiled the one-man-to-a-cell principle, they persuaded the legislature to appropriate funds to correct the situation. The state, rather than simply erecting higher walls and more strictly enforcing internal security, responded by adding cells to Sing-Sing in 1832, and to Auburn in 1833. Consequently, Auburn was able to satisfy the most basic prerequisite of the system and isolate inmates at night.[36]

Its wardens also policed convicts effectively during the day. The state-appointed prison inspectors were fully satisfied with Auburn's performance in the 1830's. Although the inspectors were not disinterested parties — having themselves selected the prison's top administrators — their reports were usually honest, candid, and to the point. When Auburn faced a crisis of overcrowding in 1830, they gave the legislature every grim detail; later, in the 1850's, when administrative diligence declined, their judgments were harsh and critical. But in these first years, they were ecstatic with Auburn's operations, convinced that internal regulation was effective. "The system of discipline which regulates this prison," they declared in 1835, "has advanced to a degree of perfection as desirable as it is difficult of attainment. . . . Our penitentiary system . . . has now become a model which the philanthropists of neighboring states, as well as of foreign countries, find it an object to follow. . . . It may now be said, without the charge of vanity, to be the best system of prison discipline in the world."[37] Even the Pennsylvania camp tacitly conceded Auburn's effectiveness. It criticized the frequency and severity of punishments and the temptations placed before the convicts, but did not contend that the prisoners were without discipline. From every indication, Auburn, like Pennsylvania, conformed to the principles of separation.

Success in the model institution did not guarantee faithful emulation, and Auburn's imitators often fell short of the program's goals. Still, they fully accepted the system's premises, and with different degrees of skill and concern enacted them. The Massachusetts and Connecticut institutions came closest to achieving Auburn's standards, rigorously enforcing the rule of silence and the separation of prisoners. Massachusetts moved quickly in the 1820's to adapt its prison at Charlestown to the congregate system, and for much of the next several

---

[36]*Ibid.*, 65. Samuel Gridley Howe also raises this image, *Prison Discipline*, 22–23, describing a "stillness . . . that of death." The construction is detailed in W. David Lewis, *From Newgate to Dannemora*, ch. 6.

[37]"Annual Report of Auburn Prison," *N.Y. Senate Docs.*, 1835, I, no. 13, p. 3. See also "Report of the Standing Committee on State Prisons," *N.Y. Senate and Assembly Docs.*, 1830, IV, no. 407, p. 1.

decades, the solitary cell and the close supervision of inmates prevented most communication. Connecticut transferred prisoners from the wretched copper mine to a newly built congregate penitentiary at Wethersfield. Its wardens during this period, Amos Pilsbury and then his son Moses, were not without faults. But frequent state prison investigations usually agreed that Wethersfield was preserving silence and separation and was certainly no seminary for vice.[38]

Conditions degenerated as one moved westward. The Ohio penitentiary was intellectually committed to maintaining rules of silence with one prisoner to a cell. "The whole system of discipline," announced the directors in the prison rules, "depends upon non-intercourse between convicts." To this end, the legislature in the 1830's appropriated funds for a new institution that would not soon become overcrowded. But the sturcture proved superior to the administration and solitary cells did not insure an effective program. In the 1840's, convicts enjoyed an almost free run of the place, communicating at will and controlling much of their routine. Guards bribed inmates with food and clothing to secure compliance — a development that seems endemic to all prisons where administration is lax and permissive, and the convicts well organized. "At the start of my duties here," declared an entering warden in the 1850's with probably only slight exaggeration, "nearly all convicts were clamorous for what *they* claimed were their rights. . . . They acted as though they were martyrs. . . . Indeed the prison seemed a perfect bedlam." So, while the principles and the physical organization of the Auburn plan reached Ohio, the end product was hardly a triumph for it.[39]

The congregate ideology made headway at Illinois, but again the final result was mixed.[40] Iowa's officials also spread the congregate program. They erected a penitentiary in 1852 and then immediately dispatched a member eastward to survey the current methods of discipline, certain that "the subject of prison construction and discipline is a specialty . . . which mechanics and architects . . . generally do not understand." Impressed with what they learned, they set out to make the state institution "as perfect" as the ones in New York and Massachusetts. But although the institution was new, and the number of convicts was small, Iowa confronted disciplinary problems. The outbreak of the Civil War, however, turned attention elsewhere, putting to rest these ambitions for at least another decade.[41]

[38]Orlando Lewis, *The Development of American Prisons*, chs. 7–8, 14–15. Moses Kimball, "Report on Prisons," *Massachusetts Senate Docs.*, January 15, 1855, no. 38, pp. 21–22; *Report of the Committee . . . on the Connecticut State Prison* (New Haven, Conn., 1842), 47. Accusations and defenses were a regular part of the Connecticut prison system; see, for example, *Report of the Committee . . . on the Connecticut State Prison* (Hartford, 1833), and the rejoinder, *Minutes of the Testimony Taken Before . . . [the] Committee . . . on the Connecticut State Prison* (Hartford, 1834).

[39]*Annual Report of the Ohio Penitentiary for 1847* (Columbus, Ohio, 1848), 142, and *Annual Report . . . for 1852* (Columbus, Ohio, 1853), 25–28; quotation is on p. 25.

[40]*Reports of the Illinois Penitentiary for 1855–1856* (Alton, Ill., 1856), 46; see too *Reports . . . for 1859–1860* (Springfield, Ill., 1861), 3–4, 12.

[41]Board of Inspectors of Iowa Penitentiary, *Reports for the Two Years ending October 1, 1859* (Des Moines, Ia., 1859), 10–11.

The problem of enforcement in the congregate system raised the dilemma of whether obedience was worth any price. Did the end of discipline justify every means of punishment? Was the cure more dangerous than the disease? The question had obvious relevance to an institution like Sing-Sing, which on the whole managed to curtail communication between convicts but with a type and frequency of correction that public investigators found cruel and sadistic. The issue, however, was not confined to one penitentiary or notorious warden. Prisons everywhere had to decide what punishments were proper for enforcing the system. Were the regular use of the whip, the yoke, the ball and chain, cold showers, or curtailed rations appropriate weapons in the battle to preserve order? Were offenders against prison law without rights, without protection from their keepers? The answer to this question offers evidence not only of the special administrative needs of penal institutions but also of the strength and implications of the concepts of deviancy and the reformatory program.

Sing-Sing officials in the 1830's were prepared to use every possible form of correction to enforce order, and justified their behavior by denigrating the whole notion of rehabilitation. Guards relied freely upon the whip, unhesitatingly using it for the smallest infraction, and their superiors defended this behavior vigorously. As Robert Wiltse, assistant to the warden, informed the state legislature in 1834: convicts "must be made to know, that *here* they must submit to every regulation, and obey every command of their keepers." Perversely insisting that most reformers had already abandoned the notion of a "general and radical reformation of offenders through a penitentiary system," Wiltse contended that a prison "should not be governed in such a manner as to induce rogues to consider it as a comfortable home. They must be *made* to *submit* to its rules, and this by the most energetic means; corporeal punishments for transgression, which to be effectual must be certain, and inflicted with as little delay as possible."[42]

Other institutions too were commonly far more intent on securing absolute obedience than on protecting convicts from cruel or unusual punishments. The whip was commonplace in Auburn and in Charlestown, in Columbus and in Wethersfield. Pennsylvania had recourse to the iron gag, Maine to the ball and chain, Connecticut to the cold shower. And officials whole-heartedly defended these punishments. Auburn's chaplain insisted that it would be "most unfortunate . . . if the public mind were to settle down into repugnance to the use of such coercive means." To isolate and rehabilitate convicts, corporal punishment was unquestionably proper and legitimate. "Only relax the reins of discipline . . .

---

[42]The quotations and the punishment methods appear in an excellent summary of Sing-Sing practices, "A Detailed Statement on the Government, Discipline, etc., of the New-York State Prison at Mount-Pleasant," appended to the "Annual Report of Mt. Pleasant Prison," *N.Y. Senate Docs.,* 1834, II, no. 92; see pp. 38, 41–42 for quotations. For the split between those intent on reform and on discipline, see W. David Lewis, *From Newgate to Dannemora,* 83–87, 101–107. But I argue below that the differences between the groups ought not to be exaggerated.

and a chaplain's labors would be of no more use here than in a drunken mob."[43] A Pennsylvania investigatory body justified using an iron gag on refractory prisoners. Convicts were "men of idle habits, vicious propensities, and depraved passions," who had to be taught obedience as the first step to reformation. Ohio's warden also considered the whip vital to a prison system. "For whenever the Penitentiary becomes a pleasant place of residence," he declared, "whenever a relaxation of discipline . . . converts it into something like an *Asylum* for the wicked, then it loses all its influence for good upon the minds of men disposed to do evil."[44]

Penal institutions' widespread and unembarrassed reliance on harsh disciplinary measures was due in part to the newness of the experiment. It reflected too a nagging concern that convicts might possibly join together to overpower their few keepers — no one was yet altogether confident that forty men could control eight hundred.[45] Yet even more fundamental was the close fit between the punitive measures and the reform perspective. The prevailing concepts of deviancy put a premium on rigorous discipline. The premises underlying the penitentiary movement placed an extraordinary emphasis on an orderly routine. Confident that the deviant would learn the lessons of discipline in a properly arranged environment, everyone agreed that prison life had to be strict and unrelenting. And with regularity a prerequisite for success, practically any method that enforced discipline became appropriate.

Reformers and prison officials agreed on the need for inmates to obey authority. Criminals, in their view, had never learned to respect limits. To correct this, the penitentiary had to secure absolute obedience, bending the convicts' behavior to fit its own rigid rules. Should wayward inmates resist, their obstinacy would have to be "broken," and as the word itself implied, the means were not nearly so important as the ends. Perhaps the most striking testimony to the influence of these ideas in legitimating disciplinary procedures came from Tocqueville and Beaumont. The visitors were under no illusions as to the nature or the extent of penitentiary punishments. "We have no doubt," they concluded, "but that the habits of order to which the prisoner is subjected for several years . . . the obedience of every moment to inflexible rules, the regularity of a uniform life, in a word, all the circumstances belonging to this severe system, are calculated to produce a deep impression upon his mind. Perhaps, leaving the prison he is

[43]"Annual Report of Auburn Prison," *N.Y. Assembly Docs.*, 1840, I, no. 18, pp. 13–14; see too Inspectors of the State Prisons of New York, *Eighth Annual Report* (New York, 1856), 322–323.

[44]*Report of the Joint Committee of the Legislature of Pennsylvania, Relative to the Eastern State Penitentiary at Philadelphia* (Harrisburg, Pa., 1835), 41; see also Thomas McElwee, *Concise History of the Eastern Penitentiary*, 19–20. For the Ohio Prisons, see *Annual Report of the Ohio Penitentiary for 1852*, 25. Examples could be endlessly added. See N.Y.P.A., *Fifth Annual Report*, 166–167, for a survey of several penitentiaries; and the observations of Beaumont and Tocqueville, *On the Penitentiary System*, 74, 77. Also, *Report of the Committee . . . on the Connecticut State Prison* (1842), 47. As the French visitors put it, the prisons were a "complete despotism."

[45]"Annual Report of Mt. Pleasant Prison," *N.Y. Senate Docs.*, 1832, I, no. 14, p. 6; John Reynolds, *Recollections of Windsor Prison*, 206.

not an honest man, but he has contracted honest habits . . . and if he is not more virtuous, he has become at least more judicious." Sing-Sing officials quoted these findings at length, and with obvious satisfaction.[46]

The commitment to a daily routine of hard and constant labor also pointed to the close correspondence between the ideas on the causes of crime and the structure of the penitentiary. Idleness was part symptom and part cause of deviant behavior. Those unwilling to work were prone to commit all types of offenses; idleness gave time for the corrupted to encourage and instruct one another in a life of crime. Proponents of a penitentiary training believed that the tougher the course, the more favorable the results. As one spokesman, Francis Gray, declared: "The object of prison discipline is to induce [the convict] not merely to form good resolutions . . . but to support himself by honest industry. The only effectual mode of leading him to do this, is to train him . . . to accustom him to work steadily and diligently from 8 to 10 hours a day, with no other respite. . . . The discipline best adapted to such men, is that which inures them to constant and vigorous toil."[47]

State legislators and wardens found these notions attractive and were eager to implement them. Secure in the knowledge that they were acting in the best interests of taxpayers and inmates alike, that they were simultaneously furthering financial and reformist goals, they had no objection to making some contracts with private manufacturers to lease convict labor to establishing a prison routine of long hours with little relief. Hoping in this way to make the penitentiary a self-supporting, even profitable venture while rehabilitating the offender, they favored a schedule that maximized work. The results in New York were not unusual: convicts were up at five o'clock for two hours of work before breakfast, then back to it for three hours and forty-five minutes; lunch was at noon for one hour and fifteen minutes, then a return to the shop for another four hours and forty-five minutes. The weekly workday averaged ten hours, from sunup to sunset six days a week. A Christian Sunday and the lack of artificial lighting prevented a lengthening of the schedule.

But prison labor never brought great returns and in many instances was unable to meet the daily expenses of operation, let alone cover the costs of construction. Some of the first prisons did claim a profit in their annual reports, but often the figures were more testimony to the jugglings of the warden than to actual

---

[46]Beaumont and Tocqueville, *On the Penitentiary System,* 90. See also *Letter of Gershom Powers,* 22–23, Francis Lieber, in his translator's preface to *On the Penitentiary System,* 184–187, and N.Y.P.A., *Fifth Annual Report,* 144–167. There were limits, as the dismissal of Lynds made clear; but that the system on the whole was despotic there can be no doubt. See also J. P. Mayer, ed., *Alexis de Tocqueville: Journey to America,* 204: "The system at Sing-Sing," claimed Tocqueville, "seems in some sense like the steamships which the Americans use so much. Nothing is more comfortable, quick, and, in a word, perfect in the ordinary run of things. But if some bit of apparatus gets out of order, the boat, the passengers and the cargo fly into the air."

[47]Francis Gray, *Prison Discipline in America,* 70–72. See too Samuel Gridley Howe, *Prison Discipline,* 26; B.P.D.S., *Fourth Annual Report,* 60–61. Also, George Smith, *A Defense of Solitary Confinement,* 24.

returns.[48] Officials gleefully cited a "profit" of ten thousand dollars at the end of the year, neglecting to mention that the costs of the institution's construction was two hundred thousand dollars. It would be decades before such a small return paid off the debt. Other agents published a favorable balance by not including officials' salaries or the cost of repairs.[49] The figures in the annual reports are generally too untrustworthy to allow firm conclusions, but it seems clear that if profit alone preoccupied the states, they could have found a better return on their investment elsewhere.[50]

External difficulties also arose constantly. Free labor bitterly and effectively protested against prison competition, and frequently secured the passage of restrictive legislation. In some states convicts were not permitted to practice a trade that they had not already learned and followed before confinement; in others the institution could not produce goods already being manufactured within the state's borders. Under these circumstances legislatures not only had to make up the deficits but bear the brunt of political protest as well. The widespread organization of convict labor was, therefore, not simply testimony to its economic rewards, any more than the persistence of penal institutions reflected their financial prowess. The idea of labor, even more than the calculations of profit and loss, made it central to the penitentiary.[51]

The doctrines of separation, obedience, and labor became the trinity around which officials organized the penitentiary. They carefully instructed inmates that their duties could be "comprised in a few words"; they were *"to labor diligently, to obey all orders,* and preserve an *unbroken silence."*[52] Yet to achieve these

[48]Orlando Lewis, *The Development of American Prisons,* brings together the data on costs and returns. See 173, 181, for Auburn and Wethersfield; Ohio also showed a profit, 259, 263. By no means, ·however, was this true for all penitentiaries. For the New York returns, see Inspectors of the State Prisons of New York, *Sixth Annual Report* (New York, 1853), 25.

[49]Despite Lewis's insistence that the prison innovation can be mostly explained in terms of its profitability, the data he gathers shows how much juggling went into the returns. See *The Development of American Prisons,* 201–202, for New Jersey's attempts, and 208–209 for Maryland. A convenient table of the costs of construction is on page 239 — and the sums make eminently clear how much greater the investment was than the returns.

[50]The verdict of an excellent survey of prisons . . . is that the profit and loss issue cannot be easily resolved. E. C. Wines and Theodore W. Dwight, *Report on the Prisons and Reformatories of the United States and Canada* (Albany, 1867), 266. "The matter," they concluded, "is present in the annual reports, in a manner so complex, confused and obscure, that we find it, in the majority of cases, quite impossible to arrive at clear and satisfactory results." The verdict is even more true for the earlier period. There is a mass of detail, as even a glance at any annual report would reveal, but the general conclusions are hardly persuasive.

[51]W. D. Lewis, *From Newgate to Dannemora,* ch. 8; Orlando Lewis, *The Development of American Prisons,* 133–146. See also, for the New York story, Walter Hugins, *Jacksonian Democracy and the Working Class* (Stanford, 1960), 155–161; "Annual Report of Auburn Prison," *N.Y. Assembly Docs.,* 1842, II, no. 31, p. 14, and "Annual Report of Mt. Pleasant Prison," *N.Y. Senate Docs.,* 1846, I, no. 16, pp. 31–32. A good discussion of the issue is in William Leggett, "The State Prison Monopoly," *Political Writings of William Leggett* (Boston, 1840), 63–64, 83, 263–271. The problems were also found in Tennessee: Jesse C. Crowe, "The Origin and Development of Tennessee's Prison Problem," *Tennessee Historical Quarterly,* 15 (1956), 111–135.

[52]"Government, Discipline of the New-York State ·Prison," (1834), 18. See too Lieber's translator's preface to *On the Penitentiary,* 14, and *Letter of Gershom Powers,* 16.

goals, officers had to establish a total routine, to administer every aspect of the institution in accord with the three guidelines, from inmates' dress to their walk, from the cells' furnishings to the guards' deportment. The common solution was to follow primarily a quasi-military model. The regulations based on this model promised to preserve isolation, to make labor efficient, and to teach men lacking discipline to abide by rules; this regimented style of life would inculcate strict discipline, precision, and instantaneous adherence to commands. Furthermore, a military model in a correctional institution seemed especially suitable for demonstrating to the society at large the right principles of organization. Here was an appropriate example for a community suffering a crisis of order.

The first designers of the prison had few other useful models to emulate. In fact, the penitentiary was not the only institution in the 1820's and 1830's facing the dilemma of organization. Such a novel economic unit as the factory was also beginning to use rigorous procedures to bring an unprecedented discipline to workers' lives. Prison designers could find the factory an interesting but limited source of inspiration, appropriating that part of it which was most regulatory and precise. Both organizations were among the first to try to take people from casual routines to rigid ones.

Regimentation became the standard mode of prison life. Convicts did not walk from place to place; rather, they went in close order and single file, each looking over the shoulder of the man in front, faces inclined to the right, feet moving in unison, in lockstep. The lockstep became the trademark of American prisons in these years, a curious combination of march and shuffle that remained standard procedure well into the 1930's. Its invention and adoption exemplified the problems and responses of the first penitentiary officials. How were they to move inmates about? Prison officials with fixed ideas on convict communication and obedience, had to reject movement. Searching for greater discipline, they turned to the military march, crossed it with a shuffle to lessen its dignity, and pointed heads to the right, rather than facing straight ahead, to prevent conversation. The result, the lockstep, was an immediate success and became the common practice.[53]

Wardens organized the convicts' daily schedule in military style. At the sound of a horn or bell, keepers opened the cells, prisoners stepped onto the deck, and then in lockstep marched into the yard. In formation they emptied their night pails, moved on and washed them, took a few more steps, and placed them on a rack to dry. Still in line they marched to the shops. There they worked at their tasks in rows on long benches until the bell rang for breakfast. They grouped again in single file, passed into the kitchen, picked up their rations (regulations admonished them not to break step), and continued on to their cells, or in some institutions, to a common messroom where they ate their meal. (Regulations again

---

[53]Gershom Powers, *A Brief Account of Auburn*, 4. The lockstep was found in practically every penitentiary. For one example, see *Rules and Regulations for the Government of the Maryland Penitentiary* (Baltimore, 1853), 15.

instructed them to sit erect with backs straight.) At the bell they stood, reentered formation, and marched back to the shops. They repeated this routine at noon, and again at six o'clock; then they returned to their cells for the night and at nine o'clock lights went out, as at a barracks. Although some institutions were more exacting than others in enforcing these procedures, almost all of them tried to impose a degree of military routine on their prisoners.[54]

The furnishings of convicts' cells also indicates the relevance of the military model. A cot and pail and tin utensils were the basic objects. Prisoners now wore uniforms of a simple, coarse, striped fabric, and all had their hair cut short to increase uniformity.[55] The military example affected keepers as well as convicts. Several wardens came to their positions directly from an army or navy career, legislators obviously eager to have them apply their former training to this setting. Guards wore uniforms, mustered at specific hours, and kept watch like sentries. Regulations ordered them to behave in a "gentlemanly manner," like officers, without laughter, ribaldry, or unnecessary conversation while on duty. As Sing-Sing's rules put it, in only a slight overstatement of a general sentiment: "They were to require from the convicts the greatest deference, and never suffer them to approach but in respectful manner; they are not to allow them the least degree of familiarity, nor exercise any towards them; they should be extremely careful to *command* as well as to compel their respect."[56]

The military style also influenced the construction and appearance of the institutions. Some were modeled after medieval fortresses. An adaptation of a structure from the Middle Ages was necessarily monumental, appropriate in size to a noble experiment like the penitentiary, capable of stimulating a citizen's pride and a visitor's respect. It also had functional qualities, for thick walls promised security against prison breaks, and turrets became posts for guarding an enclosed space. Another popular alternative was to construct the prison along factory lines — a long and low building, symmetrically arranged with closely spaced windows, all very regular and methodical. Whatever it lacked in grandeur it tried to make up in fixity and order.[57]

---

[54]Samuel Gridley Howe, *Prison Discipline*, 55, was a rare exception to the rule. "People generally admire," he unhappily concluded, "the strict discipline, the military precision of the maneuvers, and the instantaneous obedience to every order, which are seen in some congregate prisons." For another description, see B.P.D.S., *First Annual Report* (Boston, 1826), 57–58.

[55]Beaumont and Tocqueville, *On the Penitentiary*, 62, 65; for the Sing-Sing routine, see the 1834 description, "Government, Discipline of the New-York State Prison." For a similar pattern in Ohio, see J. H. Matthews, *Historical Reminiscences on the Ohio Penitentiary, from its Erection in 1835 to the Present Time* (Columbus, Ohio, 1884), 16–25, 36, 39.

[56]"Government, Discipline of the New-York State Prison" (1834), 16. Beaumont and Tocqueville also noted the military career line, *On the Penitentiary*, 62, citing Lynds in New York, Austin in Massachusetts, and Moses Pilsbury in Connecticut. Many of the careers of the prison leaders are obscure; of the several I examined, no clear pattern emerged. Unlike medical superintendents, there was no prior training or experience. Some came up through the ranks, others entered from the law, on the basis of political influence; still others left a small mercantile business, ostensibly equipped to manage the prison industries.

[57]The design and appearance of the institutions are in the annual reports and the secondary literature cited above. See also George Smith, *A Defense of Solitary Confinement*, 21.

The functioning of the penitentiary — convicts passing their sentences in physically imposing and highly regimented settings, moving in lockstep from bare
and solitary cells to workshops, clothed in common dress, and forced into standard
routines — was designed to carry a message to the community. The prison would
train the most notable victims of social disorder to discipline, teaching them to
resist corruption. And success in this particular task should inspire a general reformation of manners and habits. The institution would become a laboratory for
social improvement. By demonstrating how regularity and discipline transformed
the most corrupt persons, it would reawaken the public to these virtues. The
penitentiary would promote a new respect for order and authority.

Reformers never spelled out the precise nature and balance of this reformation.
They hoped that families, instead of overindulging or neglecting their children,
would more conscientiously teach limits and the need for obedience to them.
Assuming that social stability could not be achieved without a very personal and
keen respect for authority, they looked first to a firm family discipline to inculcate
it. Reformers also anticipated that society would rid itself of corruptions. In a
narrow sense this meant getting rid of such blatant centers of vice as taverns,
theaters, and houses of prostitution. In a broader sense, it meant reviving a social
order in which men knew their place. Here sentimentality took over, and critics
in the Jacksonian period often assumed that their forefathers had lived together
without social strain, in secure, placid, stable, and cohesive communities. In fact,
the designers of the penitentiary set out to re-create these conditions. But the
results, it is not surprising to discover, were startlingly different from anything
that the colonial period had known. A conscious effort to instill discipline through
an institutional routine led to a set work pattern, a rationalization of movement,
a precise organization of time, a general uniformity. Hence, for all the reformers'
nostalgia, the reality of the penitentiary was much closer to the values of the
nineteenth than the eighteenth century.

15. *Robert Martinson*

The Age of Treatment: Some Implications of the Custody-Treatment Dimension

Turning back, he asked the pundits about the method they followed in instructing the bird.

It was shown to him. He was immensely impressed. The method was so
stupendous that the bird looked ridiculously unimportant in comparison. The

Reprinted by permission of the publisher from *Issues in Criminology*, 2 (Fall 1966), pp. 275–293.

Raja was satisfied that there was no flaw in the arrangements. As for any complaint from the bird itself, that simply could not be expected. Its throat was so completely choked with the leaves from the books that it could neither whistle nor whisper. It sent a thrill through one's body to watch the process.

> — Rabindranath Tagore. In *The Parrot's Training
> and Other Stories.* (Calcutta, 1944.)

Early students of American corrections noted the profound discrepancy between a democratic society and a severe penal system.[1] Decades of prison reform confidently made use of this contrast. Since approximately 1870, the New Penology has attempted to reform American prisons, reformatories and correctional institutions. The stubborn advance of humanitarian impulse was ultimately successful in mitigating the worst conditions and introducing within facilities such categories as the Chaplain, the Teacher, the Psychologist, the Vocational Instructor and presently the Caseworker and the Psychiatrist.

More recently the Age of Humanitarian Reform has given way to the Age of Treatment. Simply to make prisons more liveable and inmates more comfortable is now often regarded as archaic. The ideology of treatment has gradually replaced the earlier concern with salvation or simply humanitarianism. Conservative opponents of prison reform must now confront the more complex image of the prison-as-country club. Proponents of change have gained footholds within facilities and correctional systems primarily through the incorporation of new categories of professional staff. As the helping professions entered the traditional custodial facilities, research activities multiplied. As legislative investigations declined and prison reform societies disappeared, some of their functions have fallen into the hands of staff research departments.[2] Much recent evaluation research has been delegated to University departments of sociology, social welfare, public health or criminology.

Research aimed at corrections has become entwined with vested professional interests in ideologies, job classifications and pay scales. The discrepancy between society and prison (although reduced) is now mediated through professional organizations and professional allegiances. Prison professionals are also often constrained to disregard or transform accredited doctrine and practice and substitute expedient approximations.[3] The influence of professional ideologies on the workers of the correctional system is generally feebler than for the mental hospital[4] but it is far from non-existent.

---

[1] ". . . it must be acknowledged that the penitentiary system in America is severe. While society in the United States gives the example of the most extended liberty, the prisons of the same country offer the spectacle of the most complete despotism." Gustave de Beaumont and Alexis de Tocqueville, *On the Penitentiary System in the United States and Its Application in France,* Illinois, 1964. p. 79.

[2] Thus seriously raising the problem of self-serving research. See Donald R. Cressey, "The Nature and Effectiveness of Correctional Techniques," *Law and Contemporary Problems,* 1958, 23:754–771; and Joseph W. Eaton, "Symbolic and Substantive Evaluative Research," *Administrative Science Quarterly,* 1962, 6:421–442.

[3] See Harvey Powelson and Reinhard Bendix, "Psychiatry in Prison," *Psychiatry,* 14: 73–86, February, 1951.

[4] Anselm Strauss, *et al., Psychiatric Ideologies and Institutions,* Glencoe, Ill., 1964.

The Age of Treatment has of course coincided with trends toward the dessication of publics often summarized as the "mass society." Thus the recent unfocussed concern with Crime on the Streets tends to create a crime anxiety on a nationwide basis but fails to find a persistent, knowledgeable *public* outside the network of professional groups immediately concerned.

Historically, the custody-treatment orientation should be viewed in the context of the congeries of professions which increasingly impinged upon the custodial institutions and which have not settled comfortably into the correctional harness. It provided a common-sense theoretical measuring stick against which to chart the progress toward "treatment" made in a facility or system of facilities.[5]

The Problem of Transforming Man

It would be remarkable if the doctrinal and world-political trends of recent years had no echoes within ideologically alive[6] segments of the control apparatus of a major world society. Nor are professionals immune from such trends.[7] Professions vary in the degree to which they are professionally dissatisfied with mankind and especially with its mete of scoundrels, scrooges, and fools. Some professions are oriented through doctrine, selective recruitment, idealistic graduate education, and other means toward useful endeavors to change man. In a nation which has in addition suffered the ravages of prohibition and the "Carrie Nation" syndrome this may be an especially powerful force.

What cannot be reasonably denied is this: we live in an age in which "people-changing"[8] has become a skill, a profession, indeed a moral injunction. Among other things, this is what is new. It should not be confused with the pledge, the moral campaign, or frenzied efforts to publicize virtue historically engaged in by concerned amateurs.[9]

[5]The opaque usefulness of this orientation says nothing of its theoretical clarity, cogency or adequacy. The explanatory power of the scheme, it is argued, has been outrun by newer events and impingements to be described.

[6]Erving Goffman, *Asylums,* New York, 1961, traces ideological aliveness in part to characteristics of the total institution in which the self becomes problematic and therefore subject to conflicting theories.

[7]H. L. Wilensky, "The Professionalism of Everyone?", *American Journal of Sociology,* LXX, 2, finds that solo practice encourages a "client orientation." Wilensky quotes Everett Hughes to the effect that "the quack is the man who continues through time to please his customers but not his colleagues." Wilensky does not deal with what the profession *does* to 'Serve" the client and attributes deviation from the "service ideal" to workplace pressures. From the point of view of the correctional client Hughes' aphorism might read: "A 'head-shrinker' is a tough professional gent who refuses to do his own time but keeps trying to 'blow my mind'." Such sentiments are sometimes expressed by correctional clients and some staff members as well. Richard Korn, "The Private Citizen, the Social Expert, and the Social Problem, *Mass Society in Crisis: Social Problems and Social Pathology* (edited by Bernard Rosenberg, Israel Gerver and F. William Howton), New York, 1964, cuts across professional distinctions to develop alternate models of the social expert, pp. 576–593, but does not deal at length with the sources of this new tough-minded professionalism.

[8]The term appears in quotation marks in: Robert D. Vinter and Morris Janowitz, *The Comparative Study of Juvenile Correctional Institutions: A Research Report,* School of Social Work, University of Michigan, 1961, to designate "a class of organizations more inclusive than 'treatment' institutions." (p. 659).

[9]In America today the official handling of the addict population has reached such an Alice-in-Wonderland state that the addicts band together and, in solemn conclave, give one another a merci-

Professionals who work closely with delinquents, drug addicts, parolees and street gangs have recently been dichotomized into the "hip" and the "square." The "hip" professional is excoriated for his criminogenic tendencies, his "voyeurism"! If this view were generalized the "plague" of addiction would be turned back through superior moral karma, anomie[10] reversed by the taut will of the dedicated professional unmoved by the subtle strategies of his shifty client.

If the problem of transforming man takes on such malignant forms when dealing with core areas of deviance, it may be present in less measure in the ordinary, day-to-day life of the professional worker.

In broadest compass, the custody-treatment dimension was developed to explicate what has been happening at the intersection of three processes in modern society suggested by the terms: professionalization, bureaucratization, alienation. It professed to measure, at least grossly, the penetration of professional "treatment" into a sphere hitherto ruled over by the uniformed officer class given the task of manning the correctional institutions of the nation. The penetration of professional workers has been costly. It has proceeded furthest in the larger, well-endowed state correctional systems. It is in these larger complex organizations that one is likely to find civil service, specialized facilities, advanced classification procedures, research divisions. The larger systems, historically, have taken the lead in introducing professional categories and more recently group counseling, and even more recently what has come to be summed up in the term: "correctional therapeutic community." Many threads in American (and world) correctional efforts come to rest in this term. If the Age of Treatment is beginning to give way before an emergent correctional philosophy increasingly dedicated to the transformation of man one is likely to find evidence for it in those systems with the strongest emphasis on combining technology, professional skill, managerial ardor, and rational scientific experimentation for the purpose of "changing criminals."[11] This article suggests that the custody-treatment dimension increasingly becomes a hindrance to common sense and social scientific understanding in precisely such a system.

---

less verbal drubbing aimed at a total transformation of the self. Tight and morally virtuous communities are thereby set up and crusaders are even dispatched to bring word of this new method to prisons and college communities. See Robert Martinson, "Research on Deviance and Deviant Research," *Issues in Criminology,* Vol. 1, No. 1, pp. 138–45, for a critique of Lewis Yablonsky's, *The Tunnel Back: Synanon,* New York: 1965.

[10]Perhaps the reason Durkheim's discussion of "The Normal and the Pathological," *Rules of Sociological Method,* Glencoe, Ill., 1950, pp. 65–73, rings slightly false to the modern ear is the severe theoretical limit it places on the uncontrolled passions of professional workers.

[11]There is arising within sociology a new school of tough-minded practitioners who wish to change criminals by concentrating on "the properties of groups." See, Donald R. Cressey, "Changing Criminals: The Application of the Theory of Differential Association," *American Journal of Sociology,* LXI:116–120, Sept. 1955; J. D. Grant, "The Use of Correctional Institutions as Self-Study Communities in Social Research," *British Journal of Delinquency,* (1957), 7, 4:301–307; LaMar T. Empey, "The Application of Sociological Theory to Social Problems and Research," Youth Studies Center, University of Southern California, August, 1963; Raymond J. Corsini, "Group Psychotherapy in Correctional Rehabilitation," *The British Journal of Criminology,* Jan. 1964, pp. 272–77; and "Convicted Felons as Social Therapists," *Corrective Psychiatry and Journal of Social Therapy,* 9, 3, 1963.

A correctional system is a compromise formation embedded in a larger social matrix. It is the "passive" segment of the apparatus of social control and only in exceptional historical circumstances has it been known to cut partially loose from society at large.[12] Parole systems often permit some extension of correctional influence to post-release life.[13] This influence is normally subject to political boards (Authorities, etc.) which, however, may come to function primarily as *regulating valves* matching in-put, out-put and equalizing inter-system and extra-system pressures.[14]

A correctional system will be subject to a variety of outside pressures differing in degree of access, intensity and persistence. The assessment of these pressures for any particular aspect of the system's operation is an open question to be empirically investigated in the light of organization theory. The notion that a Commonweal organization, simply because it serves the public at large, has no initiative, direction or self-actualizing tendency should be dismissed as a metaphysical postulate. Even the notion that the historical *tendencies* associated with the evolution of correctional systems must be primarily a product of congeries of *outside* social forces is a matter to be demonstrated not assumed. For the larger systems, this view would introduce considerable error. For smaller, single-facility situations in which the facility is extensively pervaded by social pressures, such a postulate might be more economical for research.

In discussing the custody-treatment dimension in this historical context, I am suggesting that we are dealing with an *emergent* process in corrections.[15] This does not void the discussion of value or empirical relevance. An emergent trend is not a fatality so long as it is recognized in time to do something about it. I would be less than frank if I were not to underline my personal rejection of the perspective of the "transformation of man."[16]

The custody-treatment dimension functions to conceal from view the emergence of a new treatment-authoritarianism and thus inhibits the assessment of the costs as well as the possible advantages of new social techniques. There are historical and social alternatives to the "correctional therapeutic community" available to

[12]See Raul Hilberg, *The Destruction of the European Jews, Chicago,* 1961; Dallin and Nicolaevsky, *Forced Labor in the Soviet Union,* New Haven, 1955.

[13]Some students have suggested a kind of parole system for mental patients released to the community. See Howard E. Freeman and O. G. Simmons, *The Mental Patient Comes Home,* New York, 1963. The aim of parole would apparently be to increase "performance levels" which the authors assert are too low for the good of society.

[14]A recent study of California's paroling boards indicates that the average time spent per case hearing was: Youth Authority, 8.7 minutes; Adult Authority, 13.7 minutes; The Board of Trustees (Women), 33.6 minutes. See, *The Paroling Boards of the Agency: An Administrative Analysis,* Youth and Adult Corrections Agency, December, 1963, Table 5, p. 158.

[15]"In 1958 less than 5 per cent of the 27,000 persons employed in American prisons were directly concerned with the administration of treatment or training," Cressey, "Prison Organizations," *op. cit.,* p. 1031, paraphrasing A. C. Schnur, "The New Penology: Fact or Fiction?", *The Journal of Criminal Law and Criminology,* 49:331–334, 1958.

[16]J. C. Spencer, "Problems in Transition: From Prison to Therapeutic Community," in: *The Sociological Review Monograph No. 9: Sociological Studies in the British Penal Services,* edited by Paul Halmost, Keele, 1965. Spencer says: "The sociological problem of the therapeutic community is how to translate the ideology of treatment into a viable social system." (p. 19.)

society. The problem of where to strike the balance can only be decided on the basis of all the evidence.

Methodological Assumptions of the Custody-Treatment Dimension

The methodology of custody-treatment appears to play the same *normative* function as did such models as the assumption of the "normality" of full employment and the null hypothesis of "perfect justice" in many recent studies in the sociology of law. It differs from these models in that it compares a hazy and little studied *past* state of affairs (custody) with a hoped for *future* state of affairs (treatment) on the assumption that what will be found in any given setting will be some mixture of the two. The custody-treatment orientation does not compare present reality with some widely held present-day norm (justice) or possible present state (perfect competition), but, on the contrary, it judges the present in terms of a projected future. Unlike other normative schemes it is unable to specify a minimum, a maximum, or the segment of the curve being measured. It implicitly contains a built-in program for reform with no maximum limit except the "logical" one of the total reduction of recidivism.[17] It might be called a methodological utopia, if its implications were not seriously connected with advances in the power of certain social segments, professions, and interests.

Historically and socially there is an intimate connection between social emphasis on the goal of reduction of recidivism[18] and movement "up" the custody-treatment dimension. As "treatment" personnel were added to custodial facilities the costs of confinement rose. These costs were partly relieved by the application of community control systems like parole and probation. Given the steady (even advancing) imput pressures on the system, experiments have been made with early release and research divisions began to develop operational research. Academics have begun to develop mathematical models of input, output and feedback. These models aim at the maximization of the correctional dollar. Some proponents propose that social science is to be utilized to transform corrections into a "learning organization," a "self-homing missile directed at the enemies of society."[19]

---

[17]Logically, if "custody" fell to zero, while "treatment" remained constant, the inmates would all escape. If "custody" fell to zero as "treatment" *increased* the need for the institution would wither away assuming no more input to the system, since all the criminals would be rehabilitated and recidivism would disappear. This "Dimension" is not a mathematical function; it has one foot in an unspecified past and the other in a projected future. Since one can only "measure" the present, and cannot specify the limits of the scale, this dimension contains within itself no limit.

[18]This is only *one* of the present goals of the correctional system but it is clearly gaining precedence over others, i.e., punishment, containment, etc. Historically, the goal of the reduction of recidivism could not become a palpable force until recidivism could be accurately *measured*. Before this could be done accurate statistics were needed on a national level. Parole also functioned to provide a feedback network for information about the parolee. Forty years of sociological analysis in the actuarial line has also helped.

[19]Leslie Wilkins, *Social Deviance: Social Policy, Action and Research*, New Jersey, 1965. One may see what could happen when these academic perspectives are further extended by California's

Much work has to be put into a "natural system" in order to further maximize even one clearly established official goal.[20] But the correctional system has *multiple* official goals. This natural system is also at the intersection of independent police, judicial, legal and legislative systems which limit its freedom in intricate ways. These systems in turn have goals and sub-goals of their own. This has become an obstacle for visionaries who wish to solve the crime problem regardless of the consequences of a particular solution on other correctional goals, the goals of connected sub-systems, and the larger goals and values of society. Some technocratic enthusiasts imagine they will solve the problem by optimizing a "mix" of costs, inputs, outputs, and values. Their envisioned matrix is a 20th Century variant of the vision behind Bentham's panopticon; it also pretends to translate human values into "costs." What is apparently envisioned is the transformation of multi-valued correctional settings in the direction of single-valued settings, i.e., the reduction of recidivism by all available means.[21]

There are many variants of the custody-treatment dimension and a growing literature devoted to it. In the hands of Donald R. Cressey, it takes the form of polar types; here custody, there treatment.[22] In Vinter and Janowitz, it takes the form of a hypothetical variable which is both cross-sectional and longitudinal. They deliberately arranged specially selected facilities to fall along the dimension for comparative purposes, and made use of the same scheme to measure longitudinal change. Attitude surveys of correctional staff have sometimes pushed a *discontinuance* variable (discrete facilities) into one that becomes continuous for all practical purposes.[23]

---

systems engineers. See, *Final Report, Prevention and Control of Delinquency,* prepared for Youth and Adult Corrections Agency, State of California, Space-General Corporation, El Monte, California, 1966. The core of this report is its proposed "Potential Offender Identification Program" which includes a "population planning program" aimed to "reduce the production of potential offenders," (p. 73) who, the report reveals, are heavily concentrated in the Negro and Mexican-American ethnic segments of the States. (Fig. A-11, p. 216).

The program will begin by requesting completely voluntary participation in recommended action, whether it entails practicing family planning or relocation in some less susceptible area. If, however, insufficient numbers are motivated by counseling, indoctrination, and other inducements, then further incentives will be developed by the committee. These might include use of incentive "bonuses" peer group influences, and social pressures as appropriate for the specific community. (p. 75)

[20]See, Philip Selznick, "Foundations of the Theory of Organizations," *American Sociological Review,* 13:25–35, 1958; and *Leadership and Administration,* Ill., 1957.

[21]Chadwick J. Haberstrom, "Organization Design and Systems Analysis," *Handbook of Organizations, op. cit.,* sees a conflict between "egocentric economizing" and Barnard's concept of "efficiency to gain currency in usage." Systems analysis need not insert any particular values into its computer simulations models, although it would appear to have an "elective affinity" for certain lofty, technocratic visions.

[22]Cressey keeps close to the tangled truth about prison organizations. In his hands the polar type of "treatment" is overlayed upon the actual reality of custody to show the conflicts, contradictions and limitations that then occur. Nevertheless, both polar types are figments. His "punitive-custodial" type assumes an equivalence between two tasks of the prison, the "punitive" task and the simple custodial task. *Custodians need not be punitive.* His "treatment prison" is an *ideal* in the *ideological* rather than the Weberian sense.

[23]Kassebaum, Ward and Wilner, *op. cit.* Here, the sliding-scale is moved up a notch. "Custodial" becomes "traditional," while "treatment" is "generally consistent with Gilbert and Levinson's con-

Recent sociological discussions of prisons and mental hospitals have attempted to put the custody-treatment dimension aside and proceed to more concrete investigations. Erving Goffman has objected to "junior psychiatry" and has constructed a typology cutting across formal distinctions. Anselm Strauss has objected to those who have "used sociological methods and analysis in the service of psychiatric assumptions and interests." Other authors have also kept close to the correctional setting without perceiving it entirely through the custody-treatment lens.[24] One difficulty with some of these empirical and descriptive studies is that they lack an overall orientation and thus do not tend to cumulate. They are like beads without a string, descriptions of discrete cases which do not add to an integrated body of knowledge. To ignore the custody-treatment orientation is not to overcome it.[25]

Professional Sources of Authoritarian Treatment Ideology

"People-changers" are not randomly distributed either in the population at large or in the professions. One might expect to find more of them in social work than in art, in psychiatry than in philology. Ultimately it is not a question of the distribution of persons but of professional *ideology* and the power to implement it.[26] Since professions are not monolithic there are sure to be ideological factions and differences both subtle and gross. One would expect the applied branches of professions and sciences to contain more than their share.

One must seriously limit a perspective which looks solely toward the seduction of professional virtue by the bureaucratic setting although this is demonstrably one significant process.[27] Of increasing importance is a growing, pervasive cynicism-*know-nothingism* — which reflects, in America at least, the widening discrepancy between a democratic, libertarian past and an increasingly authoritarian present.[28] The relation between an amoral scientism and a debunking

---

ception of the 'humanistic' orientation." (p. 24). The sole measure of personal proclivity toward "authoritarianism" is a short, ten-item version of the California F-scale. Edward A. Shils, "Authoritarianism: 'Right' and 'left,' in: *Studies in the Scope and Method of 'The Authoritarian Personality,' Continuities in Social Research*, Glencoe, Ill., 1954, has raised doubts about the conception of a conservative-liberal-radical continuum upon which this scale is based. The F-scale measures something real but it may fail to capture an unfamiliar, emergent, reality.

[24]See, for example, Stanton and Schwartz, *The Mental Hospital*, New York, 1954, Caudill, *The Psychiatric Hospital as a small Society*, Cambridge, 1958.

[25]"Overcome" in the Hegelian sense of critique through inclusion moving to a more adequate level where past error is seen as partiality. Present day social science is often eclectic in the sense of substituting statesmanship for creative conflict. Herbert Marcuse, *One-Dimensional Man*, Boston, 1964, deals with some of the sources of this "paralysis of criticism."

[26]See, George Rosen, MD, "The Evolution of Social Medicine," in: Howard E. Freeman, Sol Levine and Leo G. Reeder, *Handbook of Medical Sociology*, New Jersey, 1963, esp. the section "Mercantilism and the Concept of Medical Police."

[27]William Kornhauser, *Scientists in Industry: Conflict and Accommodation*, Berkeley, 1963.

[28]I choose the word "authoritarian" with care. Marcuse's Hegelism runs him into error at many points; the primacy he gives to thought pushes him toward the dissolution of all distinctions.

know-nothingism lays the ground for the growth of curious reactions, especially among students, intellectuals, and professionals.[29]

One is likely to find the "people-changing" ideology growing in those professional areas in which the client is especially helpless, and thus one is hardly surprised to find it associated with Skid Row, or aspects of probation, parole, social work,[30] criminology and sociology, with especially interesting forms in the small therapeutic mental hospital.[31] It is vaguely consistent with the growing public ideology of "mental health."[32]

It is at the intersection of congeries of sciences, professions, agencies and institutions that one may see the social roots of a new version of the "medical police" based not on the cameralist presuppositions of mercantilism but on more modern forms. The professions that might be empirically investigated from this orientation would be public health, psychiatry, social work, hospital and prison administration, and their para-professional helpers. The relevant agencies would be those with the more *chronic* relations with clients in which the stubbornness and intractability of the human animal may give birth to impatience, cynicism, and daring dreams. Not all aspects of social control are equally relevant, only those in which clients are stubborn, socially visible and collected together in one spot. Not all social strata are equally relevant, perhaps only those which turn away from white, middle class, Protestant, values. Class is ceasing to be the most salient distinction to make in relation to this "turning away" process. One

[29]Religious enthusiasm in modern society is as likely to be associated with professional identities as with religious associations. The growth of professional religiosity may be seen in the new "heretic," the professional deviant who makes the error of appealing to the public over the head of his colleagues. Pertinent examples which come to mind are : Thorstein Veblen, C. Wright Mills, T. S. Szasz, Rachel Carson, Hoxey, medicine; Immanuel Velikovsky; astronomy. Velikovsky's case was so extraordinary as to give birth to a special issue of *The American Behavioral Scientist*, Sept. 1963.

[30]The custody-treatment dimension shows up once again in: H. L. Wilensky and Charles N. Lebeaux, *Industrial Society and Social Welfare*, New York, 1965. Here the distinction is between the "residual" and "institutional conceptions of social welfare (Chapter VI). More recently, in his foreword, Wilensky warns that "welfare planners must be alert to the danger that in the name of improved coordination of the welfare services, in pursuit of the humane purposes of the welfare state, we may simply subject the underlying population to more efficient surveillance" (p. li). The concept "institutional" may be useful for a broad social survey of American welfare practices but it covers over nicer distinctions useful in the present context.

[31]Especially symptomatic is the frank dissolution of psychiatry into an "ideology of hopefulness" complete with a "leader who is not vulnerable to the upsets of patients." Ezra Statland and Arthur L. Kobler, *Life and Death of a Mental Hospital, Seattle*, 1965, pp. 221 ff. Chapter VII, "An Epidemic of Suicide in a Dying Hospital," makes Orwell's *1984* seem like a pleasant dream.

[32]See the interesting if troubled essay by John R. Seeley, "Social Values, the Mental Health Movement, and Mental Health," in: *Mental Health and Mental Disorder, A Sociological Approach*, New York, 1955, pp. 599–612. "Like the early church, the mental health movement unites and addresses itself to 'all sorts and conditions of men,' so only they be 'for' mental health as they were formerly for virtue and (more mildly) against sin" (p. 606). See also Kingsley Davis' article, "Mental Hygiene and Class Structure," pp. 578–598, *ibid*. Davis sees the "mental hygienist" as a "practicing moralist in a scientific, mobile world" who is vaguely buttressing the "standards of the entire society." He objects to the notion that "the mental hygienist is consciously enforcing alien class standards upon unwilling members of a lower stratum" (p. 596).

will find many candidates who are not cheerful and cooperative among the nation's five million alcoholics, one hundred thousand drug addicts, and the increasing numbers of very old people. Ethnic distinctions are not entirely relevant. American political positions are not very revealing.

I am attempting to point to what may be regarded as one of the *principia media* of our society.[33] A relatively "unique" intersection of professional ideology, medical bureaucratization, with forms of chronic alienation gives birth to our "medical police" and its project of halting the *chronic* discontent of our time.

Chronic Alienation

The distinction between acute and chronic is fundamental to this discussion and cuts across the medical-social spheres. It is usually not sufficiently appreciated that *chronic* illness as a social problem was partially a result of medical progress. The progress in halting acute disease through identifying and coping with specific infectious microorganisms has advanced steadily for the last century. Death by chronic disease — malignant neoplasms, diabetes mellitus, cardiovascular renal diseases — have doubled and tripled.[34]

While acute rapidly-spreading-spreading, infectious disorders — like the plague — have had powerful social consequences, they were more in the nature of the pre–20th Century business cycle than the structural unemployment of more recent times. The "plagues" of our day are slow, creeping processes, sometimes not even recognized as problems until they have assumed major dimensions.[35] When recognized they are usually turned over to some specialized agency or congeries of agencies.[36] As illness becomes more chronic, "public health in the community" turns from epidemiology to discussions of the "latent" function of public health in "introducing some degree of rationality into everyday life." Public

---

[33]". . . while the economic, political and ideological spheres (according to the cross-sections taken by different observers) each represent a single dimension of events as a whole, existing reality in fact consists in the mutual relationships between many such spheres and the concrete *principia media* at work in them." Karl Mannheim, *Man and Society in an Age of Reconstruction*, London, 1942.

[34]See, Saxon Graham, "Social Factors in Relation to the Chronic Illnesses," in: *Handbook of Medical Sociology, op. cit.*, pp. 65–98, especially Table 3–1. While deaths from tuberculosis have dropped from 194.4 in 1900 to 6.7 in 1959, cancer has increased from 64.0 to 147.1, heart disease from 345.2 to 519.7. Deaths from motor-vehicle accidents have climbed from nothing to 20.0 in this period.

[35]The public health research techniques summarized in the term epidemiology often raise acutely embarrassing social questions. One interesting recent example is the possible connection between circumcision and a low incidence of cancer of the cervix; another is the relation between the "gay life" and the incidence of syphilis; the smoking-cancer association, is of course, *a cause célèbre*. Value elements enter profoundly in all such situations.

[36]See, Sol Levine and Paul E. White, "The Community of Health Organizations," in: *Handbook of Medical Sociology, op. cit.*, pp. 321–347. One problem with this "community" is "interinstitutional conflict" and, of course, the answer lies in "interagency cooperation." The authors do not deal with the problem of the "unwanted client," the "multi-agency family," and the possibility of vested interest in the continuation of an on-going, chronic, situation.

health now studies its own network of functionaries, action programs, and is especially concerned with community power. Ideology is a recurrent problem.[37]

As public health becomes more political, health becomes more politicized more ideological. The problem of cost has given way to the irrational-rationality of citizens banding together to oppose fluoridation.[38] As the medical profession has gained in income, power and prestige,[39] the problem of quasi-practitioners and "quackery" continues as sub-professionals, non-professionals and religious sects borrow the prestige of medicine.[40]

As one turns toward the addictive substances such as alcohol, narcotics, and the "dangerous drugs," the emergence of the "medical police" is quite striking. Chronic alienation here received a crutch which increases incredibly the stubbornness of the client and his rejection of "treatment." Systems of social control are instituted with little success or even with a reverse effect, maintaining and sometimes increasing the problem they were instituted to solve.[41]

Large-scale industrial societies (especially the democratic ones) must wait until a process has become socially visible to act upon it. The ponderous gears of law, police, corrections and "treatment" only screw down upon such problems long after they have fixed in areas, ethnic groups, strata, and grey-markets. The deviant person joins the deviant group, subcultures, and even parallel economy. Organized crime enters and sometimes the dialectic of protracted war replaces the processualism of deviance. Since the demand for the product is quite inelastic,

[37]See, Irwin T. Sanders, "Public Health in the Community," in: *Handbook of Medical Sociology, op. cit.,* pp. 369–396. ". . . public health usually means intervening in the lives of people, often against their will. To date, those in public health have not succeeded in developing for themselves or conveying to the general public an ideology of intervention which jibes with the more widely-accepted beliefs about individual rights and the general distrust of government involvement in daily affairs" (p. 379).

[38]The attempt to dismiss this protracted, nation-wide resistance as a residual "superstition" reminds one of the manner in which the Enlightenment treated the Dark Ages. Yet it resembles the prisoner who "rejects his rejectors," the old codger who would rather die in a Skid Row hotel than live in a nice, clean zoo for old people, the fat businessman who works himself to death despite the doctor's good advice. Perhaps the ultimate in this line recently occurred in Dallas, Texas, where a Negro woman joined hands with her neighbors to prevent the white fire department from saving her six-year-old child.

[39]Drug prices, hospital prices and medical incomes have recently advanced astronomically. See, "The Rising Costs of Medical Care," Chapter 10 in: H. M. Somers and A. R. Somers, *Doctors, Patients and Health Insurance,* New York, 1961. ". . . the net *median* income of doctors rose 85 per cent from 1947 to 1955 when it reached $16,017. The 1959 *median* of $22,100 represents a 153 per cent advance over 1957." (p. 180–181).

[40]See, Walter I. Wardwell, "Limited, Marginal and Quasi-Practitioners," in *Handbook of Medical Sociology, op. cit.,* pp. 213–239. "Of course, such practitioners sometimes do effect cures among those who believe" (p. 230). See also, Ari Kiev, *Magic, Faith and Healing: Studies in Primitive Psychiatry Today,* New York, 1964; and the works of Thomas Szasz.

[41]Prohibition is the classic example. See also, Alfred Lindesmith, *The Addict and the Law,* Bloomington, Indiana, 1965. See, Edwin M. Lemert, "Social Structure, Social Control, and Deviation," in: *Anomie and Deviant Behavior,* (edited by Marchal B. Clinard),, New York, 1966, pp. 57–97. "There is a processual aspect to deviation, whose acknowledgement is forced upon us by the fact that with repetitive, persistent deviation or invidious differentiation, something happens 'inside the skin' of the deviating person" (p. 81).

the crime has no victim, and an independent judicial system stands as an obstacle to a totally efficient war against crime, an open, pluralistic society may find itself in a tragic, complex circle of effects and countereffects which operates to maintain a given permissible level of the deviance in question. The control apparatus functions in part to maintain this level. In its "war against crime" it is often forced to turn to publicity stunts, public relations, and hokum in response to an impossible task.[42]

There is an increasing recognition of the intersection of the correctional and control apparatus and the career paths of chronic deviants. For example, Wikler notes that the abstinence rate of Lexington patients compares favorably with recovery rates from diabetes, or pulmonary tuberculosis.[43] Chein sees recidivism as a constructive part of the therapeutic process.[44] Parole system use of nalline may in part function to permit addicts on parole to maintain a moderate "habit" on a working class salary.[45] Civil commitment tends to lead to a confinement, abstention, controlled re-addiction, and re-confinement.

One authority asserts: "There is no real cure for the addictive disorders, just as no cure exists for many chronic disease — there is only a slow rehabilitative process which involves continuous support and a changed way of life."[46]

The role of coercion in the "treatment" of the addictions is clearly recognized by the World Health Organization, which recommends some form of legal compulsion because "most addicts require some degree of coercion, preferably civil commitment for medical treatment, to force them to desist from what is to them often a pleasurable experience."[47] The ordinary human stubbornness of the old, the weak, the eccentric and the stupid may then be reinforced by the quality of pleasureableness. The "rehabilitative process" must then consist in tearing from the user his habitually pleasurable method for coping with his problems

---

[42]The World Health Organization argues that "the maintenance of drug addiction is not treatment," *Chronicle of the World Health Organization*, "Treatment and Care of Drug Addicts," 11:323, October, 1957. The requirements of a democratic society may hinder measures which would "ruthlessly stamp out" these practices.

[43]Abraham Wikler, "Clinical Aspects of Diagnosis and Treatment of Addictions," *Bulletin of the Meninger Clinic*, 15 (1951).

[44]Isadore Chein, et al., *The Road to H: Narcotics, Delinquency and Social Policy*, New York, 1964.

[45]See, Robert Martinson, Gene G. Kassebaum, David A. Ward, "A Critique of Research in Parole," *Federal Probation*, 28,3:34–38, Sept. 1966.

[46]Edward A. Suchman, "The Addictive Diseases as Socio-Environmental Health Problems," in *Handbook of Medical Sociology, op. cit.*, p. 139. Medicine and medical sociology is rife with such ideological injunctions. The statement should read: "Given what is meant by "cure" by upper middle-class medical practitioners in the United States *today*, there is no real cure. . . ." Even then the statement would be false. Alcoholics Anonymous, and Synanon certainly "cure" in their own way. So do the Siberian *shaman*, the Yoruba *babalawo*, the Bahalis *yanka* and *barwa*, the Iban *manang*, the Ndembu *chimbuki*, the Australian *margidbu*, the Yemenite *mori*, and so forth. See also, William Madsen, "Value Conflicts and Folk Psychotherapy in South Texas," in *Magic, Faith and Healing, op. cit.*, pp. 420–445. Madsen points to "the high degree of success the *curandero* has demonstrated and the inability of the psychiatrist or physician to communicate linguistically or culturally with this predominantly Spanish-speaking group" (p. 420).

[47]*Chronicle of the World Health Organization, op. cit.*, p. 323.

while simultaneously defining his resistance to both the first *and* the second as a "disease."[48]

In American sociology, the recent interest in alienation, social change, evolutionist perspectives, conflict theory and dialectical processes of change provides some context for the discussion.[49]

The use of the term *chronic* alienation suggest something of the process. In the largest sense, we confront the drawing apart of science and man, but in this grandiose form the process escapes definition, limit, or verification. More specifically, we must confront *medical* progress, the lengthening of human life, the healing of the sick, the halt, the blind, the essence of humanistic perspective. The technical, scientific and humanitarian revolution associated with medicine has given birth to special new forms of misery, loneliness, isolation, and suffering.

Science is capable of producing destruction on an unprecedented scale. Today the world is ambivalent about new scientific inventions. The great powers spend large sums on space. In turning toward the stars we may become more impatient with man. The sick joke, the violent gang, the search for flying saucers are associated with a partial turning away from the helpless, the victims, the dropouts. We are intensely concerned with the invisible reality just beyond our reach. We "cathect" with the starry heavens and leave our neighbors to die on the streets.[50]

We must confront the many ways in which we have kept the chronically alienated socially invisible. There are hundred of thousands if not millions of little "places" throughout America in which they are systematically tucked away. They are receiving care and "treatment." In these places, small and large, thoughts of mercy killing often arise.[51] Historically, brutal devices have been utilized in "treating" the inhabitants of these places.[52]

The health industry in America plays a most active role in producing chronic alienation. Almost all of the addicting substances are in the pharmacopeia. The opiates, heroin, *aqua vita*, the newer categories of "dangerous drugs" have been

[48]See, *Drug Addiction, Crime or Disease?* Interim and Final Reports of the Joint Committee of the American Bar Association and the American Medical Association on Narcotic Drugs, Indiana, 1963. See also, Henry D. Lederer, "How the Sick View Their World," in: Jaco, *op. cit.*, pp. 247–256. The author sees social reaction to illness moving from denial to acceptance to body interest and dependency to convalescence. Neither *chronic* illness nor addiction would seem to fit this model.

[49]See, for example, Pierre L. van den Berhe, "Dialectic and Functionalism: Toward a Theoretical Synthesis," *American Sociological Review*, 28, 5, October 1963. The specification of a "minimum dialectic" as a "residual" is not very enlightening. If a process of change is dialectical one should be able to show it to be so, empirically. The question of how "residual" it is cannot be settled by an *a priori* logic but only by following the process to its end.

[50]I am suggesting that the space emphasis has shifted mass psychology, literary perspectives, and, perhaps, our attitudes towards those who refuse the gifts of a universal, free education.

[51]See, for example, Harold Orlans, "An American Death Camp," in: Rosenberg, Gerver, and Howton, *op. cit.*, pp. 614–626. "It is in the murder by neglect of decrepit old men that, I believe, the closest analogy is to be found with death camp murders" (p. 626). The author, a Conscientious Objector, recognizes the "humanizing influence" of the CO's, but wishes also to emphasize "the brutalization of CO's by their experience" (p. 625, footnote).

[52]See, Albert Deutsch, *The Mentally Ill in America*, New York, 1949.

medically useful substances. Medical addiction is an important sub-category of addiction. Doctors and nurses have high rates of addiction. The American drug industry has poured hundreds of dangerous compounds on the market. The latest products of the most advanced industry often threaten the health and safety of the consumer.[53]

More specifically, we have to confront long-range demographic processes, such as the increase in the proportions of old people, the reduction of the extended family, the concentration and social isolation of poverty,[54] the transformation of Skid Row from "hobohemia" to a white swamp surrounded by colored areas. We are concerned with the general increase in the use of alcohol, the transformation of the major cities into Negro strongholds, and the keeping alive of the halt, lame, blind, disturbed, eccentric, and deviated.

Two perceptive students of the medical world have discussed the "paradox of medical progress."

As we preserve life at all age levels, there is more illness, more enduring disability, for the population as a whole. A great shift is taking place in the nation's morbidity and disability patterns. A relative decline in serious acute illness is accompanied by a vast increase in chronic illness of long duration and a high rate of residual disability. The control of many formerly fatal diseases, like diabetes, or disabilities, like spinal paralysis, creates a need for expensive lifetime medical supervision."[55]

The term paradox is meant to give a non-objective thrust to the process and to lay the basis for its solution through "Organization: The Perilous Imperative." For the majority of Americans organization implies the general hospital, the medical plan, medical insurance and group practice or some combination of these. For the chronically alienated a future of organization may not look so bright.

It is a symptom of our condition that the *Right to Die* is listed by the Director of the Massachusetts General Hospital as "one of the four major medical problems facing the United States."

Part of this issue . . . is keeping alive people who, not to put too fine a point upon it, would be happier if allowed to die. . . . Not long ago I heard a minister talk on the various feedoms he would like to see available to all mankind. After reviewing the more familiar ones, he added a new one: Freedom to Die. I beg of you to think that over."[56]

The chronic alienation of the aged, the crippled, the socially useless, should

---

[53]See, the muckraking and not altogether reliable report by N. Mintz, *The Therapeutic Nightmare*, Boston, 1965.

[54]Michael Harrington, *The Other America*, New York, 1962, has helped to make the more politically relevant of these areas visible. The new visibility of the poor may also give birth to unanticipated consequences. Urban renewal, the "elimination" of Skid Row, old people's hospitals, foster homes for runaways, villages for the "old folks," recovery houses for alcoholics, Synanon's, and a thousand-and-one clinics and drying-out hospitals are relevant here.

[55]Somers and Somers, *op. cit.*, p. 7.

[56]*Ibid.*, p. 7.

be carefully distinguished from the classical alienation of the worker from his product analyzed by Marx, or the alienation of man from rationality spoken of by Weber. The worker is a force of production, the chronically alienated a burden. The worker reacted to alienation through voluntary association, political and social struggle; the chronically alienated are drop-outs, a burden to themselves, their families, neighbors, and society. The worker had "nothing to lose but his chains"; the chronically alienated, as time goes on, have little to look forward to but death.[57]

Nor is the Weberian perspective too useful. The doctor, the military man, the business man, have been progressively deprived of control over their means of production through the development of the general hospital, the giant corporation, the military complex but they are not deprived of socially useful work. They are valuable. Embedded in the organizations of an organizational society they face problems peculiar to that society, some soluble, some relatively endemic. They fight for autonomy, form organizations, change policies, make alliances, preserve distance, or otherwise carry on the desperate work of the 20th Century.

The modern drop-out tends to be an *organizational reject,* a person rejected from the public school system or deprived of his livelihood at age 65. The drop-outs live in the interstices between organizations — Skid Row, the slum, the family mental ward, the small, grey cheerless houses. They are everywhere and nowhere. They are incapable of organizing, for what could they demand? The world does not want their talents, has no need of their advice, sentimentality, sensitivity, their tales of past glories, their non-automated skills.

Pessimism has never been a strong point for Americans and it is increasingly becoming unthinkable in the helping professions to the degree that the clients refuse to become the cooperative, cheerful robots of whom C. Wright Mills often spoke. Americans salt their pragmatism with a strong belief in inevitable, gradually increasing, material and social progress. In certain professions, this boyish optimism is faced with the obstreperous, eccentric, shifty, and nasty temperament of man. An unsentimental, tough-minded stance is called forth, a set of persuasions, inducements, bonuses, incentives, motivations, and coercions. This collective Hickey marches forward looking neither to the left nor the right. Something like that, I think, provides a powerful motor for our collective dealings with the drop-outs and rejects who are incapable of playing the organizational game. These drop-outs, criminals, drug fiends, sexual perverts, are not left alone. To the Ten Commandments we have added the eleventh: Thou Shalt Be Organized!

The custody-treatment dimension is thus associated with a powerful social process — the organization of the deviant, a special bringing to bear of the control

---

[57]Despite the increase in chronic illness, death as a meaningful experience is progressively blotted out or denied. In sociology, death becomes death *rate.* For example, in the *Index to the American Sociological Review,* 1936–1960, I am unable to find one article on the meaning of death; Julius Gould and William L. Kolb, *A Dictionary of the Social Sciences,* New York, 1964, list *Death Rate* but not death. Perhaps it would be speculative to suggest that the "obliteration" of death is a fitting form of alienation for the chronically ill, and perhaps for all of us, since we are all increasingly faced with this fate.

apparatus of society on those who are not permitted to drop away from the mainstream.[58]

Chronic alienation tends to evolve a career which takes different forms in the ordinary criminal, the alcoholic, the drug addict, and the very old or ill. This career often seizes upon some substance, mechanism, fantasy, some personal strategy, the aim of which is to cope with a life-plan which excludes meaningful participation in organized society. These coping mechanisms are varied but they appear to have in common the defense of consciousness from the pressures of organized society. Coping mechanisms aim to remove and isolate the reject from understanding his fate: they function to gradually extinguish his autonomy, freedom, and consciousness as a center of decision and responsibility. They may be regarded as a slow form of suicide. This career includes a set of moves, retreats, betrayals and more retreats, which is a different form of "risk-taking" than, say, the act of a soldier, or the accidental death of a hero who risks his life.

Chronic alienation is broader than that type of deviance prohibited by the legal code. The legal code is no sure guide to the process. It often provides invaluable aid to its workings. Nor am I talking about "deviance" in general. I am speaking of the widow who sips herself to death in the home of her late husband, the obese lady who eats herself to illness propped up on her bed, the businessman who works himself to extinction, the older, divorced woman who spends her former husband's declining fortune in buying a dependent relationship with a psychiatrist. What distinguishes these coping mechanisms is their concentration on relations and strategies which aim at the gradual and progressive obliteration of freedom, responsibility for self, and personal autonomy.

Criminology concentrates on those coping mechanisms for chronic alienation prohibited by the legal code; for society is not content to leave people alone to kill themselves swiftly or slowly. Society intervenes upon this process through personal appeals, the family, the Church, professional help, and legal coercion. In describing the processual nature of some deviance, Lemert distinguished *primary* from *secondary* deviance. Briefly, primary deviance was the pristine deviant act while secondary deviance was the reaction of the deviant to the social reaction called forth by the deviant act. The custody-treatment dimension forces upon us the recognition of further steps in this process.[59]

There has increasingly appeared a new, social reaction to the persistent failure of the traditional social reactions to deviance. The original deviant act has been

---

[58]Or, perhaps, become downward mobile through chronic illness. See, P. S. Lawrence, "Chronic Illness and Socio-Economic Status," in: *Patients, Physicians and Illness* (E. Gartly Jaco, editor), New York, 1958, pp. 37–49. "Families which had a reduction in socio-economic status between 1923 and 1943 had an adjusted chronic disease rate in 1943 of 87.2 per cent almost twice as high as the rate for families with an "improved status" (p. 48).

[59]Edwin M. Lemert, "Social Structure, Social Control and Deviation," in: *Anomie and Deviant Behavior, op. cit.*, pp. 57–97, speaks of "passive social control" and the act of defining behavior so as to "produce change, not to repress it" (p. 91). In the end he returns to "secondary deviation" (p. 97). One difficulty may be the social psychological bias built into the primary-secondary dichotomy. Lemert's essay moves strikingly toward a *dialectical* conception of social deviance.

partially contained, controlled, semi-organized. This process often gives birth to
secondary deviance — "rejecting the rejectors," if you like. But this rejecting
has become unacceptable to those agents of society rejected by the deviant. They
are somewhat in the position of the fanatic who might be defined as a person
who, faced with failure, redoubles his efforts. This is what treatment has become
or is becoming — a redoubling of efforts in the face of persistent failure.

There is no compelling evidence that this redoubling of efforts has as yet had
an important effect on the rate of recidivism. One powerful component of the
new "treatment" reaction is the growing social recognition that this is so. To
the daily frustrations of the correctional treatment staff member involved in the
intimate game of "shucking" the inmate who is "shucking" him, there grows
the pressure for results from central office, legislature, and society, and all those
who would narrow correctional functions to reducing recidivism. This new
urgency within the correctional system is beginning to be called: "the correctional
therapeutic community."[60] In probation and parole a similar process *can be*[61]
involved in the halfway house, the parole outpatient clinic, gathering parolees
together for nalline tests or group counseling sessions, the movement toward
smaller caseloads — situations in which the agent of society may tackle his slip-
pery client jowl-to-jowl.

I am not suggesting that this process has run its course or is even a major
component of all correctional or medical situations. It has gone further in some
areas than others. It is not a fatal drift. It is, nevertheless, a reality. It has laid
a powerful basis for even more severe redoublings of effort by those standing
in the wings with some new nostrums to sell the despairing but ever-hopeful
"treatment teams."

For Marx alienation was the antithesis to the thesis of the unregulated accumulation of capital. The synthesis would be a return of society to man. We cannot
comfort ourselves with the words. We know far too much about bureaucracy,
the State-party, forced labor, concentration camps, and a good deal more. It
should be clear that chronic alienation is a process of death not a process of
life. It apparently gives birth to little of social value.

Despite what I have said there are those who will push and preach for the
prison to become a "hospital." We are to use the iron compression chamber
of prison life to screw down upon the helpless, the aged, the misfits, the liars,

---

[60]Clemmer's use of the term "community" to refer to a total institution is discussed by George
A. Hillery, Jr., "Villages, Cities, and Total Institutions," *American Sociological Review,* 28, 5:779
–791. Hillery maintains that villages and cities are on a continuum while the total institution represents
a qualitative break. He does not deal at length with the *functions* of using this word, however. For
a discussion of the *ideology* of the "correctional therapeutic community" see: Robert Martinson with
William J. O'Brien, *Staff Training and Correctional Change, op. cit.,* Chapter 8.

[61]I will repeat this and underline it. *Can be* involved. Any new "treatment" method may involve
tertiary methods of dealing with deviance or democratic ones. For example, a "halfway house" may
be a small, intense treatment prison or a "sanctuary." See, Robert Martinson, "The California Recovery House: A Sanctuary for Alcoholics," *Mental Hygiene,* 58, 3, July 1964 and *Recovery Establishments for Alcoholics,* State of California, Department of Public Health, April 1963.

the psychopaths, the drop-outs, and those who have almost accidentally got caught up in the correctional stream. We will let these people out on parole only if they agree to continue playing the intimate and tiring games of "treatment" with us. Many practitioners wish only the best for the inmate or parolee and would be happy to see him carrying on a productive and socially useful life. That is really beside the point. If such therapy simply takes the form of a small discussion group, or larger town meeting, it is consistent with a democratic ethic. But to some degree traditional forms of "lay group therapy" are a *turning aside* of treatment authoritarianism through the inertia and perhaps good sense of many correctional personnel. If one is truly serious about "treating" the prisoner, and reducing recidivism, much more effort and work must be put into the system. The screws must be tightened, the hopefulness whipped up, efforts coordinated. All eyes shall be turned to *that rate,* all "uneconomical" expenditures reduced. This must then be coordinated to ever-new levels of dedication and intensity.

Summary

If a gloomy picture emerges from this discussion, it is a result of the method of abstraction I have used. I have also attempted to combine areas often kept apart through academic and professional specialization. Yet there appears to be some gain in explanatory power in so doing.

Chronic alienation affects only a relatively small, though growing, number of persons in all medically advanced societies. It is no respecter of different political systems. The challenge it presents may be met in a variety of ways. In America, the situation noted by Tocqueville has undergone a complex process of change. The *discrepancy* between prison tyranny and American democracy has been reduced. During the period of humanitarianism, the prison was reformed in a democratic direction. As the age of treatment begins to give way to a more vigorous assertion of the need to transform man, efforts are being made to introduce methods in fundamental opposition to the democratic ethic. These methods are more verbal than actual, more a promise than a fulfillment. Yet they are pursued by many well-intentioned persons with little thought to the consequences.

One important way in which sociology may contribute to the study of crime and the correctional process is to ask some of the right questions. One important question seldom asked in corrections is: what kind of correctional system is fitting for a democratic society? This ethical question may easily be translated into a rich variety of sociological investigations. For example, what accounts for the growth and development of the new treatment authoritarianism? Where are the professional sources of the new emphasis upon utilizing the prison for the transformation of man? Does this new ideology cut across a variety of professions? What are the social forces pressing for making the reduction of recidivism the single goal of the correctional system?

Of course, these questions may be posed and answered strictly within the compass of criminology but some may find it helpful to do so within a somewhat broader perspective. The new emphasis on the control of the use of medical substances has already produced cross-disciplinary areas and subjects. The medical profession is involved in a wide variety of activities in which social control becomes strikingly important. The increasingly chronic nature of many social ailments also tends in this direction. The chronically alienated are not the most powerful segment of a modern population. They are likely to be lost sight of in what appear to be more compelling concerns. Sociology may play a very important function in keeping them before our eyes, in describing their tribulations, and in defending their humanity.

16. *John Pallas*
Bob Barber

From Riot to Revolution

I. Introduction

The deaths of forty-one persons at Attica and six at San Quentin in 1971 brought home to America the fact that social revolution has come to the prisons. This discovery was surprising and shocking to most Americans, yet it need not have been. The social history of the country can be as well understood by examining the prison as by examining any other American institution. Indeed, American prisons are not only a microcosm of American society, with its oppression and exploitation, but also of the movement to transform that society.

Prisons are the ultimate weapon of that system of social control called the legal system, whose function it is to deal with people who are actually or potentially disruptive of the social order. The prison's capacity to achieve this goal rests largely on its ability to reduce prisoners to active accomplices or passive recipients of their own oppression. Thus, any resistance which poses a serious threat to the prison threatens the entire society as well.

The composition, ideology and constituency of resistance within prisons has changed dramatically over the past twenty years. In order to best understand these changes it is necessary to examine not only the evolution of the prison movement

Reprinted by permission of Harper & Row, Publishers, Inc., and Julian Bach Literary Agency, Inc., from *The Politics of Punishment: A Critical Analysis of Prisons in America*, edited by Erik Olin Wright, pp. 237–261. Copyright © 1973 by John Pallas and Robert Barber.

itself but also the changing conditions in the larger society. Any analysis of the "prison struggle" can only be made by examining that struggle in the context of the wider struggle within American society.

Three types of prison struggle occurred during the period 1950–1971: the traditional prison riot such as those which were widespread during the 1950's; the organizing of black prisoners by the Nation of Islam; and the revolutionary upheavals of the late 1960's and early 1970's. We are not suggesting that there has been an inevitable progression from one type to another, or that other important things have not been happening in prisons during this period. Earlier forms of prison struggle still exist and many prisoners continue to be apolitical. Nevertheless, the events at Attica and elsewhere suggest a radically new dimension in the prison struggle, a dimension which has implications for the wider revolutionary movement and for state repression.

On the one hand, participants in the prison movement such as Malcolm X and George Jackson have provided models of leadership for the movement as a whole. Their writings have illuminated the nature of American society and its legal system for millions of people. On the other hand, the repression of political rebellion in prisons is connected to the repression of other rebellious domestic groups (such as the Black Panthers) and of people's movements in Latin America and Southeast Asia. There are, therefore, practical and analytical insights to be gained from an examination of rebellion by prisoners.

Prisoners have always been limited in the options open to them for protest. They are forced to live in an institution which exercises total control over their lives, whose philosophy denies the validity of their human experience, and whose practice is dedicated to destroying their impulse to resist. As Franz Fanon has pointed out, some form of violence represents the only means by which an enslaved person can reclaim her or his humanity from the violence of oppression.[1] Beyond the rational necessity for revolt in prison lies the realm of human emotion which impels prisoners to strike out against the violence of a prison before it drives them from intolerable suffering into total madness. These factors have combined throughout history to produce numerous outbursts against prisons, outbursts that are "political" in their essence if not always in their conscious form.

Any discussion of prison riots and strikes must be conducted in the framework of a political analysis. If "political" events are those dealing with the existing arrangements of power, then clearly acts that stem from the powerlessness of prisoners are political. This powerlessnesss is rooted in the position, both within prison and in the society at large, of those people who are prisoners. Such powerlessness is rooted in the social and economic structure of the society. Consequently, the lack of a political articulation of prisoners' grievances by no means eliminates their political nature. Even acts rooted in psychological despair, such as self-mutilation, are expressions of an unarticulated political revolt.[2]

---

[1]Franz Fanon, *The Wretched of the Earth* (New York: Grove Press, 1963).
[2]Ibid., Chap. 5.

II. Riots in the The Early 1950's

Over fifty major riots occurred in American prisons between 1950 and 1953; until the disturbances of the 1970's, the early fifties were characterized as the worst period ever for American prison administration.[3] These riots and strikes were largely spontaneous uprisings against intolerable living conditions. Such uprisings have often occurred in prisons and continue to occur today. Yet the increase in their intensity in the early fifties presaged the current period of organized political rebellion, for the inability of the system to respond to their demands created the conditions in which more radical ideas could influence prisoners.

The riot of April, 1952, at Jackson State Prison in Michigan was typical of these upheavals. Two prisoners overpowered a guard, took his keys, and released the other prisoners in the maximum security wing. They smashed up several wings of the prison and liberated the canteen to provide food. For five days they held hostages at knife-point, refusing to release them until officials agreed to hear their grievances and publish them in the local newspaper. The demands, quickly formulated after the riot began, were as follows:

1. 15-block (the maximum security wing) be remodelled to provide for adequate lighting and treatment facilities.
2. Counselors have free access to the disciplinary cells in the 15-block.
3. Segregation (solitary confinement) policies be revised, and a member of the individual treatment staff be given a position on the segregation board.
4. Only guards who would not be inhumane in their treatment be picked for duty in the 12-block (reserved for epileptic, semi-mentally disturbed, blind, handicapped, and senile cases).
5. The carrying of dangerous hand weapons and inhumane restrainment equipment by guards be prohibited.
6. Adequate and competent personnel for handling mental cases, and more adequate screening of such cases.
7. A letter on prison stationery be sent to the parole board asking for a revision of procedures to give equal treatment to all parolees.
8. Post-operative care be given under the direction of the medical director (instead of by prisoner technicians).
9. Equal opportunities for dental care for all prisoners, with special regard to the elimination of special buying preferences.
10. Creation of a permanent council elected by prisoners, to confer periodically with prison officials.
11. No reprisals against any leader or participant in the revolt.

The uprising ended when officials agreed to publish the demands, allow an outside group to inspect the prison, and not take action against the participants.

---

[3]Richard McCleary, "Correctional Administration and Political Change," in Lawrence Hazelrigg (ed.), *Prison Within Society* (Garden City, N.Y.: Doubleday, 1968), p. 130.

But eventually the leaders were indicted for conspiracy and almost none of the demands were met. Things continued at Jackson much as before.

A number of generalizations can be drawn from the Jackson revolt. It was unplanned and uncoordinated. The demands put forward reflected the day-to-day needs of the prisoners. They dealt with internal conditions and problems of survival, and their accomplishment would have materially improved the prisoners' lives. Despite their narrow focus, these demands were in fact political. Because of the role of inhumane prison conditions in the degradation of prisoners, the demands for the elimination of such conditions are, in effect, political demands for social justice.

The pattern of leadership at Jackson is indicative of the level of organization in this type of riot. A white prisoner named Earl Ward imposed his leadership upon the group when it became clear that internal fighting and disorganization needed to be controlled. He prevented prisoners from attacking the hostages and supervised the formulation of the demands. He decided when the group should surrender, although a number of his fellow prisoners clearly disagreed with his decision.

In general, the leadership of such revolts was white although blacks, Puerto Ricans, and Chicanos participated. The leaders were generally prisoners feared or respected for their toughness; power accrued to them by default. Rarely, however, would they use their position to their own personal advantage. The unity of the moment usually concealed intense personal or racial hatreds, which the leaders, through force or personal persuasion, had to control in order to prevent the revolt from disintegrating.

Once such outbreaks were under way, the prisoners would often willingly negotiate with certain members of the prison staff whom they regarded as sympathetic to their cause. Such individuals were usually members of the "treatment" staff, such as psychiatrists and counselors. These trusted individuals had great influence over the leaders. At Jackson, prison psychiatrist Vernon Fox convinced the prisoners to modify some of their demands. He also convinced them that the officials were sincere in their promises of change. After the revolt was over, Fox wrote an article in *Collier's* entitled, "How I Crushed the Prison Riot."

State and prison officials faced conflicting pressures during such disruptions, but the question was a tactical one: whether to crush the revolt with force or to bring it to an end through empty negotiations. Whichever method was chosen, the results were the same, and the prisoners accomplished little or nothing. The lessons of such experiences, however, were not lost on them.

The tenor of the demands and political thrust of these riots and strikes was consistent with that of the general forms of challenge to American society which occurred in the 1950's and early 1960's. Likewise, officials of the state used essentially the same means of containing and suppressing prison revolts as they did for the larger Civil Rights movement.

During the period between 1950 and 1960 the mechanisms of social control in American society appeared to be working fairly well and few significant political groups disputed the legitimacy of the social order. To the contrary, those groups who had not yet shared in the general wealth were seeking to be included. The accompanying political style was "pluralism": various political groups attempted to bring pressure on the authorities to fulfill their obligations as defined by the prevailing system. In this sense, both the prison movement of the time and the Civil Rights movement were expressions of the same impulse. They were aimed at eliminating explicit practices and customs which were seen as antithetical to the philosophy of American democracy. They challenged the abuse of power rather than its nature.

The goal of the Civil Rights movement was the integration of black people into the mainstream of American life. In prisons, at this time, the notion of "rehabilitation" was gaining credence. This notion implied that prisoners were "deviant" and in need of treatment which would enable them to "adjust properly" to the existing society. The demands for the increase in the role of treatment officials in prison life and the trust shown those officials by prisoners during their uprisings are indicative of the fact that prisoners tended to place hope in the idea of rehabilitation. In this sense, rehabilitation and integration were identical — they both posit the adaptation of individuals to the social structure which opens up to receive them.

Although the Civil Rights movement attempted to bring change through established channels such as the courts and the legislature, its cutting edge was the use of direct action, undertaken with the faith that the federal government would back it up. Effectively closed off from the legal channels of change outside prisons, prisoners also turned to direct action to influence their institutions. Their faith in at least part of that institutional structure (the treatment staff) indicates that they still granted some legitimacy of the power exercised over them.

Both movements met with similar response from the state. Violence was used routinely to break up both Civil Rights actions and prison revolts. The Civil Rights movement, able to enlist the support of various segments of the population, achieved limited progress through the legal system. With no outside constituency at this time, prisoners were unable to prevent prison officials from revoking promised reforms after a rebellion was over. In the short run, both Civil Rights and prison dissent were crushed or co-opted, but such responses by the state only laid the groundwork for more radical challenges to the society and its prisons.

III. Black Muslims

During the time that these essentially reformist efforts were being made, political activity was being carried out in another way among black people by the Nation of Islam. A high degree of organization and discipline enabled this group to reach large numbers of blacks on both sides of the walls. Although their organizational talents were important in gaining recruits, the most significant element in their success was the fact that their philosophy spoke to the anger and frustration of poor blacks, and especially black prisoners.

This philosophy stood in sharp contrast to that of the mainstream of the Civil Rights movement, which was essentially geared to integrating middle class and professional blacks into the existing society and to bringing poor southern blacks into minimal participation in the political system. Little attention was paid to the cities of the North, where it seemed that the racism was less naked than in the South.

The Black Muslims, however, concentrated their organizing in the northern urban ghettos and in the prisons. Instead of attempting to obliterate race consciousness, they taught that black people should be aware of their group identity and collective oppression. Their ultimate objective was the creation of a separate black nation. They viewed prisons as a place of recruitment for new members of this nation, rather than as a point of political struggle in its own right. Their demands focused on the requirements of the religion, not on general prison conditions.

Central to their philosophy was the notion that blacks as a group were victims of white society, that the miseries they faced were not the result of their own personal deficiencies. Muslim organizers within prison always stressed this point:

The black prisoner, he (Elijah Muhammad, the Muslim leader) said, symbolized white society's crime of keeping black men oppressed and deprived and ignorant, and unable to get decent jobs, turning them into criminals.[4]

Muslims generally came from the same class background as most black prisoners, the unemployed or irregularly employed working class. Their philosophy appealed to this class, the class that had the least hope of benefiting from the assimilationist approach of the Civil Rights movement. The Muslims spoke more realistically to the nature of prisons for blacks than did the (white) leaders of the spontaneous uprisings of the time. Thus, the Muslims recruited large numbers of black prisoners to their movement, and fewer and fewer participated in the general riots and strikes.

Their chief mode of organizing was through personal contact. Because of their class background, many Muslims were at one time or another in prison. Once in prison they devoted their full time to contacting and organizing other blacks. Muslims on the outside wrote continuously to prisoners espousing the Muslim philosophy. Prisoners were encouraged to write to Elijah Muhammad; they always received a personal reply and literature. Malcolm X became a Muslim while in prison through continued correspondence with his family and Elijah Muhammad.[5]

Throughout the early part of the 1950's, the Muslims remained more or less "underground" in prisons, educating new recruits and building an organization. By the late fifties, they had the allegiance or sympathy of most black prisoners, and began pushing their demands. Those demands were few: the right to hold religious meetings, the right to purchase the Koran, the right to build a mosque, and the right to receive visits from Muslims outside.

The organization, discipline, and unity which backed those demands presented a threat to the prison's goal of isolating prisoners from each other. The organization was based on complete loyalty to the philosophy and way of life of the

---

[4]Malcolm X, *The Autobiography of Malcolm X* (New York: Grove Press, 1966), p. 169.
[5]*Ibid.*, Chaps. 10 & 11.

Nation. Each prison mosque was rigidly structured along the lines of the mosques outside, with clearly delineated lines of authority. The prisoner-minister was recognized both by his followers in the prison and the Muslim hierarchy outside as the leader of the Muslims in prison.

These ministers were trained to prevent violence by Muslims. No acts of violence or retaliation against white guards or inmates were permitted. Eldridge Cleaver relates,

After the death of Brother Booker T. X., who was shot dead by a San Quentin guard, and who at the time had been my cell partner and the inmate Minister of the Muslims at San Quentin, my leadership had been publically endorsed by Elijah Muhammad's west coast representative, Minister John Shabazz of Muhammad's Los Angeles Mosque. This was done because of the explosive conditions in San Quentin at the time. Muslim officials wanted to avert any Muslim-initiated violence, which had become a distinct possibility in the aftermath of Brother Booker's death. I was instructed to impose iron discipline upon the San Quentin Mosque. . . .[6]

The official policy of refraining from violence despite provocation was in part imposed because violence was seen as suicidal: they were afraid of creating a situation which could be used as an excuse for the mass killing of Muslims by guards. More importantly, however, this decision grew from Muslim attitudes towards the prisons. They wanted as many new recruits as possible to be active in their communities; the goal was to get them out on the streets safely.

Two essential tactics, strikes and lawsuits, were used by the Muslims to achieve their demands within the prison. Strikes were usually called in the aftermath of a particular incident. After the killing of a Muslim by a San Quentin guard in 1967, the Muslims called a work strike and demanded the prosecution of the guard. They also reiterated the central demands for religious freedom. Their primary tactic, however, was the use of lawsuits to force the prisons to grant them this freedom. They invariably lost the suits, but turned the losses to political advantage by pointing to the biased nature of the court system.

In dealing with the Muslims, the goal of prison officials was primarily to break up the Muslim organization. Meetings were broken up, ministers continually transferred from prison to prison, Muslims routinely placed in isolation, and communication with the outside cut off. State and prison officials publically portrayed the Muslims as violent maniacs who posed the gravest threat not only to the prison system but to the society as a whole.

Although the Muslims declined in influence in the mid-1960's, a positive legacy of their work remained. They helped destroy the barriers to political consciousness which has impeded prisoners in previous attempts to struggle against their oppression. The Muslims introduced disciplined organization among prisoners, the idea that collective action could be taken to achieve desired goals.

[6]Eldridge Cleaver, *Soul on Ice* (New York: Dell, 1968), p. 57.

They introduced the notion of collective oppression to black prisoners, which counteracted the prison ideology of individual pathology. Although they located the source of that oppression in the "white devil" and his institutions rather than in specific class-related institutions, their insistence upon the collective nature of that oppression marked an important step in the transformation of black consciousness. In addition, the Muslims brought with them the notion that outside support for a movement inside could strengthen that movement. Finally, the Muslims brought with them models of successful anti-colonial struggles in Africa. They could point to the newly independent African nations as examples of self-determination for black people in struggle against white oppression. This development was crucial for the continuing development among black prisoners of their self-conception as people involved in a world-wide struggle, and placed them firmly in the vanguard of the new prisoners' movement. As Malcolm X once pointed out, "The first thing the American power structure doesn't want Negroes to start is thinking internationally."[7]

Yet in spite of these positive contributions, the influence of the Muslims diminished considerably in the mid-1960's. The immediate causes of this decline were in the nature of the Muslim religion and movement itself. The split between Malcolm X and Elijah Muhammad in 1963 led to an uncertainty about the future of the Muslims. The Muslims had promised that Allah was coming to deliver blacks from the white devils; Allah's failure to appear caused a great deal of disillusionment with the theological analysis of the Nation of Islam. The Muslims' refusal to define prisons as a point of struggle alienated many new converts who needed legal support and wanted action in prison. As prisoners grew in political sophistication, they became increasingly aware that the Muslim philosophy of nationalism with its religious emphasis was reactionary and inappropriate for the prison struggle. The Muslim preoccupation with separatism and black racial superiority played right into the hands of the administrators who wanted nothing more than to keep black and white prisoners divided. What the black and white inmates needed, in fact, was to unite with one another in opposition to the prison administration. Malcolm's changed analysis of racism after his 1965 trip to Mecca forced many Muslims to re-examine their own attitudes towards this issue. Malcolm wrote of his changed perceptions,

The white man is not *inherently* evil, but America's racist structure influences him to act evilly. The society has produced and nourishes a psychology which brings out the lowest, most base part of human beings.[8]

Malcolm's special appeal to black prisoners gave his change of mind a special impact. Cleaver later wrote,

Many of us were shocked and outraged by these words from Malcolm X, who had been a major influence upon us all and the main factor in many of our conversions to the black Muslims, but there were those of us who

[7]Malcolm X, *The Autobiography of Malcolm X*, p. 347.
[8]*Ibid.*, p. 371.

were glad to be liberated from a doctrine of hate and racial supremacy. The onus of teaching racial supremacy and hate, which is the white man's burden, is pretty hard to bear.[9]

IV. The Revolutionary Prison Movement

In the wake of [the] Muslims' decline between 1964 and 1967, the prisoner's movement underwent fundamental changes in its nature and political thrust. The bitter lessons of the fruitless riots of the 1950's and the inability of the Muslims to relate to specific prison struggles left the prisoners open to new influences and new forms of struggle more consistent with the state of society and the general movement of opposition to it. Changing conditions in the U.S. and around the world during this period of time laid the groundwork for the rise of a revolutionary movement in prisons.

During this period the contradictions with American society had become increasingly clear. Unable to respond to the rising pressure for reform, the system turned increasingly to the repression of its challengers, the advocates of Black Power and the anti-war movement. The war in Vietnam and the intervention in the Dominican Republic revealed the roots of American foreign policy in imperialism and its concomitant racism. In this context the opposition to the state grew more radical and militant, and was met with increasing repression.

In the spiral of challenge and retrenchment, of revolution and repression, new political movements in the U.S. and around the world appeared: a black power movement expressed in ghetto riots and the growth of the Black Panther Party; an anti-imperialist movement among white students and intellectuals manifested in campus revolt; Third World Liberation groups rooted in local communities; and revolutionary movements in Indochina, Latin America, and Africa. These groups articulated an understanding of the inter-relationships of domestic and foreign repression, of the role of racism as an ideology used to divide people of different races in the interest of economic exploitation, and of the necessity for international solidarity among the victims of imperialism. They proceeded to act upon these analyses, thus providing models of both revolutionary theory and practice, and a general atmosphere of confrontation for prisoners.

The impact upon prisoners of increasing repression and successful revolution in the outside world cannot be overestimated. Third World prisoners especially made quick connections between their struggles inside and the struggles of Third World peoples around the world. These prisoners were joined by an influx of new prisoners, imprisoned for radical activities. Blacks, Puerto Ricans, Chicanos, and other Third World people active in radical movements, and an increasing number of whites arrested for offenses stemming from their opposition to the Indochina war, brought their politics and organizing talent to prisons. Women active in the women's movement and other political activities brought their perspective to women's prisons.

[9]Cleaver, *Soul on Ice*, pp. 56–57.

Since 1964, then, the prison struggle has consciously become a part of an international struggle. Among the vanguard elements inside prisons, the need for interracial unity and political education and organizing had become accepted. Putting the new precepts into practice, however, has been more difficult, for prison and state officials have not stood by to let these developments happen of their own accord. Prisoners have had to overcome their own backgrounds of hate and mistrust. This attempt is paralleled on the outside by the increasing number of street gangs of white and Third World youth who have buried their former conflicts and turned to political activity in their communities.

Prison authorities have never hesitated to exploit racism as a divisive element to further their control of prisoners. Inter-racial violence continues, often encouraged or ignored from above. Such conflict, however, has been increasingly repudiated by a growing united front of black, brown, and white prisoners.

The situation at San Quentin prison in California provides a model for the changing nature of revolt during this time of transition. A massive race riot in January, 1967, involving nearly half of the prison's 4000 prisoners, resulted in cautious attempts at reconciliation by prisoner leaders. The self-defeating nature of such violence was acknowledged and truces arranged between various black and white groups. An underground newspaper called the *Outlaw* began publication. It attacked the prison system and called for unity among the newspapers.

Within a year, open racial hostility had nearly ended and a united general strike in early 1968 caused the shutdown of nearly all the prison industries. At this point, officials moved to break up the incipient organizing by transferring suspected leaders to other prisons and increasing the general harassment of everyone. (The facilities of the *Outlaw* were discovered, although the paper continued to be occasionally published outside and smuggled in.)

The success of a second strike on Unity Day in August, 1968, in terms of prisoner participation and outside support at a rally, brought an investigation of grievances by a legislative committee and further repression by the prison administration. Guards began passing around weapons and manufacturing threats among antagonistic racial groups. They clamped down on all prison activities, and again transferred the leaders. Within months the prison had dissolved into racial killings and polarization. But the precedent of unity had been set.[10]

Three more recent prison revolts indicate a greater ability on the part of prisoners to deal with the problem of racism, and provide insights into the nature of the new prison movement. Each new revolt draws upon the experience of previous revolts and invokes the memory of earlier struggles; each revolt provides an inspiration for the next.

In early October, 1970, prisoners took over the Long Island branch of the Queens House of Detention immediately touching off similar revolts in other city jails around New York. At Long Island a number of hostages were taken and

---

[10]Robert Minton and Stephen Rice, "Race War at San Quentin," *Ramparts* 8 (January, 1970), pp. 18–24.

a list of demands issued. The central demands concerned issues of bail and speedier trials. The prisoners' negotiating committee which presented the demands, identified themselves only as "revolutionaries." The committee included four blacks, one Puerto Rican, and one white. They demanded immediate bail hearings on forty-seven cases they had selected as examples of the racism involved in the granting of bail. A group of individuals with whom the inmates had asked to meet, attempted to persuade them to give up this demand and release the hostages.[11] In addition, Mayor Lindsay attempted to assure them that such a demand was unnecessary because a complete review of the bail system was to be undertaken in the courts "within a week." He also suggested that force would be used immediately if the prisoners did not capitulate. The prisoners refused to be persuaded or intimidated. Victor Martinez of the negotiating committee told newsmen, "Unless that pig judge appears here you will never see those hostages alive".[12] Subsequently, three state supreme court judges held hearings inside the jail on thirteen cases; nine paroles and four reductions in bail were granted.

Several of the demands related to the Panther 21,[13] then in jail and unable to pay the high bail, on conspiracy charges. A number of these Panthers were involved in the revolt. After the bail hearings, the hostages were released but some prisoners continued to hold out for the demand of a "jury of peers" for the Panthers and for bail for one of the defendants. The issues of bail and lengthy pre-trial detention had been chosen not only to assist the Panthers but also to dramatize to the public the inter-relationship among political repression, racism, and the refusal to grant reasonable bail. At this point, officials ordered the police to storm the jail with tear gas and clubs, and the revolt was crushed.

Within the next month, revolts broke out in the California prison system at Soledad, Folsom, and San Luis Obispo prisons. The Folsom work-stoppage of November, 1971, was the longest and most non-violent prison strike in the history of this country. Nearly all 2400 prisoners held out in their own cells for nineteen days in the face of constant hunger and discomfort and continued psychological and physical intimidation.

They issued a 31 point "Manifesto of Demands and Anti-Oppression Platform," labelling prisons the "Fascist Concentration Camps of Modern America" and calling for "an end to the injustice suffered by all prisoners, regardless of race, creed, or color." The demands focused on the denial of political and legal rights to prisoners and the exploitation involved in the work programs inside the prison.

---

[11]Herman Badillo, a former Bronx Borough President, Rep. Shirley Chisholm of Brooklyn, Manuel Caseano, ex-executive director of the office of the Commonwealth of Puerto Rico, Louis Farakham, a Black Muslim minister, and George McGrath, New York Corrections Commissioner.

[12]*The New York Times*, October 3, 1970, p. 58.

[13]In 1969 twenty-one black men and women were arrested on 156 counts of "conspiracy to commit murder," "arson" and various other charges. The Panther 21 trial, perhaps the longest criminal trial in the history of the United States, ended when the jury acquitted all the defendants of all 156 charges after deliberating for only 90 minutes.

In the months prior to the strike, inter-racial cooperation had been building among the prisoners. The Muslim group offered their help to Chicanos in the holding of a memorial service for a Chicano journalist killed by police in Los Angeles. After the service a number of the participants were attacked by guards and the Muslim minister was officially rebuked for having conducted the service.

After the strike began, the prisoners designated certain members of the radical community outside the prison to represent them in negotiations with authorities.[14] Prison officials refused to meet with these negotiators and even refused to admit that a united strike was occurring.

After 19 days the strike was finally broken through a combination of force and deception. One prisoner described the collapse of the strike this way:

The strike was broken *not* because the prisoners had become disenchanted. The Collective Spirit and optimism were too real to make me believe that the prisoners went to work as a result of disillusionment. Two-thousand men don't strike for 19 days and then suddenly become disenchanted. Only the most naive fools would believe that such a thing could happen. Therefore it is only logical that devious means were employed to break the strike.

It is clear as crystal that Craven (the warden at Folsom) used political deception and brute force to get the prisoners to go back to work. On the 23rd of November (Monday morning the day the strike was broken) the prison pigs, armed with rifles and wooden clubs, stopped in front of each man's cell and ordered each man back to work. Of course the order was weighted down with the threat of violence. Not wanting to be shot or clubbed to death, the prisoner naturally complied with the pigs' vicious method of brute force.

In Building One, one of Craven's inmate agents drew up several reactionary leaflets and circulated them throughout the building (Building One is where "Kitchen Row" is located). The leaflets, which were passed from cell to cell by the inmates, said that the kitchen workers were supposed to go back to work so that the prisoners could start eating hot meals. Because so many legitimate leaflets and notes were being circulated throughout Building One, the inmates in that building naturally assumed that those reactionary leaflets were the real thing. This was the method used to get the kitchen workers back to work.

After the suppression of the strike, four prisoners were singled out for a brutal 14 hour ride to another prison, shackled and naked on the floor of a van. Another 52 were thrown into the hole. In spite of all this, many prisoners felt that the strike was a success. One prisoner wrote:

The strike may have fallen short of our goal, but it was not a failure. We accomplished something that has never been accomplished before. Not just the record length, but more important is that the spirit of awareness has grown, and our people begin to look around and see what's happening. The seed

[14]Sal Candelaria (Brown Berets), Huey P. Newton (Black Panther Party), Charles Garry (3rd World Legal Defense Counsel) and a representative from the California Prisoner's Union.

has been planted and grows. If we have accomplished nothing else, we have accomplished this. Let this knowledge at least console you from the disheartening news you received that the strike was broke.[15]

The demands of the Folsom strike became the model (sometimes on a word-for-word basis) for the demands of the striking prisoners at Attica State Prison in Attica, New York. The Attica Liberation Front had been formed in May, 1971, around twenty-nine demands centering on prisoners' rights to organize politically and economically, and on living and working conditions. Included was a demand that the warden be fired. A negotiating committee met with officials several times but the officials did nothing about the prisoners' grievances.

On September 9 several hundred prisoners captured the prison yard and seized numerous guards as hostages. Their numbers swelled immediately to 1500, and two demands were added to the original list: transportation to a non-imperialist country for those who wished it (later dropped), and total amnesty for participants in the action. Discipline and an operating support system were quickly organized in the yard. Leadership was chosen from the Panthers, Young Lords, Muslims, radical whites, and other groups.

Negotiations around the demands soon came down to the issues of amnesty and the resignation of the warden. These demands focus the political nature of the revolt. If granted, they would have established the precedents that prisoners have a right to participation (if not control) in the process of choosing who rules them, and that they have a right to rebel without fear of punishment. Both prisoners and officials knew that these issues were at stake and that the implications went far beyond the walls of Attica.

The demand for amnesty in particular indicates the political progression of prisoner revolts from twenty years earlier. Increasingly the demand for a guarantee against reprisal is being replaced by a demand for amnesty. The term "amnesty" denotes a relationship between political actors; the term "reprisal" implies a power relationship independent of specific political conditions. More important than the semantics is the fact that amnesty is becoming one of the central demands in prisoner revolts. It was over this demand that the Attica negotiations broke down. Inmates and administrators alike are coming to realize the political significance of this demand. Prisoners are no longer looking only for personal protection; they are seeking the legitimization of a political tool.

The prisoners at Attica had no trust in the officials they were dealing with. From past experience they knew that whatever promises were made by the warden would later be revoked; hence the demands for his removal had implications beyond his personality. The prisoners' only hope lay with whatever power the Observers Committee may have had to win concessions for them and to follow them up. In the end it was shown that the Committee had no power; they were not even informed of the impending attack by state troopers.

In the short period of its heyday, the Attica Liberation Front exemplified

---

[15]From a letter to an Oakland, California attorney.

several aspects of the new prison revolution. The overcoming of mistrust and hatred between black and white prisoners was the crucial development which allowed the Attica prisoners to live by their slogan, "The Solution is Unity." All reports indicate that there was complete racial harmony in the yard. Journalist Tom Wicker, a member of the Observers Committee, noted:

The racial harmony that prevailed among the prisoners — it was absolutely astonishing . . . That prison yard was the first place I have ever seen where there was no racism.[16]

A week after the massacre, prisoners at Attica smuggled out a statement discussing the revolt and placing it in the context of a revolutionary struggle against American capitalism. It concluded,

These brothers whose lives were taken by Rockefeller and his agents did not die in vain. Why? Because the uprising at Attica did not begin here nor will it end here.[17]

The revolutionary prison movement, still in its infancy, has several characteristics, then, which set it apart from earlier movements. To the traditional and still unwon demands for decent food, shelter, and health care, have been added demands that challenge both the ideology and structure of the prison system and larger society. Prisoners are collectively articulating what was once expressed in a less articulate way by loosely-knit groups of individuals. The leadership of these collective groups is based on mutual consent and an apportioning of responsibilities among various racial and political groups, as an indication not only of the strategy of unity but also as a concrete manifestation of its practicality. Organizing inside the prison goes on around education: education involving the acquisition of simple tools such as reading and writing and education involving the sophisticated political writings of past and present revolutionaries. The new movement addresses its demands to the people of the world, calling on them to assist in their own liberation through support for prisoners. The movement operates in conjunction with outside support groups and groups of ex-prisoners which see their task as bringing support to the prisoners in whatever way possible. As George Jackson concluded:

Only the prison movement has shown any promise of cutting across the ideological, racial, and cultural barricades that have blocked the natural coalition of left-wing forces at all times in the past. So this movement must be used to provide an example for the partisans engaged at other levels of struggle.[18]

In addition, these outside groups focus independent attacks on the prison system, the court system, the legal and medical professions, and the corporate sys-

---

[16]Tom Wicker wrote a number of articles for the New York Times about the Attica uprising in which he stressed the racial solidarity that prevailed. One of the most interesting was " 'Unity.' A Haunting Echo from Attica," *New York Times,* September 15, 1971, p. 1.

[17]*The Berkeley Tribe,* October 1–7. 1971, p. 10.

[18]George Jackson, *Blood in My Eye* (New York: Random House, 1972), p. 109.

tem, all of which contribute to and benefit from the exploitation of prisoners. For example, the Medical Committee for Human Rights is investigating the use of drugs to tranquilize and torture militant prisoners and the use of prisoners for the experimentation of new drugs by the multi-billion dollar drug industry.

The crucial measurement of the advancement represented by the current movement in prisons is its level of political articulation. The rioters of the 1950's were not conscious of the similarities between their protest and the level of protest in the larger society. Today's revolutionaries are not only conscious of that connection, but strive to make it more complete. The current movement offers a class analysis of American society which sees prisons not only as an institution for class control in the United States but also as part of the global system of class control called imperialism. The movement grounds its activity in this analysis and is based on inter-racial and international solidarity. It represents the development of the revolutionary potential of the most exploited part of the working class, the wretched of the earth, with that forsaken class providing both leadership and analysis for the larger movement. To the degree that these things are true even in the face of incredible repression, the prisoners' struggle today is in the forefront of the revolutionary movement in America.

At the same time, it is clear that many prisoners are not revolutionaries, and that those who are politicized have not solved all their own problems with racism or sexism. The movement as a whole is still grappling with these problems.

As prisoners have moved from riot towards revolution, the state has responded with an intensification of repression. At this point, the direction that this repression will take is not completely clear, although certain features can be discerned. It is linked with the intensified repression in the society in general: the death of George Jackson in San Quentin immediately brings to mind the murders of Fred Hampton and Mark Clark in Chicago.[19]

The indications are that the basic technique of preventing rebellion will continue to be the division of prisoners against each other particularly along racial lines. Promises of early parole and good treatment and threats of torture or denial of parole will be used against prisoners to prevent them from participating in political activity. When such tactics fail and a revolt does occur, the prison will continue to turn to intense repression to deal with the situation: transfers, torture, assassination, officially sponsored racial violence, and other forms of crisis-management.

However, the growth of the prisoners' movement with widespread outside support is limiting the effectiveness of these tactics of preventing and repressing

---

[19]On December 4, 1970 fourteen special police, acting on the orders of State's Attorney Edward Hanrahan, raided the Illinois Chapter of the Black Panther Party. Deputy Chairman Fred Hampton was murdered by the police while he slept, and Mark Clark, also a Black Panther, was critically wounded and died shortly thereafter. Hanrahan described the incident as a shoot-out, and said police fired only after the Black Panthers had fired several volleys at the police. However, subsequent investigations revealed that the police had fired approximately 99 shots, and that the Panthers *might* have fired one shot. As other evidence was uncovered, it became clear that Hanrahan had lied and that Hampton and Clark had not been killed in a "shoot-out" but rather had been deliberately murdered. Despite the efforts of a number of government officials to prevent any action from being taken against Hanrahan, he and eight police were indicted in August, 1971, for "obstructing justice."

revolts. The diffusion of political consciousness among prisoners is making it more difficult for officials to manipulate prisoners against each other. The use of differential rewards and punishments to prevent prisoners from cooperating with militants may still work since all prisoners are at the mercy of the system and not all are strong enough to resist completely. But an increasing number of prisoners are turning their backs on bribes and threats. And, because of increased public consciousness and alertness about prisons, especially after the murders at Attica and San Quentin, it is becoming more difficult for prison officials to hide or defend the practice of mass murder and torture behind the walls.

Because of these developments, the prison system is looking for new techniques of dealing with prison disturbances. A dim outline of the "prison of the future" is emerging. It is based on the application of sophisticated techniques of medicine and social science to solve the "problem" of prisons. These techniques include mind-altering drugs and brain surgery designed to eliminate violent, "anti-social" characteristics, and electric shocks and pain inducing drugs designed to "negatively condition" prisoners. These techniques may be clothed in the respectability of psychiatry, but they represent the same basic effort to control the lives of recalcitrant prisoners.

Along with these new techniques, we are beginning to see the rise of a new breed of penologist: liberal, academically trained and sophisticated enough to understand the revolutionary movement and its appeal to prisoners. He will attempt to undercut that revolution through "far-reaching reforms" attempting to remove the boredom and frustration from daily prison life. He will understand and sympathize with the drives of members of Third World nationalities for cultural and racial identity. He will talk about opening "lines of communication" and "sharing power with responsible inmates." Yet, all this time he will be ready and willing to use whatever force is necessary to deal with prisoners who do not coooperate with the system, and his ultimate goal will be the maintenance of a prison system whose primary purpose is the integration of prisoners into the existing social order; for him, rehabilitation will still mean passive conformity. With these new techniques and with these new prison administrators, the "liberal totalitarianism" of American prisons will become an even more pervasive reality.

The construction of such liberal horror chambers in prisons has implications for the society as a whole. Just as drugs are used on rebellious prisoners, so too tranquilizers are being used to control "troublesome and overactive" children in school. Just as prison officials have proposed the increased use of electronic technology to maintain constant surveillance of prisoners (closed-circuit television, electronic sensing devices, etc.), so too the FBI and local police have stepped up the use of "bugging" and "wire-tapping." More and more people are coming to see that they are not free, but merely prisoners in the "minimum security" wing of the same prison in which prisoners are held in "maximum security." The rise of a revolutionary movement among prisoners is inseparable from the rise of a larger revolutionary movement in America and around the world; so too is its fate.

17. Anthony Platt

The Triumph of Benevolence: The Origins of the Juvenile Justice System in the United States

Introduction: The Ideology of Criminology

This essay re-examines some myths about the origins and development of legal and institutional controls over juvenile delinquency in the United States. Special attention will be given to (1) ideological assumptions underlying traditional analysis of the juvenile justice system, (2) the importance and uses of historical analysis, and (3) the demystification of "official" history. The interpretive framework for this analysis is the child-saving movement at the end of the nineteenth century.

The prevailing ideology which underlies most research and theory in criminology is liberalism. Although there is also a tradition of more conservative thinking (typified by the work of Ernest Hooton, Edward Banfield and Ralph Schwitzgebel) as well as radical thought (exemplified by Clarence Darrow, Angela Davis and George Jackson), it is the liberals who dominate the field of criminology — writing the most influential literature, serving as governmental consultants, staffing local and national commissions, working in think tanks, and acting as brokers for large agencies and foundations. The ideology of liberalism is by no means monolithic nor consistent, but many of its domain assumptions are articulated and shared by professional and academic criminologists.

First, most writers assume a legal definition of crime, taking as their initial reference point the legal code as the subject matter of investigation and analysis.[1] Criminology has been and continues to be predominantly concerned with the background and control of legally defined and prosecuted "criminals." The "rehabilitative ideal" has so dominated American criminology that, comparatively speaking, the officially constituted agencies of the criminal law have not been subjected to serious criticism and research.[2] The positivist heritage in criminology, as David Matza has observed, serves to direct attention to the "abnormal" aspects of criminal behavior and to the construction of methods of social control.[3]

Published by permission of the author. Copyright 1974, Anthony M. Platt.

[1]For an extended discussion of this issue, see Herman & Julia Schwendinger, "Defenders of Order or Guardians of Human Rights?," 5 *Issues in Criminology*, (Summer, 1970), pp. 123–157.

[2]Francis A. Allen, *The Borderland of Criminal Justice* (Chicago: University of Chicago, 1964), pp. 125–127.

[3]David Matza, *Delinquency and Drift* (New York: John Wiley, 1964), chapter I.

Criminology as an academic discipline has typically reflected and reinforced the values of the State: in the late nineteenth century, it provided the brain trust and technical skills for major changes in legal and penal institutions; in the early part of this century, it helped to develop and legitimize bureaucratic professionalism and centralized forms of administration; and more recently, following widespread political conflict and rebellion in the 1960s, it proposed ways of refining and rationalizing the criminal justice system. In accepting the State and legal definition of crime, the scope of analysis has been constrained to exclude behavior which is not legally defined as "crime" (for example, imperialism, exploitation, racism and sexism) as well as behavior which is not typically prosecuted (for example, tax-evasion, price-fixing, consumer fraud, police homicides, etc.). The most serious crimes against the people, as the American Friends Service Committee noted, have been seriously neglected:

Actions that clearly ought to be labeled "criminal," because they bring the greatest harm to the greatest number, are in fact accomplished officially by agencies of government. The overwhelming number of murders in this century has been committed by governments in wartime. Hundreds of unlawful killings by police go unprosecuted each year. The largest forceful acquisitions of property in the United States has been the theft of lands guaranteed by treaty to Indian tribes, thefts sponsored by the government. The largest number of dislocations, tantamount to kidnapping — the evacuation and internment of Japanese-Americans during World War II — was carried out by the government with the approval of the courts. Civil rights demonstrators, struggling to exercise their constitutional rights, have been repeatedly beaten and harrassed by police and sheriffs. And in the Vietnam war America has violated its Constitution and international law.[4]

A second component of liberalism is reformism; reform of criminals, reform of the criminal justice system, and even reform of society has always been a central goal of criminology. What distinguishes liberal reformism from more fundamental criticisms of American society is the belief that it is possible to create a well-regulated, stable and humanitarian system of criminal justice under the present economic and political arrangements. While it is true that criminologists have subjected social control institutions (police, courts, prisons, etc.) to a variety of criticisms — including inefficiency, mismanagement, corruption, and brutality — their reform proposals are invariably formulated within the framework of corporate capitalism and designed to shape new adjustments to existing political and economic conditions.[5]

Liberal reformism in criminology supports the extension of welfare state capitalism and gradualist programs of amelioration, while rejecting radical and violent forms of social and political change. This is often accompanied by a

---

[4]American Friends Service Committee, *Struggle for Justice*, (New York: Hill & Wang, 1971), pp. 10–11.

[5]See, generally, Alvin W. Gouldner, "The Sociologist as Partisan: Sociology and the Welfare State," 3 *American Sociologist*, (May, 1968), pp. 103–116.

reliance on technocratic solutions to social problems and a belief that progress will occur through enlightening managers and policy-makers rather than by organizing the oppressed.[6] This kind of reformism has helped to create probation and parole, the juvenile court system, reformatories and half-way houses, the indeterminate sentence, adjustment and diagnostic centers, public defenders, youth service bureaus and many other "reforms" which have served to strengthen the power of the State over the poor, Third World communities and youth. As the American Friends Service Committee has observed, "the legacy of a century of reform effort is an increasingly repressive penal system and overcrowded courts dispensing assembly-line justice."[7]

A third quality of liberalism in criminology is a rejection of general theory and macroscopic historical analysis, in favor of an emphasis on behaviorism, pragmatism and social engineering. The pragmatic perspective, as Stanley Cohen has observed in a critique of British criminology, is typically anti-theoretical and relativistic, seeing some good in all approaches and adopting an indiscriminate eclecticism.[8] This has led to a narrowing of scientific interest, to provincialism and parochialism, and even to a certain amount of anti-intellectualism in much criminological research.

In an analysis of a recent book of essays on nineteenth-century urban history, Norman Birnbaum notes that "the United States, insofar as major aspects of its past are concerned, remains an unknown country."[9] Our ignorance of urban history is perhaps only surpassed by our ignorance of the origins and development of the criminal justice system and its relationship to economic and political conditions. The field of criminology is long overdue for serious historical scholarship. The history of the police is unwritten, with the exception of "house" histories and a few microscopic case studies; the history of the criminal courts has been systematically neglected; we know very little about the modern prison system, its variations over time, its relationship to other institutions, or its impact on the lives of prisoners; finally, we know even less about the nature and range of "criminal" behavior in the United States before the twentieth century, even though European scholars have demonstrated the value and insight of such studies.[10]

Finally, liberalism in criminology is often characterized by an underlying cynicism and a lack of passion. The technocratic tradition in criminology, typified by the *Journal of Criminal Law, Criminology and Police Science*, characteristi-

[6]Irving Louis Horowitz (Ed.), *The Rise and Fall of Project Camelot*, (Cambridge: M.I.T. Press, 1967), p. 353.

[7]American Friends Service Committee, *op. cit.*, p. 9.

[8]See, generally, Stanley Cohen, "Criminology and the Sociology of Deviance in Britain: A Recent History and a Current Report," Unpublished paper presented to the annual conference of the British Sociological Association, April 1971.

[9]Stephan Thernstrom and Richard Sennett (Eds.), *Nineteenth-Century Cities: Essays in the New Urban History* (New Haven: Yale University Press, 1969), p. 422.

[10]See, for example, George Rudé, *The Crowd in History: A Study of Popular Disturbances in France and England, 1730–1848*, (New York: John Wiley, 1964); E. P. Thompson, *The Making of the English Working Class*, (Middlesex, England: Pelican Books, 1968), especially pp. 59–83 and Eric J. Hobsbawm, *Primitive Rebels*, (New York: Norton, 1959).

cally encourages narrowly conceived, microscopic studies which fail to raise general moral and political questions about the nature of society. Even the more socially sensitive interactionist theorists are prone to a preoccupation with trivia and politically irresponsible hipsterism.[11] The criminological literature is for the most part dry, without passion, and replete with technical jargon. Criminologists are not reaching the general public with vital and exciting ideas, preferring instead to maintain an incestuous and closed discipline among professionals and academics. The most imaginative criminology has been written by "criminals" — Brendan Behan, Claude Brown, Eldridge Cleaver, Angela Davis, George Jackson and Sam Melville, to name a few.

The liberal emphasis on pragmatism, short-range solutions and ameliorism reveals an attitude of cynicism and defeatism concerning human potentiality and the possibility of far-ranging changes in society. This focus serves to exclude or underestimate the possibility of a radically different society in which cooperation replaces competition, where human values takes precedence over property values, where exploitation, racism and sexism are eliminated, and where basic human needs are fulfilled. Liberal cynicism serves to reinforce the malevolent view that radical change is utopian and visionary, thereby helping to impede the development of revolutionary social and political movements.

These four values — a legalistic definition of crime, a "weak" reformism, an anti-theoretical and anti-historical framework, and a susceptibility to cynicism — are not the accident of academic fashion but rather reflect fundamental relationships between the State, social institutions and the academic community. Of the many complex reasons for the prevalence of these values, the following four structural conditions appear to play an influential role.

(1) As Howard Zinn has pointed out, "there is an underside to every age about which history does not often speak, because history is written from the records left by the privileged. We learn about politics form the political leaders, about economics from the entrepreneurs, about slavery from the plantation owners, about the thinking of an age from its intellectual elite."[12] Similarly, we learn about the criminal justice system from judges, prison wardens, the police and government consultants. This is especially true of the earlier development of American criminology when research and study were for the most part monopolized by persons intimately concerned with the regulation of crime. This scholar-technician tradition helped to produce a great deal of managerially oriented research and "official" history, that is a history written by the managers of and spokesmen for the criminal justice agencies. The emphasis in liberal analysis on pragmatism, professionalism and technocratic solutions is partly explained by this scholar-technician relationship.

(2) The source and conditions of contemporary research funding are a significant indicator of liberal analysis. Much criminological research is "agency-

---

[11]See, for example, critiques by Gouldner, *loc. cit.* and in Barry Krisberg's book review of Laud Humphreys, *Tearoom Trade* in 7 *Issues in Criminology*, (Winter, 1972), pp. 126–127.

[12]Howard Zinn, *The Politics of History* (Boston: Beacon Press, 1970), p. 102.

determined'' and subordinated to institutional interests, whereby the formulation of research problems, the scope of inquiry, and the conditions of funding are determined by the ''agency'' rather than by scholars.[13] The Ford Foundation has poured millions of dollars into carefully specified action-research in various criminal justice centers throughout the country. President Johnson's Crime Commission and several ''riot'' commissions provided work and predetermined problems for hundreds of lawyers and social scientists.[14] Another example of agency-determined research is the Law Enforcement Assistance Administration in the Department of Justice, created by the Safe Streets Act in 1968 with a budget of 63 million dollars, which is scheduled to be funding ''acceptable'' research and programs with an estimated budget of 1.75 billion dollars in 1973.[15]

The rise of the ''multiversity'' in recent years as a broker between scholars and funding agencies has served to strengthen and institutionalize relationships in which scholars are encouraged to formulate research programs which are of interest and politically acceptable to established agencies.[16] The research marketplace, dominated by large foundations and the government, is thus structured in such a way that research grants, prestige, facilities and other fringe benefits are more easily achieved by scholars who are willing to work on behalf of the State and its official institutions.

There are at least three major ethical dangers in agency-determined research, as Herbert Blumer has pointed out. First, it imposes restrictions on the freedom of scientific inquiry by predetermining the problems to be studied and by inhibiting academics from examining distasteful or controversial issues outside a particular range of possibilities. Secondly, notes Blumer, it is ''prone to treat lightly the interests and claims of people who are the objects of study or whose lives are to be changed by applying the results of the study. The interests and needs of the agency on whose behalf the research is to be undertaken have priority in governing the research enterprise.'' And, thirdly, agency-determined research tends to have a corrupting influence on scholars through the lure of research grants, travel, prestige and other benefits.[17] Accordingly, much of what passes as scholarly research in criminology tends to avoid issues which may lead to structural criticisms of American society and instead caters to facilitating the efficient and smooth operation of established systems.

(3) While it is true that criminological research has been dominated by professional and funding interests, it should also be recognized that academics have generally been willing, even enthusiastic, victims of this kind of relationship.

---

[13]Herbert Blumer, ''Threats from Agency-Determined Research: The Case of Camelot,'' in Horowitz (Ed.), *op. cit.*, pp. 153–74.

[14]On the role of social scientists in riot commissions, see Anthony Platt, *The Politics of Riot Commissions, 1917–1970*, (New York: Macmillan, 1971), pp. 3–54.

[15]Joseph C. Goulden, ''The Cops Hit the Jackpot,'' *The Nation* (November 23, 1970), pp. 520–533.

[16]See, for example, Clark Kerr, *The Uses of the University*, (New York: Anchor, 1961).

[17]Blumer, *op. cit.*, p. 165.

The image of social scientists as value-free technical experts ready for hire is one which social scientists have themselves helped to build. There are many criminologists who are not only willing to do "agency-determined" research but also share the agency's perspective on the problem to be studied.[18] The "diluted liberalism," to use C. Wright Mills' apt term, of most research on juvenile delinquency, for example, results from the fact that researchers are typically prepared to accept prevailing (i.e., State) definitions of crime, to work within the premises of the criminal law, and to concur at least implicitly with those who make and enforce laws as to the nature and distribution of the "criminal" population.

Compared with the role played by economists, political scientists and anthropologists in the formulation of domestic and foreign policies, criminologists have traditionally had minimum influence on national policy-making. This is quickly changing, however, as foundations and government agencies are now turning to criminologists for their expert help in developing new forms of social control following the political rebellions of the 1960s.[19] The willingness of academics to lend themselves to these kinds of demands arises from their occupational marginality and insecurity, as well as from their limited and specialized view of the world. The marginality of criminology as an academic discipline makes it vulnerable to "agency-determined" research and cooptation by funding agencies. Furthermore, the training of most criminologists, with its emphasis on technical virtuosity and narrow specialization, serves to insulate them from broader considerations about the ethical and political consequences of their work.

(4) Finally, it should be remembered that many agencies within the criminal justice system (especially the police and prisons) are politically sensitive communities which resist intrusions from academic outsiders unless the proposed research is likely to serve their best interests. Research which undermines established policy is generally viewed as insensitive or subversive, aside from the fact that it serves to justify and harden administrators' suspicions of "intellectuals."[20] Most workers in the criminal justice system are linked to a professional system that relegates them to the lowest status in occupational and political hierarchies but also makes them vulnerable to public and political scandals. They are society's "dirty workers," according to Lee Rainwater, who are "increasingly caught between the silent middle class, which wants them to do the dirty work and keep quiet about it, and the objects of that dirty work, who refuse to continue to take it lying down."[21] They are doomed to annual investigations, blue-ribbon commis-

---

[18]For an analogous critique of the impact of intellectuals on American foreign policy, see Noam Chomsky, *American Power and the New Mandarins* (New York: Pantheon Books, 1967).

[19]See, for example, Lee Webb, "Back Home: The Campus Beat" and Mike Klare, "Bringing It Back: Planning for the City," in National Action/Research on the Military-Industrial Complex, *Police on the Homefront,* (Philadelphia: American Friends Service Committee, 1971), pp. 1–20, 66–73.

[20]Controversial studies of official criminal justice agencies run the risk of hampering further academic investigations, as was apparently the case with Jerome Skolnick's study of a California police department, *Justice Without Trial* (New York: John Wiley, 1966).

[21]Lee Rainwater, "The Revolt of the Dirty-Workers," 5 *Trans-action* (November, 1967), p. 2.

sions, ephemeral research studies, and endless volumes of propaganda and muck-raking. They live with the inevitability of professional mediocrity, poor salaries, uncomfortable living conditions, ungrateful "clients," and tenuous links with established institutions. It is understandable why they protect their fragile domain from intrusive research which is not supportive of their policies.

These four structural conditions — the scholar-technician tradition, agency-determined research, the acquiescence and vulnerability of academics, and the resistance of criminal justice agencies to critical research — underlie criminological ideology in general and play a specific role in legitimizing the juvenile justice system. This essay examines liberal criminological stereotypes about the history of the juvenile system and offers some alternative interpretations.

Accurate historical analysis should, *inter alia*, demystify the past by explaining how false ideologies are used to legitimize oppression and exploitation.[22] This is often a difficult and challenging enterprise, for economic and political elites have been very successful in using the mass media and educational systems for celebrating and mystifying prevailing ideologies.[23] But criminologists can learn a great deal from historians in other fields who have committed themselves to demystifying the past. For example, Herbert Aptheker's *American Negro Slave Revolts* refuted myths about the systematic passivity and apathy of slaves;[24] Melville Herskovits' study of *The Myth of the Negro Past* similarly refuted sterotypes about the inferior and deficient cultural background of Black Americans;[25] in the field of economics and political theory, the work of persons like C. Wright Mills, Paul Baran, Paul Sweezy, James Weinstein, Gabriel Kòlko, Harry Magdoff, and Ralph Miliband (to name a few) has begun to offer alternative explanations to standard glorifications of the American past,[26] and in foreign policy, anti-war protest has helped to produce radically new understandings of imperialism and economic expansion,[27] as well as revelations about governmental duplicity at home.[28]

Traditional Perspectives on Juvenile Justice

The modern system of crime control in the United States has many roots in penal and judicial reforms at the end of the nineteenth century. Contemporary programs

[22]*Zinn, op. cit.*, pp. 35–55.

[23]On the social control functions of high school, see Edgar Z. Friedenberg, *Coming of Age in America*, (New York: Random House, 1965); on cultural indoctrination, see Norman Birnbaum, *The Crisis of Industrial Society*, (New York: Oxford University, 1969).

[24]Herbert Aptheker, *American Negro Slave Revolts*, (New York: Columbia University Press, 1943).

[25]Melville J. Herskovits, *The Myth of the Negro Past,* (Boston: Beacon Press, 1941).

[26]In addition to those cited elsewhere, see C. Wright Mills, *The Power Elite*, (New York: Oxford University Press, 1956); Paul A. Baran and Paul M. Sweezy, *Monopoly Capital*, (New York: Monthly Review Press, 1966); and Harry Magdoff, *The Age of Imperialism*, (New York: Monthly Review Press, 1968).

[27]See, for example, Felix Greene, *The Enemy: What Every American Should Know about Imperialism*, (New York: Vintage, 1971).

[28]The New York Times (ed.), *The Pentagon Papers*, (New York: Bantam Books, 1971).

which we commonly associate with the "war on poverty" and the "great society" can be traced in numerous instances to the programs and ideas of nineteenth century reformers who helped to create and develop probation and parole, the juvenile court, strategies of crime prevention, the need for education and rehabilitative programs in institutions, the indeterminate sentence, the concept of "half-way" houses, and "cottage" systems of penal organization.

The creation of the juvenile court and its accompanying services is generally regarded by scholars as one of the most innovative and idealistic products of the age of reform. It typified the "spirit of social justice," and, according to the National Crime Commission, represented a progressive effort by concerned reformers to alleviate the miseries of urban life and to solve social problems by rational, enlightened and scientific methods.[29] The juvenile justice system was widely heralded as "one of the greatest advances in child welfare that has ever occurred" and "an integral part of total welfare planning."[30] Charles Chute, an enthusiastic supporter of the child-saving movement, claimed that "no single event has contributed more to the welfare of children and their families. It revolutionized the treatment of delinquent and neglected children and led to the passage of similar laws throughout the world."[31] Scholars from a variety of disciplines, such as the American sociologist George Herbert Mead and the German psychiatrist August Aichhorn, agreed that the juvenile court system represented a triumph of progressive liberalism over the forces of reaction and ignorance.[32] More recently, the juvenile court and related reforms have been characterized as a "reflection of the humanitarianism that flowered in the last decades of the 19th century"[33] and an indication of "America's great sense of philanthropy and private concern about the common weal."[34]

Histories and accounts of the child-saving movement tend either to represent an "official" perspective or to imply a gradualist view of social progress.[35] This

---

[29]See, for example, The President's Commission on Law Enforcement and Administration of Justice, *Juvenile Delinquency and Youth Crime* (Washington D.C.: U.S. Government Printing Office, 1967), pp. 2–4.

[30]Charles L. Chute, "The Juvenile Court in Retrospect," 13 *Federal Probation* (September, 1949), p. 7; Harrison A. Dobbs, "In Defense of Juvenile Court," *Ibid.*, p. 29.

[31]Charles L. Chute, "Fifty Years of the Juvenile Court," *National Probation and Parole Association Yearbook* (1949), p. 1.

[32]George H. Mead, "The Psychology of Punitive Justice," 23 *American Journal of Sociology* (March, 1918), pp. 577–602; August Aichhorn, "The Juvenile Court: Is It a Solution?", in *Delinquency and Child Guidance: Selected Papers* (New York: International Universities Press, 1964), pp. 55–79.

[33]Murray Levine and Adeline Levine, *A Social History of Helping Services: Clinic, Court, School, and Community* (New York: Appleton-Century-Crofts, 1970), p. 156.

[34]Gerhard O. W. Mueller, *History of American Criminal Law Scholarship* (New York: Walter E. Meyer Research Institute of Law, 1962), p. 113.

[35]See, for example, Herbert H. Lou, *Juvenile Courts in the United States* (Chapel Hill: University of North Carolina Press, 1927); Negley K. Teeters and John Otto Reinmann, *The Challenge of Delinquency* (New York: Prentice-Hall, 1950); and Ola Nyquist, *Juvenile Justice* (London: Macmillan, 1960).

latter view is typified in Robert Pickett's study of the House of Refuge movement in New York in the middle of the last century:

In the earlier era, it had taken a band of largely religiously motivated humanitarians to see a need and move to meet that need. Although much of their vision eventually would be supplanted by more enlightened policies and techniques and far more elaborate support mechanisms, the main outlines of their program, which included mild discipline, academic and moral education, vocational training, the utilization of surrogate parents, and probationary surveillance, have stood the test of time. The survival of many of the notions of the founders of the House of Refuge testifies, at least in part, to their creative genius in meeting human needs. Their motivations may have been mixed and their oversights many, but their efforts contributed to a considerable advance in the care and treatment of wayward youth.[36]

This view of the nineteenth century reform movement as fundamentally benevolent, humanitarian and gradualist is shared by most historians and criminologists who have written about the Progressive era. They argue that this reform impulse has its roots in the earliest ideals of modern liberalism and that it is part of a continuing struggle to overcome injustice and fulfill the promise of American life.[37] At the same time, these writers recognize that reform movements often degenerate into crusades and suffer from excessive idealism and moral absolutism.[38] The faults and limitations of the child-saving movement, for example, are generally explained in terms of the psychological tendency of its leaders to adopt attitudes of rigidity and moral righteousness. But this form of criticism is misleading because it overlooks larger political issues and depends too much on a subjective critique.

Although the Progressive era was a period of considerable change and reform in all areas of social, legal, political and economic life, its history has been garnished with various myths. Conventional historical analysis, typified by the work of American historians in the 1940s and 1950s, promoted the view that American history consisted of regular confrontations between vested economic interests and various popular reform movements.[39] For Arthur Schlesinger, Jr., "liberalism in America has been ordinarily the movement of the other sections of society to restrain the power of the business community."[40] Similarly, Louis Hartz characterizes "liberal reform" as a "movement which emerged toward the end

[36]Robert S. Pickett, *House of Refuge: Origins of Juvenile Reform in New York State, 1815–1857* (Syracuse: Syracuse University Press, 1969), p. 188.
[37]See, for example, Arthur M. Schlesinger, *The American as Reformer* (Cambridge: Harvard University Press, 1950).
[38]See, for example, Richard Hofstadter, *The Age of Reform* (New York: Vintage Books, 1955) and Joseph R. Gusfield, *Symbolic Crusade: Status Politics and the American Temperance Movement* (Urbana: University of Illinois Press, 1963).
[39]R. Jackson Wilson (Ed.) *Reform, Crisis, and Confusion, 1900–1929* (New York: Random House, 1970), especially pp. 3–6.
[40]Arthur M. Schlesinger, Jr., *The Age of Jackson* (Boston: Little, Brown, 1946), p. 505.

of the nineteenth century to adapt classical liberalism to the purposes of small propertied interests and the labor class and at the same time which rejected socialism.''[41]

Conventional histories of progressivism argue that the reformers, who were for the most part drawn from the urban middle classes, were opposed to big business and felt victimized by the rapid changes in the economy, especially the emergence of the corporation as the dominant form of financial enterprise.[42] Their reform efforts were aimed at curbing the power of big business, eliminating corruption from the urban political machines, and extending the powers of the state through federal regulation of the economy and the development of a vision of "social responsibility" in local government. They were joined in this mission by sectors of the working class who shared their alienation and many of their grievances. For liberal historians like Richard Hofstadter, this alliance represented part of a continuing theme in American politics:

It has been the function of the liberal tradition in American politics, from the time of Jeffersonian democracy down through Populism, Progressivism, and the New Deal, at first to broaden the numbers of those who could benefit from the great American bonanza and then to humanize its workings and help heal its casualties. Without this sustained tradition of opposition and protest, and reform, the American system would have been, as in times and places it was, nothing but a jungle, and would probably have failed to develop into the remarkable system for production and distribution that it is.[43]

The political and racial crises of the 1960s, however, provoked a reevaluation of this earlier view of the liberal tradition in American politics, a tradition which appeared bankrupt in the face of rising crime rates, ghetto rebellions, and widespread protests against the state and its agencies of criminal justice. In the field of criminology, this reevaluation took place in national commissions such as the Kerner Commission and President Johnson's Commission on Law Enforcement and the Administration of Justice. Johnson's Crime Commission, as it is known, included a lengthy and detailed analysis of the juvenile justice system and its ineffectiveness in dealing with juvenile delinquency.

The Crime Commission's view of the juvenile justice system is cautious and pragmatic, designed to "shore up" institutional deficiencies and modernize the system's efficiency and accountability. Noting the rising rate of juvenile delinquency, increasing disrespect for constituted authority and the failure of reformatories to rehabilitate offenders, the Commission attributes the failures of the juvenile justice system to the "grossly overoptimistic" expectations of nineteenth century reformers and the "community's continuing unwillingness to provide the resources — the people and facilities and concern — necessary to permit [the

---

[41]Louis Hartz, *The Liberal Tradition in America* (New York: Harcourt, Brace & World, 1955), p. 228.
[42]Hofstadter, *op. cit.,* chapter IV.
[43]*Ibid.,* p. 18.

juvenile courts] to realize their potential. . . .''[44] This view of the *unrealistic* quality of American liberalism was observed earlier by Richard Hofstadter:

My criticism . . . is . . . not that the Progressives most typically undermined or smashed standards, but that they set impossible standards, that they were victimized, in brief, by a form of moral absolutism. . . . A great part of both the strength and the weaknesses of our national existence lies in the fact that Americans do not abide very quietly the evils of life. We are forever restlessly pitting ourselves against them, demanding changes, improvements, remedies, but not often with sufficient sense of the limits that the human condition will in the end insistently impose upon us.[45]

Or as the Crime Commission stated it, ''failure is most striking when hopes are highest.''[46]

In the following pages we will argue that the above views and interpretations of juvenile justice are factually inaccurate and suffer from a serious misconception about the functions of modern liberalism. The prevailing myths about the juvenile justice system can be summarized as follows: (1) The child-saving movement in the late nineteenth century was successful in humanizing the criminal justice system, rescuing children from jails and prisons, developing humanitarian judicial and penal institutions for juveniles, and defending the poor against economic and political exploitation. (2) The child-savers were ''disinterested'' reformers, representing an enlightened and socially responsible urban middle class, and opposed to big business. (3) The failures of the juvenile justice system are attributable partly to the overoptimism and moral absolutism of earlier reformers and partly to bureaucratic inefficiency and a lack of fiscal resources and trained personnel.

These myths are grounded in a liberal conception of American history which characterizes the child-savers as part of a much larger reform movement directed at restraining the power of political and business elites. In contrast, we will offer evidence that the child-saving movement was a coercive and conservatizing influence, that liberalism in the Progressive era was the conscious product of policies initiated or supported by leaders of major corporations and financial institutions, and that many social reformers wanted to secure existing political and economic arrangements, albeit in an ameliorated and regulated form.

The Child-Saving Movement

Although the modern juvenile justice system can be traced in part to the development of various charitable and institutional programs in the early nineteenth century,[47] it was not until the close of the century that the modern system was sys-

---

[44]The President's Commission on Law Enforcement and Administration of Justice, *op cit.*, pp. 7, 8.

[45]Hofstadter, *op. cit.*, p. 16.

[46]The President's Commission on Law Enforcement and Administration of Justice, *op. cit.*, p. 7.

[47]For discussions of earlier reform movements, see Pickett, *loc. cit.* and Sanford J. Fox, ''Juvenile Justice Reform: An Historical Perspective,'' 22 *Stanford Law Review*, (June, 1970), pp. 1187–1239.

tematically organized to include juvenile courts, probation, child guidance clinics, truant officers, and reformatories. The child-saving movement — an amalgam of philanthropists, middle-class reformers and professionals — was responsible for the consolidation of these reforms.[48]

The 1890s represented for many middle-class intellectuals and professionals a period of discovery of "dim attics and damp cellars in poverty-stricken sections of populous towns" and "innumerable haunts of misery throughout the land."[49] The city was suddenly discovered to be a place of scarcity, disease, neglect, ignorance, and "dangerous influences." Its slums were the "last resorts of the penniless and the criminal"; here humanity reached the lowest level of degradation and despair.[50] These conditions were not new to American urban life and the working class had been suffering such hardships for many years. Since the Haymarket Riot of 1886, the centers of industrial activity had been continually plagued by strikes, violent disruptions, and widespread business failures.

What distinguished the late 1890s from earlier periods was the recognition by some sectors of the privileged classes that far-reaching economic, political and social reforms were desperately needed to restore order and stability. In the economy, these reforms were achieved through the corporation which extended its influence into all aspects of domestic and foreign policies so that by the 1940s some 139 corporations owned 45 percent of all the manufacturing assets in the country. It was the aim of corporate capitalists to limit traditional laissez-faire business competition and to transform the economy into a rational and interrelated system, characterized by extensive long-range planning and bureaucratic routine.[51] In politics, these reforms were achieved nationally by extending the regulatory powers of the federal government and locally by the development of commission and city manager forms of government as an antidote to corrupt machine politics. In social life, economic and political reforms were paralleled by the construction of new social service bureaucracies which regulated crime, education, health, labor and welfare.

The child-saving movement tried to do for the criminal justice system what industrialists and corporate leaders were trying to do for the economy — that is, achieve order, stability and control while preserving the existing class system and distribution of wealth. While the child-saving movement, like most Progressive reforms, drew its most active and visible supporters from the middle class and professions, it would not have been capable of achieving significant reforms with-

---

[48]The child-saving movement was broad and diverse, including reformers interested in child welfare, education, reformatories, labor and other related issues. This paper is limited primarily to child-savers involved in anti-delinquency reforms and should not be interpreted as characterizing the child-saving movement in general.

[49]William P. Letchworth, "Children of the State," National Conference of Charities and Correction, *Proceedings* (St. Paul, Minnesota, 1886), p. 138.

[50]R.W. Hill, "The Children of Shinbone Alley," National Conference of Charities and Correction, *Proceedings* (Omaha, 1887), p. 231.

[51]William Appleman Williams, *The Contours of American History* (Chicago: Quadrangle Books, 1966), especially pp. 345–412.

out the financial and political support of the wealthy and powerful. Such support was not without precedent in various philanthropic movements preceding the child-savers. New York's Society for the Reformation of Juvenile Delinquents benefited in the 1820s from the contributions of Stephen Allen, whose many influential positions included Mayor of New York and president of the New York Life Insurance and Trust Company.[52] The first large gift to the New York Children's Aid Society, founded in 1853, was donated by Mrs. William Astor.[53] According to Charles Loring Brace, who helped to found the Children's Aid Society, "a very superior class of young men consented to serve on our Board of Trustees; men who, in their high principles of duty, and in the obligations which they feel are imposed by wealth and position, bid fair hereafter to make the name of New York merchants respected as it was never before throughout the country."[54] Elsewhere, welfare charities similarly benefited from the donations and wills of the upper class.[55] Girard College, one of the first large orphanages in the United States, was built and furnished with funds from the banking fortune of Stephen Girard;[56] and the Catholic bankers and financiers of New York helped to mobilize support and money for various Catholic charities.[57]

The child-saving movement similarly enjoyed the support of propertied and powerful individuals. In Chicago, for example, where the movement had some of its most notable successes, the child-savers included Louise Bowen and Ellen Henrotin who were both married to bankers;[58] Mrs. Potter Palmer, whose husband owned vast amounts of land and property, was an ardent child-saver when not involved in the exclusive Fortnightly Club, the elite Chicago Woman's Club or the Board of Lady Managers of the World's Fair;[59] another child-saver in Chicago, Mrs. Perry Smith, was married to the vice-president of the Chicago and Northwestern Railroad. Even the more radically-minded child-savers came from upper-class backgrounds. The fathers of Jane Addams and Julia Lathrop, for example, were both lawyers and Republican senators in the Illinois legislature. Jane Addams' father was one of the richest men in northern Illinois, and her stepbrother, Harry Haldeman, was a socialite from Baltimore who later amassed a large fortune in Kansas City.[60]

The child-saving movement was not simply a humanistic enterprise on behalf of the lower classes against the established order. On the contrary, its impetus

---

[52]Pickett, *op. cit.*, pp. 50–55.

[53]Committee on the History of Child-Saving Work, *History of Child-Saving in the United States* (National Conference of Charities and Correction, 1893), p. 5.

[54]Charles Loring Brace, *The Dangerous Classes of New York and Twenty Years' Work Among Them* (New York: Wynkoop and Hallenbeck, 1880), pp. 282–83.

[55]Committee on the History of Child-Saving Work, *op. cit.*, pp. 70–73.

[56]*Ibid.*, pp. 80–81.

[57]*Ibid.*, p. 270.

[58]For more about these child-savers, see Anthony Platt, *The Child-Savers: The Invention of Delinquency*, (Chicago: University of Chicago Press, 1969), pp. 75–100.

[59]Louise C. Wade, *Graham Taylor: Pioneer for Social Justice, 1851–1938* (Chicago: University of Chicago Press, 1964), p. 59.

[60]G. William Domhoff, *The Higher Circles: The Governing Class in America* (New York: Random House, 1970), p. 48 and Platt, *op. cit.*, pp.92–98.

came primarily from the middle and upper classes who were instrumental in devising new forms of social control to protect their privileged positions in American society. The child-saving movement was not an isolated phenomenon but rather reflected massive changes in productive relationships, from laissez-faire to monopoly capitalism, and in strategies of social control, from inefficient repression to welfare state benevolence.[61] This reconstruction of economic and social institutions, which was not achieved without conflict within the ruling class, represented a victory for the more "enlightened" wing of corporate leaders who advocated strategic alliances with urban reformers and support of liberal reforms.[62]

Many large corporations and business leaders, for example, supported federal regulation of the economy in order to protect their own investments and stabilize the marketplace. Business leaders and political spokesmen were often in basic agreement about fundamental economic issues. "There was no conspiracy during the Progressive Era," notes Gabriel Kôlko. "There was basic agreement among political and business leaders as to what was the public good, and no one had to be cajoled in a sinister manner."[63] In his analysis of liberal ideology in the Progressive era, James Weinstein similarly argues that "few reforms were enacted without the tacit approval, if not the guidance, of the large corporate interests." For the corporation executives, liberalism meant "the responsibility of all classes to maintain and increase the efficiency of the existing social order."[64]

Progressivism was in part a businessmen's movement and big business played a central role in the Progressive coalition's support of welfare reforms. Child labor legislation in New York, for example, was supported by several groups, including upper-class industrialists who did not depend on cheap child labor. According to Jeremy Felt's history of that movement, "the abolition of child labor could be viewed as a means of driving out marginal manufacturers and tenement operators, hence increasing the consolidation and efficiency of business."[65] The rise of compulsory education, another welfare state reform, was also closely tied to the changing forms of industrial production and social control. Charles Loring Brace, writing in the mid-nineteenth century, anticipated the use of education as preparation for industrial discipline when, "in the interests of

[61]"The transformation in penal systems cannot be explained only from changing needs of the war against crime, although this struggle does play a part. Every system of production tends to discover punishments which correspond to its productive relationships. It is thus necessary to investigate the origin and fate of penal systems, the use or avoidance of specific punishments, and the intensity of penal practices as they are determined by social forces, above all by economic and then fiscal forces." Georg Rusche and Otto Kirchheimer, *Punishment and Social Structure,* (New York: Russell & Russell, 1968), p. 5.

[62]See, for example, Gabriel Kolko, *The Triumph of Conservatism: A Reinterpretation of American History, 1900–1916* (Chicago: Quadrangle Books, 1967); James Weinstein, *The Corporate Ideal in the Liberal State, 1900–1918* (Boston: Beacon Press, 1969); Samuel Haber, *Efficiency and Uplift: Scientific Management in the Progressive Era, 1890–1920* (Chicago: University of Chicago Press, 1964); and Robert H. Wiebe, *Businessmen and Reform: A Study of the Progressive Movement* (Cambridge: Harvard University Press, 1962).

[63]Kolko, *op. cit.,* p. 282.

[64]Weinstein, *op. cit.,* pp. ix, xi.

[65]Jeremy P. Felt, *Hostages of Fortune: Child Labor Reform in New York State* (Syracuse: Syracuse University Press, 1965), p. 45.

public order, of liberty, of property, for the sake of our own safety and the endurance of free institutions here,'' he advocated ''a strict and careful law, which shall compel every minor to learn and read and write, under severe penalties in case of disobedience.''[66] By the end of the century, the working class had imposed upon them a sterile and authoritarian educational system which mirrored the ethos of the corporate workplace and was designed to provide ''an increasingly refined training and selection mechanism for the labor force.''[67]

While the child-saving movement was supported and financed by corporate liberals, the day-to-day work of lobbying, public education and organizing was undertaken by middle-class urban reformers, professionals and special interest groups. The more moderate and conservative sectors of the feminist movement were especially active in anti-delinquency reforms.[68] Their successful participation derived in part from public stereotypes of women as the ''natural caretakers'' of ''wayward children.'' Women's claim to the public care of children had precedent during the nineteenth century and their role in child rearing was paramount. Women, generally regarded as better teachers than men, were more influential in child-training and discipline at home. The fact that public education also came more under the direction of women teachers in the schools served to legitimize the predominance of women in other areas of ''child-saving.''[69]

The child-saving movement attracted women from a variety of political and class backgrounds, though it was dominated by the daughters of the old landed gentry and wives of the upper-class nouveau riche. Career women and society philanthropists, elite women's clubs and settlement houses, and political and civic organizations worked together on the problems of child care, education and juvenile delinquency. Professional and political women's groups regarded child-saving as a problem of women's rights, whereas their opponents seized upon it as an opportunity to keep women in their ''proper place.'' Child-saving became a reputable task for any woman who wanted to extend her ''housekeeping'' func-

---

[66]Brace, *op. cit.*, p. 352.

[67]David K. Cohen and Marvin Lazerson, ''Education and the Corporate Order,'' 8 *Socialist Revolution*, (March–April, 1972), p. 50. See, also Michael B. Katz, *The Irony of Early School Reform: Educational Innovation in Mid-Nineteenth Century Massachusetts*, (Cambridge: Harvard University Press, 1968), and Lawrence A. Cremin, *The Transformation of the School: Progressivism in American Education, 1876–1957*, (New York: Vintage, 1961).

[68]It should be emphasized that child-saving reforms were predominantly supported by more privileged sectors of the feminist movement, especially those who had an interest in developing professional careers in education, social work and probation. In recent years, radical feminists have emphasized that ''we must include the oppression of children in any program for feminist revolution or we will be subject to the same failing of which we have so often accused men: of not having gone deep enough in our analysis, of having missed an important substratum of oppression merely because it didn't directly concern *us*.'' Shulamith Firestone, *The Dialectic of Sex: The Case for Feminist Evolution*, (New York: Bantam, 1971), p. 104.

[69]Robert Sunley, ''Early Nineteenth Century American Literature on Child-Rearing,'' in Margaret Mead and Martha Wolfenstein (Eds.), *Childhood in Contemporary Cultures* (Chicago: University of Chicago Press, 1955), p. 152; see, also, Orville G. Brim, *Education for Child-Rearing* (New York: Free Press, 1965), pp. 321–49.

tions into the community without denying anti-feminist stereotypes of woman's nature and place.[70]

For traditionally educated women and daughters of the landed and industrial genty, the child-saving movement presented an opportunity for pursuing socially acceptable public roles and for restoring some of the authority and spiritual influence which many women felt they had lost through the urbanization of family life. Their traditional functions were dramatically threatened by the weakening of domestic roles and the specialized rearrangement of the family.[71] The child-savers were aware that their championship of social outsiders such as immigrants, the poor and children, was not wholly motivated by disinterested ideals of justice and equality. Philanthropic work filled a void in their own lives, a void which was created in part by the decline of traditional religion, increased leisure and boredom, the rise of public education, and the breakdown of communal life in large, crowded cities. "By simplifying dress and amusements, by cutting off a little here and there from our luxuries," wrote one child-saver, "we may change the whole current of many human lives."[72] Women were exhorted to make their lives useful by participating in welfare programs, by volunteering their time and services, and by getting acquainted with less privileged groups. They were also encouraged to seek work in institutions which were "like family-life with its many-sided development and varied interests and occupations, and where the woman-element shall pervade the house and soften its social atmosphere with motherly tenderness."[73]

While the child-saving movement can be partly understood as a "symbolic crusade"[74] which served ceremonial and status functions for many women, it was by no means a reactionary and romantic movement, nor was it supported only by women and members of the old gentry. Child-saving also had considerable instrumental significance for legitimizing new career openings for women. The new role of social worker combined elements of an old and partly fictitious role — defender of family life — and elements of a new role — social servant. Social work and professional child-saving provided new opportunities for career-minded women who found the traditional professions dominated and controlled by men.[75] These child-savers were members of the emerging bourgeoisie created by the new industrial order.

It is not surprising that the professions also supported the child-saving movement, for they were capable of reaping enormous economic and status rewards

---

[70]For an extended discussion of this issue, See Platt, *loc. cit.* and Christopher Lasch, *The New Radicalism in America, 1889–1963: The Intellectual as a Social Type,* (New York: Alfred A. Knopf, 1965), pp. 3–68.

[71]Talcott Parsons and Robert F. Bales, *Family, Socialization and Interaction Process* (Glencoe, Illinois: Free Press, 1955), pp. 3–33.

[72]Clara T. Leonard, "Family Homes for Pauper and Dependent Children," Annual Conference of Charities, *Proceedings* (Chicago, 1879), p. 175.

[73]W.P. Lynde, "Prevention in Some of its Aspects," *Ibid.,* pp. 165–166.

[74]Joseph R. Gusfield, *Symbolic Crusade, loc. cit.*

[75]See, generally, Roy Lubove, *The Professional Altruist: The Emergence of Social Work as a Career, 1880–1930* (Cambridge: Harvard University Press, 1965).

from the changes taking place. The clergy had nothing to lose (but more of their rapidly declining constituency) and everything to gain by incorporating social services into traditional religion. Lawyers were needed for their technical expertise and to administer new institutions. And academics discovered a new market which paid them as consultants, elevated them to positions of national prestige and furnished endless materials for books, articles and conferences. As Richard Hofstadter has noted:

> The development of regulative and humane legislation required the skills of lawyers and economists, sociologists and political scientists, in the writing of laws and in the staffing of administrative and regulative bodies. Controversy over such issues created a new market for the books and magazine articles of the experts and engendered a new respect for their specialized knowledge. Reform brought with it the brain trust.[76]

While the rank and file reformers in the child-saving movement worked closely with corporate liberals, it would be inaccurate to simply characterize them as lackeys of big business. Many were principled and genuinely concerned about alleviating human misery and improving the lives of the poor. Moreover, many women who participated in the movement were able to free themselves from male domination and participate more fully in society. But for the most part, the child-savers and other Progressive reformers defended capitalism and rejected socialist alternatives. Most reformers accepted the structure of the new industrial order and sought to moderate its cruder inequities and reduce inharmonies in the existing system.[77] Though many child-savers were "socialists of the heart" and ardent critics of society, their programs were typically reformist and did not alter basic economic inequalities.[78] Rhetoric and righteous indignation were more prevalent than programs of radical action.

The intellectual and professional communities did little to criticize Progressive reforms, partly because so many benefited from their new role as government consultants and experts, and partly because their conception of social change was limited and elitist. As Jackson Wilson observed, many intellectuals in the Progressive movement were "interested in creating a system of government which would allow the people to rule only at a carefully kept distance and at infrequent intervals, reserving most real power and planning to a corps of experts and professionals."[79] Those few reformers who had a genuine concern for liberating the lives of the poor by considering socialist alternatives were either coopted by their allies, betrayed by their own class interests, or became the prisoners of social and economic forces beyond their control.[80]

---

[76]Hofstadter, *op. cit.*, p. 155.
[77]Williams, *op. cit.*, p. 373 and Weinstein, *op. cit.*, p. 254.
[78]Williams, *op. cit.*, pp. 374, 395–402.
[79]R. Jackson Wilson, "United States: the Reassessment of Liberalism," *Journal of Contemporary History* (January, 1967), p. 96.
[80]Ralph Miliband, *The State in Capitalist Society*, (New York: Basic Books, 1969), pp. 265–277.

Images of Crime and Delinquency

The child-saving reformers were part of a much larger movement to readjust institutions to conform to the requirements of corporate capitalism and the modern welfare state. As the country emerged from the depressions and industrial violence of the late nineteenth century, efforts were made to rescue and regulate capitalism through developing a new political economy, designed to stabilize production and profits. The stability and smooth functioning of this new order depended heavily on the capacity of welfare state institutions, especially the schools, to achieve cultural hegemony and guarantee loyalty to the State. As William Appleman Williams has commented, "it is almost impossible to overemphasize the importance of the very general — yet dynamic and powerful — concept that the country faced a fateful choice between order and chaos."[81] In order to develop support for and legitimize the corporate liberal State, a new ideology was promoted in which chaos was equated with crime and violence, and salvation was to be found in the development of new and more extensive forms of social control.

The child-savers viewed the "criminal classes" with a mixture of contempt and benevolence. Crime was portrayed as rising from the "lowest orders" and threatening to engulf "respectable" society like a virulent disease. Charles Loring Brace, a leading child-saver, typified popular and professional views about crime and delinquency:

> As Christian men, we cannot look upon this great multitude of unhappy, deserted, and degraded boys and girls without feeling our responsibility to God for them. The class increases: immigration is pouring in its multitudes of poor foreigners who leave these young outcasts everywhere in our midst. These boys and girls . . . will soon form the great lower class of our city. They will influence elections; they may shape the policy of the city; they will assuredly, if unreclaimed, poison society all around them. They will help to form the great multitude of robbers, thieves, and vagrants, who are now such a burden upon the law-respecting community. . . .[82]

This attitude of contempt derived from a view of criminals as less-than-human, a perspective which was strongly influenced and aggravated by nativist and racist ideologies.[83] The "criminal class" was variously described as "creatures" living in "burrows," "dens," and "slime"; as "little Arabs" and "foreign childhood that floats along the streets and docks of the city — vagabondish, thievish, familiar with the vicious ways and places of the town";[84] and as "ignorant," "shiftless," "indolent," and "dissipated."[85]

---

[81]Williams, *op. cit.*, p. 356.

[82]Committee on the History of Child-Saving Work, *op. cit.*, p. 3.

[83]See, generally, John Higham, *Strangers in the Land: Patterns of American Nativism, 1860–1925* (New York: Atheneum, 1965).

[84]Brace, *op. cit.*, pp. 30, 49; Bradford Kinney Peirce, *A Half Century with Juvenile Delinquents* (Montclair, New Jersey: Patterson Smith, 1969, originally published 1869), p. 253.

[85]Nathan Allen, "Prevention of Crime and Pauperism," Annual Conference of Charities, *Proceedings* (Cincinnati, 1878), pp. 111–24.

The child-savers were alarmed and frightened by the "dangerous classes" whose "very number makes one stand aghast," noted the urban reformer Jacob Riis.[86] Law and order were widely demanded:

> The "dangerous classes" of New York are mainly American-born, but the children of Irish and German immigrants. They are as ignorant as London flashmen or costermongers. They are far more brutal than the peasantry from whom they descend, and they are much banded together, in associations, such as "Dead Rabbit," "Plug-ugly," and various target companies. They are our *enfant perdus*, grown up to young manhood. . . . They are ready for any offense or crime, however degraded or bloody. . . . Let but Law lift its hand from them for a season, or let the civilizing influences of American life fail to reach them, and, if the opportunity offered, we should see an explosion from this class which might leave this city in ashes and blood.[87]

These views derived considerable legitimacy from prevailing theories of social and reform Darwinism which, *inter alia*, proposed that criminals were a dangerous and atavistic class, standing outside the boundaries of morally regulated relationships. Herbert Spencer's writings had a major impact on American intellectuals and Cesare Lombroso, perhaps the most significant figure in nineteenth century criminology, looked for recognition in the United States when he felt that his experiments on the "criminal type" had been neglected in Europe.[88]

Although Lombroso's theoretical and experimental studies were not translated into English until 1911, his findings were known by American academics in the early 1890s, and their popularity, like that of Spencer's works, was based on the fact that they confirmed widely-held stereotypes about the biological basis and inferior character of a "criminal class." A typical view was expressed by Nathan Allen in 1878 at the National Conference of Charities and Correction: "If our object is to prevent crime in a large scale, we must direct attention to its main sources — to the materials that make criminals; the springs must be dried up; the supplies must be cut off."[89] This was to be achieved, if necessary, by birth control and eugenics. Similar views were expressed by Hamilton Wey, an influential physician at Elmira Reformatory, who argued before the National Prison Association in 1881 that criminals had to be treated as a "distinct type of human species."[90]

Literature on "social degradation" was extremely popular during the 1870s and 1880s, though most such "studies" were little more than crude and racist

---

[86]Jacob A. Riis, *How the Other Half Lives* (New York: Hill and Wang, 1957, originally published in 1890), p. 134.

[87]Brace, *op. cit.*, pp. 27, 29.

[88]See, for example, Lombroso's comments in the Introduction to Arthur MacDonald, *Criminology* (New York: Funk and Wagnalls, 1893).

[89]Allen, *loc. cit.*

[90]Hamilton D. Wey, "A Plea for Physical Training of Youthful Criminals," National Prison Association, *Proceedings* (Boston, 1888), pp. 181–93. For further discussion of this issue, see Platt, *op. cit.*, pp. 18–28 and Arthur E. Fink, *Causes of Crime: Biological Theories in the United States, 1800–1915* (New York: A. S. Barnes, 1962).

polemics, padded with moralistic epithets and preconceived value judgments. Richard Dugdale's series of papers on the Jukes family, which became a model for the case-study approach to social problems, was distorted almost beyond recognition by anti-intellectual supporters of hereditary theories of crime.[91] Confronted by the evidence of Darwin, Galton, Dugdale, Caldwell and many other disciples of the biological image of behavior, many child-savers were compelled to admit that "a large proportion of the unfortunate children that go to make up the great army of criminals are not born right."[92] Reformers adopted and modified the rhetoric of social Darwinism in order to emphasize the urgent need for confronting the "crime problem" before it got completely out of hand. A popular proposal, for example, was the "methodized registration and training" of potential criminals, "or these failing, their early and entire withdrawal from the community."[93]

Although some child-savers advocated drastic methods of crime control — including birth control through sterilization, cruel punishments, and life-long incarceration — more moderate views prevailed. This victory for moderation was related to the recognition by many Progressive reformers that short-range repression was counter-productive as well as cruel and that long-range planning and amelioration were required to achieve economic and political stability. The rise of more benevolent strategies of social control occurred at about the same time that influential capitalists were realizing that existing economic arrangements could not be successfully maintained only through the use of private police and government troops.[94] While the child-savers justified their reforms as humanitarian, it is clear that this humanitarianism reflected their class background and elitist conceptions of human potentiality. The child-savers shared the view of more conservative professionals that "criminals" were a distinct and dangerous class, indigenous to working-class culture, and a threat to "civilized" society. They differed mainly in the procedures by which the "criminal class" should be controlled or neutralized.

Gradually, a more "enlightened" view about strategies of control prevailed among the leading representatives of professional associations. Correctional workers, for example, did not want to think of themselves merely as the custodians of a pariah class. The self-image of penal reformers as "doctors" rather than "guards," and the medical domination of criminological research in the United States at that time facilitated the acceptance of "therapeutic" strategies in prisons and reformatories.[95] Physicians gradually provided the official rhetoric of penal reform, replacing cruder concepts of social Darwinism with a new optimism.

[91]Richard L. Dugdale, *The Jukes: A Study in Crime, Pauperism, Disease, and Heredity* (New York: G.P. Putnam's Sons, 1877).

[92]Sarah B. Cooper, "The Kindergarten as Child-Saving Work," National Conference of Charities and Correction, *Proceedings* (Madison, 1883), pp. 130–38.

[93]I.N. Kerlin, "The Moral Imbecile," National Conference of Charities and Correction, *Proceedings* (Baltimore, 1890), pp. 244–50.

[94]Williams, *op. cit.*, p. 354.

[95]Fink, *op. cit.*, p. 247.

Admittedly, the criminal was "pathological" and "diseased," but medical science offered the possibility of miraculous cures. Although there was a popular belief in the existence of a "criminal class" separated from the rest of humanity by a "vague boundary line," there was no good reason why this class could not be identified, diagnosed, segregated, changed and incorporated back into society.[96]

By the late 1890s, most child-savers agreed that hereditary theories of crime were overfatalistic. The superintendent of the Kentucky Industrial School of Reform, for example, told delegates to a national conference on corrections that heredity is "unjustifiably made a bugaboo to discourage efforts at rescue. We know that physical heredity tendencies can be neutralized and often nullified by proper counteracting precautions."[97] E. R. L. Gould, a sociologist at the University of Chicago, similarly criticized biological theories of crime as unconvincing and sentimental. "Is it not better," he said, "to postulate freedom of choice than to preach the doctrine of the unfettered will, and so elevate criminality into a propitiary sacrifice?"[98]

Charles Cooley, writing in 1896, was one of the first American sociologists to observe that criminal behavior depended as much upon social and economic circumstances as it did upon the inheritance of biological traits. "The criminal class," he observed, "is largely the result of society's bad workmanship upon fairly good material." In support of this argument, he noted that there was a "large and fairly trustworthy body of evidence" to suggest that many "degenerates" could be converted into "useful citizens by rational treatment."[99]

Although there was a wide difference of opinion among experts as to the precipitating causes of crime, it was generally agreed that criminals were abnormally conditioned by a multitude of biological and environmental forces, some of which were permanent and irreversible. Strictly biological theories of crime were modified to incorporate a developmental view of human behavior. If, as it was believed, criminals are conditioned by biological heritage and brutish living conditions, then prophylactic measures must be taken early in life. "We must get hold of the little waifs that grow up to form the criminal element just as early in life as possible," exhorted an influential child-saver. "Hunt up the children of poverty, of crime, and of brutality, just as soon as they can be reached."[100] Efforts were needed to reach the criminals of future generations. "They are born to crime," wrote the penologist Enoch Wines, "brought up for it. They must

[96]See, for example, Illinois Board of State Commissioners of Public Charities, *Second Biennial Report* (Springfield: State Journal Steam Print, 1873), pp. 195–96.

[97]Peter Caldwell, "The Duty of the State to Delinquent Children," National Conference of Charities and Correction, *Proceedings* (New York, 1898), pp. 404–10.

[98]E.R.L. Gould, "The Statistical Study of Hereditary Criminality," National Conference of Charities and Correction, *Proceedings* (New Haven, 1895), pp. 134–43.

[99]Charles H. Cooley, " 'Nature' v. 'Nurture' in the Making of Social Careers," National Conference of Charities and Correction, *Proceedings* (Grand Rapids, 1896), pp. 399–405.

[100]Committee on the History of Child-Saving Work, *op. cit.,* p. 90.

be saved."[101] New institutions and new programs were required to meet this challenge.

Juvenile Court and the Reformatory System

The essential preoccupation of the child-saving movement was the recognition and control of youthful deviance. It brought attention to, and thus "invented" new categories of youthful misbehavior which had been hitherto unappreciated. The efforts of the child-savers were institutionally expressed in the juvenile court which, despite recent legislative and constitutional reforms, is generally acknowledged as their most significant contribution to progressive penology. There is some dispute about which state first created a special tribunal for children. Massachusetts and New York passed laws, in 1874 and 1892 respectively, providing for the trials of minors apart from adults charged with crimes. Ben Lindsey, a renowned judge and reformer, also claimed this distinction for Colorado where a juvenile court was, in effect, established through an educational law of 1899. However, most authorities agree that the Juvenile Court Act, passed by the Illinois legislature in the same year, was the first official enactment to be recognized as a model statute by other states and countries.[102] By 1917, juvenile court legislation had been passed in all but three states and by 1932 there were over 600 independent juvenile courts throughout the United States.[103]

The juvenile court system was part of a general movement directed towards developing a specialized labor market and industrial discipline under corporate capitalism by creating new programs of adjudication and control for "delinquent," "dependent" and "neglected" youth. This in turn was related to augmenting the family and enforcing compulsory education in order to guarantee the proper reproduction of the labor force. For example, underlying the juvenile court system was the concept of *parens patriae* by which the courts were authorized to handle with wide discretion the problems of "its least fortunate junior citizens."[104] The administration of juvenile justice, which differed in many important respects from the criminal court system, was delegated extensive powers of control over youth. A child was not accused of a crime but offered assistance and guidance; intervention in the lives of "delinquents" was not supposed to carry the stigma of criminal guilt. Judicial records were not generally available to the press or public, and juvenile hearings were typically conducted in private. Court procedures were informal and inquisitorial, not requiring the presence of

---

[101]Enoch C. Wines, *The State of Prisons and of Child-Saving Institutions in the Civilized World,* (Cambridge: Harvard University Press, 1880).

[102]Helen Page Bates, "Digest of Statutes Relating to Juvenile Courts and Probation Systems," 13 *Charities* (January, 1905), pp. 329–36.

[103]Joel F. Handler, "The Juvenile Court and the Adversary System: Problems of Function and Form," 1965 *Wisconsin Law Review* (1965), pp. 7–51.

[104]Gustav L. Schramm, "The Juvenile Court Idea," 13 *Federal Probation* (September, 1949), p. 21.

a defense attorney. Specific criminal safeguards of due process were not applicable because juvenile proceedings were defined by statute as civil in character.[105]

The judges of the new court were empowered to investigate the character and social background of "predelinquent" as well as delinquent children; they concerned themselves with motivation rather than intent, seeking to identify the moral reputation of problematic children. The requirements of preventive penology and child-saving further justified the court's intervention in cases where no offense had actually been committed, but where, for example, a child was posing problems for some person in authority, such as a parent or teacher or social worker.

The role model for juvenile court judges was doctor-counselor rather than lawyer. "Judicial therapists" were expected to establish a one-to-one relationship with "delinquents" in the same way that a country doctor might give his time and attention to a favorite patient. Juvenile courtrooms were often arranged like a clinic and the vocabulary of its participants was largely composed of medical metaphors. "We do not know the child without a thorough examination," wrote Judge Julian Mack. "We must reach into the soul-life of the child."[106] Another judge from Los Angeles suggested that the juvenile court should be a "laboratory of human behavior" and its judges trained as "specialists in the art of human relations." It was the judge's task to "get the whole truth about a child" in the same way that a "physician searches for every detail that bears on the condition of the patient."[107] Similarly, the judges of the Boston juvenile court liked to think of themselves as "physicians in a dispensary."[108]

The unique character of the child-saving movement was its concerns for predelinquent offenders — "children who occupy the debatable ground between criminality and innocence" — and its claim that it could transform potential criminals into respectable citizens by training them in "habits of industry, self-control and obedience to law."[109] This policy justified the diminishing of traditional procedures and allowed police, judges, probation officers and truant officers to work together without legal hindrance. If children were to be rescued, it was important that the rescuers be free to pursue their mission without the interference of defense lawyers and due process. Delinquents had to be saved, transformed and reconstituted. "There is no essential difference," noted a prominent child-saver, "between a criminal and any other sinner. The means and methods of restoration are the same for both."[110]

[105]Monrad G. Paulsen, "Fairness to the Juvenile Offender," 41 *Minnesota Law Review* (1957), pp. 547–67.

[106]Julian W. Mack, "The Chancery Procedure in the Juvenile Court," in Jane Addams (Ed.), *The Child, the Clinic and the Court* (New York: New Republic, 1925), p. 315.

[107]Miriam Van Waters, "The Socialization of Juvenile Court Procedure," 21 *Journal of Criminal Law and Criminology* (1922), pp. 61, 69.

[108]Harvey H. Baker, "Procedure of the Boston Juvenile Court," 23 *Survey* (February, 1910), p. 646.

[109]Illinois Board of State Commissioners of Public Charities, *Sixth Biennial Report* (Springfield: H. W. Rokker, 1880), p. 104.

[110]Frederick H. Wines, "Reformation as an End in Prison Discipline," National Conference of Charities and Correction, *Proceedings* (Buffalo, 1888), p. 198.

The juvenile court legislation enabled the state to investigate and control a wide variety of behaviors. As Joel Handler has observed, "the critical philosophical position of the reform movement was that no formal, legal distinctions should be made between the delinquent and the dependent or neglected."[111] Statutory definitions of "delinquency" encompassed (1) acts that would be criminal if committed by adults; (2) acts that violated county, town, or municipal ordinances; and (3) violations of vaguely worded catch-alls — such as "vicious or immoral behavior," "incorrigibility," and "truancy" — which "seem to express the notion that the adolescent, if allowed to continue, will engage in more serious conduct."[112]

The juvenile court movement went far beyond a concern for special treatment of adolescent offenders. It brought within the ambit of governmental control a set of youthful activities that had been previously ignored or dealt with on an informal basis. It was not by accident that the behavior subject to penalties — drinking, sexual "license," roaming the streets, begging, frequenting dance halls and movies, fighting, and being seen in public late at night — was especially characteristic of the children of working-class and immigrant families. Once arrested and adjudicated, these "delinquents" became wards of the court and eligible for salvation.

It was through the reformatory system that the child-savers hoped to demonstrate that delinquents were capable of being converted into law-abiding citizens. Though the reformatory was initially developed in the United States during the middle of the nineteenth century as a special form of prison discipline for adolescents and young adults, its underlying principles were formulated in Britain by Matthew Davenport Hill, Alexander Maconochie, Walter Crofton and Mary Carpenter. If the United States did not have any great penal theorists, it at least had energetic administrators — like Enoch Wines, Zebulon Brockway and Frank Sanborn — who were prepared to experiment with new programs.

The reformatory was distinguished from the traditional penitentiary in several ways: it adopted a policy of indeterminate sentencing; it emphasized the importance of a countryside location; and it typically was organized on the "cottage" plan as opposed to the traditional congregate housing found in penitentiaries. The ultimate aim of the reformatory was reformation of the criminal, which could only be achieved "by placing the prisoner's fate, as far as possible, in his own hand, by enabling him, through industry and good conduct to raise himself, step by step, to a position of less restraint. . . ."[113]

Based on a crude theory of rewards and punishments, the "new penology" set itself the task of re-socializing the "dangerous classes." The typical resident of a reformatory, according to one child-saver, had been "cradled in infamy,

---

[111]Joel F. Handler, *op. cit.*, p. 9.

[112]Joel F. Handler and Margaret K. Rosenheim, "Privacy and Welfare: Public Assistance and Juvenile Justice," 31 *Law and Contemporary Problems* (1966), pp. 377–412.

[113]From a report by Enoch Wines and Theodore Dwight to the New York legislature in 1867, quoted by Max Grünhut, *Penal Reform* (Oxford: Clarendon Press, 1948), p. 90.

imbibing with its earliest natural nourishment the germs of a depraved appetite, and reared in the midst of people whose lives are an atrocious crime against natural and divine law and the rights of society." In order to correct and reform such a person, the reformatory plan was designed to teach the value of adjustment, private enterprise, thrift and self-reliance. "To make a good boy out of this bundle of perversities, his entire being must be revolutionized. He must be taught self-control, industry, respect for himself and the rights of others."[114] The real test of reformation in a delinquent, as William Letchworth told the National Conference of Charities and Correction in 1886, was his uncomplaining adjustment to his former environment. "If he is truly reformed in the midst of adverse influences," said Letchworth, "he gains that moral strength which makes his reform permanent."[115] Moreover, reformed delinquents were given every opportunity to rise "far above the class from which they sprang," especially if they were "patient" and "self-denying."[116]

Reformation of delinquents was to be achieved in a number of different ways. The trend from congregate housing to group living represented a significant change in the organization of penal institutions. The "cottage" plan was designed to provide more intensive supervision and to reproduce, symbolically at least, an atmosphere of family life conducive to the re-socialization of youth. The "new penology" also urged the benefits of a rural location, partly in order to teach agricultural skills, but mainly in order to guarantee a totally controlled environment. This was justified by appealing to the romantic theory that corrupt delinquents would be spiritually regenerated by their contact with unspoiled nature.[117]

Education was stressed as the main form of industrial and moral training in reformatories. According to Michael Katz, in his study on nineteenth-century education, the reformatory provided "the first form of compulsory schooling in the United States."[118] The prominence of education as a technique of reform reflected the widespread emphasis on socialization and assimilation instead of cruder methods of social control. But as Georg Rusche and Otto Kirchheimer observed in their study of the relationship between economic and penal policies, the rise of "rehabilitative" and educational programs was "largely the result of opposition on the part of free workers," for "wherever working-class organizations were powerful enough to influence state politics, they succeeded in obtaining complete abolition of all forms of prison labor (Pennsylvania in 1897, for example), causing much suffering to the prisoners, or at least in obtaining very considerable limitations, such as work without modern machinery, conventional rather than modern types of prison industry, or work for the government instead of for the free market."[119]

---

[114]Peter Caldwell, "The Reform School Problem," National Conference of Charities and Correction, Proceedings (St. Paul, 1886), pp. 71–76.

[115]Letchworth, op. cit., p. 152.

[116]Committee on the History of Child-Saving Work, op. cit., p. 20.

[117]See Platt, op. cit., pp. 55–66.

[118]Katz, op. cit., p. 187.

[119]Rusche and Kirchheimer, op. cit., pp. 131–132.

Although the reformatory system, as envisioned by urban reformers, suffered in practice from overcrowding, mismanagement, inadequate financing and staff hiring problems, its basic ideology was still tough-minded and uncompromising. As the American Friends Service Committee noted, "if the reformers were naive, the managers of the correctional establishment were not. Under the leadership of Zebulon R. Brockway of the Elmira Reformatory, by the latter part of the nineteenth century they had co-opted the reformers and consolidated their leadership and control of indeterminate sentence reform."[120] The child-savers were not averse to using corporal punishment and other severe disciplinary measures when inmates were recalcitrant. Brockway, for example, regarded his task as "socialization of the anti-social by scientific training while under completest governmental control."[121] To achieve this goal, Brockway's reformatory became "like a garrison of a thousand prisoner soldiers" and "every incipient disintegration was promptly checked and disinclination of individual prisoners to conform was overcome."[122] Child-saving was a job for resolute professionals who realized that "sickly sentimentalism" had no place in their work.[123]

"Criminals shall either be cured," Brockway told the National Prison Congress in 1870, "or kept under such continued restraint as gives guarantee of safety from further depredations."[124] Restraint and discipline were an integral part of the "treatment" program and not merely expediencies of administration. Military drill, "training of the will," and long hours of tedious labor were the essence of the reformatory system and the indeterminate sentencing policy guaranteed its smooth operation. "Nothing can tend more certainly to secure the most hardened and desperate criminals than the present system of short sentences," wrote the reformer Bradford Kinney Peirce in 1869.[125] Several years later, Enoch Wines was able to report that "the sentences of young offenders are wisely regulated for their amendment; they are not absurdly shortened as if they signified only so much endurance of vindictive suffering."[126]

Since the child-savers professed to be seeking the "best interests" of their "wards" on the basis of corporate liberal values, there was no need to formulate legal regulation of the right and duty to "treat" in the same way that the right and duty to punish had been previously regulated. The adversary system, therefore, ceased to exist for youth, even as a legal fiction.[127] The myth of the child-saving movement as a humanitarian enterprise is based partly on a superficial interpretation of the child-savers' rhetoric of rehabilitation and partly on a miscon-

---

[120]American Friends Service Committee, *op. cit.,* p. 28.

[121]Zebulon R. Brockway, *Fifty Years of Prison Service* (New York: Charities Publication Committee, 1912), p. 393.

[122]*Ibid.,* pp. 310, 421.

[123]*Ibid.,* pp. 389–408.

[124]*Ibid.*

[125]Peirce, *op. cit.,* p. 312.

[126]Enoch Wines, *op. cit.,* p. 81.

[127]On informal cooperation in the criminal courts, see Jerome H. Skolnick, "Social Control in the Adversary System," 11 *Journal of Conflict Resolution,* (March, 1967), pp. 52–70.

ception of how the child-savers viewed punishment. While it is true that the child-savers advocated minimal use of corporal punishment, considerable evidence suggests that this recommendation was based on managerial rather than moral considerations. William Letchworth reported that "corporal punishment is rarely inflicted" at the State Industrial School in Rochester because "most of the boys consider the lowering of their standing the severest punishment that is inflicted."[128] Mrs. Glendower Evans, commenting on the decline of whippings at a reform school in Massachusetts, concluded that "when boys do not feel themselves imprisoned and are treated as responsible moral agents, they can be trusted with their freedom to a surprising degree."[129] Officials at another state industrial school for girls also reported that "hysterics and fits of screaming and of noisy disobedience, have of late years become unknown. . . ."[130]

The decline in the use of corporal punishment was due to the fact that indeterminate sentencing, the "mark" or "stage" system of rewards and punishments, and other techniques of "organized persuasion" were far more effective in maintaining order and compliance than cruder methods of control. The chief virtue of the "stage" system, a graduated system of punishments and privileges, was its capacity to keep prisoners disciplined and submissive.[131] The child-savers had learned from industrialists that persuasive benevolence backed up by force was a far more effective device of social control than arbitrary displays of terrorism. Like an earlier generation of penal reformers in France and Italy, the child-savers stressed the efficacy of new and indirect forms of social control as a "practical measure of defense against social revolution as well as against individual acts."[132]

Although the child-saving movement had far-reaching consequences for the organization and administration of the juvenile justice system, its overall impact was conservative in both spirit and achievement. The child-savers' reforms were generally aimed at imposing sanctions on conduct unbecoming "youth" and disqualifying youth from the benefit of adult privileges. The child-savers were prohibitionists, in a general sense, who believed that social progress depended on efficient law enforcement, strict supervision of children's leisure and recreation, and enforced education. They were primarily concerned with regulating social behavior, eliminating "foreign" and radical ideologies, and preparing youth as a disciplined and devoted work force. The austerity of the criminal law and penal institutions was only of incidental concern; their central interest was in the normative outlook of youth and they were most successful in their efforts to extend governmental control over a whole range of youthful activities which had previously been handled locally and informally. In this sense, their reforms were aimed at defining, rationalizing and regulating the dependent status of youth.[133]

---

[128]Committee on the History of Child-Saving Work, *op. cit.*, p. 20.

[129]*Ibid.*, p. 237.

[130]*Ibid.*, p. 237.

[130]*Ibid.* p. 251.

[131]Rusche and Kirchheimer, *op. cit.*, pp. 155–156.

[132]*Ibid.*, p. 76. For a similar point, see American Friends Service Committee, *op. cit.*, p. 33.

[133]See, generally, Frank Musgrove, *Youth and the Social Order* (London: *Routledge and Kegan Paul*, 1964).

Although the child-savers' attitudes to youth were often paternalistic and romantic, their commands were backed up by force and an abiding faith in the benevolence of government.

The child-saving movement had its most direct impact on the children of the urban poor. The fact that "troublesome" adolescents were depicted as "sick" or "pathological," imprisoned "for their own good," addressed in paternalistic vocabulary, and exempted from criminal law processes, did not alter the subjective experiences of control, restraint and punishment. It is ironic, as Philippe Ariès observed in his historical study of European family life, that the obsessive solicitude of family, church, moralists and administrators for child welfare served to deprive children of the freedoms which they had previously shared with adults and to deny their capacity for initiative, responsibility and autonomy.[134]

The child-savers' rhetoric of benevolence should not be mistaken for popular, democratic programs. Paternalism was a typical ingredient of most reforms in the Progressive era, legitimizing imperialism in foreign policy and extensive state control at home. Even the corporate rich, according to William Appleman Williams, "revealed a strikingly firm conception of a benevolent feudal approach to the firm and its workers" and "were willing to extend — to provide in the manner of traditional beneficence — such things as new housing, old age pensions, death payments, wage and job schedules, and bureaus charged with responsibility for welfare, safety, and sanitation."[135] But when benevolence failed — in domestic institutions such as schools and courts or in economic policies abroad — government officials and industrial leaders were quick to resort to massive and overwhelming force.[136]

This is not to suggest that the child-savers and other Progressive movements did not achieve significant reforms. They did in fact create major changes. In the arena of criminal justice they were responsible for developing important new institutions which transformed the character of the administration of juvenile justice. But these reforms, to use André Gorz's distinctions, were "reformist" rather than "structural":

> [S]tructural reform . . . does not mean a reform which rationalizes the existing system while leaving intact the existing distribution of powers; this does not mean to delegate to the (capitalist) State the task of improving the system.
>
> Structural reform is by definition a reform implemented or controlled by those who demand it. Be it in agriculture, the university, property relations, the

---

[134]Philippe Ariès, *Centuries of Childhood: A Social History of Family Life* (New York: Vintage Books, 1965).

[135]Williams, *op. cit.*, p. 382.

[136]On benevolence and repression in foreign policy, see Felix Greene, *The Enemy; What Every American Should Know about Imperialism* (New York Vintage Books, 1971). For examples of domestic repression, see William Preston, Jr.., *Aliens and Dissenters: Federal Suppression of Radicals, 1903–1933* (New York: Harper Torchbooks, 1966) and Jacobus tenBroek, Edward N. Barnhart and Floyd W. Matson, *Prejudice, War and the Constitution* (Berkeley: University of California Press, 1968).

region, the administration, the economy, etc., a structural reform *always* requires the creation of new centers of democratic power. Whether it be at the level of companies, schools, municipalities, regions, or of the national Plan, etc., structural reform always requires a *decentralization* of the decision making power, a *restriction on the powers of State or Capital*, an *extension of popular power*, that is to say, a victory of democracy over the dictatorship of profit.[137]

By this definition, then, the child-saving movement was a "reformist reform." It was not controlled by those whom it was supposed to benefit; it did not create new centers of democratic power; it extended and consolidated the powers of the state; and it helped to preserve existing economic and political relationships.

New Strategies of Control

During the last seventy years, the juvenile justice system has grown into a massive and complex bureaucratic organization, staffed by judges, prosecutors, public defenders, probation and parole officers, counselors, child guidance experts, correctional officers, guards and bailiffs. It is significant that the exclusion of "amateurs" and volunteers from decision-making positions was one of the first tasks undertaken by "professional" child-savers at the beginning of this century.[138] With the exception of a few attempts to develop community controlled anti-delinquency programs — for example, the Cincinnati experiment in 1917 and the Chicago Area Project in the 1930s[139] — the job of controlling delinquency has become an esoteric craft reserved for specialists and outside the competence of ordinary citizens.[140] In addition to the earlier problems of the child-saving movement — its class exploitation, repressive benevolence and elitism — the modern juvenile justice system also helps to maintain racism, sexism and working-class powerlessness.

Even by its own standards, the juvenile justice system has seriously failed. One out of every nine persons under the age of eighteen years is referred by the police to the juvenile court on delinquency charges; one out of every six boys (boys are arrested five times more than girls) is referred to juvenile court.[141] Arrests of young persons for crimes increased 47 percent between 1960 and 1965, while each year, according to a conservative estimate, 100,000 youths are held

[137]André Gorz, *Strategy for Labor: A Radical Proposal* (Boston: Beacon Press, 1964), p. 8.
[138]Platt, *op. cit.*, p. 148.
[139]See, for example, Anatole Shaffer, "The Cincinnati Social Unit Experiment: 1917–19," 45 *Social Service Review*, (June, 1971), pp. 159–172 and Ernest Burgess, Joseph D. Lohman and Clifford R. Shaw, "The Chicago Area Project," *Yearbook of the National Probation Association*, (1937), pp. 21–23.
[140]This issue is treated more fully in Anthony Platt, "Saving and Controlling Delinquent Youth: A Critique," 5 *Issues in Criminology*, (Winter, 1970), pp. 1–24.
[141]The facts and figures cited in the following discussion are taken from President's Commission on Law Enforcement and Administration of Justice, *Juvenile Delinquency and Youth Crime*, (Washington, D.C.: Government Printing Office, 1967) and Howard James, *Children in Trouble*, (New York: Simon & Schuster, 1969), pp. 162–171.

in custody institutions. Youth arrests exceed adult arrests and in the large urban centers literally millions of young persons are arrested annually. A high proportion — as much as 75 percent in some cities — of the victims of the juvenile justice system are Third World.

On purely utilitarian grounds, reformatories and detention centers are also a dismal failure in deterring or reducing crime.[142] The task of these institutions is to educate or coerce youth into conformity and submission, to make them accept society's prevailing values, and to prepare them for future roles as punctual and disciplined workers, contented housewives and secretaries, and competitors for "service" jobs as maids, janitors, garbage collectors and other forms of "dirty work." Under the present system, successful "rehabilitation" is impossible because people cannot have their basic needs met in a society practicing class exploitation, racism and sexism. It is not surprising, then, that the "graduates" of reformatories invariably return to crime as a means of survival and that many eventually end up in Folsom, Attica, Soledad and other heavy security prisons.

The increases in delinquency and ineffectiveness of the juvenile justice system are not simply attributable to "youth" or "generational problems." This description obscures the class and racial composition of youth processed through the system. While it is true that middle-class youths are being arrested in increasing numbers, especially for drug-related offenses, the overwhelming majority of arrestees are poor and Third World. Middle-class youth are kept out of state institutions with the help of expensive attorneys, private psychiatrists, and (in extreme cases) referrals to private military schools. Most white middle-class residents have community control of their suburban police and are able to prevent officials from channeling their children to juvenile court.

The most serious and militant challenge to established authority in recent years has come from urban black youth.[143] The Kerner Report observed that there was enough evidence by 1966 to indicate that a large proportion of "riot" participants were youths. It also suggested that "increasing race pride, skepticism about their job prospects, and dissatisfaction with the inadequacy of their education, caused unrest among students in Negro colleges and high schools."[144] The events of recent years support and go beyond this finding, especially in urban schools which are more and more becoming the locus of youthful protest.

Young blacks between the ages of fifteen and twenty-four were the most active participants in the urban riots of the 1960s.[145] These youths were not known to be psychologically impaired or suffering from any special personality problems.

---

[142]See, for example, Henry D. McKay, "Report on the Criminal Careers of Male Delinquents in Chicago," in *Juvenile Delinquency and Youth Crime, op. cit.,* pp. 107–113.

[143]The following discussion is adapted from a paper prepared for Jerome H. Skolnick (Director), *The Politics of Protest,* (New York: Simon & Schuster, 1969), pp. 162–171.

[144]National Advisory Commission on Civil Disorders, *Report,* (Washington, D.C.: Government Printing Office, 1968), p. 21.

[145]See, for example, Robert M. Fogelson and Robert B. Hill, "Who Riots? A Study of Participation in the 1967 Riots," in *Supplemental Studies for the National Advisory Commission on Civil Disorders,* (Washington, D.C.: Government Printing Office, (1968), pp. 221–248.

Juveniles arrested in the 1967 Detroit riot were found by a psychological team to be less emotionally disturbed than typical arrestees.[146] Furthermore, the recent riots not only were viewed by non-rioting blacks as a legitimate form of protest but they also served to mobilize the younger segments of the black community and educate them to the realities of their caste position in American society. As William Grier and Price Cobbs observed:

> Today it is the young men who are fighting the battles, and for now, their elders, though they have given their approval, have not joined in. The time seems near, however, for the full range of the black masses to put down the broom and buckle on the sword. And it grows nearer day by day. Now we see skirmishes, sputtering erratically, evidence if you will that the young men are in a warlike mood. But evidence as well that the elders are watching closely and may soon join the battle.[147]

One of the most significant features of the new black militancy is the increased political consciousness of youth who are developing Afro-American organizations in high schools, forming youth chapters in political organizations, demanding cultural autonomy and community control in education, and challenging arbitrary authority. Massive student boycotts occurred in Chicago and New York in 1968 in support of extensive demands, including locally controlled schools and holidays to commemorate the birthdays of Martin Luther King, Malcolm X, Marcus Garvey and W. E. B. DuBois. White high school youth, notably in New York and Berkeley, developed union organizations to oppose the war and to express their solidarity with the struggles of Third World youth. High school activists have generally impressed school officials with the sophistication and legitimacy of their demands; some ameliorative concessions were made to students while more fundamental disputes over school control and decentralization are still being contested.

The militant activities of black and other Third World youth, the development of political organizations in high schools, opposition to the war and draft, the increasing rebelliousness and use of drugs, opposition to stereotypes about the immaturity of youth, and the recruitment of young persons into militant political organizations — all these events in the 1960s indicated that a radical political movement was developing and that agencies of social control were both ineffective and counter-productive. In the same way that the child-savers created the juvenile justice system at the end of the last century in order to rescue capitalism and avert radical change, the State has begun to develop new strategies of control and amelioration in response to recent militancy.

Following the 1967 National Crime Commission and various riot and violence commissions, efforts are currently under way to streamline and professionalize the administration of criminal justice by introducing rational management procedures, removing private citizens from the affairs of specialists, and developing

---

[146]Richard Komisaruk and Carol Pearson, "Children of the Detroit Riots," 44 *Journal of Urban Law*, (Spring and Summer, 1968), pp. 599–626.

[147]William H. Grier and Price M. Cobbs, *Black Rage*, (New York: Basic Books, 1968), p. 211.

techniques for managing an increasingly recalcitrant and hostile youth population. A cautious pragmatism guides the contemporary reformer, for crime control has become a task for hard-headed professionals attempting to rescue antiquated criminal justice bureaucracies with methods engineering and an updated Taylorism.

As in the child-saving movement, the new strategies of control are two-pronged — some are benevolent, ameliorative and reformist, while some are explicitly coercive and authoritarian. The Crime Commission, which represents the more "enlightened" wing of the contemporary reform movement, primarily focuses on ways of extending controls over "hard-to-reach" youth and devising new methods of control within existing institutions.[148] The "two-pronged" approach proceeds upon the premise that the solution to delinquency lies in creating more systematic and pervasive institutions of control, together with making conventional and legal activities more attractive to youth.

The more benevolent strategies of reform presently under development include youth service bureaus, community relations programs, and the provision of lawyers in juvenile court. Public officials have in some instances recognized the potential power of youth by agreeing to negotiate student demands, creating special programs of job training, and consulting with youth and gang leaders in the development of community projects. Often this recognition is motivated by an awareness that youth organizations, like the Blackstone Rangers in Chicago, are becoming more and more capable of mobilizing vast numbers of young people with a view to political or even guerilla action.

The most significant ameliorative reform in recent years is the "constitutional domestication" of the juvenile court. For several years, critics have pointed out that the juvenile court violates constitutional guarantees of due process and stigmatizes youths as "delinquents," thereby performing functions similar to those of the criminal courts. The United States Supreme Court recognized the constitutional argument for the first time in 1967 when it delivered an opinion on the Juvenile court in the *Gault Case*. The Court added clear procedural guidelines to its earlier statement in the *Kent Case* (1966) that the "admonition to function in a 'parental' relationship is not an invitation to procedural arbitrariness." Speaking for the majority in the *Gault Case*, Justice Fortas held that juveniles are entitled to (1) timely notice of the specific charges against them; (2) notification of the right to be represented by counsel in proceedings which "may result in commitment to an institution in which the juvenile's freedom is curtailed;" (3) the right to confront and cross-examine complainants and other witnesses; and (4) adequate warning of the privilege against self-incrimination and the right to remain silent. The right to counsel is the fundamental issue in the *Gault Case* (1967:36) because exercise of the right is designed to aussure procedural regularity and implementation of related principles:

> A proceeding where the issue is whether the child will be found to be "delinquent" and subjected to the loss of his liberty for years is comparable in

[148]See, generally, Platt, "Saving and Controlling Delinquent Youth: A Critique," *loc. cit.*

seriousness to a felony prosecution. The juvenile needs the assistance of counsel to cope with problems of law, to make skilled inquiry into facts, to insist upon the regularity of the proceedings, and to ascertain whether he has
a defense and to prepare and submit it.[149]

The *Gault* decision followed shortly after the President's Crime Commission
had made even stronger recommendations concerning the right to counsel:

> Counsel must be appointed where it can be shown that failure to do so would
> prejudice the rights of the person involved. . . . Nor does reason appear for
> the argument that counsel should be provided in some situations but not in
> others; in delinquency proceedings, for example, but not in neglect.
> Whereever coercive action is a possibility, the presence of counsel is impera-
> tive. . . . [W]hat is urgent and imperative is that counsel be provided in
> the juvenile courts at once and as a regular matter for all who cannot afford
> to retain their own. . . . Counsel should be appointed . . . without requiring
> any affirmative choice by child or parent.[150]

Although the *New York Times* greeted *Gault* as a landmark decision demanding
"radical changes,"[151] it seems unlikely that the decision will generate anything
more than a few modest alterations in existing arrangements for handling delinquents. Whereas the *Gault* decision may introduce some measure of due process
in juvenile court, it also runs the risk of making juvenile court more orderly and
efficient at the expense of substantive fairness. The "constitutional domestication" of the juvenile court will mean, *inter alia*, that the intake of delinquency
cases will be sharply reduced, but it is unlikely to have much impact on the
mechanical expediency of lower-court justice or on the penal character of juvenile
institutions. Furthermore, studies of defense lawyers in juvenile court suggest that
the implementation of due process will fall far short of the ideal adversary system
suggested by the Supreme Court. Lawyers in juvenile court bring to their job
common-sense notions about adolescence and "troublesome" behavior. Their
views on youth and delinquency are really no different from those of other adult
officials (teachers, social workers, youth officers, etc.) who are charged with regulating youthful behavior. Juveniles get the same kind of treatment in court that
they get in school or at home, and lawyers accept this as one of the inevitable
and appropriate consequences of adolescence.[152]

While the provision of lawyers for youth represents one of the ameliorative
concessions of the contemporary reform movement, the main focus has been on
improving efficiency in the juvenile court through narrowing its formal jurisdic-

---

[149]*In re Gault*, 387 U.S. 1, 41, (1967).

[150]President's Commission on Law Enforcement and Administration of Justice, *The Challenge of
Crime in a Free Society* (Washington, D.C.: Government Printing Office, 1967), p. 87 and *Juvenile
Delinquency and Youth Crime, op. cit.*, pp. 31, 33.

[151]*New York Times*, (May 16, 1967), p. 1.

[152]Anthony Platt and Ruth Friedman, "The Limits of Advocacy: Occupational Hazards in Juvenile
Court," 116 *Pennsylvania Law Review*, (1968), pp. 1156–1184; and Anthony Platt, Howard Schech-
ter and Phyllis Tiffany, "In Defense of Youth: A Case Study of the Public Defender in Juvenile
Court," 43 *Indiana Law Journal*, (1968), pp. 619–640.

tion, developing more refined classification systems, and creating new institutional arrangements (Youth Service Bureaus, for example) to handle less serious crimes on a local and informal basis. At the same time, however, the creation of police gang intelligence units, infiltration of youth groups by police spies, the presence of heavily armed riot and "tactical" units, and the routine patroling of urban schools by police guarantee the availability of coercive measures to support benevolent policies. Rather than increasing opportunities for self-determination by youth, public officials have opted for closer supervision in order to decrease opportunities for the exercise of illegal or collective power.[153] Intelligence units are expanding and developing counter-insurgency techniques to manage gangs.[154] The size of the gang intelligence unit in Chicago, for example, increased from 38 to 200 within a few years.[155] In many cities, schools have taken hard-line action against organizers since some authorities feel that "riots are unleashed against the community" from high schools and the granting of concessions to students might encourage further rebellions.[156] As in Vietnam, authorities quickly resort to the use of force when "pacification" fails; and as the contradictions become more apparent and the control system more unsuccessful, the methods of coercion become similarly more explicit and more desperate.

Contemporary efforts to re-structure the juvenile justice system have many parallels with the child-saving movement, though the State today has far more technological resources and a capacity to create more sophisticated and dangerous strategies of control. Academics have in general helped to legitimize and provide technical assistance to these new developments, albeit in the name of liberal ideology. They continue to accept State definitions of crime, to promote reforms within the framework of corporate capitalism, to underestimate the importance of historical and macroscopic analysis, and to encourage defeatist attitudes about the possibility of radical change. The answer to economic and political oppression is not to be found in such liberal reforms as youth service bureaus or the provision of public defenders. The old models need to be completely dismantled and replaced by institutions which serve and are democratically controlled by the people. While undertaking this task, we must also discard false ideologies and break free from the myths which distort our views of the past and limit our vision of the future.

[153]Gerald Marwell, "Adolescent Powerlessness and Delinquent Behavior," 14 *Social Problems,* (Summer, 1966), pp. 35–47.

[154]Edwin Lemert, "Juvenile Justice — Quest and Reality," 4 *Trans-action,* (1967), p. 32.

[155]*Chicago Tribune,* (November 8, 1968), p. 4.

[156]Ray Momboisse, *Riot and Civil Emergency Guide for City and County Officials,* (Sacramento, California: MSM Enterprises, 1968), p. 11.

Chapter Seven

PROSPECTS

The nature of criminal justice in America is a reflection of the larger
political and economic system — the advanced capitalist society. In
order for that system to survive, challenges to it have to be controlled.
Repression — especially legal repression — becomes the chief
weapon of control. Crime control in America today can be seen as
the response of the state and the ruling class to the crisis of the capitalist order.

The contradiction within modern capitalism is that a system which
violates human essence leads to resistance and rebellion by the people.
And the more the people attempt to remove the oppression, the more
the capitalist state brings repressive measures to bear on them. Today
in America we are experiencing the repression of a society that refuses
to use its resources to solve its own problems. In order to protect
the system from its own victims, a war on crime is being waged.

The crime control programs of the last ten years have been constructed within the framework of "reform." This is to be expected, since
reform is the capitalist state's way of adjusting the system so that
it will survive according to its own terms. Many of the crime programs
have been an integral part of programs confronting poverty, racial
inequality, and campus disorders. Under the guise of liberal reforms,
measures have been instituted that serve to preserve the existing social
and economic arrangements. At the same time, measures have been
established to control resistance to the reforms and to prevent changes
that would go beyond the reforms. The state thus uses repression in
the administration of its reforms. Reform and repression are not alternative options for the state but complementary ones: "As reform reveals itself incapable of subduing pressure and protest, so does the

emphasis shift towards repression, coercion, police power, law and order, the struggle against subversion, etc. . . . The state must arm itself with more extensive and more efficient means of repression, seek to define more stringently the area of 'legitimate' dissent and opposition, and strike fear in those who seek to go beyond it."[1]

Therefore, the prospects for our future, as they appear in our critical understanding, revolve around the contradictions of modern capitalism. The existing system, even with its reforms, must respond to the increasing internal challenges by designing and administering further repression. Crime control thus increasingly serves as an instrument of state authoritarianism. The transition to a new kind of authoritarian society is a distinct possibility. An alternative to this future is liberation of the capitalist state and achievement of our authentic being in a socialist society.

The selections in this last chapter present an analysis of the crisis in the capitalist system in America, relating particularly to crime and justice, and the prospects for the future. In "Law, the Breakdown of Order, and Revolution," Stanley Aronowitz begins by noting that although repression is rooted in the institutions of capitalism — always having been a weapon of the ruling class to protect its property and reinforce the legal system — repression today is "fast becoming the central adhesive for disintegrating political and social institutions." Aronowitz goes on to show that the disintegration in institutions is a result of a crisis in the institutions themselves and a demystification of the official ideology. Not only have the institutions failed to respond to the challenges and needed changes, but many people no longer accept the legitimacy of these institutions. Hence, the hegemony of ruling class ideas and capitalist relations is being eroded.

So it is that people today question the legitimacy of the law. Aronowitz writes that "the revolt of ordinary people against all forms of legitimate authority controlling the institutions of daily life and their simultaneous efforts to establish their own authority over these institutions takes the law from its position of preeminence in society and reveals it as an arm of class rule." Consequently there is a breakdown of the legal order itself. The author goes on to document the many ways in which the legal order has been demystified, and he observes the development of an authoritarian state as a reaction to this demystification.

Aronowitz's final concern is with a radical strategy to confront both the void in the legitimacy of institutions and the authoritarian bid to save them. The answer certainly is neither to modify the existing institutions nor to replace them with a new system of domination. Rather, the answer is in the liberation of all hierarchical authority.

---

[1]Ralph Miliband, *The State in Capitalist Society*, pp. 271–272. Reprinted by permission of the publishers. © 1969 by George Weidenfield & Nicolson Ltd., London. Basic Books Inc., Publishers, New York.

With a new understanding of our conditions, we can arrive at ideas that are appropriate to this liberation. The author's final remark indicates the nature of the new ideas and our liberation: "But we must be the advocates of direct popular democracy — of the reconstruction of society from below, of popular power over all institutions, and the creation of institutions to meet human needs — not to serve the interests of profit and domination."

On a cautionary note, Bertram Gross informs us about the counter-revolutionary forces in the United States. In "Friendly Fascism, A Model for America," Gross suggests that the United States is well on the way to becoming a "new-style" facism, one that involves no major changes from what is already occurring in America. This "new-style" fascism is based on a complex of modernized control mechanisms, a pervasive, insidious form of control: indeed, a managed society. Gross describes this new order as follows: "A managed society rules by a faceless and widely dispersed complex of warfare-welfare-industrial-communications-police bureaucracies caught up in developing a new-style empire based on a technocratic ideology, a culture of alienation, multiple scapegoats, and competing control networks." Not only will the economy be managed, but the total society will be managed by the modern state.

The police component of the new state will involve, as we know from present experience, a network of law enforcement systems decentralized on a geographical basis yet guided by federal agencies. "It will include the Attorney General's office, the FBI, the CIA, the military intelligence agencies, federal-aid crime agencies, and new computer-based dossier facilities tied in with the Internal Revenue Service, the Census Bureau, and credit-rating offices." This control complex will, of course, be integrated into an expanding welfare system which itself malignly controls the population. We will be bound, finally, by a communications network for manipulation and surveillance of the people.[2]

Can there be an alternative to this future? Certainly the liberal reform solutions are not the answer; they lead to further repression and open the way for the neofascist state. Only a vision that goes beyond reform of the capitalist system can provide us with a human existence and a world free of the authoritarian state. Crime control in modern America is a crucial indication of the world that can emerge under present images and theories of society and human nature.

One alternative to capitalist society and its forms of oppression is a socialist society. We learn from a critical reading of Marx that only under appropriate conditions can human possibilities be realized.[3] An authentic human being should be able to reach his or her full potential

---

[2]On other aspects of the authoritarian response in advanced capitalism, see Herbert Marcuse, *Counterrevolution and Revolt* (Boston: Beacon Press, 1972).

[3]Karl Marx, *The Grundrisse*, translated by David McLellan (New York: Harper & Row, 1971).

as the result of a socialist revolution. In the movement from a capitalist society to a socialist society, the human being no longer suffers from the alienation otherwise inherent in the relations of capitalism. The socialist revolution is one of human liberation.

The last selection concludes this book with the hope of a truly human existence. "Toward a Socialist Alternative" is a concise statement of a democratic alternative to the contradictions of capitalism. The authors, Richard C. Edwards, Michael Reich, and Thomas E. Weisskopf, drawing from their analysis of American society, discuss the need for the radical transformation of capitalism. Capitalism will be changed as a political consciousness and revolutionary movement develop in reaction to the present system. They write: "Fundamental social change will occur only if a self-conscious class emerges and engages in organized political struggle around the contradictions of capitalism in such a way as to challenge the basic capitalist relations of production, for capitalism will not 'evolve' or 'develop naturally' into the transformed society we desire."

A vision of a decent, humane, socialist society must be developed. It is in the struggle to transcend capitalist society that the details of an alternative existence will emerge. The values that characterize a truly decent society will be based on equality and cooperation. Socialism, as a process, means the democratic, decentralized, and participatory control of the activities that affect one's life. Alienating, destructive forms of production, consumption, and social relations will be eliminated. Our task, in the political struggle, is to develop forms that will promote equality, nonalienating activity, and the other requirements of a decent society.[4]

Finally, it is in the creation of a critical understanding of our condition that we can begin to suggest a possible future. This has been the purpose of our discussion of crime and justice in American society. We must think and act in a way that will bring about a world quite different from the one we are now experiencing and the one which we are presently moving towards. We are capable of an existence that makes us human. Never before has our understanding of crime and justice been so crucial. Never before has that understanding been so related to the way we must live our lives. To think critically and radically today is to be revolutionary.

---

[4]The nature of law in a socialist society is discussed in Michael E. Tigar, "Socialist Law and Legal Institutions," in Robert Lefcourt (ed.), *Law Against the People: Essays To Demystify Law, Order and the Courts* (New York: Random House, 1971), pp. 327–347.

18. Stanley Aronowitz

Law, the Breakdown of Order, and Revolution

Repressive violence is no longer an occasional tool employed by the state to quell political dissenters. It has become a pervasive and a routine feature of bourgeois rule. Its deployment is so widespread, the number of persons murdered, in jail, or awaiting imprisonment as a result of political and social acts deemed dangerous to the prevailing system of power is so large that the time has come for reassessing its significance.

Of course, political and social repression is rooted in the institutions of capitalism. Repression has always been a weapon used by the ruling class to protect its property or to reinforce the legal system. But the contemporary situation suggests that, far from being just another weapon in the arsenal of class rule, repression is fast becoming the central adhesive for disintegrating political and social institutions. For the victims of state repression and others concerned with the preservation of traditional liberties, there has been a qualitative shift in the modes of rule, lending legitimacy to talk of a fascist or "authoritarian" country.

The use of violence as a mode of rule is a sign of profound weakness. Otherwise the mediations between consciousness and real social relations would remain effective. But it is precisely the inability of ideologies and institutions to disguise corporate control over all property and resources which has required the large-scale deployment of armies, police, and the courts to thwart popular movements contesting the prevailing organs of power.

This is not to claim that the revolutionary project has gripped the consciousness of large sections of the underlying population. On the contrary. Yet even though the struggle remains within the institutions and has not succeeded in transcending their limits, the feebleness and disfunctionality of all the primary social institutions are such that even attempts merely to wrest concessions threaten the fabric of social life.

The notion that advanced capitalist societies, owing to their surfeit of resources and technological capacities, can coopt any demand for sectoral reform seems to be losing its force in a period when the fiscal crises afflicting major social welfare and educational institutions have created severe limits to the options available to bureaucracies. It is important not to overstate the case. It is still true that any individual challenge to a particular institution can be granted if the pres-

Reprinted by permission of the author from *Law Against the People*, edited by Robert Lefcourt (Random House, 1971), pp. 150–182.

sure mounted is sufficient to offset the political deficits of denying another sector. But massive concessions seem no longer possible. A general challenge to the resources of institutions is no more likely to be met with substantial concessions than a challenge to their juridical and moral legitimacy. We are experiencing the merger of these challenges; that is, the distinction between the struggle for more resources and the struggle for power within institutions is disappearing.

The rise of repression in America cannot be separated from the disintegration of the institutions of daily life. The breakdown has reached crisis proportions, the most significant of which is the ideological crisis, the demystification of morals, values and norms. Ideology is more than a series of rationales for legitimating existing property and power relations. It is not merely false consciousness. To the extent that ideology is transformed into social and personal conduct, to the extent that ideas such as laws, having been produced by underlying social relations, become guides to practical action, they become part of social reality. The ideological crisis undermines the capacity of institutions to perform their assigned roles. Moreover, the tenuous state of ideological apparatuses has produced a void for the ruling class. Repression in its ideological cloak, law and order, has attempted to fill that void. This is the basis of the rise of authoritarian modes of rule in our society.

The law is but one moment of the codes of conduct governing social intercourse. More generally, it is part of the social norms which arise from the divisions within society — the division between public and private, rulers and the ruled, ownership and nonownership of property. Insofar as social divisions exist, the law serves as a regulator of social and economic relations. The mutual contract, including the labor and marriage contract, is the formal expression of the division of labor and provides a universal code to guide various transactions within the system of production and exchange. The rule of law insures social order, the smooth operation of all social institutions resting on class divisions. Its effectiveness presupposes its legitimacy in consciousness.

Law must retain its independence of the interests of any sector of the capitalist class if it is to remain the final arbiter of all social conflict. The universality of laws derives from the laws' alienation from real production relations and their autonomous form. As one of the most important ideological apparatuses of the state, law appears as an independent force standing above all institutions and the sphere of production and exchange. Its autonomy is the condition of its permeation into all social spheres.

The hidden hand of law is embodied in moral codes, administrative rules, and institutional values. More than laws which are mandated by the state, these norms constitute the ideological underpinnings of all social relations. Children are socialized to specific standards of conduct, systems of moral behavior, and respect for hierarchical authority through the family and the school. Although the legal institutions of the state provide public sanctions for the institutions of civil society which govern everyday life, no system of law actually encompasses everyday behavior. Yet the institutions at the base of society, those dealing with family, education and work, impose norms which are consistent with those of more formal legality. The laws governing institutions, in short, are not confined to the ideological or state spheres. They operate as morals, rules, and values in the institutions of everyday life.

The challenges to the division between public and private, to the authority of the state and the institutions of civil society, and more profoundly, to the ideas which maintain the legitimacy of prevailing hierarchies within these institutions, have become the greatest threat to the viability of capitalist society. This does not mean that the hegemony of ruling class ideas and capitalist institutions will necessarily be challenged, even if the society experiences profound economic crisis. On the other hand, in the 1960s and early 1970s America underwent profound social crisis amid relative economic boom. The social crisis consists precisely in the challenge of sectors of the ruled classes to the legitimacy of social institutions, including the state. College students are challenging the power of school administrations to determine curriculum, the hiring and firing of teachers, and the use of facilities. High school students are refusing to observe even the elementary rules of decorum. Blacks particularly are demanding control over public education and a greater influence in determining the policies of colleges which exist adjacent to ghetto communities. Health institutions, especially hospitals, face demands from consumers of health services for a voice in, if not sole determination of, hospital policy. It is doubtful whether these demands would be made if the costs of medical services had not become prohibitive to working class people or if the quality of the services was not deteriorating rapidly. But the demands of health groups have gone beyond simply asking for expansion of health care. They are demanding representation on hospital boards. More important, they are evincing distrust of the sanctity of medical authority.

The crisis of institutions is the objective side of a revolutionary process, the crisis of bourgeois culture and ideology the subjective side. Together they constitute the necessary, but not the sufficient conditions for the emergence of a revolutionary situation. Revolutionary action requires the development of new social relations within the old society, a new hegemony of ideas, values and norms — a widespread belief among the ruled class that the old institutions and ideologies have lost their legitimacy.

The demystification of the law, in this respect, goes deeper than the beginnings of revolt by radical lawyers and clients against legal institutions or of law students against their education and indoctrination. Rather, the revolt of ordinary people against all forms of legitimate authority controlling the institutions of daily life and their simultaneous efforts to establish their own authority over these institutions takes the law from its position of preeminence in society and reveals it as an arm of class rule.

The process of demystification is complex and contradictory. Often the revolt remains confined to a single sphere of social life. Popular consciousness is often unable to transcend the concrete conditions within a particular institution and penetrate the universal character of all institutions. In other words, the challenge to institutions has not yet reached class consciousness, if we mean by this the capacity of workers to join the alienated conditions of their own labor and the struggle against a particular employer to the general class essence of domination in all social institutions.

But the demand for popular control itself poses all the questions about the neutrality of law and the legitimacy of bureaucracies and hierarchies to manage our lives. If law is not merely an ideological apparatus of the state for the coercive preservation of external social relations but rather permeates all aspects of public conduct, then the challenge to the institutions is the challenge to patterns of ordinary life and the legitimacy of those institutions which govern it. The breakdown of institutions is the breakdown of their legitimacy and consequently the breakdown of the legal order and its functional efficacy.

Capitalism depends on three kinds of institutions to enforce its hegemony over society. These institutions are: first, the work place itself and those institutions which organize the division of labor, the conditions of work, and the production and distribution of commodities. The corporation is the decisive form of organization in contemporary capitalist society. Within its framework, the relations of capitalist production and exchange are mediated. The trade unions act as a disciplinary force among the workers and serve as a contractor of labor according to an established price.

Second, the coercive and administrative institutions of the state, particularly the police, the army, and the social overhead or public service institutions. In contemporary American society, many of these services, particularly power, transportation and communications, are owned directly by the private sector but regulated publicly. The same condition applies to health and education.

Third, the ideological apparatuses, which include law, education, trade unions, and cultural functions. Here one can observe a great deal of overlap with other institutions. For example, educational institutions are both administrative and ideological apparatuses of bourgeois society. Law serves a regulatory function in all institutions and an ideological role as well. Trade unions are important ideological apparatuses because they provide legitimacy for the prevailing political parties as representatives of the working class; they support the principle of private ownership and state intervention into institutions of class conflict; and they appear as instruments of class struggle because of their bargaining role.

Historically, the separation of the state from the underlying economic and social relations has facilitated the illusion of popular sovereignty. To the extent that civil society remained sharply demarcated in form and function from the state, the ideology of popular control and representative democracy was consistent with the notion of the bourgeois state. Within civil society, the system of private appropriation of the means of production was legitimated by the doctrine of individual liberty, and its corollary, free competition.

The corporations have destroyed the whole ideological and institutional foundation of their authority. By taking over and "colonizing" civil society, they have plunged the third group of institutions necessary for the preservation of their authority into crisis. Capitalism does not merely rely on its force or its administrative capacity for survival. Equally, it requires ideological apparatuses to diffuse and channel social discontent and to return industrial and social discipline. The rebellion which transcends established channels of negotiation is a sign that institutions created as buffers between the subject and the dominant classes have lost their legitimacy, at least temporarily. The challenge to institutions has exacerbated the crisis.

The crisis is manifested most sharply in the disintegration of the structures of everyday life, especially the primary institutions of acculturation and socialization, the first of which is the family. The rise in the divorce rate, the breakdown of family solidarity in wide social strata and classes, and the spread of common law marriage are all symptoms of the decline of the authority of the family and its growing disutility as an instrument to successfully integrate children into the prevailing norms, values, and rules of conduct.

Law sanctions sexual relations between men and women under specific conditions, that is, provided that people agree to reproduce a new generation of workers. For example, the law requires children to attend school. This requirement arose historically from capitalism's need for a highly trained labor force. The state, representing the general interest of the capitalist class, was invested with the responsibility of training the new labor force, by transmitting technical knowledge required as a prerequisite for productive labor and by inculcating approved social values and norms to the new generation.

The family is the only legitimate form for cohabitation between men and women, although the state will tolerate other forms as long as these do not materially threaten the existing social norms. In advanced capitalist societies where there is chronic overproduction of the work force relative to the capacity of the forces of production, the degree of social toleration of "deviant" sexual behavior is greater, although subject to more or less repression depending on social and political circumstances.

The disintegration of the family threatens contemporary capitalism not because a new labor force is not being produced, but because the family is the chief instrument for the transmission of approved values. The habit structures of the individual are formed within the family. Work discipline may be enforced in part by the material requirements of human survival; indeed, the slogan "He who does not work, neither shall he eat" applies to every working-class person. But industrial discipline is not sufficient to insure proper adaptation to the world of work. Indeed, discipline involves at least two elements: the capacity to perform sustained work over the prescribed length of the working day, and respect for authority, the ability to act on external command, to internalize the legitimacy of the prevailing hierarchy.

The family is among the authoritarian institutions of capitalist society and is organized on principles which mirror the hierarchies of all institutions. The male "head of household" reigns as "lord of the castle." The position of the working class man at the head of the family serves the dual role of preparing children for industrial labor and mediating the alienation of the worker at the work place by restoring his sense of personal, if not social, power. If the man's position in the family teaches children the inevitability of authority supported by financial power and coercion, the woman is charged with the task of moral persuasion. The woman brings the children to school and church and is the line supervisor of the child's everyday existence, teaching children right from wrong in the pragmatic daily confrontations with life.

The development of mass transit and communication, the mobility of industrial plants, regional depressions, wars, and the permanent inflationary spiral in the post–World War era have all contributed to the decline of the nuclear family. Concomitant with these changes is the new status of the woman in the labor force. Unlike previous periods of industrial expansion, where the role of women was circumscribed within clerical and light factory occupations, the configuration of American capitalist economy placed women at the center of the expansion. In the postwar period, rising labor productivity and the growing concentration of capital were two of the major results of the acceleration of capital investment and the spread of U.S. hegemony to the entire capitalist world. During the years 1947–65, the manufacturing labor force grew by only thirteen percent, although the labor force as a whole increased by nearly fifty percent. The entrance of women into the retail and wholesale industries, into the vastly expanded clerical work force, which grew by forty-three percent, and, most important, into the employment explosion in the public sector, radically altered their status and the stability of the nuclear family.

Most adult women hold full-time or part-time jobs. Their income is essential for their own support and that of their family. Although women are still responsible for maintaining the home, their role as wage earner is equally important. The rapid increase of the divorce rate means that many women have become sole or primary supporters of their children. Few working class families can survive in the inflationary economy without the income of the working woman.

The challenge to the efficacy of the family and especially its hierarchical mode of organization derives chiefly from from the objective changes which have been forced on the family structure by the demographic and economic changes in capitalist economy. Working women, confronted by the reality of their everyday situation, refuse to remain subordinate to men. The revolt of women extends beyond the organizations which articulate the rebellion. In the first place, the cycle of marriage and divorce and the proliferation of common law marriages represent the refusal of women to accept their historical role in capitalist culture. In the second place, the phenomenon of women as heads of household has had a profound impact on the consciousness of children, who can no longer rationalize the myth of the bourgeois family with their own situation. Respect for authority is weakened by the changing role of women. Even though women often reproduce the command patterns of the bourgeois family, the preoccupation with work and the more democratic role they have begun to play within the family mean that the ability of the family structure to deal effectively with its traditional socialization role is limited.

The loosening of family ties is observed especially when both parents are employed. It is not uncommon for a father to be employed on two or more jobs and for a mother to be fully employed as well, and for young children to perform most of their essential life functions themselves. Children are being thrown upon their own resources in typical working class families to a greater degree than at any time in history. Attempts of absent parents to enforce discipline break down under the sheer weight of work responsibility.

Another development which has changed the traditional role of the family is the emergence of youth society, a phenomenon partly attributable to the absent parents. Children are as likely to be socialized by peer groups as they are by parents. These peer groups are not immune to the norms and value systems of the dominant culture. Approved values are learned through organs of mass communication as much as they are in school or in family life. The television culture has become a real influence on youth consciousness. Internally, peer groups often observe rules of conduct which are patterned after canons of bourgeois morality. But youth have great difficulty emulating authoritarian power relations from the larger society. If the development of consciousness is not a passive process; if the consumption of information from mass media or school is not sufficient to *determine* behavior, but can only influence it, social practice is the central way in which consciousness is formed. The young gang or group may not have thrown out leaders and hierarchy, but the law of the peer group, of the hippie culture, which represents a significant break with family and institutional authority, is arrived at in a more democratic manner than any institution of capitalist society. In a sense, the peer group and the youth culture become an alternate institution to the family and the school.

The loosening of family ties has been recognized by the ruling class for some time, and has resulted in the expansion of the school's role in transmitting approved social values. But the education system itself has been plunged into crisis. Materially, its dysfunction is rooted in the fiscal crisis of the state, that is, in the chronic incapacity of the public sector to finance the elementary public services. In turn, the shortage of funds reflects the enlargement of corporate prerogatives over public functions and resources and their consequent diversion to private hands. Thus at the same time as the education system has been endowed with this enlarged responsibility, it has lost the ability to perform the task. This contradiction is based not only on the economic crisis, but on the general crisis of confidence in the legitimacy of public bureaucracies. In part this crisis orginates in the schools' failure to successfully transmit knowledge and technique, especially to Black and Brown children. But beyond the decline in the quality of education measured by traditional standards, another more pervasive crisis is growing — the opposition by the students themselves to the norms and values of contemporary capitalist society.

Students in secondary and higher educational institutions have begun to doubt the efficacy of the objects of education. The jobs offered as payoff for completion of school no longer seem worthwhile in comparison to the length of school time required. In contemporary America good jobs have been intimately linked with educational achievement. The decline of interest in jobs as a valid life ambition is a measure of the estrangement of large sectors of young people from capitalist culture.

But student disaffection goes beyond vocational alienation. It is not merely a question of making jobs more attractive by offering higher pay. A generation reared not on scarcity but on the culture of consumption cannot be socialized into work with a promise of more and better gadgets. College students offered nothing but a chance to serve corporations and the state when they do not accept the underlying values and norms of bourgeois society will work only if material necessity forces them to.

The proletarianization of students is expressed in the mass character of higher education. The proliferation of degrees granted by colleges and universities has transformed college education from an experience reserved for managerial and petty-bourgeois professional strata into a prerequisite for technical labor. The Bachelor's and Master's degrees are now widely diffused among the labor force and have lost their special connotations.

In the 1960s it was students who first challenged the legitimacy of the state and its ideological apparatuses. The recognition that the university, long regarded as an academic market-place, was in fact a knowledge factory subordinate to the research needs of the corporate war machine, was both the cause and the consequence of student demands for power to change the university into a partisan of its own stated values. It was not that students attacked the universities and colleges because they felt betrayed by the revelation that schools served the imperialist interests of the state and its corporate masters. Students first demanded power to control their own lives in school, to make their educational experience relevant to the contemporary world. The boredom and monotony of the classroom in the midst of social turbulence on the one hand, and the perception by students that the work for which they were being prepared was instrumental for consumption of waste or production for destruction rather than the advancement of human needs on the other, were at the bottom of the student revolt. Students of the 1950s could not accep tthe fate of their parents or thier quiescent predecessors.

As all educational institutions, universities and colleges serve a twofold function. The first function is to produce skilled labor for manufacturing, government, and service industries. During periods of economic growth, higher education plays an important part in the development of the forces of production. The importance of machinery for modern industry has placed knowledge itself at the center of the productive forces. From the universities private corporations derive practical applications of scientific research as well as cadres for their own plants and laboratories. Moreover, colleges produce teachers, health workers, and others engaged in the provision of social overheads. It is no accident that those engaged in scientific, technical, and medical studies have been the most ambivalent about the worth of their education. Some of these students have joined in the protests but, in the main, scientists and engineers have been least involved in contesting the quality and objects of higher education. To the extent that the economy has made provisions for their employment in *productive* work and the content of science itself remains unquestioned, radicalism has not sunk deep roots among this stratum of students.

Academic unemployment has further eroded the legitimacy of higher education. The public and service sectors have failed to expand fast enough to absorb the tremendous growth of credentialed workers leaving the academy. Concurrently, the production sector is faced with stagnating output on the one hand, and higher output per worker on the other. Layoffs among engineers and scientists have begun to occur in private corporations, and schools and health institutions have cut back in hiring because of fiscal crises.

The requirement demanded by many employers for higher education as a prerequisite for administrative and technical jobs is not rooted in the level of development of the productive forces, particularly modern machinery. Operation of these machines is much less complex than formerly. Automation has destroyed traditional skills, even at the level of operation. Employers demand higher qualifications precisely because increased productivity has created vast labor surpluses as the general level of literacy has advanced. Much of the stratification of the labor force and the relatively minute division of labor in industry are not primarily caused by the new technologies, but by the requirements of corporate and government hierarchies to disguise the community of interest among all workers and to serve their own economic interest. The point is that automation and other modern forms of mechanization require fewer skills than the older industrial processes, except for a few highly trained employees. Yet, institutions demand higher educational qualifications than ever before.

The second function of education is to socialize students into work in general and the hierarchical form of alienated labor in particular. During the era of economic scarcity the work ethic was deeply ingrained into social consciousness, and material necessity has remained a powerful instrument of social integration, despite the appearance of material plenty in society at large. But the contradiction between the technical capacity of the U.S. production system to end scarcity and the persistent need to work at boring, meaningless jobs substantially erodes work discipline. The ideological imperative that liberation can only come through self-sacrifice and hard work has lost its legitimacy. However, the coercive aspect of alienated work still remains the most powerful drive to enforce the system of industrial discipline since technical innovation has been stifled and people must work in order to eat.

Of course Blacks, Puerto Ricans and impoverished whites experience the deterioration of education at a much earlier age. Many Blacks are barred from participation in skilled labor by the school system. The tracking system, according to which students are classified at the very beginning of their school life by intelligence tests based on discriminatory cultural criteria, acts as a demoralizing influence on students and parents alike. The rise of Black militancy in the early '60s was reflected in the demands of Black parents and students for community control over the hiring of teachers, administration of schools, and curriculum. The quest for Black control over public institutions providing services to Black communities was a rejection of the authority of municipal government over crucial institutions in the Black, Puerto Rican and Mexican-American areas.

At first, the struggle to impose forms of popular power over the schools appeared merely to rearrange or "reform" the power structure. But the impulse went much deeper. The struggle for popular control arises side by side with the attempt to create new institutions which go outside the prevailing system. Young people do not simply reproduce the family — they consider the value of communal living, a new way to organize their personal lives outside the old nuclear family. Parents and students try to create their own schools without substantial public support or, if they choose to develop new educational practice within the public sector, they refuse to accept the old structure of authority and simply make themselves new masters over the old institution.

The disintegration of the primary institutions has affected trade unions, which, once viewed as workers' instruments for the defense and extension of class interests, now play a new role at the work place. In part, they have been charged with tasks which primary institutions such as the family and the school have failed to perform. The labor union has been converted, in part, into an ideological apparatus of the state, an institution performing primary socialization functions by collaborating with employers to codify rewards for loyal performance of labor. The union contract not only represents the outcome of industrial struggle; it also helps to reinforce bourgeois ideological and cultural hegemony: it embodies a value system.

The role of unions as bargaining agents for workers is an integral part of the administrative structure of the modern corporation and represents an auxiliary method by which the state establishes control over wages and working conditions. One of the key mechanisms of trade union–government collaboration is the mediation and arbitration procedures of most union contracts, which remove the settlement of disputes from the bargaining table or the picket line to the courts. Arbitration is a quasi-judicial procedure — the arbitrator is usually a private individual or agency rather than an official of the state courts. But the principle of a neutral party making final and binding decisions in labor disputes is parallel to the role played by courts in the judicial system. The fact that we do not have labor courts in the United States is ideologically efficient for corporate capitalism, since it avoids placing the onus for antilabor decisions on the state itself.

In most labor agreements the right to strike is restricted so that strikes can be called only at the expiration of the contract or for a limited number of issues during the life of the agreement. And in the majority of instances strikes can be called during the term of a contract only after the union has exhausted a rather prolonged series of grievance procedures. But no contract formally recognizes the "right" to strike at any time, for any reason. Under the Taft-Hartley Law unions are accountable for abrogation of the "no strike" provision of the labor agreement by any of its members. Thus it is in the union's interest to quell wildcat strikes and to maintain fundamental work discipline.

The role of the union as policeman reflects itself in day-to-day issues. Lateness and absenteeism are usually the mutual concerns of management and the union. It is not uncommon for union stewards and other officials to administer warnings to workers who do not come to work on time, fail to meet production standards, or are insubordinate. Union officials often view themselves as intermediaries between the rank and file, whom they regard as undisciplined and ignorant of broader issues and the management. In many industries, particularly those in which the strength of the union is greater than the individual employer's, such as garment and construction, the union itself takes responsibility for many important industry decisions. Unions use union welfare funds to help tottering employers and union lobbying power to support industry's concern with imports or government contracts for military expenditures and construction. More fundamentally, where the union controls the supply of labor in industries, such as construction and shipping, its power over the individual worker as well as within the industry itself gives it the appearance of an independent force. Actually, many union officials boast that they are responsible for the economic health of the industry as well as the welfare of the members, although politically they are forced to enter into the management of industry for the ostensible purpose of safeguarding their members' interests.

During the '50s, liberal union officials' complicity in corporate capitalism's drive for maximum profits in the midst of economic stagnation caused an outbreak of wildcat strikes in the auto and steel industries and long strikes in other sectors of the economy. The trade union reaction was swift and sure. It deplored the anarchic strike movements and agreed with employers that militants should be fired and that the injunctive procedures of the Taft-Hartley Law should be applied. At the same time unions and employers took steps to meet the demands of the workers. The no-strike provision of the auto workers' contract was modified to permit strikes over production standards under certain conditions. The steelworkers' union bureaucracy reaffirmed its determination to enforce the provision of the basic steel agreement which prohibited technological change without union consultation.

The wildcat strikes were smashed, but the challenge to the unions did not abate. Workers attempted to capture control over their own working conditions through mushrooming rank-and-file movements to replace the old leadership. Beginning in the late '50s and early '60s, there was a parade of electoral challenges to the leaders of many key industrial unions. Although most of the pretenders to the thrones were middle-rank leaders, they rode to power on the strength of membership discontent. Such contests took place in the steelworkers', rubber workers', textile workers', oil and chemical workers', teachers', state, county and municipal workers', the electrical workers' and in many locals of the auto workers' union, where each collective bargaining defeat was followed by the defeat of a raft of local union incumbents. Another manifestation of the emergence of rank-and-file discontent in the '60s was the rise of the teamsters' unions as a major challenger to traditional union jurisdictions. The apparent militancy of this "outlawed" union meshed neatly with rank-and-file disgust with the softness of the middle-aged CIO labor statemen. The merger of the AFL and the CIO had prevented workers from seeking alternative representation when their unions engaged in company union practices. The expulsion of the teamsters from the House of Labor in 1957 provided disgruntled workers with a powerful alternative to the old labor unions.

But by the late '60s the initial enthusiasm of the workers for competitive unionism and internal union reform had ebbed. After 1967 real wages declined each year and, after a period of economic growth due to the Vietnam War, the economy began to slow down. The first effects of the slowdown were reflected in rising layoffs and the elimination of overtime, which took the gloss from pay envelopes. Meanwhile prices kept rising.

The last two years of the '60s and the oepning of the '70s were marked by a reawakening of rank-and-file militancy, which took different forms in different sectors. Among public workers and workers in voluntary institutions such as hospitals, there was a wave of union organizing and strike movements, led by teachers. The impact of public employee organizing was peculiar because every strike of this group of workers is, perforce, a strike against the state. In many places the pent-up frustrations of these workers, who had borne the worst effects of the inflation and the fiscal crisis of the public sector, caused widespread disrespect for laws prohibiting strikes by public employees and court injunctions aimed at enforcing these laws. In many cities, particularly on the Eastern seaboard, the leaders riding the crest of the wave of militancy became important political figures and were absorbed by municipal governments as warm allies and important sources of political power. Although the fiscal crisis afflicting all public organs prevents a secure alliance of the workers with government authority, the unions do represent the newly discovered power of the membership. Chances of upheaval against the leadership, until the state shows its inability and unwillingness to come through on workers' demands, seem remote for the near future.

But the picture is far from uniform. The 1970 wildcat strike of postal workers took place over the heads of union leadership and became a national strike without central coordination and direction. Even more dramatic was the extraordinary wildcat strike by 100,000 teamsters in the Middle West and the West Coast in rejection of a contract negotiated by their national leaders. The vaunted authority of the union over the membership, its reputation for militancy and toughness at the bargaining table, its myth of invincibility, collapsed beneath the insurgent rank and file which for the first time acted independently of the bureaucracy.

The new form of the labor revolt is not found in rank-and-file protests against specific union leaders. It is expressed in the disbelief in the legitimacy of the unions as well as their leaders to "represent the workers" and the growing disrespect for the old, legally sanctioned bargaining mechanisms. Less dramatic, but equally significant, has been the phenomenal rise of members' contract rejections against the wishes of the bureaucracy. In the older unions, having attempted internal reform of the leadership structure, the members are experimenting with new forms of class struggle. They are not likely to abandon the unions, because in many cases the union has become the chief dispenser of social benefits. But the impulse to dual forms of struggle — shop committees, wildcat strikes, stewards' movements — may become important in the future. New instruments of workers' struggle would have to reject the institutionalization of the class contract represented by the legally sanctioned labor agreement administered by trade union bureaucracies. Workers would have to consciously reject limitations on their freedom to take direct action to meet their elementary needs at the work place. Although many wildcat strikes are implicitly caused by issues which go beyond wage demands, these remain hidden beneath the economic struggles.

Labor unions are not likely to become formally committed to the ideas of workers' control over working conditions, investment decisions, and the objects of labor. On the contrary, they will remain "benefits" oriented, fighting incessantly to improve the economic position of their own membership in relation to other sections of the work force rather than relative to the employers. They will bitterly oppose workers' efforts to take direct action beyond the scope of the union agreement and to make agreements with the boss on the informal basis of power relations rather than within the limitations imposed by a legally sanctioned contract. Trade unions are likely to remain both a deterrent to the workers' initiative and a "third party" force at the work place, objectively serving corporate interests both ideologically and in the daily life of the shop, and diminishing as an instrument of workers' struggle, to be employed only selectively by them.

Anti-union consciousness is confused by the inability of workers to organize on an independent basis. Trade unionism still appears a progressive force to the mass of working poor, such as farm and hospital workers, who labor under conditions of severe degradation. At first unionization seems to be deliverance from bondage. But after the initial upsurge has been spent, most of these unions fall back into patterns of class collaboration and repression, and defend the union contract with all the coercive powers at their command. At the point when grinding poverty has been overcome and the unions have settled into their conservative groove, their bureaucratic character becomes clear to workers.

We are now in the midst of a massive reevaluation by organized industrial workers of the viability of the unions. As already indicated, it is an action critique rather than an ideological criticism. In the end, the spontaneous revolt will have to develop its own demands and forms of struggle. It is still too early to predict their precise configuration in the United States. The European experience suggests that workers' councils and committees or autonomous creations of workers at the point of production will not replace the unions immediately, but will exist side by side with them for some time.

The crisis of values in America has affected religious institutions also. The church has always played a political and economic role in addition to its ideological function. Separation of church and state was always more formal than actual. The importance of religious teaching during the rise of capitalism cannot be underestimated. Religion legitimated private property, the alienation of labor, and industrial progress. As long as the church represented eternal values reinterpreted in the context of capitalist social relations, its status as a universal institution was secure. But the development of capitalism itself deprived the church of its functional legitimacy. The bourgeois revolution stripped the church of its property and its power as the official religion and relegated it to the role of guardian of ideological treasures, and then the industrial revolution required a system of free public education under secular authority. Having become a subsidiary political and economic influence, the church's ideological role was diminished because it was relegated to the spiritual realm and denied material functions to provide social legitimacy. The erosion of religious authority corresponds to the decline of its functions in contemporary capitalism.

However, it would be a mistake to discount religious influences entirely. The church remains an important social institution in America. Churches, especially the Catholic Church, have a growing role in economic and social life. Their ownership of property, especially real estate, makes them an important capitalist institution participating in many major decisions affecting sectors of the political economy. But as a political and economic force the church is forced to deal with secular issues — often against the interests of its constituency — and thus, through its exposure as an economic interest, the vaunted neutrality of the church from earthly affairs, regarded as the necessary basis of its moral and juridical authority, has been considerably weakened. To counter its ideological weakness, the church, especially the Catholic Church, has vastly expanded its educational system — parochial education in America has grown enormously in many areas over the past ten years. But the reversion to secular functions has demystified the church. It now must be judged by the canons of civil society.

This trend can be observed in all advanced capitalist countries. An indication of the crisis of religious authority is the massive defections of young priests and ministers from Christian churches, the decline of church attendance and income, and the desperate attempts of religious hierarchies to become more relevant to the secular crises which have contributed to their isolation.

Organized oppositon to the church hierarchy is most dramatic in the Catholic Church. Having perceived that the Church has become another corporate institution and has lost its unification on the ideological plane, young priests have demanded that the employees of the company be integrated into secular life on its own terms. They have challenged celibacy, Church litany, and other hallowed customs designed to reinforce the spirituality of the Church, its status as a higher moral force. The resistance of the Church hierarchy to the most radical demands aimed at demystification is attenuated by concessions to radical priests who wish the Church to be relevant to contemporary political and social issues. To a certain extent, these concessions are in the interest of the hieararchy, which is desperately attempting to hold on to its young cadre while at the same time enlarging its own political influence. Priests are being encouraged to run for public office, to participate in popular struggles within health and educational institutions, to fight for more housing. In New York, the Catholic Church emerged as a major force in the School decentralization battle in 1966. Many Church officials as well as active Catholic laymen were successful candidates for local school board seats in 1970.

It would be an error to assume that the church's active role in the affairs of urban life is entirely venal. It is propelled by complex motives. On the one hand, church involvement in politics reflects its struggle to win legislative approval for public funds for parochial schools since they, too, face a deep fiscal crisis. On the other hand, the hierarchy has been forced to be more permissive with its activist cadre, many of whom are influenced by radical ideologies or humanist philosophies. But the church cannot solve the fundamental conflict between its growing secular role as an integral part of corporate capitalism and its need for moral and juridical legitimacy, which supposedly rests on its status as a neutral arbiter of all earthly affairs. The institutional interests of the church have become incompatible with its ideological functions.

The breakdown of institutions is the breakdown of values, norms, and rules of conduct. Law, a system of rules and regulations, provides the cohesion necessary for the preservation of institutional structures. As a system of morality, a lexicon of rights and responsibilities, it establishes the legitimacy for the exercise of institutional functions. It is the critical ideological apparatus of the state. As a mediation between consciousness and the actual character of social relations, juridical relations are the most crucial for the preservation of class society because they embody simultaneously a system of beliefs and rules of conduct.

If law were only operable in its institutional form, that is, as a branch of the state, its power would be limited to political relations. Since man is not a political animal but a social animal, the concept of law must permeate all social institutions. It is called upon to provide standards of behavior in the factory and all other institutions of daily life. In its juridical form, it provides sanction for entering into certain relations. But as a system of rules and regulations it governs the daily activity of institutional relations, prescribing orderly procedures for the business of production and exchange of commodities and for the functions of all intermediate institutions between the state and civil society.

The phenomenon of divorce, the inability of the schools to transmit knowledge and values, the breakdown of industrial discipline and the decline in church authority pose a grave threat to the life of capitalist society. The challenge of mass movements to institutions such as the school, the family, the trade unions, and the church, which constitute the critical mediations between individuals and the class nature of production relations, rips the reified mask from these man-made institutions and shows the bare face of the ruling class. Without ideologies and apparatuses representing them, there can be no class society, unless its power is maintained by repressive violence. Repression is no longer a last resort; it is transformed into a mode of rule.

The fascism of the 1920s and the 1930s based itself on the attempt of a bourgeoisie to save itself from extinction in the wake of the most massive economic and political crisis in the history of capitalism. The bourgeoisie of Germany and Italy were prepared to surrender their autonomy over all basic decisions to a state which, owing to its capacity to suppress the working class movement and direct economic as well as social life, could unify the bourgeoisie. The German industrialists learned that the old parliamentary conservative and social democratic majorities were no match for inexorable social forces which were beyond the control of private interests or the liberal state.

Fascism was an able representative of capitalist interests because it did not advocate them in a period when capitalism as a system had reached its moral nadir. Instead, the fascists presented themselves as critics of capitalism and upholders of a socialism ensconced in the rhetoric and the ethos of imperialism and racism. The fascists were the most articulate critics of bourgeois values and liberal political and social institutions. Parliamentary democracy was the cruelest hoax ever perpetrated upon the working classes, they argued, because it gave the workers no genuine voice in the conduct of political affairs. Instead, the intellectual and political elites who controlled the political parties manipulated popular demands to advance their own special interests. The parliamentary process was nothing but a series of deals between politicians in search of power.

Private corporate interests did not escape the ideological thrusts of the fascists, who declared competition archaic and untrammeled capitalism a detriment to the national good. Fascism proposed to unify the German nation in its quest for its own historic destiny — the civilizing of the world. National reconstruction would proceed without the constraints imposed by a state legislative and administrative bureaucracy hopelessly entangled in bitter internecine warfare. The Nazis promised an end to strife within the German nation. Harmony between workers and capitalists, between men and women, between man and the state would be established under the hegemony of the party and its leader. The enemy was redefined within the socialist tradition — international bankers who had made Germany poor. But Hitler introduced a profound racist strain into his ideological anticapitalist appeal. The real bankers were also Jews. Existing social relations need not be disturbed except that Jews must be separated from their property and their political influence. Thus did the fascists attempt to coopt the traditional anticapitalist traditions of the socialist movement in order to win a mass base among large sections of the working class who had, during the 1920s, experienced the denouement of bourgeois pretensions of democracy, even its social democratic variety.

But the fascists did not renounce all capitalist institutions. They did not define socialism as expropriation of private property by the working class. Instead, in the traditions of the Second and the Third Internationals, socialism was the direction by the state of all economic and political life. Turning to a deformed version of Hegel's *Rechtsphilosophie*, the state was presumed to be the expression of the reconciliation of conflicting interests within the economic and social spheres. Nazi ideologists did not proclaim the end of conflict, but they did reassert in its authoritarian mask the concept of the state as an instrument of social harmony and stability. Stripped of its mystical form, this is simply an ideology of state capitalism according to which the neutral state is transformed into the command and the leadership state — an activist and organizer of social and economic life.

Fascism in the United States is developing under different circumstances, based on its own needs and history. In the first place, the elements of state capitalism, intrinsic in fascist evolution, already exist within the uncomfortable framework of liberal institutions. It is no longer possible to deny the centrality of the state to capitalist survival. No longer merely a coercive instrument for the protection of private property, or a regulator of relations among the capitalists themselves, the newest function of the state is its direct intervention in the economy, particularly its role as investor. In all advanced capitalist societies this development has taken place to a greater or lesser degree. In the United States state capitalism is characterized not only by the accretion of the planning functions of the state, but by the intervention of the state into all institutional life. Institutions, including production, literally depend on the support of the state for their survival. Corporate power is wielded decisively in all organs of the state which, in turn, have been enlisted as economic institutions.

Second, having coopted liberal institutions for authoritarian ends, there is no reason to believe that parliamentary forms must be destroyed to establish an authoritarian state. In fact, the reverse is true. The corporation, in consequence of its inability to survive without the state, did surrender much of its autonomy to it. In the process the corporation colonized the state and brought it fully into its service, although it left the state with its own prerogatives. To a certain extent the state retains autonomous functions and institutions which operate, at least in part, independently of direct corporate power lest the vital regulatory functions of the state be undermined. The destruction of the autonomy of the state is not in the interest of the corporate bourgeoisie in the long run even though it has been forced to impress public authority directly in its service. But the process of absorption of the public by the private is rather advanced in America. Parliamentary institutions have been reduced to little more than debating bodies at worst, veto bodies at best. During the past half-century, Congress has initiated virtually no major legislation. It acts occasionally to balance the most centralist actions of the executive branch, which has, with impunity, kept Congress only imperfectly informed of its actions. America has no articulate parliamentary opposition nor a mass left movement capable of checking the organizational and stabilizing functions of the state.

Third, unlike Germany, where the rise of fascism was a response to visible economic catastrophe afflicting the country and the chaos which it produced, American authoritarianism is growing amidst a social crisis which arises from the long-term crisis of the capitalist system as a whole. Chiefly, the crisis is a crisis of the superstructure — the breakdown of institutions and of ideologies. Although these crises are not separate from the underlying instability of the economy and its reliance on the state for coherence and for growth, the American crisis has a different configuration from the world economic crisis forty years ago.

Liberal institutions, for example, have revealed their disintegration. Liberals still propose that the end of the Indochina war will be a first step in reordering national priorities so that the center cities can be rebuilt, school and health facilities expanded, and local services broadened. A more advanced group asks for new forms of popular participation in order to guarantee a broad base for institutional reform. But their program of social reconstruction to fill the void of legitimate authority has come into conflict with the hierarchies which control social institutions and necessary corporate requirements. Since the consciousness of men does not, in the last analysis, determine being, the reconstructionist wing of corporate interests has entered its nadir and a more authoritarian wing has gained ascendency. The old liberal values, products of a bygone era, can no longer be successfully reconstructed. The polarization of American society has sharpened. The "law and order" forces now dominant in the government and among a section of the bourgeoisie are building a mass base among sections of workers, intellectuals, and small businessmen who have become disillusioned with the old liberal program. The ideological strength of the Right is its critique of bourgeois liberalism, its attack against the bankrupt welfarism of the Democratic Party, and the inability of the liberal bourgeoisie to solve the underlying economic crisis maturing within American society. Indeed, fascism disguises itself in the cloak of a conservative defense of traditional liberalism. In order to reconstruct the existing social institutions, which have failed in their appointed mission, the authoritarians appear as the other side of the coin: the Right criticizes bourgeois values while defending bourgeois institutions.

It is the authoritarians who defend the family as ideology even as capitalism destroys its material basis, who uphold the hierarchies of education and credentials even as capitalism renders traditional skills obsolete and assigns large numbers of the labor force to the historic dustbin. But instead of a material reconstruction of these institutions, the authoritarians seek to superimpose discipline upon them. They dream of schools which train people but do not educate them; families which prepare youth for steady work but do not transmit the old individualistic and humanistic values; religion which teaches obedience not love; trade unions which act as disciplinary forces for the corporations, not instruments of workers' struggles. Law becomes hypostatized as an end of human conduct. Order is a value instead of the outcome of human endeavor. Fascism in America is the form of law without its content.

Liberals themselves have gone over to the forces of law and order. No less a bourgeois liberal ideologist than John Kenneth Galbraith can simultaneously defend the old civil libertarian values and attack the fundamental right of workers to struggle for higher wages. The necessity of preserving the capitalist economy makes necessary measures to abrogate workers' ability to strike, and to deny, in practice, the myth of free competition by calling for price controls. No more revealing instance of the bankruptcy of liberalism in America exists than the support rendered by the Democratic majority of the Senate and the House to the new administration's "no-knock" legislation which permits, among other things, law enforcement officers to circumvent constitutional guarantees regarding search and seizure and habeas corpus. Together with growing "left" liberal support for wage freeze measures to counter inflation and thus preserve economic values, these indicate the merger of liberal and more openly authoritarian methods to preserve capitalist institutions. No liberal can deny the need to fight chaos, riots, and other instances of social disorder. The ultimate law of a state is to defend itself against those who would overthrow it. Herein lies the identity of interest among both wings of the capitalist class.

We now arrive at the question of radical strategy to confront the emergence of both the void in the legitimacy of institutions and the authoritarian bid to save them. The burden of the ancestral left strategy to combat fascism was the alliance of the social democratic and communist movements in defense of traditional bourgeois liberties. The Communists reacted to the breakdown of institutions in the 1930s by attempting to preserve them, against the right-wing attempt to reconstitute them on an absolutist basis. Everywhere the attempt failed. For beneath the political alliance of left parties was the presumption that there were on the one hand viable elements in bourgeois institutions worth saving, and "progressive" elements of the bourgeoisie with whom to form alliances on the other. The pact made by the left in France and Germany was that the condition for socialism was the defeat of fascism. Fascism, in turn, could only be overcome on the basis of the existing liberal social relations and institutional arrangements. The Communists argued against the "lefts" who insisted that the only way to defeat fascism was the revolutionary action of the working class itself in behalf of its own socialist demands. According to the popular front proponents, socialist activity would only splinter the antifascist forces and insure the victory of fascism.

History has passed judgment on this strategy in France and Spain. The militant defense of bourgeois legality by the Communists in France in 1936 and their opposition to and suppression of revolutionary movements in Spain was consistent with their policy of making alliances with the bourgeoisie to defeat fascism in Greece in 1945, in France and Italy in 1968, and elsewhere. In each case, the ephemeral character of the bourgeois ally was revealed. The collapse of the liberal bourgeoisie in the prewar popular front period, the inability of the popular front to stem the fascist tide, showed the mythological character of the alliance. In the end, the bourgeoisie went over to the Nazis. But not before the juridical and political institutions showed themselves as trusted instruments of class oppression. In fact, in Spain the Communists became themselves instruments of the capitalist state.

In the United States, the Communists and Socialists loyally followed the policy of alliances with the liberal wing of the capitalist class. Within the workers' movement where there were no mass socialist forces, the alliance took the form of the "center-left" coalition between left wing and pro—New Deal trade unionists which, for a time, dominated the CIO. The left played the role of loyal opposition to the Roosevelt administration, its most friendly and persistent critic. During the late 1930s and the World War II period, the Communist Party and the Socialst Party advocated more government intervention into the economy and social life. In the name of social welfare, it prepared the ground for workers' acceptance of government regulation of labor relations. Objectively, the left strengthened the role of the state in the political economy and facilitated the emergence of nascent authoritarianism. The main allies of the popular front, the liberal corporatists, used the left as a means to save capitalism from its economic crisis. The popular front left contributed to the development of new institutions of capitalist stability — social welfare, a powerful labor bureaucracy, and a reinvigorated state machinery.

Another consideration in a determination of radical strategy is the history of the parties on the left themselves. They would replace the capitalist dictatorship with the proletarian power represented by a centralist party at the helm of a socialist state. But these parties have been without significant influence among the underlying population. One factor contributing to the decline of state socialism has been the periodic repression of political dissent in our country. But repression is not powerful enough to explain away the sect-like character of all state socialist movements. Other working class movements, including state socialist movements, have experienced such hardship and managed to gain support among the oppressed classes and strata. Two key developments in America may be decisive in explaining the failure of American socialism. The first is the ethnic, occupational, and racial diversity of the American working class and the consequent racist and elitist ideologies among the American workers. The second is the authoritarianism of the state socialist program and organizations. Leninist and social democratic movements have operated on the principle of bureaucratic hegemony and hierarchical authority, mirroring the prevailing corporate and state structures which they seek to replace. Workers who face the power of bureaucratic corporations every day are not likely to transfer their allegiance o a new bureaucracy, although they will join movements for social change in order to wring concessions from the prevailing system.

The older, sect-like socialist organizations, including the Communist Party, seem to forget that today's institutions are being challenged for just their authoritarian, elitist, corporatist character. The students know that schools do not exist as centers of free inquiry. They have become instrumental to the forces of domination. The trade unions cannot be reconstructed by the rank and file as if they were voluntary organizations. They are now creatures of law, with specific tasks within corporate hierarchies. The internal challenge to the unions simply results in a reproduction of the old leadership. If the new leaders cannot be integrated into the old framework, they are eliminated, by violence if necessary. The courts have their marching orders. The end of the last of the liberal Supreme Courts was accomplished by force. The resignation of Fortas, the elimination of Goldberg, the retirement of Warren and the selection of conservatives, despite liberal rejections of early choices, were no accidents. They were the results of a concerted effort to remove the last barriers to the new authoritarianism.

Therefore, it is extremely important that we make the distinction between bourgeois institutions and bourgeois values. The proposal to defend bourgeois institutions against the bourgeoisie lacks the same material basis as it did forty years ago. These institutions, backed by a legitimacy derived from laws and by force, are under withering criticism and attack by new generations who can no longer live within them. But the challenge to institutions, significantly, has taken place in the name of some of the traditional values, specifically individual liberty, humanism, and democracy.

The radicals and militants, Black and white, today seek neither to modify nor replace the existing institutions with a new system of domination. They reject the Old Left notion that a transitional state as an organ of class oppression is necessary as a transition to communism. The student, youth, and Black movements are a revolt against domination itself. They represent, in embryo, the impulse to liberation from all hierarchical authority — from the concept of right, that is, from the legitimation of rules of conduct from above.

Further, they will not accept the family, the education system, the trade unions, and the state as legitimate institutions, They have begun an action critique to demystify them. The law, which presently represents the repressive power of the bourgeoisie, is losing its mediating role. The law *is* against the people.

In essence, radicals must be the defenders of the values inherent in the unfulfilled promise of the great bourgeois revolutions. The radical movement may not have established the hegemony of its ideas or culture throughout society or even among its constituents. But we must be the advocates of direct popular democracy — of the reconstruction of society from below, of popular power over all institutions, and the creation of institutions to meet human needs — not to serve the interests of profit and domination.

19. Bertram Gross

Friendly Fascism, a Model for America

Before World War II many American liberals and radicals — myself included — voiced alarm over the rise of fascism in Mussolini's Italy and Hitler's Germany. For our indiscretion in detecting future foreign enemies we were later branded "prematurely antifascist."

As I look back on those days — they seem centuries ago — I cannot help but feel "How easy it was to be boldly antifascist then!" We applauded Sinclair Lewis' wryly titled *It Can't Happen Here* (1935) because of his barbs against fascist tendencies in America's white racism, anti-Semitism, and populism. But

Reprinted by permission of the publisher from *Social Policy*, 1 (November/December 1970), pp. 44–52. © Social Policy 1970.

we never *seriously* thought it could happen here. Fascism was something that happened in other countries.

Today, in the 1970s, it is easy to talk about the dangers of repression in America. "Hard-hats," Birchers, police extremists, and George Wallace are viewed with alarm as the cutting edge of a new repression. Left-wingers and Black militants are solemnly warned that extremism in opposition to war or on behalf of justice will trigger repressive action. But it is much harder to analyze the nature of the repression we fear. It is extremely difficult to face up to the question, *"Could a new-style fascism happen here?"*

There are many reasons for this difficulty.

First, the media have focused much more on left-wing dissidents than on the more widespread acitivites of right-wing subversives, particularly those within the citadels of formal governmental authority.

Second, the terms "fascist" and "fascism" have at times been used by the Black Panthers and others as quick terms of abuse — without the conceptual foundations that might make the labels stick.

Above all, most of us have lost what Gunther Anders[1] calls the "courage to fear"! For a quarter of a century, under the threat of nuclear annihilation, we have been developing our ability to repress justified fear. If it seems there's nothing to be done, why think about the unthinkable — either the nuclear holocaust or the fascist horror?

Today, as Anders has suggested, we must strive not so much for the freedom from *fear* as for the freedom *to* fear. We need greater capacity to develop articulated fears that match the magnitude of tomorrow's dangers. We must accept *the possibility that in this decade our America — despite all that we may love or admire in it — may have a rendezvous with fascism.* And we must be aware that if fascism comes to the United States, as Huey Long suggested back in the 1930s, it will come under the slogans of democracy and 100 percent Americanism; it will come in the form of an advanced technological society, supported by its techniques — a techno-urban fascism, American style.

"Flabby" Futurism

"If repression is not yet as blatant or as flamboyant as it was during the McCarthy years," wrote Henry Steele Commager[2] in a recent article, "it is in many ways more pervasive and more formidable. For it comes to us now with official sanction and is imposed upon us by officials sworn to uphold the law: the Attorney General, the FBI, state and local officials, the police and even judges." Vice President Spiro Agnew's proposal to "separate [the protest leaders] from our society — with no more regret than we should feel over discarding rotten apples from a barrel" is described by Commager as "precisely the philosophy that

---

[1]Gunther Anders, "Theses for the Atomic Age," *The Massachusetts Review*, Spring 1962, pp. 493–505.

[2]Henry Steele Commager, "Is Freedom Dying in America?" *Look*, July 14, 1970.

animated the Nazis." He concluded that "it would be an exaggeration to say that the United States is a garrison state, but none to say that it is in danger of becoming one."

The idea of a "garrison state" has thus far been the most explicit model for examining future political developments in a grand style First described in 1941 by Harold Lasswell, a garrison state is defined as a military-police society that differs from previous military dictatorships in three ways:

1. It integrates militarism and modern technology.
2. It continues to use the symbols of "mystic democracy" while promoting a deep and general sense of participation in the total enterprise of the state.
3. It suppresses or controls legislative assemblies and opposition political parties.[3]

Reviewing the subject in 1965, Lasswell restated his earlier judgment that we are entering a world of garrison states, a "world of ruling castes (or a single caste) learning how to maintain ascendancy against internal challenge by the ruthless exploitation of hitherto unapplied instruments of modern science and technology."[4]

Most recent discussion of fascism, regrettably, lack Lasswellian vigor. William Ebenstein describes fascism as "the totalitarian way of resolving conflicts within an industrially advanced society."[5] He suggests that its principal elements are (*1*) a distrust of reason, (*2*) a denial of basic human equality, (*3*) a code of behavior based on lies and violence, (*4*) government by an elite, (*5*) totalitarianism, (*6*) racialism and imperialism, and (*7*) opposition to international law and order.[6] In his analysis of right-wing extremist attacks on church liberalism in America, Franklin H. Littell offers a longer list of elements and maintains that "fascism" is the most appropriate term to apply to the Radical Right.[7] But both Ebenstein and Littell derive their elements from other countries. The same is true of John Weiss, who — in contrast to Ebenstein — suggests that "the greatest potential for fascism lies not in the liberal West, but rather in the dialectical polarities even now increasing in non-Western or underdeveloped societies."[8]

If we look to explicit futurism, we get even less help. The bulk of "future-casting" is, of course, still in science fiction, in which scores of authors have developed endless variations on the theme of science-based dictatorships. Some are in the spirit of Huxley's *Brave New World* (1931), featuring the systematic reinforcement of desirable behavior. Others are modeled after Orwell's *1984* (1948), a society controlled almost exclusively by punishment.

[3]Harold Lasswell, "The Garrison State," *The American Journal of Sociology*, January 1941.
[4]Harold Lasswell, "The Garrison-State Hypothesis Today," in Samuel P. Huntington, Ed., *Changing Patterns of Military Politics*, New York: Free Press, 1962.
[5]William Ebenstein, *Today's Isms*, Englewood Cliffs, N.J.: Prentice-Hall, 1954.
[6]William Ebenstein, *Totalitarianism: New Perspectives*, New York: Holt, Rinehart and Winston, 1962, p. 32.
[7]Franklin H. Littell, *Wild Tongues, a Handbook of Social Pathology*, New York: Macmillan, 1969.
[8]John Weiss, *The Fascist Tradition*, New York: Harper and Row, 1967.

By contrast, the official "future-casting" of Daniel Bell's Commission on the Year 2000 and *The Futurist* magazine is rather insipid. Both have concentrated on the gadgetry of technology and on the more trivial aspects of the social system. With but few exceptions, most of htis work has represented escapism from contemporary political issues or even such "middle-range" questions as the quality of freedom in 1976 or 1984. Bell's own analysis of "postindustrialism," although opening up vital questions concerning current societal change, greatly exaggerates the power of the new "knowledge elites." Like Galbraith in his discussion of the "technostructure," he has developed a romantic fantasy that, though flattering to the egos of grateful colleagues, pushes into the background the unpleasant realities of militarism, repression, and neo-imperialism.

In my own work on postindustrialism I have thus far focused on current societal changes: from the production of goods to the provision of services, from big organizations to macrosystems, from white-collar work to extended professionalism, from metropolis to megalopolis, and the fragmentation resulting from all these trends.[9] In my work on social systems accounting, while tracing the transformations from agriculturalism and industrialism to postindustrial service societies,[10] I have not yet explored the new "grand alternatives" facing service societies.

The "social indicator movement," unfortunately, has thus far avoided indicators of major institutional change. With support from both the White House and the Bureau of the Budget, the emphasis has been on routinized "management indicators," major attention being diverted away from "critical societal indicators" and the new concepts required to illuminate changing conditions. Wilbur Cohen and Mancur Olsen's *Toward a Social Report* (1969), submitted in the last days of the Johnson administration, dodged all important indicators of racism, injustice, police corruption, and the alienation of the young. Based mainly on outworn concepts, it studiously ignored future potentialities and goal alternatives.

Under Raymond A. Bauer, President Nixon's National Goals Research Staff aimed higher, but achieved still less. Its first goals report, *Toward Balanced Growth: Quantity with Quality* (July 4, 1970),[11] dealt directly with future potentialities, but confined itself to "safe and sane" subjects, avoiding any discussion of civil liberties, racism, urban decay, or war.

Probably the most significant hints for the study of future styles of fascism are contained in various forms of social and artistic criticism aimed at the present. For example, Jules Henry, in his *Culture Against Man*, has provided a passionate description of a culture of death, fear, and conformity. In his *One Dimensional*

[9]Bertram M. Gross, "Some Questions for Presidents," in Bertram M. Gross, Ed., *A Great Society?*, New York: Basic Books, 1968, Chapter 13.

[10]Bertram M. Gross, *The State of the Nation: Social Systems Accounting*, London: Tavistock, 1966.

[11]National Goals Research Staff, *Toward Balanced Growth: Quantity with Quality*, Washington, D.C., U.S. Government Printing Office, 1970.

Man and other writings, Herbert Marcuse has identified new forms of control and repression in a "faceless," bureaucratized society moving toward new forms of totalitarianism. The "literature of the absurd" — e.g., Franz Kafka's *The Castle* and *The Trial*, or Beckett's *Waiting for Godot* — ushers us into a strange world in which groping individuals are at the mercy of all-powerful forces that cannot be seen or understood.

Techno-Urban Fascism, American Style

To do justice to the subject, we must realize that reactionary repression at home and expansion abroad, the essence of full-fledged fascism, cannot be identified by any single element or dimension. We need a model dealing with the many interrelated elements of a *fascist society* operating under the new conditons of cybernetic technology, electronic mass media, nationwide urbanism, and a new structure of world power. To emphasize the pervasive roles of modern technology and urban and suburban life-styles, I use the term "techno-urban fascism," a new form of garrison state, or totalitarianism, built by older elites to resolve the growing conflicts of postindustrialism. More specifically: *A managed society rules by a faceless and widely dispersed complex of warfare welfare-industrial-communications-police bureaucracies caught up in developing a new-style empire based on a technocratic ideology, a culture of alienation, multiple scapegoats, and competing control networks.*

In examining these elements we can readily find similarities to the bureaucratic regimes of the ancient river valley empires of Mesopotamia, China, and Egypt and the later empires of Persia, Rome, and Byzantium. We can also find certain roots or antecedents in German and Japanese fascism, to a lesser extent in the Italian, Spanish, and Argentinian varieties, and in Soviet communism. On the other hand, the differences are rather striking. Under techno-urban fascism, certain elements previously regarded as inescapable earmarks of fascism would no longer be essential. Pluralistic in nature, techno-urban fascism would need no charismatic dictator, no one-party rule, no mass fascist party, no glorification of the state, no dissolution of legislatures, no discontinuation of elections, no distrust of reason. It would probably be a cancerous growth *within* and *around* the White House, the Pentagon, and the broader political establishment.

Let us now examine some of the major elements in the model.

A Managed Society. In industrial societies, the managed or planned economy was a conspicuous aspect of earlier fascism. Centralized management and control were invariably attempted — with varying degrees of success — through some system of "command economics."

In the postindustrial era, management practices (and, at a slower rate, management theory) have undergone fundamental changes:

1. Substantial decentralization, dispersion, and devolution have become the prerequisites of truly large-scale management.

2. Market-style rewards and punishments through the manipulation of prices, taxes, transfer payments, credit, and money supply have become indispensable accompaniments of direct control and regulation.
3. The Big Organization of the past has been encapsulated in the "complex": the macrosystem composed of overlapping networks of large private and public bureaucracies, trade associations, unions, friendly officials in all branches and levels of government, and specialized law firms, research groups, and consultants.
4. Macrosystem structure is characterized not only by formal hierarchy (which has received most attention in management theory) but also by multiple hierarchy and "polyarchic" forms of shared and diffused responsibility.
5. Macrosystem management, impossible through any single, central, planning agency, requires a "central guidance cluster" composed of partially competing elites performing overlapping roles in general leadership, financial management, general and special staff service, and the handling of critical problems.

Under techno-urban fascism, this style of management and planning would not be limited to the economy: it would deal with the political, social, cultural, and technological aspects of society as well. It would use the skills not only of economists but also of social and natural scientists, professionals, technicians, and assorted intellectuals. The focus of control would be not the economy, but the national society conceived of as a total system operating in the world environment. The key theme, therefore, would be not the managed economy, but rather, the *managed society*.

Obviously, this would be totalitarianism, but not in the older sense. Ebenstein, for example, distinguishes a totalitarian from an authoritarian regime on the ground that the latter (prevalent throughout history) "leaves the citizen a wide sphere of private life, in which he can still retain some of his dignity and self-respect." Totalitarianism, in contrast, means "all-encompassing control and unrestrained ruthlessness" as the "totalitarian ruler . . . seeks to dominate all aspects of life, nonpolitical as well as political."[12]

Even in the industrial era, this concept greatly exaggerated the extent of central omnipotence, an exaggeration that proved useful to both fascist propagandists and antifascist critics.[13] Under postindustrialist fascism, this concept would no longer be operational. Efforts to control *all* aspects of life would be scotched — just as the managers of large, multiproduct corporations and holding companies long ago learned that detailed control would interfere with comprehensive control. The "total" in the new totalitarianism would refer to the totality of the society being managed rather than to the details of tight central control. Above all, the management system would be *faceless* — without a single dictator or a single party.

---

[12]Ebenstein, *Totalitarianism: New Perspectives*, p. 15.
[13]See discussion of "The Myth of Central Omnipotence," in Bertram M. Gross, *The Managing of Organizations*, New York: Free Press, 1964, pp. 65–72.

With many rotating "faces," any one of them could be sacrificed when necessary without the system's losing face.

A   Warfare-Welfare-Industrial-Communications-Police   Complex. Under techno-urban fascism the central guidance cluster would be a loose but enormously powerful, five-part complex extending far beyond the old-style military-industrial complex.

The warfare-business establishment, of course, would still be of central importance. A sizable — and perhaps larger — proportion of the federal budget would still be automatically available to supply it with investment funds, working capital, pork-barrel contracts, and political slush funds. Sophisticated control systems — perceptively analyzed in Seymour Melman's *Pentagon Capitalism* — would continue the McNamara tradition of consolidating selective power over thousands of subcontractors in the name of alleged cost-cutting.[14] The symbiotic relationship between the White House and the Pentagon — which started slowly under Roosevelt and matured under Truman, Eisenhower, Kennedy, Johnson, and Nixon — would become still closer.

But the concept of a warfare-industrial complex is too limited to describe the commanding heights of postindustrialism's new modes of production and performance. Nor is it enough even to accept Melman's idea of the transformation of the military expenditure aspect of the complex into a more tightly managed "state administration." Indeed, to focus too much on the possibility of tighter expenditure management might be to detract attention from the possibility of a major enlargement of the complex itself from two to five components.

The first enlargement lies in the direction of Lasswell's original definition of the garrison state: the addition of *police*. But the police component of the complex would itself be far from unidimensional. It would involve far more than the expansion of the Pentagon's Directorate of Civil Disturbance Planning, set up in 1968, given a major role in Luttwak's *coup d'état* scenario.[15] It would include the Attorney General's office, the FBI, the CIA, the military intelligence agencies, federal-aid crime agencies, and new computer-based dossier facilities tied in with the Internal Revenue Service, the Census Bureau, and credit-rating offices.

The second enlargement is equally terrifying, though less obvious: the addition of the major control elements in an expanding *welfare* establishment. In the industrial past, there has never been a successful empire or a successful fascist regime without a major program of domestic welfare. Under Hitler, for example, Bismarckian welfare measures were continued in new forms, accounting for a major part of the Nazis' appeal to rank-and-file workers and to the lower middle class. Under postindustrial neofascism, we might well expect guaranteed minimum subsistence programs, expanded social security, improved medical care, and enlarged

[14]Seymour Melman, *Pentagon Capitalism: The Political Economy of War*, New York: McGraw-Hill, 1970.

[15]Edward Luttwak, "A Scenario for a Military *Coup d'Etat* in the United States," *Esquire*, July 1970.

housing and educational programs. Together, these programs would provide major forms of control and placation outside the area reachable through war contracts. Like William H. Whyte's organization men "imprisoned by brotherhood," millions of people would be imprisoned by the malign beneficence of an enlarged welfare state. Above all, under the combined blessings of HEW, HUD, OEO, and new coordinating agencies, ever-new and changing community participation games and carnivals would be staged to allow low-income and low-status leaders — from both white and Black ethnic groups — to work off their steam harmlessly without endangering the system.

The third enlargement — *communications* — would complete the five-part complex. This would include not only the central staffs of the major TV networks but also the wire services, the AT&T, and the FCC. A central role would be played by the new cable-based "narrowcasting" networks that will soon replace a major part of broadcasting and usher in the "wired society," with multichannels linked with almost every household and office in the country.

In toto, the warfare-welfare-industrial-communication-police complex would be the supramodern fascist form of what has hitherto been described as "oligopolistic state capitalism." Its products would be: (*1*) increasingly differentiated armaments (including more outer-space and under-sea instruments of destruction) that in the name of defense and security would contribute to world insecurity; (*2*) increasingly specialized medical, education, housing, and welfare programs that would have a declining relation to health, learning, community, or social justice; (*3*) industrial products to serve warfare-welfare purposes and provide consumer incentives for acceptance of the system; (*4*) communication services that would serve as instruments for the manipulation, surveillance, and suppression — or prettifying — of information on domestic and foreign terrorism; and (*5*) police activities designed to cope with the new "crime" of opposing the system, probably enlisting organized crime in the effort.

Unlike earlier forms of large-scale domination, the warfare-welfare-industrial-communications-police complex would have no single headquarters that could be seized, no central junta or executive committee that could be nationalized or liquidated, no set of orderly accounts that would keep track of all assets and activities, and no single, central, planning staff. Corporate profit-making and loss-avoidance would still be important objectives, but not within the framework of the old-fashioned balance sheet. Above all, they would be subordinated to more fundamental considerations of bureaucratic competition and system growth and maintenance as the basis for expanding power, prestige, and careerism.

As befits a complex, the social background of the key elites would be diverse. The hard core would doubtless be composed of middle-aged, male WASPs from both the older aristocracies of the social register and the new managerial "technopols." Tactical "mop-up" roles would be played by "knowledge elites," "hard-hat" storm troops, John Birchers, and "blockheads" or "know nothing" officials of the Lester Maddox or George Wallace variety. Each would have tactical missions to perform and would probably perform better if under the illusion of enjoying greater power and less subservience. Any effort to push too far or fast, however, would run the risk of quick liquidation.

Similarly, a selective sprinkling of "inferior" types would be conspicuous in middle-range positions: showpiece Blacks, Jews, Italians, Irish, and East Europeans, along with defeminized women and middle-aged "youth." It may also be confidently predicted that conspicuous advisory or public relations positions would be provided for former left-wingers of a previous generation — recanting Rudds, switching Savios, and penitent Panthers.

Neo-imperialism. Imperialism is an old phenomenon that has altered its form with changing social systems. In pastoral-nomadic societies, imperialist efforts were oriented mainly to hunting down and gathering in other people's wealth — in the form of land, slaves, women, tribute, and trophies. Under city-based agriculturalism, these efforts became consolidated in empires based on the forced import of capital. Under industrialism, imperialism concentrated on the export of capital to underdeveloped countries, the import of needed raw materials, the creation of new markets, and — above all — the consolidation of rival power blocs.

In postindustrial America, thus far, the course of empire has been more political, military, and ideological, with major emphasis on the development of anti-Soviet and anti-China blocs. The geographical orientation has been divided, some interests pressing mainly toward Europe, some mainly toward Asia or the Middle East, some mainly toward Latin America.

Under postindustrial American fascism, these cross-currents would probably be brought together in the *grand design of an Atlantic-Pacific anticommunist alliance* that would include the United States, the European Community, and Japan — with support from the Organization of American States and assorted satellite and client states in Southeast Asia and the Middle East. Economic operations would be handled not only by the Pentagon and the largest private corporations but also by quasi-public corporations such as COMSAT. Above all, the huge American-dominated, multinational corporations and conglomerates would complete the process — the beginnings of which are vividly described in J. J. Servan-Schreiber's *The American Challenge* — of seizing economic power in Europe. With European satellites as bases and fronts, the American power complex could more easily control and exploit Third World countries in which a fully open American presence would be more forcefully resisted. Thus, the Atlantic-Pacific anticommunist alliance would become the dreaded form of imperialism long ago predicted by Rudolf Hilferding and systematically ridiculed by Russian Marxists: ultra-imperialism.

Under the banner of a *Pax Americana*, the new ultra-imperialsim would seek full domination of the non-Soviet and non-Chinese world. This would probably involve successive deals with the Russians and the Chinese, in an effort to play one against the other. In the process, nuclear or biological confrontations would be risked.

Multiple Scapegoats. In Nazi Germany the Jews served as "societal scapegoats," an official objects of hatred and aggression. Organized anti-Semitism became a way of relieving the pent-up, hostile emotions of people in all classes and of channeling such emotions away from the harsh realities of the system. But the frenzy of Nazi anti-Semitism and the attempted "final solution" have partially obscured the fact that there were other scapegoats as well, namely, almost anyone who would not play ball with the Nazis and who could be tarred as "non-Aryan" or "bolshevik."

Under techno-urban fascism in America, the scapegoat role would be a double one: not only to divert aggressive energies and emotions but also to provide deterrents against the growth of effective opposition to the warfare-welfare state. But these deterrents, including the control networks to be discussed, could not be designed in the style of "those wonderful people who gave us Auschwitz and Belsen" (to paraphrase the title of a recent book on American advertising). Over-attention to one group in a heterogeneous society would hardly meet cost effectiveness standards. Even concentration on a few fixed groups would hardly comport with either principles of managerial flexibility or the necessity of building up an outward façade of a pluralistic, all-American, "friendly fascism."

Black people, of course, would be major scapegoats. But not *all* — as it was with *all* the Jews under the Nazis. Only Black traitors, Black criminals, Black deviants, and Black "effete snobs." Nor would there be any need whatever for costly concentration camps (despite current Black fears along these lines). Black ghettos in the central cities and in the older suburbs would serve apartheid purposes more cheaply and efficiently. Incursions across the lines into white areas would be met not only with suppression but also with retaliation.

In accordance with some of the worst of America's old traditions, there would also be a considerable amount of interethnic "scapegoatery." America's ethnic and religious diversity would be systematically exploited — the emphasis shifting back and forth between "melting pot" suppression of differences and the promotion of a seething cauldron of prejudice. Major roles would be played — particularly in the Black suburbs — by Black-Jewish conflicts, the inner-city cauldron being heated by Black–Puerto Rican and Black–East European conflicts.

Above all, a new invective would almost surely be invented — far sharper than that of Spiro Agnew recently, or of the "old" Richard Nixon and Joseph McCarthy — to stigmatize the traitors, foreign agents, criminals, and sniveling cowards among us: student rebels, intellectual protesters, and dropouts. From time to time, the official *Zeitgeist* would be revised to include additional targets. A menacing foreign enemy, it may be presumed, would figure centrally in this dramaturgy.

Old methods of pillorying scapegoats would not only be brought back but would be retooled and modernized. Security-risk blacklists would be both expanded and computerized, rating systems being introduced to calculate the extent to which each person had become a "rotten apple" and to provide opportunities for appropriate rehabilitation. Plots and conspiracies against the "public security" would be dramatically uncovered, usually just in the nick of time. Selected schools (or even specific courses or classes) would be closed down for considerable periods. Preventive detention would be extended to the "mentally unstable," who would be incarcerated in mental institutions. Finally, political assassiantions would be used more widely, but with more frequent resort to presumably "accidental" means.

In its use of these methods, America's "friendly fascism" would strive for an efficient balance between the secrecy that allows large-scale action with minimum resistance and the public symbolism that can get a pound of terror from an ounce of violence. It may be presumed that a "revitalized" Rand Corporation would prepare special manuals on the staging of "optimal show trials" and on a minimax strategy for crucifying opponents without converting them, dead or alive, into martyrs.

At the crabgrass roots of various suburb-dominated states, we might also expect some state governments to assume their old role of serving as laboratories for "advanced" ideas in the arts of repression. State-supported universities would probably be among the first victims. In this way the older "creative federalism" and "new federalism" would be converted into a "fascist federalism."

A Technocratic Ideology. Ebenstein[16] wrote, concerning the Hitler and Mussolini regimes:

> The distrust of reason is perhaps the most significant trait of fascism. The rational tradition of the West stems from Greece, and is one of the three basic components (the other two being Jewish monotheism and Christian love) that have given the West its characteristic culture and outlook. Fascism rejects this Greek root of Western civilization and is frankly *antirationalist*, distrusting reason in human affairs and stressing the irrational, sentimental, uncontrollable elements of man.

However, in this now commonly accepted analysis, Ebenstein fails to distinguish among various aspects of the rational tradition. In particular, he misses the distinction between what both Weber and Mannheim referred to as "substantive rationality" and "formal rationality." Substantive rationality is broad-gauged, transcends narrow means-ends distinctions, and deals more boldly and controversially with the good, the desirable, and the improbable. Formal rationality is narrowly instrumental and technocratic, emphasizing feasibilities and probabilities and disdaining basic human values or higher objectives.

In the formal sense, techno-urban fascism — particularly in America — would be frankly rationalist. Under it, nonsubstantive rationality would be raised to the level of a full-blown — if not authoritatively articulated — technocratic ideology. Stressing the controllable and nonsentimental, this essential component of new fascism would provide a continuing illusion of human progress in the form of new technological gadgets for killing people, controlling their behavior, elimina-

---

[16]Ebenstein, *Today's Isms*, p. 105.

ting mental and physical labor, and wasting natural resources. It would expand the principles of R-and-D-ology, i.e., the theory that any problem can be solved quickly, given enough investment of high-quality research-and-development hours with appropriate provisions for controlled testing and evaluation. Also, it would develop nationalistic rivalries in science and technology, with the continuing discovery of science-technology gaps that (as Russia's Sputnik once did) threaten the science-technology foundations of empire. Finally, it would provide elaborate rituals of certification, credentialism, and meritocracy. Huey Long's old slogan "Every man a king" would be converted into the more powerful "Every properly processed man or woman a technician or professional."

With such developments the two essential elements of rationality would be burst asunder. Emphasizing functions, roles, operationalism, and abstracted empiricism, the technocratic ideology would put aside rational analyses of human beings and personalities, of human groups as more than the sum or product of their parts, of totally new forms of social organization. With the accumulation of indigestible mountains of isolated facts, the proliferation of technical jargons and subspecializations, and declining interest in judgment, wisdom, and understanding, this new *Zeitgeist* would lead to a new *ignorance explosion*. Purportedly "value free," it would tend to be valueless apart from its vital role in buttressing a neo-imperialist warfare-welfare state. Above all, in encouraging new ways to waste resources on changing forms of overkill technocratic ideology would carry instrumental rationality to the lowest depths of substantive irrationality: bureaucratized madness.

A Culture of Alienation. In every period of confusing historical change and dislocation, older values and beliefs break down. In the Third Reich, an effort was made to develop a *Volkskultur* based on a mythical past, racial lies, and the social passions of a large, lower middle class. This fitted well into a situation in which millions of people were being prepared for active warfare.

Under techno-urban fascism, with different societal modes of behavior, a mass culture would be inappropriate. Active warfare would exist only on the fringes of the empire, with "coolie labor" used for most of the mass armies on the ground. At home, with huge populations concentrated in a few urban regions and huge numbers of young people in schools and universities, mass movements and mass culture would represent potentially uncontrollable elements. Under these conditions the appropriate milieu of neofascism would be a *culture of alienation*.

The major characteristics of a fascist culture of alienation would be social aphasis, loneliness, materialism, homogenized pluralism, and hopelessness. "Aphasis," writes Franklin H. Littell, in an effort to identify totalitarian movements in America, "is that condition, either physical or psychological, which hampers or prevents a person from communicating with his fellows."[17] Fascist politics, he points out, would fatten on the breakdown of trust. Similarly, loneli-

---

[17]Littel, op. cit., p. 83.

ness is better than shared feelings. The "lonely crowd" is better than an organized crowd, unless the organization itself — as with both bureaucracies and labor unions — is designed to focus attention on career ambitions and individual grievances.

Materialist "goodies" in unending kinds and quantities would become the symbols of achievement, dissenters being subtly encouraged to fight for slightly larger slices rather than a new recipe for the pie. Every effort to develop a more humanist "counterculture" would itself be countered by profit-making or bureaucratic takeovers. The deviant drug culture of the 1960s could probably be taken over as a new instrument of conformity through "opium for part of the people." All this would contribute to a pluralistic variety of approved art forms — with no slowdown in the cycles of fad and fashion, but a greater homogeneity underlying the apparent differences.

The great majority of the people would be repressed isolates with very little to live for and nothing they would consciously be willing to die for. Nonetheless, death itself would be stripped of its human qualities, the victims of distant wars and domestic oppression being viewed as either nonhuman or subhuman. Large-scale violence in the hands of the Pentagon-police complex would be legitimated as a technical activity to be conducted by experts. Thus, to use the prescient words of Jules Henry's *Culture Against Man*, the new culture of alienation would lead to the "culture of death."

Competing Control Networks. Under previous forms of totalitarianism, behind the carefully promoted myths of central omnipotence and omniscience, competing systems of surveillance and espionage were invariably used to repress opposition, even to liquidate possible sources of future opposition.

Under techno-urban fascism, the range of competitive control systems would be much wider. There would be much more of what Herbert Marcuse, in *One Dimensional Man* and *Soviet Marxism*, refers to as "the pleasant forms of social control and cohesion," including what he calls "repressive tolerance" and "repressive desublimation."

Direct repression would, of course, be a major characteristic of the new managed society, as it is in all forms of totalitarianism. But it would be *selective repression operating through and around the established constitutional system*. It would destroy any confidence that the constitutional freedoms set forth in the U.S. Bill of Rights would be allowed to operate on behalf of any serious dissent or seriously organized opposition to the warfare-welfare-industrial-communications-police complex, to neo-imperialism, to the technological ideology, or to the culture of alienation. Preventive detention, "no-knock" and "quick entry" practices, "martial law" lawlessness, and out-and-out domestic *Schrecklichkeit* would be used callously, but not indiscriminately.

The economizing on direct repression would be made possible only through the sophisticated development of indirect control and manipulation. The ordinary forms of indirect control, apart from ideology and culture, would be these:

1. *rationed welfare state benefits*, with categorical aid programs in health, housing, education, and subsistence contributions made conditional upon good behavior;
2. *accelerated consumerism*, with new services as well as new goods rewarding conformity;
3. *"credentialized" meritocracy*, with people moving from Marx's wage slavery to a post-Marxian form of status slavery; and
4. *market administration*, with incentive manipulation increasingly used to supplement the direct control of private corporations, mixed corporations, public authorities, and ordinary public bureaucracies.

But *co-optation* would be the most powerful form of indirect control. In Philip Selznick's older terms, co-optation was "the process of absorbing new elements into the leadership or policymaking structure of an organization as a means of averting threats to its stability or existence."[18] Under American-style techno-urban fascism, co-optation would be *the process of absorbing new elements into the interstices of the managed society as a means not only of averting threats but of strengthening the system.*

In the warfare-welfare components of the larger fascist complex, there would be many thousands of juicy, lower-level plumbs available for dissidents and rebels demanding "a piece of the action." Some of these would go preemptively in advance to those showing exceptional promise; others would be held out as prizes. In either case, choices would be available — as a well-organized vice ring allows star call girls to choose one city or another. Positions close to "the leadership or policymaking structure," however, would be available only after considerable effort and intra-system coalition-building and politicking. Often, entire organizations or subsystems would be co-opted. In what might be called "subsystem co-optation," liberal and purportedly radical organizations would be used to provide young people with opportunities to "work off their steam" harmlessly or to provide the backdrop for the system's normal compromising in the resolution of routine conflicts.

Still less conspicuously, "fifth column co-optation" would capitalize on the age-old policy strategy of the *agent provocateur*. But instead of relying on the individual undercover agent, this form of co-optation would involve the direct organization and financing of revolutionary groups that would trigger off whatever acts of violence might be needed as a pretext for quick and violent repression. A continuing task for the Judston Institute, in friendly competition with the Rand Corporation, would be the simulation of revolutionary movements in the United States — as a guide to a variety of undercover ventures to take control of them at early stages.

[18]Philip Selznick, *TVA and the Grass Roots*, Berkeley: University of California Press, 1949, p. 259.

Hydra-like System Maintenance

How long could mature techno-urban fascism be maintained in America?

Here, unfortunately, we have little choice but to look back at the record of mature fascism in Germany, Japan, and Italy. In each of these — with more primitive forms of domestic control — all serious internal resistance was liquidated. The only effective antifascism was defeat by external powers.

Looking at the future of a neofascist America, we find a picture that is both similar and different. One similarity is the *improbability of any effective internal resistance*. The new managed society would be like the mythical hydra of antiquity. Cut off one head, and another grows elsewhere. Strike here, and you will be struck from behind. Even organized disruption of water supply and power plants would not go very far. The system would heal itself quickly, and probably come back stronger than before.

One difference is the *impossibility of overthrowing fascism through war*. The only war that could defeat a fascist America would be a nuclear war, a holocaust from which no antifascist victors would emerge.

This brings us back to another similarity and another difference — the war-orientation of techno-urban fascism. The drive toward military conquest might not be so open as that of the German, Japanese, and Italian fascists. But the orientation toward worldwide destruction through the eventual use of nuclear weapons — whether "tactically" or "accidentally" — is unmistakable. Once neofascism arrives, the only choice would be *fascist or dead*.

In presenting his earlier model of the garrison state, Lasswell stated that he would "prefer it to be a self-disconfirming hypothesis"; I share this preference.

But in this new and more terrifying context, I cannot so readily adopt Lasswell's thought that "the master challenge of modern politics . . . is to civilize a garrisoning world, thereby cultivating the conditions for its eventual dissolution."[19] Techno-urban fascism in America would already be largely civilized. Indeed, as Lasswell himself foresaw in his original article, the neofascist form of the garrison state would in large part "abolish the distinction between civilian and military functions."[20]

The alternative to neofascism and nuclear annihilation, I am convinced, is far more exhilarating than minor ameliorism. It lies in the historic potentialities of human growth as mankind moves from the epoch of industrialism into an as-yet-uncharted postindustrial future, potentialities for a reconstructed world society based on more humanistic forms, ideologies, and cultures.

But any hope of such far-going social reconstruction depends, among other things, on increasing our capacity to fear. Thus, the purpose of this essay has been to frighten my neighbor as well as myself. I have tried to promote what Gunther Anders has called "a fearless fear, since it excludes fearing those who might deride us as cowards; a stirring fear, since it should drive us into the streets

[19]Lasswell, "The Garrison-State Hypothesis Today."
[20]Lasswell, "The Garrison State."

instead of under cover; and a loving fear, not fear *of* danger ahead but *for* the generations to come.''[21]

By itself, of course, fear would lead to inaction, spreading the intangible terror that would be the secret weapon of creeping fascism.

It is my hope that this article may contribute to a widespread discussion of neofascist tendencies in the United States, their societal roots, and their possible forms of expansion. Such a dialogue will unquestionably reveal that older styles of antifascism are obsolete and that we need new-style antifascist strategies, tactics, and coalitions.

20. Richard C. Edwards
Michael Reich
Thomas E. Weisskopf

Toward a Socialist Alternative

I

At the present time the capitalist system is under severe attack from many quarters. Victims of inequality, alienation, racism, sexism, irrationality, and imperialism are engaged in simultaneous struggles to overcome their oppression, and they are finding that capitalism is one of their principal enemies. The very existence of such challenges suggests that capitalism is neither a smoothly operating system in which little protest is heard nor a system unsusceptible to any change. On the contrary, the entire history of the capitalist era has been marked by resistance from those whom capitalism has sought to subordinate. Often this resistance has been overcome only through the use of violent force and coercion by the state.

The social oppression which capitalism perpetuates and generates, and the protests and challenges that arise in response, lead us to the question: Is it ultimately possible to bring about a radical social transformation of capitalism, one that would result in a more humane society? We already know that to achieve a better society, a *radical* transformation of capitalism is necessary; . . . each of the forms of oppression . . . [is] *functional* to the capitalist mode of production and will persist unless capitalism itself is fundamentally transformed.

[21]Gunther Anders, op. cit.

Reprinted by permission of Prentice-Hall, Inc., Englewood Cliffs, New Jersey, from *The Capitalist System: A Radical Analysis of American society*, by Richard C. Edwards, Michael Reich, and Thomas E. Weisskopf, pp. 462–464, 520–521. © 1972.

Social systems do not fall simply because they are oppressive or considered by some to be unjust. Dynamic forces within capitalist society insure that *some* social change will take place; but this social change will not necessarily nor inevitably take the form of a fundamental transformation of the capitalist mode of production into a better society. Capitalism can be radically transformed only if it produces dysfunctional social forces that have the potential for fundamental change. Equally important, a radical transformation of capitalism can occur only if men and women understand the historical social forces at work in a capitalist society and intervene actively and collectively in a conscious attempt to direct and control those forces and turn them to desired human ends. In short, a strategy for radical social change must be based on an understanding of the *contradictions* at work in a capitalist society. . . .

What is meant by the term contradiction? By contradiction we mean more than simply a flaw in the logic of an argument or a conflict of interests. A contradiction of capitalism results when the very process of capitalist development produces simultaneously the conditions needed to transform it fundamentally; that is, when the successes of capitalist development create situations which are fundamentally antagonistic to capitalism itself. Contradictions tend to intensify with time and cannot be resolved within the existing social framework. In the following paragraphs we shall outline some of the domestic and international contradictions of advanced capitalism.

We have already noted that capitalism is not a static society. The production process itself is constantly being revolutionized and capital continually attempts to extend its area of influence and domination. But these developments contain major contradictions: They produce changes that ultimately call into question the social desirability of the capitalist drive for profits and the necessity of capitalist production relations. Capitalism has reached a stage where it is incompatible with and holds back the further development of human potentials and capacities.

On the one hand, capitalism promises to meet basic human needs but is increasingly unable to deliver on that promise. Throughout the underdeveloped world, and among the oppressed minorities in the developed countries — such as Blacks and Chicanos in the United States, Quebeçois (French-Canadians) in Canada, and Catholics in Northern Ireland — it is apparent that real economic and social development is impossible within the confines of the international capitalist system. Capitalism by its very nature creates unequal development and is unable to institute economic reforms that would co-opt burgeoning anti-imperialist struggles for national liberation. Yet it is capitalism itself which, in attempting to extend its area of domination, promised economic development in these areas and created an awareness of the possiblity of development. Capitalism thus becomes caught in a web of international contradictions.

In the developed world, where modern capitalism has delivered a wealth of material goods, it has sought to define well-being in terms of individual commodity consumption. But with continued economic growth, the desirability of more individual material consumption fades in comparison to other dimensions of well-being, such as the availability of creative and socially useful work, meaningful community, and liberating education for individual development. Yet, because capitalism must constantly expand, the realization of these needs is incompatible with capitalist relations of production. Instead, capitalist economic growth deepens the alienation of work and community, and poisons the environment, and commercializes all social relationships. People increasingly recognize that well-being consists of more than the individual acquisition and consumption of commodities, and that capitalism cannot meet their felt needs.

Moreover, capitalist economic growth itself becomes increasingly predicated on irrationality and production of waste (e.g., military and space expenditures and planned obsolescence in consumer goods) as production for profit increasingly subordinates production for use. Continued economic growth threatens the ecological balance of the earth, and the expanding role of the state in direct production and maintenance of economic growth both undermines the ideological legitimacy of private ownership of capital and politicizes the issue of economic priorities.

Equally important, the expansion of capitalist production draws an ever-increasing share of the population into alienating wage and salary work. Modern capitalist production has become incredibly complex and interdependent, requiring the drawing together and cooperation of labor from all over the globe. An enormous expansion in the size of the proletariat occurs within the United States as blacks and women increasingly join the ranks of wage and salary workers, and small entrepreneurial businessmen and professional white-collar workers are subordinated to large capital. The proletarianization of these groups produces an awareness of the constraints of capitalist production relations; the oppression of women and blacks becomes linked to their oppression as workers.

At the same time, the internationalization of capital, accelerated by developments in high-speed communications and transportation, creates a worldwide proletariat and necessarily heightens the awareness within the United States of social interdependence with the Third World. The interrelationships between the logic of capitalism at home and abroad become clearer. Thus, the war in Vietnam exposed the destructive effect of U.S. foreign policy on poor nations and revealed the linkages between poverty, racism, and sexism at home and imperialism abroad.

Finally, as production has grown in complexity, capitalism requires a more skilled work force — workers with more developed capabilities. The simple rote tasks of the past are replaced by work which involves a certain degree of initiative and autonomy, some ability to conceptualize, analyze, and synthesize, and a more active involvement of workers in the production process; but by educating workers capitalism provides them both with a greater awareness of their material and emotional needs and the capacity to grasp the system's essential irrationality. This leads very quickly to questioning the present hierarchical social division of labor and distribution of power.

In these ways capitalism becomes increasingly caught in its own contradictions. Capitalist development generates expectations that it cannot fulfill. As the impoverishment of daily life deepens, the gap between people's felt needs and what capitalism can deliver grows wider, and both the necessity for and feasibility of radical social change become widely recognized. As the capitalist class appears more and more parasitic and the capitalistic system less and less instrumental to the welfare of society as a whole, each of the oppressive social problems . . . becomes a locus around which opposition to capitalist society can develop. It is not surprising that the revolts from the Third World, blacks, women, students, and factory and office workers against inequality, alienation, racism, sexism, irrationality, and imperialism have grown in frequency and intensity in recent years.

However, the emergence of contradictions in advanced capitalism is not sufficient by itself to insure the fundamental transformation of capitalism. Indeed, there are countless examples of spontaneous individual protests and rebellions that are either self-destructive, because they strike at wrong targets, or strike in a purely symbolic and ineffectual way, or become co-opted and commercialized as part of the capitalist system itself. Fundamental social change will occur only if a self-conscious class emerges and engages in organized political struggle around the contradictions of capitalism in such a way as to challenge the basic capitalist relations of production, for capitalism will not "evolve" or "develop naturally" into the transformed society we desire.

The capitalist class is a privileged and exploiting class, and it is not about to give up its special place without resistance. In the absence of a conscious political movement, the capitalist class will always be able to obfuscate and mystify discontent, offer sham concessions, co-opt leaders and causes, divide the movement, and suppress movement organizations. What it cannot do, however, is to resolve the contradictions of advanced capitalism. Only a change in the mode of production can do that.

One final implication of our analysis should be noted. Precisely because advanced capitalism has sought to reorganize and commercialize every aspect of daily life, the transformation of capitalism cannot be separated from the overthrow of all forms of oppression with which capitalism has associated itself. Purely economic exploitation, as we have argued, is significantly intertwined by capitalist development with dehumanization in psychological, cultural, racial, sexual, and other dimensions. All oppressed groups share a certain solidarity in that each is struggling for self-determination. At any one time the contradictions around particular forms of oppression may be sharper than around others. But the revolutionary process is not reducible to struggle against economic explotation or the alienation of labor; it must incorporate simultaneous struggles against dehumanization in *all* its forms. That is, it must articulate and struggle for a vision of a liberated society, in which all social relations are transformed and all hierarchical divisions of labor are abolished.

● ● ●

II

. . . But what kind of society might replace capitalism? What is our vision of a more decent, humane, *socialist* society?

We cannot present a blueprint or an exact specification of how a socialist "utopia" would work; nor should we attempt to do so, since constructing imaginary utopias bears little relation to the actual task of building a decent society. Any *real* alternatives to capitalism will be historically linked to the forces and movements generated by the contradictions of capitalist society itself. New institutions which liberate rather than oppress can only be created by real people confronting concrete problems in their lives and developiing new means to overcome oppression. The political movements arising from capitalism's contradictions therefore constitute the only means for society to move from its present condition to a new and more decent form, and only out of these movements will humane as well as practical new institutions be generated.

We can, however, explain what *values* would characterize a truly decent society and what *goals* should motivate the political movement for a more decent society. . . . In a sense, the values underlying a decent society have been implicit throughout our anlysis of capitalism. A truly socialist society would be characterized by equality: equality in sharing the material benefits of the society; equality rather than hierarchy in making social decision; and equality in society's encouragement to develop one's full potentials. Work must cease to be a means of "making one's living" and become non-alienated, a *part* of one's living. Arbitrary distinctions by race and sex (or language or eye color) would cease to be criteria for particular forms of oppression or for tracking people into limited opportunities. The irrationality of production for profits would be transformed into the rationaltiy of production to satisfy people's needs, and the unequal relations of imperialism would be replaced by a cooperative ethic recognizing people's responsibility to each other.

But more importantly, socialism is more than a set of humane values; it is a *process*. And defining and describing this process is more difficult than defining the goals of a socialist society. Most fundamentally, socialism means democratic, decentralized and *participatory* control for the individual: it means having a say in the decisions that affect one's life. Such a participatory form of socialism certainly requires equal access for all to material and cultural resources, which in turn requires the abolition of private ownership of capital and the redistribution of wealth. But it also calls for socialist men and women to eliminate alienating, destructive forms of production, consumption, education and social relations. Participatory socialism requires the elimination of bureaucracies and all hierarchical forms and their replacement, not by new state or party bureaucracies, but by a self-governing and self-managing people with directly chosen representatives subject to recall and replacement. Participatory socialism entails a sense of egalitarian cooperation, of solidarity of people with one another; but at the same time it respects individual and group differences and guarantees individual rights.

It affords to all individuals the freedom to exercise human rights and civil liberties that are not mere abstractions but have concrete day-to-day meaning.

These socialist values and process — and the institutions which would encourage and promote them — must grow out of specific struggles against alienation and other forms of oppression. Hence one part of our struggle against concrete problems and forms of oppression that face us *now* must be to develop institutions which promote equality, nonalienating production, and the other requisites of a decent society.

We must stress that this development is not automatic: Just as the existence of oppression does not guarantee the emergence of oppositional forces (hence our analysis of contradictions), so oppositional forces do not inevitably lead to the creation of liberating institutions. The progression can occur only on the basis of a self-conscious and self-educated *political* movement.

INDEX OF AUTHORS

INDEX OF SUBJECTS